Lecture Notes in Computer Science   10139

Commenced Publication in 1973
Founding and Former Series Editors:
Gerhard Goos, Juris Hartmanis, and Jan van Leeuwen

Advanced Research in Computing and Software Science
Subline of Lecture Notes in Computer Science

More information about this series at http://www.springer.com/series/7407

Bernhard Steffen · Christel Baier
Mark van den Brand · Johann Eder
Mike Hinchey · Tiziana Margaria (Eds.)

SOFSEM 2017:
Theory and Practice
of Computer Science

43rd International Conference on Current Trends
in Theory and Practice of Computer Science
Limerick, Ireland, January 16–20, 2017
Proceedings

 Springer

Editors
Bernhard Steffen
TU Dortmund
Dortmund
Germany

Christel Baier
TU Dresden
Dresden
Germany

Mark van den Brand
Eindhoven University of Technology
Eindhoven
The Netherlands

Johann Eder
Alpen Adria University Klagenfurt
Klagenfurt
Austria

Mike Hinchey
Lero - Irish Software Research Center
Limerick
Ireland

Tiziana Margaria
Lero - Irish Software Research Center
Limerick
Ireland

ISSN 0302-9743   ISSN 1611-3349 (electronic)
Lecture Notes in Computer Science
ISBN 978-3-319-51962-3   ISBN 978-3-319-51963-0 (eBook)
DOI 10.1007/978-3-319-51963-0

Library of Congress Control Number: 2016962027

LNCS Sublibrary: SL1 – Theoretical Computer Science and General Issues

Printed on acid-free paper

This Springer imprint is published by Springer Nature
The registered company is Springer International Publishing AG
The registered company address is: Gewerbestrasse 11, 6330 Cham, Switzerland

Preface

This volume contains the invited and contributed papers selected for presentation at the 43rd Conference on Current Trends in Theory and Practice of Computer Science (SOFSEM 2017), held January 16–20, 2017, in Limerick, Ireland.

SOFSEM (originally SOFtware SEMinar) is devoted to leading research and fosters cooperation among researchers and professionals from academia and industry in all areas of computer science. SOFSEM started in 1974 in the former Czechoslovakia as a local conference and winter school combination. The renowned invited speakers and the growing interest of the authors from abroad gradually turned SOFSEM in the mid-1990s into an international conference with proceedings published in the Springer LNCS series, in the last two years in their prestigious subline ARCoSS: *Advanced Research in Computing and Software Science*. SOFSEM became a well-established and fully international conference maintaining the best of its original winter school aspects, such as a higher number of invited talks and an in-depth coverage of novel research results in selected areas of computer science. SOFSEM 2017, accordingly, was organized around the following three thematic tracks:

- Foundations of Computer Science (chaired by Christel Baier, TU Dresden)
- Software Engineering: Methods, Tools, Applications (chaired by Mark van den Brand, TU Eindhoven)
- Data, Information, and Knowledge Engineering (chaired by Johann Eder, U. Klagenfurt)

With its three tracks, SOFSEM 2017 covered the latest advances in research, both theoretical and applied, in selected areas of computer science. The SOFSEM 2017 Program Committee consisted of 62 international experts from 22 different countries, representing the track areas with outstanding expertise. After a detailed reviewing process, 34 papers were selected for presentation, namely: 27 in the Foundations of Computer Science, four in the Software Engineering, and three in the Data, Information, and Knowledge Engineering tracks.

As usual, SOFSEM 2017 comprised seven invited talks There was unifying talk:

- "Dependable and Optimal Cyber-Physical Systems," by Kim Guldstrand Larsen (Aalborg University, Denmark)

And two talks for each thematic track:

- "Trends and Challenges in Predictive Analytics," by Jaakko Hollmèn (Aalto University, Finland)
- "On Featured Transition Systems," by Axel Legay (Rennes University and Inria, France)
- "Domain-Specific Languages: A Systematic Mapping Study," by Marjan Mernik (University of Maribor, Slovenia)

- "Model-Driven Development in Practice: From Requirements to Code," by Óscar Pastor López (Polytechnic University of Valencia, Spain)
- "Network Constructors: A Model for Programmable Matter," by Paul G. Spirakis (University of Liverpool, UK)
- "Verifying Parametric Thread Creation," by Igor Walukiewicz (Bordeaux University and CNRS, France).

An integral part of SOFSEM 2017 was the traditional SOFSEM Student Research Forum (chaired by Anila Mjeda, University of Limerick and Lero, Ireland), organized with the aim of presenting student projects in both the theory and practice of computer science, and to give the students feedback on the originality of their results. The papers presented at the Student Research Forum were published in separate local proceedings, available as the *Lero Technical Report*.

In addition, this year's edition introduced an industry track that included a full-day track ASE@SOFSEM organized by Yaping Luo of Altran, The Netherlands, and several demonstrations and presentations.

Moreover, five tutorials profiled emergent and established technologies:

- "Cinco: A Simplicity-Focused Language Workbench for Domain-Specific Graphical Modeling Environments," by Stefan Naujokat, Johannes Neubauer, Bernhard Steffen (TU Dortmund, Germany)
- "Unifying Theories of Programming: Principles, Theories and Tools," by Andrew Butterfield (Trinity College Dublin and Lero, Ireland)
- "Verification and Test-case Generation from Architectural Models of Automotive Systems," by Cristina Seceleanu (Mälardalen Technical University, Sweden)
- "Plasma Lab Statistical Model Checker: Architecture, Usage, and Extension," by Axel Legay and Louis-MarieTraonouez (Rennes University and Inria, France)
- "Becoming Goldilocks: Privacy and Data Sharing in 'Just Right' Conditions for Software Engineering," by Fayola Peters (University of Limerick and Lero, Ireland) – the Early Career Researcher tutorial

As editors of these proceedings, we are grateful to everyone who contributed to the scientific program of the conference, especially the invited speakers and all the authors of contributed papers. We would like to express our special thanks to:

- The members of the SOFSEM 2017 Program Committee and all external reviewers for their careful reviewing of the submissions
- Anila Mjeda for her preparation and handling of the Student Research Forum
- The SOFSEM Steering Committee, chaired by Július Štuller and supported by Jan van Leeuwen, for guidance and support throughout the preparation of the conference
- The local Organizing Committee, chaired by Anna-Lena Lamprecht (University of Limerick and Lero), with Pavel Tyl (TU Liberec, Czech Republic) as Website Chair and the help and support of Susan Mitchell and Dara O'Connor (Lero), Andrew Butterfield, Brian Fitzgerald, Clare McInerney and Brian O'Donnellan (Lero), Gerard Mulligan and Denis Hogan (Lero, tech support), Colm Mc Gettrick and Tony Irwin (CSIS, tech support)

- The OCS team in Dortmund for their support with the OCS conference management system and their immediate reaction to requests
- Springer for their continued support of the SOFSEM conferences
- Lero for publishing the second volume of the proceedings (at conference)

We are greatly indebted to Easy Conferences, in particular Petros Stratis, Melita Rolandi Stratis, Boyana Slavova, Sotia Demetriou, Marios Christou, and Kyriakos Georgiadis, for the event management of SOFSEM 2017.

We received generous sponsoring: We thank the Science Foundation Ireland, whose support through the SFI Conference and Workshops program made this rich program and in particular the many keynotes possible, and Altran (Eindhoven, The Netherlands) for their industrial sponsorship of the ASE@SOFSEM track. The generosity of the Slovak Society for Computer Science sponsored again the Best Student Paper Award.

We hope the readers of the proceedings gain valuable new insights that hopefully contribute to their research and its uptake.

November 2017

Bernhard Steffen
Christel Baier
Mark van den Brand
Johann Eder
Mike Hinchey
Tiziana Margaria

Organization

Program Chair

Bernhard Steffen   TU Dortmund, Germany

Track Chairs

Christel Baier	TU Dresden, Germany
Johann Eder	Alpen-Adria University Klagenfurt, Austria
Mark van den Brand	Eindhoven University of Technology, The Netherlands

Program Committee

Alessandro Abate	University of Oxford, UK
Andreas Abel	Gothenburg University, Sweden
Erika Abraham	RWTH Aachen University, Germany
Christel Baier	TU Dresden, Germany
Marko Bajec	University of Ljubljana, Slovenia
Ion Barosan	Eindhoven University of Technology, The Netherlands
Ladjel Bellatreche	LIAS/ISAE-ENSMA, France
Maria Bielikova	Slovak University of Technology in Bratislava, Slovakia
Armin Biere	Johannes Kepler University Linz, Austria
Hans Bodlaender	University of Utrecht, The Netherlands
Patricia Bouyer	CNRS, France
Gerth Stølting Brodal	Aarhus University, Denmark
Sergio Cabello	University of Ljubljana, Slovenia
Barbara Catania	University of Genoa, Italy
Loek Cleophas	TU Eindhoven, The Netherlands
Pedro D'Argenio	Universidad Nacional de Córdoba, Argentina
Yuxin Deng	East China Normal University, China
Uwe Egly	TU Wien, Austria
Gregor Engels	Paderborn University, Germany
Zoltan Esik	University of Szeged, Hungary
Uli Fahrenberg	LIX, École Polytechnique, France
Bernd Fischer	University of Stellenbosch, South Africa
Johann Gamper	Free University of Bozen-Bolzano, Italy
Tibor Gyimothy	University of Szeged, Hungary
Görel Hedin	Lund University, Sweden
Zoltán Horváth	Eötvös Loránd University, Hungary
Juraj Hromkovic	ETH Zurich, Switzerland
Theo Härder	University of Kaiserslautern, Germany

Mirjana Ivanovic	University of Novi Sad, Serbia
Kazuo Iwama	Kyoto University, Japan
Rolf Klein	University of Bonn, Germany
Georgia Koutrika	HP Labs, USA
Stanislav Krajci	UPJ, Slovakia
Jan Kretinsky	Technische Universität München, Germany
Rastislav Královič	Comenius University, Slovakia
Antonín Kučera	Masaryk University, Czech Republic
Barbara König	Universität Duisburg-Essen, Germany
Yannis Manolopoulos	Aristotle University, Greece
Rainer Manthey	University of Bonn, Germany
Kaminski Marcin	University of Warsaw, Poland
Elvira Mayordomo	Universidad de Zaragoza, Spain
Pierre-Etienne Moreau	Université de Lorraine - LORIA, France
Anca Muscholl	LaBRI, France
Boris Novikov	St. Petersburg State University, Russia
Claus Pahl	Free University of Bozen-Bolzano, Italy
Alfonso Pierantonio	University of L'Aquila and MDH, Italy
Evaggelia Pitoura	University of Ioannina, Greece
Andrei Popescu	Middlesex University, London, UK
Tomasz Radzik	King's College London, UK
Paolo Rosso	Technical University of Valencia, Spain
Serguei Roubtsov	Eindhoven University of Technology, The Netherlands
Gunter Saake	Otto-von-Guericke-University Magdeburg, Germany
Ina Schaefer	TU Braunschweig, Germany
Bran Selic	Malina Software Corp., Canada
Alexandra Silva	UCL, UK
Jiri Srba	Aalborg University, Denmark
Miroslaw Staron	University of Gothenburg, Sweden
Krzysztof Stencel	University of Warsaw, Poland
Emma Söderberg	Google, Denmark
Morzy Tadeusz	Poznan University of Technology, Poland
Bogdan Vasilescu	Carnegie Mellon University, USA
Marina Waldén	Åbo Akademi University, Finland

Additional Reviewers

Dieky Adzkiya	Hans-Joachim	Søren Enevoldsen
Mustaq Ahmed	Böckenhauer	Johan Ersfolk
Kadir Akbudak	Jérémie Chalopin	Panos Giannopoulos
Eric Badouel	Yu-Fang Chen	Thomas Given-Wilson
Harsh Beohar	Dmitry Chistikov	Luca Grilli
Benedikt Bollig	Vincenzo Ciancia	Magnus Halldorsson
Guillaume Bonfante	Raymond Devillers	Tomas Horvath
Broňa Brejová	Tom Durrant	Rasmus Ibsen-Jensen

Trends and Challenges in Predictive Analytics
(Abstract of Invited Talk)

Jaakko Hollmén

Department of Computer Science, Helsinki Institute for Information Technology
(HIIT), Aalto University, P.O. Box 15400, FI-00076 Aalto, Espoo, Finland
jaakko.hollmen@aalto.fi

Abstract. Predictive analytics is one of the most popular areas in machine
learning and data mining. I will start by reviewing some fundamentals in data
science and then focus on time series analysis and prediction. In the talk, I will
present recent trends in predictive analytics, covering reducing dimensionality
of the data space, stream processing, learning interpretable models, and connections to multi-label classification. I will also speak about patterns of missing
data and its implications on predictive analytics in stream processing where no
missing data imputation is possible. The solutions will be demonstrated in the
areas of environmental informatics, medical science and transportation areas.

Introduction

The research fields of machine learning [1] and data mining [3] have enjoyed increased
attention in recent years, thanks to their ability to generalize beyond recorded past
experience in the form of individual cases. The generalized laws can be deployed to
function as part of an operational data processing systems to make estimations of
unknown quantities or predictions.

In the talk, I will review fundamentals of data analysis, including the curse of
dimensionality and the concept of generalization. Then, I will speak about recent trends
in predictive analysis, including highlights from my own research. Making predictive
models transparent and understandable has high priority in many domains such as
medical diagnostics. One approach is to reduce the number of variables in the prediction model, or to make the model representation compact, or sparse. Sparsity can be
enforced by a search procedure in the space of regressors [10, 12] or by optimizing a
penalized cost function that enforces sparsity [2, 11]. Reporting of results in a compact
and understandable form has been the topic our previous pattern mining research in the
context of cancer genomics application [4]. Prediction models could very well be
described in natural language [9] as well. Recent work in multi-label classification and
its connections to sequence prediction will be reviewed [5, 7, 8].

Although the popular discussion around Big Data has emphasized the power of
fusing data from many sources to improve results, the heterogeneity of the data poses
many challenges. The missing data found in many practical data sources is so prevalent
that only a rather small portion of the data contains valid values. If we select variables

to be included in the analysis by the prevalence of missing data, we may end up with only a handful of variables, despite the large number of original data sources. This provides an immediate motivation for investigating missing data in the context of predictive models. Our theoretical studies [13] and applications in predicting quantities in environmental monitoring context [14] show how the prediction results rapidly deteriorate when missing values are present and when missing value imputation [6] is not possible. We provide novel optimization criteria for learning linear predictive models, when the prevalence of missing data is known.

References

1. David, B.: Bayesian Reasoning and Machine Learning. Cambridge University Press (2012)
2. Bradley, E., Trevor, H., Iain, J., Robert, T.: Least angle regression. Ann. Stat. **32**(2), 407–499 (2004)
3. David, H., Heikki, M., Padhraic, S.: Principles of Data Mining. Adaptive Computation and Machine Learning Series. MIT Press (2001)
4. Jaakko, H., Jarkko, T.: Compact and understandable descriptions of mixture of Bernoulli distributions. In: Berthold, M.R., Shawe-Taylor, J., Lavrač, N. (eds.) IDA 2007. LNCS, vol. 4723, pp. 1–12. Springer, Berlin (2007)
5. Liisa, K., Jesse, R., Pekka, N., Cyrille, B.K.R., Henri, E.C., Jaakko, H., Harri, M.: Identifying the main drivers for the production and maturation of scots pine tracheids along a temperature gradient. Agric. For. Meteorol. **232**, 210–224 (2017)
6. Roderick, J.A.L., Donald, B.R.: Statistical Analysis with Missing Data. Wiley Series in probability and mathematical statistics. John Wiley & Sons (1986)
7. Jesse, R., Luca, M., Jaakko, H.: Multi-label methods for prediction with sequential data. Pattern Recogn. **63**, 45–55 (2017)
8. Jesse, R., Indrė, Ž., Jaakko, H.: Labeling sensing data for mobility modeling. Inf. Syst. **57**, 207–222 (2016)
9. Ehud, R., Robert, D.: Building Natural Language Generation Systems. Cambridge University Press (1999)
10. Mika, S., Jarkko, T., Jaakko, H.: Sparse regression for analyzing the development of foliar nutrient concentrations in coniferous trees. Ecol. Model. **191**(1), 118–130 (2006)
11. Robert, T.: Regression shrinkage and selection via the lasso. J. J. Roy. Stat. Soc. B **58**(1), 267–288 (1996)
12. Jarkko, T., Jaakko, H.: A sequential input selection algorithm for long-term prediction of time series. Neurocomputing **71**(13–15), 2604–2615 (2008)
13. Indrė, Ž., Jaakko, H.: Optimizing regression models for data streams with missing values. Mach. Learn. **99**(1), 47–73 (2015)
14. Indrė, Ž., Jaakko, H., Heikki, J.: Regression models tolerant to massively missing data: a case study in solar radiation nowcasting. Atmos. Meas. Tech. **7**(12), 4387–4399 (2014)

Contents

Petri Nets, Games and Relaxed Data Structures

Graph Theory and Scheduling Algorithms

Quantum and Matrix Algorithms

Planar and Molecular Graphs

Coloring and Vertex Covers

Algorithms for Strings and Formal Languages

Data, Information and Knowledge Engineering

Software Engineering: Methods, Tools, Applications

Foundations in Computer Science

Dependable and Optimal Cyber-Physical Systems

Kim Guldstrand Larsen[✉]

Department of Computer Science, Aalborg University, Selma Lagerlöfs Vej 300,
9220 Aalborg East, Denmark
kgl@cs.aau.dk

1 Cyber-Physical Systems

Cyber-Physical Systems (CPS) describe systems combining computing elements with dedicated hardware and software having to monitor and control a particular physical environment. This combination of the physical with a virtual world provides the digital foundation for smart solutions throughout society and within all sectors. The constant demand for increased functionality and performance that needs to be produced with tight time schedules and cost budges challenges without compromising dependability of the final products constitutes a significant challenge.

What is needed are improved, scalable methods, tools and techniques that support the development of CPS. For this we propose a model-based approached for the design of dependable and optimal CPS, powered by the tool UPPAAL (www.uppaal.org) [8]. The underlying formalism of UPPAAL of timed automata with support for so-called model checking. However, the most recent branches of the UPPAAL tool suite – UPPAAL SMC and UPPAAL STRATEGO– allows for performance evaluation as well as automatic synthesis of optimal and safe controllers for the much richer formalisms of stochastic hybrid automata and games.

The importance of CPS is clear within the domains of energy and transport with the emergence Smart Grid, Home Automation, Autonomous Driving and Advanced Driver Assistance, where optimizing yet critical functionality is provided by intelligent and flexible software components.

To illustrate the usage of UPPAAL STRATEGO within these two domains we first describe in Sect. 2 the formalism of (weighted and stochastic) timed automata and games by means of a small Route Choosing Problem. In Sect. 3 we summarize the application of UPPAAL STRATEGO to the synthesis of a safe and optimal adaptive cruise control [7], and in Sect. 4 we summarize the applicaiton of UPPAAL STRATEGO to the synthesis of optimal floor heating system [6].

2 Stochastic Priced Timed Games

UPPAAL STRATEGO [2,3] is a novel branch of the UPPAAL tool suite that allows to generate, optimize, compare and explore consequences and performance of

© Springer International Publishing AG 2017
B. Steffen et al. (Eds.): SOFSEM 2017, LNCS 10139, pp. 3–10, 2017.
DOI: 10.1007/978-3-319-51963-0_1

strategies synthesized for stochastic priced timed games (SPTG) in a user-friendly manner. In particular, UPPAAL STRATEGO comes with an extended query language (see Table 1), where strategies are first class objects that may be constructed, compared, optimized and used when performing (statistical) model checking of a game under the constraints of a given synthesized strategy.

Table 1. Various types of UPPAAL STRATEGO queries: "`strategy S =`" means strategy assignment and "`under S`" is strategy usage via strategy identifier S. Here the variables NS, DS and SS correspond to non-deterministic, deterministic and stochastic strategies respectively; **bound** is a bound expression on time or cost like `x<=100` and n is the number of simulations.

Strategy generators using [2]:	
Minimize objective:	`strategy DS = minE (expr) [bound]: <> prop`
Maximize objective:	`strategy DS = maxE (expr) [bound]: <> prop under NS`
Strategy generators using UPPAAL TIGA:	
Guarantee objective:	`strategy NS = control: A<> prop`
Guarantee objective:	`strategy NS = control: A[] prop`
Statistical Model Checking Queries:	
Hypothesis testing:	`Pr[bound](<> prop)>=0.1 under SS`
Evaluation:	`Pr[bound](<> prop) under SS`
Comparison:	`Pr[bound](<> prop1) under SS1 >= Pr[<=20](<> prop2) under SS2`
Expected value:	`value E[bound;n](min: prop) under SS`
Simulations:	`simulate n [bound] { expr1, expr2 } under SS`
Symbolic model checking queries:	
Safety:	`A[] prop under NS`
Liveness:	`A<> prop under NS`
Infimum of value:	`inf { condition } : expression`
Supremum of value:	`sup { condition } : expression`

To illustrate the features of UPPAAL STRATEGO, let us look at the example in Fig. 1, providing an "extended" timed automata based model of a car, that needs to make it from its initial position Start to the final position End. In fact the model constitutes a timed *game*, where the driver of the car twice needs to make a decision as to whether (s)he wants to use a high road (H1 and H2) or a low road (L1 and L2). The four roads differ in their required travel-time (up to 100 min respectively 50 min as reflected by the invariants on the clock x). Also the roads differ in fuel-consumption reflected by the difference in the rate of the continuous variable fc (representing the total amount of fuel consumed).

Whereas the choice of road is up to the driver of the car to control (indicated by the solid transitions), the actual travel-time of the road is uncontrollable (indicated by the dashed transitions) reflecting the uncertainty of the amount of traffic on the particular day. In one scenario, the objective of the car it to choose the combination of roads that will ensure the shortest overall travel-time even

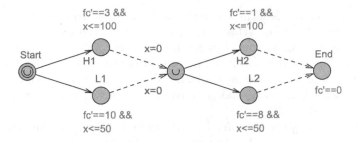

Fig. 1. The route choice problem for a car.

in the most hostile traffic situation on the four roads. Under this interpretation, Fig. 1 represents a timed game. However, it may also be seen as a stochastic priced timed game (SPTG), assuming that the travel-times of the four roads are chosen by uniform distributions, and the objective of the control strategy is to minimize the expected overall travel-time, or the expected overall fuel-consumption (e.g. the rate or fuel-consumption `fc'==3` on the first high road `H1` indicates that the cost variable `fc` grows with rate 3 in this location).

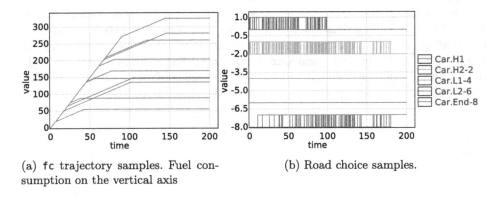

(a) `fc` trajectory samples. Fuel consumption on the vertical axis

(b) Road choice samples.

Fig. 2. Evaluation of strategy `Opt` via simulation.

We are interested in synthesizing strategies for various objectives. Being primarily concerned with fuel-consumption, the query

$$\texttt{strategy Opt = minE (fc) [<=200] : <> Car.End}$$

will provide (by reinforcement learning[1]) the strategy `Opt`, that minimizes the expected total fuel-consumption, learning from runs which are maximally 200 time units long. The relativized query `E[<=200 ; 1000] (max: fc) under Opt`,

---

[1] The reinforcement learning uses machine learning techniques to learn strategies from sets of randomly generated runs. See [2] for more details.

generates 1000 runs of length 200 time units and then averages the maximum value of `fc` from each run. this is used to estimate the expected cost to be 200.39. Figure 2a summarizes 10 random runs according `Opt` illustrating fuel-consumption. None of the runs had a fuel consumption of 400 indicating that we always choose the energy-efficient roads. In Fig. 2b we see that this is actually the case as the simulations always choose to go to locations `H1` and `H2`, which models the energy-efficient roads.

Now, assume that the task *must* be completed before 150 time-units. From Fig. 2 it can be seen that the strategy `Opt` unfortunately does not guarantee this, as there are a few runs which exceeds 150 before reaching `End`. However, the query

> `strategy Safe = control: A<> Car.End and time<=150`

will generate the most permissive (non-deterministic) strategy `Safe` that guarantees this bound but unfortunately with a high expected total fuel-consumption of 342.19. However, the relativized learning query

> `strategy OptSafe = minE (fc) [<=200] : <> Car.End under Safe`

will provide a sub-strategy `OptSafe` that minimizes the expected total fuel-consumption – here found to be 279.87 – subject to the constraints of `Safe`. Figure 3 summarizes 10 random runs according to `SafeOpt`, incidating that only road `L1` is never choosen. Also, the failed model checking of `E<> Car.H2 and time>=51 and Car.x==0 under Safe` reveals that the high road `H2` may only be choosen in case the first phase is completed before 50 time-units, confirming the observations from the simulations.

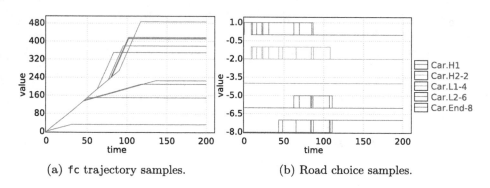

(a) `fc` trajectory samples.   (b) Road choice samples.

Fig. 3. Evaluation of strategy `OptSafe` via simulation.

In general, as shown in the overview Fig. 4, UPPAAL STRATEGO will start from a SPTG $\mathcal{P}$. It can then abstract $\mathcal{P}$ into a timed game (TGA) $\mathcal{G}$ by simply ignoring prices and stochasticity in the model. Using $\mathcal{G}$, UPPAAL TIGA [1] may

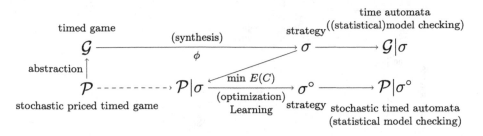

Fig. 4. Overview of UPPAAL STRATEGO

now be used to (symbolically) synthesize a (most permissive) strategy σ meeting a required safety or (time-bounded) liveness constraint ϕ. The TGA $\mathcal{G}$ under σ (denoted $\mathcal{G}|\sigma$) may now be subject to additional (statistical) model checking using classical UPPAAL[8] and UPPAAL SMC [4,5]. Similarly, the original STGA $\mathcal{P}$ under σ may be subject to statistical model checking. Now using reinforcement learning [2], we may synthesize near-optimal strategies that minimizes (maximizes) the expectation of a given cost-expression *cost*. In case the learning is performed from $\mathcal{P}|\sigma$, we obtain a sub-strategy σ^o of σ that optimizes the expected value of *cost* subject to the hard constraints guaranteed by σ. Finally, given σ^o, one may perform additional statistical model checking of $\mathcal{P}|\sigma^o$.

3   Adaptive Cruise Control

These days the Google Self-Driving car is about to become a reality: legislation has been passed in several U.S. states allowing driverless cars, in April 2014, Google announced that their vehicles had been logging nearly 1.1 million km, and it is forecast that Google's self-driving cars will hit the roads this summer. Also, in Europe driverless cars have been actively pursued, both by the automotive industry itself and within a number of national and European research projects (e.g. FP7 and Horizon2020). With more and more traffic, European roads are becoming increasingly congested, polluted and unsafe. One potential solution to this growing problem is seen to be the use of small, automated, low-polluting vehicles for driverless transport in (and between) cities. Within the last decade, a number of European projects have been launched for making transport systems capable of fully automated driving, energy efficient and environmentally friendly while performing. In addition, many individual driving assistant systems based on suitable sensors have been developed for cars.

In [7], we have considered a small part of lane-change manoeuvres, namely the existence of a safe-distance controller (assumed in the above work of Olderog et al.). In particular, we demonstrated how UPPAAL STRATEGO may be applied to automatically obtain a safe yet optimal adaptive strategy `safe` for the cruice control. Modelling the cruice control as a game with a car in front a *safe* strategy was synthezed ensuring that the distance to the front care would never get below 5 m. In fact utilizing the distinct feature of UPPAAL STRATEGO– allowing

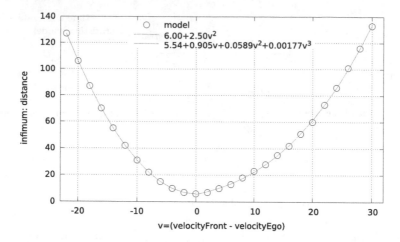

Fig. 5. Smallest distance possible under the `safe` strategy as a function of speed difference computed using `inf{velocityFront-velocityEgo==v}`: `distance under safe`
for each v value. Connecting lines are from linear regression analysis.

additional properties to be verified of a synthesized strategy – we may verify the
smallest distance possible to the front care which will not violate the `safe` as
shown in Fig. 5.

Now asking for a sub-strategy `safeFast` of `safe` that will minimize the
expected accumulated distance to the front care yields a substantial improvement as seen in Fig. 6.

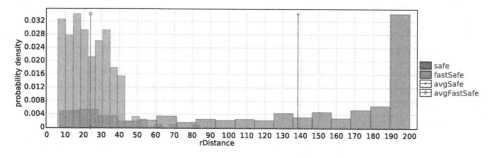

Fig. 6. The probability density distribution over `rDistance` at `time >= 100` thus after
100 time units under the strategies `safe` and `safeFast`. The (dark) red bars for `safe`
and the (light) green bars for `safeFast`. (Color figure online)

4   Home Automation

Home automation includes the centralized control of a number of functionalities
in a house such as lighting, HVAC (heating, ventilation and air conditioning),

appliances, security locks of gates and doors as well as other systems. The overall goal is to achieve improved convenience, comfort, energy efficiency as well as security. The popularity of home automation has increased significantly in recent years through affordable smartphone and tablet connectivity. Also the emergence of "Internet of Things" has tied in closely with the popularization of home automation.

In [6] we collaborated with the Danish company Seluxit within the European project CASSTING[2]. The focus was on the floorheating system of a family house, where each room of the house has its own hot-water pipe circuit. These are controlled through a number of valves based on information about room temperatures communicated wirelessly (periodically due to energy considerations) from a number of temperature sensors. In the existing system, a simple "Bang-Bang"-like strategy is applied, however, there are though several problems with this strategy, as experienced by the house owner: it completely disregards the interaction between rooms in terms of heat-exchange, the impact of the outside temperature and weather forecast as well as information about movements in the house. Taking this knowledge into account should potentially enable the synthesis of significantly improved control strategies. Unfortunately, direct application of UPPAAL STRATEGO does not scale: due to the enormous number of control modes it is virtually impossible to learn optimal control. Instead, we proposed a novel on-line synthesis methodology, where we periodically—and on-line—learn the optimal controller for the near future based on the current sensor readings. For additional scalability, we proposed and applied a novel compositional synthesis approach.

In particular, the strategy provided by UPPAAL STRATEGO takes weather information into account, as illustrated by Fig. 7 showing the spring stability scenario. From points of time between 0 and 500 min, the outside temperature increases and exceeds the target temperature. We observe that since the controller synthesized by UPPAAL STRATEGO is able to look at the weather forecast for the next 45 min, it shuts down the valves much earlier than the other controllers. This results in energy savings and increased comfort.

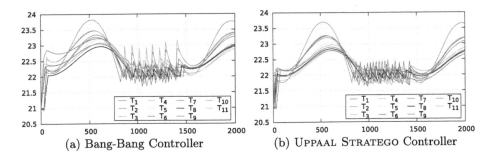

(a) Bang-Bang Controller   (b) UPPAAL STRATEGO Controller

Fig. 7. Room temperatures in the spring stability scenario

---

[2] http://www.cassting-project.eu/.

References

1. Behrmann, G., Cougnard, A., David, A., Fleury, E., Larsen, K.G., Lime, D.: UPPAAL-Tiga: time for playing games!. In: Damm, W., Hermanns, H. (eds.) CAV 2007. LNCS, vol. 4590, pp. 121–125. Springer, Berlin (2007). doi:10.1007/978-3-540-73368-3_14

2. David, A., Jensen, P.G., Larsen, K.G., Legay, A., Lime, D., Sørensen, M.G., Taankvist, J.H.: On time with minimal expected cost!. In: Cassez, F., Raskin, J.-F. (eds.) ATVA 2014. LNCS, vol. 8837, pp. 129–145. Springer, Heidelberg (2014). doi:10.1007/978-3-319-11936-6_10

3. David, A., Jensen, P.G., Larsen, K.G., Mikučionis, M., Taankvist, J.H.: UPPAAL STRATEGO. In: Baier, C., Tinelli, C. (eds.) TACAS 2015. LNCS, vol. 9035, pp. 206–211. Springer, Heidelberg (2015). doi:10.1007/978-3-662-46681-0_16

4. David, A., Larsen, K.G., Legay, A., Mikucionis, M., Poulsen, D.B.: Uppaal SMC tutorial. STTT 17(4), 397–415 (2015)

5. David, A., Larsen, K.G., Legay, A., Mikučionis, M., Wang, Z.: Time for statistical model checking of real-time systems. In: Gopalakrishnan, G., Qadeer, S. (eds.) CAV 2011. LNCS, vol. 6806, pp. 349–355. Springer, Heidelberg (2011). doi:10.1007/978-3-642-22110-1_27

6. Larsen, K.G., Mikučionis, M., Muñiz, M., Srba, J., Taankvist, J.H.: Online and compositional learning of controllers with application to floor heating. In: Chechik, M., Raskin, J.-F. (eds.) TACAS 2016. LNCS, vol. 9636, pp. 244–259. Springer, Heidelberg (2016). doi:10.1007/978-3-662-49674-9_14

7. Larsen, K.G., Mikučionis, M., Taankvist, J.H.: Safe and optimal adaptive cruise control. In: Meyer, R., Platzer, A., Wehrheim, H. (eds.) Correct System Design. LNCS, vol. 9360, pp. 260–277. Springer, Heidelberg (2015). doi:10.1007/978-3-319-23506-6_17

8. Larsen, K.G., Pettersson, P., Yi, W.: UPPAAL in a nutshell. STTT 1(1–2), 134–152 (1997)

Verifying Parametric Thread Creation

Igor Walukiewicz

CNRS, LaBRI, University of Bordeaux, Bordeaux, France

Abstract. Automatic verification of concurrent systems is an active area of research since at least a quater of a century. We focus here on analyses of systems designed to operate with an arbitrary number of processes. German and Sistla, already in 1992, initiated in depth investigation of this problem for finite state systems. For infinite state systems, like pushdown systems, extra care is needed to avoid undecidability, as reachability is undecidable even for two identical pushdown processes communicating via single variable. Kahlon and Gupta in 2006 have proposed to use parametrization as means of bypassing this undecidability barrier. Indeed when instead of two pushdown processes we consider some unspecified number of them, the reachability problem becomes decidable. This idea of parametrization as an abstraction has been pursued further by Hague, who in 2011 has shown that the problem is still decidable when one of the pushdown processes is made different from the others: there is one leader process and many contributor processes. We discuss how the idea of parametrization as an abstraction leads to decidability, and in some cases even efficient algorithms, for verification of systems which combine recursion with dynamic thread creation.

1 An Overview

We consider recursive programs with thread creation. A thread can be abstracted as a pushdown process. Communication between threads is via global variables as well as via local variables that are shared between a thread and its sub-threads. This setting is an abstraction of a situation found today in many programming languages such as Java, Scala, or Erlang.

While this setting can model many phenomena in programming languages, it is not adapted to automatic verification. Reachability is not decidable even for the case when there are two threads communicating over a 2-bit shared variable. In absence of global variables, reachability becomes undecidable already for two pushdown threads if a rendez-vous primitive is available [19]. A similar result holds if finitely many locks are allowed [11].

We obtain a decidable setting by relaxing the semantics of thread creation operation. Instead of creating one thread the operation creates some unspecified number of threads. The general idea goes back to Kahlon, who observed that various verification problems become decidable for multi-pushdown systems that are *parametric* [10], i.e., systems consisting of an arbitrary number of indistinguishable pushdown threads. Later, Hague extended this result by showing that

© Springer International Publishing AG 2017
B. Steffen et al. (Eds.): SOFSEM 2017, LNCS 10139, pp. 11–14, 2017.
DOI: 10.1007/978-3-319-51963-0_2

an extra designated leader thread can be added without sacrificing decidability [9]. All threads communicate here over a shared, bounded register *without* locking. It is crucial for decidability that only one thread has an identity, and that the operations on the shared variable do not allow to elect a second leader.

The setting of Hague has attracted some attention in recent years. Esparza et al. established the complexity of deciding reachability in that model [7]. La Torre et al. generalized these results to hierarchically nested models for a fixed nesting depth [14]. Durand-Gasselin et al. [6] have shown decidability of the liveness problem for this model. It turns out that the problem has a surprisingly low complexity, namely it is PSPACE-complete [8]. Another problem that has been considered is universal reachability: this is the question of deciding if on every maximal execution trace of the system, the leader reaches some designated state. In terms of temporal logics, reachability is about EF properties, while universal reachability is about AF properties. While still decidable, this problem has very different nature and it turns out to be coNEXPTIME-complete [8]. Indeed, generalizing this result we obtain that all stuttering LTL properties of the leader process can be decided in coNEXPTIME.

The results above concern the case with one leader process that issues one thread creation operation resulting in some number of sub-processes who do not create any new sub-processes. It turns out that we can go even further and have a decidable model for recursive programs with parametric thread creation [18]. Reachability is decidable for a very general class of processes. Every sub-process can maintain a local pushdown store, spawn new sub-processes, and communicate over global variables, as well as via local variables with its sub-processes and with its parent. As in [7,9,14], all variables have bounded domains and no locks are allowed.

The algorithm for deciding reachability in this expressive model relies on well-quasi-orders, so its complexity is very high. Yet, there are simpler instances where we know algorithms of a reasonable complexity [18]. As one such instance, we consider the situation where communication between sub-processes is through global variables only. We show that reachability for this model can be effectively reduced to reachability in the model of Hague [7,9], giving us a precise characterization of the complexity for pushdown threads as PSPACE. As another instance, we consider a parametric variant of *generalized futures* where spawned sub-processes may not only return a single result but create a stream of answers. For that model, we obtain complexities between NP and DEXPTIME. This opens the venue to apply e.g. SAT-solving to check safety properties of such programs.

2   Related Work

There are other approaches than parametrization to get a decidable model of recursive programs with thread creation.

One approoach is to consider systems with locks. As we have mentioned, the model with locks is undecidable even if there are no shared variables, no rendez-vous, or other means of communication between processes. Interestingly, decidability is regained if locking is performed in a disciplined way. This is, e.g., the case for nested [11] and contextual locking [5]. These decidability results have been extended to dynamic pushdown networks as introduced by Bouajjani et al. [4]. This model combines pushdown threads with dynamic thread creation by means of a spawn operation, while it ignores any exchange of data between threads. Indeed, reachability of dedicated states or even regular sets of configurations stays decidable in this model, if finitely many global locks together with nested locking [15,17] or contextual locking [16] are allowed. Such regular sets allow, e.g., to describe undesirable situations such as concurrent execution of conflicting operations.

Another approach is to bound the number of switches of execution contexts. A simple definition of an execution context is a part of an execution when only one process reads from its stack. A context switch is when some other process starts reading from its stack. So the reachability problem now asks for an execution with a given fixed number of context switches. Many decidability results have been established in the last decade for more and more refined notions of context switching [1–3,12,13]. In [1,3], dynamic thread creation is allowed.

References

1. Atig, M.F., Bouajjani, A., Qadeer, S.: Context-bounded analysis for concurrent programs with dynamic creation of threads. Logical Meth. Comput. Sci. **7**(4), 1–48 (2011)
2. Bollig, B., Gastin, P., Schubert, J.: Parameterized verification of communicating automata under context bounds. In: Ouaknine, J., Potapov, I., Worrell, J. (eds.) RP 2014. LNCS, vol. 8762, pp. 45–57. Springer, Heidelberg (2014). doi:10.1007/978-3-319-11439-2_4
3. Bouajjani, A., Esparza, J., Schwoon, S., Strejcek, J.: Reachability analysis of multithreaded software with asynchronous communication. In: Sarukkai, S., Sen, S. (eds.) FSTTCS 2005. LNCS, vol. 3821, pp. 348–359. Springer, Heidelberg (2005). doi:10.1007/11590156_28
4. Bouajjani, A., Müller-Olm, M., Touili, T.: Regular symbolic analysis of dynamic networks of pushdown systems. In: Abadi, M., Alfaro, L. (eds.) CONCUR 2005. LNCS, vol. 3653, pp. 473–487. Springer, Heidelberg (2005). doi:10.1007/11539452_36
5. Chadha, R., Madhusudan, P., Viswanathan, M.: Reachability under contextual locking. In: Flanagan, C., König, B. (eds.) TACAS 2012. LNCS, vol. 7214, pp. 437–450. Springer, Heidelberg (2012)
6. Durand-Gasselin, A., Esparza, J., Ganty, P., Majumdar, R.: Model checking parameterized asynchronous shared-memory systems. In: Kroening, D., Păsăreanu, C.S. (eds.) CAV 2015. LNCS, vol. 9206, pp. 67–84. Springer, Heidelberg (2015). doi:10.1007/978-3-319-21690-4_5
7. Esparza, J., Ganty, P., Majumdar, R.: Parameterized verification of asynchronous shared-memory systems. J. ACM **63**(1), 10 (2016)
8. Fortin, M., Muscholl, A., Walukiewicz, I.: On parametrized verification of asynchronous, shared-memory pushdown systems. CoRR, abs/1606.08707 (2016)

9. Hague, M.: Parameterised pushdown systems with non-atomic writes. In: Chakraborty, S., Kumar, A. (eds.) IARCS Annual Conference on Foundations of Software Technology and Theoretical Computer Science, FSTTCS 12–14, 2011, Mumbai, India, vol. 13 of LIPIcs, pp. 457–468. Schloss Dagstuhl - Leibniz-Zentrum für Informatik, December 2011

10. Kahlon, V.: Parameterization as abstraction: a tractable approach to the dataflow analysis of concurrent programs. In: Proceedings of the Twenty-Third Annual IEEE Symposium on Logic in Computer Science, LICS 2008, 24–27 , Pittsburgh, PA, USA, pp. 181–192. IEEE Computer Society, June 2008

11. Kahlon, V., Ivančić, F., Gupta, A.: Reasoning about threads communicating via locks. In: Etessami, K., Rajamani, S.K. (eds.) CAV 2005. LNCS, vol. 3576, pp. 505–518. Springer, Heidelberg (2005). doi:10.1007/11513988_49

12. La Torre, S., Madhusudan, P., Parlato, G.: Model-checking parameterized concurrent programs using linear interfaces. In: Touili, T., Cook, B., Jackson, P. (eds.) CAV 2010. LNCS, vol. 6174, pp. 629–644. Springer, Heidelberg (2010). doi:10.1007/978-3-642-14295-6_54

13. La Torre, S., Madhusudan, P., Parlato, G.: Sequentializing parameterized programs. In: FIT 2012, EPTCS, vol. 87, pp. 34–47 (2012)

14. La Torre, S., Muscholl, A., Walukiewicz, I.: Safety of parametrized asynchronous shared-memory systems is almost always decidable. In: Aceto, L., de Frutos-Escrig, D. (eds.) 26th International Conference on Concurrency Theory, CONCUR, LIPIcs, Madrid, Spain, September 1.4, vol. 42, pp. 72–84. Schloss Dagstuhl - Leibniz-Zentrum für Informatik (2015)

15. Lammich, P., Müller-Olm, M.: Conflict analysis of programs with procedures, dynamic thread creation, and monitors. In: Alpuente, M., Vidal, G. (eds.) SAS 2008. LNCS, vol. 5079, pp. 205–220. Springer, Heidelberg (2008)

16. Lammich, P., Müller-Olm, M., Seidl, H., Wenner, A.: Contextual locking for dynamic pushdown networks. In: Logozzo, F., Fähndrich, M. (eds.) SAS 2013. LNCS, vol. 7935, pp. 477–498. Springer, Heidelberg (2013). doi:10.1007/978-3-642-38856-9_25

17. Lammich, P., Müller-Olm, M., Wenner, A.: Predecessor sets of dynamic pushdown networks with tree-regular constraints. In: Bouajjani, A., Maler, O. (eds.) CAV 2009. LNCS, vol. 5643, pp. 525–539. Springer, Heidelberg (2009). doi:10.1007/978-3-642-02658-4_39

18. Muscholl, A., Seidl, H., Walukiewicz, I.: Reachability for dynamic parametric processes. CoRR, abs/1609.05385 (2016)

19. Ramalingam, G.: Context-sensitive synchronization-sensitive analysis is undecidable. ACM Trans. Program. Lang. Syst. **22**(2), 416–430 (2000)

Network Constructors: A Model
for Programmable Matter

Othon Michail[1,2(✉)] and Paul G. Spirakis[1,2]

[1] Department of Computer Science, University of Liverpool, Liverpool, UK
{Othon.Michail,P.Spirakis}@liverpool.ac.uk
[2] Computer Technology Institute and Press "Diophantus" (CTI), Patras, Greece

Abstract. We discuss recent theoretical models for programmable matter operating in a dynamic environment. In the basic *Network Constructors* model, all devices are finite automata, begin from the same initial state, execute the same protocol, and can only interact in pairs. The interactions are scheduled by a *fair* (or uniform random) scheduler, in the spirit of *Population Protocols*. When two devices interact, the protocol takes as input their states and the state of the connection between them (*on/off*) and updates all of them. Initially all connections are *off*. The goal of such protocols is to eventually construct a desired stable network, induced by the edges that are *on*. We present protocols and lower bounds for several basic network construction problems and also universality results. We next highlight minimal strengthenings of the model, that can be exploited by appropriate network-transformation protocols in order to achieve *termination* and the *maximum computational power* that one can hope for in this family of models. Finally, we discuss a more applied version of these abstract models, enriched with geometric constraints, aiming at capturing some first physical restrictions in potential future programmable matter systems operating in dynamic environments.

1 Introduction

The realization of computing systems and computer networks was indisputably one of the most outstanding achievements of science and engineering of the last century. The impact of Information and Communication Technologies on society, industry, and everyday life was incomparable. Digital communications and the Internet have made the world look much smaller, personal computers radically changed office work, largely simplifying it, high processing speeds made it possible for the first time to simulate and accurately predict a wide range of physical phenomena, from weather forecast to chemical reactions and whole-cell simulations [KSM+12], and combined to increased storage capabilities, transformed the

Supported in part by the School of EEE/CS of the University of Liverpool, NeST initiative, and the EU IP FET-Proactive project MULTIPLEX under contract no 317532.

B. Steffen et al. (Eds.): SOFSEM 2017, LNCS 10139, pp. 15–34, 2017.
DOI: 10.1007/978-3-319-51963-0_3

world of paper to a world of digital information, where everything, from a data-trace of successful collisions in CERN that produced the Higgs boson [CKS+12] to the human genome, can be stored and retrieved. Computing and Information Sciences have been extremely successful in revealing the laws underlying all possible ways of manipulating information. Every possible object, system or problem can be encoded in an appropriate binary representation, which can then be stored, processed, retrieved and transmitted. It would be reasonable to say that the 20th century was *the century of information*.

However, the story does not seem to end here. The established knowledge of manipulating information seems to have opened the road towards a vision that will further reshape society to an unprecedented degree. This vision concerns our ability to *manipulate matter* via information-theoretic and computing mechanisms and principles. It will be the jump from amorphous information to the *incorporation of information to the physical world*. Information will not only be part of the physical environment: it will constantly interact with the surrounding environment and will have the ability to reshape it. *Matter will become programmable* [GCM05] which is a plausible future outcome of progress in high-volume nanoscale assembly that makes it feasible to inexpensively produce millimeter-scale units that integrate computing, sensing, actuation, and locomotion mechanisms. This will enable the astonishing possibility of transferring the discrete dynamics from the computer memory black-box to the real world and to achieve a *physical realization of any computer-generated object*. "It will have profound implications for how we think about chemistry and materials. Materials will become user-programmed and smart, adapting to changing conditions in order to maintain, optimize or even create a whole new functionality using means that are intrinsic to the material itself. It will even change the way we think about engineering and manufacturing. We will for the first time be capable of building smart machines that adapt to their surroundings, such as an airplane wing that adjusts its surface properties in reaction to environmental variables" [Zak07], or even further realize machines that can self-built autonomously.

This vision is not a human invention. It is an inspiration from a property that pervades the biological world. Every biological organism is a collection of relatively simple units of matter (the cells) coupled with information storing, processing, and transmission capabilities. Moreover, the effort to realize this vision has already begun and the first outcomes are more than promising. For example, it has been already demonstrated that it is possible to fold long, single-stranded DNA molecules into arbitrary nanoscale two-dimensional shapes and patterns [Rot06]. Also, a system was recently reported that demonstrates programmable self-assembly of complex two-dimensional shapes with a thousand-robot swarm [RCN14]. "This was enabled by creating small, cheap, and simple autonomous robots designed to operate in large groups and to cooperate through local interactions and by developing a collective algorithm for shape formation that is highly robust to the variability and error characteristic of large-scale decentralized systems" [RCN14]. Other systems for programmable matter include the

Robot Pebbles [GKR10], consisting of 1 cm cubic programmable matter modules able to form 2-dimensional (abbreviated "2D" throughout) shapes through self-disassembly, and the Millimotein [KCL+12], a chain of programmable matter which can fold itself into digitized approximations of arbitrary 3-dimensional (abbreviated "3D" throughout) shapes.

Apart from the fact that systems work is still in its infancy, there is also an apparent lack of unifying formalism and theoretical treatment. The following are some of the very few exceptions aiming at understanding the fundamental possibilities and limitations of this prospective. The area of *algorithmic self-assembly* tries to understand how to program molecules (mainly DNA strands) to manipulate themselves, grow into machines and at the same time control their own growth [Dot12]. The theoretical model guiding the study in algorithmic self-assembly is the Abstract Tile Assembly Model (aTAM) [Win98, RW00] and variations. Recently, a model, called the *nubot* model, was proposed for studying the complexity of self-assembled structures with active molecular components [WCG+13]. This model "is inspired by biology's fantastic ability to assemble biomolecules that form systems with complicated structure and dynamics, from molecular motors that walk on rigid tracks and proteins that dynamically alter the structure of the cell during mitosis, to embryonic development where large-scale complicated organisms efficiently grow from a single cell" [WCG+13]. Another very recent model, called the *Network Constructors* model, studied what stable networks can be constructed by a population of finite-automata that interact randomly like molecules in a well-mixed solution and can establish bonds with each other according to the rules of a common small protocol [MS16b]. Interestingly, the special case of the model that cannot create bonds (known as the *Population Protocol* model [AAD+06]) is known to be formally equivalent to *chemical reaction networks* (CRNs), which model chemistry in a *well-mixed solution* and are widely used to describe information processing occurring in natural cellular regulatory networks [Dot14]. Also the recently proposed *Amoebot* model, offers a versatile framework to model self-organizing particles and facilitates rigorous algorithmic research in the area of programmable matter [DDG+14, DGP+16].

At the same time, recent research in distributed computing theory and practice is taking its first timid steps on the pioneering endeavor of investigating the possible *relationships of distributed computing systems to physical and biological systems*. The first main motivation for this is the fact that a wide range of physical and biological systems are governed by underlying laws that are essentially *algorithmic*. The second is that the higher-level physical or behavioral properties of such systems are usually the outcome of the coexistence, which may include both cooperation and competition, and constant interaction of *very large numbers of relatively simple distributed entities* respecting such laws. This effort, to the extent that its perspective allows, is expected to promote our understanding on the algorithmic aspects of our (distributed) natural world and to develop innovative artificial systems inspired by them.

In the present paper, we shall focus on the Network Constructors model and its existing variations. In Sect. 2, we present the basic Network Constructors model and give the main definitions to be used in the sequel. In Sect. 3, we present protocols for the spanning line construction problem and bounds for other basic network construction problems. Section 4 goes one step further, showing how one can establish universality results. In Sect. 5, we show how network-transformation protocols can exploit minimal strengthenings of the basic model, in order to maximize the computational power. Section 6 discusses a geometric variant of the basic model, in which the nodes can be programmed to self-assemble into complex 2D or 3D shapes. Finally, Sect. 7 highlights some promising directions for future research.

2   The Network Constructors Model

Suppose a set of tiny computational devices (possibly at the nanoscale) are injected into a human circulatory system for the purpose of monitoring or even treating a disease. The devices are incapable of controlling their mobility. The mobility of the devices, and consequently the interactions between them, stems solely from the dynamicity of the environment, the blood flow inside the circulatory system in this case. Additionally, each device alone is incapable of performing any useful computation, as the small scale of the device highly constrains its computational capabilities. The goal is for the devices to accomplish their task via cooperation. To this end, the devices are equipped with a mechanism that allows them to create bonds with other devices (mimicking nature's ability to do so). So, whenever two devices come sufficiently close to each other and interact, apart from updating their local states, they may also become connected by establishing a physical connection between them. Moreover, two connected devices may at some point choose to drop their connection. In this manner, the devices can organize themselves into a desired global structure. This network-constructing self-assembly capability allows the artificial population of devices to evolve greater complexity, better storage capacity, and to adapt and optimize its performance to the needs of the specific task to be accomplished.

Our goal in [MS16b] was to study the fundamental problem of *network construction* by a distributed computing system. The system consists of a set of n processes that are capable of performing local computation (via pairwise interactions) and of forming and deleting connections between them. Connections between processes can be either *physical* or *virtual* depending on the application. In the most general case, a connection between two processes can be in one of a finite number of possible states. For example, state 0 could mean that the connection does not exist while state $i \in \{1, 2, \ldots, k\}$, for some finite k, that the connection exists and has strength i. We considered the simplest case, which we call the *on/off* case, in which, at any time, a connection can either exist or not exist; that is, there are just two states for the connections, 1 and 0, respectively. If a connection exists we also say that it is *active* and if it does not exist we say that it is *inactive*. Initially all connections are inactive and the goal is for the processes, after interacting and activating/deactivating connections for a while, to end up with a desired *stable network*. In the simplest case, the output-network is the one induced by the active connections and it is stable when no connection changes state any more.

Our aim in [MS16b] was to initiate this study by proposing and studying a very *simple*, yet sufficiently generic, model for distributed network construction. To this end, we assumed the computationally weakest type of processes. In particular, the processes are finite automata that all begin from the same initial state and all execute the same finite program which is stored in their memory (i.e., the system is *homogeneous*). The communication model that we considered is also very minimal. In particular, we considered processes that are inhabitants of an *adversarial environment* that has total control over the inter-process interactions. Such an environment is modeled by an adversary scheduler that operates in discrete steps, selecting in every step a pair of processes which then interact according to the common program. This represents very well systems of (not necessarily computational) entities that interact in pairs whenever two of them come sufficiently close to each other. When two processes interact, the program takes as input the states of the interacting processes and the state of their connection and outputs a new state for each process and a new state for the connection. The only restriction that we imposed on the scheduler, in order to study the constructive power of the model, is that it is *fair*, by which we mean the weak requirement that, at every step, it assigns to every reachable configuration of the system a non-zero probability to occur. In other words, a fair scheduler cannot forever conceal an always reachable configuration of the system. Note that under such a generic scheduler, we cannot bound the running time of our constructors. To estimate the efficiency of our solutions, we assume a *uniform random scheduler*, one of the simplest fair probabilistic schedulers. The uniform random scheduler selects in every step independently and uniformly at random a pair of processes to interact from all such pairs. What renders this model interesting is, as we shall see, its ability to achieve complex global behavior via a set of notably simple, uniform (i.e., with codes that are independent of the size of the system), homogeneous, and cooperative entities.

We now give a simple illustration of the above. Assume a set of n very weak processes that can only be in one of two states, "black" or "red". Initially, all processes are black. We can think of the processes as small particles that move randomly in a fair solution. The particles are capable of forming and deleting physical connections between them, by which we mean that, whenever two particles interact, they can read and write the state of their connection. To keep this first model as simple as possible, we assume that fairness of the solution is independent of the states of the connections.[1] In particular, we assume, for

---

[1] This is in contrast to schedulers that would take into account the geometry of the active connections and would, for example, forbid two non-neighboring particles of the same component to interact with each other. Such a geometrically restricted variant, studied in [Mic15], shall be discussed in Sect. 6.

the time being, that, throughout the execution, every pair of processes may be selected for interaction.

Consider now the following simple problem. We want to identically program the initially disorganized particles so that they become self-organized into a *spanning star*. In particular, we want to end up with a unique black particle connected (via active connections) to $n-1$ red particles and all other connections (between red particles) being inactive. Conversely, given a (possibly physical) system that tends to form a spanning star we would like to unveil the code behind this behavior.

Consider the following program. When two black particles that are not connected interact, they become connected and one of them becomes red. When two connected red particles interact they become disconnected (i.e., reds repel). Finally, when a black and a red that are not connected interact they become connected (i.e., blacks and reds attract).

The protocol forms a spanning star as follows. As whenever two blacks interact only one survives and the other becomes red, eventually a unique black will remain and all other particles will be red (we say "eventually", meaning "in finite time", because we do not know how much time it will take for all blacks to meet each other, but, from fairness, we know that this has to occur in a finite number of steps). As blacks and reds attract while reds repel, it is clear that eventually the unique black will be connected to all reds while every pair of reds will be disconnected. Moreover, no rule of the program can modify such a configuration, so the constructed spanning star is stable (see Fig. 1). It is worth noting that this very simple protocol is optimal both with respect to (abbreviated "w.r.t." throughout) the number of states that it uses and w.r.t. the time it takes to construct a stable spanning star under the uniform random scheduler.

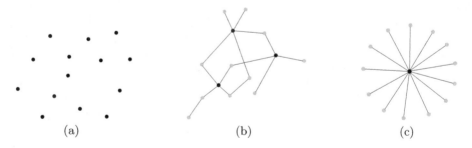

(a)   (b)   (c)

Fig. 1. (a) Initially all particles are black and no active connections exist. (b) After a while, only 3 black particles have survived each having a set of red neighbors (red particles appear as gray here). Note that some red particles are also connected to red particles. The tendency is for the red particles to repel red particles and attract black particles. (c) A unique black has survived, it has attracted all red particles, and all connections between red particles have been deactivated. The construction is a stable spanning star.

Our model for network construction has been strongly inspired by the Population Protocol model [AAD+06] and the Mediated Population Protocol model [MCS11]. In the former, connections do not have states. States on the connections were first introduced in the latter. The main difference to the present model is that *in those models the focus was on the computation of functions of some input values and not on network construction.* Another important difference is that we now allow the edges to choose between *only two possible states* which was not the case in [MCS11]. As already mentioned, when operating under a uniform random scheduler, population protocols are formally equivalent to *chemical reaction networks* (CRNs). "With upcoming advances in synthetic biology, CRNs are a promising programming language for the design of artificial molecular control circuitry" [Dot14]. However, CRNs and population protocols can only capture the dynamics of molecular counts and not of structure formation. Our model then may be also viewed as an extension of population protocols and CRNs aiming to capture the stable structures that may occur in a well-mixed solution. From this perspective, our goal is to determine what stable structures can result in such systems (natural or artificial), how fast, and under what conditions (e.g., by what underlying codes/reaction-rules).

2.1   Definitions

Definition 1. A *Network Constructor* (NET) is a distributed protocol defined by a 4-tuple $(Q, q_0, Q_{out}, \delta)$, where Q is a finite set of *node-states*, $q_0 \in Q$ is the *initial node-state*, $Q_{out} \subseteq Q$ is the set of *output node-states*, and $\delta : Q \times Q \times \{0, 1\} \rightarrow Q \times Q \times \{0, 1\}$ is the *transition function*.

The system consists of a population V_I of n distributed *processes/nodes*. In the generic case, there is an underlying *interaction graph* $G_I = (V_I, E_I)$ specifying the permissible interactions between the nodes. Interactions are always pairwise. In the basic model, G_I is a *complete undirected interaction graph*, i.e., $E_I = \{uv : u, v \in V_I \text{ and } u \neq v\}$, where $uv = \{u, v\}$. Initially, all nodes in V_I are in the initial node-state q_0. A central assumption of the model is that edges have binary states. An edge in state 0 is said to be *inactive* while an edge in state 1 said to be *active*. All edges are initially inactive.

Execution of the protocol proceeds in discrete steps. In every step, a pair of nodes uv from E_I is selected by an *adversary scheduler* and these nodes interact and update their states and the state of the edge joining them according to the transition function δ.

A *configuration* is a mapping $C : V_I \cup E_I \rightarrow Q \cup \{0, 1\}$ specifying the state of each node and each edge of the interaction graph. An *execution* is a finite or infinite sequence of configurations $C_0, C_1, C_2, \ldots$, where C_0 is an initial configuration and $C_i \rightarrow C_{i+1}$ ('$\rightarrow$' meaning "goes via a single interaction to"), for all $i \geq 0$. A *fairness condition* is imposed on the adversary to ensure the protocol makes progress. An infinite execution is *fair* if for every pair of configurations C and C' such that $C \rightarrow C'$, if C occurs infinitely often in the execution then so does C'. In what follows, every execution of a NET will by definition considered to be fair.

Whenever we study the running time (counted in number of sequential interactions) of a NET, we assume that interactions are chosen by a *uniform random scheduler* which, in every step, selects independently and uniformly at random one of the $|E_I| = n(n-1)/2$ possible interactions. In this case, the running time becomes a random variable (abbreviated "r.v." throughout) X and our goal is to obtain bounds on the expectation $E[X]$ of X. Note that the uniform random scheduler is fair with probability 1. We say that an execution of a NET on n processes *constructs a graph* (or *network*) G, if its output stabilizes to a graph isomorphic to G. We say that a NET $\mathcal{A}$ *constructs a graph language L with useful space $g(n) \leq n$*, if $g(n)$ is the greatest function for which: (i) for all n, every execution of $\mathcal{A}$ on n processes constructs a $G \in L$ of order at least $g(n)$ (provided that such a G exists) and, additionally, (ii) for all $G \in L$ there is an execution of $\mathcal{A}$ on n processes, for some n satisfying $|V(G)| \geq g(n)$, that constructs G. Equivalently, we say that $\mathcal{A}$ *constructs L with waste $n - g(n)$*. Define **REL**$(g(n))$ to be the class of all graph languages that are constructible with useful space $g(n)$ by a NET. We call **REL**$(\cdot)$ the *relation* or *on/off* class. Also define **PREL**$(g(n))$ in precisely the same way as **REL**$(g(n))$ but in the extension of the above model in which every pair of processes is capable of tossing an unbiased coin during an interaction between them. In this case, we additionally require that all graphs have the same probability to be constructed by the protocol. We denote by **DGS**$(f(l))$ (for "Deterministic Graph Space") the class of all graph languages that are decidable by a Turing Machine (abbreviated "TM" throughout) of (*binary*) space $f(l)$, where l is the length of the adjacency matrix encoding of the input graph.

3   Basic Constructors

Probably the most fundamental network-construction problem, is the problem of constructing a spanning line, i.e., a connected graph in which 2 nodes have degree 1 and $n-2$ nodes have degree 2. Its importance lies in the fact that a spanning line provides an ordering on the processes which can then be exploited (as discussed in Sect. 4) to simulate a TM and, in this way, to establish universality of the model.

We begin with a lower bound on the expected time required by any NET to construct a spanning line.

Theorem 1 (Line Lower Bound [MS16b]). *The expected time to convergence of any protocol that constructs a spanning line is $\Omega(n^2)$.*

Take any protocol $\mathcal{A}$ that constructs a spanning line and any execution of $\mathcal{A}$ on n nodes. It suffices to show that any execution necessarily passes through a "bottleneck" transition, by which we mean a transition that requires $\Omega(n^2)$ expected number of steps to occur. Observe that, in any execution, the set of active edges eventually stabilizes (in this case, to a spanning line), which implies that there is always a *last* activation/deactivation of an edge. The idea is to focus on this last operation before stabilization, and show that either this operation is a bottleneck transition or an immediately previous operation is a bottleneck transition. In both cases, any execution passes through a bottleneck transition, thus paying at that point an $\Omega(n^2)$ expected number of steps. Indeed, if the last modification was an activation, then the construction just before this modification was either a line on $n - 1$ nodes and an isolated node or two disjoint lines spanning all nodes. In both cases, the expected number of steps until the last edge becomes activated is $\Omega(n^2)$. On the other hand, if the last modification was a deactivation, then this implies that the construction just before this modification was a spanning line with an additional active edge between two nodes, u and v, that are not neighbors on the line. The only interesting case is the one in which the construction was actually a spanning ring. Then, by considering the last modification of an edge that resulted in the ring, we obtain again an expected number of $\Omega(n^2)$ interactions.

We present now our simplest protocol for the spanning line problem.

Simple-Global-Line. $Q = \{q_0, q_1, q_2, l, w\}$, δ: $(q_0, q_0, 0) \rightarrow (q_1, l, 1)$, $(l, q_0, 0) \rightarrow (q_2, l, 1)$, $(l, l, 0) \rightarrow (q_2, w, 1)$, $(w, q_2, 1) \rightarrow (q_2, w, 1)$, $(w, q_1, 1) \rightarrow (q_2, l, 1)$.

In the initial configuration C_0, all nodes are in state q_0 and all edges are inactive, i.e., in state 0. Every configuration C that is reachable from C_0 consists of a collection of lines and isolated nodes. Additionally, every line has a unique leader which either occupies an endpoint and is in state l or occupies an internal node, is in state w, and moves randomly along the line. Lines can expand towards isolated nodes and two lines can connect their endpoints to get merged into a single line (with total length equal to the sum of the lengths of the merged lines plus one). Both of these operations only take place when the corresponding endpoint of every line that takes part in the operation is in state l. A line resulting from merging, has a w internal-leader and only waits until the random walk of w reaches one endpoint and becomes an l leader. Figure 2 gives an illustration of a typical configuration of the protocol.

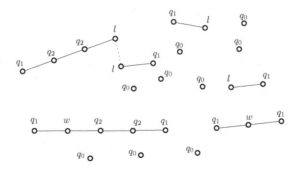

Fig. 2. A typical configuration of *Simple-Global-Line* (after some time has passed).

Theorem 2 ([MS16b]). *Protocol* Simple-Global-Line *constructs a spanning line. It uses 5 states and its expected running time is $\Omega(n^4)$ and $O(n^5)$.*

For correctness, we have to prove two things: (i) there is a set $\mathcal{S}$ of output-stable configurations whose active network is a spanning line, (ii) for every reachable configuration C it holds that $C \rightsquigarrow C_s$ ('$\rightsquigarrow$' meaning "goes in one or more steps to") for some $C_s \in \mathcal{S}$.

For the running time upper bound, we have an expected number of $O(n^2)$ steps until progress is made (i.e., for another merging to occur given that at least two l-leaders exist) and $O(n^4)$ steps for the resulting random walk (walk of state w until it reaches one endpoint of the line) to finish and to have the system again ready for progress. This is because the state actually walks only if it interacts with one of its (at most) two neighbors on the line. As only 2 interactions over the $\Theta(n^2)$ possible interactions allow the state to walk, the otherwise $O(n^2)$-time walk is delayed by a factor of $O(n^2)$. As progress must be made $n - 2$ times, we conclude that the expected running time of the protocol is bounded from above by $(n - 2)[O(n^2) + O(n^4)] = O(n^5)$.

Next, it can be proved that we cannot hope to improve the upper bound on the expected running time by a better analysis by more than a factor of n. For this, we can prove by a Chernoff bound, that the protocol with high probability (abbreviated "w.h.p." throughout) constructs $\Theta(n)$ disjoint lines of length 1 during its course. A set of k disjoint lines implies that $k - 1 = \Theta(n)$ distinct merging processes have to be executed in order to merge them all into a common line and each single merging results in the execution of another random walk. Let t_{min} be the first time at which there is a line L of length $h \geq k/4$. It holds that $k/4 \leq h \leq k/2 - 1$, so there is a remaining length of at least $k - h \geq k - (k/2 - 1) = k/2 + 1$ to get merged to L via distinct sequential mergings. Now, if d_i denotes the length of the ith line merged to L, Y the r.v. of the duration of all random walks, and Y_i the r.v. of the duration of the i-th random walk, we have $\mathrm{E}[Y] = \mathrm{E}[\sum_{i=1}^{j} Y_i] = \sum_{i=1}^{j} \mathrm{E}[Y_i] = \sum_{i=1}^{j} n^2(h + d_1 + \ldots + d_{i-1})d_i \geq n^2 \sum_{i=1}^{j} h d_i = n^2 h \sum_{i=1}^{j} d_i \geq n^2 \cdot (k/4) \cdot (k/2 + 1) = n^2 \cdot \Theta(n) \cdot \Theta(n) = \Theta(n^4)$. This proves the desired $\Omega(n^4)$ lower bound.

By using more states, we can develop an alternative protocol that constructs a spanning line much faster. The main difference between this and the previous protocol is that we now totally avoid mergings as they seem to consume much time. As before, when the leaders of two lines interact, one of them becomes eliminated and the edge is activated. But now, the leader that has survived does not initiate a merging process. Instead, it steals a node from the eliminated leader's line and disconnects the two new lines: its own line, which has increased by one and is called *awake*, and the eliminated leader's line, which has decreased by one and is called *sleeping*. The code follows:

Fast-Global-Line. $Q = \{q_0, q_1, q_2, q_2', l, l', l'', f_0, f_1\}$, δ: $(q_0, q_0, 0) \rightarrow (q_1, l, 1)$, $(l, q_0, 0) \rightarrow (q_2, l, 1)$, $(l, l, 0) \rightarrow (q_2', l', 1)$, $(l', q_2, 1) \rightarrow (l'', f_1, 0)$, $(l', q_1, 1) \rightarrow (l'', f_0, 0)$, $(l'', q_2', 1) \rightarrow (l, q_2, 1)$, $(l, f_0, 0) \rightarrow (q_2, l, 1)$, $(l, f_1, 0) \rightarrow (q_2', l', 1)$.

In more detail, when two lines L_1 and L_2 interact via their l-leader endpoints, one of the leaders, say w.l.o.g. that of L_2, becomes l' and the other becomes q_2'. We can interpret this operation as expanding L_1 on the endpoint of L_2 and obtaining two new lines (still attached to each other): L_1' which is awake and L_2' which is sleeping. Now, the l'-leader of L_1' waits to interact with its neighbor from L_2' (which is either a q_2 or a q_1) to deactivate the edge between them and disconnect L_1' from L_2'. This operation leaves L_1' with an l''-leader and L_2' with a sleeping leader f_1 (it can also be the case that L_2' is just a single isolated f_0, in case L_2 consisted only of 2 nodes). Then l'' waits to meet its q_2' neighbor to convert it to q_2 and update itself to l. This completes the operation of a line growing one step towards another line and making the other line sleep. A sleeping line cannot increase any more and only loses nodes to lines that are still awake by a similar operation as the one just described. A single leader is guaranteed to always win and this occurs quite fast. Then the unique leader does not need much time to collect all nodes from the sleeping lines to its own line and make the latter spanning.

Theorem 3 ([MS16b]). *Protocol* Fast-Global-Line *constructs a spanning line. It uses 9 states and its expected running time under the uniform random scheduler is* $O(n^3)$.

A variant that backtracks many "sleeping" lines in parallel, is an immediate improvement of *Fast-Global-Line*. The improvement is due to the fact that instead of having the awake leader backtrack sleeping lines node-by-node, we now have any sleeping line backtrack itself, so that many backtrackings occur in parallel. We have some first experimental evidence showing a small improvement in the running time [ALMS15], but we do not yet have a proof of whether this is also an asymptotic improvement. For example, is it the case that the running time of this improvement is $O(n^3/\log n)$ (or even smaller)? This question is open.

Table 1 summarizes a variety of protocols and the corresponding upper and lower bounds that are known for several basic construction problems [MS16b].

4   Generic Constructors

An immediate next question is whether there is a generic constructor capable of constructing a large class of networks. In [MS16b], we answered this in the affirmative by presenting constructors that simulate a TM. The idea is to program the nodes to organize themselves into a network that can serve as a memory of size $O(n^2)$, which is asymptotically maximum and can only be achieved by exploiting the presence or absence of bonds between nodes as the bits of the memory (if only the nodes' local space was used, then the total memory could not exceed $O(n)$). Then the population draws a random network and simulates on the distributed memory a TM that decides whether the network belongs to the target ones. If yes, the population stabilizes to it, otherwise the random

Table 1. Some established upper and lower bounds [MS16b]. *kRC* (standing for *k-regular connected*) protocol solves a generalization of global ring in which every node has degree $k \geq 2$, *c-cliques* partitions the processes into $\lfloor n/c \rfloor$ cliques of order c each, and *Graph-Replication* constructs a copy of a given input graph.

Protocol	# states	Expected time	Lower bound
Simple-Global-Line	5	$\Omega(n^4)$ and $O(n^5)$	$\Omega(n^2)$
Fast-Global-Line	9	$O(n^3)$	$\Omega(n^2)$
Cycle-Cover	3	$\Theta(n^2)$ (opt.)	$\Omega(n^2)$
Global-Star	2 (opt.)	$\Theta(n^2 \log n)$ (opt.)	$\Omega(n^2 \log n)$
Global-Ring	9		$\Omega(n^2)$
2RC	6		$\Omega(n \log n)$
kRC	$2(k+1)$		$\Omega(n \log n)$
c-cliques	$5c - 3$		$\Omega(n \log n)$
Graph-Replication	12	$\Theta(n^4 \log n)$	

experiment and the simulation are repeated (see Fig. 3). What makes the construction intricate is that all the sub-routines have to be executed in parallel and potential errors due to this to be corrected by global resets throughout the course of the protocol. This is summarized in the following theorem.

Theorem 4 (Linear Waste-Two Thirds [MS16b]). $\mathbf{DGS}(O(n^2)+O(n)) \subseteq \mathbf{PREL}(\lfloor n/3 \rfloor)$. *In words, for every graph language L that is decidable by a $(O(n^2) + O(n))$-space TM, there is a protocol that constructs L equiprobably with useful space $\lfloor n/3 \rfloor$.*

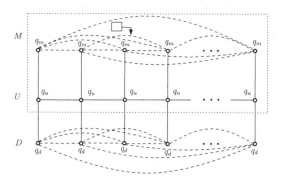

Fig. 3. A partitioning into three equal sets U, D, and M. The line of set U plays the role of an ordering that will be exploited both by the random graph drawing process and by the TM-simulation. The line of set U uses the $\Theta(n^2)$ memory of set M as the memory of the TM. Set D is the useful space on which the output-network will be constructed. Sets U and M constitute the waste.

5   Network Transformations

We shall now consider minimal strengthenings of network constructors that can maximize their computational power, also rendering them capable to terminate. To this end, we now assume that the initial configuration of the edges can be any configuration in which the active edges form *a connected graph spanning the set of processes*. This choice is motivated by the fact that, without some sort of initial connectivity (or bounded disconnectivity) we can only hope for global computations and constructions that are *eventually stabilizing* (and not *terminating*), roughly because a component can guess neither the number of components not encountered yet nor an upper bound on the time needed to interact with another one of them.[2] The initial configuration of the nodes is either, again, the one in which all nodes are initially in the same state, q_0, or (if needed) the one in which all nodes begin from q_0 apart from a pre-elected unique leader that begins from a distinct initial leader-state l. Unfortunately, even with the additional assumption of bounded initial disconnectivity, it can be proved that non-trivial terminating computation is still impossible.

We now add to the picture a very minimal and natural, but extremely powerful, additional assumption that, combined with our assumptions so far, will lead us to a stronger model. In particular, we equip the nodes with the ability to detect some small local degrees. For a concrete example, assume that a node can detect when its active degree is equal to 0 (otherwise it only knows that its degree is at least 1). A first immediate gain, is that we can now directly simulate any constructor that assumes an empty initial network (like those presented in the previous section): every node initially deactivates the active edges incident to it until its local active degree becomes for the first time 0, and only when this occurs the node starts participating in the simulation.

Our main finding in [MS16a], was that the initial connectivity guarantee together with the ability to modify the network and to detect small local degrees (combined with either a pre-elected leader or a natural mechanism that allows two nodes to tell whether they have a neighbor in common), are sufficient to obtain the *maximum computational power* that one can hope for in this family of models. In particular, the resulting model can compute *with termination* any symmetric predicate[3] computable by a *TM of space* $\Theta(n^2)$, and no more than this, i.e., it is an *exact characterization*. The symmetricity restriction can only be dropped by UIDs or by any other means of knowing and maintaining an ordering of the nodes' inputs. This power is maximal because the distributed space of the system is $\Theta(n^2)$, so we cannot hope for computations exploiting more space. The substantial improvement is that the universal computations are now *terminating* and not just *eventually stabilizing*. It is interesting to point out

---

[2] Alternative ways to overcome this are to assume that the nodes know some upper bound on this time [MS15], or, as we shall discuss in the next section, to assume a uniform random scheduler and a unique leader and restrict correctness to be w.h.p..

[3] Essentially, a predicate in this type of models is called *symmetric* (or *commutative*) if permuting the input symbols does not affect the predicate's outcome. This restriction is imposed by the fact that, in general, the nodes cannot be distinguished initially.

that the additional assumptions and mechanisms are minimal, in the sense that the removal of each one of them leads to either an impossibility of termination or to a substantial decrease in computational power.

The approach to arriving at the above characterization is to develop protocols that exploit the knowledge of the initial connectivity of the active topology and try to transform it to a less symmetric and detectable active topology, without ever breaking its connectivity. The knowledge of initial connectivity and its preservation throughout the transformation process, ensure that the protocol always has all nodes of the network in a single component. Still, if the target-network is symmetric, then there might be no way for the transformation to determine when it has managed to form the network. Instead, the protocols *transform any spanning connected initial topology into a spanning line while preserving connectivity throughout the transformation process*. The spanning line has the advantage that it can be detected under the minimal assumption that a node can detect whether its local degree is in $\{1, 2\}$ and that it is minimally symmetric and, therefore, capable of serving as a linear memory. Preservation of connectivity allows the protocol to be certain that the spanning line contains all processes. So, the protocol can detect the formation of the spanning line and then count (on the $O(\log n)$ cells, i.e., the nodes, of the linear distributed memory) the size of the system. Then the protocol can use the spanning line as it is, for simulating (on the nodes of the line) TMs of space $\Theta(n)$. Going one step further, it is not hard for a protocol to exploit all this obtained information and perform a final transformation that increases the simulation space to $\Theta(n^2)$ (in the spirit of the universal construction of the previous section).

In particular, given an initially connected active topology and the ability of the protocol to transform it, the following set of results can be proved [MS16a]:

- The running time of any protocol that transforms any initial active topology to a spanning line and terminates is $\Omega(n^2 \log n)$.
- If there is a unique leader and a node can detect whether its degree is equal to 1, then there is a time-optimal protocol, with running time $\Theta(n^2 \log n)$ (now defined as the maximum/worst-case expected running time over all possible initial active topologies), that transforms any initial active topology to a spanning line and terminates. This implies a full-power TM simulation as described above.
- If all nodes are initially identical (and even if small local degrees can be detected) then there is no protocol that can transform any initial active topology to an acyclic topology without ever breaking connectivity. The impossibility result is quite strong, proving that, for any initial topology G, there is an infinite family $\mathcal{G}$, such that if the protocol makes G acyclic then it disconnects every $G' \in \mathcal{G}$ in $\Theta(|V(G')|)$ parts. The latter implies that it is impossible to transform to a spanning line with termination.
- There is a plausible additional strengthening that allows the problem to become solvable with initially identical nodes. In particular, the assumption that two interacting nodes can tell whether they have a neighbor in common (*common neighbor detection* mechanism). It can be proved that, with

this additional assumption, initially identical nodes can transform any connected spanning initial active topology to a spanning line and terminate in time $O(n^3)$. This implies a full-power TM simulation as described above.

We now describe the aforementioned time-optimal protocol for the simplest case in which there is initially a pre-elected unique leader that handles the transformation. Recall that the initial active topology is connected and the goal is for the protocol to transform the active topology to a spanning line and when this occurs to detect it and terminate (called the Terminating Line Transformation problem). Ideally, the transformation should preserve connectivity of the active topology during its course (or break connectivity in a controlled way). The minimal additional assumption to make the problem solvable, is that a node can detect whether it has local degree 1 or 2 (otherwise it knows that it has degree in $\{0, 3, 4, ..., n-1\}$ without being able to tell its precise value).

Line-Around-a-Star. There is initially a unique leader in state l and all other nodes are in state q_0. Nodes can detect when their degree is 1.

The leader starts connecting with the q_0s (by activating the connection between them in case it was inactive and by preserving it in case it was already active) and converts them to p' trying to form a star with itself at the center. When two p's interact, if the edge is active they deactivate it, trying to become the peripherals of the star. Additionally, if after such a deactivation the degree of a p' is 1, then the p' becomes p to represent the fact that it is now connected only to the leader and has become a normal peripheral. The same occurs if after the interaction of the leader with a q_0, the degree of the q_0 is 1, i.e., the q_0 immediately becomes a normal peripheral p.

When the leader first encounters a p, it starts constructing a line which has as its "left" endpoint the center of the star and that will start expanding over the peripherals until it covers them all. Whenever the leader interacts with an internal node of the line, it disconnects from it (but it never disconnects from the second node of the line, counting from the center; to ensure this, the protocol has that node in a distinguished state i' while all other internal nodes of the line are in state i). The protocol terminates when the degree of the center becomes 1 for the first time (note that it could be 1 also at the very beginning of the protocol but this early termination can be trivially avoided).

Theorem 5 ([MS16a]). *By assuming a pre-elected unique leader and the ability to detect local degree 1, Protocol* Line-Around-a-Star *solves the Terminating Line Transformation problem. Its running time is* $\Theta(n^2 \log n)$, *which is optimal.*

For correctness, observe that every q_0 eventually becomes p, because the center forever attracts the q_0s making them p' and a p' only disconnects from other peripherals until it becomes p. This implies that eventually each non-leader node will become available for the line to expand over it and thus the line will eventually become spanning. Also, the protocol never disconnects the topology because it performs only two types of edge eliminations, (p', p') and (center, node $3 \leq i \leq k$ of the line of length k), which cannot lead to disconnection.

Finally it can be shown that the protocol terminates iff the active topology has become a spanning line, by showing that after the line formation subroutine has performed at least on step, the degree of the center first becomes 1 when the active topology becomes a spanning line.

For the running time, the time needed for the leader to connect to every q_0 (and convert all q_0 to p'), is equivalent to the time needed for a particular node to meet every other node, which takes $\Theta(n^2 \log n)$ expected time. Next consider the time for all peripherals to disconnect from one another and become p. If we study this after the time all q_0 have become p', it is the time (in the worst case) needed for all edges to be picked by the scheduler, which takes $\Theta(n^2 \log n)$ expected time. After the completion of both the above, we have a star with the leader at the center and all peripherals are only connected to the leader. Next consider the formation of the line over the peripherals. The right endpoint of the line is always ready for expansion towards another available peripheral. The time needed for the line to cover all peripherals is again the time to meet every other node, therefore takes time $\Theta(n^2 \log n)$ to complete. We finally take into account the time needed for the center to disconnect from the peripherals that are part of the line. We can study this after the line has become spanning. This is simply a star deformation, i.e., the time needed until the center meets all peripherals in order to disconnect from them, taking again time $\Theta(n^2 \log n)$. Putting all these together, we conclude that the running time of the protocol is $\Theta(n^2 \log n)$, which matches the $\Omega(n^2 \log n)$ lower bound mentioned above, therefore the protocol is time-optimal.

6   A Geometric Variant

We shall now discuss a more applied version of network constructors, that may be obtained by adjusting some of the abstract parameters of the general model. In particular, [Mic15] introduced some physical (or geometrical) constraints on the connections that the processes are allowed to form. In the general network constructors model, there were no such imposed restrictions, in the sense that, at any given step, any two processes were candidates for an interaction, independently of their relative positioning in the existing structure/network. For example, even two nodes hidden in the middle of distinct dense components could interact and, additionally, there was no constraint on the number of active connections that a node could form (could be up to the order of the system). This was very convenient for studying the capability of such systems to self-organize into abstract networks and, as we discussed, it helped us show that arbitrarily complex networks are in principle constructible. On the other hand, this is not expected to be the actual mechanism of at least the first potential implementations. First implementations will most probably be characterized by physical and geometrical constraints. To capture this, it was assumed in [Mic15] that each device can connect to other devices only via a very limited (finite and independent of the size of the system) number of ports, usually four or six, which implies that, at any given time, a device has only a bounded number of neighbors. Moreover, the connections are further restricted to be always made at unit distance and to be perpendicular to connections of neighboring ports. Though such a model can no longer form abstract networks, we will see that it is still capable of forming very practical 2D or 3D shapes. This is also in agreement with natural systems, where the complexity and physical properties of a system are rarely the result of an unrestricted interconnection between entities.

It can be immediately observed that the universal constructors of Sect. 4 do not apply in this case. In particular, those constructors cannot be adopted in order to characterize the constructive power of the present variant. The reason is that they work by arranging the nodes in a long line and then exploiting the fact that connections are elastic and allow any pair of nodes of the line to interact independently of the distance between them. In contrast, no elasticity is allowed in the more local model that we now consider, where a long line can still be formed, but only adjacent nodes of the line are allowed to interact with each other. As a result, new techniques have to be developed for determining the computational and constructive capabilities of this model. Another main novelty of [Mic15], concerns an alternative approach to overcome the inability of such systems to terminate, by exploiting the ability of nodes to self-assemble into larger structures that can then be used as distributed memories of any desired length and the existence of a uniform random scheduler. Achieving termination is crucial here, as it allows us to develop terminating subroutines that can be sequentially composed to form larger modular protocols. Such protocols are more efficient, more natural, and more amenable to clear proofs of correctness, compared to protocols that are based on composing all subroutines in parallel and "sequentializing" them eventually by perpetual reinitializations (like the one in Sect. 4).

Now, every node has a bounded number of ports which it uses to interact with other nodes. In the 2D case, there are four ports p_y, p_x, p_{-y}, and p_{-x}, which for notational convenience are usually denoted u, r, d, and l, respectively (for up, right, down, and left, respectively). Similarly, in the 3D case there are 6 ports. Neighboring ports are perpendicular to each other, forming local axes. For example, in the 2D case, $u \perp r, r \perp d, d \perp l, and l \perp u$. An important remark is that the above coordinates are only for local purposes and do not necessarily represent the actual orientation of a node in the system. A node may be arbitrarily rotated so that, for example, its x local coordinate is aligned with the y real coordinate of the system or it is not aligned with any real coordinate. Nodes may interact in pairs, whenever a port of one node w is at unit distance and in straight line (w.r.t. to the local axes) from a port of another node v.

The transition function is now of the form $\delta : (Q \times P) \times (Q \times P) \times \{0,1\} \rightarrow Q \times Q \times \{0,1\}$, where $P = \{u, r, d, l\}$ ($P = \{p_y, p_z, p_x, p_{-y}, p_{-z}, p_{-x}\}$, respectively, for the 3D case) is the set of ports. In every step, a pair of node-ports $(v_1, p_1)(v_2, p_2)$ is selected by an adversary scheduler and these nodes interact via the corresponding ports and update their states and the state of the edge joining them according to the transition function δ. A configuration is called valid, if any connected component defined by it (when arranged according to the geometrical constraints) is a subnetwork of the *2D grid network with unit distances*. Valid configurations restrict the possible selections of the scheduler at each step. In particular, $(v_1, p_1)(v_2, p_2) \in E_I$ can be selected for interaction (or *is permitted*) at step t iff the configuration that would result after an activation between (v_1, p_1) and (v_2, p_2) is valid. The interactions are chosen by a uniform random scheduler, which in every step selects independently and uniformly at random one of the permitted interactions. The output shapes of a configuration consist of those nodes that are in output or halting states and those edges between them that are active. We are usually interested in obtaining a single shape as the final output of the protocol. We say that an execution of a protocol on n processes *constructs (stably constructs) a shape G*, if it terminates (stabilizes, resp.) with output G.

The following theorem gives a partial characterization of the constructive power of the 2D version of this model.

Theorem 6 ([Mic15]). *Let $\mathcal{L} = (S_1, S_2, \ldots)$ be a connected 2D shape language, such that $\mathcal{L}$ is TM-computable in space d^2. Then there is a protocol that w.h.p. constructs $\mathcal{L}$. In particular, for all $d \geq 1$, whenever the protocol is executed on a population of size $n = d^2$, w.h.p. it constructs S_d and terminates. In the worst case, the waste is $(d-1)d = O(d^2) = O(n)$.*

The idea is again to organize the population in such a way that it can simulate appropriate TMs; in this case, a type of shape-constructing TMs that will realize their output-shape in the distributed system. Such a TM M constructs a shape on the pixels of a $\sqrt{n} \times \sqrt{n}$ square, which are indexed in a zig-zag way. M takes as input an integer $i \in \{0, 1, \ldots, n-1\}$ and the size n or the dimension $\sqrt{n}$ of the square (all in binary) and decides whether pixel i should belong or not to the final shape, i.e., if it should be *on* or *off*, respectively. In order, to self-organize and simulate the TM, the population first executes a *counting* subroutine, which constructs w.h.p. a line of length $\Theta(\log n)$, containing n in binary. To do this, the protocol requires a pre-elected unique leader. The leader maintains two distributed n-counters and uses them to implement two competing processes, running in parallel. The first process counts the number of nodes that have been encountered once by the leader and the second process counts the number of nodes that have been encountered twice. The game ends when the second counter catches up the first. It can be proved, via a probabilistic analysis of random walks on lines with time and position dependencies, that when this occurs, the leader will almost surely have already counted at least half of the nodes.[4] Then the leader exploits its knowledge of n to construct a $\sqrt{n} \times \sqrt{n}$ square and successfully detect termination of the construction. When it is done, it simulates the TM on the square n distinct times, one for each pixel. As already mentioned, the input to the TM is each time the index of the corresponding pixel and $\sqrt{n}$, in binary, while its output is an *on* or *off* decision for that pixel. Finally,

---

[4] In practice, this estimation is expected to be much closer to n than to $n/2$. A first indication is that, in all of our experiments for up to 1000 nodes the estimation was always close to $(9/10)n$ and usually higher.

the protocol releases the connected shape consisting of the *on* pixels. It is worth mentioning that it is still open whether the pre-elected leader assumption can be dropped.

7 Further Research

An obvious first target is to achieve complete characterizations of the constructible networks both in the basic and in the geometric model. It is also worth noting that existing results on universal construction indicate that the constructive power increases as a function of the available waste. A complete characterization of this dependence would be of special value. Another intriguing question is whether there exists a network constructor for global line that is asymptotically faster than $O(n^3)$. We also do not know yet whether counting the size of the population w.h.p. and with termination is still possible if all nodes are initially identical. Towards refining and extending the existing models, considering hybrid models of active and passive mobility seems interesting. Also, it seems plausible, apart from geometric constraints, to take further physical considerations into account, like mass, strength of bonds, rigid and elastic structure, and collisions. It would also be worth studying structures that optimize some global property or that achieve a desired behavior or functionality. Regarding fault-tolerance capabilities of programmable matter systems, protocols that efficiently reconstruct broken parts of the structure would be of special value. Moreover, we should draw more connections to natural processes and to self-assembly and programmable matter models coming from other research areas (e.g., by comparing the various models via formal simulations). Finally, we believe that more real systems of collectives of large numbers of simple interacting entities (e.g., devices) are needed in order to inspire theory and highlight the feasible mechanisms and, thus, the realistic modeling assumptions.

References

[AAD+06] Angluin, D., Aspnes, J., Diamadi, Z., Fischer, M.J., Peralta, R.: Computation in networks of passively mobile finite-state sensors. Distrib. Comput. **18**(4), 235–253 (2006)

[ALMS15] Amaxilatis, D., Logaras, M., Michail, O., Spirakis, P.G.: NETCS: a new simulator of population protocols and network constructors (2015). arXiv preprint arXiv:1508.06731

[CKS+12] Chatrchyan, S., Khachatryan, V., Sirunyan, A.M., Tumasyan, A., Adam, W., Aguilo, E., Bergauer, T., Dragicevic, M., Erö, J., Fabjan, C., et al.: Observation of a new boson at a mass of 125 GEV with the CMS experiment at the LHC. Phys. Lett. B **716**(1), 30–61 (2012)

[DDG+14] Derakhshandeh, Z., Dolev, S., Gmyr, R., Richa, A.W., Scheideler, C., Strothmann, T.: Brief announcement: amoebot-a new model for programmable matter. In: Proceedings of the 26th ACM Symposium on Parallelism in Algorithms and Architectures (SPAA), pp. 220–222 (2014)

[DGP+16] Derakhshandeh, Z., Gmyr, R., Porter, A., Richa, A.W., Scheideler, C., Strothmann, T.: On the runtime of universal coating for programmable matter. In: Rondelez, Y., Woods, D. (eds.) DNA 2016. LNCS, vol. 9818, pp. 148–164. Springer, Heidelberg (2016). doi:10.1007/978-3-319-43994-5_10

[Dot12] Doty, D.: Theory of algorithmic self-assembly. Commun. ACM **55**, 78–88 (2012)

[Dot14] Doty, D.: Timing in chemical reaction networks. In: Proceedings of the 25th Annual ACM-SIAM Symposium on Discrete Algorithms (SODA), pp. 772–784 (2014)

[GCM05] Goldstein, S.C., Campbell, J.D., Mowry, T.C.: Programmable matter. Computer **38**(6), 99–101 (2005)

[GKR10] Gilpin, K., Knaian, A., Rus, D.: Robot pebbles: one centimeter modules for programmable matter through self-disassembly. In: IEEE International Conference on Robotics and Automation (ICRA), pp. 2485–2492. IEEE (2010)

[KCL+12] Knaian, A.N., Cheung, K.C., Lobovsky, M.B., Oines, A.J., Schmidt-Neilsen, P., Gershenfeld, N.A.: The milli-motein: a self-folding chain of programmable matter with a one centimeter module pitch. In: IEEE/RSJ International Conference on Intelligent Robots and Systems, pp. 1447–1453. IEEE (2012)

[KSM+12] Karr, J.R., Sanghvi, J.C., Macklin, D.N., Gutschow, M.V., Jacobs, J.M., Bolival Jr., B., Assad-Garcia, N., Glass, J.I., Covert, M.W.: A whole-cell computational model predicts phenotype from genotype. Cell **150**(2), 389–401 (2012)

[MCS11] Michail, O., Chatzigiannakis, I., Spirakis, P.G.: Mediated population protocols. Theor. Comput. Sci. **412**(22), 2434–2450 (2011)

[Mic15] Michail, O.: Terminating distributed construction of shapes and patterns in a fair solution of automata. In: Proceedings of the 34th ACM Symposium on Principles of Distributed Computing (PODC), pp. 37–46. ACM (2015)

[MS15] Michail, O., Spirakis, P.G.: Terminating population protocols via some minimal global knowledge assumptions. J. Parallel Distrib. Comput. **81**, 1–10 (2015)

[MS16a] Michail, O., Spirakis, P.G.: Connectivity preserving network transformers. Theor. Comput. Sci. (TCS) (2016). Elsevier. doi:10.1016/j.tcs.2016.02.040

[MS16b] Michail, O., Spirakis, P.G.: Simple and efficient local codes for distributed stable network construction. Distrib. Comput. **29**(3), 207–237 (2016)

[RCN14] Rubenstein, M., Cornejo, A., Nagpal, R.: Programmable self-assembly in a thousand-robot swarm. Science **345**(6198), 795–799 (2014)

[Rot06] Rothemund, P.W.: Folding dna to create nanoscale shapes and patterns. Nature **440**(7082), 297–302 (2006)

[RW00] Rothemund, P.W.K., Winfree, E.: The program-size complexity of self-assembled squares. In: Proceedings of the 32nd Annual ACM Symposium on Theory of Computing (STOC), pp. 459–468 (2000)

[WCG+13] Woods, D., Chen, H.-L., Goodfriend, S., Dabby, N., Winfree, E., Yin, P.: Active self-assembly of algorithmic shapes and patterns in polylogarithmic time. In: Proceedings of the 4th Conference on Innovations in Theoretical Computer Science, pp. 353–354. ACM (2013)

[Win98] Winfree, E.: Algorithmic Self-Assembly of DNA. Ph.D. thesis. California Institute of Technology, June 1998

[Zak07] Zakin, M.: The next revolution in materials. In: DARPA's 25th Systems and Technology Symposium (DARPATech) (2007)

Semantics, Specification and Compositionality

Logical Characterisations and Compositionality of Input-Output Conformance Simulation

Luca Aceto[1], Ignacio Fábregas[1,2(✉)], Carlos Gregorio-Rodríguez[2], and Anna Ingólfsdóttir[1]

[1] School of Computer Science, ICE-TCS, Reykjavik University, Reykjavik, Iceland
[2] Departamento de Sistemas Informáticos y Computación,
Universidad Complutense de Madrid, Madrid, Spain
`fabregas@ucm.es`

Abstract. Input-output conformance simulation (ioco͟s) has been proposed by Gregorio-Rodríguez, Llana and Martínez-Torres as a simulation-based behavioural preorder underlying model-based testing. This relation is inspired by Tretman's classic ioco relation, but has better worst-case complexity than ioco and supports stepwise refinement. The goal of this paper is to develop the theory of ioco͟s by studying logical characterisations of this relation and its compositionality. More specifically, this article presents characterisations of ioco͟s in terms of modal logics and compares them with an existing logical characterisation for ioco proposed by Beohar and Mousavi. A precongruence rule format for ioco͟s and a rule format ensuring that operations take quiescence properly into account are also given. Both rule formats are based on the GSOS format by Bloom, Istrail and Meyer.

1 Introduction

Model-based testing (MBT) is an increasingly popular technique for validation and verification of computing systems, and provides a compromise between formal verification approaches, such model checking, and manual testing. MBT uses a model to describe the aspects of system behaviour that are considered to be relevant at some suitable level of abstraction. This model is employed to generate test cases automatically, while guaranteeing that some coverage criterion is met. Such test cases are then executed on the actual system in order to check whether its behaviour complies with that described by the model.

A formal notion of compliance relation between models (specifications) and systems (implementations) provides a formal underpinning for MBT. The

Research partially supported by the Spanish projects DArDOS (TIN2015-65845-C3-1-R), TRACES (TIN2015-67522-C3-3-R) and SICOMORo-CM (S2013/ICE-3006), the project 001-ABEL-CM-2013 within the NILS Science and Sustainability Programme and the project Nominal SOS (project nr. 141558-051) of the Icelandic Research Fund.

© Springer International Publishing AG 2017
B. Steffen et al. (Eds.): SOFSEM 2017, LNCS 10139, pp. 37–48, 2017.
DOI: 10.1007/978-3-319-51963-0_4

de-facto standard compliance relation underlying MBT for labelled transition systems with input and output actions is the classic ioco relation proposed by Tretmans, for which a whole MBT framework and tools have been developed. (See, for instance, [16] and the references therein.)

An alternative conformance relation that can be used to underlie MBT is *input-output conformance simulation* (iocos). This relation shares with ioco many of its ideas and rationale. However, iocos is a branching-time semantics based on simulation, whereas ioco is a trace-based semantics. iocos has been introduced, motivated and proved to be an adequate conformance relation for MBT in [8–10].

Since iocos has been proposed as an alternative, branching-time touchstone relation for MBT, it is natural to investigate its theory in order to understand its properties. The goal of this paper is to contribute to this endeavour by studying the discriminating power of iocos and its compositionality. More precisely, in Sect. 3, we provide modal characterisations of iocos in the style of Hennessy and Milner [11]. We offer two modal chacterisations of iocos, which are based on the use of either a 'non-forcing diamond modality' (Theorem 1) or of a 'forcing box modality' (Theorem 2), and compare them with an existing logical characterisation for ioco proposed by Beohar and Mousavi in [3] (Sect. 4). We also show, by means of an example, that, contrary to what is claimed in [13, Theorem 2], ioco and iocos do *not* coincide even when implementations are input enabled (Sect. 4.1).

As argued in [2,17] amongst other references, MBT can benefit from a compositional approach whose goal is to increase the efficiency of the testing activity. The above-mentioned references study compositionality of ioco with respect to a small collection of well-chosen operations. Here we take a general approach to the study of compositionality of iocos, which is based on the theory of rule formats for structural operational semantics [1]. In Sect. 5, we present a congruence rule format for iocos based on the GSOS format proposed by Bloom, Istrail and Meyer [5] (Theorem 4). Since operations preserving iocos need to take quiescence properly into account, we also propose a rule format guaranteeing that operations preserve coherent quiescent behaviour (Theorem 5 in Sect. 5.1).

Section 6 concludes the paper and presents avenues for future research.

2   Preliminaries

The input-output conformance simulation preorder presented in [8–10,13] (henceforth referred to as iocos) is a semantic relation developed under the assumption that systems have two kinds of transitions: input actions, namely those that the systems are willing to admit or respond to, and output actions, which are those produced by the system and that can be seen as responses or results.

We use I to denote the alphabet of input actions, which are written with a question mark $(a?, b?, c? \ldots)$. We call O the alphabet of output actions, which are annotated with an exclamation mark $(a!, b!, \delta! \ldots)$. In many cases we want to name actions in a general sense, inputs and outputs indistinctly. We will consider the set $L = I \cup O$ and we will omit the exclamation or question marks when naming generic actions, $a, b, x, y, z \in L$.

A state with no output actions cannot proceed autonomously; such a state is called *quiescent*. Following Tretmans (see, for instance, [14,16]), we directly introduce the event of quiescence as a special output action denoted by $\delta! \in O$ in the definition of our models.

Definition 1. *A labelled transition system with inputs and outputs, LTS for short, is a quadruple $(S, I, O, \longrightarrow)$ such that*

- *S is a set of states, processes, or behaviours.*
- *I and O are disjoint sets of input and output actions, respectively. Output actions include the quiescence symbol $\delta! \in O$. We define $L = I \cup O$.*
- *$\longrightarrow \subseteq S \times L \times S$ is the transition relation. As usual we write $p \xrightarrow{x} q$ instead of $(p, x, q) \in \longrightarrow$ and $p \xrightarrow{x}$, for $x \in L$, if there exists some $q \in S$ such that $p \xrightarrow{x} p \xrightarrow{x} q$. Analogously, we will write $p \xrightarrow{x}\!\!\!\!\!/$, for $x \in L$, if there is no q such that $p \xrightarrow{x} q$.*

  In order to allow only for coherent quiescent systems, the set of transitions $\longrightarrow$ should also satisfy the following requirement: $p \xrightarrow{\delta!} p'$ iff $p = p'$ and $p \xrightarrow{o!}\!\!\!\!\!/$ for each $o! \in O \backslash \{\delta!\}$.

The extension of the transition relation to sequences of actions is defined as usual.

Contrary to the classic ioco testing theory, in the theory of iocos presented in [8–10], all actions are assumed to be observable. In this paper, we follow those references and consider only concrete actions.

In general we use $p, q, p', q' \dots$ for states or behaviours, but also i, i', s and s' when we want to emphasise the concrete role of a behaviour as an implementation or a specification, respectively. We consider implementations and specifications, or, more generally, behaviours under study, as states of the same LTS.

The following functions over states of an LTS will be used in the remainder of the paper:

$$\mathsf{outs}(p) = \{o! \mid o! \in O, \ p \xrightarrow{o!}\}, \text{the set of initial outputs of a state } p.$$

$$\mathsf{ins}(p) = \{a? \mid a? \in I, \ p \xrightarrow{a?}\}, \text{the set of initial inputs of a state } p.$$

Definition 2. *We say that a binary relation R over states in an LTS is an iocos-relation if, and only if, for each $(p, q) \in R$ the following conditions hold:*

1. *$\mathsf{ins}(q) \subseteq \mathsf{ins}(p)$.*
2. *For all $a? \in \mathsf{ins}(q)$ and $p' \in S$, if $p \xrightarrow{a?} p'$ then there exists some q' such that $q \xrightarrow{a?} q'$ with $(p', q') \in R$.*
3. *For all $o! \in O$ and $p' \in S$, if $p \xrightarrow{o!} p'$ then there exists some q' such that $q \xrightarrow{o!} q'$ with $(p', q') \in R$.*

We define the input-output conformance simulation (iocos) as the largest iocos-relation. We write p iocos q instead of $(p, q) \in$ iocos. As proven in [8], iocos is a preorder.

Example 1. Consider the following processes:

$$\delta! \leftrightarrows i \leftrightarrows a? \qquad s \leftrightarrows \delta!$$

It is easy to see that i iocos s. Indeed, $\text{ins}(s) = \emptyset$ and therefore the specification s does not prevent the implementation i from offering the input transition $i \xrightarrow{a?} i$.

Throughout the paper we make extensive use of modal logics. A logic over processes is defined by a language to express the formulae and a satisfaction relation that defines when a process (that is, a state of an LTS) has the property described by some formula. A classic example and a reference for the rest of the paper is Hennessy-Milner Logic [11].

Definition 3. *Hennessy-Milner Logic over the set of actions L (abbreviated to HML) is the collection of formulae defined by the following BNF grammar:*

$$\phi ::= \mathbf{tt} \mid \mathbf{ff} \mid \phi \wedge \phi \mid \phi \vee \phi \mid [\,a\,]\phi \mid \langle a \rangle \phi,$$

where $a \in L$. HML is interpreted over an LTS by defining a satisfaction relation $\models$ relating states to formulae. The semantics of the boolean constants $\mathbf{tt}$ and $\mathbf{ff}$ and of the boolean connectives $\wedge$ and $\vee$ is defined as usual. The satisfaction relation for the modalities $\langle a \rangle$ and $[\,a\,]$ is as follows:

- $p \models \langle a \rangle \varphi$ *iff there exists some p' such that $p \xrightarrow{a} p'$ and $p' \models \varphi$.*
- $p \models [\,a\,]\varphi$ *iff $p' \models \varphi$ for all p' such that $p \xrightarrow{a} p'$.*

Every subset of HML naturally induces a preorder on a given set of behaviours.

Definition 4. *Given a logic $\mathcal{L}$ included in HML and a set S of states in an LTS, we define $\leq_{\mathcal{L}}$ as the binary relation over S given by*

$$p \leq_{\mathcal{L}} q \quad \textit{iff} \quad \forall \phi \in \mathcal{L} \ (p \models \phi \Rightarrow q \models \phi).$$

Remark 1. Since the logics we use in this paper to give modal characterisations of iocos have binary conjunctions and disjunctions, in what follows we will consider only *image-finite* LTSs, that is, LTSs where for each p and each $a \in I \cup O$ there are only finitely many p' such that $p \xrightarrow{a} p'$. Also, we will consider both I and O to be finite sets.

3   Logic for iocos

In this section we present a logic that characterises the iocos relation. This logic is a subset of Hennessy-Milner Logic (HML) and is rather minimal, but is convenient to characterize clearly the discriminating power of the iocos relation.

Definition 5. *The syntax of the logic for iocos, denoted by $\mathcal{L}_{\text{iocos}}$, is defined by the following BNF grammar:*

$$\phi ::= \mathbf{tt} \mid \mathbf{ff} \mid \phi \wedge \phi \mid \phi \vee \phi \mid \langle\!\langle a? \rangle\!\rangle \phi \mid \langle x! \rangle \phi,$$

where $a? \in I$ and $x! \in O$. The semantics of the constants $\mathbf{tt}$ and $\mathbf{ff}$, of the boolean connectives $\wedge$ and $\vee$, and of the modality $\langle x! \rangle$ is defined as usual. The satisfaction relation for the modality $\langle\!\langle a? \rangle\!\rangle$ is given below:

$- p \models \langle\!|a?|\!\rangle\phi$ iff $p \xrightarrow{a?}$ or $p' \models \phi$ for some $p \xrightarrow{a?} p'$.

The new modal operator $\langle\!|a?|\!\rangle$ can be read as a *non forcing* diamond modality: if the action specified in the modality is not possible in a given state then the formula is satisfied. This operator can be expressed with the classic modalities in HML; indeed, $\langle\!|a?|\!\rangle\phi$ is equivalent to $\langle a?\rangle\phi \vee [\,a?\,]\mathbf{ff}$. The need for this special modality arises because, in order for $i\mathsf{iocos}s$ to hold, s need only match the input transitions of i that are labelled with input actions that s affords.

According to Definition 4, the logic $\mathcal{L}_{\mathsf{iocos}}$ induces the preorder $\leq_{\mathcal{L}_{\mathsf{iocos}}}$. Next we prove that this logical preorder coincides with the input output conformance simulation preorder, iocos, over an arbitrary (image-finite) LTS.

Theorem 1. *For all states i, s in some LTS,*

$$i\ \mathsf{iocos}\ s \quad \textit{iff} \quad i \leq_{\mathcal{L}_{\mathsf{iocos}}} s.$$

The logic for iocos we have presented in Definition 5 follows a standard approach to the logical characterisation of simulation semantics; see, for instance, [6,18]. However, the iocos relation originated in the model-based testing environment where the natural reading for a logical characterisation would be *'every property satisfied by the specification should also hold in the implementation'*. Next we define an alternative logic that better matches this specification/implementation view.

Definition 6. *The syntax of the logic $\widetilde{\mathcal{L}}_{\mathsf{iocos}}$ is defined by the following BNF grammar:*

$$\phi ::= \mathbf{tt} \mid \mathbf{ff} \mid \phi \wedge \phi \mid \phi \vee \phi \mid [\![a?]\!]\phi \mid [\,x!\,]\phi,$$

where $a? \in I$ and $x! \in O$. The semantics of the constants $\mathbf{tt}$ and $\mathbf{ff}$, of the boolean connectives $\wedge$ and $\vee$, and of the modality $[\,x!\,]$ is defined as usual. The satisfaction relation for the modalities $[\![a?]\!]$ is as follows:

$- p \models [\![a?]\!]\phi$ iff $p \xrightarrow{a?}$ and $p' \models \phi$, for each $p \xrightarrow{a?} p'$.

The new modal operator, denoted by $[\![a?]\!]$, can be read as a *forcing* box modality: the action specified in the modality must be possible in order for a process to satisfy the formula. This operator can be described with the classic modalities in HML: $[\![a?]\!]\phi$ is equivalent to $\langle a?\rangle\mathbf{tt} \wedge [\,a?\,]\phi$.

Now with this logic, we can define a preorder $\leq_{\widetilde{\mathcal{L}}_{\mathsf{iocos}}}$ in terms of the formulae that the specification satisfies: $s \leq_{\widetilde{\mathcal{L}}_{\mathsf{iocos}}} i$ iff $\forall\phi \in \widetilde{\mathcal{L}}_{\mathsf{iocos}}\ (s \models \phi \Rightarrow i \models \phi)$.

We note that the logics $\mathcal{L}_{\mathsf{iocos}}$ and $\widetilde{\mathcal{L}}_{\mathsf{iocos}}$ are dual. In fact, there exist mutual transformations between both sets of formulae such that a behaviour satisfies one formula if, and only if, it does *not* satisfy the transformed formula. These statements are at the heart of the proof of the following result.

Theorem 2. *For all states i, s in some LTS, $i\ \mathsf{iocos}\ s$ iff $s \leq_{\widetilde{\mathcal{L}}_{\mathsf{iocos}}} i$.*

4   The Relation with a Logic for ioco

Input-output conformance (ioco) was introduced by Tretmans in [15]. The intuition behind ioco is that a process i is a correct implementation of a specification s if, for each sequence of actions σ allowed by the specification, all the possible outputs from i after having performed σ are allowed by the specification. This is formalized below in a setting in which all actions are observable.

Definition 7. *Let $(S, I, O, \longrightarrow)$ be an LTS with inputs and outputs. We define the traces of a state $p \in S$ as* $\mathsf{traces}(p) = \{\sigma \mid \exists p'.\ p \xrightarrow{\sigma} p'\}$. *Given a trace σ, we define p after $\sigma = \{p' \mid p' \in S,\ p \xrightarrow{\sigma} p'\}$. For each $T \subseteq S$, we set* $\mathsf{Out}(T) = \bigcup_{p \in T} \mathsf{outs}(p)$. *Finally, the relation* $\mathsf{ioco} \in S \times S$ *is defined as:*

$$i \text{ ioco } s \text{ iff } \mathsf{Out}(i \text{ after } \sigma) \subseteq \mathsf{Out}(s \text{ after } \sigma), \text{ for all } \sigma \in \mathsf{traces}(s).$$

As shown in [8, Theorem 1], iocos is included in ioco.

In the setting of Tretmans' standard ioco theory [15], only input-enabled implementations are considered. A state i in an LTS is input enabled if every state i' that is reachable from i is able to perform every input action, that is, $i' \xrightarrow{a?}$ holds for each $a? \in I$ and for each state i' that is reachable from i.

In [3] Beohar and Mousavi introduced an explicit logical characterization of ioco. This characterization uses a non-standard modal operator reminiscent of our $[\![\cdot]\!]$, denoted by $\|\cdot\|$[1]. However, output actions can also be used as labels of $\|\cdot\|$. This modality can be extended to traces σ as follows: $p \models \|\sigma\|\phi$ if, and only if, $p \xrightarrow{\sigma}$ and $p' \models \phi$, for each p' such that $p \xrightarrow{\sigma} p'$. (Note that, for the particular case of input actions $a?$, the semantics of $\|a?\|$ coincides with that of $[\![a?]\!]$.)

The explicit logical characterization of ioco given in [3] is defined by means of two different subclasses of logical formulae. The first subclass permits only formulae of the form $\|\sigma\|[b]\mathbf{ff}$, where σ is a trace and b is an output action.

For the second subclass of formulae, Beohar and Mousavi consider an extension of the operator $[\cdot]$ to traces, defined as: $p \models [\sigma]\phi$ if, and only if, $p' \models \phi$ for each p' such that $p \xrightarrow{\sigma} p'$. This second subclass permits only formulae of the form $[\sigma][b]\mathbf{ff}$, where σ is a trace and b is an output action.

The formulae in each of these two subclasses characterize one defining property of the ioco-relation. This intuition is made precise in the following lemma.

Lemma 1 ([3]). *For each sequence of actions σ, output action b and process p the following statements hold:*

1. *$\sigma \in \mathsf{traces}(p)$ and $b \notin \mathsf{Out}(p$ after $\sigma)$ iff $p \models \|\sigma\|[b]\mathbf{ff}$.*
2. *$b \notin \mathsf{Out}(p$ after $\sigma)$ iff $p \models [\sigma][b]\mathbf{ff}$.*

---

[1] In fact, the symbol used to denote the operator $\|\cdot\|$ in [3] is $\langle\!\langle\cdot\rangle\!\rangle$, but we prefer to use an alternative notation in order to avoid confusion with our modal operator $\langle\!\langle\,\cdot\,\rangle\!\rangle$.

The resulting logical characterization theorem for ioco is as follows,

Theorem 3 ([3]). *i ioco s iff, for all $\sigma \in L^*$, $b \in O$, if $s \models \lVert \sigma \rVert [b]$ff, then $i \models [\sigma][b]$ff.*

The above result is the counterpart of Theorem 2 in the setting of ioco. Note, however, that Theorem 3 is not a classic modal characterization result (as it is the case of, for example, Theorem 2) where if the implementation i is correct with respect to the specification s and s satisfies a formula, then also i satisfies it. Here the implementation does not need to satisfy the properties that hold for the specification. By way of example, implementations need not exhibit all the traces of a specification they correctly implement.

4.1   Relation with iocos

Theorem 2 in [13] states that if i is input enabled, i ioco s implies i iocos s. This means that, when restricted to input-enabled implementations, ioco and iocos coincide, and therefore the logics characterizing iocos presented in this paper also characterize ioco over that class of LTSs. Unfortunately, however, Theorem 2 in [13] does *not* hold, as shown in the following example.

Example 2. Let s and i be defined as follows, where we assume that $I = \{a?, b?\}$.

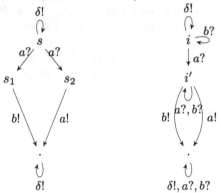

Note that i is input-enabled, as required by the theory of ioco. It is easy to see that i ioco s. On the other hand, i iocos s because each iocos relation containing the pair (i, s) would also have to contain the pair (i', s_1) or the pair (i', s_2). However, no relation including either of those pairs is an iocos-relation because $i' \xrightarrow{a!}$ and $i' \xrightarrow{b!}$, but $s_1 \xrightarrow{a!} \!\!\!/$ and $s_2 \xrightarrow{b!} \!\!\!/$.

As we will now argue, the logics for ioco and iocos are incomparable in terms of their expressive power. First of all, note that, if we consider only input-enabled implementations, the formulae of the form $[\sigma][b]$ff, with σ a trace, can be expressed in $\widetilde{\mathcal{L}}_{\text{iocos}}$ since in an input-enabled scenario $[\![a?]\!]$ has the same semantics as $[a?]$. On the other hand, it is not possible to define a formula $\phi \in \tilde{\mathcal{L}}_{\text{iocos}}$ that captures Lemma 1(1). Indeed, by way of example, consider $\phi = \|x!\|[b!]\mathbf{ff}$. Any specification s would have to satisfy ϕ iff $s \xrightarrow{x!}$ and $s' \models [b!]\mathbf{ff}$, for all $s \xrightarrow{x!} s'$. Now, assume that we have in $\tilde{\mathcal{L}}_{\text{iocos}}$ a formula ψ whose semantics coincides with that of $\|x!\|[b!]\mathbf{ff}$. Let

$$a! \mathrel{\subset\!\!\!\cdot} s \mathrel{\cdot\!\!\!\supset} x! \qquad\qquad a! \mathrel{\subset\!\!\!\cdot} i$$

It is easy to see that i iocos s, but $s \models \psi$ and $i \not\models \psi$. In other words, ψ is a formula that distinguishes processes related by iocos. Hence, such a formula ψ cannot be in any logic that characterizes iocos.

On the other hand, let us consider the two processes of Example 2 and the formula $\phi = [a?]([a!]\mathbf{ff} \vee [b!]\mathbf{ff}) \in \tilde{\mathcal{L}}_{\text{iocos}}$. As we already stated in Example 2, i ioco s, but $s \models \phi$ and $i \not\models \phi$. Hence, ϕ can distinguish processes that are ioco-related.

5   A Rule Format for Iocos

In this section we study compositionality for iocos and present a congruence rule format for the input-output conformance simulation preorder based on the GSOS format proposed by Bloom, Istrail and Meyer [5]. The restriction to GSOS rules is partly justified by our wish to have a purely syntactic rule format and by the undecidability results presented in [12]. In what follows, we assume that the reader is familiar with the standard notions of signature and of term over a signature.

We recall that a deduction rule for an operator f of arity n in some signature Σ is in the *GSOS format* if, and only if, it has the following form:

$$\frac{\{x_i \xrightarrow{a_{ij}} y_{ij} \mid 1 \leq i \leq n, 1 \leq j \leq m_i\} \cup \{x_i \xrightarrow{b_{ik}} \mid 1 \leq i \leq n, 1 \leq k \leq \ell_i\}}{f(\boldsymbol{x}) \xrightarrow{a} C[\boldsymbol{x}, \boldsymbol{y}]} \tag{1}$$

where the x_i's and the y_{ij}'s ($1 \leq i \leq n$ and $1 \leq j \leq m_i$) are all distinct variables, m_i and ℓ_i are natural numbers, $C[\boldsymbol{x}, \boldsymbol{y}]$ is a term over Σ with variables including at most the x_i's and y_{ij}'s, and the a_{ij}'s, b_{ik}'s and a are actions from L. The above rule is said to be *f-defining* and *a-emitting*. Its *positive trigger for variable x_i* is the set $\{a_{ij} \mid 1 \leq j \leq m_i\}$ and its *negative trigger for variable x_i* is the set $\{b_{ik} \mid 1 \leq k \leq \ell_i\}$. The *source of the conclusion* of the rule is $f(\boldsymbol{x})$.

A GSOS language is a triple (Σ, L, D) where Σ is a finite signature, L is a finite set of labels and D is a finite set of deduction rules in the GSOS format. In what follows, we assume, without loss of generality, that all f-defining rules have the same source of their conclusions.

A GSOS language naturally defines a set of transitions over the variable-free terms over Σ by structural induction: for vectors of such terms $\boldsymbol{p}$ (with typical entry p_i) and $\boldsymbol{q}$ (with entries q_{ij}), there is a transition $f(\boldsymbol{p}) \xrightarrow{a} C[\boldsymbol{p}, \boldsymbol{q}]$ if, and only if, there is an f-defining rule of the form (1) such that

- $p_i \xrightarrow{a_{ij}} q_{ij}$ for each $1 \leq i \leq n$ and $1 \leq j \leq m_i$ and
- $p_i \xrightarrow{b_{ik}} \!\!\!\!\!/ \ $ for each $1 \leq i \leq n$ and $1 \leq k \leq \ell_i$.

Note that GSOS rules define operations over states in an arbitrary LTS with inputs and outputs. In what follows, we apply derived operations built over the signature of a GSOS language to states in the collection of LTSs with input and output actions.

Definition 8. *An operation f in a GSOS language is in* iocos*-format if the collection of f-defining rules satisfies the following conditions:*

1. *Each a?-emitting rule, where a? is an input action, has only output actions as labels of negative premises and input actions as labels of positive premises.*
2. *For each input action a? and each pair of rules $r = \dfrac{H}{f(x_1,\dots,x_n) \xrightarrow{a?} t}$ and $r' = \dfrac{H'}{f(x_1,\dots,x_n) \xrightarrow{a?} t'}$, there is a rule $r'' = \dfrac{H''}{f(x_1,\dots,x_n) \xrightarrow{a?} t'}$ such that*
   (a) *for each $1 \leq i \leq n$, the positive trigger for variable x_i in r'' is included in the positive trigger for variable x_i in r;*
   (b) *for each $1 \leq i \leq n$, the negative trigger for variable x_i in r'' is included in the negative trigger for variable x_i in r;*
   (c) *if $x_i \xrightarrow{b?} z$ is contained in H'' and z occurs in t', then $x_i \xrightarrow{b?} z$ is also contained in H'.*
3. *Each a!-emitting rule, where a! is an output action, has only input actions as labels of negative premises and output actions as labels of positive premises.*

A GSOS language is in iocos*-format if so is each of its operations.*

Theorem 4. iocos *is a precongruence for each GSOS language in* iocos *format.*

As an example of application of the above result, we show that the merge operator from [2] can be expressed in our rule format.

Example 3. Merge, or conjunction, is a composition operator from the theory of ioco. It acts as a logical conjunction of requirements, that is, it describes systems by a conjunction of sub-systems, or sub-specifications. We denote by $\bigwedge_{i=1}^{n} s_i$ the result of the merge of the states s_i, with $1 \leq i \leq n$. In [2] it is noted that, in general, the merge of two systems can lead to invalid states (for example the merge of a quiescent state with another with some output). The solution is to add a pruning algorithm after calculating the merge. Here we just show the merge operator and not that pruning algorithm. (See also Example 4.)

The merge operator can be formalized using the following GSOS rules (one such rule for each $a \in L$):

$$\frac{\{x_i \xrightarrow{a} y_i \mid 1 \leq i \leq n\}}{\bigwedge_{i=1}^{n} x_i \xrightarrow{a} \bigwedge_{i=1}^{n} y_i}.$$

It is immediate to check that the above rules are in iocos-format. Therefore the above theorem yields that the merge operator preserves iocos.

5.1   A Rule Format for Coherent Quiescent Behaviour

Operators for constructing LTSs with inputs and outputs should ensure 'coherent quiescent behaviour' in the sense of Definition 1. This means that each operator f, when applied to a vector of states $\boldsymbol{p}$ in an LTS, should satisfy the following property:

$$f(\boldsymbol{p}) \xrightarrow{\delta!} p' \text{ iff } p' = f(\boldsymbol{p}) \text{ and, for each } a! \in O \backslash \{\delta!\}, \ f(\boldsymbol{p}) \xrightarrow{a!} \not. \qquad (2)$$

In what follows, we will isolate sufficient conditions on the GSOS rules that define f that guarantee the above-mentioned property.

Definition 9. *We say that the following sets of formulae contradict each other:*

- $\{x \xrightarrow{a} y\}$ *and* $\{x \xrightarrow{a} \not\}$ *for* $a \in L$,
- $\{x \xrightarrow{b!} y\}$ *and* $\{x \xrightarrow{\delta!} z\}$ *for* $b! \in O \backslash \{\delta!\}$, *and*
- H *and* H' *when* H *and* H' *are non-empty and* $H \cup H' = \{x \xrightarrow{b!} \not | \ b! \in O\}$.

Formulae $x \xrightarrow{a} y$ *and* $x \xrightarrow{a} \not$ *are said to negate each other.*
We say that two sets of formulae H_1 *and* H_2 *are* contradictory *if there are* $H_1' \subseteq H_1$ *and* $H_2' \subseteq H_2$ *such that* H_1' *and* H_2' *contradict each other.*

Intuitively, two sets of contradictory formulae cannot be both satisfied by states in an LTS. For example, in the light of the requirement on quiescent behaviour in Definition 1, there is no state p in an LTS such that $p \xrightarrow{b!} \not$ for each $b! \in O$. This observation motivates the third requirement in Definition 9.

Definition 10. *We say that an operation* f *is* quiescent consistent *if the set of rules for* f *satisfies the following two constraints:*

[δ_1] If $H/f(\boldsymbol{x}) \xrightarrow{\delta!} t$ *is a rule for* f *then*
   1. *for each* f-*defining rule* $H'/f(\boldsymbol{x}) \xrightarrow{b!} t'$ *with* $b! \in O \backslash \{\delta!\}$, *the sets* H *and* H' *are contradictory, and*
   2. $t = f(\boldsymbol{y})$ *for some vector of variables* $\boldsymbol{y}$ *such that, for each index* i, *either* $y_i = x_i$ *or* $x_i \xrightarrow{\delta!} y_i \in H$.

[δ_2] Let $\{r_1, \ldots r_n\}$ *be the set of output-emitting rules for* f *not having* $\delta!$ *as label of their conclusions. Then the set of rules for* f *contains all rules of the form* $\{l_1, \ldots, l_n\}/f(\boldsymbol{x}) \xrightarrow{\delta!} f(\boldsymbol{x})$, *where* l_i *negates some premise of* r_i *and no two sets of formulae included in* $\{l_1, \ldots l_n\}$ *contradict each other.*

A GSOS language is quiescent consistent *if so is each operation in it.*

Theorem 5. *If* f *is quiescent consistent then Eq. 2 holds for* f.

Example 4. Consider the merge, or conjunction, operator from [2] described in Example 3. As remarked in [2, Example 2], the merge operator may produce an invalid LTS when applied to states from an LTS. Note that the set of rules for the n-ary merge operator satisfy constraint $[\delta_1]$ in Definition 10, but not constraint $[\delta_2]$. Constraint $[\delta_2]$ also suggests how to add rules to those of the merge operator so that it preserves consistent quiescent behaviour. By way of example, consider the binary version of the merge operator, and assume that $a!$ and $b!$ are the only two output actions different from $\delta!$. Then one should add the following four rules to those for the binary merge given in Example 3:

$$\frac{\{x_1 \xrightarrow{a!} y_1, \; x_2 \xrightarrow{b!} y_2\}}{x_1 \wedge x_2 \xrightarrow{\delta!} x_1 \wedge x_2} \; (a! \neq b!) \; .$$

The resulting operation is quiescent consistent and, by Theorem 5, satisfies Eq. 2.

6   Conclusion

In this paper, we have developed the theory of iocos [8–10] by studying logical characterisations of this relation and its compositionality. We have also compared the proposed logical characterisation of iocos with an existing logical characterisation for ioco proposed by Beohar and Mousavi. The article also offers a precongruence rule format for iocos and a rule format ensuring that operations take quiescence properly into account. Both rule formats are based on the GSOS format by Bloom, Istrail and Meyer.

Avenues for future research we are currently pursuing include an extension of the logic for iocos with fixed points, a characteristic formula construction for finite-state behaviours with respect to iocos, an application of the divide and congruence approach from [7] to the definition of a congruence rule format for iocos (as done in [4] for the XY-simulation preorder) and a compositionality result for the logic characterising iocos over languages in iocos format.

References

1. Aceto, L., Fokkink, W.J., Verhoef, C.: Structural operational semantics. In: Bergstra, J.A., Ponse, A., Smolka, S.A. (eds.) Handbook of Process Algebra, pp. 197–292. Elsevier, Amsterdam (2001)
2. Benes, N., Daca, P., Henzinger, T.A., Kretínský, J., Nickovic, D., Complete composition operators for IOCO-testing theory. In: Proceedings of the 18th International ACM SIGSOFT Symposium on Component-Based Software Engineering, CBSE, pp. 101–110 (2015)
3. Beohar, H., Mousavi, M.R.: Two logical characterizations for input-output conformance. In: Preproceedings of EXPRESS/SOS 2014 (Short Paper), July 2014
4. Beohar, H., Mousavi, M.R.: A pre-congruence format for XY-simulation. In: Dastani, M., Sirjani, M. (eds.) FSEN 2015. LNCS, vol. 9392, pp. 215–229. Springer, Heidelberg (2015)

5. Bloom, B., Istrail, S., Meyer, A.R.: Bisimulation can't be traced. J. ACM **42**(1), 232–268 (1995)
6. de Frutos-Escrig, D., Gregorio-Rodríguez, C., Palomino, M., Romero-Hernández, D.: Unifying the linear time-branching time spectrum of process semantics. Log. Methods Comput. Sci. **9**(2:11), 1–74 (2013)
7. Fokkink, W., Glabbeek, R.J., Wind, P.: Compositionality of Hennessy-Milner logic by structural operational semantics. Theor. Comput. Sci. **354**(3), 421–440 (2006)
8. Gregorio-Rodríguez, C., Llana, L., Martínez-Torres, R.: Input-output conformance simulation (iocos) for model based testing. In: Beyer, D., Boreale, M. (eds.) FMOODS/FORTE -2013. LNCS, vol. 7892, pp. 114–129. Springer, Berlin (2013). doi:10.1007/978-3-642-38592-6_9
9. Gregorio-Rodríguez, C., Llana, L., Martínez-Torres, R.: Effectiveness for input output conformance simulation iocos. In: Ábrahám, E., Palamidessi, C. (eds.) FORTE 2014. LNCS, vol. 8461, pp. 100–116. Springer, Berlin (2014). doi:10.1007/978-3-662-43613-4_7
10. Gregorio-Rodríguez, C., Llana, L., Martínez-Torres, R.: Extending mCRL2 with ready simulation and iocos input-output conformance simulation. In: Wainwright, R.L., Corchado, J.M., Bechini, A., Hong, J. (eds.) Proceedings of the 30th Annual ACM Symposium on Applied Computing, Salamanca, Spain, 13–17 April 2015, pp. 1781–1788. ACM (2015)
11. Hennessy, M., Milner, R.: Algebraic laws for nondeterminism and concurrency. J. ACM **32**, 137–161 (1985)
12. Klin, B., Nachyła, B.: Some undecidable properties of SOS specifications. J. Log. Algebraic Methods Program. (2016). http://dx.doi.org/10.1016/j.jlamp.2016.08.005
13. Llana, L., Martínez-Torres, R.: IOCO as a simulation. In: Counsell, S., Núñez, M. (eds.) SEFM 2013. LNCS, vol. 8368, pp. 125–134. Springer, Cham (2014). doi:10.1007/978-3-319-05032-4_10
14. Stokkink, G., Timmer, M., Stoelinga, M., Talking quiescence: a rigorous theory that supports parallelcomposition, action hiding and determinisation. In: Petrenko, A.K., Schlingloff, H. (eds.) MBT. EPTCS, vol. 80, pp. 73–87 (2012)
15. Tretmans, J.: Test generation with inputs, outputs and repetitive quiescence. Softw. Concepts Tools **17**(3), 103–120 (1996)
16. Tretmans, J.: Model Based testing with labelled transition systems. In: Hierons, R.M., Bowen, J.P., Harman, M. (eds.) Formal Methods and Testing. LNCS, vol. 4949, pp. 1–38. Springer, Berlin (2008). doi:10.1007/978-3-540-78917-8_1
17. Bijl, M., Rensink, A., Tretmans, J.: Compositional testing with IOCO. In: Petrenko, A., Ulrich, A. (eds.) FATES 2003. LNCS, vol. 2931, pp. 86–100. Springer, Heidelberg (2004)
18. van Glabbeek, R.J.: The linear time -branching time spectrum I: the semantics of concrete, sequential processes. In: Bergstra, J.A., Ponse, A., Smolka, S.A. (eds.) Handbook of Process Algebra, pp. 3–99. Elsevier, Amsterdam (2001)

A Linear-Time–Branching-Time Spectrum of Behavioral Specification Theories

Uli Fahrenberg[1(✉)] and Axel Legay[2]

[1] École polytechnique, Palaiseau, France
uli@lix.polytechnique.fr
[2] Inria, Rennes, France

Abstract. We propose behavioral specification theories for most equivalences in the linear-time–branching-time spectrum. Almost all previous work on specification theories focuses on bisimilarity, but there is a clear interest in specification theories for other preorders and equivalences. We show that specification theories for preorders cannot exist and develop a general scheme which allows us to define behavioral specification theories, based on disjunctive modal transition systems, for most equivalences in the linear-time–branching-time spectrum.

1 Introduction

Models and specifications are central objects in theoretical computer science. In model-based verification, models of computing systems are held up against specifications of their behaviors, and methods are developed to check whether or not a given model satisfies a given specification.

In recent years, behavioral specification theories have seen some popularity [1,3,4,7,10–12,21,22,24,29]. Here, the specification formalism is an extension of the modeling formalism, so that specifications have an operational interpretation and models are verified by comparing their operational behavior against the specification's behavior. Popular examples of such specification theories are modal transition systems [3,11,21], disjunctive modal transition systems [7,10,24], and acceptance specifications [12,29]. Also relations to contracts and interfaces have been exposed [4,28], as have extensions for real-time and quantitative specifications and for models with data [5,6,8,13,14].

Except for the work by Vogler *et al.* in [10,11], behavioral specification theories have been developed only to characterize bisimilarity. While bisimilarity is an important equivalence relation on models, there are many others which also are of interest. Examples include nested and k-nested simulation [2,17], ready or $\frac{2}{3}$-simulation [23], trace equivalence [19], impossible futures [33], or the failure semantics of [9–11,27,32] and others.

In order to initiate a systematic study of specification theories for different semantics, we exhibit in this paper specification theories for most of the equivalences in van Glabbeek's linear-time–branching-time spectrum [31].

Most of this work was carried out while the first author was still employed at Inria Rennes, France.

To develop our systemization, we first have to clarify what precisely is meant by a specification theory. This is similar to the attempt at a uniform framework of specifications in [4], but our focus is more general. Inspired by the seminal work of Pnueli [27], Larsen [22], and Hennessy and Milner [18], we develop the point of view that a behavioral specification theory is an expressive specification formalism equipped with a mapping from models to their characteristic formulae and with a refinement preorder which generalizes the satisfaction relation between models and specifications.

We then introduce a general scheme of linear and branching relation families and show that variants of these characterize most of the preorders and equivalences in the linear-time–branching-time spectrum (notably also all of the ones mentioned above). We transfer our scheme to disjunctive modal transition systems and use it to define a linear-time–branching-time spectrum of refinement preorders, each giving rise to a specification theory for a different equivalence in the linear-time–branching-time spectrum.

Specification theories as we define them here are useful for incremental design and verification, as specifications can be refined until a sufficient level of detail is reached. The specification theories developed for bisimilarity in [1,3,7,12,21,22,24,29] also include operations of conjunction and composition, hence allowing for compositional design and verification. What we present here is a first fundamental study of specification theories for equivalences other than bisimilarity, and we leave compositionality for future work.

To sum up, the contributions of this paper are as follows:

- a clarification of the basic theory of behavioral specification theories;
- a uniform treatment of most of the relations in the linear-time–branching-time spectrum;
- a uniform linear-time–branching-time spectrum of specification theories.

The paper is accompanied by a technical report [16] which contains some of the proofs of our results and extra material to provide context.

2   Specification Theories

We start this paper by introducing and clarifying some concepts related to models and specifications from [18,22,27].

Let Mod be a set (of models). A *specification formalism* for Mod is a structure $(\mathsf{Spec}, \models)$, where Spec is a set of specifications and $\models \subseteq \mathsf{Mod} \times \mathsf{Spec}$ is the satisfaction relation. The models in Mod serve to represent computing systems, and the specifications in Spec represent properties of such systems. The model-checking problem is, given $\mathcal{I} \in \mathsf{Mod}$ and $\mathcal{S} \in \mathsf{Spec}$, to decide whether $\mathcal{I} \models \mathcal{S}$.

For $\mathcal{S} \in \mathsf{Spec}$, let $[\![\mathcal{S}]\!] = \{\mathcal{I} \in \mathsf{Mod} \mid \mathcal{I} \models \mathcal{S}\}$ denote its set of *implementations*, that is, the set of models which adhere to the specification. Note that $\models$ and $[\![\cdot]\!]$ are inter-definable: for $\mathcal{I} \in \mathsf{Mod}$ and $\mathcal{S} \in \mathsf{Spec}$, $\mathcal{I} \models \mathcal{S}$ iff $\mathcal{I} \in [\![\mathcal{S}]\!]$.

There is a preorder of *semantic refinement* on Spec, denoted $\preceq$, defined by

$$\mathcal{S}_1 \preceq \mathcal{S}_2 \quad \text{iff} \quad [\![\mathcal{S}_1]\!] \subseteq [\![\mathcal{S}_2]\!].$$

Hence $S_1 \preceq S_2$ iff every implementation of S_1 is also an implementation of S_2, that is, if it holds for every model that once it satisfies S_1, it automatically also satisfies S_2. The corresponding equivalence relation $\approx = \preceq \cap \succeq$ is called *semantic equivalence*: $S_1 \approx S_2$ iff $[\![S_1]\!] = [\![S_2]\!]$.

For a model $\mathcal{I} \in \mathsf{Mod}$, let $\mathsf{Th}(\mathcal{I}) = \{S \in \mathsf{Spec} \mid \mathcal{I} \models S\}$ denote its set of *theories*: the set of all specifications satisfied by $\mathcal{I}$. As [22] notes, the functions $[\![\cdot]\!] : \mathsf{Spec} \to 2^{\mathsf{Mod}}$ and $\mathsf{Th} : \mathsf{Mod} \to 2^{\mathsf{Spec}}$ can be extended to functions on sets of specifications and models by $[\![A]\!] = \bigcap_{S \in A}[\![S]\!]$ and $\mathsf{Th}(B) = \bigcap_{\mathcal{I} \in B} \mathsf{Th}(\mathcal{I})$, and then $[\![\cdot]\!] : 2^{\mathsf{Spec}} \rightleftarrows 2^{\mathsf{Mod}} : \mathsf{Th}$ forms a Galois connection.

Let $\sqsubseteq$ be the preorder on Mod defined by

$$\mathcal{I}_1 \sqsubseteq \mathcal{I}_2 \quad \text{iff} \quad \mathsf{Th}(\mathcal{I}_1) \subseteq \mathsf{Th}(\mathcal{I}_2),$$

and let $\sqsubseteq\!\!\sqsupseteq = \sqsubseteq \cap \sqsupseteq$. Hence $\mathcal{I}_1 \sqsubseteq\!\!\sqsupseteq \mathcal{I}_2$ iff $\mathsf{Th}(\mathcal{I}_1) = \mathsf{Th}(\mathcal{I}_2)$, that is, iff $\mathcal{I}_1$ and $\mathcal{I}_2$ satisfy precisely the same specifications.

In terminology first introduced in [18], the specification formalism $(\mathsf{Spec}, \models)$ is said to be *adequate* for $\sqsubseteq\!\!\sqsupseteq$. In fact, the usual point of view is sightly different: normally, Mod comes equipped with some equivalence relation $\sim$, and then one says that $(\mathsf{Spec}, \models)$ is adequate for $(\mathsf{Mod}, \sim)$ if $\sqsubseteq\!\!\sqsupseteq = \sim$. It is clear that $\sim$ is not needed to reason about specification formalisms; we can simply declare that $(\mathsf{Spec}, \models)$ is adequate for whatever model equivalence $\sqsubseteq\!\!\sqsupseteq$ it *induces*.

Using the terminology of [27], a specification $S \in \mathsf{Spec}$ is a *characteristic formula* for a model $\mathcal{I} \in \mathsf{Mod}$ if $\mathcal{I} \models S$ and for all $\mathcal{I}' \models S$, $\mathcal{I}' \sqsubseteq\!\!\sqsupseteq \mathcal{I}$. Hence S characterizes precisely all models which are equivalent to $\mathcal{I}$.

Again following [27], the specification formalism $(\mathsf{Spec}, \models)$ is said to be *expressive* for Mod if every $\mathcal{I} \in \mathsf{Mod}$ admits a characteristic formula. Our first result seems to have been overlooked in [18,22,27]: in an expressive specification formalism, the preorder $\sqsubseteq$ is, in fact, an equivalence.

Proposition 1. *If* Spec *is expressive for* Mod, *then* $\sqsubseteq = \sqsubseteq\!\!\sqsupseteq$.

Proof. Let $\mathcal{I}_1, \mathcal{I}_2 \in \mathsf{Mod}$ and assume $\mathcal{I}_1 \sqsubseteq \mathcal{I}_2$. Let $S_1 \in \mathsf{Spec}$ be a characteristic formula for $\mathcal{I}_1$, then $S_1 \in \mathsf{Th}(\mathcal{I}_1)$. But $\mathsf{Th}(\mathcal{I}_1) \subseteq \mathsf{Th}(\mathcal{I}_2)$, hence $S_1 \in \mathsf{Th}(\mathcal{I}_2)$, *i.e.* $\mathcal{I}_2 \models S_1$. As S_1 is characteristic, this implies $\mathcal{I}_2 \sqsubseteq\!\!\sqsupseteq \mathcal{I}_1$.   □

Example. A very simple specification formalism is $\mathsf{Spec} = 2^{\mathsf{Mod}}$, that is, specifications are sets of models. In that case, $\models \,=\, \in$ is the element-of relation, and $[\![S]\!] = S$, thus $S_1 \preceq S_2$ iff $S_1 \subseteq S_2$ and $S_1 \approx S_2$ iff $S_1 = S_2$. Every $\mathcal{I} \in \mathsf{Mod}$ has characteristic formula $\{\mathcal{I}\} \in \mathsf{Spec}$, hence 2^{Mod} is expressive for Mod, so that $\sqsubseteq = \sqsubseteq\!\!\sqsupseteq$. Further, if $\mathcal{I}_1 \sqsubseteq\!\!\sqsupseteq \mathcal{I}_2$, then $\mathcal{I}_2 \in \{\mathcal{I}_1\}$, hence $\mathcal{I}_1 = \mathcal{I}_2$. We have shown that 2^{Mod} is adequate for equality $=$.

3   Behavioral Specification Theories

We are ready to introduce what we mean by a behavioral specification theory: an expressive specification formalism with extra structure. This mainly sums up and clarifies ideas already present in [4,22], but we make a connection between specification theories and characteristic formulae which is new. Specifically, we will see that a central ingredient in a specification theory is a function χ which maps models to their characteristic formulae.

Definition 2. *A (behavioral)* specification theory *for* Mod *is a specification formalism* (Spec, $\models$) *for* Mod *together with a mapping* χ : Mod $\rightarrow$ Spec *and a pre-order* $\leq$ *on* Spec, *called* modal refinement, *subject to the following conditions:*

– *for every* $\mathcal{I} \in$ Mod, $\chi(\mathcal{I})$ *is a characteristic formula for* $\mathcal{I}$;
– *for all* $\mathcal{I} \in$ Mod *and all* $\mathcal{S} \in$ Spec, $\mathcal{I} \models \mathcal{S}$ *iff* $\chi(\mathcal{I}) \leq \mathcal{S}$.

The equivalence relation $\equiv\, =\, \leq \cap \geq$ on Spec is called *modal equivalence*. Note that specification theories are indeed expressive; also, $\models$ is fully determined by $\leq$.

Remark 3. In a categorical sense, the function χ : Mod $\rightarrow$ Spec is a *section* of the Galois connection $\llbracket \cdot \rrbracket : 2^{\mathsf{Spec}} \rightleftarrows 2^{\mathsf{Mod}} :$ Th. Indeed, we have $\chi(\mathcal{I}) \in \mathsf{Th}(\mathcal{I})$ for all $\mathcal{I} \in$ Mod and $\mathcal{I}' \sqsubseteq \mathcal{I}$ for all $\mathcal{I}' \in \llbracket \chi(\mathcal{I}) \rrbracket$, and these properties are characterizing for χ.

We sum up a few consequences of the definition: modal refinement (equivalence) implies semantic refinement (equivalence), and on characteristic formulae, all refinements and equivalences collapse.

Proposition 4. *Let* (Spec, χ, $\leq$) *be a specification theory for* Mod.

1. *For all* $\mathcal{S}_1, \mathcal{S}_2 \in$ Spec, $\mathcal{S}_1 \leq \mathcal{S}_2$ *implies* $\mathcal{S}_1 \preceq \mathcal{S}_2$ *and* $\mathcal{S}_1 \equiv \mathcal{S}_2$ *implies* $\mathcal{S}_1 \approx \mathcal{S}_2$.
2. *For all* $\mathcal{I}_1, \mathcal{I}_2 \in$ Mod, *the following are equivalent:* $\chi(\mathcal{I}_1) \leq \chi(\mathcal{I}_2)$, $\chi(\mathcal{I}_2) \leq \chi(\mathcal{I}_1)$, $\chi(\mathcal{I}_1) \preceq \chi(\mathcal{I}_2)$, $\chi(\mathcal{I}_2) \preceq \chi(\mathcal{I}_1)$, $\mathcal{I}_1 \sqsubseteq \mathcal{I}_2$.

Proof. The first claim follows from transitivity of $\leq$: if $\mathcal{I} \in \llbracket \mathcal{S}_1 \rrbracket$, then $\chi(\mathcal{I}) \leq \mathcal{S}_1 \leq \mathcal{S}_2$, hence $\chi(\mathcal{I}) \leq \mathcal{S}_2$, thus $\mathcal{I} \in \llbracket \mathcal{S}_2 \rrbracket$.
For the second claim, let $\mathcal{I}_1, \mathcal{I}_2 \in$ Mod.

– If $\chi(\mathcal{I}_1) \leq \chi(\mathcal{I}_2)$, then $\chi(\mathcal{I}_1) \preceq \chi(\mathcal{I}_2)$ by the first part.
– If $\chi(\mathcal{I}_1) \preceq \chi(\mathcal{I}_2)$, then $\llbracket \chi(\mathcal{I}_1) \rrbracket \subseteq \llbracket \chi(\mathcal{I}_2) \rrbracket$. But $\mathcal{I}_1 \in \llbracket \chi(\mathcal{I}_1) \rrbracket$, hence $\mathcal{I}_1 \in \llbracket \chi(\mathcal{I}_2) \rrbracket$, which, as $\chi(\mathcal{I}_2)$ is characteristic, implies $\mathcal{I}_1 \sqsubseteq \mathcal{I}_2$. Also, $\mathcal{I}_1 \in \llbracket \chi(\mathcal{I}_2) \rrbracket$ implies $\chi(\mathcal{I}_1) \leq \chi(\mathcal{I}_2)$.
– Assume $\mathcal{I}_1 \sqsubseteq \mathcal{I}_2$ and let $\mathcal{I} \in \llbracket \chi(\mathcal{I}_1) \rrbracket$. Then $\mathcal{I} \sqsubseteq \mathcal{I}_1$, hence $\mathcal{I} \sqsubseteq \mathcal{I}_2$, which implies $\mathcal{I} \in \llbracket \chi(\mathcal{I}_2) \rrbracket$. We have shown that $\chi(\mathcal{I}_1) \preceq \chi(\mathcal{I}_2)$.

We have shown that $\chi(\mathcal{I}_1) \leq \chi(\mathcal{I}_2)$ iff $\chi(\mathcal{I}_1) \preceq \chi(\mathcal{I}_2)$ iff $\mathcal{I}_1 \sqsubseteq \mathcal{I}_2$, and reversing the roles of $\mathcal{I}_1$ and $\mathcal{I}_2$ gives the other equivalences.   □

The second part of the proposition means that the mapping χ : Mod $\rightarrow$ Spec is an *embedding* up to equivalence: for all $\mathcal{I}_1, \mathcal{I}_2 \in$ Mod, $\mathcal{I}_1 \sqsubseteq \mathcal{I}_2$ iff $\chi(\mathcal{I}_1) \equiv \chi(\mathcal{I}_2)$ iff $\chi(\mathcal{I}_1) \approx \chi(\mathcal{I}_2)$. Because of this, most work in specification theories *identifies* models $\mathcal{I}$ with their characteristic formulae $\chi(\mathcal{I})$; for reasons of clarity, we will not make this identification here.

We finish this section with a lemma which shows that the property of $\chi(\mathcal{I})$ being characteristic formulae follows when $\leq$ is symmetric on models.

Lemma 5. *Let* Spec *be a set,* $\chi : $ Mod $\rightarrow$ Spec *a mapping and* $\leq \subseteq$ Spec $\times$ Spec *a preorder. If the restriction of* $\leq$ *to the image of* χ *is symmetric, then* (Spec, $\chi, \leq$) *is a specification theory for* Mod.

Example. For our other example, Spec $= 2^{\mathsf{Mod}}$, we can let $\chi(\mathcal{I}) = \{\mathcal{I}\}$ and $\leq \ = \ \subseteq$. Then $\mathcal{I} \in \mathcal{S}$ iff $\{\mathcal{I}\} \subseteq \mathcal{S}$, *i.e.* $\mathcal{I} \models \mathcal{S}$ iff $\chi(\mathcal{I}) \leq \mathcal{S}$. This shows that $(2^{\mathsf{Mod}}, \chi, \subseteq)$ is a specification theory for Mod (which is adequate and expressive for equality).

4 Disjunctive Modal Transition Systems

We proceed to recall disjunctive modal transition systems and how these can serve as a specification theory for bisimilarity. The material in this section is well-known, but our definitions from the previous sections allow for much more succinctness, for example in Proposition 6 below.

From now on, Mod will be the set **LTS** of *finite labeled transition systems*, *i.e.* tuples (S, s^0, T) consisting of a finite set of states S, an initial state $s^0 \in S$, and transitions $T \subseteq S \times \Sigma \times S$ labeled with symbols from some fixed finite alphabet Σ.

Recall [25,26] that two LTS (S_1, s_1^0, T_1) and (S_2, s_2^0, T_2) are *bisimilar* if there exists a relation $R \subseteq S_1 \times S_2$ such that $(s_1^0, s_2^0) \in R$ and for all $(s_1, s_2) \in R$,

- for all $(s_1, a, t_1) \in T_1$, there is $(s_2, a, t_2) \in T_2$ with $(t_1, t_2) \in R$,
- for all $(s_2, a, t_2) \in T_2$, there is $(s_1, a, t_1) \in T_1$ with $(t_1, t_2) \in R$.

A *disjunctive modal transition system* (DMTS) [24] is a tuple $\mathcal{D} = (S, S^0, \dashrightarrow, \longrightarrow)$ consisting of finite sets $S \supseteq S^0$ of states and initial states, a *may*-transition relation $\dashrightarrow \ \subseteq S \times \Sigma \times S$, and a *disjunctive must-transition relation* $\longrightarrow \ \subseteq S \times 2^{\Sigma \times S}$. It is assumed that for all $(s, N) \in \longrightarrow$ and all $(a, t) \in N$, $(s, a, t) \in \dashrightarrow$. Note that we permit several (or no) initial states, in contrast to [24]. The set of DMTS is denoted **DMTS**.

As customary, we write $s \overset{a}{\dashrightarrow} t$ instead of $(s, a, t) \in \dashrightarrow$ and $s \longrightarrow N$ instead of $(s, N) \in \longrightarrow$. The intuition is that may-transitions $s \overset{a}{\dashrightarrow} t$ specify which transitions are permitted in an implementation, whereas a must-transition $s \longrightarrow N$ stipulates a disjunctive requirement: at least one of the choices $(a, t) \in N$ has to be implemented.

A *modal refinement* [24] of two DMTS $\mathcal{D}_1 = (S_1, S_1^0, \dashrightarrow_1, \longrightarrow_1)$, $\mathcal{D}_2 = (S_2, S_2^0, \dashrightarrow_2, \longrightarrow_2)$ is a relation $R \subseteq S_1 \times S_2$ for which it holds of all $(s_1, s_2) \in R$ that

- $\forall s_1 \overset{a}{\dashrightarrow}_1 t_1 : \exists s_2 \overset{a}{\dashrightarrow}_2 t_2 : (t_1, t_2) \in R$;
- $\forall s_2 \longrightarrow_2 N_2 : \exists s_1 \longrightarrow_1 N_1 : \forall (a, t_1) \in N_1 : \exists (a, t_2) \in N_2 : (t_1, t_2) \in R$;

and such that for all $s_1^0 \in S_1^0$, there exists $s_2^0 \in S_2^0$ for which $(s_1^0, s_2^0) \in R$. Let $\leq \ \subseteq$ DMTS $\times$ DMTS be the relation defined by $\mathcal{D}_1 \leq \mathcal{D}_2$ iff there exists a modal refinement as above (a *witness* for $\mathcal{D}_1 \leq \mathcal{D}_2$). Clearly, $\leq$ is a preorder.

LTS are embedded into DMTS as follows. For an LTS $\mathcal{I} = (S, s^0, T)$, let $\chi(\mathcal{I}) = (S, \{s^0\}, \dashrightarrow, \longrightarrow)$ be the DMTS with $\dashrightarrow = T$ and $\longrightarrow = \{(s, \{(a,t)\}) \mid (s,a,t) \in T\}$. The following proposition reformulates well-known facts about DMTS and modal refinement.

Proposition 6. (DMTS, $\chi, \leq$) *is a specification theory for* LTS *adequate for bisimilarity.*

Proof. In lieu of Lemma 5, we show that $\leq$ is bisimilarity, hence symmetric, on the image of χ. Let $\mathcal{I}_1, \mathcal{I}_2 \in$ LTS and assume $\chi(\mathcal{I}_1) \leq \chi(\mathcal{I}_2)$. Write $\mathcal{I}_1 = (S_1, s_1^0, T_1)$, $\mathcal{I}_2 = (S_2, s_2^0, T_2)$, $\chi(\mathcal{I}_1) = (S_1, \{s_1^0\}, \dashrightarrow_1, \longrightarrow_1)$, and $\chi(\mathcal{I}_2) = (S_2, \{s_2^0\}, \dashrightarrow_2, \longrightarrow_2)$.

We have a relation $R \subseteq S_1 \times S_2$ such that $(s_1^0, s_2^0) \in R$ and for all $(s_1, s_2) \in R$, $\forall s_1 \overset{a}{\dashrightarrow}_1 t_1 : \exists s_2 \overset{a}{\dashrightarrow}_2 t_2 : (t_1, t_2) \in R$ and $\forall s_2 \longrightarrow_2 N_2 : \exists s_1 \longrightarrow_1 N_1 : \forall (a, t_1) \in N_1 : \exists (a, t_2) \in N_2 : (t_1, t_2) \in R$. Let $(s_1, s_2) \in R$. We show that R is a bisimulation.

Let $(s_1, a, t_1) \in T_1$. Then $s_1 \overset{a}{\dashrightarrow}_1 t_1$, so that we have a transition $s_2 \overset{a}{\dashrightarrow}_2 t_2$ with $(t_1, t_2) \in R$. By definition of $\chi(\mathcal{I}_1)$, $(s_2, a, t_2) \in T_2$.

Let $(s_2, a, t_2) \in T_2$. Then $s_2 \longrightarrow_2 N_2 = \{(a, t_2)\}$, hence there is $s_1 \longrightarrow_1 N_1$ such that $\forall (a, t_1) \in N_1 : \exists (a, t_2') \in N_2 : (t_1, t_2') \in R$. But then $t_2' = t_2$, and by definition of $\chi(\mathcal{I}_2)$, $N_1 = \{(a, t_1)\}$ must be a one-element set, hence $(s_1, a, t_1) \in T_1$ and $(t_1, t_2) \in R$.

We have shown that $\chi(\mathcal{I}_1) \leq \chi(\mathcal{I}_2)$ implies that $\mathcal{I}_1$ and $\mathcal{I}_2$ are bisimilar; the proof of the other direction is similar.   □

5   A Specification Theory for Simulation Equivalence

We want to construct specification theories for other interesting relations in the linear-time–branching-time spectrum [31]. Given Proposition 1 and the fact that specification theories are expressive, we know that it is futile to look for specification theories for *preorders* in the spectrum. What we *can* do, however, is find specification theories for the *equivalences* in the spectrum. To warm up, we start out by a specification theory for simulation equivalence.

Recall [20] that a *simulation* of LTS (S_1, s_1^0, T_1), (S_2, s_2^0, T_2) is a relation $R \subseteq S_1 \times S_2$ such that $(s_1^0, s_2^0) \in R$ and for all $(s_1, s_2) \in R$,

- for all $(s_1, a, t_1) \in T_1$, there is $(s_2, a, t_2) \in T_2$ with $(t_1, t_2) \in R$.

LTS (S_1, s_1^0, T_1) and (S_2, s_2^0, T_2) are said to be *simulation equivalent* if there exist a simulation $R^1 \subseteq S_1 \times S_2$ *and* a simulation $R^2 \subseteq S_2 \times S_1$.

Definition 7. *Let* $\mathcal{D}_1 = (S_1, S_1^0, \dashrightarrow_1, \longrightarrow_1), \mathcal{D}_2 = (S_2, S_2^0, \dashrightarrow_2, \longrightarrow_2) \in$ DMTS. *A simulation refinement consists of two relations* $R_1, R_2 \subseteq S_1 \times S_2$ *such that*

1. $\forall s_1^0 \in S_1^0 : \exists s_2^0 \in S_2^0 : (s_1^0, s_2^0) \in R_1$ *and* $\forall s_2^0 \in S_2^0 : \exists s_1^0 \in S_1^0 : (s_1^0, s_2^0) \in R_2$;
2. $\forall (s_1, s_2) \in R_1 : \forall s_1 \overset{a}{\dashrightarrow}_1 t_1 : \exists s_2 \overset{a}{\dashrightarrow}_2 t_2 : (t_1, t_2) \in R_1$;

3. $\forall (s_1, s_2) \in R_2 : \forall s_2 \longrightarrow_2 N_2 : \exists s_1 \longrightarrow_1 N_1 : \forall (a, t_1) \in N_1 : \exists (a, t_2) \in N_2 :$ $(t_1, t_2) \in R_2.$

Intuitively, R_1 is a simulation of may-transitions from $\mathcal{D}_1$ to $\mathcal{D}_2$, whereas R_2 is a simulation of disjunctive must-transitions from $\mathcal{D}_2$ to $\mathcal{D}_1$. Let $\leq_s \subseteq$ DMTS × DMTS be the relation defined by $\mathcal{D}_1 \leq_s \mathcal{D}_2$ iff there exists a simulation refinement as above. Clearly, $\leq_s$ is a preorder. A direct proof of the following theorem, similar to the one of Proposition 6, is given in [16], but it also follows from Theorem 12.

Theorem 8. (DMTS, $\chi, \leq_s$) *forms a specification theory for* LTS *adequate for simulation equivalence.*

6 Specification Theories for Branching Equivalences

We proceed to generalize the work in the preceding section and develop DMTS-based specification theories for all *branching* equivalences in the linear-time–branching-time spectrum. Examples of such branching equivalences include the bisimilarity and simulation equivalence which we have already seen, but also ready simulation equivalence [23] and nested simulation equivalence [2, 17] are important. We will treat the linear part of the spectrum, which includes relations such as trace equivalence [19], impossible-futures equivalence [33] or failure equivalence [9–11, 27, 32], in the next section.

We start by laying out a scheme which systematically covers all branching relations in the spectrum.

Definition 9. *Let* $k \in \mathbb{N} \cup \{\infty\}$ *and* $\mathcal{I}_1 = (S_1, s_1^0, T_1), \mathcal{I}_2 = (S_2, s_2^0, T_2) \in$ LTS. *A* branching k-switching relation family *from* $\mathcal{I}_1$ *to* $\mathcal{I}_2$ *consists of relations* $R^0, \ldots, R^k \subseteq S_1 \times S_2$ *such that* $(s_1^0, s_2^0) \in R^0$ *and*

- *for all even* $j \in \{0, \ldots, k\}$ *and* $(s_1, s_2) \in R^j$:
  • $\forall (s_1, a, t_1) \in T_1 : \exists (s_2, a, t_2) \in T_2 : (t_1, t_2) \in R^j$;
  • *if* $j < k$, *then* $\forall (s_2, a, t_2) \in T_2 : \exists (s_1, a, t_1) \in T_1 : (t_1, t_2) \in R^{j+1}$;
- *for all odd* $j \in \{0, \ldots, k\}$ *and* $(s_1, s_2) \in R^j$:
  • $\forall (s_2, a, t_2) \in T_2 : \exists (s_1, a, t_1) \in T_1 : (t_1, t_2) \in R^j$;
  • *if* $j < k$, *then* $\forall (s_1, a, t_1) \in T_1 : \exists (s_2, a, t_2) \in T_2 : (t_1, t_2) \in R^{j+1}$.

Clearly, a simulation is the same as a branching 0-switching relation family. Also, a branching 1-switching relation family is a *nested simulation*: the initial states are related in R^0; any transition in $\mathcal{I}_1$ from a pair $(s_1, s_2) \in R^0$ has to be matched recursively in $\mathcal{I}_2$; and at any point in time, the sense of the matching can switch, in that now transitions in $\mathcal{I}_2$ from a pair $(s_1, s_2) \in R^1$ have to be matched recursively by transitions in $\mathcal{I}_1$. In general, a branching k-switching relation family is a k-nested simulation, see also [17, Definition 8.5.2] which is similar to ours. A branching ∞-switching relation family is a bisimulation: any transition in $\mathcal{I}_1$ has to be matched recursively by one in $\mathcal{I}_2$ and vice versa. We refer to [15] for more motivation.

Definition 10. *Let $k \in \mathbb{N} \cup \{\infty\}$ and $\mathcal{I}_1 = (S_1, s_1^0, T_1), \mathcal{I}_2 = (S_2, s_2^0, T_2) \in$ LTS. A* branching k-ready relation family *from $\mathcal{I}_1$ to $\mathcal{I}_2$ is a branching k-switching relation family $R^0, \ldots, R^k \subseteq S_1 \times S_2$ with the extra property that for all $(s_1, s_2) \in R^k$:*

- *if k is even, then $\forall(s_2, a, t_2) \in T_2 : \exists(s_1, a, t_1) \in T_1$;*
- *if k is odd, then $\forall(s_1, a, t_1) \in T_1 : \exists(s_2, a, t_2) \in T_2$.*

Hence a branching 0-ready relation family is the same as a *ready simulation*: any transition in $\mathcal{I}_1$ has to be matched recursively by one in $\mathcal{I}_2$; and at any point in time, precisely the same actions have to be available in the two states. A branching 1-ready relation family would be a nested ready simulation, and so on. Branching k-switching and k-ready relation families cover all branching relations in the linear-time–branching-time spectrum.

Because of Proposition 1, we are only interested in equivalences. For $k \in \mathbb{N} \cup \{\infty\}$ and $\mathcal{I}_1, \mathcal{I}_2 \in$ LTS, we write $\mathcal{I}_1 \sim_k \mathcal{I}_2$ if there exist a branching k-switching relation family from $\mathcal{I}_1$ to $\mathcal{I}_2$ and another from $\mathcal{I}_2$ to $\mathcal{I}_1$. We write $\mathcal{I}_1 \sim_k^r \mathcal{I}_2$ if there exist a branching k-ready relation family from $\mathcal{I}_1$ to $\mathcal{I}_2$ and another from $\mathcal{I}_2$ to $\mathcal{I}_1$. Then $\sim_0$ is simulation equivalence, $\sim_1$ is nested simulation equivalence, $\sim_\infty$ is bisimilarity, $\sim_0^r$ is ready simulation equivalence, etc.

We proceed to devise specification theories for LTS which are adequate for $\sim_k$ and $\sim_k^r$.

Definition 11. *Let $k \in \mathbb{N} \cup \{\infty\}$ and $\mathcal{D}_1 = (S_1, S_1^0, \dashrightarrow_1, \longrightarrow_1), \mathcal{D}_2 = (S_2, S_2^0, \dashrightarrow_2, \longrightarrow_2) \in$ DMTS. A* branching k-switching relation family *from $\mathcal{D}_1$ to $\mathcal{D}_2$ consists of relations $R_1^0, \ldots, R_1^k, R_2^0, \ldots, R_2^k \subseteq S_1 \times S_2$ such that*

- *$\forall s_1^0 \in S_1^0 : \exists s_2^0 \in S_2^0 : (s_1^0, s_2^0) \in R_1^0$ and $\forall s_2^0 \in S_2^0 : \exists s_1^0 \in S_1^0 : (s_1^0, s_2^0) \in R_2^0$;*
- *for all even $j \in \{0, \ldots, k\}$ and $(s_1, s_2) \in R_1^j$:*
  - *$\forall s_1 \dashrightarrow_1^a t_1 : \exists s_2 \dashrightarrow_2^a t_2 : (t_1, t_2) \in R_1^j$;*
  - *if $j < k$, then $\forall s_2 \longrightarrow_2 N_2 : \exists s_1 \longrightarrow_1 N_1 : \forall(a, t_1) \in N_1 : \exists(a, t_2) \in N_2 : (t_1, t_2) \in R_1^{j+1}$;*
- *for all odd $j \in \{0, \ldots, k\}$ and $(s_1, s_2) \in R_1^j$:*
  - *$\forall s_2 \longrightarrow_2 N_2 : \exists s_1 \longrightarrow_1 N_1 : \forall(a, t_1) \in N_1 : \exists(a, t_2) \in N_2 : (t_1, t_2) \in R_1^j$;*
  - *if $j < k$, then $\forall s_1 \dashrightarrow_1^a t_1 : \exists s_2 \dashrightarrow_2^a t_2 : (t_1, t_2) \in R_1^{j+1}$;*
- *for all even $j \in \{0, \ldots, k\}$ and $(s_1, s_2) \in R_2^j$:*
  - *$\forall s_2 \longrightarrow_2 N_2 : \exists s_1 \longrightarrow_1 N_1 : \forall(a, t_1) \in N_1 : \exists(a, t_2) \in N_2 : (t_1, t_2) \in R_2^j$;*
  - *if $j < k$, then $\forall s_1 \dashrightarrow_1^a t_1 : \exists s_2 \dashrightarrow_2^a t_2 : (t_1, t_2) \in R_2^{j+1}$.*
- *for all odd $j \in \{0, \ldots, k\}$ and $(s_1, s_2) \in R_2^j$:*
  - *$\forall s_1 \dashrightarrow_1^a t_1 : \exists s_2 \dashrightarrow_2^a t_2 : (t_1, t_2) \in R_2^j$;*
  - *if $j < k$, then $\forall s_2 \longrightarrow_2 N_2 : \exists s_1 \longrightarrow_1 N_1 : \forall(a, t_1) \in N_1 : \exists(a, t_2) \in N_2 : (t_1, t_2) \in R_2^{j+1}$;*

A branching k-ready relation family *from $\mathcal{D}_1$ to $\mathcal{D}_2$ is a branching k-switching relation family as above with the extra property that if k is even, then*

- $\forall (s_1, s_2) \in R_1^k : \forall s_2 \longrightarrow_2 N_2 : \exists s_1 \longrightarrow_1 N_1 : \forall (a, t_1) \in N_1 : \exists (a, t_2) \in N_2;$
- $\forall (s_1, s_2) \in R_2^k : \forall s_1 \overset{a}{\dashrightarrow}_1 t_1 : \exists s_2 \overset{a}{\dashrightarrow}_2 t_2;$

and if k is odd, then

- $\forall (s_1, s_2) \in R_1^k : \forall s_1 \overset{a}{\dashrightarrow}_1 t_1 : \exists s_2 \overset{a}{\dashrightarrow}_2 t_2;$
- $\forall (s_1, s_2) \in R_2^k : \forall s_2 \longrightarrow_2 N_2 : \exists s_1 \longrightarrow_1 N_1 : \forall (a, t_1) \in N_1 : \exists (a, t_2) \in N_2.$

For $k \in \mathbb{N} \cup \{\infty\}$ and $\mathcal{D}_1, \mathcal{D}_2 \in \mathsf{DMTS}$, we write $\mathcal{D}_1 \leq_k \mathcal{D}_2$ if there exist a branching k-switching relation family from $\mathcal{D}_1$ to $\mathcal{D}_2$. We write $\mathcal{D}_1 \leq_k^r \mathcal{D}_2$ if there exist a branching k-ready relation family from $\mathcal{D}_1$ to $\mathcal{D}_2$. Note that $\leq_0$ is the relation $\leq_s$ from the preceding section.

Theorem 12. *For any $k \in \mathbb{N} \cup \{\infty\}$, $(\mathsf{DMTS}, \chi, \leq_k)$ is a specification theory for LTS adequate for $\sim_k$, and $(\mathsf{DMTS}, \chi, \leq_k^r)$ is a specification theory for LTS adequate for $\sim_k^r$.*

Remark 13. There is a setting of *generalized simulation games*, based on Stirling's bisimulation games [30], which generalizes the above constructions and gives them a natural context. We have developed these in a quantitative setting in [15], and we provide an exposition of the approach in [16]. Generalized simulation games can be lifted to games on DMTS which can be used to define the relations of Definition 11, see again [16].

7   Specification Theories for Linear Equivalences

We develop a scheme similar to the one of the previous section to cover all linear relations in the linear-time–branching-time spectrum. For $\mathcal{I} = (S, s^0, T) \in \mathsf{LTS}$, we let $T^* \subseteq S \times \Sigma^* \times S$ be the reflexive, transitive closure of T; a recursive definition is as follows:

- $(s, \varepsilon, s) \in T^*$ for all $s \in S$;
- for all $(s, \tau, t) \in T^*$ and $(t, a, u) \in T$, also $(s, \tau.a, u) \in T^*$.

Definition 14. *Let $k \in \mathbb{N} \cup \{\infty\}$ and $\mathcal{I}_1 = (S_1, s_1^0, T_1), \mathcal{I}_2 = (S_2, s_2^0, T_2) \in \mathsf{LTS}$. A linear k-switching relation family from $\mathcal{I}_1$ to $\mathcal{I}_2$ consists of relations $R^0, \dots, R^k \subseteq S_1 \times S_2$ such that $(s_1^0, s_2^0) \in R^0$ and*

- *for all even $j \in \{0, \dots, k\}$ and $(s_1, s_2) \in R^j$:*
  - $\forall (s_1, \tau, t_1) \in T_1^* : \exists (s_2, \tau, t_2) \in T_2^*;$
  - *if $j < k$, then $\forall (s_1, \tau, t_1) \in T_1^* : \exists (s_2, \tau, t_2) \in T_2^* : (t_1, t_2) \in R^{j+1};$*
- *for all odd $j \in \{0, \dots, k\}$ and $(s_1, s_2) \in R^j$:*
  - $\forall (s_2, \tau, t_2) \in T_2^* : \exists (s_1, \tau, t_1) \in T_1^*;$
  - *if $j < k$, then $\forall (s_2, \tau, t_2) \in T_2^* : \exists (s_1, \tau, t_1) \in T_1^* : (t_1, t_2) \in R^{j+1};$*

Hence a linear 0-switching relation family is a *trace inclusion*, and a linear 1-switching relation family is a *impossible-futures inclusion*: any trace in $\mathcal{I}_1$ has to be matched by a trace in $\mathcal{I}_2$, and then any trace from the end of the second trace has to be matched by one from the end of the first trace.

Definition 15. Let $k \in \mathbb{N} \cup \{\infty\}$ and $\mathcal{I}_1 = (S_1, s_1^0, T_1), \mathcal{I}_2 = (S_2, s_2^0, T_2) \in \mathsf{LTS}$. A linear k-ready relation family *from $\mathcal{I}_1$ to $\mathcal{I}_2$ is a linear k-switching relation family* $R^0, \ldots, R^k \subseteq S_1 \times S_2$ with the extra property that for all $(s_1, s_2) \in R^k$:

- *if k is even, then* $\forall (s_1, \tau, t_1) \in T_1^* : \exists (s_2, \tau, t_2) \in T_2^* : \forall (t_2, a, u_2) \in T_2 : \exists (t_1, a, u_1) \in T_1$;
- *if k is odd, then* $\forall (s_2, \tau, t_2) \in T_2^* : \exists (s_1, \tau, t_1) \in T_1^* : \forall (t_1, a, u_1) \in T_1 : \exists (t_2, a, u_2) \in T_2$.

Thus a linear 0-ready relation family is a *failure inclusion*: any trace in $\mathcal{I}_1$ has to be matched by a trace in $\mathcal{I}_2$ such that there is an inclusion of *failure sets* of non-available actions. For $k \in \mathbb{N} \cup \{\infty\}$ and $\mathcal{I}_1, \mathcal{I}_2 \in \mathsf{LTS}$, we write $\mathcal{I}_1 \approx_k \mathcal{I}_2$ if there exist a branching k-switching relation family from $\mathcal{I}_1$ to $\mathcal{I}_2$ and another from $\mathcal{I}_2$ to $\mathcal{I}_1$. We write $\mathcal{I}_1 \approx_k^r \mathcal{I}_2$ if there exist a branching k-ready relation family from $\mathcal{I}_1$ to $\mathcal{I}_2$ and another from $\mathcal{I}_2$ to $\mathcal{I}_1$.

For $\mathcal{D} = (S, S^0, \dashrightarrow, \longrightarrow) \in \mathsf{DMTS}$, we define $\dashrightarrow^*, \longrightarrow^* \subseteq S \times \Sigma^* \times S$ recursively as follows:

- $s \xdashrightarrow{\varepsilon}{}^* s$ and $s \xrightarrow{\varepsilon}{}^* s$ for all $s \in S$;
- for all $s \xdashrightarrow{\tau}{}^* t$ and $t \xdashrightarrow{a} u$, also $s \xdashrightarrow{\tau.a}{}^* u$;
- for all $s \xrightarrow{\tau}{}^* t$, $t \longrightarrow N$, and $(a, u) \in N$, also $s \xrightarrow{\tau.a}{}^* u$.

Definition 16. Let $k \in \mathbb{N} \cup \{\infty\}$ and $\mathcal{D}_1 = (S_1, S_1^0, \dashrightarrow_1, \longrightarrow_1), \mathcal{D}_2 = (S_2, S_2^0, \dashrightarrow_2, \longrightarrow_2) \in \mathsf{DMTS}$. A linear k-switching relation family *from $\mathcal{D}_1$ to $\mathcal{D}_2$ consists of relations* $R_1^0, \ldots, R_1^k, R_2^0, \ldots, R_2^k \subseteq S_1 \times S_2$ such that

- $\forall s_1^0 \in S_1^0 : \exists s_2^0 \in S_2^0 : (s_1^0, s_2^0) \in R_1^0$ *and* $\forall s_2^0 \in S_2^0 : \exists s_1^0 \in S_1^0 : (s_1^0, s_2^0) \in R_2^0$;
- *for all even* $j \in \{0, \ldots, k\}$ *and* $(s_1, s_2) \in R_1^j$:
  - $\forall s_1 \xdashrightarrow{\tau}{}^*_1 t_1 : \exists s_2 \xdashrightarrow{\tau}{}^*_2 t_2$;
  - *if $j < k$, then* $\forall s_1 \xdashrightarrow{\tau}{}^*_1 t_1 : \exists s_2 \xdashrightarrow{\tau}{}^*_2 t_2 : (t_1, t_2) \in R_1^{j+1}$;
- *for all odd* $j \in \{0, \ldots, k\}$ *and* $(s_1, s_2) \in R_1^j$:
  - $\forall s_2 \xrightarrow{\tau}{}^*_2 t_2 : \exists s_1 \xrightarrow{\tau}{}^*_1 t_1$;
  - *if $j < k$, then* $\forall s_2 \xrightarrow{\tau}{}^*_2 t_2 : \exists s_1 \xrightarrow{\tau}{}^*_1 t_1 : (t_1, t_2) \in R_1^{j+1}$;
- *for all even* $j \in \{0, \ldots, k\}$ *and* $(s_1, s_2) \in R_2^j$:
  - $\forall s_2 \xrightarrow{\tau}{}^*_2 t_2 : \exists s_1 \xrightarrow{\tau}{}^*_1 t_1$;
  - *if $j < k$, then* $\forall s_2 \xrightarrow{\tau}{}^*_2 t_2 : \exists s_1 \xrightarrow{\tau}{}^*_1 t_1 : (t_1, t_2) \in R_1^{j+1}$;
- *for all odd* $j \in \{0, \ldots, k\}$ *and* $(s_1, s_2) \in R_2^j$:
  - $\forall s_1 \xdashrightarrow{\tau}{}^*_1 t_1 : \exists s_2 \xdashrightarrow{\tau}{}^*_2 t_2$;
  - *if $j < k$, then* $\forall s_1 \xdashrightarrow{\tau}{}^*_1 t_1 : \exists s_2 \xdashrightarrow{\tau}{}^*_2 t_2 : (t_1, t_2) \in R_2^{j+1}$.

A linear k-ready relation family *from $\mathcal{D}_1$ to $\mathcal{D}_2$ is a linear k-switching relation family as above with the extra property that if k is even, then*

- $\forall (s_1, s_2) \in R_1^k : \forall s_1 \xdashrightarrow{\tau}{}^*_1 t_1 : \exists s_2 \xdashrightarrow{\tau}{}^*_2 t_2 : \forall t_2 \longrightarrow_2 N_2 : \exists t_1 \longrightarrow_1 N_1 : \forall (a, u_1) \in N_1 : \exists (a, u_2) \in N_2$;
- $\forall (s_1, s_2) \in R_2^k : \forall s_2 \xrightarrow{\tau}{}^*_2 t_2 : \exists s_1 \xrightarrow{\tau}{}^*_1 t_1 : \forall t_1 \xdashrightarrow{a}_1 u_1 : \exists t_2 \xdashrightarrow{a}_2 u_2$;

and if k is odd, then

- $\forall (s_1, s_2) \in R_1^k : \forall s_2 \xrightarrow{\tau}{}^*_2 t_2 : \exists s_1 \xrightarrow{\tau}{}^*_1 t_1 : \forall t_1 \xdashrightarrow{a}_1 u_1 : \exists t_2 \xdashrightarrow{a}_2 u_2;$
- $\forall (s_1, s_2) \in R_2^k : \forall s_1 \xdashrightarrow{\tau}{}^*_1 t_1 : \exists s_2 \xdashrightarrow{\tau}{}^*_2 t_2 : \forall t_2 \xrightarrow{}_2 N_2 : \exists t_1 \xrightarrow{}_1 N_1 :$
  $\forall (a, u_1) \in N_1 : \exists (a, u_2) \in N_2;$

For $k \in \mathbb{N} \cup \{\infty\}$ and $\mathcal{D}_1, \mathcal{D}_2 \in \mathsf{DMTS}$, we write $\mathcal{D}_1 \preccurlyeq_k \mathcal{D}_2$ if there exists a linear k-switching relation family from $\mathcal{D}_1$ to $\mathcal{D}_2$ and $\mathcal{D}_1 \preccurlyeq_k^{\mathrm{r}} \mathcal{D}_2$ if there exists a linear k-ready relation family from $\mathcal{D}_1$ to $\mathcal{D}_2$.

Theorem 17. *For any $k \in \mathbb{N} \cup \{\infty\}$, $(\mathsf{DMTS}, \chi, \preccurlyeq_k)$ is a specification theory for LTS adequate for $\approx_k$, and $(\mathsf{DMTS}, \chi, \preccurlyeq_k^{\mathrm{r}})$ is a specification theory for LTS adequate for $\approx_k^{\mathrm{r}}$.*

Remark 18. In the setting of generalized simulation games, *cf.* Remark 13, the linear relations can be characterized by introducing a notion of *blind* strategy. This gives a correspondence between linear and branching relations which splits the linear-time–branching-time spectrum in two halves: trace inclusion corresponds to simulation; failure inclusion corresponds to ready simulation, etc. We refer to [15,16] for details. Whether a similar notion of blindness can yield the linear relations of Definition 16 is open.

8 Conclusion

We have in this paper extracted a reasonable and general notion of (behavioral) specification theory, based on previous work by a number of authors on concrete specification theories in different contexts and on the well-established notions of characteristic formulae, adequacy and expressivity.

Using this general concept of specification theory, we have introduced new concrete specification theories, based on disjunctive modal transition systems, for most equivalences in van Glabbeek's linear-time–branching-time spectrum. Previously, only specification theories for bisimilarity have been available, and recent work by Vogler *et al.* calls for work on specification theories for failure equivalence. Both failure equivalence and bisimilarity are part of the linear-time–branching-time spectrum, as are nested simulation equivalence, impossible-futures equivalence, and many other useful relations. We develop specification theories for all branching equivalences in the spectrum, but we miss some of the linear equivalences; notably, possible futures and ready trace equivalence are missing. We believe that these can be captured by small modifications to our setting, but leave this for future work.

Our new specification theories should be useful for example in the setting of the failure semantics of Vogler *et al.*, but also in many other contexts where bisimilarity is not the right equivalence to consider. Using our own previous work on the quantitative linear-time–branching-time spectrum and on quantitative specification theories for bisimilarity, we also plan to lift our work presented here to the quantitative setting.

Specification theories for bisimilarity admit notions of conjunction and composition which enable compositional design and verification, and also the specification theories of Vogler *et al.* have (different) such notions. Using the game-based setting in [16], we believe one can define general notions of conjunction and composition defined by games played on the involved disjunctive modal transition systems. This is left for future work.

References

1. Aceto, L., Fábregas, I., de Frutos-Escrig, D., Ingólfsdóttir, A., Palomino, M.: On the specification of modal systems. Sci. Comput. Program. **78**(12), 2468–2487 (2013)
2. Aceto, L., Fokkink, W., van Glabbeek, R.J., Ingólfsdóttir, A.: Nested semantics over finite trees are equationally hard. Inf. Comput. **191**(2), 203–232 (2004)
3. Antonik, A., Huth, M., Larsen, K.G., Nyman, U., Wąsowski, A.: 20 years of modal and mixed specifications. Bull. EATCS **95**, 94–129 (2008)
4. Bauer, S.S., David, A., Hennicker, R., Guldstrand Larsen, K., Legay, A., Nyman, U., Wąsowski, A.: Moving from specifications to contracts in component-based design. In: Lara, J., Zisman, A. (eds.) FASE 2012. LNCS, vol. 7212, pp. 43–58. Springer, Heidelberg (2012). doi:10.1007/978-3-642-28872-2_3
5. Bauer, S.S., Fahrenberg, U., Juhl, L., Larsen, K.G., Legay, A., Thrane, C.: Weighted modal transition systems. Form. Meth. Syst. Design **42**(2), 193–220 (2013)
6. Bauer, S.S., Juhl, L., Larsen, K.G., Legay, A., Srba, J.: Extending modal transition systems with structured labels. Math. Struct. Comput. Sci. **22**(4), 581–617 (2012)
7. Beneš, N., Černá, I., Křetínský, J.: Modal transition systems: composition and LTL model checking. In: Bultan, T., Hsiung, P.-A. (eds.) ATVA 2011. LNCS, vol. 6996, pp. 228–242. Springer, Berlin (2011). doi:10.1007/978-3-642-24372-1_17
8. Bertrand, N., Legay, A., Pinchinat, S., Raclet, J.: Modal event-clock specifications for timed component-based design. Sci. Comput. Program. **77**(12), 1212–1234 (2012)
9. Brookes, S.D., Hoare, C.A.R., Roscoe, A.W.: A theory of communicating sequential processes. J. ACM **31**(3), 560–599 (1984)
10. Bujtor, F., Sorokin, L., Vogler, W.: Testing preorders for dMTS: deadlock- and the new deadlock/divergence-testing. In: IEEE Computer Society, ACSD (2015)
11. Bujtor, F., Vogler, W.: Failure semantics for modal transition systems. ACM Trans. Embed. Comput. Syst. **14**(4), 67 (2015)
12. Caillaud, B., Raclet, J.-B.: Ensuring reachability by design. In: Roychoudhury, A., D'Souza, M. (eds.) ICTAC 2012. LNCS, vol. 7521, pp. 213–227. Springer, Berlin (2012). doi:10.1007/978-3-642-32943-2_17
13. David, A., Larsen, K.G., Legay, A., Nyman, U., Traonouez, L., Wasowski, A.: Real-time specifications. STTT **17**(1), 17–45 (2015)
14. Fahrenberg, U., Legay, A.: General quantitative specification theories with modal transition systems. Acta Inf. **51**(5), 261–295 (2014)
15. Fahrenberg, U., Legay, A.: The quantitative linear-time-branching-time spectrum. Theor. Comput. Sci. **538**, 54–69 (2014)
16. Fahrenberg, U., Legay, A.: A linear-time branching-time spectrum of behavioral specification theories (2016). http://arxiv.org/abs/1604.06503

17. Groote, J.F., Vaandrager, F.W.: Structured operational semantics and bisimulation as a congruence. Inf. Comput. **100**(2), 202–260 (1992)
18. Hennessy, M., Milner, R.: Algebraic laws for nondeterminism and concurrency. J. ACM **32**(1), 137–161 (1985)
19. Hoare, C.A.R.: Communicating sequential processes. Commun. ACM **21**(8), 666–677 (1978)
20. Larsen, K.G.: A context dependent equivalence between processes. Theor. Comput. Sci. **49**, 184–215 (1987)
21. Larsen, K.G.: Modal specifications. In: Sifakis, J. (ed.) CAV 1989. LNCS, vol. 407, pp. 232–246. Springer, Berlin (1990). doi:10.1007/3-540-52148-8_19
22. Guldstrand Larsen, K.: Ideal specification formalism = expressivity + compositionality + decidability + testability +. In: Baeten, J.C.M., Klop, J.W. (eds.) CONCUR 1990. LNCS, vol. 458, pp. 33–56. Springer, Heielberg (1990). doi:10.1007/BFb0039050
23. Larsen, K.G., Skou, A.: Bisimulation through probabilistic testing. In: POPL, ACM Press (1989)
24. Larsen, K.G., Xinxin, L.: Equation solving using modal transition systems. In: LICS. IEEE Computer Society (1990)
25. Milner, R.: Calculi for synchrony and asynchrony. Theor. Comput. Sci. **25**(3), 267–310 (1983)
26. Park, D.: Concurrency and automata on infinite sequences. In: Deussen, P. (ed.) GI-TCS 1981. LNCS, vol. 104, pp. 167–183. Springer, Heidelberg (1981). doi:10.1007/BFb0017309
27. Pnueli, A.: Linear and branching structures in the semantics and logics of reactive systems. In: Brauer, W. (ed.) ICALP 1985. LNCS, vol. 194, pp. 15–32. Springer, Heidelberg (1985). doi:10.1007/BFb0015727
28. Raclet, J., Badouel, E., Benveniste, A., Caillaud, B., Legay, A., Passerone, R.: A modal interface theory for component-based design. Fund Inf **108**(1–2), 119–149 (2011)
29. Raclet, J.-B.: Residual for component specifications. Electr. Notes Theor. Comput. Sci. **215**, 93–110 (2008)
30. Stirling, C.: Modal and temporal logics for processes. In Banff Higher Order Workshop. LNCS, 1043. Springer, Heidelberg (1995)
31. van Glabbeek, R.J.: The linear time - branching time spectrum I. In: Handbook of Process Algebra, Chap. 1. Elsevier (2001)
32. Vogler, W.: Failures semantics and deadlocking of modular Petri nets. Acta Inf. **26**(4), 333–348 (1989)
33. Vogler, W.: Modular Construction and Partial Order Semantics of Petri Nets. LNCS, vol. 625. Springer, Heidelberg (1992)

Symbolic Semantics for Multiparty Interactions in the Link-Calculus

Linda Brodo[1] and Carlos Olarte[2($\boxtimes$)]

[1] Dipartimento di Scienze Politiche, Scienze della Comunicazione e Ingegneria dell'Informazione, Università di Sassari, Sassari, Italy
brodo@uniss.it
[2] ECT - Universidade Federal do Rio Grande do Norte, Natal, Brazil
carlos.olarte@gmail.com

Abstract. The link-calculus is a model for concurrency that extends the point-to-point communication discipline of Milner's CCS with multiparty interactions. Links are used to build chains describing how information flows among the different agents participating in a multiparty interaction. The inherent non-determinism in deciding both, the number of participants in an interaction and how they synchronize, makes it difficult to devise efficient verification techniques for this language. In this paper we propose a symbolic semantics and a symbolic bisimulation for the link-calculus which are more amenable to automating reasoning. Unlike the operational semantics of the link-calculus, the symbolic semantics is finitely branching and it represents, compactly, a possibly infinite number of transitions. We give necessary and sufficient conditions to efficiently check the validity of symbolic configurations. We also implement an interpreter based on this semantics and we show how to use such implementation for verification.

1 Introduction

Distributed systems are evolving in complex ways and adequate modeling languages are needed to specify and verify properties such as resources consuming, security, privacy, among several others. Multiparty interactions are commonplace in this new era of distributed systems. Take for instance an on-line payment service where a shopper contacts the vendor's webpage and fills a form with its credit card information. Then, the vendor's webpage automatically contacts the cashier's service that completes the payment and sends the needed confirmations. At a certain abstract level, all the previous operations can be seen as a unique multi-party communication, as if one of the steps fails, the whole transaction is canceled.

In order to have a more comprehensive representation of the system's dynamics, it would be convenient to consider multiparty interactions instead of binary ones. In the literature there are multi-way synchronization calculi [6,10,11] that seem to be adequate to be applied in different areas such as distributed computing, web applications and Systems Biology. Here we shall focus on the link-calculus [1,2] to model multiparty communications.

© Springer International Publishing AG 2017
B. Steffen et al. (Eds.): SOFSEM 2017, LNCS 10139, pp. 62–75, 2017.
DOI: 10.1007/978-3-319-51963-0_6

The link-calculus is a new multiparty process algebra where the number of participants in each synchronization is not fixed a priori. It extends the binary communication discipline of CCS [9] with *links*, e.g., $^a\backslash_b$, that can be thought of as the forwarding of a message received on channel a (the input channel) to another channel b (the output channel). It could be the case that a link exposes only an output $(^\tau\backslash_b)$, or an input $(^a\backslash_\tau)$; these particular actions are the ends of a *link chain*.

A link chain allows for the synchronize of several entities. Each entity must offer a link that have to match with an adjacent link offered by another entity. For instance, if three processes offer, respectively, the links $^a\backslash_b$, $^b\backslash_c$ and $^c\backslash_d$, they can synchronize and produce the link chain $^a\backslash_b^b\backslash_c^c\backslash_d$, where information flow from a to d through b and c.

The multiparty synchronization mechanism of the link-calculus brings interesting challenges for devising automatic reasoning tools. The main technical problem is that the number of participants in an interaction is not known a priori. Then, the operational semantics (SOS) must consider all the possible synchronizations among the agents running in parallel. For instance, consider two processes offering, respectively, the links $^a\backslash_b$ and $^b\backslash_a$. They may synchronize and produce the link chain $^a\backslash_b^b\backslash_a$, but also $^b\backslash_a^a\backslash_b$. They may also produce the link chain $^a\backslash_b^\square\backslash_\square^b\backslash_a$, where the free space $^\square\backslash_\square$ (called virtual link) can be used by a third participant offering the proper link.

We propose a symbolic semantics which is more amenable for reasoning about link processes. The semantics collects together all the possible synchronizations that can be composed with a multiset of links (e.g., $\langle ^a\backslash_b, ^b\backslash_a\rangle$ for the example above). We thus abstract from the order of the links and we represent, compactly, a possibly infinite number of transitions in the SOS. Moreover, unlike the SOS, the proposed semantics is finitely branching (if guarded recursive definitions are considered).

The presence of restricted names makes more interesting the definition of symbolic configurations. In fact, internal (multiparty) synchronizations play an important role in the definition of network bisimulation [1,2]. We give a symbolic representation of transitions involving restricted names and we give efficient procedures to check the validity of such configurations. Furthermore, we define a symbolic bisimulation and we show that it is a congruence and it coincides with network bisimulation.

Finally, we present a prototypical implementation of our semantics in Maude (available at http://subsell.logic.at/links/). We illustrate the semantics and the tool with the classical problem of the dining philosophers. We show that this problem has a simple implementation in the link-calculus. Furthermore, we use our tool to show that the model is deadlock free. We then contribute with a theoretical framework, that may help to better understand multiparty interactions, and a tool to enact it.

Contributions and Plan of the Paper. Section 2 recalls the theory of the link-calculus. In Sect. 3 we define our symbolic semantics and we give polynomial procedures to check whether a symbolic configuration is valid or not. We then show that the symbolic semantics is sound and complete wrt the SOS. We define a procedure to extract a symbolic configuration from a trace in the SOS and we show that the resulting configuration is an upper bound for the symbolic semantics. In Sect. 3.3 we define a symbolic bisimulation that coincides with network bisimulation and has the property to be a congruence. In Sect. 3.4 we present the implementation of simulation and verification techniques for the link-calculus based on the symbolic semantics. Section 4 concludes the paper and discusses related work. Due to space restrictions, auxiliary results and the detailed proofs are given in the companion technical report of this paper available at tool's web page.

2   Background on Link-calculus

A *link* is a pair $^{\alpha}\backslash_{\beta}$ where $\alpha, \beta \in \mathcal{C} \cup \{\tau, \square\}$. $\mathcal{C}$ denotes the set of channels, ranged over by $a, b, c, ...$; τ is the silent action and $\square$ is a virtual action. Intuitively, $^{a}\backslash_{b}$ is a prefix that executes an input on channel a and an output on b. The τ action is used to represent a link where no interaction is required (on the left or on the right) as in $^{a}\backslash_{\tau}$. A virtual link $^{\square}\backslash_{\square}$ represents a non specified interaction that will be later completed. The link $^{\alpha}\backslash_{\beta}$ is *solid* if $\alpha, \beta \neq \square$, and it is virtual if $\alpha, \beta = \square$. A link is *valid* if it is solid or virtual. For instance, $^{\square}\backslash_{\square}$, $^{a}\backslash_{a}$, $^{\tau}\backslash_{a}$, $^{b}\backslash_{a}$ are valid links whereas $^{\square}\backslash_{a}$, $^{\tau}\backslash_{\square}$ are not.

Links can be combined in *link chains* that record the source and the target sites of each hop of the interaction. Formally, a link chain is a non-empty finite sequence $s = \ell_1...\ell_n$ of valid links $\ell_i =^{\alpha_i} \backslash_{\beta_i}$ such that:

1. for any $i \in 1..n - 1$, $\begin{cases} \beta_i, \alpha_{i+1} \in \mathcal{C} & \text{implies } \beta_i = \alpha_{i+1} \\ \beta_i = \tau & \text{iff } \alpha_{i+1} = \tau \end{cases}$
2. $\exists i \in 1..n.\ \ell_i \neq^{\square} \backslash_{\square}$.

The first condition says that two adjacent solid links must match on their adjacent sites. Moreover, the silent action τ can not be matched by a virtual action $\square$. This last condition is required since, as we shall see, a τ action can be only matched with τ when processes synchronize on restricted channels. The second condition says that a valid link must have at least one solid link. We shall use VC to denote the set of valid chains and we write $|s|$ to denote the *length* of the chain s.

Some examples of valid link chains are: $^{\square}\backslash_{\square}^{a}\backslash_{b}^{b}\backslash_{\tau}$, $^{a}\backslash_{b}^{\square}\backslash_{\square}^{c}\backslash_{d}$, and $^{\tau}\backslash_{a}^{a}\backslash_{\tau}$. The first chain represents an interaction where there is a pending synchronization on the left of $^{a}\backslash_{b}$; similarly, the second chain represents an interaction where a third-party process must offer a link joining b and c (i.e., $^{b}\backslash_{c}$). Finally, the last chain is the result of a binary interaction between a process performing the output $^{\tau}\backslash_{a}$ and a process performing the input $^{a}\backslash_{\tau}$. Examples of non valid link chains are: $^{a}\backslash_{b}^{c}\backslash_{d}$, $^{\square}\backslash_{\square}^{\tau}\backslash_{a}$, and $^{a}\backslash_{\tau}^{c}\backslash_{d}$.

Processes in the link-calculus are built from the syntax

$$P, Q ::= \mathbf{0} \mid \ell.P \mid P + Q \mid P|Q \mid (\nu a)P \mid A$$

where ℓ is a solid link (i.e. $\ell =^{\alpha} \backslash_{\beta}$ with $\alpha, \beta \neq \square$) and A is a process identifier for which we assume a (possibly recursive) definition $A \triangleq P$.

The nil process $\mathbf{0}$ does nothing. The process $\ell.P$ first performs ℓ and then behaves as P. The non-deterministic process $P+Q$ can either behave as P or Q. Parallel composition is denoted as $P \mid Q$. The process $(\nu\, a)P$ behaves as P but it cannot exhibit any unmatched action a. Finally, A behaves as P if $A \triangleq P$.

As usual, $(\nu\, a)P$ binds the occurrences of a in P. The sets of free and of bound names of a process P are defined in the obvious way and denoted, respectively, by $fn(P)$ and $bn(P)$. Processes are taken up to alpha-conversion of bound names. We shall often omit a trailing $\mathbf{0}$, e.g. by writing $^{a}\backslash_b$ instead of $^{a}\backslash_b.\mathbf{0}$.

Operational Semantics. The operational semantics is given by the labeled transition system $(\mathcal{P}, \mathcal{L}, \longrightarrow)$ where states $\mathcal{P}$ are link-processes, labels $\mathcal{L}$ are valid chains (i.e., $\mathcal{L} = VC$) and the transition relation $\longrightarrow$ is the minimal transition relation generated by the rules in Fig. 1. In the following we explain the rules.

The presence of virtual links in a link chain suggests that an interaction is not completed and it allows for more processes to synchronize by offering the correct links. A process $\ell.P$ can take part in any interaction where ℓ can be placed in an admissible position of a (larger) chain. Hence, in order to join in a communication, $\ell.P$ should suitably enlarge its link ℓ to a link chain s including ℓ and some virtual links. Formally, Rule *Act* says that $\ell.P \xrightarrow{s} P$ for any link chain s such that $s \bowtie \ell$ where $\bowtie$ is the least equivalence relation on valid link chains closed under the following axioms:

$$s^{\square}\backslash_{\square} \bowtie s \qquad s_1{}^{\square}\backslash_{\square}^{\square}\backslash_{\square}s_2 \bowtie s_1{}^{\square}\backslash_{\square}s_2$$
$$^{\square}\backslash_{\square}s \bowtie s \qquad s_1{}^{\alpha}\backslash_a{}^{\square}\backslash_a^a\backslash_{\beta}s_2 \bowtie s_1{}^{\alpha}\backslash_a^a\backslash_{\beta}s_2$$

Note that the link $^{\tau}\backslash_a$ (resp. $^{a}\backslash_{\tau}$) can be only enlarged with virtual links on the right (resp. left). Moreover, if $s \bowtie^{\tau}\backslash_{\tau}$ then $s =^{\tau}\backslash_{\tau}$.

Rules *Lsum*, *Lpar* and *Ide* are standard. If P is able to exhibit a transition to P' with label s, then $P + Q \xrightarrow{s} P'$ (Rule *Lsum*). Similarly for Q with Rule *Rsum* omitted in Fig. 1. If P can exhibit a transition, it can also exhibit the same transition when running in parallel with Q (Rules *Lpar* and *Rpar*). Finally, A moves to P' if its body definition P can move to P' (Rule *Ide*).

The synchronization mechanism (Rule *Com*) works by merging two link chains, say s and s'. We require that the chains are of the same length (i.e., $|s| = |s'|$) and that every solid link of s must correspond to a virtual link in s' in the same position, and vice versa. Then we make the two link chains collapse in one link chain where some of the virtual links have been substituted with the corresponding solid links. More precisely, let α, β be actions. We define

$\alpha \bullet \beta = \alpha$ if $\beta = \square$ $\qquad \alpha \bullet \beta = \beta$ if $\alpha = \square$ $\qquad \alpha \bullet \beta = \bot$ otherwise Let $l_1 =^{\alpha_1} \backslash_{\beta_1}$ and $l_2 =^{\alpha_2} \backslash_{\beta_2}$ be valid links and $\alpha_1 \bullet \alpha_2 = x_\alpha$, $\beta_1 \bullet \beta_2 = x_\beta$. If $x_\alpha, x_\beta \neq \bot$, then $l_1 \bullet l_2 =^{x_\alpha} \backslash_{x_\beta}$. Otherwise, $l_1 \bullet l_2 = \bot$. Let $s = \ell_1...\ell_n$ and $s' = \ell'_1...\ell'_n$ be valid chains with $\ell_i =^{\alpha_i} \backslash_{\beta_i}$ and $\ell'_i =^{\alpha'_i} \backslash_{\beta'_i}$. If $l_i \bullet l'_i \neq \bot$ for all $i \in 1..n$ and $(l_1 \bullet l'_1)...(l_n \bullet l_n)$ is a valid chain, then $s \bullet s' = (l_1 \bullet l'_1)...(l_n \bullet l_n)$. Otherwise, $s \bullet s' = \bot$.

$$\frac{}{\ell.P \xrightarrow{s} P} \; Act \qquad \frac{P \xrightarrow{s} P'}{P+Q \xrightarrow{s} P'} \; Lsum \qquad \frac{P \xrightarrow{s} P'}{P\,|\,Q \xrightarrow{s} P'\,|\,Q} \; Lpar \qquad \frac{P \xrightarrow{s} P' \quad A \triangleq P}{A \xrightarrow{s} P'} \; Ide$$

$$\frac{P \xrightarrow{s} P'}{(\nu a)P \xrightarrow{(\nu a)s} (\nu a)P'} \; Res \qquad \frac{P \xrightarrow{s} P' \quad Q \xrightarrow{s'} Q'}{P\,|\,Q \xrightarrow{s \bullet s'} P'\,|\,Q'} \; Com$$

Fig. 1. SOS semantic rules. Rules $Rsum$ and $Rpar$ are omitted. All the rules have, as a side condition, that the link chains in the conclusion and premises are valid (i.e., different from $\perp$).

As an example, the chains ${}^\square\backslash{}^\square_\square\backslash{}^a_\square\backslash_b$ and ${}^c\backslash{}^\square_a\backslash_\square$ cannot merge, as they have different length; ${}^a\backslash{}^\square_b\backslash_\square$ and ${}^\square\backslash{}^c_\square\backslash_d$ cannot merge since ${}^a\backslash{}^c_b\backslash_d$ is not a valid chain; a chain s cannot merge with itself; finally, ${}^c\backslash{}^\square_a\backslash{}^b_\square\backslash_d$ and ${}^\square\backslash{}^a_\square\backslash{}^\square_b\backslash_\square$ merges into ${}^c\backslash{}^a_a\backslash{}^b_b\backslash_d$.

We note that, contrary to CCS, the Rule Com can appear several times in the proof tree of a transition since $s \bullet s'$ can still contain virtual links (if s and s' have a virtual link in the same position). Hence, $s \bullet s'$ can possibly be merged with other link chains. However, when $s \bullet s'$ is solid, no further synchronization is possible.

As usual in process calculi, names are restricted in order to force an interaction. Let α be an action and $a \in C$. Then,

$$(\nu a)\alpha = \begin{cases} \tau & \text{if } \alpha = a \\ \alpha & \text{otherwise} \end{cases} \qquad \text{and} \qquad (\nu a)^\alpha\backslash_\beta = {}^{((\nu a)\alpha)}\backslash_{((\nu a)\beta)}$$

Let $s = \ell_1...\ell_n$, with $\ell_i = {}^{\alpha_i}\backslash_{\beta_i}$ and $i \in 1..n$. We say that a is *matched* in s if:

1. $a \neq \alpha_1, \beta_n$ (i.e., a cannot occur in the extremes of the chain), and
2. for any $i \in 1..n-1$, either $\beta_i = \alpha_{i+1} = a$ or $\beta_i, \alpha_{i+1} \neq a$.

Otherwise, we say that a is *unmatched* (or *pending*) in s. We define,

$$(\nu a)s = \begin{cases} ((\nu a)\ell_1)...((\nu a)\ell_n) & \text{if } a \text{ is } matched \text{ in } s \\ \perp & \text{otherwise} \end{cases}$$

As an example, all the names are matched in the valid link chain ${}^\tau\backslash_\tau$. Instead, neither a nor b are matched in ${}^a\backslash{}^a_a\backslash_b$. In $s = {}^\tau\backslash{}^a_a\backslash{}^\square_b\backslash_\square$, the name a can be restricted and $(\nu a)s = {}^\tau\backslash{}^\tau_\tau\backslash{}^\square_b\backslash_\square$; whereas $(\nu b)s$ is undefined since b is pending in s.

The Rule Res can serve different aims: (i) *floating*, if a does not occur in s, then $(\nu a)s = s$ and $(\nu a)P \xrightarrow{s} (\nu a)P'$; (ii) *hiding*, if a is matched in s, then all occurrences of a in s are replaced with τ in $(\nu a)s$; (iii) *blocking*, if a is pending in s (i.e., there is some unmatched occurrence of a in s), then $(\nu a)s = \perp$ and the rule cannot be applied.

3 Symbolic Semantics

As mentioned in the introduction, the system ${}^a\backslash_b.\mathbf{0} \mid {}^b\backslash_a.\mathbf{0}$ can synchronize in different ways, i.e., we can use the rule *Com* to observe different link chains such as ${}^a\backslash_b^{\,b}\backslash_a$, ${}^b\backslash_a^{\,a}\backslash_b$, ${}^\square\backslash_\square^{\,a}\backslash_b^{\,\square}\backslash_a$, etc. In this section we propose a novel symbolic semantics that represents, in a unique configuration, all these link-chains. Hence, the non-determinism of the operational semantics (due to *Com* and *Act*) is completely replaced with a deterministic transition collecting all the possible interactions the process may engage. We also give sufficient and necessary conditions for testing the validity on configuration.

3.1 Symbolic Configurations

Definition 1 (Link configurations). *Let L be a multiset of solid links. We define the (symbolic) configuration $\langle L \rangle$ as the set*

$$\langle L \rangle = \{ s \in VC \mid \text{ there exists } s_i \blacktriangleright\!\!\blacktriangleleft l_i \text{ for all } l_i \in L \text{ s.t. } s = s_1 \bullet s_2 \bullet \cdots \bullet s_n \}$$

We say that $\langle L \rangle$ is a valid configuration if the set above is not empty.

Intuitively, the configuration $\langle L \rangle$ accumulates the links that can be merged in an application of the rule *Com*. As an example, the configuration $\langle {}^a\backslash_b \rangle$ represents, for instance, ${}^a\backslash_b$ (and the process does not interact any more), ${}^\square\backslash_\square^{\,a}\backslash_b$ where there are no further interaction on b and a is still pending, ${}^\square\backslash_\square^{\,a}\backslash_b^{\,\square}\backslash_\square$ where both a and b are pending. The configuration $\langle {}^a\backslash_b, {}^b\backslash_a \rangle$ represents, e.g., the following chains: ${}^a\backslash_b^{\,b}\backslash_a$, ${}^b\backslash_a^{\,a}\backslash_b$, ${}^b\backslash_a^{\,\square}\backslash_\square^{\,\square}\backslash_\square^{\,a}\backslash_b$, ${}^\square\backslash_\square^{\,b}\backslash_a^{\,a}\backslash_b^{\,\square}\backslash_\square$, etc. Finally, the configuration $\langle {}^\tau\backslash_a, {}^a\backslash_\tau \rangle$ contains the chains ${}^\tau\backslash_a^{\,a}\backslash_\tau$, ${}^\tau\backslash_a^{\,\square}\backslash_\square^{\,a}\backslash_\tau$, ${}^\tau\backslash_a^{\,\square}\backslash_\square^{\,\square}\backslash_\square^{\,a}\backslash_\tau$, etc. (recall that matched τ-actions can be only introduced by the restriction operator).

Next proposition gives us an algorithm, linear on the number of elements in L, to check whether $\langle L \rangle$ is valid or not.

Proposition 1 (Valid Configurations). *Let L be a non-empty multiset of solid links. Then, $\langle L \rangle$ is valid iff τ appears at most once in L as input and at most once as output.*

Definition 2 (Hiding). *Let γ be a configuration and $a \in C$. We define the configuration*

$$(\nu a)\gamma = \{ s \in VC \mid \text{ there exists } s' \in \gamma \text{ and } s = (\nu a)s' \}$$

We say that $(\nu a)\gamma$ is valid if the set above is not empty.

If γ is not valid, by definition, $(\nu a)\gamma$ is not valid. The other direction is not necessarily true. For instance, $L_1 = \langle {}^a\backslash_a \rangle$ and $L_2 = \langle {}^\tau\backslash_a, {}^a\backslash_\tau, {}^b\backslash_c \rangle$ are valid configurations but neither $(\nu a)\langle L_1 \rangle$ nor $(\nu a)\langle L_2 \rangle$ are valid. In the first case, observe that $(\nu a)(s)$ is not valid for any $s \blacktriangleright\!\!\blacktriangleleft {}^a\backslash_a$ (since a cannot appear in the extremes and it must be matched). In the second case, if $s \in \langle L_2 \rangle$, then s must be of the shape $^\tau\backslash_a^\Box\backslash_\Box^\Box\ldots^\Box\backslash_c^b\backslash_\Box^\Box\backslash_\Box\ldots^\Box\backslash_\tau^a\backslash_\tau$. Since a is not matched, $(\nu a)s = \bot$ and $(\nu a)\langle L_2\rangle$ is empty.

We shall use $\gamma, \gamma', \psi, \psi'$ to denote configurations (with and without restricted names). Given a multiset L of solid links, we shall use $names(L)$ to denote the set of names occurring in the links in L. Let $\gamma = (\nu a_1)\ldots(\nu a_n)\langle L\rangle$. We define the free names of γ as $fn(\gamma) = names(L)\backslash\{a_1, \ldots, a_n\}$ and its bound names as $bn(\gamma) = \{a_1, \ldots, a_n\}$. Given a sequence of distinct names $\boldsymbol{a} = a_1, \ldots, a_n$, we shall use $(\nu a_1, \ldots, a_n)\langle L\rangle$ to denote the configuration $(\nu a_1)\ldots(\nu a_n)\langle L\rangle$. If $\boldsymbol{a}$ is empty, then we write $\langle L\rangle$ instead of $(\nu\boldsymbol{a})\langle L\rangle$. Finally, we shall write $\gamma \equiv_s \gamma'$ when $\gamma = \gamma'$ (i.e., $\gamma \subseteq \gamma'$ and $\gamma' \subseteq \gamma$).

As a direct consequence of the corresponding equivalences on chains [2], we can show that (1) $(\nu a)\gamma \equiv_s \gamma$ if $a \notin fn(\gamma)$; (2) $(\nu a)(\nu b)\gamma \equiv_s (\nu b)(\nu a)\gamma$; (3) $(\nu a)\gamma \equiv_s (\nu b)\gamma[b/a]$ is $b \notin names(\gamma)$ (α-conversion).

Now we give necessary and sufficient conditions for testing if a configuration of the shape $(\nu a)\gamma$ is valid or not. Such checking can be performed in linear time on the number of links in the configuration γ.

Proposition 2 (Valid Configuration). *Let* $\gamma = (\nu\boldsymbol{x})\langle L\rangle$ *be a valid configuration and* $a \in fn(\gamma)$. $(\nu a)\gamma$ *is valid iff the three conditions below hold:*

1. **Matched:** *a occurs the same number of times as input and as output in L.*
2. **Extremes:** *there exist two links $^\alpha\backslash_\beta, ^{\alpha'}\backslash_{\beta'}$ in L where $\alpha, \beta' \neq a$.*
3. **Synchronizations:** *if both $^\tau\backslash_a$ and $^a\backslash_\tau$ occur in L, then either $names(L) = \{a, \tau\}$ or there exist two links $^a\backslash_\beta, ^{\beta'}\backslash_a$ in L s.t. $\beta, \beta' \notin \{a, \tau\}$.*

The following definition shows how to merge two valid configurations. This definition will be useful to define the rule *Com* in the symbolic semantics.

Definition 3 (Merging). *Let* $(\nu a_1, \ldots, a_n)\langle L\rangle$ *and* $(\nu b_1, \ldots b_m)\langle L'\rangle$ *be two valid configurations. By alpha conversion, we assume that the names $a_1, \ldots, a_n$ (resp. $b_1, \ldots, b_m$) do not occur in L' (resp. L). We define*

$$(\nu a_1, \ldots, a_n)\langle L\rangle \bullet (\nu b_1, \ldots b_m)\langle L'\rangle = (\nu a_1, \ldots, a_n, b_1, \ldots, b_m)\langle L \uplus L'\rangle$$

where $\uplus$ denotes multiset union.

It is easy to see that $\bullet$ is a commutative and associative (partial) operator.

3.2 Semantic Rules

The rules of the symbolic semantics are given in Fig. 2 and explained below.

We note that the equivalence relation $\blacktriangleright\!\blacktriangleleft$ relates two valid link chains when they only differ on the number of virtual links. This relation is central to the definition of configurations. In fact, it is easy to see that if $s \in \gamma$, then $s'\blacktriangleright\!\blacktriangleleft s$ iff $s' \in \gamma$. Rule Act_s builds a configuration containing only the solid link l. Then, as we shall see, any move of the operational rule Act can be mimicked by Act_s.

Rules $Lsum_s$, $Lpar_s$ and Ide_s are self-explanatory and Rule Res_s, as expected, makes use of the restriction operator on configurations.

$$\frac{P \overset{\gamma}{\Longrightarrow} P'}{P + Q \overset{\gamma}{\Longrightarrow} P'} \; Lsum_s \qquad \frac{P \overset{\gamma}{\Longrightarrow} P'}{P \mid Q \overset{\gamma}{\Longrightarrow} P' \mid Q} \; Lpar_s \qquad \frac{P \overset{\gamma}{\Longrightarrow} P' \quad A \triangleq P}{A \overset{\gamma}{\Longrightarrow} P'} \; Ide_s$$

$$\frac{}{\ell.P \overset{\{\{\ell\}\}}{\Longrightarrow} P} \; Act_s \qquad \frac{P \overset{\gamma}{\Longrightarrow} P'}{(\nu a)P \overset{(\nu a)\gamma}{\Longrightarrow} (\nu a)P'} \; Res_s \qquad \frac{P \overset{\gamma}{\Longrightarrow} P' \quad Q \overset{\gamma'}{\Longrightarrow} Q'}{P \mid Q \overset{\gamma \bullet \gamma'}{\Longrightarrow} P' \mid Q'} \; Com_s$$

Fig. 2. Symbolic semantics for the `link`-calculus. All the rules have, as a side condition, that the configurations in the conclusion and premises are valid. Rules $Rpar_s$ and $Rsum_s$ are omitted.

Rule Com_s merges the symbolic configurations γ and γ'. Recall that the merge operator simply computes the union (resp. multiset union) of the bounded names (resp. links) in γ and γ'. Unlike the operational rule, Com_s does not need to know in advance the length of the chains to be merged. Instead, it only checks whether $\gamma \bullet \gamma'$ is valid (by using the algorithms in Propositions 1 and 2). Moreover, from the definition of the merge operator, we can show that,

1. **Composition:** if $s \in \gamma$, $s' \in \gamma'$ and $s \bullet s'$ is defined then $s \bullet s' \in \gamma \bullet \gamma'$.
2. **Splitting:** if $w \in \gamma \bullet \gamma'$ then there exist s, s' s.t. $w = s \bullet s'$ and $s \in \gamma$ and $s' \in \gamma'$.

Now we are ready to show the desired adequacy results.

Theorem 1 (Soundness). *Let P be a process and assume that $P \overset{s}{\longrightarrow} P'$. Then, there exists γ s.t. $P \overset{\gamma}{\Longrightarrow} P'$ and $s \in \gamma$.*

Theorem 2 (Completeness). *Let P be a process and assume that $P \overset{\gamma}{\Longrightarrow} P'$. Then, for all $s \in \gamma$, $P \overset{s}{\longrightarrow} P'$.*

The above results can be easily extended to sequences of transitions. Given a sequence of symbolic configurations $\Gamma = \gamma_1, ..., \gamma_n$, we say that the sequence of chains $s_1, ..., s_n$ is an instance of Γ if $s_i \in \gamma_i$ for all $i \in 1..n$.

Corollary 1 (Adequacy). *Let P be a process. Then,*

1. *if $P \overset{s_1}{\longrightarrow} P_1 \overset{s_2}{\longrightarrow} P_2 \cdots \overset{s_n}{\longrightarrow} P_n$ then there exists $\gamma_1, ..., \gamma_n$ s.t. $P \overset{\gamma_1}{\Longrightarrow} P_1 \cdots \overset{\gamma_n}{\Longrightarrow} P_n$ and for all $i \in 1..n$, $s_i \in \gamma_i$.*
2. *if $P \overset{\gamma_1}{\Longrightarrow} P_1 \cdots \overset{\gamma_n}{\Longrightarrow} P_n$. Then, for all instance $s_1, ..., s_n$ of $\gamma_1, ..., \gamma_n$, we have $P_1 \overset{s_1}{\longrightarrow} P_2 \cdots \overset{s_n}{\longrightarrow} P_n$.*

Extraction and Soundness. We can strength Theorem 1 and give an upper bound to γ. If $P \overset{s}{\longrightarrow} P'$, one may be tempted to think that such upper bound is $\gamma = solid(s)$ where $solid(s)$ denotes the multiset of solid links in s. We note that this does not work under the presence of restriction. For instance, $s = (\nu a)(^\tau\backslash_a^a\backslash_\tau) =^\tau \backslash_\tau^\tau\backslash_\tau$ if a valid label for a transition $P \overset{s}{\longrightarrow} P'$ but $\langle ^\tau\backslash_\tau, ^\tau\backslash_\tau \rangle$ is not a valid configuration.

Next definition shows how to extract a valid configuration from a link chain, that we later show to be a suitable over approximation of the symbolic semantics.

Definition 4 (Extraction). *Let* $s =^{x_1} \big\backslash^{x_2}_{x_1'}\big\backslash_{x_2'} \cdots^{x_n} \big\backslash_{x_n'}$ *be a valid chain and* $\alpha \in C$ *be a name not occurring in* s. *We define* $\mathbf{ext}(s) = (\nu\,\alpha)\langle L \rangle$ *where* L *is the multiset of solid links of* s *subject to the following substitutions:*

   $\forall\, i \in 1 \ldots n - 1$, *substitute* x_i' *and* x_{i+1} *with* α *if* $x_i' = x_{i+1} = \tau$.

For instance, if $s =^a \big\backslash^\tau_\tau\big\backslash^c_c\big\backslash_d$ then $\mathbf{ext}(s) = (\nu x)\langle^a\big\backslash_x,^x\big\backslash_c,^c\big\backslash_d\rangle$.

The $\mathbf{ext}(s)$ function satisfies the following properties: if s is a valid chain without occurrences of matched τ's, then $\mathbf{ext}(s) \equiv_s \langle solid(s)\rangle$; if $|s| = 1$, i.e., $s = \ell$ for some solid link ℓ, then $\mathbf{ext}(s) \equiv \langle \ell \rangle$; for any valid chain s, $s \in \mathbf{ext}(s)$. Moreover,

- If $s \bullet s'$ is a valid chain then $\mathbf{ext}(s) \bullet \mathbf{ext}(s') \subseteq \mathbf{ext}(s \bullet s')$.
- If $(\nu a)s$ be a valid chain. Then,
    1. if $\mathbf{ext}(s) = (\nu\beta)\langle L\rangle$ then $\mathbf{ext}((\nu a)s) \equiv_s (\nu\beta)\langle L[\beta/a]\rangle$; and
    2. $(\nu a)\mathbf{ext}(s) \subseteq \mathbf{ext}((\nu a)s)$.

Theorem 3 (Soundness). *Let* P *be a process and assume that* $P \xrightarrow{\;s\;} P'$. *Then, there exists* $\gamma \subseteq \mathbf{ext}(s)$ *s.t.* $P \overset{\gamma}{\Longrightarrow} P'$.

We note that $\mathbf{ext}(s)$ over approximates the output of the symbolic semantics since $\mathbf{ext}(s)$ identifies τ actions that may come from different synchronizations. For instance, consider the operational transition $(\nu a)(^b\big\backslash_a|^a\big\backslash_b) \mid (\nu c)(^d\big\backslash_c|^c\big\backslash_d) \xrightarrow{\;s \bullet s'\;} \mathbf{0}$ where

$$s =^\Box \big\backslash_\Box \big\backslash^\Box_\Box \big\backslash^b_\Box \big\backslash^\tau_\tau \big\backslash_b \qquad s' =^d \big\backslash^\tau_\tau \big\backslash_d \big\backslash^\Box_\Box \big\backslash^\Box_\Box \big\backslash_\Box \qquad w = s \bullet s' =^d \big\backslash^\tau_\tau \big\backslash_d \big\backslash^\Box_\Box \big\backslash^b_\Box \big\backslash^\tau_\tau \big\backslash_b$$

In the symbolic semantics we have $(\nu a)(^b\big\backslash_a|^a\big\backslash_b) \mid (\nu c)(^d\big\backslash_c|^c\big\backslash_d) \xrightarrow{\;\gamma \bullet \gamma'\;} \mathbf{0}$ where

$$\gamma = (\nu a)\langle^b\big\backslash_a,^a\big\backslash_b\rangle \qquad \gamma' = (\nu c)\langle^d\big\backslash_c,^c\big\backslash_d\rangle \qquad \psi = \gamma \bullet \gamma' = (\nu\,a,c)\langle^b\big\backslash_a,^a\big\backslash_b,^d\big\backslash_c,^c\big\backslash_d\rangle$$

Note that $\mathbf{ext}(w) = (\nu x)\langle^b\big\backslash_x,^x\big\backslash_b,^d\big\backslash_x,^x\big\backslash_d\rangle$ and $w' =^b \big\backslash^\tau_\tau \big\backslash_d \big\backslash^d_\tau \big\backslash^\tau_b \in \mathbf{ext}(w)$. Note also that w' is not part of the operational semantics and $w' \notin \psi$.

Let $\gamma = (\nu x)\langle L\rangle$ and $a = \{a_1, ..., a_n\}$ be a set of names s.t. $x \cap a = \emptyset$. We say that $(\nu a)\langle L'\rangle$ is a ν-variant of γ if L' is the least set satisfying:

- if $^\alpha\big\backslash_\beta \in L$, $\alpha, \beta \notin x$ then $^\alpha\big\backslash_\beta \in L'$;
- if $^\alpha\big\backslash_\beta \in L$ and $\alpha \in x$, $\beta \notin x$ then $^a\big\backslash_\beta \in L'$ for some $a \in a$;
- if $^\alpha\big\backslash_\beta \in L$ and $\alpha \notin x$, $\beta \in x$ then $^\alpha\big\backslash_a \in L'$ for some $a \in a$.
- if $^\alpha\big\backslash_\beta \in L$ and $\alpha, \beta \in x$ then $^a\big\backslash_{a'} \in L'$ for some $a, a' \in a$.

Intuitively, a ν-variant of γ may discriminate, using different local names, some synchronizations in γ (take for instance a, c in ψ and x in $\mathbf{ext}(w)$ in the example above).

Theorem 4 (Soundness). *Let* P *be a process and assume that* $P \xrightarrow{\;s\;} P'$. *Then, there exists a* ν-variant γ *of* $\mathbf{ext}(s)$ *s.t.* $P \overset{\gamma}{\Longrightarrow} P'$.

3.3   Symbolic Bisimulation

In this section we show that network bisimulation, [1,2] coincides with the symbolic bisimulation as defined below in Definition 7. Let us recall some definitions from [1].

Let $\bowtie$ be the least equivalence relation over VC closed under the inference rules:

$$\frac{s \,\blacktriangleright\!\!\blacktriangleleft\, s'}{s \bowtie s'} \qquad\qquad s_1{}^\alpha\backslash_\tau^\tau\backslash_\beta s_2 \bowtie s_1^\alpha\backslash_\beta s_2$$

The relation $\bowtie$ allows us to enlarge/contract chains by adding/removing matched τ actions (similar to $\blacktriangleright\!\!\blacktriangleleft$ for virtual actions). This means that $\bowtie$ abstracts away also from internal (restricted) communications. A link chain is *essential* if it is composed by alternating solid and virtual links, and has solid links at its extremes. It is immediate to check that, by orienting the axioms of $\blacktriangleright\!\!\blacktriangleleft$ and $\bowtie$ from left to right, we have a procedure to transform any link chain s to a unique essential link chain s' such that $s \bowtie s'$. We write $\mathsf{e}(s)$ to denote such unique representative.

Lemma 1 ([1]). *For any link chains s, s' we have $s \bowtie s'$ iff $\mathsf{e}(s) = \mathsf{e}(s')$.*

Definition 5. *A network bisimulation [1]* **R** *is a binary relation over* **link** *processes such that, if P **R** Q then:*

- *if $P \xrightarrow{s} P'$, then $\exists\, s', Q'$ such that $\mathsf{e}(s) = \mathsf{e}(s')$, $Q \xrightarrow{s'} Q'$, and P' **R** Q';*
- *if $Q \xrightarrow{s} Q'$, then $\exists\, s', P'$ such that $\mathsf{e}(s) = \mathsf{e}(s')$, $P \xrightarrow{s'} P'$, and P' **R** Q'.*

We let $\sim_n$ denote the largest network bisimulation and we say that P is *network bisimilar* to Q if $P \sim_n Q$.

Theorem 5 (Congruence [1]). *Network bisimilarity is a congruence.*

Symbolic Bisimulation. Let $s =^a \backslash_\tau^\tau\backslash_a$ and $s' =^a \backslash_a$. We know that $s\bowtie s'$. However, there is no a symbolic configuration γ such that $s \in \gamma$ and also $s' \in \gamma$. On the other side, let $\gamma = \langle^a\backslash_a\rangle$ and $\gamma' = (\nu b)\langle^a\backslash_b,{}^b\backslash_a\rangle$. We know that $\gamma \not\equiv_s \gamma'$ but, if $w \in \gamma$ and $w' \in \gamma'$, it must be the case that $w\bowtie w'$.

Next definition introduces the relation $\bowtie$ on configurations.

Definition 6. *Let $\bowtie$ be the least symmetric relation on valid configurations s.t. $\gamma\bowtie\gamma'$ iff for all $s \in \gamma$ there exists $s' \in \gamma'$ s.t. $s'\bowtie s$.*

Note that $\gamma \equiv_s \gamma'$ implies, of course, that $\gamma\bowtie\gamma'$. Moreover, it is easy to see that $\bowtie$ is an equivalence relation.

Intuitively, if $\gamma\bowtie\gamma'$, then from γ we can build the same chains as in γ' but adding/removing τ synchronizations. For instance, let $\gamma = (\nu x)\langle^a\backslash_x,{}^x\backslash_b\rangle$ and $\gamma' = \langle^a\backslash_b\rangle$. If $s \in \gamma$ (resp. $s' \in \gamma'$) then s must be of the shape $...^\Box\backslash_\Box^a\backslash_\tau^\tau\backslash_b^\Box\backslash_\Box...$ (resp. s' must be of the shape $...^\Box\backslash_\Box^a\backslash_b^\Box\backslash_\Box...$). Hence, $\gamma\bowtie\gamma'$.

Definition 7 (Symbolic Bisimulation). *A symbolic network bisimulation* **R** *is a binary relation over* link *processes such that, if P***R***Q then:*

- *If* $P \overset{\gamma}{\Longrightarrow} P'$, *then, there exists* $\gamma' \bowtie \gamma$ *s.t.* $Q \overset{\gamma'}{\Longrightarrow} Q'$ *and* P'**R**Q'.
- *If* $Q \overset{\gamma}{\Longrightarrow} Q'$, *then, there exists* $\gamma' \bowtie \gamma$ *s.t.* $P \overset{\gamma'}{\Longrightarrow} P'$ *and* Q'**R**P'.

We let $\sim_s$ *be the largest symbolic network bisimulation and we say that P and Q are bisimilar if* $P \sim_s Q$.

Testing whether $\gamma \bowtie \gamma'$, according to Definition 6, requires to check for every sequence $s \in \gamma$ the existence of $s' \in \gamma'$ s.t. $s' \bowtie s$ and vice versa. It turns out that there is a more efficient procedure to decide $\gamma \bowtie \gamma'$ using the next definition and lemma.

Definition 8 (Capabilities). *Let* $\gamma = (\nu \boldsymbol{x})\langle L \rangle$ *be a valid configuration. Let* $a, b \notin \boldsymbol{x}$. *We say that* $[a \cdot b]$ *is a capability of* γ, *notation* $[a \cdot b] \in \gamma$, *if* $^a\backslash_b \in L$ *or, it is possible to use the links in L to form a chain of the shape* $^a\backslash^{x_1}_{x_1}\backslash^{x_2} \cdots {}^{x_{n-1}}\backslash^{x_n}_{x_n}\backslash_b$ *where* $x_1, ..., x_n \in \boldsymbol{x}$. *We shall use* $\mathsf{cap}(\gamma)$ *to denote the multiset of capabilities in* γ.

Lemma 2. *Let* $s \in \gamma$. *For all solid link* $^a\backslash_b$, $^a\backslash_b \in \mathsf{e}(s)$ *iff* $[a \cdot b] \in \gamma$. *Moreover, let* γ, γ' *be valid configurations. Then,* $\gamma \bowtie \gamma'$ *iff* $\mathsf{cap}(\gamma) = \mathsf{cap}(\gamma')$.

Therefore, checking $\gamma \bowtie \gamma'$ can be done in polynomial time by extracting and comparing the capabilities of the configurations.

Next theorem shows that network and symbolic bisimulations coincides. Moreover, since network bisimulation is a congruence [1], so the symbolic bisimulation.

Theorem 6. *Let P and Q be processes. Then,* $P \sim_n Q$ *iff* $P \sim_s Q$.

Corollary 2. $\sim_s$ *is a congruence.*

3.4   Implementation

As we saw in the previous sections, the symbolic semantics allows for simple mechanisms to generate traces and check whether a configuration is valid or not. Moreover, it is finitely branching (if guarded recursive definitions are considered) unlike the operational semantics. We have implemented the symbolic semantics in Maude (http://maude.cs.illinois.edu) and it is available at http://subsell.logic. at/links. In this section, relaying on the multiparty synchronization mechanism of the link-calculus, we model the classical problem of dining philosophers. We show how the semantics, and our tool, allow for the verification of such system.

The dining philosophers is a classical example introduced to study interactions between independent and distributed entities that want to share resources. The problem relates n philosopher sitting around a table, where each one has its own dish, and they can only eat or think. When they, independently, decide to eat, they need two forks. On the table, there is only one fork between two dishes, i.e. exactly n forks.

A solution to this problem in a binary synchronization calculus such as CCS leads to a deadlock exactly when all the philosophers take the fork at their left at the same time [8]. Hence, the system reaches a state where no further transition is possible. The multiparty synchronization mechanism of the link-calculus allows us to overcome this problem. The idea is that, atomically, the philosopher willing to eat has to synchronize with both, the fork on his right and the one on his left. Then he can eat. The link-calculus model is: $(\nu\ dw_0, \ldots, dw_{n-1}, up_0, \ldots, up_{n-1})(Phil_0\ |\ \cdots\ |\ Phil_{n-1}\ |\ Fork_0\ |\ \cdots\ |$ $Fork_{n-1})$ where processes $Phil_i$ and $Fork_i$ are defined as:

$$Phil_i \quad \triangleq {}^\tau\backslash_{think_i}.Phil_i\ +^{up_i}\backslash_{up_{(i+1)\bmod n}}.PhilEat_i$$
$$PhilEat_i \triangleq {}^\tau\backslash_{eat_i}.^{dw_i}\backslash_{dw_{(i+1)\bmod n}}.Phil_i$$
$$Fork_i \quad \triangleq {}^\tau\backslash_{up_i}.^\tau\backslash_{dw_i}.Fork_i\ +\ {}^{up_i}\backslash_\tau.^{dw_i}\backslash_\tau.Fork_i$$

Let us show a trace generated with our tool for the system with $n = 2$ philosophers:

```
(tau \ 'tk_1) --> (tau \ 'tk_0) --> ('up_0 \ 'up_1 ; 'up_1 \ tau ; tau \ 'up_0) -->
(tau \ 'eat_0) --> (tau \ 'tk_1) --> ('dw_0 \ 'dw_1 ; 'dw_1 \ tau ; tau \ 'dw_0) -->
('up_0 \ tau ; 'up_1 \ 'up_0 ; tau \ 'up_1) --> (tau \ 'eat_1) --> (tau \ 'tk_0) -->
('dw_0 \ tau ; 'dw_1 \ 'dw_0 ; tau \ 'dw_1)
```

In the first line, $Phil_1$ thinks and then $Phil_0$ thinks. Later, $Phil_0$ grabs the two forks, as shown in the last configuration of the first line. Such output represents the symbolic configuration $(\nu up_0, up_1)\langle L\rangle$ where $L = \{{}^{up_0}\backslash_{up_1}, {}^{up_1}\backslash_\tau, {}^\tau\backslash_{up_0}\}$. This configuration is a three-party interaction involving $Phil_0$ and the two forks. Note that the chain $(\nu\ up_0, up_1)^\tau\backslash_{up_0}^{up_0}\backslash_{up_1}^{up_1}\backslash_\tau = {}^\tau\backslash_\tau^\tau\backslash_\tau^\tau\backslash_\tau$ is the only chain that belongs to the configuration (due to the restriction on up_i). Hence, in one transition, we observe the atomic action of grabbing the two forks. In the second line, we observe $Phil_0$ eating, then $Phil_1$ thinking again and, in the end of the line, $Phil_0$ releases the two forks with a multiparty synchronization. The third and forth lines represent the transitions where $Phil_1$ grabs the forks, eats and then releases the forks.

Our tool can also compute the label transition system with all the reachable states that, in the case of the dinning philosophers, is finite (note that this is not always the case since the link-calculus is a conservative extension of CCS where Turing Machines can be encoded [4]). The output of the tool and the resulting graph can be found at the tool's site. The transition system is deadlock-free, i.e., all the states have at least one transition. Moreover, using the search procedures in Maude, we can verify that the system cannot reach a configuration containing both ${}^\tau\backslash_{eat_0}$ and ${}^\tau\backslash_{eat_1}$.

4   Concluding Remarks

We proposed a symbolic semantics and bisimulation for an open and multiparty interaction process calculus. We gave efficient procedures to check whether a symbolic configuration is valid or not and proved adequate our semantics wrt the operational semantics. We implemented also a tool based on this semantics to simulate and verify systems modeled in the calculus. We are currently implementing a procedure to check (symbolic) bisimulation in the link-calculus. We are also planning to use the extraction procedure (ext(s)), that over approximates the semantics, as basis for abstract debugging and analysis of link-calculus specifications.

Related Work. Multiparty calculi with different synchronization mechanisms have been proposed, e.g., in CSP [7], PEPA [6] and full Lotos [3]. These calculi offer parallel operators that exhibit a set of action names (or channel names), and all the parallel processes offering that action (or an input/output action along that channel) can synchronize by executing it. In [11], a binary form of input allows for a three-way communication. MultiCCS [4] is equipped with a new form of prefix to execute atomic sequences of actions and the resulting parallel operator allows for multi-synchronizations. The multiparty calculus most related to the link-calculus is in [10], where links are named and are distinct from usual input/output actions: there is one sender and one receiver (the output includes the final receiver name).

Symbolic semantics in processes calculi are used to represent compactly the possibly infinitely many transitions a process may exhibit. For instance, [5] proposes a symbolic semantics for the π-calculus to avoid the problem of considering the possibly infinite number of values a process can send/receive along a channel. We are currently considering such techniques to give a symbolic semantics for the link-calculus with value-passing [1]. The only symbolic semantics for a multiparty calculus we are aware of is [3,12] where the authors present the definition of a symbolic semantics for the full Lotos language and its implementation.

References

1. Bodei, C., Brodo, L., Bruni, R.: Open multiparty interaction. In: Martí-Oliet, N., Palomino, M. (eds.) WADT 2012. LNCS, vol. 7841, pp. 1–23. Springer, Heidelberg (2013). doi:10.1007/978-3-642-37635-1_1
2. Bodei, C., Brodo, L., Bruni, R., Chiarugi, D.: A flat process calculus for nested membrane interactions. Sci. Ann. Comp. Sci. **24**(1), 91–136 (2014)
3. Calder, M., Shankland, C.: A symbolic semantics and bisimulation for full LOTOS. In: Kim, M., Chin, B., Kang, S., Lee, D. (eds.) IFIP Conference Proceedings, FORTE, vol. 197, pp. 185–200. Kluwer (2001)
4. Gorrieri, R., Versari, C.: Introduction to Concurrency Theory - Transition Systems and CCS. Texts in Theoretical Computer Science. An EATCS Series. Springer, Cham (2015)
5. Hennessy, M., Lin, H.: Symbolic bisimulations. Theor. Comput. Sci. **138**(2), 353–389 (1995)
6. Hillston, J.: A Compositional Approach to Performance Modelling. Cambridge University Press, New York (1996)
7. Hoare, C.A.R.: Communicating Sequential Processes. Prentice-Hall Inc, Upper Saddle River (1985)

8. Lehmann, D.J., Rabin, M.O.: On the advantages of free choice: a symmetric and fully distributed solution to the dining philosophers problem. In: White, J., Lipton, R.J., Goldberg, P.C. (eds.) POPL, pp. 133–138. ACM Press (1981)
9. Milner, R.: A Calculus of Communicating Systems. LNCS, vol. 92. Springer, Heidelberg (1980)
10. Montanari, U., Sammartino, M.: Network conscious pi-calculus: a concurrent semantics. In: Proceedings of Mathematical Foundations of Programming Semantics (MFPS), Electronic Notes in Theoretical Computer Science, vol. 286, pp. 291–306. Elsevier (2012)
11. Nestmann, U.: On the expressive power of joint input. Electron. Notes Theor. Comput. Sci. **16**(2), 145–152 (1998)
12. Verdejo, A.: Building tools for LOTOS symbolic semantics in maude. In: Peled, D.A., Vardi, M.Y. (eds.) FORTE 2002. LNCS, vol. 2529, pp. 292–307. Springer, Heidelberg (2002). doi:10.1007/3-540-36135-9_19

Theory of Mobile and Distributed Systems

Different Speeds Suffice for Rendezvous of Two Agents on Arbitrary Graphs

Evangelos Kranakis[1]([✉]), Danny Krizanc[2], Euripides Markou[3],
Aris Pagourtzis[4], and Felipe Ramírez[2]

[1] School of Computer Science, Carleton University, Ottawa, ON, Canada
kranakis@scs.carleton.ca
[2] Department of Mathematics and Computer Science, Wesleyan University,
Middletown, USA
{dkrizanc,framirez}@wesleyan.edu
[3] Department of Computer Science and Biomedical Informatics,
University of Thessaly, Volos, Greece
emarkou@ucg.gr
[4] School of Electronic and Computer Engineering,
National Technical University of Athens, Zografou, Greece
pagour@cs.ntua.gr

Abstract. We consider the rendezvous problem for two robots on an arbitrary connected graph with n vertices and all its edges of length one. Two robots are initially located on two different vertices of the graph and can traverse its edges with different but constant speeds. The robots do not know their own speed. During their movement they are allowed to meet on either vertices or edges of the graph. Depending on certain conditions reflecting the knowledge of the robots we show that a rendezvous algorithm is always possible on a general connected graph.

More specifically, we give new rendezvous algorithms for two robots as follows. (1) *In unknown topologies.* We provide a polynomial time rendezvous algorithm based on *universal exploration sequences*, assuming that n is known to the robots. (2) *In known topologies.* In this case we prove the existence of more efficient rendezvous algorithms by considering the special case of the two-dimensional torus.

Keywords: Graph · Mobile agents · Rendezvous · Speeds · Universal exploration sequence

1 Introduction

Rendezvous is an important primitive in distributed computing which enables remote and mobile entities in a distributed network to meet, coordinate and exchange information. It is also important in robotics for establishing connectivity and exchanging information in a geometric environment which is being traversed by the robots. As such it has been the focus of numerous studies from dynamic symmetry breaking problem [20], operations research [2], and distributed computing in general [16] and specific [15] distributed topologies.

© Springer International Publishing AG 2017
B. Steffen et al. (Eds.): SOFSEM 2017, LNCS 10139, pp. 79–90, 2017.
DOI: 10.1007/978-3-319-51963-0_7

In this paper we study the rendezvous problem under a deterministic model first introduced in [11] concerning rendezvous in a ring topology of two robots which have different speeds but are otherwise identical. The authors in [11] give an optimal time rendezvous algorithm (expressed as a function of the speed ratio c and size n of the ring) in a ring network for two robots which do not know their own speeds. This line of research has been extended to randomized rendezvous in [14] and to deterministic rendezvous for many agents in a ring in [12]. In this paper we study for the first time the rendezvous problem for two robots having speed ratio $c > 1$ in the most general setting of an arbitrary graph of n nodes.

1.1   Model

In the sequel the terms *agent* and *robot* will be considered interchangeable. We generalize to arbitrary graphs the model first introduced in [11]. There are two mobile agents placed at different nodes of an unknown arbitrary network. The network is modelled as a simple undirected connected graph with all its edges of equal length and the agents are deterministic mobile entities with unlimited memory; from the computational point of view they are modelled as Turing machines. The agents are anonymous (i.e., they do not have labels) and identical except for their speeds which are unknown to them. Each agent moves at all times at its own same fixed speed. The speed of an agent is the inverse of the time it takes that agent to traverse one unit of length in the network. For simplicity we set as unit speed, the speed required by the slow robot to traverse a unit length edge of the graph, in which case, the length of an edge is also the time it takes the slow robot to traverse it. Thus, without loss of generality, we normalize the speed of the slowest agent to 1, and denote by $c > 1$ the speed of the faster agent.

The agents start the execution of the rendezvous algorithm simultaneously. An agent can detect when it encounters another agent at a node or inside an edge. The agents have to meet at a node or inside an edge of the graph. We consider two situations below, one in which the topology of the network is unknown to the agents and one in which it is known. They cannot mark the visited nodes in any way. The nodes of the network are anonymous but the edges incident to a node v have distinct labels in $\{0, ..., d-1\}$, where d is the degree of v. Therefore, every undirected edge $\{u, v\}$ of the graph has two labels, which are called its port numbers at u and at v. The port numbering is local, i.e., there is no relation between port numbers at u and at v. An agent entering a node u learns the port of entry and the degree of the node and can see the exit port-labels at u. An agent at a node u can decide to stop or move to an adjacent node by selecting an exit port-label leaving u. The movement of an agent is always at its own constant speed. The edges of the network are of the same length which we normalize to 1. As the agents move, they can count the visited nodes. We note here that in the model of [11] each agent is equipped with a pedometer and by using it, an agent is capable of measuring the distance travelled and take decisions depending on its value. However, the algorithms in our model only use the agent's capability to count the visited nodes and detect whether an agent occupies a node or not (in order to select its next destination). Hence the agents in our model can only take decisions (stop or change direction) at a node and not inside an edge. The agents cannot communicate at all (except when they meet) and each agent does not know either its own or the other agent's speed.

When discussing running-time and feasibility of rendezvous, we take an adversarial model where the adversary can choose the network, the initial position of each agent and their speeds. The network can be considered as a graph where all edges have the same length given by the adversary. Although, as we mentioned above, we normalize the distance of every edge to 1 for the sake of the presentation, our algorithms work when the edges of the network have been associated with any (same) distance value.

The time complexity of an algorithm solving the rendezvous problem for two agents with different speeds and ratio $c > 1$ in an arbitrary network of size n, is defined as the worst case time to rendezvous, taken over all pairs of initial positions of the two agents, over all networks (of a particular type) of size n and over all pairs of different speeds with ratio c.

1.2 Related Work

The rendezvous problem for mobile agents (or robots) has been studied extensively in many topologies (or domains) and under various assumptions on system synchronicity and capabilities of the agents [7–9,15]. A critical distinction in the models is whether the agents must all run the same algorithm, which is generally known as the *symmetric rendezvous problem* [3]. If agents can execute different algorithms, generally known as the *asymmetric rendezvous problem*, then the problem is typically much easier, though not always trivial.

In quite a few of those models, rendezvous cannot be achieved without symmetry breaking. For example, in the simple case of two deterministic identical agents on a ring graph, rendezvous cannot be achieved since the agents, no matter how they move, they will always maintain the same distance apart. Even in cases where rendezvous can be achieved without it, breaking symmetry often leads to much more efficient algorithms. One studied method for breaking symmetry is to use random bits to make probabilistic choices. An extensive survey of randomized rendezvous in various scenarios can be found in [4]. Although such algorithms may provide reasonable expected time to rendezvous, in most cases they have poor worst-case behaviour. Another studied symmetry breaking mechanism is to let the agents drop tokens and count inter-token distances [18]. In arbitrary anonymous graphs with identical agents, the problem was solved (when it is feasible) in [6], for synchronous agents. A third studied symmetry breaking mechanism is to let agents have distinct labels [9,19]. In the asynchronous case, an almost complete solution for rendezvous in networks using distinct labels has been provided in [10].

In asynchronous scenarios the speed of any agent's traversal is controlled by an adversary. Hence even the traversals of the same edge by the same agent at two different times, take finite, but maybe different times. Under this assumption rendezvous in a node cannot be guaranteed even in very simple graphs, and therefore the rendezvous requirement in that case is usually relaxed to allow the agents to meet at a node or inside an edge. In our model, although any two traversals of the same edge by the same agent last the same fixed time, this time is controlled by the adversary (by selecting the speed of the agent and the length of the edges) and it is not the same for the two agents. It is easy to see that rendezvous in the same node also cannot be guaranteed even in simple networks (e.g., rings). Hence we also adopt in our model the relaxed requirement for rendezvous, i.e., allow the agents to meet at a node or inside an edge. Note that in our model since the agents initially have exactly the same information about themselves and the network, they cannot assign to themselves distinct labels. Hence the agents must exploit their different speeds (whose values are unknown to the agents) in order to meet.

The difference in speed between two otherwise identical agents, is a source of asymmetry that has recently received more attention. While agent speeds have been considered as a problem parameter before, the traditional assumption for synchronous agents has been that all agents move at a common fixed speed. Even when agent speed has been allowed to vary, as in [5], agents have typically had a uniform range of possible speeds and have been required to choose their speed deterministically, maintaining the symmetry of the problem.

The rendezvous problem is also related to the exploration problem, since both agents have to traverse (explore) some (the same) node or edge in order to meet. The exploration problem of an anonymous arbitrary network by an agent has been extensively studied. An important tool for exploration of anonymous arbitrary networks is the *Universal Traversal Sequence (UTS)* which has been suggested in [1]. A UTS for n-vertex graphs is a predetermined sequence of instructions that when executed on any n-vertex graph, from any starting vertex, defines a walk that visits all the vertices of the graph. The authors of [1] showed the existence of a UTS of a polynomial length for any graph of at most n nodes. However, to date it remains unknown whether a UTS of a polynomial length can be constructed in polynomial time. In [13] a tool closely related to UTS was proposed, called *Universal Exploration Sequence (UXS)*. Roughly speaking, exploration sequences can replace traversal sequences when backtracking is allowed. Reingold showed in [17] that a UXS of a polynomial length can be constructed in log-space and therefore in polynomial time. In [19], they defined and constructed in polynomial time the so called *strongly* universal exploration sequence, which is a possibly infinite sequence σ with the property that every contiguous subsequence of σ of some fixed length $p(n)$ (where $p(n)$ is a polynomial) is a UXS for any graph of at most n nodes.

1.3   Outline and Results of the Paper

Section 2 studies rendezvous in unknown topologies and includes preliminaries on Universal Exploration Sequences in Subsect. 2.1, and a rendezvous algorithm for known n in Subsect. 2.2. Section 3 deals with rendezvous when the network topology is known; we discuss rendezvous in a torus.

2   Rendezvous in Unknown Topologies

In this section we present algorithms for accomplishing rendezvous in unknown graph topologies by using universal exploration sequences. We begin by mentioning relevant results on universal exploration sequences and then proceed to give a new rendezvous algorithm that solves the problem in any graph consisting of n nodes, when n is known.

2.1   Preliminaries on Universal Exploration Sequences

Let us briefly explain the notion of the universal exploration sequence. Let $(a_1, a_2, ..., a_k)$ be a sequence of integers and let G be a graph and u be a node of G. Let also $w = succ(v, x)$ be the node reached by taking the exit-port x from node v. A sequence of nodes $(u_0, \ldots, u_{k+1})$ of G can be obtained as follows: $u_0 = u$, $u_1 = succ(u_0, 0)$; for any $1 \leq i \leq k$, $u_{i+1} = succ(u_i, (p + a_i)$ mod $d(u_i))$, where p is the entry-port number at u_i corresponding to the edge $\{u_{i-1}, u_i\}$. A sequence $(a_1, a_2, \ldots, a_k)$ which can be applied to any node u of a graph G and produces a sequence of nodes containing all nodes of G is called a *Universal Exploration Sequence (UXS)* for graph G. A UXS for a class of graphs is a UXS for all graphs in this class. The following important result, based on universal exploration sequences introduced by Koucký [13], is due to Reingold [17].

Proposition 1 ([17]). *For any positive integer n, a Universal Exploration Sequence.$Y(n) = (a_1, a_2, \ldots, a_M)$ can be constructed in polynomial time with respect to n (thus, the agents will be using $O(\log n)$ bits of memory) for the class of all graphs with at most n nodes, where M is polynomial in n.*

The length of such a log-space constructive universal exploration sequence is on the order of at least n^{100} in Reingold's [17] original implementation (though still polynomial in n). Aleliunas et al. proved in [1] the existence of Universal *Traversal* Sequences of shorter length.

Proposition 2 ([1]). *For any positive integers n, d, $d < n$, there exists a universal traversal sequence of length $O(n^3 d^2 \log n)$ for the family of all graphs with at most n nodes and maximum degree at most d.*

Koucký has shown in [13] in exactly the same way as in Proposition 2, a similar result for universal exploration sequences. Note that the traversal (or exploration) sequences in Proposition 2 above are not necessarily constructible in logarithmic memory[1] (and hence not constructible in polynomial time).

Given any positive integer n, the UXS leads one agent to visit all nodes of any graph of size at most n, starting from any node of the graph, using at most $T(n)$ edge traversals, where T is some polynomial. Upon entering a node of degree d by some port p, the agent can compute the port q by which it has to exit; more precisely $q = (p + x_i)$ mod d, where x_i is the corresponding term of the UXS.

---

[1] In fact they are (deterministically) constructible in polylogarithmic space, but to date it is unknown whether a universal traversal (or exploration) sequence of length $O(n^3 d^2 \log n)$ can be constructed in polynomial time.

2.2   Rendezvous in Arbitrary Graphs When n is Known

Suppose that the two agents only know the size n of the graph. We will show that they can rendezvous within at most polynomial time with respect to n. To this end, we first need to convert a UXS U to a walk that traverses all edges of the graph; let us call such a walk *Full Edge Traversal (FET)*. This can be easily done by having each robot traversing back and forth all incident edges of each node visited by U before it continues with the next term of U. Let $\mathcal{S}_U$ be this modified sequence. The total number of edge traversals in $\mathcal{S}_U$ is $|\mathcal{S}_U| \leq |U| + 2(n-1)|U|$. If we additionally instruct the agents to traverse back and forth exactly $n-1$ incident edges of each node (if a node has $t < n-1$ incident edges, then the agent additionally traverses one edge, randomly chosen, back and forth $(n-1)-t$ times), then the total number of edge traversals is exactly $|U| + 2(n-1)|U|$.

Proposition 3. *Given an arbitrary graph G consisting of n nodes and a universal exploration sequence U of G, of length $|U|$, an agent knowing U can construct and follow a full edge traversal $\mathcal{S}_U$ of G of length $O(n|U|)$.*

We will now show how to achieve rendezvous between two robots of different speeds that are able to compute and follow a full edge traversal with a known bound on its length.

Theorem 1. *Consider an arbitrary graph G consisting of n nodes, and two anonymous agents that have different speeds and (except for their speeds) are identical. The agents start moving at the same time on their own constant speeds and they know n.*

1. *If the agents follow full edge traversals $\mathcal{S}_c$ and $\mathcal{S}_1$, respectively, where $|\mathcal{S}_c| = |\mathcal{S}_1| = B(n)$, then rendezvous is always possible within time at most $O\left(\frac{B(n)}{c-1}\right)$.*
2. *If the agents can construct a universal exploration sequence of length $T(n)$ then rendezvous is always possible within time at most $O\left(\frac{n \cdot T(n)}{c-1}\right)$.*

Proof. We present Algorithm 1; the idea is to make the slow robot stay long enough at the first edge of its traversal during each round, so as to allow the fast robot to arrive and rendezvous[2].

Observe that on the one hand, the fast robot finishes its graph traversal in time $\frac{2B(n)+|\mathcal{S}_c|}{c} = \frac{3B(n)}{c}$. On the other hand, the slow robot finishes the back and forth traversals of the chosen edge in time $2B(n)$. Therefore the fast robot will catch up with slow robot while the latter is still traversing its chosen edge provided that

$$2B(n) \geq \frac{3B(n)}{c}. \tag{1}$$

If $c \geq \frac{3}{2}$ then relation (1) is satisfied, which means that the robots meet during their first round within time $\frac{3B(n)}{c}$. If $c < \frac{3}{2}$, then we have:

The slow robot proceeds in each round $i \geq 1$ as follows:

---

[2] This algorithm builds on an idea proposed (without its analysis) by an unknown reviewer based on an algorithm appearing in an earlier version of this paper.

Algorithm 1. Rendezvous Algorithm for n known. The two robots stop immediately when they meet.

1: **Input:** Graph G, FETs $\mathcal{S}_c, \mathcal{S}_1$ of G for robots $R(c), R(1)$ respectively, where $|\mathcal{S}_c| = |\mathcal{S}_1| = B(n)$;
2: **Goal:** Rendezvous of the two robots;
3: **repeat**
4:     let u be your current node; choose an adjacent node v;
5:     zig-zag $B(n)$ times between nodes u, v of edge $\{u, v\}$;
6:     traverse the edges of the graph in the order specified by your FET sequence;
7: **until** you meet the other robot

- zig-zags a chosen edge in the time interval $[3iB(n), 3iB(n) + 2B(n)]$,
- traverses the graph in the time interval $[3iB(n) + 2B(n), 3iB(n) + 3B(n)]$,

The fast robot proceeds in each round $j \geq 1$ as follows:

- zig-zags a chosen edge in the time interval $[\frac{3jB(n)}{c}, \frac{3jB(n)+2B(n)}{c}]$,
- traverses the graph in the time interval $[\frac{3jB(n)+2B(n)}{c}, \frac{3jB(n)+3B(n)}{c}]$,

If during a round j the fast robot starts its FET after the slow robot (which is at a round i) has started traversing back and forth its chosen edge and the fast robot finishes its FET before the slow robot finishes its zig-zags, then the two robots will meet. Hence the robots meet when:

$$\frac{3j+3}{3i+2} \leq c \leq \frac{3j+2}{3i} \tag{2}$$

The robots would meet at the same round if relation (2) is satisfied for $i = j$:

$$\frac{3i+3}{3i+2} \leq c \leq \frac{3i+2}{3i} \tag{3}$$

It is easy to see that for every $i \geq 1$ it holds:

$$\frac{3(i+1)+3}{3(i+1)+2} < \frac{3i+3}{3i+2} < \frac{3(i+1)+2}{3(i+1)} < \frac{3i+2}{3i} \tag{4}$$

The above relation (4) implies that the sequence of intervals $[\frac{3i+3}{3i+2}, \frac{3i+2}{3i}]$, $\forall i \geq 1$, covers any value of c when $1 < c < \frac{3}{2}$ and therefore for any such value of c there is a round i for which relation (3) is satisfied. The number of rounds needed for relation (3) to be satisfied (and thus the robots to meet) can be calculated by the second part of relation (3):

$$i \leq \frac{2}{3(c-1)} \tag{5}$$

Therefore the meeting will occur within time $\frac{2B(n)}{c(c-1)} + \frac{3B(n)}{c} = O(\frac{B(n)}{c-1})$, since $c > 1$. The second claim is obtained as a corollary of the first, using Proposition 3 with $|U| = T(n)$. This completes the proof of Theorem 1. □

Combining Theorem 1 with the result of Proposition 2 we derive easily the following corollary.

Corollary 1. *Consider an arbitrary graph G consisting of n nodes, and two anonymous agents having different speeds with ratio $c > 1$. The agents start moving at the same time on their own constant speeds and they know n. There is an algorithm which accomplishes rendezvous in at most $O\left(\frac{n^6 \log n}{c-1}\right)$ time.* □

Comments: One could possibly think of whether the algorithm could be modified in order to work for unknown n (e.g., by letting the agents test varying values of n in an appropriate manner). Unfortunately, since the number of zigzags depends on $B(n)$, there seems to be no obvious way to make the algorithm work correctly; in particular, the agents would not generally test the same n at the same time and therefore their delays due to zig-zags would vary considerably.

3   Rendezvous in a $n \times m$ Torus When the Agents Do Not Know n or m

In this section we investigate whether rendezvous can be done faster when more knowledge is available about the network topology. We focus on rendezvous in a $n \times m$ torus when the agents do not know n or m. As usual there are two robots with different speeds starting from arbitrary vertices. Let us imagine that the two robots are located on a $n \times m$ torus with n rows, m columns, and thus a total of nm vertices. The first result presented in this section assumes no knowledge of n or m; the only requirement is $\gcd(n, m) = 1$. For the second result knowledge of $\mathrm{lcm}(n, m)$ and $\gcd(n, m)$ is assumed.

3.1   Rendezvous in a $n \times m$ Torus When $\gcd(n, m) = 1$

Consider an $n \times m$ torus with n rows, m columns, and nm vertices. Further assume that $\gcd(n, m) = 1$. Construct a sequence of coordinates starting from any arbitrary vertex (x, y) as follows:

▷ $x_0 \leftarrow x$; $y_0 \leftarrow y$
▷ **for** $i = 0, 1, \ldots$ **set**
    $x_{i+1} \leftarrow x_i + 1 \bmod m$
    $y_{i+1} \leftarrow y_i + 1 \bmod n$

For each $i = 0, 1, \ldots$ consider the L-shaped walk (L-walk in short) L_i defined as follows: $L_i = \langle (x_i, y_i), (x_{i+1}, y_i), (x_{i+1}, y_{i+1}) \rangle$. That is, L_i starts at point $P_i = (x_i, y_i)$, continues to point $C_i = (x_{i+1}, y_i)$ and ends at point $P_{i+1} = (x_{i+1}, y_{i+1})$, thus traversing two edges, the first 'horizontal' and the second 'vertical'.

Let us now consider the following simple algorithm: Each robot follows the trajectory resulting from the concatenation of walks $L_0, L_1, \ldots$. Then the following theorem holds:

Theorem 2. *Consider a $n \times m$ torus with n rows, m columns, and nm vertices. Further assume that $\gcd(n, m) = 1$. Then rendezvous between two robots with different speeds, 1 and $c > 1$, can be accomplished in time $\frac{2nm}{c-1}$.*

Proof. Suppose that each robot follows the trajectory resulting from the concatenation of walks $L_0, L_1, \ldots$. We will show that every vertex of the torus appears in this trajectory as starting point of some L-walk, and as middle point of some other L-walk. Indeed, by definition we get that $(x_i, y_i) = (x_0 + i \bmod m, y_0 + i \bmod n)$. Therefore, for any $x_i, x_j \in \{0, \ldots, m-1\}, y_i, y_j \in \{0, \ldots, n-1\}$ it holds $(x_i, y_i) = (x_j, y_j)$ if and only if, $i \equiv j \bmod m$ and $i \equiv j \bmod n$. Since $\gcd(n, m) = 1$, by applying the Chinese Remainder Theorem we get that $i \equiv j \bmod (nm)$.

To sum up we have shown that the trajectory $L_0, L_1, \ldots, L_{nm-1}$ starting from the vertex (x, y) must traverse all the vertices of the torus and also return to its original position. Moreover the length of this trajectory is exactly $2mn$. In fact, each vertex is visited twice, once as a starting point of some L-walk (and ending point of the previous one) and once as middle point of some other L-walk. This is not unnecessary; the fact that each point is visited as a starting of some trajectory is crucial, as it guarantees that both robots follow exactly the same trajectory, differing only in their starting point.

Therefore, both robots move along the same cycle of length $2mn$, in the same direction. Thus, directly applying the result of the analysis of this rendezvous algorithm of [11] (i.e., when the robots move in the same direction, not knowing the length of the cycle or c), we obtain the claimed bound $\frac{2nm}{c-1}$. This concludes the proof of Theorem 2. □

3.2   Rendezvous in a $n \times m$ Torus When $\gcd(n, m) > 1$

Assuming $\gcd(n, m) = 1$, the previous trajectory passes from every vertex of the torus (see the proof of Theorem 2) and the success of the previous algorithm heavily relies on this.

If $\gcd(n, m) = d > 1$ then the trajectory $L_0, L_1, \ldots, L_{\mathrm{lcm}(n,m)-1}$ returns to the initial point P_0. It thus visits only $2 \, \mathrm{lcm}(n, m)$ nodes (and an equal number of edges). Therefore, the previous algorithm does not work in this case. A different algorithm which works when $\gcd(n, m) > 1$ is presented below.

Consider coordinates similar to those previously defined (the superscript refers to the round number, with respect to the algorithm defined below). Recall that (x, y) are the initial coordinates of a robot.

> $\triangleright$ $x_0^{(0)} \leftarrow x; y_0^{(0)} \leftarrow y$
> $\triangleright$ **for** $k = 0, 1, \ldots, i = 0, 1, \ldots,$ **set**
> $\qquad x_{i+1}^{(k)} \leftarrow x_i^{(k)} + 1 \bmod m$
> $\qquad y_{i+1}^{(k)} \leftarrow y_i^{(k)} + 1 \bmod n$
> $\triangleright$ **for** $k = 0, 1, \ldots,$ **set**
> $\qquad x_0^{(k+1)} \leftarrow x_0^{(k)} + 1 \bmod m$
> $\qquad y_0^{(k+1)} \leftarrow y_0^{(k)}$

Let us also define the corresponding L-walk $L_i^{(k)}$:

$$L_i^{(k)} = \langle (x_i^{(k)}, y_i^{(k)}), (x_{i+1}^{(k)}, y_i^{(k)}), (x_{i+1}^{(k)}, y_{i+l}^{(k)}) \rangle$$

We denote the points of walk $L_i^{(k)}$ by $P_i^{(k)}, C_i^{(k)}, P_{i+1}^{(k)}$, respectively. We propose the following algorithm:

Algorithm 2. Rendezvous Algorithm for the torus $n \times m$ with $\gcd(n, m) > 1$

1: **Input:** $\mathrm{lcm}(n, m), \gcd(n, m)(> 1)$;
2: **Goal:** Rendezvous of the two robots;
3: **repeat**
4:     zig-zag $\gcd(n, m)(2\mathrm{lcm}(n, m) + 1)$ times on edge $P_0^{(0)}, C_0^{(0)}$;
5:     **for** round $k = 0$ to $\gcd(n, m)$ **do**
6:         follow trajectory $T^{(k)} = L_0^{(k)}, L_1^{(k)}, \ldots, L_{\mathrm{lcm}(n,m)-1}^{(k)}$;
7:         traverse edge $P_0^{(k)}, C_0^{(k)}$;
8: **until** You meet the other robot

Theorem 3. *Consider an $n \times m$ torus with n rows, m columns, and nm vertices. Further assume that $\gcd(n, m)$ and $\mathrm{lcm}(n, m)$ are known and that $\gcd(n, m) > 1$. Two robots with different speeds, 1 and $c > 1$, can rendezvous in time $O\left(\frac{nm}{c-1}\right)$.*

Proof. We will first show that the trajectories $T^{(k)}, 0 \le k < d = \gcd(n, m)$, partition the torus into d edge-disjoint cycles, and that the cycle corresponding to $T^{(k)}$ coincides with the cycle corresponding to $T^{(k+d)}$. Indeed, we can extend arguments used in the proof of Theorem 2 as follows. We first observe that $(x_i^{(k)}, y_i^{(k)}) = (x_0^{(k)} + i \bmod m, y_0^{(k)} + i \bmod n)$. Therefore for any $x_i^{(k)}, x_j^{(k)} \in \{0, \ldots, m-1\}, y_i^{(k)}, y_j^{(k)} \in \{0, \ldots, n-1\}$ it holds $(x_i^{(k)}, y_i^{(k)}) = (x_j^{(k)}, y_j^{(k)})$ iff:

$$i \equiv j \pmod{m}$$
$$i \equiv j \pmod{n}.$$

Since $\gcd(n, m) = d > 1$, by applying a more general form of the Chinese Remainder Theorem (for non coprime moduli) we get that $i \equiv j \pmod{\mathrm{lcm}(n, m)}$; therefore each $T^{(k)}$ trajectory visits exactly $\mathrm{lcm}(n, m)$ distinct points as starting points of L-walks and exactly $\mathrm{lcm}(n, m)$ distinct points as middle points of L-walks.

Next, in order to have (starting) point coincidence among different trajectories $T^{(k)}, T^{(k')}$ it should hold that $(x_i^{(k)}, y_i^{(k)}) = (x_j^{(k')}, y_j^{(k')})$ for some $i, j \in \{0, \ldots, \mathrm{lcm}(n, m) - 1\}$. This in turn is equivalent to:

$$(x_0^{(k)} + i \bmod m, y_0^{(k)} + i \bmod n) = (x_0^{(k)} + k' - k + j \bmod m, y_0^{(k)} + j \bmod n),$$

where we use the fact that the x-coordinate of the starting point of $T^{(k')}$ is equal to the x-coordinate of the starting point of $T^{(k)}$ shifted by $k' - k \mod m$, while their y-coordinates coincide. Clearly, the above condition holds iff:

$$i \equiv k' - k + j \pmod{m}$$
$$i \equiv j \pmod{n}.$$

Since $\gcd(n, m) = d > 1$, by applying the general form of the Chinese Remainder Theorem we get that this can happen iff $k' \equiv k \pmod{d}$, and that for given i, k, k' there is a unique solution $j \in \{0, \ldots, \operatorname{lcm}(n, m) - 1\}$ to the above system.

This means that, as already mentioned, every d rounds a robot repeats the same cycle, usually starting from a different point of the cycle each time (if $m = d$, trajectories $T^{(k)}$ and $T^{(k+d)}$ are completely identical). In addition, cycles $T^{(k)}$ and $T^{(k+t)}$ with $t \bmod d \neq 0$ are completely disjoint with respect to starting points of their L-walks, hence are edge-disjoint.

Consequently, during a number of $d = \gcd(n, m)$ rounds a robot visits all vertices of the torus twice (once as a starting point and once as a middle point of some L-walk) and traverses all edges of the torus. Note that all edges are traversed once, except for horizontal edges $(P_0^{(i)}, P_0^{(i+1)})$ which are traversed twice, the second time providing a transfer of the robot to a different cycle.

Therefore, the concatenation of trajectories $T^{(i)}, 0 \leq i \leq d - 1$ performed in the second step of the algorithm is in fact a full edge traversal (FET) of length $\gcd(n, m)(2\operatorname{lcm}(n, m) + 1) = 2nm + \gcd(n, m)$, and by applying Theorem 1 we get the claim.

Note that the fact that $T^{(k)}$ is not (in most cases) completely identical to $T^{(k+d)}$ (due to different starting point) does not affect rendezvous time, since all edges of the torus are traversed. This completes the proof of Theorem 3.   □

4   Open Questions

It would be interesting to investigate rendezvous algorithms for two robots which require even less knowledge. In particular, it would be nice to remove the requirement of knowledge of the size of the graph, potentially by using an appropriate guessing strategy. Another important open question would be to address the case of equal speeds, possibly by introducing delays after certain number of rounds. Finally, the study of rendezvous for many robots of different speeds would also be of great interest.

References

1. Aleliunas, R., Karp, R.M., Lipton, R.J., Lovasz, L., Rackoff, C.: Random walks, universal traversal sequences, and the complexity of maze problems. In: FOCS, pp. 218–223. IEEE (1979)

2. Alpern, S.: The rendezvous search problem. SIAM J. Control Optim. **33**(3), 673–683 (1995)
3. Alpern, S.: Rendezvous search: a personal perspective. Oper. Res. **50**(5), 772–795 (2002)
4. Alpern, S., Gal, S.: The Theory of Search Games and Rendezvous. Kluwer Academic Publishers, New York (2002). International Series in Operations Research and Management Science
5. Czyzowicz, J., Ilcinkas, D., Labourel, A., Pelc, A.: Asynchronous deterministic rendezvous in bounded terrains. TCS **412**(50), 6926–6937 (2011)
6. Czyzowicz, J., Kosowski, A., Pelc, A.: How to meet when you forget: log-space rendezvous in arbitrary graphs. Distrib. Comput. **25**(2), 165–178 (2012)
7. Czyzowicz, J., Kosowski, A., Pelc, A.: Deterministic rendezvous of asynchronous bounded-memory agents in polygonal terrains. Theor. Comput. Syst. **52**(2), 179–199 (2013)
8. Marco, G., Gargano, L., Kranakis, E., Krizanc, D., Pelc, A., Vaccaro, U.: Asynchronous deterministic rendezvous in graphs. Theoret. Comput. Sci. **355**(3), 315–326 (2006)
9. Dessmark, A., Fraigniaud, P., Kowalski, D., Pelc, A.: Deterministic rendezvous in graphs. Algorithmica **46**, 69–96 (2006)
10. Dieudonné, Y., Pelc, A., Villain, V.: How to meet asynchronously at polynomial cost. In: Proceedings of the ACM Symposium on Principles of Distributed Computing, PODC 2013, pp. 92–99 (2013)
11. Feinerman, O., Korman, A., Kutten, S., Rodeh, Y.: Fast rendezvous on a cycle by agents with different speeds. In: Chatterjee, M., Cao, J., Kothapalli, K., Rajsbaum, S. (eds.) ICDCN 2014. LNCS, vol. 8314, pp. 1–13. Springer, Heidelberg (2014). doi:10.1007/978-3-642-45249-9_1
12. Huus, E., Kranakis, E.: Rendezvous of many agents with different speeds in a cycle. In: Papavassiliou, S., Ruehrup, S. (eds.) ADHOC-NOW 2015. LNCS, vol. 9143, pp. 195–209. Springer, Heidelberg (2015). doi:10.1007/978-3-319-19662-6_14
13. Koucky, M.: Universal traversal sequences with backtracking. J. Comput. Syst. Sci. **65**, 717–726 (2002)
14. Kranakis, E., Krizanc, D., MacQuarrie, F., Shende, S.: Randomized rendezvous on a ring for agents with different speeds. In: Proceedings of the 15th International Conference on Distributed Computing and Networking (ICDCN) (2015)
15. Kranakis, E., Krizanc, D., Markou, E.: The mobile agent rendezvous problem in the ring: an introduction. Synthesis Lectures on Distributed Computing Theory Series. Morgan and Claypool Publishers, San Rafael (2010)
16. Pelc, A.: Deterministic rendezvous in networks: a comprehensive survey. Networks **59**, 331–347 (2012)
17. Reingold, O.: Undirected connectivity in log-space. J. ACM **55**(4), 17 (2008)
18. Sawchuk, C.: Mobile Agent Rendezvous in the Ring. Ph.D. thesis, Carleton University (2004)
19. Ta-Shma, A., Zwick, U.: Deterministic rendezvous, treasure hunts, strongly universal exploration sequences. ACM Trans. Algorithms **10**(3), 12 (2014)
20. Yu, X., Yung, M.: Agent rendezvous: a dynamic symmetry-breaking problem. In: Meyer, F., Monien, B. (eds.) ICALP 1996. LNCS, vol. 1099, pp. 610–621. Springer, Heidelberg (1996). doi:10.1007/3-540-61440-0_163

Deciding Structural Liveness of Petri Nets

Petr Jančar[(✉)]

Department of Computer Science, FEI, Technical University, Ostrava, Czech Republic
petr.jancar@vsb.cz

Abstract. Place/transition Petri nets are a standard model for a class of distributed systems whose reachability spaces might be infinite. One of well-studied topics is the verification of safety and liveness properties in this model; despite the extensive research effort, some basic problems remain open, which is exemplified by the open complexity status of the reachability problem. The liveness problems are known to be closely related to the reachability problem, and many structural properties of nets that are related to liveness have been studied.

Somewhat surprisingly, the decidability status of the problem if a net is structurally live, i.e. if there is an initial marking for which it is live, has remained open, as also a recent paper (Best and Esparza, 2016) emphasizes. Here we show that the structural liveness problem for Petri nets is decidable.

A crucial ingredient of the proof is the result by Leroux (LiCS 2013) showing that we can compute a finite (Presburger) description of the reachability set for a marked Petri net if this set is semilinear.

1 Introduction

Petri nets are a standard tool for modeling and analysing a class of distributed systems; we can name [15] as a recent introductory monograph for this area. A natural part of the analysis of such systems is checking the safety and/or liveness properties, where the question of deadlock-freeness is just one example.

The classical version of place/transition Petri nets (exemplified by Fig. 1) is used to model systems with potentially infinite state spaces; here the decidability and/or complexity questions for respective analysis problems are often intricate. E.g., despite several decades of research the complexity status of the basic problem of *reachability* (can the system get from one given configuration to another?) remains unclear; we know that the problem is EXPSPACE-hard due to a classical construction by Lipton (see, e.g., [4]) but the known upper complexity bounds are not primitive recursive (we can refer to [12] and the references therein for further information).

The *liveness* of a transition (modelling a system action) is a related problem; its complementary problem asks if for a given initial marking (modelling an initial system configuration) the net enables to reach a marking in which the transition is dead, in the sense that it can be never performed in the future.

Supported by the Grant Agency of the Czech Rep., project GAČR:15-13784S.

© Springer International Publishing AG 2017
B. Steffen et al. (Eds.): SOFSEM 2017, LNCS 10139, pp. 91–102, 2017.
DOI: 10.1007/978-3-319-51963-0_8

A marked net (N, M_0), i.e. a net N with an initial marking M_0, is live if all its transitions are live.

The close relationship of the problems of reachability and liveness has been clear since the early works by Hack [8,9]. Nevertheless, the situation is different for the problem of *structural* liveness that asks, given a net N, if there is a marking M_0 such that (N, M_0) is live. While semidecidability of structural liveness is clear due to the decidability of (reachability and) liveness, the decidability question has been open: see, e.g., the overview [16] and in particular the recent paper [3] where this problem (STLP) is discussed in Concluding Remarks.

Here we show the decidability of structural liveness, by showing the semidecidability of the complementary problem. The idea is to construct, for a given net N, a marked net (N', M_0') (partly sketched in Fig. 2) that works in two phases (controlled by places added to N): in the first phase, an arbitrary marking M from the set $\mathcal{D}$ of markings with at least one dead transition is generated, and then N is simulated in the reverse mode from M. If N is not structurally live, then the projection of the reachability set of (N', M_0') to the set P of places of N is the whole set $\mathbb{N}^P$; if N is structurally live, then there is $M \in \mathbb{N}^P$ such that the projection of any marking reachable from M_0' differs from M.

In the first case (with the whole set $\mathbb{N}^P$) the reachability set of (N', M_0') is semilinear, i.e. Presburger definable. Due to a result by Leroux [11], there is an algorithm that finishes with a Presburger description of the reachability set of (N', M_0') when this set is semilinear (while it runs forever when not). This yields the announced semidecidability.

The construction of the above mentioned (downward closed) set $\mathcal{D}$ is standard; the crucial ingredient of our proof is thus the mentioned result by Leroux. Though we use the decidability of reachability (for semidecidability of the positive case), it is not clear if reachability reduces to structural liveness, and the complexity of the structural liveness problem is left open for future research.

Section 2 provides the formal background, and Sect. 3 shows the decidability result. In Sect. 4 a few comments are added, and in particular an example of a net is given where the set of live markings is not semilinear.

2   Basic Definitions

By $\mathbb{N}$ we denote the set $\{0, 1, 2, \ldots\}$. For a set A, by A^* we denote the set of finite sequences of elements of A, and ε denotes the empty sequence.

Nets. A *Petri net*, or just a *net* for short, is a tuple $N = (P, T, W)$ where P and T are two disjoint finite sets of *places* and *transitions*, respectively, and $W : (P \times T) \cup (T \times P) \to \mathbb{N}$ is the *weighted flow function*. A *marking* M of N is an element of $\mathbb{N}^P$, a mapping from P to $\mathbb{N}$, often also viewed as a vector with $|P|$ components (i.e., an element of $\mathbb{N}^{|P|}$).

Figure 1 presents a net $N = (\{p_1, p_2, p_3\}, \{t_1, t_2, t_3\}, W)$ where $W(p_1, t_1) = 2$, $W(p_1, t_2) = 1$, $W(p_1, t_3) = 0$, etc.; we do not draw an arc from x to y when $W(x, y) = 0$, and we assume $W(x, y) = 1$ for the arcs (x, y) with no depicted

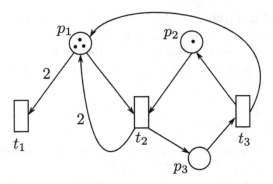

Fig. 1. Example of a net $N = (P, T, W)$, with marking $M = (3, 1, 0)$

numbers. Figure 1 also depicts a marking M by using black tokens, namely $M = (3, 1, 0)$, assuming the ordering (p_1, p_2, p_3) of places.

Reachability. Assuming a net $N = (P, T, W)$, for each $t \in T$ we define the following relation $\xrightarrow{t}$ on $\mathbb{N}^P$:

$$M \xrightarrow{t} M' \Leftrightarrow_{\mathrm{df}} \forall p \in P : M(p) \geq W(p, t) \wedge M'(p) = M(p) - W(p, t) + W(t, p).$$

By $M \xrightarrow{t}$ we denote that t is *enabled in* M, i.e., that there is M' such that $M \xrightarrow{t} M'$. The relations $\xrightarrow{t}$ are inductively extended to $\xrightarrow{u}$ for all $u \in T^*$: $M \xrightarrow{\varepsilon} M$; if $M \xrightarrow{t} M'$ and $M' \xrightarrow{u} M''$, then $M \xrightarrow{tu} M''$. The *reachability set for a marking* M is the set

$$[M\rangle = \{M' \mid M \xrightarrow{u} M' \text{ for some } u \in T^*\}.$$

For the net of Fig. 1 we have, e.g., $(3, 1, 0) \xrightarrow{t_2} (4, 0, 1) \xrightarrow{t_1} (2, 0, 1) \xrightarrow{t_1} (0, 0, 1) \xrightarrow{t_3} (1, 1, 0)$; we can check that the reachability set for $(3, 1, 0)$ is

$$\{(x, 1, 0) \mid x \text{ is odd }\} \cup \{(y, 0, 1) \mid y \text{ is even}\}. \tag{1}$$

Liveness. For a net $N = (P, T, W)$, a *transition* t is *dead in a marking* M if there is no $M' \in [M\rangle$ such that $M' \xrightarrow{t}$. (Such t can be never performed in N when we start from M.)

A *transition* t is *live in* M_0 if there is no $M \in [M_0\rangle$ such that t is dead in M. (Hence for each $M \in [M_0\rangle$ there is $M' \in [M\rangle$ such that $M' \xrightarrow{t}$.) A *set* $T' \subseteq T$ *of transitions is live in* M_0 if each $t \in T'$ is *live in* M_0. (Another natural definition of liveness of a set T' is discussed in Sect. 4.)

A *marked net* is a pair (N, M_0) where $N = (P, T, W)$ is a net and M_0 is a marking, called *the initial marking*. A *marked net* (N, M_0) is *live* if each transition (in other words, the set T) is live in M_0 (in the net N). A *net* N is *structurally live* if there is M_0 such that (N, M_0) is live.

E.g., the net in Fig. 1 is structurally live since it is live for the marking $(3, 1, 0)$, as can be easily checked by inspecting the transitions enabled in the elements of the reachability set (1). We can also note that the net is not live for $(4, 1, 0)$, we even have that no transition is live in $(4, 1, 0)$, since $(4, 1, 0) \xrightarrow{t_1 t_1} (0, 1, 0)$ where all transitions are dead.

Liveness decision problems.

- The *partial liveness problem*, denoted PLP, asks, given a marked net (N, M_0) and a set T' of its transitions, if T' is live in M_0.
- The *liveness problem*, denoted LP, is a special case of PLP: it asks, given a marked net (N, M_0), if (N, M_0) is live (i.e., if all its transitions are live in M_0).
- The *partial structural liveness problem*, denoted PSLP, asks, given a net N and a set T' of its transitions, if there is M in which T' is live.
- The *structural liveness problem*, denoted SLP, is a special case of PSLP: it asks, given a net N, if there is M such that (N, M) is live.

3   Structural Liveness of Nets Is Decidable

We aim to show the decidability of PSLP, and thus also of SLP:

Theorem 1. *The partial structural liveness problem (PSLP) is decidable.*

We prove the theorem in the rest of this section. We first recall the famous decidability result for reachability. The *reachability problem*, denoted RP, asks if $M \in [M_0\rangle$ when given N, M_0, M.

Lemma 2. *[13] The reachability problem (RP) is decidable.*

In Petri net theory this is a fundamental theorem; we call it a "lemma" here, since it is one ingredient used in proving the theorem of this paper (i.e. Theorem 1). The first proof of Lemma 2 was given by E.W. Mayr (see [13] for a journal publication), and there is a row of further papers dealing with this problem; we can refer to a recent paper [12] and the references therein for further information. As already mentioned, the complexity of the reachability problem remains far from clear.

There are long known, and straightforward, effective reductions among the reachability problem RP and the (partial) liveness problems (PLP and LP); we can find them already in Hack's works from 1970s [8,9]. This induces semidecidability of the partial structural liveness problem (PSLP): given N and T', we can systematically generate all markings of N, always deciding if T' is live in the currently generated M (and halt when the answer is positive). Hence the main issue is to establish the semidecidability of the complementary problem of PSLP; roughly speaking, we need to find a finite witness when (N, M) is non-live for all M.

We further assume a fixed net $N = (P, T, W)$ if not said otherwise.

Sets of "dead" markings are downward closed. A natural first step for studying (partial) liveness is to explore the sets

$$\mathcal{D}_{T'} = \{M \in \mathbb{N}^P \mid \text{ some } t \in T' \text{ is dead in } M\}$$

for $T' \subseteq T$. We note that the definition entails $\mathcal{D}_{T'} = \bigcup_{t \in T'} \mathcal{D}_{\{t\}}$. E.g., in the net of Fig. 1 we have $\mathcal{D}_{\{t_1\}} = \{(x,0,0) \mid x \leq 1\} \cup \{(0,x,0) \mid x \in \mathbb{N}\}$, $\mathcal{D}_{\{t_2,t_3\}} = \{(x,0,0) \mid x \in \mathbb{N}\}$, and

$$\mathcal{D}_T = \{(0,x,0) \mid x \in \mathbb{N}\} \cup \{(x,0,0) \mid x \in \mathbb{N}\}. \tag{2}$$

Due to the monotonicity of Petri nets (by which we mean that $M \xrightarrow{u} M'$ implies $M + \delta \xrightarrow{u} M' + \delta$ for all $\delta \in \mathbb{N}^P$), each $\mathcal{D}_{T'}$ is obviously downward closed. We say that $\mathcal{D} \subseteq \mathbb{N}^P$ is *downward closed* if $M \in \mathcal{D}$ implies $M' \in \mathcal{D}$ for all $M' \leq M$, where we refer to the component-wise order:

$$M' \leq M \Leftrightarrow_{\text{df}} \forall p \in P : M'(p) \leq M(p).$$

It is standard to characterize any downward closed subset $\mathcal{D}$ of $\mathbb{N}^P$ by the set of its maximal elements, using the extension $\mathbb{N}_\omega = \mathbb{N} \cup \{\omega\}$ where ω stands for an "arbitrarily large number" satisfying $\omega > n$ for all $n \in \mathbb{N}$. Formally we extend a downward closed set $\mathcal{D} \subseteq \mathbb{N}^P$ to the set

$$\widehat{\mathcal{D}} = \{M \in (\mathbb{N}_\omega)^P \mid \forall M' \in \mathbb{N}^P : M' \leq M \Rightarrow M' \in \mathcal{D}\}.$$

We thus have

$$\mathcal{D} = \{M' \in \mathbb{N}^P \mid M' \leq M \text{ for some } M \in \text{MAX}(\widehat{\mathcal{D}})\}$$

where $\text{MAX}(\widehat{\mathcal{D}})$ is the set of maximal elements of $\widehat{\mathcal{D}}$. By (the standard extension of) Dickson's Lemma, the set $\text{MAX}(\widehat{\mathcal{D}})$ is finite. (We can refer, e.g., to [5] where such completions by "adding the limits" are handled in a general framework.)

E.g., for the set $\mathcal{D}_T$ in (2) we have $\text{MAX}(\widehat{\mathcal{D}_T}) = \{(0,\omega,0),(\omega,0,0)\}$.

Proposition 3. *Given $N = (P,T,W)$ and $T' \subseteq T$, the set $\mathcal{D}_{T'}$ is downward closed and the finite set $\text{MAX}(\widehat{\mathcal{D}_{T'}})$ is effectively constructible.*

Proof. We consider a net $N = (P,T,W)$ and a set $T' \subseteq T$. As discussed above, the set $\mathcal{D}_{T'}$ is downward closed.

Instead of a direct construction of the finite set $\text{MAX}(\widehat{\mathcal{D}_{T'}})$, we first show that the set $\mathcal{S}_{T'} = \text{MIN}(\mathbb{N}^P \smallsetminus \mathcal{D}_{T'})$, i.e. the set of minimal elements of the (upward closed) complement of $\mathcal{D}_{T'}$, is effectively constructible.

For each $t \in T'$, we first compute $\mathcal{S}_t = \text{MIN}(\mathbb{N}^P \smallsetminus \mathcal{D}_{\{t\}})$, i.e. the set of minimal markings in which t is not dead. One standard possibility for computing $\mathcal{S}_t$ is to use the following backward algorithm, where

$\text{MINPRE}(t', M)$ is the unique marking in $\text{MIN}(\{M' \mid \exists M'' \geq M : M' \xrightarrow{t'} M''\})$.

(For each $p \in P$, $\text{MINPRE}(t', M)(p) = W(p,t') + \max\{M(p) - W(t',p), 0\}$.)

An algorithm for computing $\mathcal{S}_t$:

1. Initialize the variable $\mathcal{S}$, containing a finite set of markings, by

$$\mathcal{S} := \{\text{MINPRE}(t, \mathbf{0})\}$$

where $\mathbf{0}$ is the zero marking ($\mathbf{0}(p) = 0$ for each $p \in P$).

2. Perform the following step repeatedly, as long as possible:
   if for some $t' \in T$ and $M \in \mathcal{S}$ the marking $M' = \text{MINPRE}(t', M)$ is not in the upward closure of $\mathcal{S}$ (hence $M' \not\geq M''$ for each $M'' \in \mathcal{S}$), then put

$$\mathcal{S} := \mathcal{S} \cup \{M'\} \smallsetminus \{M'' \in \mathcal{S} \mid M' \leq M''\}.$$

Termination is clear by Dickson's Lemma, and the final value of $\mathcal{S}$ is obviously the set $\mathcal{S}_t$ (of all minimal markings from which t can get enabled). We can remark that related studies in more general frameworks can be found, e.g., in [1,6].

Having computed the sets $\mathcal{S}_t = \text{MIN}(\mathbb{N}^P \smallsetminus \mathcal{D}_{\{t\}})$ for all $t \in T'$, we can surely compute the set $\mathcal{S}_{T'} = \text{MIN}(\mathbb{N}^P \smallsetminus \mathcal{D}_{T'})$ since

$$\mathcal{S}_{T'} = \text{MIN}(\{M \in \mathbb{N}^P \mid (\forall t \in T')(\exists M' \in \mathcal{S}_t) : M \geq M'\}).$$

This also entails that the maximum $\text{B} \in \mathbb{N}$ of values $M(p)$ where $M \in \mathcal{S}_{T'}$ (and $p \in P$) is bounded by the maximum value $M(p)$ where $M \in \mathcal{S}_t$ for some $t \in T'$. Since the finite (i.e., non-ω) numbers $M(p)$ in the elements M of $\text{MAX}(\widehat{\mathcal{D}_{T'}})$ are obviously less than B, the set $\text{MAX}(\widehat{\mathcal{D}_{T'}})$ can be constructed when given $\mathcal{S}_{T'}$. $\square$

Remark. Generally we must count with at least exponential-space algorithms for constructing $\text{MAX}(\widehat{\mathcal{D}_{T'}})$ (or $\text{MIN}(\mathbb{N}^P \smallsetminus \mathcal{D}_{T'})$), due to Lipton's EXPSPACE-hardness construction that also applies to the coverability (besides the reachability). On the other hand, by Rackoff's results [14] the maximum B mentioned in the proof is at most doubly-exponential w.r.t. the input size, and thus fits in exponential space. Nevertheless, the precise complexity of computing $\text{MAX}(\widehat{\mathcal{D}_{T'}})$ is not important in our context.

Sets of "live" markings are more complicated. Assuming $N = (P, T, W)$, for $T' \subseteq T$ we define

$$\mathcal{L}_{T'} = \{M \in \mathbb{N}^P \mid T' \text{ is live in } M\}.$$

The set $\mathcal{L}_{T'}$ is not the complement of $\mathcal{D}_{T'}$ in general, but our definitions readily yield the following equivalence:

Proposition 4. $M \in \mathcal{L}_{T'}$ *iff* $[M\rangle \cap \mathcal{D}_{T'} = \emptyset$.

We note that $\mathcal{L}_{T'}$ is not upward closed in general. We have already observed this on the net in Fig. 1, where $\mathcal{D}_T = \{(0, x, 0) \mid x \in \mathbb{N}\} \cup \{(x, 0, 0) \mid x \in \mathbb{N}\}$ (i.e., $\text{MAX}(\widehat{\mathcal{D}_T}) = \{(0, \omega, 0), (\omega, 0, 0)\}$). It is not difficult to verify that in this net we have

$$\mathcal{L}_T = \{ M \in \mathbb{N}^{\{p_1, p_2, p_3\}} \mid M(p_2) + M(p_3) \geq 1 \text{ and } M(p_1) + M(p_3) \text{ is odd} \}. \quad (3)$$

Proposition 4 has the following simple corollary:

Proposition 5. *The answer to an instance* $N = (P, T, W)$, T' *of* PSLP *(the partial structural liveness problem) is*

1. *YES if* $\mathcal{L}_{T'} \neq \emptyset$, *i.e., if* $\{M \in \mathbb{N}^P ; [M\rangle \cap \mathcal{D}_{T'} \neq \emptyset\} \neq \mathbb{N}^P$.
2. *NO if* $\mathcal{L}_{T'} = \emptyset$, *i.e., if* $\{M \in \mathbb{N}^P ; [M\rangle \cap \mathcal{D}_{T'} \neq \emptyset\} = \mathbb{N}^P$.

It turns out important for us that in the case 2 (NO) the set $\{M \in \mathbb{N}^P ; [M\rangle \cap \mathcal{D}_{T'} \neq \emptyset\}$ is semilinear. We now recall the relevant notions and facts, and then we give a proof of Theorem 1.

Semilinear sets. For a fixed (dimension) $d \in \mathbb{N}$, a *set* $\mathcal{L} \subseteq \mathbb{N}^d$ is *linear* if there is a (basic) vector $\rho \in \mathbb{N}^d$ and (period) vectors $\pi_1, \pi_2, \ldots, \pi_k \in \mathbb{N}^d$ (for some $k \in \mathbb{N}$) such that

$$\mathcal{L} = \{ \rho + x_1\pi_1 + x_2\pi_2 + \cdots + x_k\pi_k \mid x_1, x_2, \ldots, x_k \in \mathbb{N} \}.$$

Such vectors $\rho, \pi_1, \pi_2, \ldots, \pi_k$ constitute a *description* of the set $\mathcal{L}$.

A *set* $\mathcal{S} \subseteq \mathbb{N}^d$ is *semilinear* if it is the union of finitely many linear sets; a *description* of $\mathcal{S}$ is a collection of descriptions of $\mathcal{L}_i$, $i = 1, 2, \ldots, m$ (for some $m \in \mathbb{N}$), where $\mathcal{S} = \mathcal{L}_1 \cup \mathcal{L}_2 \cup \cdots \cup \mathcal{L}_m$ and $\mathcal{L}_i$ are linear.

It is well known that an equivalent formalism for describing semilinear sets are Presburger formulas [7], the arithmetic formulas that can use addition but no multiplication (of variables); we also recall that the truth of (closed) Presburger formulas is decidable. E.g., all downward (or upward) closed sets $\mathcal{D} \subseteq \mathbb{N}^P$ are semilinear, and also the above sets (1) and (3) are examples of semilinear sets. Moreover, given the set $\mathrm{MAX}(\widehat{\mathcal{D}})$ for a downward closed set $\mathcal{D}$, constructing a description of $\mathcal{D}$ as of a semilinear set is straightforward.

It is also well known that the reachability sets $[M\rangle$ are not semilinear in general; similarly the sets $\mathcal{L}_{T'}$ (of live markings) are not semilinear in general. (We give an example in Sect. 4.) But we have the following result by Leroux [11]; it is again an important theorem in Petri net theory that we call a "lemma" in our context (since it is an ingredient for proving Theorem 1).

Lemma 6. *[11] There is an algorithm that, given a marked net* (N, M_0), *halts iff the reachability set* $[M_0\rangle$ *is semilinear, in which case it produces a description of this set.*

Roughly speaking, the algorithm guaranteed by Lemma 6 generates the reachability graph for M_0 while performing certain "accelerations" when possible (which captures repeatings of some transition sequences by simple formulas); this process is creating a sequence of descriptions of increasing semilinear subsets of the reachability set $[M_0\rangle$ until the subset is closed under all steps $\xrightarrow{t}$ (which can be effectively checked); in this case the subset (called an inductive invariant in [11]) is equal to $[M_0\rangle$, and the process is guaranteed to reach such a case when $[M_0\rangle$ is semilinear. (A consequence highlighted in [11] is that in such a case all reachable markings can be reached by sequences of transitions from a bounded language.)

Proof of Theorem 1 (decidability of PSLP).

Given $N = (P, T, W)$ and $T' \subseteq T$, we will construct a marked net (N', M_0') where $N' = (P \cup P_{new}, T \cup T_{new}, W')$ so that we will have:

(a) if $\mathcal{L}_{T'} = \emptyset$ in N (i.e., T' is non-live in each marking of N) then $[M_0'\rangle$ is semilinear and the projection of $[M_0'\rangle$ to P is equal to $\mathbb{N}^P$;

(b) if $\mathcal{L}_{T'} \neq \emptyset$, then the projection of $[M_0'\rangle$ to P is not equal to $\mathbb{N}^P$ (and might be non-semilinear).

This construction of (N', M_0') yields the required decidability proof, since we can consider two algorithms running in parallel:

- One is the algorithm of Lemma 6 applied to (N', M_0'); if it finishes with a semilinear description of $[M_0'\rangle$, which surely happens in the case (a), then we can effectively check if the projection of $[M_0'\rangle$ to P is $\mathbb{N}^P$, i.e. if $\mathcal{L}_{T'} = \emptyset$. (A projection of a semilinear set is effectively semilinear, the set-difference of two semilinear set is also effectively semilinear [7], and checking emptiness of a semilinear set is trivial.)
- The other algorithm generates all $M \in \mathbb{N}^P$ and for each of them checks if there is $M' \in [M_0'\rangle$ such that $M'_{\restriction P}$ (i.e., M' projected to P) is equal to M. It thus finds some M with the negative answer if, and only if, $\mathcal{L}_{T'} \neq \emptyset$ (the case (b)). The existence of the algorithm checking the mentioned property for M follows from a standard extension of the decidability of reachability (Lemma 2); for our concrete construction below this extension is not needed, and just the claim of Lemma 2 will suffice.

The construction of (N', M_0') is illustrated in Fig. 2; we create a marked net that first generates an element of $\mathcal{D}_{T'}$ on the places P, and then simulates N in the reverse mode. More concretely, we assume the ordering $(p_1, p_2, \ldots, p_n)$ of the set P of places in N, and compute a description of the semilinear set $\mathcal{D}_{T'} \subseteq \mathbb{N}^{|P|}$ (by first constructing the set $\mathrm{MAX}(\widehat{\mathcal{D}_{T'}})$; recall Proposition 3). We thus get

$$\mathcal{D}_{T'} = \mathscr{L}_1 \cup \mathscr{L}_2 \cup \cdots \cup \mathscr{L}_m,$$

given by descriptions $\rho_i, \pi_{i1}, \pi_{i2}, \ldots, \pi_{ik_i}$ of the linear sets $\mathscr{L}_i$, for $i = 1, 2, \ldots, m$.

Remark. We choose this description of $\mathcal{D}_{T'}$ to make clear that the construction can be applied to any semilinear set, not only to a downward closed one.

The construction of (N', M_0'), where $N' = (P \cup P_{new}, T \cup T_{new}, W')$, is now described in detail:

1. Given $N = (P, T, W)$, create the "reversed" net $N_{rev} = (P, T, W_{rev})$, where $W_{rev}(p, t) = W(t, p)$ and $W_{rev}(t, p) = W(p, t)$ for all $p \in P$ and $t \in T$. (By induction on the length of u it is easy to verify that $M \xrightarrow{u} M'$ in N iff $M' \xrightarrow{u_{rev}} M$ in N_{rev}, where u_{rev} is defined inductively as follows: $\varepsilon_{rev} = \varepsilon$ and $(tu)_{rev} = u_{rev}t$.)

2. To get N', extend N_{rev} as described below; we will have $W'(p, t) = W_{rev}(p, t)$ and $W'(t, p) = W_{rev}(t, p)$ for all $p \in P$ and $t \in T$.

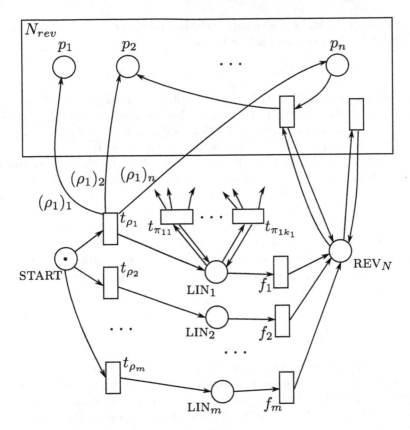

Fig. 2. Construction of (N', M_0') for deciding the (partial) structural liveness (PSLP)

3. Create the set P_{new} of additional places

$$P_{new} = \{\text{START}, \text{LIN}_1, \text{LIN}_2, \ldots, \text{LIN}_m, \text{REV}_N\}$$

and the set T_{new} of additional transitions

$$T_{new} = \bigcup_{i \in \{1,2,\ldots,m\}} \{t_{\rho_i}, f_i, t_{\pi_{i1}}, t_{\pi_{i2}}, \ldots, t_{\pi_{ik_i}}\}$$

(as partly depicted in Fig. 2.)

4. Put $M_0'(\text{START}) = 1$ and $M_0'(p) = 0$ for all other places $p \in P \cup P_{new}$.

5. For each $i \in \{1, 2, \ldots, m\}$, put $W'(\text{START}, t_{\rho_i}) = W'(t_{\rho_i}, \text{LIN}_i) = 1$, and $W'(t_{\rho_i}, p_j) = (\rho_i)_j$ for all $j \in \{1, 2, \ldots, n\}$, where $(\rho_i)_j$ is the j-th component of the vector $\rho_i \in \mathbb{N}^n$. (We tacitly assume that the value of W' is 0 for the pairs (p, t) and (t, p) that are not mentioned.)

6. For each $t_{\pi_{i\ell}}$ ($i \in \{1, 2, \ldots, m\}$, $\ell \in \{1, 2, \ldots, k_i\}$) put $W'(\text{LIN}_i, t_{\pi_{i\ell}}) = W'(t_{\pi_{i\ell}}, \text{LIN}_i) = 1$, and $W'(t_{\pi_{i\ell}}, p_j) = (\pi_{i\ell})_j$ for all $j \in \{1, 2, \ldots, n\}$.

7. For each f_i put $W'(\text{LIN}_i, f_i) = W'(f_i, \text{REV}_N) = 1$.

8. For each transition $t \in T$ in N_{rev} put $W'(\text{REV}_N, t) = W'(t, \text{REV}_N) = 1$.

In the resulting (N', M_0') we have only one token moving on P_{new}; more precisely, the set $[M_0'\rangle$ can be expressed as the union

$$[M_0'\rangle = \mathcal{S}_{\text{START}} \cup \mathcal{S}_{\text{LIN}_1} \cup \cdots \cup \mathcal{S}_{\text{LIN}_m} \cup \mathcal{S}_{\text{REV}_N}$$

of the disjoint sets $\mathcal{S}_p = \{M \mid M \in [M_0'\rangle$ and $M(p) = 1\}$, for $p \in \{\text{START}, \text{LIN}_1, \ldots, \text{LIN}_m, \text{REV}_N\}$. It is clear that each of the sets $\mathcal{S}_{\text{START}}$, $\mathcal{S}_{\text{LIN}_1}$, $\ldots$, $\mathcal{S}_{\text{LIN}_m}$ is linear, and that the projection of $\mathcal{S}_{\text{REV}_N}$ to $P = \{p_1, p_2, \ldots, p_n\}$ is the set $\{M \in \mathbb{N}^P; [M\rangle \cap \mathcal{D}_{T'} \neq \emptyset\}$ where $[M\rangle$ refers to the net N.

The constructed (N', M_0') clearly satisfies the above conditions (a) and (b). In the algorithm verifying b), it suffices to generate the markings M of N' that satisfy $M(\text{REV}_N) = 1$, $M(\text{START}) = M(\text{LIN}_1) = \cdots = M(\text{LIN}_m) = 0$, and to check the (non)reachability from M_0' for each of them (recall Lemma 2).

Remark. We also have another option (than Lemma 2) for establishing the non-reachability of M from M_0', due to another result by Leroux (see, e.g., [10]): namely to find a description of a semilinear set that contains M_0', does not contain M, and is closed w.r.t. all steps $\xrightarrow{t}$ (being thus an inductive invariant in the terminology of [10]).

4   Additional Remarks

Sets of live markings can be non-semilinear. In Petri net theory, there are many results that relate liveness to specific structural properties of nets. We can name [2] as an example of a cited paper from this area. Nevertheless, the general structural liveness problem is still not fully understood; one reason might be the fact that *the set of live markings of a given net is not semilinear in general.*

We give an example. If the set $\mathcal{L}_T$ of live markings for the net $N = (P, T, W)$ in Fig. 3 was semilinear, then also its intersection with the set $\{(x_1, 0, 1, 0, 1, x_6) \mid x_1, x_6 \in \mathbb{N}\}$ would be semilinear (i.e., definable by a Presburger formula). But is is straightforward to verify that the markings in this set are live if, and only if, $x_6 > 2^{x_1}$, which makes the set clearly non-semilinear. Indeed, any marking M where p_4 is marked (forever), i.e. $M(p_4) \geq 1$, is clearly live, and we can get at most 2^{x_1} tokens in p_5 as long as p_4 is unmarked; if $x_6 \leq 2^{x_1}$, then there is a reachable marking where all transitions are dead, but otherwise p_4 gets necessarily marked.

Another version of liveness of a set of transitions. Given $N = (P, T, W)$, we defined that a set T' of transitions is live in a marking M if each $t \in T'$ is live in M. Another option is to view T' as live in M if in each $M' \in [M\rangle$ at least one $t \in T'$ is not dead. But the problem if T' is live in M in this sense can be easily reduced to the problem if a specific transition is live. (We can add a place $\bar{p}$ and a transition $\bar{t}$, putting $W(\bar{p}, \bar{t}) = 1$. For each $t \in T'$ we then add t' and put $W(t', \bar{p}) = 1$ and $W(p, t') = W(t', p) = W(p, t)$ for each $p \in P$. Then T' is live in M in the new sense iff $\bar{t}$ is live in M.) The above nuances in definitions thus make no substantial difference.

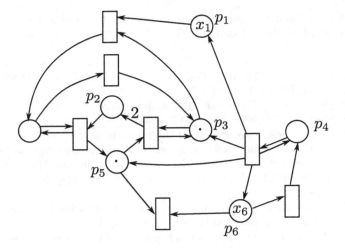

Fig. 3. Sets of live markings can be non-semilinear

Open complexity status. We have not clarified the complexity of the (partial) structural liveness problem (PSLP, SLP). The complexity of the (partial) liveness problem (PLP, LP) is "close" to the complexity of the reachability problem RP (as follows already by the constructions in [8]), but it seems natural to expect that the *structural* liveness problem might be easier. (E.g., the boundedness problem, asking if $[M_0\rangle$ is finite when given (N, M_0), is ExpSpace-complete, by the results of Lipton and Rackoff, but the structural boundedness problem is polynomial; here we ask, given N, if (N, M_0) is bounded for all M_0, or in the complementary way, if (N, M_0) is unbounded for some M_0.)

Acknowledgement. I would like to thank Eike Best for drawing my attention to the problem of structural liveness studied in this paper. I also thank the anonymous reviewers for helpful comments.

References

1. Abdulla, P.A., Cerans, K., Jonsson, B., Tsay, Y.: Algorithmic analysis of programs with well quasi-ordered domains. Inf. Comput. **160**(1–2), 109–127 (2000). http://dx.doi.org/10.1006/inco.1999.2843
2. Barkaoui, K., Pradat-Peyre, J.: On liveness and controlled siphons in Petri nets. Application and Theory of Petri Nets 1996. LNCS, vol. 1091, pp. 57–72. Springer, Heidelberg (1996). doi:10.1007/3-540-61363-3_4
3. Best, E., Esparza, J.: Existence of home states in Petri nets is decidable. Inf. Process. Lett. **116**(6), 423–427 (2016). http://dx.doi.org/10.1016/j.ipl.2016.01.011
4. Esparza, J.: Decidability and complexity of Petri net problems—an introduction. In: Reisig, W., Rozenberg, G. (eds.) ACPN 1996. LNCS, vol. 1491, pp. 374–428. Springer, Heidelberg (1998). doi:10.1007/3-540-65306-6_20

5. Finkel, A., Goubault-Larrecq, J.: Forward analysis for WSTS, Part II: complete WSTS. Logical Methods Comput. Sci. 8(3) (2012). http://dx.doi.org/10.2168/LMCS-8(3:28)2012

6. Finkel, A., Schnoebelen, P.: Well-structured transition systems everywhere!. Theor. Comput. Sci. **256**(1–2), 63–92 (2001). http://dx.doi.org/10.1016/S0304-3975(00)00102-X

7. Ginsburg, S., Spanier, E.H.: Semigroups, presburger formulas, and languages. Pacific J. Math. **16**(2), 285–296 (1966)

8. Hack, M.: The recursive equivalence of the reachability problem and the liveness problem for Petri nets and vector addition systems. In: 15th Annual Symposium on Switching and Automata Theory, New Orleans, Louisiana, USA, October 14–16, 1974, pp. 156–164. IEEE Computer Society (1974). http://dx.doi.org/10.1109/SWAT.1974.28

9. Hack, M.: Decidability Questions for Petri Nets. Outstanding Dissertations in the Computer Sciences. Garland Publishing, New York (1975)

10. Leroux, J.: Vector addition systems reachability problem (A simpler solution). In: Voronkov, A. (ed.) Turing-100 - The Alan Turing Centenary, Manchester, UK, June 22–25, 2012. EPiC Series in Computing, vol. 10, pp. 214–228. EasyChair (2012). http://www.easychair.org/publications/?page=1673703727

11. Leroux, J.: Presburger vector addition systems. In: 28th Annual ACM/IEEE Symposium on Logic in Computer Science, LICS 2013, New Orleans, LA, USA, June 25–28, 2013, pp. 23–32. IEEE Computer Society (2013). http://dx.doi.org/10.1109/LICS.2013.7

12. Leroux, J., Schmitz, S.: Demystifying reachability in vector addition systems. In: 30th Annual ACM/IEEE Symposium on Logic in Computer Science, LICS 2015, Kyoto, Japan, July 6–10, 2015, pp. 56–67. IEEE Computer Society (2015). http://dx.doi.org/10.1109/LICS.2015.16

13. Mayr, E.W.: An algorithm for the general petri net reachability problem. SIAM J. Comput. **13**(3), 441–460 (1984). http://dx.doi.org/10.1137/0213029

14. Rackoff, C.: The covering and boundedness problems for vector addition systems. Theor. Comput. Sci. **6**, 223–231 (1978)

15. Reisig, W.: Understanding Petri Nets (Modeling Techniques, Analysis Methods, Case Studies). Springer, Heidelberg (2013). 230 pp

16. Wimmel, H.: Entscheidbarkeit bei Petri Netzen: Überblick und Kompendium. Springer, Heidelberg (2008). 242 pp

Distributed Network Generation Based on Preferential Attachment in ABS

Keyvan Azadbakht[(✉)], Nikolaos Bezirgiannis, and Frank S. de Boer

Centrum Wiskunde & Informatica (CWI), Amsterdam, Netherlands
{k.azadbakht,n.bezirgiannis,f.s.de.boer}@cwi.nl

Abstract. Generation of social networks using Preferential Attachment (PA) mechanism is proposed in the Barabasi-Albert model. In this mechanism, new nodes are introduced to the network sequentially and they attach to the existing nodes preferentially where the preference can be based on the degree of the existing nodes. PA is a classical model with a natural intuition, great explanatory power and interesting mathematical properties. Some of these properties only appear in large-scale networks. However generation of such extra-large networks can be challenging due to memory limitations. In this paper, we investigate a distributed-memory approach for PA-based network generation which is scalable and which avoids low-level synchronization mechanisms thanks to utilizing a powerful programming model and proper programming constructs.

Keywords: Distributed programming · Social network · Preferential Attachment · Actor model · Synchronization

1 Introduction

Social networks appear in many domains, e.g., communication, friendship, and citation networks. These networks are different from random networks as they demonstrate structural features like power-law degree distribution. There exist certain models which generate artificial graphs that preserve the properties of real world networks (e.g., [1–3]), among which Barabasi-Albert model of scale-free networks, which is based on Preferential Attachment (PA) [3], is one of the most widely-used ones, mainly because of its natural intuition, great explanatory power and simple mechanism [4].

Generating network based on PA is inherently a sequential task as there is a sequence among the nodes in terms of their addition to the network. The nodes are added preferentially to the graph. The preference is the node degrees in the graph, i.e., the higher a node degree, the higher probability with which the new node makes connection.

Massive networks are structurally different from small networks synthesized by the same algorithm. Furthermore there are many patterns that emerge only in massive networks [5]. Analysis of such networks is also of importance in many

© Springer International Publishing AG 2017
B. Steffen et al. (Eds.): SOFSEM 2017, LNCS 10139, pp. 103–115, 2017.
DOI: 10.1007/978-3-319-51963-0_9

areas, e.g. data-mining, network sciences, physics, and social sciences [6]. Nevertheless, generation of such extra-large networks necessitates an extra-large memory in a single server in the centralized algorithms.

The major challenge is generating large-scale social networks utilizing distributed-memory approaches where the graph, generated by multiple processes, is distributed among multiple corresponding memories. Few existing methods are based on a distributed implementation of the PA model among which some methods are based on a version of the PA model which does not fully capture its main characteristics. In contrast, we aim for a distributed solution which follows the original PA model, i.e., preserving the same probability distribution as the sequential one. The main challenge of a faithful distributed version of PA is to manage the complexity of the communication and synchronization involved.

In a distributed version, finding a target node in order for the new node to make connection with may cause an unresolved dependency, i.e., the target itself is not yet resolved. However this kind of dependencies must be preserved and the to-be-resolved target will be utilized when it is resolved. How to preserve these dependencies and their utilization give rise to low-level explicit management of the dependencies or, by means of powerful programming constructs, high-level implicit management of them.

The main contribution of this paper is a new scalable distributed implementation of an ABS (Abstract Behavioral Specification) [7] model of PA. The ABS language is a high-level actor-based executable modeling language which is tailored towards modeling distributed applications and which supports a variety of tool-supported techniques for, e.g., verification [8] and resource analysis [9]. In this paper, we show that ABS also can be used as a powerful programming language for efficient implementation of cloud-based distributed applications. The underlying runtime system and compiler are written in the Haskell language integrating the Cloud Haskell API [10].

The paper is organized as follows: The description of ABS language and its Haskell backend is given in Sect. 2. Section 3 elaborates on the high-level proposed distributed algorithm using the notion of cooperative scheduling and futures. In Sect. 4, implementation-specific details and experimental results are presented. Finally, Sect. 5 concludes the paper.

Related Work. Efficient implementation of PA model has been investigated in, e.g., [4,11–15]. Some of these works still focus on the sequential approach (e.g., [4,11,12]). The main proposal of such methods is to adopt data structures which improve time and memory complexity. There are also parallel and distributed proposals: [13,14] do not fully capture the main properties expected in the original model of graph generation; [15] also requires complex synchronization and communication management.

Our work was inspired by the work in [15] where a low-level distributed implementation of PA is given in MPI: the implementation code remains closed source (even after contacting the authors) and, as such, we cannot validate their presented results (e.g., there are certain glitches in their weak scaling demonstration), nor compare them to our own implementation. Since efficient implementation of PA is an important and challenging topic, further research is called for. Moreover, our experimental data are based on a high-level model of the PA which abstracts from low-level management of process queues and corresponding synchronization mechanism as used in [15].

In [16] a high-level distributed model of the PA in ABS has been presented together with a high-level description of its possible implementation in Java. However, as we argue in Sect. 4, certain features of ABS pose serious problems to an efficient distributed implementation in Java. In this paper, we show that these problems can be solved by a runtime system for ABS in Haskell and a corresponding source-to-source translation. We do so by providing an experimental validation of a scalable distributed implementation based on Haskell.

2   ABS: The Modeling Framework

The Abstract Behavioral Specification language (ABS for short) [7] is a modeling language for concurrent systems. Its formal operational semantics permit the analysis [9], and verification [8] of complex concurrent models. Moreover, the ABS language is executable which means the user can generate executable code and integrate it to production—currently backends have been written to target Java, Erlang and Haskell [17] and ProActive [18] software.

ABS at its core is a purely functional programming language, with support for pure functions (functions that disallow side-effects), parametrically polymorphic algebraic datatypes (e.g. Maybe<A>) and pattern matching over those types. At the outside sits the imperative layer of the language with the Java-reminiscing class, interface, method and attribute definitions. Unlike Java, the objects in ABS are typed exclusively by interface with the usual nominal subtyping relations— ABS does not provide any means for class (code) inheritance. It also attributes the notion of *concurrent object group*, which is essentially a group of objects which share control [7]. Note that a complement to this notion where the active objects share the data, i.e., the message queue, instead of control is studied in [19].

Besides the common synchronous method calls to passive objects $o.m(\bar{e})$, ABS introduces the notion of concurrent objects (also known as active objects). These concurrent objects interact primarily via asynchronous method invocations and futures. An asynchronous method invocation is of the form $f = o!m(\bar{e})$, where f is a future used as a reference to the return value of the asynchronous method call m. The method call itself will generate a process which is stored in the process queue of the callee object of the call. Futures can be passed around and can be queried for the value they contain. The query $r = f.get$ blocks the execution of the active object until the future f is resolved, and returns its value. On the other hand, the statement *await f?* additionally releases control. This allows for scheduling of another process of the same active object and as such gives rise to the notion of *cooperative scheduling*: releasing the control cooperatively so another enabled process can be (re)activated. ABS provides two other forms of releasing control: the `await` b statement which will only re-activate the process when the given boolean condition b becomes true (e.g. `await this.field==3`), and the `suspend` statement which will unconditionally release control to the active object. Note that the ABS language specification does not fix a particular scheduling strategy for the process queue of active objects as the ABS analysis and verification tools will explore many (if all) schedulability options; however, ABS backends commonly implement such process queues with FIFO ordering.

Since we are interested in the implementation of a distributed ABS model, we utilize the cloud extension to the ABS standard language, as implemented in [17]. This extension introduces the *Deployment Component* (DC), which abstracts over the resources for which the ABS program gets to run on. In the simplest case, the DC corresponds to a Cloud Virtual Machine executing some ABS code, though this could be extended to include other technologies as well (e.g. containers, microkernels). The DC, being a first class citizen of the language, can be created (`DC dc1 = new AmazonDC(cpuSpec,memSpec)`) and called for (`dc1 ! shutdown()`) as any other ABS concurrent object. The DC interface tries to stay as abstract as possible by declaring only two methods `shutdown` to stop the DC from executing ABS code while freeing its resources, and `load` to query the utilization of the DC machine (e.g. UNIX load). Concrete class implementations to the DC interface are (cloud) machine provider specific and thus may define further specification (cpu, memory, or network type) or behaviour.

Initially, the Deployment Component will remain idle until some ABS code is assigned to it by creating a new object inside using the expression `o = [DC: dc1] new Class(...)`, where o is a so-called remote object reference. Such references are indistinguishable to local object references and can be normally passed around or called for their methods. The ABS language specification and its cloud extension do not dictate a particular Garbage Collection policy, but we assume that holding a reference to a remote object or future means that the object is alive, if its DC is alive as well.

3   Distributed PA

In this section, we present a high-level distributed solution for PA which is similar to the ones proposed for multicore architectures in [20] and distributed architectures in [15,16], in a sense that they adopt *copy model* introduced in [21] to represent the graph. To this aim, the description of the main data structure used to model the graph which represents the social network is given. Next we present the basic synchronization and communication mechanism underlying our approach and its advantages over existing solutions.

3.1   Array Representation of the Network Graph

In this paper, the social network is represented by the notion of graph, where the members of the network are the nodes and the connection between them are the edges. Generating a network based on Preferential Attachment is realized by means of adding new nodes to the network preferentially. The preference is usually the degree of the nodes, that is, the higher the degree of a node, the higher probability that it makes connection with the new node. We assume there is a sequence between the nodes to be added to the network starting from 1 to n, each of which makes m connections with the nodes in the existing graph. It implies that the initial state is a complete graph composed of the nodes 1 to $m + 1$. m is usually a small number.

Suppose node $u \in [m + 2, n]$ is going to be attached to the existing graph with the nodes $[1, u - 1]$. It is done by randomly selecting m *distinct* nodes from $1, ..., u - 1$, so that the probability of each node to be selected is proportional to its degree (to follow the PA model), that is, respectively $[p_1, ..., p_{u-1}]$ where

$$p_i = \frac{degree(i)}{\sum_{j=1}^{u-1} degree(j)} \qquad \sum_{i=1}^{u-1} p_i = 1$$

Figure 1 illustrates the array representation of the graph. Given the number of nodes n and the number of connections per node m, the size of the array is known. As shown, $2m$ slots are allocated for the edges sourcing from a node, u (in the figure, $m = 3$). The targets of u, represented by question mark (or later in implementation with 0), are determined from the slots representing the edges sourcing from the nodes $[1, u - 1]$ which are located previous to the node u. In order to generate the graph based on PA, the unresolved slots are resolved by randomly selecting the slots previous to the current node. The obtained values are then written as the targets of the current node, provided that there is no conflict between them. In case of conflict, the algorithm simply retries until all the targets are distinct for a specific node.

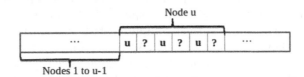

Fig. 1. The array representation of social network graph

The above-mentioned probability distribution is naturally applied through randomly selecting the slots with a uniform chance, since the number of slots keeping the value of a node is equal to its degree.

The sequential algorithm is fairly straightforward and the unresolved slots of the array are resolved from left to right. The distributed algorithms however introduce more challenges. First of all, the global array should be distributed over multiple machines as local arrays. The indices of the global array are also mapped to the ones in the local arrays according to the partitioning policy. Secondly, there is the challenge of *unresolved dependencies*, the one marked by e in Fig. 2, a kind of dependency where the target itself is not resolved yet since either

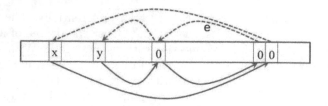

Fig. 2. Dependency and computation directions in the array

the process responsible for the target has not processed the target slot yet or the target slot itself is dependent on another target slot (chain of dependencies). Synchronization between the processes to deal with the unresolved dependencies is the main focus of this paper.

3.2   The Distributed ABS Model of PA

Two approaches are represented in Fig. 3 which illustrate two different schemes of dealing with the unresolved dependencies in a distributed setting. In order to remain consistent with the original PA, both schemes must keep the unresolved dependencies and use the value of the target when it is resolved. Scheme A (used in [15]) utilizes message passing. If the target is not resolved yet, actor b explicitly stores the request in a data structure until the corresponding slot is resolved. Then it communicates the value with actor a. Actor b must also make sure the data structure remains consistent (e.g., it does not contain a request for a slot which is already responded).

In addition to message passing, scheme B utilizes the notion of *cooperative scheduling*. Instead of having an explicit data structure, scheme B simply uses the *await* statement on *(target $\neq$ 0)*. It suspends the request process until the target is resolved. The value is then communicated through the return value to actor a. The above-mentioned await construct eliminates the need for an explicit synchronization of the requests. The following section describes an ABS implementation of the scheme B and presents the performance results.

An ABS-like pseudo code which represents scheme B in the above section is given in Fig. 4. The main body of the program, which is not mentioned in the figure, is responsible to set up the actors by determining their partitions, and sending them other parameters of the problem, e.g., n and m. Each actor then processes its own partition via *run* method. The function *whichActor* returns the index of the actor containing the target slot. The request for the slot is then sent asynchronously to the actor and the future variable is sent as a parameter to the *delegate* function where the future value is obtained and checked for conflict. If there is no conflict, i.e., the new target is not previously taken by the source, then the slot is written with the target value. The *request* method is responsible to map the global index of the target to the local index via *whichLocal* function and *await* on it and returns the value once the slot is resolved.

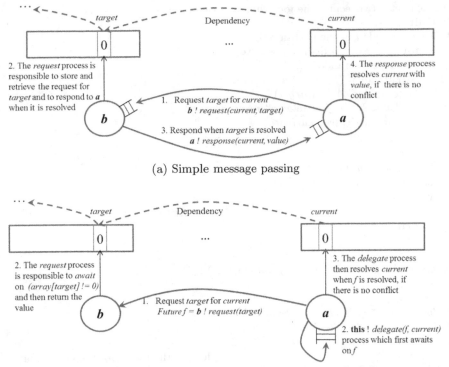

(a) Simple message passing

(b) Message passing with futures and cooperative scheduling

Fig. 3. The process of dealing with unresolved dependencies in an actor-based distributed setting

4 Implementation

The distributed algorithm of Fig. 4 is implemented directly in ABS, which is subsequently translated to Haskell code, by utilizing the ABS-Haskell [17] transcompiler (source-to-source compiler). The translated Haskell code is then linked against a Haskell-written parallel and distributed runtime API. Finally, the linked code is compiled by a Haskell compiler (normally, GHC) down to native code and executed directly.

The parallel runtime treats ABS active objects as Haskell's lightweight threads (also known as green threads), each listening to its own concurrently-modifiable process queue: a method activation pushes a new continuation to the end of the callee's process queue. Processes awaiting on futures are lightweight threads that will push back their continuation when the future is resolved; processes awaiting on boolean conditions are continuations which will be put back to the queue when their condition is met. The parallel runtime strives to avoid busy-wait polling both for futures by employing the underlying OS asynchronous event notification system (e.g. epoll, kqueue), and for booleans by

1: Each actor O executes the following in parallel
2: **Unit** run(...)
3: **for** each node i in the partition **do**
4:      **for** $j = 2$ to $2m$ **do** $j = j + 2$ **step**
5:          $target \leftarrow \text{random}[1..(i-1)*2m]$
6:          $current = (i-1)*2m + j$
7:          $x = whichActor(target)$
8:          $Fut < Int > \ f = actor[x]! \ request(target)$
9:          **this**! $delegate(f, current)$

10:
11:
12: Int request($Int \ target$)
13: $localTarget = whichSlot(target)$
14: **await** $(arr[localTarget] \neq 0)$
15:                                      ▷ At this point the target is resolved
16: **return** $arr[localTarget]$
17:
18:
19: **Unit** delegate($Fut < Int > \ f, Int \ current$) :
20: **await** $f?$
21: $value = f.get$
22: $localCurrent = whichSlot(current)$
23: **if** $duplicate(value, localCurrent)$ **then**
24:      $target = \text{random}[1..current/(2m)*2m]$
25:                                      ▷ Calculate the target for the current again
26:      $x = whichActor(target)$
27:      $Fut < Int > \ f = actor[x]! \ request(target)$
28:      **this**. $delegate(f, current)$
29: **else**
30:      $arr[localCurrent] = value$ ▷ Resolved
31:
32:
33: $boolean$ duplicate($Int \ value, Int \ localCurrent$)
34: **for** each i in (indices of the node to which $localCurrent$ belongs) **do**
35:      **if** $arr[i] == value$ **then**
36:          **return** True
37: **return** False

Fig. 4. The sketch of the proposed approach

retrying the continuations that have part of its condition modified (by mutating fields) since the last release point.

For the distributed runtime we rely on Cloud Haskell [10], a library framework that tries to port Erlang's distribution model to the Haskell language while adding type-safety to messages. Cloud Haskell code is employed for remote method activation and future resolution: the library provides us means to serialize a remote method call to its arguments plus a static (known at compile time) pointer to the method code. No actual code is ever transferred; the active objects are serialized to unique among the whole network identifiers and futures to unique identifiers to the caller object (simply a counter). The serialized data, together with their types, are then transferred through a network transport layer (TCP, CCI, ZeroMQ); we opted for TCP/IP, since it is well-established and easier to debug. The data are de-serialized on the other end: a de-serialized method call corresponds to a continuation which will be pushed to the end of the process queue of the callee object, whereas a de-serialized future value will wake up all processes of the object awaiting on that particular future.

The creation of Deployment Components is done under the hood by contacting the corresponding (cloud) platform provider to allocate a new machine, usually done through a REST API. The executable is compiled once and placed on each created machine which is automatically started as the 1st user process after kernel initialization of the VM has completed.

The choice of Haskell was made mainly for two reasons: the ABS-Haskell backend seems to be currently the fastest in terms of speed and memory use, attributed perhaps to the close match of the two languages in terms of language features: Haskell is also a high-level, statically-typed, purely functional language. Secondly, compared to the distributed implementation sketched in Java [16], the ABS-Haskell runtime utilizes the support of Haskell's lightweight threads and first-class continuations to efficiently implement multicore-enabled cooperative scheduling; Java does not have built-in language support for algebraic datatypes, continuations and its system OS threads (heavyweight) makes it a less ideal candidate to implement cooperative scheduling in a straightforward manner. On the distributed side, layering our solution on top of Java RMI (Remote Method Invocation) framework was decided against for lack of built-in support for asynchronous remote method calls and superfluous features to our needs, such as code-transfer and fully-distributed garbage collection.

4.1   Implementing Delegation

The distributed algorithm described in Sect. 3 uses the concept of a *delegate* for asynchronicity: when the worker actor demands a particular slot of the graph array, it will spawn asynchronously an extra delegate process (line 9) that will only execute when the requested slot becomes available. This execution scheme may be sufficient for preemptive scheduling concurrency (with some safe locking on the active object's fields), since every delegate process gets a fair time slice to execute; however, in cooperative scheduling concurrency, the described scheme yields sub-optimal results for sufficient large graph arrays. Specifically, the worker actor traverses its partition from left to right (line 3), spawning continuously a new delegate in every step; all these delegates cannot execute until the worker actor has released control, which happens upon reaching the end of its run method (finished traversing the partition). Although at first it may seem that the worker actors do operate in parallel to each other, the accumulating delegates are a space leak that puts pressure on the Garbage Collector and, most importantly, delays execution by traversing the partitioned arrays "twice", one for the creation of delegates and one for "consuming them".

A naive solution to this space leak is to change lines 8, 9 to a synchronous instead method call (i.e. `this.delegate(f, current)`). However, a new problem arises where each worker actors (and thus its CPU) continually blocks waiting on the network result of the request. This intensely sequentializes the code and defeats the purpose of distributing the workload, since most processors are idling on network communication. The intuition is that modern CPUs operate in much larger speeds than commodity network technologies. To put it differently, the worker's main calculation is much faster than the round-trip time of a request method call to a remote worker. Theoretically, a synchronous approach could only work in a parallel setting where the workers are homogeneous processors and requests are exchanged through shared memory with memory speed near that of the CPU processor. This hypothesis requires further investigation.

We opted instead for a middle-ground, where we allow a window size of delegate processes: the worker process continues to create delegate processes until their number reaches the upper bound of the window size; thereafter the worker process releases control so the delegates have a chance to execute. When only the number of alive delegate processes falls under the window's lower bound, the worker process is allowed to resume execution. This algorithmic description can be straightforwardly implemented in ABS with boolean awaiting and a integer counter field (named *this.aliveDelegates*). The modification of the `run` is shown in Fig. 5; Similarly the `delegate` method must be modified to decrease the *aliveDelegates* counter when the method exits.

Interestingly, the size of the window is dependent on the CPU/Network speed ratio, and the Preferential Attachment model parameters: nodes (n) and degree (d). We empirically tested and used a fixed window size of $[500, 2000]$. Finding the optimal window size that keeps the CPUs busy while not leaking memory by keeping too much delegates alive, for a specific setup (cpu, network, n, d) is planned for future work.

```
1: Unit  run(...)
2: for each node i in the partition do
3:     for  j = 2 to 2m do j = j + 2 step
4:         target ← random[1..(i − 1) ∗ 2m]
5:         current = (i − 1) ∗ 2m + j
6:         x = whichActor(target)
7:         Fut < Int >  f = actor[x]! request(target)
8:         aliveDelegates = aliveDelegates + 1
9:         this! delegate(f, current)
10:        if aliveDelegates == maxBoundWindow then
11:            await aliveDelegates <= minBoundWindow
```

Fig. 5. The modified run method with window of delegates.

4.2 Experimental Results

We ran the ABS-Haskell implementation of the PA algorithm by varying the graph size, on a distributed cloud environment kindly provided by the SURF foundation. The hardware consisted of identical virtual machines interconnected over a 10 Gbps ethernet network; each Virtual Machine (VM) was a single-core Intel Xeon E5-2698, 16 GB RAM running Ubuntu 14.04 Server edition. The runtime execution results are shown in Fig. 6; the execution time decreases while we add more VMs to the distributed system, which suggests that the distributed algorithm scales. However, still with 8 Virtual Machines the implementation cannot "beat" the execution time of 1 VM running PA sequentially; to achieve this we may need to include more VMs. The reason for this can be attributed to the significant communication overhead, since each worker will send a network packet for every request call made.

On the other hand, the memory consumption (Table 1) is more promising: a larger distributed system requires less memory per VM. For example with the largest tested graph size, a distributed system of 8 VMs requires approx. 2.5 times less memory per VM than a local system. This allows the generation of much larger PA graphs than would otherwise fit in a single machine, since the graph utilizes and is "distributed" over multiple memory locations. Finally, the repository at http://github.com/abstools/distributed-PA contains the ABS code for PA and instructions for installing the ABS-Haskell backend.

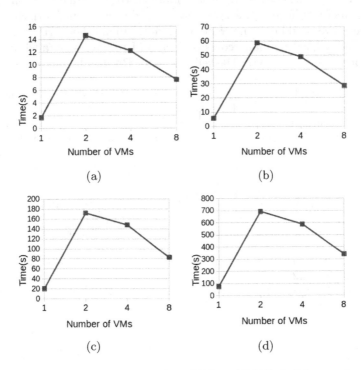

Fig. 6. Performance results of the distributed PA in ABS-Haskell for graphs of $n = 10^6$ nodes with degree $d =$ (a) 3, (b) 10 and $n = 10^7$ nodes with degree $d =$ (c) 3, (d) 10.

Table 1. Maximum memory residency (in MB) per Virtual Machine.

Graph size	Total number of VMs			
	1	2	4	8
$n = 10^6, d = 3$	306	423	313	229
$n = 10^6, d = 10$	899	1058	644	411
$n = 10^7, d = 3$	1943	2859	1566	874
$n = 10^7, d = 10$	6380	9398	4939	2561

5   Conclusion and Future Work

In this paper, we have presented a scalable, high-level distributed-memory algorithm that implements synthesizing artificial graphs based on Preferential Attachment mechanism. The algorithm avoids low-level synchronization complexities thanks to ABS, an actor-based modeling framework, and its programming abstractions which support *cooperative scheduling*. The experimental results suggest that the implementation scales with the size of the distributed system, both in time but more profoundly in memory, a fact that permits the generation of PA graphs that cannot fit in memory of a single system.

For future work, we are considering combining multiple request messages in a single TCP segment; this change would increase the overall execution speed by having a smaller overhead of the TCP headers and thus less network communication between VMs, and better network bandwidth. In another (orthogonal) direction, we could utilize the many cores of each VM to have a parallel-distributed hybrid implementation in ABS-Haskell for faster PA graph generation.

Acknowledgments. Partly funded by the EU project FP7-612985 UpScale (http://www.upscale-project.eu) and the EU project FP7-610582 ENVISAGE (http://www.envisage-project.eu). This work was carried out on the Dutch national HPC cloud infrastructure, a service provided by the SURF Foundation (http://surf.nl).

References

1. Erdös, P., Rényi, A.: On the central limit theorem for samples from a finite population. Publ. Math. Inst. Hungar. Acad. Sci **4**, 49–61 (1959)
2. Watts, D.J., Strogatz, S.H.: Collective dynamics of 'small-world' networks. Nature **393**(6684), 440–442 (1998)
3. Barabási, A.L., Albert, R.: Emergence of scaling in random networks. Science **286**(5439), 509–512 (1999)
4. Tonelli, R., Concas, G., Locci, M.: Three efficient algorithms for implementing the preferential attachment mechanism in Yule-Simon stochastic process. WSEAS Trans. Inf. Sci. Appl. **7**(2), 176–185 (2010)
5. Leskovec, J.: Dynamics of Large Networks. ProQuest, Ann Arbor (2008)
6. Bader, D., Madduri, K., et al.: Parallel algorithms for evaluating centrality indices in real-world networks. In: International Conference on Parallel Processing, ICPP 2006, pp. 539–550. IEEE (2006)

7. Johnsen, E.B., Hähnle, R., Schäfer, J., Schlatte, R., Steffen, M.: ABS: a core language for abstract behavioral specification. In: Aichernig, B.K., Boer, F.S., Bonsangue, M.M. (eds.) FMCO 2010. LNCS, vol. 6957, pp. 142–164. Springer, Heidelberg (2011). doi:10.1007/978-3-642-25271-6_8

8. Din, C.C., Bubel, R., Hähnle, R.: KeY-ABS: a deductive verification tool for the concurrent modelling language ABS. In: Felty, A.P., Middeldorp, A. (eds.) CADE 2015. LNCS, vol. 9195, pp. 517–526. Springer, Heidelberg (2015). doi:10.1007/978-3-319-21401-6_35

9. Albert, E., Arenas, P., Correas, J., Genaim, S., Gómez-Zamalloa, M., Puebla, G., Román-Díez, G.: Object-sensitive cost analysis for concurrent objects. Softw. Test. Verification Reliab. **25**(3), 218–271 (2015)

10. Epstein, J., Black, A.P., Peyton-Jones, S.: Towards haskell in the cloud. In: ACM SIGPLAN Notices, vol. 46, pp. 118–129. ACM (2011)

11. Atwood, J., Ribeiro, B., Towsley, D.: Efficient network generation under general preferential attachment. Comput. Soc. Netw. **2**(1), 1 (2015)

12. Batagelj, V., Brandes, U.: Efficient generation of large random networks. Phys. Rev. E **71**(3), 036113 (2005)

13. Yoo, A., Henderson, K.: Parallel generation of massive scale-free graphs. arXiv preprint arXiv:1003.3684 (2010)

14. Lo, Y.C., Li, C.T., Lin, S.D.: Parallelizing preferential attachment models for generating large-scale social networks that cannot fit into memory. In: Privacy, Security, Risk and Trust (PASSAT), 2012 International Conference on and 2012 International Confernece on Social Computing (SocialCom), pp. 229–238. IEEE (2012)

15. Alam, M., Khan, M., Marathe, M.V.: Distributed-memory parallel algorithms for generating massive scale-free networks using preferential attachment model. In: Proceedings of SC13: International Conference for High Performance Computing, Networking, Storage and Analysis, p. 91. ACM (2013)

16. Şerbănescu, V., Azadbakht, K., de Boer, F.: A java-based distributed approach for generating large-scale social network graphs. In: Pop, F., Kołlodziej, J., Di Martino, B. (eds.) Resource Management for Big Data Platforms, pp. 401–417. Springer, Cham (2016)

17. Bezirgiannis, N., Boer, F.: ABS: a high-level modeling language for cloud-aware programming. In: Freivalds, R.M., Engels, G., Catania, B. (eds.) SOFSEM 2016. LNCS, vol. 9587, pp. 433–444. Springer, Heidelberg (2016). doi:10.1007/978-3-662-49192-8_35

18. Henrio, L., Rochas, J.: From modelling to systematic deployment of distributed active objects. In: Lluch Lafuente, A., Proença, J. (eds.) COORDINATION 2016. LNCS, vol. 9686, pp. 208–226. Springer, Heidelberg (2016). doi:10.1007/978-3-319-39519-7_13

19. Azadbakht, K., de Boer, F.S., Serbanescu, V.: Multi-threaded actors. arXiv preprint arXiv:1608.03322 (2016)

20. Azadbakht, K., Bezirgiannis, N., de Boer, F.S., Aliakbary, S.: A high-level and scalable approach for generating scale-free graphs using active objects. In: Proceedings of the 31st Annual ACM Symposium on Applied Computing, pp. 1244–1250. ACM (2016)

21. Kumar, R., Raghavan, P., Rajagopalan, S., Sivakumar, D., Tomkins, A., Upfal, E.: Stochastic models for the web graph. In: 2000 Proceedings of 41st Annual Symposium on Foundations of Computer Science, pp. 57–65. IEEE (2000)

Verification and Automated System Analysis

Completeness of Hoare Logic Relative to the Standard Model

Zhaowei Xu[1,2]([✉]), Wenhui Zhang[1], and Yuefei Sui[3]

[1] State Key Laboratory of Computer Science, Institute of Software,
Chinese Academy of Sciences, Beijing, China
xuzw@ios.ac.cn
[2] University of Chinese Academy of Sciences, Beijing, China
[3] Key Laboratory of Intelligent Information Processing,
Institute of Computing Technology, Chinese Academy of Sciences, Beijing, China

Abstract. The general completeness problem of Hoare logic relative to the standard model N of Peano arithmetic has been studied by Cook, and it allows for the use of arbitrary arithmetical formulas as assertions. In practice, the assertions would be simple arithmetical formulas, e.g. of a low level in the arithmetical hierarchy. This paper further studies the completeness of Hoare Logic relative to N with assertions restricted to subclasses of arithmetical formulas. Our completeness results refine Cook's result by reducing the complexity of the assertion theory.

Keywords: Hoare logic · Peano arithmetic · Arithmetical hierarchy · The standard model · Relative completeness

1 Introduction

Hoare logic, first introduced by Hoare [1] and further studied by Cook [2] and many other researchers, lays the foundation of program verification [3–5]. For an introduction to Hoare logic, the reader should refer to [6–9]. Let L be the language of Peano arithmetic PA [10], let N be the standard model of PA, and let $Th(N)$ be the set of all true sentences in N. Hoare logic for the set WP of while-programs with the language L and the assertion theory $T \subset L$ is denoted $HL(T)$ [11]. The set $\{\varphi \in L : T \vdash \varphi\}$ of all theorems of $T \subset L$ is denoted $Thm(T)$. By Cook's completeness theorem, it follows that $Th(N)$ is the only extension T of PA such that $HL(T)$ is complete relative to N: for any $p, q \in L$ and $S \in WP$, if $N \models \{p\}S\{q\}$ then $HL(Th(N)) \vdash \{p\}S\{q\}$; for any $T' \supseteq PA$ with $Thm(T') \subsetneqq Th(N)$ (note that $Thm(PA) \subsetneqq Th(N)$ follows from Gödel's incompleteness theorem), there exist $p, q \in L$ and $S \in WP$ such that $N \models \{p\}S\{q\}$ but $HL(T') \nvdash \{p\}S\{q\}$. Note that $Th(N)$ is not recursively enumerable, and even not arithmetical [12, Lemma 17.3]. That $Th(N)$ is the only extension of PA for this completeness result to hold is due to the fact that it allows for the use of arbitrary arithmetical formulas as pre- and postconditions. In practice, the pre- and postconditions would be simple arithmetical formulas, e.g. of a

© Springer International Publishing AG 2017
B. Steffen et al. (Eds.): SOFSEM 2017, LNCS 10139, pp. 119–131, 2017.
DOI: 10.1007/978-3-319-51963-0_10

low level in the arithmetical hierarchy [13, Chap. IV]. The set $\{true, false\}$ of logical constants $true$ and $false$ is denoted Cnt. Apt's survey paper [6, p. 437] has shown that, for no recursively enumerable extension T of PA, can $HL(T)$ derive all true Hoare's triples with pre- and postconditions restricted to Cnt. A natural question is whether there exists an arithmetical extension T of PA such that $HL(T)$ derives all true Hoare's triples with pre- and postconditions restricted to Cnt. Furthermore, we shall investigate the completeness of Hoare logic relative to N with pre- and postconditions restricted to the arithmetical hierarchy.

The rest of this paper is organized as follows: the related work is given in Sect. 2; the basic preliminary results are presented in Sect. 3; completeness of $HL(T)$ with pre- and postconditions restricted to Cnt is given in Sect. 4; completeness of $HL(T)$ with pre- and postconditions restricted to the arithmetical hierarchy is shown in Sect. 5; Sect. 6 concludes the paper.

2   Related Work

We call a set of assertions A complete w.r.t. a class of programs C if for any $p, q \in A$ and $S \in C$, whenever $\{p\}S\{q\}$ holds, then all intermediate assertions can be chosen from A. Apt et al. [14] studied the problem which sets of assertions are complete in the above sense. They have shown that Σ_1 is complete w.r.t. WP; Δ_1 is not complete w.r.t. WP; and by allowing the use of an 'auxiliary' coordinate, Δ_1 is complete w.r.t. WP.

Clarke [15] exhibited programming language structures for which Hoare logic is not complete relative to the finite structures, and observed that if a programming language possesses a relatively complete Hoare logic for partial correctness (relative to the finite structures) then the halting problem for finite interpretations must be decidable (Clarke's Observation). Lipton [16], Clarke et al. [17], and Grabowski [18] investigated under what circumstances the converse of Clarke's Observation holds. For the detailed relationship among their results, the reader refers to the Introduction of [18]. Note that their completeness results hold under the assumption that the halting problem for finite interpretations is decidable, whereas ours holds relative to the fixed structure N; and their axiom systems for Hoare logic are determined by the decision (or enumeration) procedures, while ours is given by Cook [2].

Bergstra and Tucker [19] studied the logical completeness of Hoare logic with nonstandard inputs: $Th(N)$ is the only extension T of PA such that $HL(T)$ is logically complete. Xu et al. [20] studied the logical completeness of Hoare logic without nonstandard inputs: PA^+ (cf. Definition 4.2.1) is the minimal extension T of PA such that $HL(T)$ is logically complete when inputs range over N. To establish this completeness result, the technical line of reducing from $HL(T)$ to T (cf. Subsect. 3.3) has been adopted, which will also be followed in this paper. Kozen and Tiuryn [21] investigated the completeness of propositional Hoare logic with assertions and programs abstracted to propositional symbols.

3   Preliminaries

First some notations are introduced: in syntax, we write $\neg$, $\wedge$, $\vee$, $\rightarrow$, $\leftrightarrow$, $\forall$, $\exists$ to denote the negation, conjunction, disjunction, conditional, biconditional connectives and the universal, existential quantifiers; in semantics, we write $\sim$, $\&$, $\mid$, $\Rightarrow$, $\Leftrightarrow$, **A**, **E** to denote the corresponding connectives and quantifiers.

3.1   Peano Arithmetic

Let $\Sigma = \{0, 1, +, \cdot, <\}$ be the signature of L. For simplicity, the sum of 1 with itself n times is abbreviated n. We use n to denote both a closed term and a natural number, and use M to denote both a model and its domain. Besides the standard model N, PA has nonstandard models. From PA, one can deduce the least-number principle $\exists x \; \varphi(x, \boldsymbol{y}) \rightarrow \exists z(\varphi(z, \boldsymbol{y}) \wedge \forall u < z \; \neg\varphi(u, \boldsymbol{y}))$, where $\varphi(x, \boldsymbol{y}) \in L$.

Generalized Σ_n-formulas and generalized Π_n-formulas of L are defined as follows: a generalized Σ_0-formula (or a generalized Π_0-formula) is a formula built up from atomic formulas using only negation, conjunction, disjunction, and bounded quantifications $\forall x < t$ and $\exists x < t$, where t is a term of L; a generalized Σ_{n+1}-formula is a formula obtainable from generalized Π_n-formulas by conjunction, disjunction, bounded quantifications, and unbounded existential quantification; a generalized Π_{n+1}-formula is a formula obtainable from generalized Σ_n-formulas by conjunction, disjunction, bounded quantifications and unbounded universal quantification. Σ_n-formulas and Π_n-formulas of L are defined as follows: a Σ_0-formula (or a Π_0-formula) is a generalized Σ_0-formula; a Σ_{n+1}-formula is a formula of the form $\exists x \; \psi$ with ψ being a Π_n-formula; a Π_{n+1}-formula is a formula of the form $\forall x \; \psi$ with ψ being a Σ_n-formula. The set of all Σ_n-formulas is denoted Σ_n, and similarly for Π_n. Σ_n-sentences are Σ_n-formulas without free variables, and similarly for Π_n-sentences. The set of all true Σ_n-sentences in N is denoted $Tr^N(\Sigma_n)$, and similarly for $Tr^N(\Pi_n)$.

It holds, in PA, that every generalized Σ_n-formula (resp. generalized Π_n-formula) is logically equivalent to a Σ_n-formula (resp. Π_n-formula) [13, Chap. IV]. For the membership relation $\in$, besides the standard meaning, we sometimes adopt a nonstandard meaning: by $\varphi \in A$ (the nonstandard meaning) is meant that there exists $\psi \in A$ (the standard meaning) such that $PA \vdash \varphi \leftrightarrow \psi$. Only when the standard meaning of $\in$ is inapplicable, can the nonstandard meaning be adopted. The reader should keep this in mind. Then $\varphi \in \Sigma_n$ implies $\neg\varphi \in \Pi_n$, and $\varphi \in \Pi_n$ implies $\neg\varphi \in \Sigma_n$. Both Σ_n and Π_n are closed under conjunction and disjunction. For any $i \geq 0$, $\Sigma_i, \Pi_i \subset \Sigma_{i+1}, \Pi_{i+1}$, and $\Sigma_i \not\subseteq \Pi_i, \Pi_i \not\subseteq \Sigma_i$. For the truth of these results, the reader refers to [13, Chap. IV].

We say that a set of natural numbers is Σ_n (resp. Π_n) if it is arithmetically definable (or arithmetical for short) by a Σ_n-formula (resp. by a Π_n-formula); a set of natural numbers is Δ_n if it is both Σ_n and Π_n. Note that a set of natural numbers is recursively enumerable (or r.e. for short) iff it is Σ_1, and that a set of natural numbers is recursive iff it is Δ_1 [12, Sect. 7.2]. Theorem 16.13 in [12] says that for all Σ_1-sentences φ, $N \models \varphi$ iff $PA \vdash \varphi$. Let $\ulcorner\varphi\urcorner$ be a fixed Gödel's numbering function [12, Chap. 15]. By arithmetical definability of the theory $T \subset L$ is meant that the set $\{ \ulcorner \varphi \urcorner : \varphi \in T \}$ of natural numbers is arithmetical. Gödel's diagonal lemma [12, Lemma 17.1] says that for any $T \supseteq PA$ and any $\varphi(x) \in L$ there is a sentence $G \in L$ such that $T \vdash G \leftrightarrow \varphi(\ulcorner G \urcorner)$.

3.2   Hoare Logic

Based on the language L, together with the program constructs $\{ :=, ;, if, then,$ $else, fi, while, do, od \}$, a while-program S is defined by $S ::= x := E \mid S_1; S_2 \mid$ $if\ B\ then\ S_1\ else\ S_2\ fi \mid while\ B\ do\ S_0\ od$, where an expression E is defined by $E ::= 0 \mid 1 \mid x \mid E_1 + E_2 \mid E_1 \cdot E_2$, and a boolean expression B is defined by $B ::= E_1 < E_2 \mid \neg B_1 \mid B_1 \rightarrow B_2$. The set of all such while-programs is denoted WP. The set of all assignment programs $x := E$ is denoted AP. For $S \in WP$, the vector $(x_1, x_2, \ldots, x_m)$ of all m program variables $x_1, x_2, \ldots, x_m$ occurring in S will be denoted $\boldsymbol{x}$; the vector $(n_1, n_2, \ldots, n_m)$ of m natural numbers $n_1, n_2, \ldots,$ $n_m \in N$ will be denoted $\boldsymbol{n}$; the connectives will be assumed to distribute over the components of the vectors (for instance, $\boldsymbol{n} \in N$ means $n_1, n_2, \ldots, n_m \in N$, and $\boldsymbol{x} = \boldsymbol{n}$ means $\bigwedge_{i=1}^{m} x_i = n_i$). Let the program variables considered below occur among $\boldsymbol{x}$, the vector of all program variables of the target program. For a model M of L, let v be an assignment over M for all the first order variables (including $\boldsymbol{x}$), let $v(\boldsymbol{x})$ be the vector of elements of M assigned to $\boldsymbol{x}$ at v, and let $v(\boldsymbol{a}/\boldsymbol{x})$ be an assignment as v except that $v(\boldsymbol{a}/\boldsymbol{x})(\boldsymbol{x}) = \boldsymbol{a}$.

For any $S \in WP$ and any model M of L, the input-output relation R_S^M of S in M is a binary relation on the set of all assignments over M defined as follows:

- $(v, v') \in R_{x:=E}^M \Leftrightarrow v' = v(E^{M,v}/x)$, where $E^{M,v}$ receives the standard meaning;
- $(v, v') \in R_{S_1;S_2}^M \Leftrightarrow (v, v') \in R_{S_1}^M \circ R_{S_2}^M$, where $(z, z') \in R_1 \circ R_2 \Leftrightarrow \mathbf{E}z''((z, z'') \in R_1\ \&\ (z'', z') \in R_2)$;
- $(v, v') \in R_{if\ B\ then\ S_1\ else\ S_2\ fi}^M \Leftrightarrow M, v \models B\ \&\ (v, v') \in R_{S_1}^M \mid M, v \not\models B\ \&\ (v, v') \in R_{S_2}^M$;
- $(v, v') \in R_{while\ B\ do\ S_0\ od}^M \Leftrightarrow \mathbf{E}i \in N, \mathbf{E}a_0, \ldots, a_i \in M\ (v(\boldsymbol{x}) = a_0\ \&\ \mathbf{A}j < i(M, v(a_j/\boldsymbol{x}) \models B\ \&\ (v(a_j/\boldsymbol{x}), v(a_{j+1}/\boldsymbol{x})) \in R_{S_0}^M)\ \&\ v' = v(a_i/\boldsymbol{x})\ \&\ M, v' \not\models B)$.

Given $S \in WP$ and a model M of L, R_S^M defines in M a vectorial function $\boldsymbol{y} = f_S^M(\boldsymbol{x})$ such that for every $\boldsymbol{a}, \boldsymbol{b} \in M$, $f_S^M(\boldsymbol{a}) = \boldsymbol{b}$ iff $\mathbf{E}v, v'(v(\boldsymbol{x}) = \boldsymbol{a}\ \&\ v'(\boldsymbol{x}) = \boldsymbol{b}\ \&\ (v, v') \in R_S^M)$. Given a model M of L and an asserted program $\{p\}S\{q\}$, $\{p\}S\{q\}$ is satisfied at M, denoted $M \models \{p\}S\{q\}$, iff $\mathbf{A}v[M, v \models p \Rightarrow \mathbf{A}v'((v, v') \in R_S^M \Rightarrow M, v' \models q)]$. Given a theory $T \subset L$ and an asserted program $\{p\}S\{q\}$, $\{p\}S\{q\}$ is satisfied at T, denoted $HL(T) \models \{p\}S\{q\}$, iff $\mathbf{A}M(M \models T \Rightarrow M \models \{p\}S\{q\})$. $HL(T)$ has the usual axiom system [11]; the derivability of $\{p\}S\{q\}$ in $HL(T)$ is denoted $HL(T) \vdash \{p\}S\{q\}$. By the logical completeness of $HL(T)$ we mean that for all asserted programs $\{p\}S\{q\}$, $HL(T) \vdash \{p\}S\{q\}$ iff $HL(T) \models \{p\}S\{q\}$. We say that $HL(T)$ is logically complete when inputs range over N if for every $S \in WP$ with program variables $\boldsymbol{x}$, every $p, q \in L$ (p, q could contain other first-order variables than those in $\boldsymbol{x}$), and every $\boldsymbol{n} \in N$, $HL(T) \vdash \{p \wedge \boldsymbol{x} = \boldsymbol{n}\} S \{q\}$ iff $HL(T) \models \{p \wedge \boldsymbol{x} = \boldsymbol{n}\} S \{q\}$.

Let P and Q denote respectively the levels of choices of preconditions and postconditions (i.e. Cnt or Σ_i, Π_i, $i \geq 0$), and let R denote the sets of programs (i.e. AP or WP). The completeness of $HL(T)$ relative to N for $\{P\}R\{Q\}$ is defined as follows.

Definition 3.2.1. $HL(T)$ is complete relative to N for $\{P\}R\{Q\}$ if for any $p \in P$, $S \in R$, and $q \in Q$, $N \models \{p\}S\{q\}$ implies $HL(T) \vdash \{p\}S\{q\}$.

3.3   Reduction from $HL(T)$ to T

Let $\langle x, y \rangle$, $L(z)$ and $R(z)$ be the pairing functions with $\langle L(z), R(z) \rangle = z$, $L(\langle x, y \rangle) = x$ and $R(\langle x, y \rangle) = y$ [22, Theorem 2.1]. For notational convenience, we denote $(L(z), R(z))$ by $\bar{z}$. The functions $\langle x, y \rangle$ and $\bar{z}$ can be extended to n-tuples (for each $n \in N$) by setting $\langle x_1, x_2, \ldots, x_n \rangle = \langle x_1, \langle x_2, \ldots, x_n \rangle \rangle$ and $\overline{\langle x_1, x_2, \ldots, x_n \rangle} = (x_1, \overline{\langle x_2, \ldots, x_n \rangle})$. Let $(x)_i$ be Gödel's β-function such that for each finite sequence $a_0, a_1, \ldots, a_n$ of natural numbers, there exists a natural number w such that $(w)_i = a_i$ for all $i \leq n$ [22, Theorem 2.4]. Note that the graph relations of these functions are all Σ_1.

Definition 3.3.1 (The definition of α_S, cf. [20, Definition 3.1.1]). For every $S \in WP$ with program variables $\boldsymbol{x}$, the generalized Σ_1-formula $\alpha_S(\boldsymbol{x}, \boldsymbol{y}) \in L$, where $\boldsymbol{y} = (y_1, y_2, \ldots, y_m)$ is disjoint from $\boldsymbol{x} = (x_1, x_2, \ldots, x_m)$, is defined inductively as follows.
Assignment: $S \equiv x_i := E$

$$\alpha_S(\boldsymbol{x}, \boldsymbol{y}) ::= y_i = E(\boldsymbol{x}) \wedge \bigwedge_{\substack{1 \leq j \leq m \\ j \neq i}} y_j = x_j;$$

Composition: $S \equiv S_1; S_2$

$$\alpha_S(\boldsymbol{x}, \boldsymbol{y}) ::= \exists \boldsymbol{z}(\alpha_{S_1}(\boldsymbol{x}, \boldsymbol{z}/\boldsymbol{y}) \wedge \alpha_{S_2}(\boldsymbol{z}/\boldsymbol{x}, \boldsymbol{y}));$$

Conditional: $S \equiv$ *if* B *then* S_1 *else* S_2 *fi*

$$\alpha_S(\boldsymbol{x}, \boldsymbol{y}) ::= (B(\boldsymbol{x}) \wedge \alpha_{S_1}(\boldsymbol{x}, \boldsymbol{y})) \vee (\neg B(\boldsymbol{x}) \wedge \alpha_{S_2}(\boldsymbol{x}, \boldsymbol{y}));$$

Iteration: $S \equiv$ *while* B *do* S_0 *od*. We first let

$$A_S(i, w, \boldsymbol{x}, \boldsymbol{y}) ::= \boldsymbol{x} = \overline{(w)_0} \wedge \forall j < i(B(\overline{(w)_j}/\boldsymbol{x}) \\ \wedge \alpha_{S_0}(\overline{(w)_j}/\boldsymbol{x}, \overline{(w)_{j+1}}/\boldsymbol{y})) \wedge \boldsymbol{y} = \overline{(w)_i}$$

then set

$$\alpha_S^*(i, \boldsymbol{x}, \boldsymbol{y}) ::= \exists w \, A_S(i, w, \boldsymbol{x}, \boldsymbol{y})$$

and finally define

$$\alpha_S(\boldsymbol{x}, \boldsymbol{y}) ::= \exists i \, \alpha_S^*(i, \boldsymbol{x}, \boldsymbol{y}) \wedge \neg B(\boldsymbol{y}/\boldsymbol{x}).$$

Lemma 3.3.2 (Arithmetical definability of recursive functions, cf. [20, Lemma 3.1.2]). *For every $S \in WP$ and every $a, b \in N$, $f_S^N(a) = b$ iff $N \models \alpha_S(a, b)$.*

Theorem 3.3.3 (Reduction from $HL(T)$ to T, cf. [20, Theorem 3.1.3]). *For every $T \supseteq PA$, every $p, q \in L$ and every $S \in WP$,*

$$HL(T) \vdash \{p\}S\{q\} \text{ iff } T \vdash p(\boldsymbol{x}) \wedge \alpha_S(\boldsymbol{x}, \boldsymbol{y}) \to q(\boldsymbol{y}/\boldsymbol{x}).$$

Corollary 3.3.4. *$HL(PA)$ is complete relative to N for $\{Cnt\}AP\{Cnt\}$.*

Proof. Immediate from Definition 3.2.1 and Theorem 3.3.3. ☐

4   Completeness of $HL(T)$ for $\{Cnt\}WP\{Cnt\}$

This section devotes to the completeness of $HL(T)$ for $\{Cnt\}WP\{Cnt\}$: in Subsect. 4.1, a particular extension PA^* of PA is defined and, by using PA^*, the completeness of $HL(T)$ relative to N for $\{Cnt\}WP\{Cnt\}$ is established; in Subsect. 4.2, the relationship of PA^*, PA^+ and $PA \cup Tr^N(\Pi_1)$ is investigated.

4.1   Completeness of $HL(T)$ for $\{Cnt\}WP\{Cnt\}$

Lemma 4.1.1. *There exists $S \in WP$ such that $N \models \forall \boldsymbol{x}, \boldsymbol{y} \neg \alpha_S(\boldsymbol{x}, \boldsymbol{y})$ and $PA \nvdash \forall \boldsymbol{x}, \boldsymbol{y} \neg \alpha_S(\boldsymbol{x}, \boldsymbol{y})$.*

Proof. Note that the set of Hoare's triples $\{\{true\}S\{false\} : S \in WP, N \models \{true\}S\{false\}\}$ represents the complement of the halting problem, and hence is not r.e. (cf. the Fact in [6, p. 437]). On the other hand, the set of Hoare's triples $\{\{true\}S\{false\} : S \in WP, HL(PA) \vdash \{true\}S\{false\}\}$ is r.e. By soundness of Hoare logic, it follows that $\{\{true\}S\{false\} : S \in WP, HL(PA) \vdash \{true\}S\{false\}\} \subsetneqq \{\{true\}S\{false\} : S \in WP, N \models \{true\}S\{false\}\}$. Then we have that there exists $S \in WP$ such that $N \models \{true\}S\{false\}$ but $HL(PA) \nvdash \{true\}S\{false\}$. By Lemma 3.3.2, jointly with Theorem 3.3.3, it follows that there exists $S \in WP$ such that $N \models \forall \boldsymbol{x}, \boldsymbol{y} \neg \alpha_S(\boldsymbol{x}, \boldsymbol{y})$ and $PA \nvdash \forall \boldsymbol{x}, \boldsymbol{y} \neg \alpha_S(\boldsymbol{x}, \boldsymbol{y})$. ☐

Definition 4.1.2. We define PA^* to be

$$PA^* ::= PA \cup \{\forall \boldsymbol{x}, \boldsymbol{y} \neg \alpha_S(\boldsymbol{x}, \boldsymbol{y}) : S \in WP$$
$$\& N \models \forall \boldsymbol{x}, \boldsymbol{y} \neg \alpha_S(\boldsymbol{x}, \boldsymbol{y}) \& PA \nvdash \forall \boldsymbol{x}, \boldsymbol{y} \neg \alpha_S(\boldsymbol{x}, \boldsymbol{y})\}.$$

Proposition 4.1.3. *PA^* is Σ_2.*

Proof. Consider the statement $\varphi \in PA^*$ as follows: by definition of PA^*, it is equivalent to saying that $\varphi \in PA$, or there exists $S \in WP$ such that $\varphi = \forall \boldsymbol{x}, \boldsymbol{y} \neg \alpha_S(\boldsymbol{x}, \boldsymbol{y})$, $N \nvDash \neg \varphi$ and $PA \nvdash \varphi$; since $\neg \forall \boldsymbol{x}, \boldsymbol{y} \neg \alpha_S(\boldsymbol{x}, \boldsymbol{y})$ is logically equivalent to a Σ_1-sentence, and a Σ_1-sentence is true in N iff it is a theorem of PA, it is equivalent to saying that $\varphi \in PA$, or there exists $S \in WP$ such that $\varphi = \forall \boldsymbol{x}, \boldsymbol{y} \neg \alpha_S(\boldsymbol{x}, \boldsymbol{y})$, $\neg \varphi \notin Thm(PA)$ and $\varphi \notin Thm(PA)$. Note that the set $\{\varphi : \varphi = \forall \boldsymbol{x}, \boldsymbol{y} \neg \alpha_S(\boldsymbol{x}, \boldsymbol{y})$ & $S \in WP\}$ is Δ_1 and hence Σ_2. Since $Thm(PA)$ is Σ_1, we have that the set $\{\varphi : \varphi \notin Thm(PA)\}$ is Π_1 and hence Σ_2, and the set $\{\varphi : \neg \varphi \notin Thm(PA)\}$ is Π_1 and hence Σ_2. By closure of Σ_2 under conjunction, it follows that the set $\{\varphi : \varphi = \forall \boldsymbol{x}, \boldsymbol{y} \neg \alpha_S(\boldsymbol{x}, \boldsymbol{y})$ & $S \in WP$ & $\neg \varphi \notin Thm(PA)$ & $\varphi \notin Thm(PA)\}$ is Σ_2. Moreover, since PA is Δ_1, we have that the set $\{\varphi : \varphi \in PA\}$ is Σ_2. By closure of Σ_2 under disjunction, it follows that PA^* is Σ_2. $\qquad\square$

Definition 4.1.4. T' is the minimal extension T of PA such that the property $p(T)$ of T holds if

(i) $p(T')$ holds; and
(ii) for any $T'' \supseteq PA$ with $Thm(T'') \subsetneqq Thm(T')$, $p(T'')$ doesn't hold.

Theorem 4.1.5. PA^* *is the minimal extension* T *of* PA *such that* $HL(T)$ *is complete relative to* N *for* $\{Cnt\}WP\{Cnt\}$.

Proof. We first show that $HL(PA^*)$ is complete relative to N for $\{Cnt\}WP\{Cnt\}$. By Definition 3.2.1, we have to prove that for any $p, q \in Cnt$, and $S \in WP$, $N \models \{p\}S\{q\}$ implies $HL(PA^*) \vdash \{p\}S\{q\}$. Let $N \models \{p\}S\{q\}$ with $p, q \in Cnt$ and $S \in WP$. It remains to prove that $HL(PA^*) \vdash \{p\}S\{q\}$. For $p \equiv false$ or $q \equiv true$, it's easy to see that $PA^* \vdash p(\boldsymbol{x}) \wedge \alpha_S(\boldsymbol{x}, \boldsymbol{y}) \to q(\boldsymbol{y}/\boldsymbol{x})$; by Theorem 3.3.3, it follows that $HL(PA^*) \vdash \{p\}S\{q\}$. For $p \equiv true$ and $q \equiv false$, we have that $N \models \{true\}S\{false\}$; by Lemma 3.3.2, it follows that $N \models \forall \boldsymbol{x}, \boldsymbol{y} \neg \alpha_S(\boldsymbol{x}, \boldsymbol{y})$; by Definition 4.1.2, it follows that $PA^* \vdash \forall \boldsymbol{x}, \boldsymbol{y} \neg \alpha_S(\boldsymbol{x}, \boldsymbol{y})$; then $PA^* \vdash p(\boldsymbol{x}) \wedge \alpha_S(\boldsymbol{x}, \boldsymbol{y}) \to q(\boldsymbol{y}/\boldsymbol{x})$ follows; by Theorem 3.3.3, it follows that $HL(PA^*) \vdash \{p\}S\{q\}$.

   We then show that for any $T \supseteq PA$ with $Thm(T) \subsetneqq Thm(PA^*)$, $HL(T)$ is not complete relative to N for $\{Cnt\}WP\{Cnt\}$. By Definition 3.2.1, we have to prove that for any $T \supseteq PA$ with $Thm(T) \subsetneqq Thm(PA^*)$, there exist $p, q \in Cnt$, and $S \in WP$ such that $N \models \{p\}S\{q\}$ but $HL(T) \nvdash \{p\}S\{q\}$. Let $T \supseteq PA$ with $Thm(T) \subsetneqq Thm(PA^*)$. By Definition 4.1.2, it follows that there exists $S \in WP$ such that $N \models \forall \boldsymbol{x}, \boldsymbol{y} \neg \alpha_S(\boldsymbol{x}, \boldsymbol{y})$ and $T \nvdash \forall \boldsymbol{x}, \boldsymbol{y} \neg \alpha_S(\boldsymbol{x}, \boldsymbol{y})$. Let $p ::= true$, $q ::= false$, and $S \in WP$ such that $N \models \forall \boldsymbol{x}, \boldsymbol{y} \neg \alpha_S(\boldsymbol{x}, \boldsymbol{y})$ and $T \nvdash \forall \boldsymbol{x}, \boldsymbol{y} \neg \alpha_S(\boldsymbol{x}, \boldsymbol{y})$; by Lemma 3.3.2, it follows that $N \models \{p\}S\{q\}$; since $T \nvdash p(\boldsymbol{x}) \wedge \alpha_S(\boldsymbol{x}, \boldsymbol{y}) \to q(\boldsymbol{y}/\boldsymbol{x})$, by Theorem 3.3.3, it follows that $HL(T) \nvdash \{p\}S\{q\}$. $\qquad\square$

4.2   Comparison of PA^*, PA^+ and $PA \cup Tr^N(\Pi_1)$

In our previous work [20], a particular extension PA^+ of PA has been defined, and, by using PA^+, the condition under which $HL(T)$ is logically complete when inputs range over N has been shown. For an explicit citation, PA^+ is redefined as follows.

Definition 4.2.1 (cf. [20, Definition 3.2.2]). We define PA^+ to be

$$PA^+ ::= PA \cup \{\forall \boldsymbol{y} \neg \alpha_S(\boldsymbol{n}, \boldsymbol{y}) : \boldsymbol{n} \in N \ \& \ S \in WP$$
$$\& \ N \models \forall \boldsymbol{y} \neg \alpha_S(\boldsymbol{n}, \boldsymbol{y}) \ \& \ PA \nvdash \forall \boldsymbol{y} \neg \alpha_S(\boldsymbol{n}, \boldsymbol{y})\}.$$

For the validity of Definition 4.2.1, the reader refers to [20, Theorem 3.2.1]. Note that the newly added formulas to PA^* and PA^+ are similar: both describe nonterminating computations (one for all inputs while the other for one input) and are logically equivalent to Π_1-sentences. It would be interesting to relate PA^* to PA^+. We achieve this by relating them to $PA \cup Tr^N(\Pi_1)$.

In what follows, for while-programs, we should distinguish between the input variables and non-input variables. Let $S \in WP$ have the program variables $\boldsymbol{x} = (\boldsymbol{p}, \boldsymbol{q})$ with $\boldsymbol{p}$ and $\boldsymbol{q}$ being the vectors of input and non-input variables respectively. Define $\alpha_S^{(i)}(\boldsymbol{p}, y)$ by

$$\alpha_S^{(i)}(\boldsymbol{p}, y) ::= \exists \boldsymbol{q}, \boldsymbol{y}(\alpha_S(\boldsymbol{x}, \boldsymbol{y}) \wedge y = y_i),$$

where y is the designated output variable.

Lemma 4.2.2. *For every $\varphi(\boldsymbol{x}, y) \in \Sigma_1$ with $PA \vdash \forall \boldsymbol{x}, y, z(\varphi(\boldsymbol{x}, y) \wedge \varphi(\boldsymbol{x}, z) \to y = z)$, there exists $S \in WP$ such that $PA \vdash \forall \boldsymbol{p}, y(\alpha_S^{(1)}(\boldsymbol{p}, y) \leftrightarrow \varphi(\boldsymbol{p}, y))$.*

Proof. It follows from recursion theory that for every $\varphi(\boldsymbol{x}, y) \in \Sigma_1$ with $N \models \forall \boldsymbol{x}, y, z(\varphi(\boldsymbol{x}, y) \wedge \varphi(\boldsymbol{x}, z) \to y = z)$, there exists $S \in WP$ such that $N \models \forall \boldsymbol{p}, y(\alpha_S^{(1)}(\boldsymbol{p}, y) \leftrightarrow \varphi(\boldsymbol{p}, y))$. In order to extend this result from N to PA, partial recursive functions should be redefined in PA, and recursion theory will be rebuilt correspondingly. Due to space constraints, the detailed work is left to the reader as an exercise. □

Theorem 4.2.3. $Thm(PA^*) = Thm(PA^+) = Thm(PA \cup Tr^N(\Pi_1))$.

Proof. Since $\forall \boldsymbol{x}, \boldsymbol{y} \neg \alpha_S(\boldsymbol{x}, \boldsymbol{y})$ and $\forall \boldsymbol{y} \neg \alpha_S(\boldsymbol{n}, \boldsymbol{y})$ are logically equivalent to Π_1-sentences, it follows that $Thm(PA^*), Thm(PA^+) \subseteq Thm(PA \cup Tr^N(\Pi_1))$. Then we have to prove that $Thm(PA^*), Thm(PA^+) \supseteq Thm(PA \cup Tr^N(\Pi_1))$. It suffices to prove that $PA^* \vdash Tr^N(\Pi_1)$ and $PA^+ \vdash Tr^N(\Pi_1)$. Fix $\varphi \in Tr^N(\Pi_1)$. It remains to show that $PA^* \vdash \varphi$ and $PA^+ \vdash \varphi$. By definition of $Tr^N(\Pi_1)$, there exists $\psi(y) \in \Sigma_0$ such that $\varphi \equiv \forall y \ \psi(y)$ and $N \models \forall y \ \psi(y)$. Define $\phi(x, y) \in \Sigma_0$ by $\phi(x, y) ::= x = x \wedge \neg \psi(y) \wedge \forall i < y \ \psi(i)$. By the least number principle, it follows that $PA \vdash \exists y \ \neg \psi(y) \leftrightarrow \exists y(\neg \psi(y) \wedge \forall i < y \ \psi(i))$. Negating both sides of $\leftrightarrow$, we have that $PA \vdash \forall y \ \psi(y) \leftrightarrow \forall y \neg(\neg \psi(y) \wedge \forall i < y \ \psi(i))$. By inserting the valid formula $x = x$ into the right side of $\leftrightarrow$, it follows that $PA \vdash \forall y \ \psi(y) \leftrightarrow \forall y \neg(x = x \wedge \neg \psi(y) \wedge \forall i < y \ \psi(i))$. By definition of φ and ϕ, it follows that $PA \vdash \varphi \leftrightarrow \forall y \neg \phi(x, y)$. On the other hand, it's easy to see that $PA \vdash \forall x, y, z(\phi(x, y) \wedge \phi(x, z) \to y = z)$. By Lemma 4.2.2, there exists $S \in WP$ such that $PA \vdash \forall x, y(\alpha_S^{(1)}(x, y) \leftrightarrow \phi(x, y))$. Then $PA \vdash \forall y \neg \alpha_S^{(1)}(x, y) \leftrightarrow \forall y \neg \phi(x, y)$ follows. Since $PA \vdash \varphi \leftrightarrow \forall y \neg \phi(x, y)$, we have that $PA \vdash \varphi \leftrightarrow \forall y \neg \alpha_S^{(1)}(x, y)$. By definition of $\alpha_S^{(1)}(x, y)$ (note that $\boldsymbol{p} = x$), it follows that $PA \vdash$

$\varphi \leftrightarrow \forall \boldsymbol{x}, \boldsymbol{y} \neg \alpha_S(\boldsymbol{x}, \boldsymbol{y})$. By soundness of first-order logic, it follows that $N \models \varphi \leftrightarrow \forall \boldsymbol{x}, \boldsymbol{y} \neg \alpha_S(\boldsymbol{x}, \boldsymbol{y})$. Since $N \models \varphi$, we have that $N \models \forall \boldsymbol{x}, \boldsymbol{y} \neg \alpha_S(\boldsymbol{x}, \boldsymbol{y})$. By definition of PA^*, it follows that $PA^* \vdash \forall \boldsymbol{x}, \boldsymbol{y} \neg \alpha_S(\boldsymbol{x}, \boldsymbol{y})$. Since $PA \vdash \varphi \leftrightarrow \forall \boldsymbol{x}, \boldsymbol{y} \neg \alpha_S(\boldsymbol{x}, \boldsymbol{y})$, we have that $PA^* \vdash \varphi \leftrightarrow \forall \boldsymbol{x}, \boldsymbol{y} \neg \alpha_S(\boldsymbol{x}, \boldsymbol{y})$. Then $PA^* \vdash \varphi$ follows. Fix $\boldsymbol{n} \in N$. Since $N \models \forall \boldsymbol{x}, \boldsymbol{y} \neg \alpha_S(\boldsymbol{x}, \boldsymbol{y})$, we have that $N \models \forall \boldsymbol{y} \neg \alpha_S(\boldsymbol{n}, \boldsymbol{y})$. By definition of PA^+, it follows that $PA^+ \vdash \forall \boldsymbol{y} \neg \alpha_S(\boldsymbol{n}, \boldsymbol{y})$. Since $PA \vdash \varphi \leftrightarrow \forall \boldsymbol{y} \neg \alpha_S(\boldsymbol{n}, \boldsymbol{y})$, we have that $PA^+ \vdash \varphi \leftrightarrow \forall \boldsymbol{y} \neg \alpha_S(\boldsymbol{n}, \boldsymbol{y})$. Then $PA^+ \vdash \varphi$ follows. $\qquad\square$

Observe from Theorem 4.2.3 that PA^*, PA^+ and $PA \cup Tr^N(\Pi_1)$ have the same set of theorems. Hence Theorem 4.1.5 can be reformulated as an alternative form: $PA \cup Tr^N(\Pi_1)$ (or PA^+) is the minimal extension T of PA such that $HL(T)$ is complete relative to N for $\{Cnt\}WP\{Cnt\}$.

5   Completeness of $HL(T)$ for $\{P\}WP\{Q\}$

We now turn our attention to the completeness of $HL(T)$ with pre- and postconditions restricted to the arithmetical hierarchy: letting P, Q be $\Sigma_i, \Pi_i, i \geq 0$, to what extension T of PA, $HL(T)$ is complete relative to N for $\{P\}WP\{Q\}$. As is established above, only for extension T of PA with $Thm(PA \cup Tr^N(\Pi_1)) \subseteq Thm(T) \subseteq Th(N)$, can $HL(T)$ be complete relative to N for $\{P\}WP\{Q\}$. Note that if P or Q is expanded to a larger level in the arithmetical hierarchy, then T will correspondingly be expanded to "a larger level in the hierarchy of $Th(N)$". Hence the hierarchy of $Th(N)$ will be studied: whether $Tr^N(\Sigma_{n+1})$ and $Tr^N(\Pi_{n+1})$ can be derived from $PA \cup Tr^N(\Pi_n)$. In Subsect. 5.1, the hierarchy of $Th(N)$ is given; in Subsect. 5.2, the completeness of $HL(T)$ relative to N for $\{P\}WP\{Q\}$ is studied.

5.1   Hierarchy of $Th(N)$

Lemma 5.1.1. *For any $n \geq 0$, $PA \cup Tr^N(\Pi_n) \vdash Tr^N(\Sigma_{n+1})$.*

Proof. Fix $n \geq 0$, and fix $\varphi \in Tr^N(\Sigma_{n+1})$. It remains to prove that $PA \cup Tr^N(\Pi_n) \vdash \varphi$. By definition of Σ_{n+1}, there exists a $\psi(x) \in \Pi_n$ such that $\varphi \equiv \exists x \, \psi(x)$. Since $N \models \varphi$, it follows that there exists $m \in N$ such that $N \models \psi(m)$. Since $\psi(m)$ is a Π_n-sentence, it follows that $PA \cup Tr^N(\Pi_n) \vdash \psi(m)$. By introducing the existential quantifier $\exists x$, it follows that $PA \cup Tr^N(\Pi_n) \vdash \exists x \, \psi(x)$. By definition of φ, we have that $PA \cup Tr^N(\Pi_n) \vdash \varphi$. $\qquad\square$

Lemma 5.1.2. *For any $n > 0$, the sets of sentences $Tr^N(\Sigma_n)$, $Tr^N(\Pi_n)$, and $Thm(PA \cup Tr^N(\Pi_n))$ are Σ_n, Π_n, and Σ_{n+1}, respectively.*

Proof. The argument can be done by using mathematical induction. Due to space constraints, the detailed proof is omitted. $\qquad\square$

Theorem 5.1.3. *For any $n \geq 0$, $PA \cup Tr^N(\Pi_n) \nvdash Tr^N(\Pi_{n+1})$.*

Proof. The case for $n = 0$ follows from Gödel's first completeness theorem, together with the fact that $PA \vdash Tr^N(\Pi_0)$. It remains to consider the cases for $n > 0$. Fix $n > 0$. By Lemma 5.1.2, $Thm(PA \cup Tr^N(\Pi_n))$ is Σ_{n+1}. Then there exists $\varphi(x) \in \Sigma_{n+1}$ such that for any $\psi \in L$,

$$\psi \in Thm(PA \cup Tr^N(\Pi_n)) \text{ iff } N \models \varphi(\ulcorner\psi\urcorner). \tag{1}$$

By Gödel's diagonal lemma, there exists a sentence $G \in L$ such that

$$PA \cup Tr^N(\Pi_n) \vdash G \leftrightarrow \neg\varphi(\ulcorner G\urcorner). \tag{2}$$

Assume for a contradiction that $PA \cup Tr^N(\Pi_n) \vdash G$. Then $G \in Thm(PA \cup Tr^N(\Pi_n))$ and hence by assertion (1) we have $N \models \varphi(\ulcorner G\urcorner)$. On the other hand, by assertion (2), it follows that $PA \cup Tr^N(\Pi_n) \vdash \neg\varphi(\ulcorner G\urcorner)$. Since $N \models PA \cup Tr^N(\Pi_n)$, by soundness of first-order logic, we have that $N \models \neg\varphi(\ulcorner G\urcorner)$, contrary to $N \models \varphi(\ulcorner G\urcorner)$. So we have that $PA \cup Tr^N(\Pi_n) \nvdash G$. Then $G \notin Thm(PA \cup Tr^N(\Pi_n))$ follows. By assertion (1), it follows that $N \models \neg\varphi(\ulcorner G\urcorner)$. Since $\neg\varphi(\ulcorner G\urcorner) \in \Pi_{n+1}$, we have that $\neg\varphi(\ulcorner G\urcorner) \in Tr^N(\Pi_{n+1})$. By assertion (2), together with the fact $PA \cup Tr^N(\Pi_n) \nvdash G$, it follows that $PA \cup Tr^N(\Pi_n) \nvdash \neg\varphi(\ulcorner G\urcorner)$. Finally we have that $PA \cup Tr^N(\Pi_n) \nvdash Tr^N(\Pi_{n+1})$.   □

5.2   Completeness of $HL(T)$ for $\{P\}WP\{Q\}$

To investigate the completeness of $HL(T)$ relative to N for $\{P\}WP\{Q\}$, we remark that if P or Q is too large, or $Thm(T)$ is too small, then $HL(T)$ might not be complete relative to N for $\{P\}WP\{Q\}$.

Definition 5.2.1. If $HL(T)$ is complete relative to N for $\{P\}WP\{Q\}$, then we say that

(i) pre-P (resp. post-Q) is maximal w.r.t. T if for any $P' \nsubseteq P$ (resp. $Q' \nsubseteq Q$), $HL(T)$ is not complete relative to N for $\{P'\}WP\{Q\}$ (resp. for $\{P\}WP\{Q'\}$).

(ii) T is minimal w.r.t. pre-P (resp. w.r.t. post-Q) if for any $T' \supseteq PA$ with $Thm(T') \subsetneqq Thm(T)$, $HL(T')$ is not complete relative to N for $\{P\}AP\{Cnt\}$ (resp. for $\{Cnt\}AP\{Q\}$).

Note that in Definition 5.2.1 (ii), in case $HL(T')$ is not complete relative to N for $\{P\}AP\{Cnt\}$ (resp. for $\{Cnt\}AP\{Q\}$), we can see that P (resp. Q) is the only factor leading to this, since $HL(PA)$ is complete relative to N for $\{Cnt\}AP\{Cnt\}$ (cf. Corollary 3.3.4).

Lemma 5.2.2. *For any $i > 0$, $HL(PA \cup Tr^N(\Pi_i))$ is complete relative to N for $\{\Sigma_i\}WP\{\Pi_i\}$.*

Proof. Fix $i > 0$. Let $N \models \{p\}S\{q\}$ with $S \in WP$ (having program variables $\boldsymbol{x}$), $p(\boldsymbol{u}, \boldsymbol{x}) \in \Sigma_i$ and $q(\boldsymbol{u}, \boldsymbol{x}) \in \Pi_i$. By Definition 3.2.1, it remains to prove that $HL(PA \cup Tr^N(\Pi_i)) \vdash \{p\}S\{q\}$. By Lemma 3.3.2, it follows that $N \models \forall\boldsymbol{u}, \boldsymbol{x}, \boldsymbol{y}(p(\boldsymbol{u}, \boldsymbol{x}) \wedge \alpha_S(\boldsymbol{x}, \boldsymbol{y}) \rightarrow q(\boldsymbol{u}, \boldsymbol{y}/\boldsymbol{x}))$. By pure logic, we have that $N \models$

$\forall \boldsymbol{u}, \boldsymbol{x}, \boldsymbol{y}(\neg p(\boldsymbol{u}, \boldsymbol{x}) \vee \neg \alpha_S(\boldsymbol{x}, \boldsymbol{y}) \vee q(\boldsymbol{u}, \boldsymbol{y}/\boldsymbol{x}))$. Since $p(\boldsymbol{u}, \boldsymbol{x})$, $\alpha_S(\boldsymbol{x}, \boldsymbol{y}) \in \Sigma_i$, it follows that $\neg p(\boldsymbol{u}, \boldsymbol{x})$, $\neg \alpha_S(\boldsymbol{x}, \boldsymbol{y}) \in \Pi_i$. By closure of Π_i under disjunction, it follows that $\neg p(\boldsymbol{u}, \boldsymbol{x}) \vee \neg \alpha_S(\boldsymbol{x}, \boldsymbol{y}) \vee q(\boldsymbol{u}, \boldsymbol{y}/\boldsymbol{x}) \in \Pi_i$. Then $\forall \boldsymbol{u}, \boldsymbol{x}, \boldsymbol{y}(p(\boldsymbol{u}, \boldsymbol{x}) \wedge \alpha_S(\boldsymbol{x}, \boldsymbol{y}) \to q(\boldsymbol{u}, \boldsymbol{y}/\boldsymbol{x})) \in Tr^N(\Pi_i)$ and hence $PA \cup Tr^N(\Pi_i) \vdash \forall \boldsymbol{u}, \boldsymbol{x}, \boldsymbol{y}(p(\boldsymbol{u}, \boldsymbol{x}) \wedge \alpha_S(\boldsymbol{x}, \boldsymbol{y}) \to q(\boldsymbol{u}, \boldsymbol{y}/\boldsymbol{x}))$. By Theorem 3.3.3, it follows that $HL(PA \cup Tr^N(\Pi_i)) \vdash \{p\}S\{q\}$. □

Lemma 5.2.3. *Let $S ::= y := 0; while \ y < x \ do \ y := y + 1 \ od$, and let $PA \subseteq T \subseteq Th(N)$, $\psi(x) \in L$ such that $N \models \forall x \ \psi(x)$ and $T \not\vdash \forall x \ \psi(x)$. It is the case that $HL(T) \not\vdash \{\neg \psi(x)\}S\{false\}$.*

Proof. Follows from the proof of Theorem 4.3 of [19]. □

Lemma 5.2.4. *Pre-Σ_i (resp. post-Π_i) is maximal w.r.t. $PA \cup Tr^N(\Pi_i)$.*

Proof. Proof of pre-Σ_i being maximal w.r.t. $PA \cup Tr^N(\Pi_i)$. Recalling Definition 5.2.1 (i), we have to prove that there exist $p \in \Pi_i$ (the minimal level $\not\subseteq \Sigma_i$), $S \in WP$, and $q \in \Pi_i$ such that $N \models \{p\}S\{q\}$ but $HL(PA \cup Tr^N(\Pi_i)) \not\vdash \{p\}S\{q\}$. By Theorem 5.1.3, it follows that $PA \cup Tr^N(\Pi_i) \not\vdash Tr^N(\Pi_{i+1})$. Then there exists a Π_{i+1}-sentence φ such that $N \models \varphi$ and $PA \cup Tr^N(\Pi_i) \not\vdash \varphi$. By definition of Π_{i+1}, we have that, for some $\psi(x) \in \Sigma_i$, $\varphi \equiv \forall x \ \psi(x)$. Let $p ::= \neg \psi(x) \ (\in \Pi_i)$, $S ::= y := 0; while \ y < x \ do \ y := y + 1 \ od$, and $q ::= false$. It's easy to check that $N \models \{p\}S\{q\}$. By Lemma 5.2.3, it follows that $HL(PA \cup Tr^N(\Pi_i)) \not\vdash \{p\}S\{q\}$.

Proof of post-Π_i being maximal w.r.t. $PA \cup Tr^N(\Pi_i)$. Recalling Definition 5.2.1 (i), we have to prove that there exist $p \in \Sigma_i$, $S \in WP$, and $q \in \Sigma_i$ (the minimal level $\not\subseteq \Pi_i$) such that $N \models \{p\}S\{q\}$ but $HL(PA \cup Tr^N(\Pi_i)) \not\vdash \{p\}S\{q\}$. Let $p ::= true$, let $S ::= x := x$, and let $q ::= \psi(x)$ with $\psi(x)$ being as defined in the proof of pre-Σ_i being maximal w.r.t. $PA \cup Tr^N(\Pi_i)$. It's easy to see that $N \models \{p\}S\{q\}$. It remains to show that $HL(PA \cup Tr^N(\Pi_i)) \not\vdash \{p\}S\{q\}$. By Theorem 3.3.3, it suffices to prove that $PA \cup Tr^N(\Pi_i) \not\vdash \forall x, y(true \wedge \alpha_S(x, y) \to \psi(y))$. By definition of $\alpha_S(x, y)$, it suffices to prove that $PA \cup Tr^N(\Pi_i) \not\vdash \forall x \ \psi(x)$. This is the case due to the choice of $\psi(x)$. □

By Lemma 5.2.2, together with Definition 3.2.1, it follows that $HL(PA \cup Tr^N(\Pi_i))$ is complete relative to N for $\{\Pi_{i-1}\}WP\{\Sigma_{i-1}\}$.

Lemma 5.2.5. *$PA \cup Tr^N(\Pi_i)$ is minimal w.r.t. pre-Π_{i-1} (resp. w.r.t. post-Σ_{i-1}).*

Proof. Proof of $PA \cup Tr^N(\Pi_i)$ being minimal w.r.t. pre-Π_{i-1}. Recalling Definition 5.2.1 (ii), we have to prove that for any $T \supseteq PA$ with $Thm(T) \subsetneq Thm(PA \cup Tr^N(\Pi_i))$, there exist $p \in \Pi_{i-1}$, $S \in AP$, and $q \in Cnt$ such that $N \models \{p\}S\{q\}$ but $HL(T) \not\vdash \{p\}S\{q\}$. Let $T \supseteq PA$ with $Thm(T) \subsetneq Thm(PA \cup Tr^N(\Pi_i))$. Then there exists a Π_i-sentence φ such that $N \models \varphi$ and $T \not\vdash \varphi$. By definition of Π_i, we have that, for some $\psi(x) \in \Sigma_{i-1}$, $\varphi \equiv \forall x \ \psi(x)$. Let $p ::= \neg \psi(x) \ (\in \Pi_{i-1})$, $S ::= x := x$, and $q ::= false$. It's easy to see that $N \models \{p\}S\{q\}$. It remains to show that $HL(T) \not\vdash \{p\}S\{q\}$. By Theorem 3.3.3, it suffices to prove that $T \not\vdash \forall x, y(\neg \psi(x) \wedge \alpha_S(x, y) \to false)$. Since $N \models \varphi$ and $T \not\vdash \varphi$, by completeness of first-order logic, there exists nonstandard

$M \models T$ such that $M \models \exists x \ \neg\psi(x)$. Since $M \models \forall x \exists y \ \alpha_S(x, y)$, we have that $M \not\models \forall x, y(\neg\psi(x) \wedge \alpha_S(x, y) \rightarrow false)$. By completeness of first-order logic, it follows that $T \not\vdash \forall x, y(\neg\psi(x) \wedge \alpha_S(x, y) \rightarrow false)$.

Proof of $PA \cup Tr^N(\Pi_i)$ being minimal w.r.t. post-Σ_{i-1}. Recalling Definition 5.2.1 (ii), we have to prove that for any $T \supseteq PA$ with $Thm(T) \subsetneq Thm(PA \cup Tr^N(\Pi_i))$, there exist $p \in Cnt$, $S \in AP$, and $q \in \Sigma_{i-1}$ such that $N \models \{p\}S\{q\}$ but $HL(T) \not\vdash \{p\}S\{q\}$. Let $T \supseteq PA$ with $Thm(T) \subsetneq Thm(PA \cup Tr^N(\Pi_i))$. Then there exists a Π_i-sentence φ such that $N \models \varphi$ and $T \not\vdash \varphi$. By definition of Π_i, we have that, for some $\psi(x) \in \Sigma_{i-1}$, $\varphi \equiv \forall x \ \psi(x)$. Let $p ::= true$, $S ::= x := x$, and $q ::= \psi(x)$. It's easy to see that $N \models \{p\}S\{q\}$. It remains to show that $HL(T) \not\vdash \{p\}S\{q\}$. By Theorem 3.3.3, it suffices to prove that $T \not\vdash \forall x, y(true \wedge \alpha_S(x, y) \rightarrow \psi(y))$. Since $N \models \varphi$ and $T \not\vdash \varphi$, by completeness of first-order logic, there exists nonstandard $M \models T$ such that $M \models \exists x \ \neg\psi(x)$. Since $M \models \forall x \ \alpha_S(x, x)$, we have that $M \not\models \forall x, y(true \wedge \alpha_S(x, y) \rightarrow \psi(y))$. By completeness of first-order logic, it follows that $T \not\vdash \forall x, y(true \wedge \alpha_S(x, y) \rightarrow \psi(y))$.   □

Theorem 5.2.6. *For any $i > 0$, it is the case that*

(i) $HL(PA \cup Tr^N(\Pi_i))$ is complete relative to N for $\{P\}WP\{Q\}$ iff $P \subseteq \Sigma_i$ and $Q \subseteq \Pi_i$;

(ii) if $\Sigma_i \supseteq P \supseteq \Pi_{i-1}$ or $\Pi_i \supseteq Q \supseteq \Sigma_{i-1}$, then $HL(T)$ is complete relative to N for $\{P\}WP\{Q\}$ iff $Thm(T) \supseteq Thm(PA \cup Tr^N(\Pi_i))$.

Proof. Follows from Definition 3.2.1, together with Lemmas 5.2.2, 5.2.4 and 5.2.5.   □

6   Conclusion

In this paper, we have shown that $PA \cup Tr^N(\Pi_1)$ is the minimal extension T of PA such that $HL(T)$ is complete relative to N for $\{Cnt\}WP\{Cnt\}$. We have shown that for any $i > 0$, $HL(PA \cup Tr^N(\Pi_i))$ is complete relative to N for $\{P\}WP\{Q\}$ iff $P \subseteq \Sigma_i$ and $Q \subseteq \Pi_i$; and if $\Sigma_i \supseteq P \supseteq \Pi_{i-1}$ or $\Pi_i \supseteq Q \supseteq \Sigma_{i-1}$, then $HL(T)$ is complete relative to N for $\{P\}WP\{Q\}$ iff $Thm(T) \supseteq Thm(PA \cup Tr^N(\Pi_i))$. Considering $Thm(PA) \subsetneq Thm(PA \cup Tr^N(\Pi_i)) \subsetneq Th(N)$ and $Th(N) = \bigcup_{i=1}^{\infty} Thm(PA \cup Tr^N(\Pi_i))$, the completeness gap between $HL(PA)$ and $HL(Th(N))$ has been bridged.

Cook's completeness result allows for the whole set of arithmetical formulas as assertions, at the price of using $Th(N)$ as an oracle for the assertion theory. By restricting assertions to subclasses of arithmetical formulas, we show that arithmetical extensions of PA suffice to act as the assertion theory, and the lower the level of the assertions in the arithmetical hierarchy the lower the level of the required assertion theory is. In conclusion, our completeness results refine Cook's one by reducing the complexity of the assertion theory.

Acknowledgement. The authors would thank the 973 Program of China (Grant No. 2014CB340701), the National Natural Science Foundation of China (Grant Nos. 61672504 and 61472474), and the CAS-SAFEA International Partnership Program for Creative Research Teams for the financial support.

References

1. Hoare, C.A.R.: An axiomatic basis for computer programming. Commun. ACM **12**, 576–580 (1969)
2. Cook, S.A.: Soundness and completeness of an axiom system for program verification. SIAM J. Comput. **7**, 70–90 (1978)
3. Mirkowska, G., Salwicki, A.: Algorithmic Logic. Springer, Dordrecht (1987)
4. Harel, D., Kozen, D., Tiuryn, J.: Dynamic Logic. MIT Press, Cambridge (2000)
5. Reynolds, J.C.: Separation logic: a logic for shared mutable data structures. In: LICS, pp. 55–74 (2002)
6. Apt, K.R.: Ten years of Hoare's logic: a survey - Part I. ACM Trans. Program. Lang. Syst. **3**(4), 431–483 (1981)
7. Apt, K.R.: Ten years of Hoare's logic: a survey - Part II: nondeterminism. Theoret. Comput. Sci. **28**, 83–109 (1984)
8. Kleymann, T.: Hoare logic and auxiliary variables. Formal Aspects Comput. **11**, 541–566 (1999)
9. Nipkow, T.: Hoare logics in Isabelle, HOL. In: Proof and System-Reliability, pp. 341–367, Kluwer Academic Publishers (2002)
10. Kaye, R.: Models of Peano Arithmetic. Oxford University Press, New York (1991)
11. Bergstra, J.A., Tucker, J.V.: Hoare's logic and Peano's arithmetic. Theoret. Comput. Sci. **22**, 265–284 (1983)
12. Boolos, G.S., Burgess, J.P., Jeffrey, R.C.: Computability and Logic, 5th edn. Cambridge University Press, Cambridge (2007)
13. Soare, R.I.: Recursively Enumerable Sets and Degrees. Springer, Heidelberg (1987)
14. Apt, K., Bergstra, J.A., Meertens, L.G.L.T.: Recursive assertions are not enough-or are they? Theoret. Comput. Sci. **8**, 73–87 (1979)
15. Clarke, E.M.: Programming language constructs for which it is impossible to obtain good Hoare axiom systems. J. ACM **26**, 129–147 (1979)
16. Lipton, R.J.: A necessary and sufficient condition for the existence of Hoare logics. In: IEEE Symposium on Foundations of Computer Science, pp. 1–6 (1977)
17. Clarke, E.M., German, S.M., Halpern, J.Y.: Effective axiomatizations of Hoare logics. J. ACM **30**, 612–636 (1983)
18. Grabowski, M.: On relative completeness of Hoare logics. Inf. Control **66**, 29–44 (1985)
19. Bergstra, J.A., Tucker, J.V.: Expressiveness and the completeness of Hoare's logic. J. Comput. Syst. Sci. **25**, 267–284 (1982)
20. Xu, Z., Sui, Y., Zhang, W.: Completeness of Hoare logic with inputs over the standard model. Theoret. Comput. Sci. **612**, 23–28 (2016)
21. Kozen, D., Tiuryn, J.: On the completeness of propositional Hoare logic. Inf. Sci. **139**, 187–195 (2001)
22. Davis, M.: Computability & Unsovability. Courier Dover Publications, New York (1982)

Configuration- and Residual-Based Transition Systems for Event Structures with Asymmetric Conflict

Eike Best[1]([✉]), Nataliya Gribovskaya[2], and Irina Virbitskaite[2,3]

[1] Department of Computing Science, Carl von Ossietzky Universität Oldenburg,
26111 Oldenburg, Germany
eike.best@informatik.uni-oldenburg.de

[2] A.P. Ershov Institute of Informatics Systems, SB RAS, 6, Acad. Lavrentiev av.,
630090 Novosibirsk, Russia
{gribovskaya,virb}@iis.nsk.su

[3] Novosibirsk State University, 2, Pirogov av., 630090 Novosibirsk, Russia

Abstract. In order to associate a transition system with an event structure, it is customary to use configurations, constructing a transition system by repeatedly adding executable events. It is also possible to use residuals, constructing a transition system by repeatedly deleting non-executable events. The present paper proposes a systematic investigation of how the two methods are interrelated. The focus will be on asymmetric versions of prime, bundle, and dual event structures. For each of them, configuration-based and residual-based transition system semantics will be defined. The pairwise bisimilarity of the resulting transition systems will be proved, considering interleaving, multiset, and pomset semantics.

Keywords: Bisimilarity · Event structures with asymmetric conflict · Labelled transition systems · Interleaving/Multiset/Pomset semantics

1 Introduction

Event structures, first defined in [16], consist of a set of events and three binary relations between events: *precedence*, basically meant to be a transitive relation, understood in a causal (or temporal) way; *conflict*, broadly construed as a symmetric relation, and understood as a relation of mutual exclusion; and *concurrency*, which is generally symmetric and informally understood as the absence of one of the other relationships. In the literature, several modifications and generalisations of the original definition can be found, often depending on the domain of application [6,7,9,19]. In this paper, we shall be particularly interested in event structures whose conflict relations are not necessarily symmetric

E. Best, N. Gribovskaya and I. Virbitskaite—Supported by DFG (German Research Foundation) and by RFBR (Russian Foundation for Basic Research) through the grant CAVER (Be 1267/14-1 and 14-01-91334, respectively).

B. Steffen et al. (Eds.): SOFSEM 2017, LNCS 10139, pp. 132–146, 2017.
DOI: 10.1007/978-3-319-51963-0_11

(e.g., [1, 8, 15]), and which we shall uniformly call *asymmetric*. Such event structures allow, amongst other things, the description of weak causality.

Event structures are usually required to satisfy some basic properties. For example, infinite pasts are generally disallowed. Hence there is always an initial configuration, which can usually be taken as the empty set. By adding executable events to a configuration, new configurations can be reached, until this is no longer possible (or forever, if infinite executions are possible). In interleaving semantics, only one executable event is added at a time; in multiset semantics, a set of executable events (without any relation) is added; in step semantics, a set of concurrently executable events is added; in pomset semantics, a partially ordered set of executable events is added. This method is commonly used in order to define transition system semantics of event structures. Another way of associating a transition system to an event structure has a more "structural" appeal. The entire event structure is initially considered as the initial state of a transition system. Then, in each step, an initial part of the event structure is executed, and the new state of the transition system consists of the residual event structure, in which all parts that have become non-executable (e.g., all events that are in conflict with an already executed one) are neglected. This method has mostly been investigated in connection with operational and algebraic semantics.

The question, to be considered in the present paper, is whether the transition systems obtainable by these two methods are related, in some way. The question has already been answered, for prime event structures with symmetric binary conflict, by Majster-Cederbaum and Roggenbach in [12]. It is shown there that for interleaving, step, and pomset semantics, bisimilar transition systems are obtained. [12] also demonstrates that such a result is not permitted by (strong) history preserving semantics, and that one cannot, in general, expect more than bisimilarity (in particular, no isomorphism). The authors know of no other results of this kind, even though both types of semantics have been defined in other circumstances, e.g., configuration semantics in [3–5, 11, 13, 17], and residual semantics in [2, 8, 14]. In this paper, we extend the work of [12] for asymmetric versions of three types of event structures: prime event structures [13, 16], bundle event structures [9], and dual event structures [10]. Our main results are that – with judicious but intuitively justifiable definitions, whenever possible – bisimilarity can be achieved for three types of semantics: interleaving, multisets, and pomsets. The proofs of the results can be found at www.iis.nsk.su/virb/proofsketches-SOFSEM-FOCS-2017.

2   Models of Event Structures

A prime event structure is a set of events, together with a causality relation (denoted by $<$) and a conflict relation (denoted by $\sharp$) which satisfy the principles of finite causes and hereditary conflict, respectively. Two events that are neither in causality relation nor in conflict relation are considered to be concurrent. Prime event structures are useful in order to study relationships between different models of concurrent processes, such as Mazurkewicz trace languages, pomsets, occurrence nets, Petri nets, configuration structures, and Scott domains [5,13,16,17].

Definition 1. *A* (symmetric) *prime event structure over* L *is a tuple* $\mathcal{E} = (E, \sharp, \leq, L, l)$, *where* E *is a set of events;* $\leq\ \subseteq E \times E$ *is a partial order (the* causality relation*), satisfying the* principle of finite causes: $\forall e \in E\colon \lfloor e \rfloor = \{e' \in E \mid e' \leq e\}$ *is finite;* $\sharp \subseteq E \times E$ *is an irreflexive and symmetric relation (the* conflict relation*), satisfying the* principle of hereditary conflict: $\forall e, e', e'' \in E\colon e \leq e'$ *and* $e \sharp e''$ *then* $e' \sharp e''$; L *is a set of labels; and* $l\colon E \to L$ *is a labeling function.*

Let $\mathbb{E}_L^p$ denote the class of prime event structures over L. In the graphical representation of a prime structure, pairs of events related by a causality relation are connected by arrows (for the pairs derivable from the transitivity property, the arrows are not shown), and pairs of the events included in a conflict relation are marked by a symbol $\sharp$ (for the pairs derivable from the hereditary conflict principle, symbols $\sharp$ are not depicted).

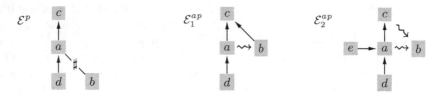

Fig. 1. A symmetric (l.h.s.) and two asymmetric (r.h.s.) prime event structures

Example 1: Figure 1(l.h.s.) shows the prime event structure $\mathcal{E}^p$ over $L = \{a, b, c, d\}$, with $E_{\mathcal{E}^p} = \{a, b, c, d\}$, $<_{\mathcal{E}^p} = \{(d, a), (a, c), (d, c)\}$, $\sharp_{\mathcal{E}^p} = \{(a, b), (b, a), (c, b), (b, c)\}$, and the identity labeling function $l_{\mathcal{E}^p}$.

The behavior of prime structures is described in terms of *configurations*, subsets of conflict-free events left-closed with respect to the causality relation. Call a set $X \subseteq E$ a *configuration* of a prime event structure $\mathcal{E}$ iff X is a finite set, left-closed in E (i.e., $\lfloor e \rfloor \subseteq X$, for all $e \in X$) and conflict-free (i.e., $\neg(e \sharp e')$, for all $e, e' \in X$). The set of the configurations of $\mathcal{E}$ is denoted as $Conf(\mathcal{E})$. For $X, X' \in Conf(\mathcal{E})$, we write $X \to X'$ iff $X \subseteq X'$. Further, for $X \in Conf(\mathcal{E})$, we define the following sets:

$$\sharp(X) = \{e \in E \mid e \sharp e', \text{ for some } e' \in X\} \qquad \text{(strong syntactic conflict)}$$
$$\dagger(X) = \{e \in E \mid \exists e' \in \lfloor e \rfloor \text{ s.t. } e' \in \sharp(X)\} \qquad \text{(weak syntactic conflict)}$$
$$\ddagger(X) = \{e \in E \mid \not\exists X' \in Conf(\mathcal{E}) \text{ containing } X \text{ and } e\} \quad \text{(semantic conflict)}$$

For symmetric prime event structures, these sets coincide:

Lemma 1. *For a prime event structure* $\mathcal{E}$ *and* $X \in Conf(\mathcal{E})$, $\sharp(X) = \dagger(X) = \ddagger(X)$.

In [12,14], for a prime event structure $\mathcal{E}$ and a configuration $X \in Conf(\mathcal{E})$, a removal operator being used in constructing residuals has been defined as follows: $\mathcal{E} \backslash X = (E', \leq \cap (E' \times E'), \sharp \cap (E' \times E'), L, l\mid_{E'})$, with $E' = E \backslash (X \cup \sharp(X))$. Due to Lemma 1, we can use any of the conflict sets of X, in the removal operator. We write $\mathcal{E} \rightsquigarrow_X \mathcal{E}'$ iff there exists $X \in Conf(\mathcal{E})$ such that $\mathcal{E}' = \mathcal{E} \backslash X$.

Based on Lemma 1 together with Lemma 1 of [12], the lemma below states some correctness criteria for the removal operator with any conflict set. The meaning of the correctness properties is that the obtained residuals are prime event structures which do not allow configurations that are disallowed by an original prime event structure. In some sense, this signifies some compositionality properties of the removal operator.

Lemma 2. *Let $\mathcal{E}$ be a prime event structure.*

(i) For any $X \in Conf(\mathcal{E})$, $\mathcal{E}' = \mathcal{E} \backslash X$ is a prime event structure.
(ii) For any $\mathcal{E}' = \mathcal{E} \backslash X$ with $X \in Conf(\mathcal{E})$ and $\mathcal{E}'' = \mathcal{E}' \backslash X'$ with $X' \in Conf(\mathcal{E}')$,
   (a) $X \cup X' \in Conf(\mathcal{E})$,
   (b) if $X \rightarrow X''$ in $\mathcal{E}$, then $X'' \backslash X \in Conf(\mathcal{E}')$,
   (c) $\mathcal{E}'' = \mathcal{E} \backslash (X \cup X')$.

The results in items (a)–(c) are crucial for establishing bilimilarities between different kinds of transition systems obtained from prime event structures (see Proposition 1 and Theorem 1).

Asymmetric prime event structures have a causal relation similar to that of prime event structures, but replace the symmetric conflict with a relation, denoted by $\rightsquigarrow$, modelling asymmetric conflict or weak causality. Such a relation allows one to represent a new kind of dependency between events arising in contextual nets [1] (an extension of place/transition Petri nets where transitions can also have context conditions, modelling resources that can be read without being consumed). Intuitively, $e_0 \rightsquigarrow e_1$ means that e_0 cannot occur once e_1 has occurred, and if e_0 and e_1 both occur in a single system run, then e_0 causally precedes e_1. So, in this setting, the symmetric binary conflict is no more a primitive relation, but it is represented via "cycles" of asymmetric conflict. As a consequence, prime event structures can be identified with a special subclass of asymmetric (prime) event structures where all conflicts are actually symmetric.

Definition 2. *An asymmetric (prime) event structure over L is a tuple $\mathcal{E} = (E, \leq, \rightsquigarrow, L, l)$, where E is a set of events; $\leq \subseteq E \times E$ is a partial order (the causality relation), satisfying the principle of finite causes: $\forall e \in E$: $\lfloor e \rfloor = \{e' \in E \mid e' \leq e\}$ is finite; $\rightsquigarrow \subseteq (E \times E)$ is a disabling relation such that $\forall e \in E$: $\nearrow_{\lfloor e \rfloor}{}^1$ is acyclic[2], with $\nearrow = (\rightsquigarrow \cup <)$; L is a set of actions; and $l : E \rightarrow L$ is a labeling function.*

Let $\mathbb{E}_L^{ap}$ denote the class of asymmetric prime event structures over L. An asymmetric prime event structure $\mathcal{E}$ is called *with hereditary conflict* iff whenever

---

[1] For a set $Y \subseteq X$ and a relation $r \subseteq X \times X$, r_Y denotes the restriction of r to Y.
[2] A relation $r \subseteq X \times X$ is *acyclic* if it has no "cycles" of the form $e_0 \, r \, e_1 \, r \, \ldots \, r \, e_n \, r \, e_0$, with $n \geq 1$ and $e_i \in X$ for all $0 \leq i \leq n$.

$e \rightsquigarrow e'$ and $e < e''$, then $e'' \rightsquigarrow e'$. In the graphical representation of an asymmetric prime structure, pairs of events related by a causality relation are connected by arrows (for the pairs derivable from the transitivity property, the arrows are not shown), and the pairs of the events included in a disabling relation are connected by squiggly arrows.

Example 2: Figure 1(r.h.s.) shows the asymmetric prime event structures $\mathcal{E}_1^{ap}$ and $\mathcal{E}_2^{ap}$. For instance, consider the syntax of $\mathcal{E}_1^{ap}$ over $L = \{a, b, c, d\}$: $E_{\mathcal{E}_1^{ap}} = \{a, b, c, d\}$; $<_{\mathcal{E}_1^{ap}} = \{(d, a), (a, c), (d, c), (b, c)\}$; $\rightsquigarrow_{\mathcal{E}_1^{ap}} = \{(a, b)\}$; and the labeling function $l_{\mathcal{E}_1^{ap}}$ is the identity.

A *configuration* of an asymmetric prime event structure $\mathcal{E}$ is a finite set $C \subseteq E$ such that: (i) $\nearrow_C$ is well-founded,[3] and (ii) C is left-closed w.r.t. $\leq$, i.e. for all $e \in C$, $e' \leq e$ implies $e' \in C$. Condition (i) guarantees that $\nearrow$ has no infinite descending chains in C, and thus ensures that in C there are no $\nearrow$-cycles, i.e. excludes the possibility of having in C a subset of conflicting events. Condition (ii) requires that all the causes of each event are present. The set of all configurations of $\mathcal{E}$ is denoted by $Conf(\mathcal{E})$. For $X \in Conf(\mathcal{E})$, the causality relation on X, $\leq_X$, is defined as the reflexive and transitive closure of $\nearrow_X$.

Conventions. For a sequence $t = e_1 \ldots e_n$ of events, let $\bar{t} := \{e_1, \ldots e_n\}$, and $t_i := e_1 \ldots e_i$, for all $1 \leq i \leq n$. we write $t \rightarrow t'$ iff t is a prefix of t' and, further, $t'' = t' \backslash t$ iff t'' is a suffix of t', with $t' = tt''$.

A *trace* of an asymmetric prime event structure $\mathcal{E}$ is a sequence $t = e_1 \ldots e_n$ ($n \geq 0$) of distinct events from E such that for all $1 \leq i, j \leq n$ if $e_i \rightsquigarrow e_j$, then $i < j$, and for all $1 \leq i \leq n$ if $e \leq e_i$ for some $e \in E$, then there is $1 \leq j \leq n$ such that $e = e_j$ and $j \leq i$. The set of all traces of $\mathcal{E}$ is denoted by $Traces(\mathcal{E})$. Clearly, $\bar{t}$ is a configuration of $\mathcal{E}$, for any $t \in Traces(\mathcal{E})$, and for any configuration $X \in Conf(\mathcal{E})$ there is a trace t such that $X = \bar{t}$. For $X, X' \in Conf(\mathcal{E})$, we write $X \rightarrow X'$ iff there are $t, t' \in Traces(\mathcal{E})$ such that $X = \bar{t}$, $X' = \bar{t'}$, and $t \rightarrow t'$. For $t \in Traces(\mathcal{E})$, define the sets:

$$\rightsquigarrow (t) = \{e \in E \backslash \bar{t} \mid e \rightsquigarrow e' \text{ for some } e' \in \bar{t}\} \quad \text{(strong syntactic conflict)}$$
$$\dagger(t) = \{e \in E \mid \exists e' \in \lfloor e \rfloor \text{ s.t. } e' \in \rightsquigarrow (t)\} \quad \text{(weak syntactic conflict)}$$
$$\ddagger(t) = \{e \in E \mid \nexists t' \in Traces(\mathcal{E}) \text{ s.t. } t \rightarrow t' \text{ and } e \in \bar{t'}\} \quad \text{(semantic conflict)}$$

Crucially, we define the conflict sets for a trace, but not for a configuration, because the former allows for keeping the order of event occurrences that is essential for event structures with asymmetric conflict. The following lemma establishes the interrelations between these sets.

Lemma 3. *Let $\mathcal{E}$ be an asymmetric prime event structure and $t \in Traces(\mathcal{E})$. Then $\rightsquigarrow (t) \subseteq \dagger(t) = \ddagger(t)$; and $\rightsquigarrow (t) = \dagger(t) = \ddagger(t)$, if $\mathcal{E}$ is with hereditary conflict.*

---

[3] A relation $r \subseteq X \times X$ is *well-founded* if it has no infinite descending chains, i.e., $\langle e_i \rangle_{i \in \mathbb{N}}$ such that $e_{i+1} \, r \, e_i$, $e_i \neq e_{i+1}$, for all $i \in \mathbb{N}$.

Example 3: To illustrate the $\subseteq$ in this lemma, consider the asymmetric prime event structures $\mathcal{E}_1^{ap}$ and $\mathcal{E}_2^{ap}$ shown in Fig. 1(r.h.s.). Clearly, $\mathcal{E}_1^{ap}$ is not with hereditary conflict, but $\mathcal{E}_2^{ap}$ is. It is easy to see that $\leadsto_{\mathcal{E}_1^{ap}}(t_1) = \{a\} \subsetneq \{a,c\} = \dagger_{\mathcal{E}_1^{ap}}(t_1)$, for the trace $t_1 = db$, and $\leadsto_{\mathcal{E}_2^{ap}}(t_2) = \{a,c\} = \dagger_{\mathcal{E}_2^{ap}}(t_2)$, for the trace $t_2 = db$.

For an asymmetric prime event structure $\mathcal{E}$, we say that $t, t' \in \textit{Traces}(\mathcal{E})$ are *equivalent* if $\overline{t} = \overline{t'}$, and use $[t]$ to denote the equivalence class of t. For $\mathcal{E}$ and $t \in \textit{Traces}(\mathcal{E})$, define a removal operator as follows: $\mathcal{E}\backslash[t] = (E', \leq' = \leq \cap (E' \times E'), \leadsto' = \leadsto \cap (E' \times E'), L, l \mid_{E'})$, with $E' = E\backslash(\overline{t} \cup \dagger(t))$. Notice that semantic conflict can be used as well. We write $\mathcal{E} \xrightarrow{\hspace{0.3cm}}_{\overline{t}} \mathcal{E}'$ iff there exists $t \in \textit{Traces}(\mathcal{E})$ such that $\mathcal{E}' = \mathcal{E}\backslash[t]$.

Bundle event structures were introduced in [8,9] for the description of formal semantics of the specification language LOTOS for parallel systems and the corresponding algebra of processes. Unlike in prime event structures, the events in bundle structures can be initiated by different sets of events. Causality is not a binary relation anymore; instead, it is represented by the bundle relation $\mapsto$ between a finite set of pairwise conflicting events W and an event e. This relation can be interpreted as follows: in the system's functioning, an event e can occur only if one of the events from the set W has already occurred. A pair (W, e) such that $W \mapsto e$ is called a bundle, and W is called a bundle set. In asymmetric bundle event structures, the conflict relation $\sharp$ is replaced by a disabling relation $\leadsto$. As in asymmetric prime structures, an event e_1 disabling another event e_0 means that once e_1 occurs, e_0 cannot occur anymore. Clearly, asymmetric bundle event structures are a generalisation of bundle event structures, since the symmetric conflict can be modelled through mutual disabling (i.e., $e \leadsto e'$ and $e' \leadsto e$). Moreover, any asymmetric prime event structure $\mathcal{E}^{ap}$ can be considered as a special asymmetric bundle event structure $\mathcal{E}^{ab}$, with $\{e'\} \mapsto_{\mathcal{E}^{ab}} e$, if $e' <_{\mathcal{E}^{ap}} e$, and $e' \leadsto_{\mathcal{E}^{ab}} e$, if $e' \leadsto_{\mathcal{E}^{ap}} e$; the irreflexivity of $\leadsto_{\mathcal{E}^{ab}}$ is guaranteed by the restriction on $\nearrow_{\mathcal{E}^{ap}}$ in the syntax of $\mathcal{E}^{ap}$.

Definition 3. *An* asymmetric bundle event structure *over L is a tuple $\mathcal{E} = (E, \leadsto, \mapsto, L, l)$, where E is a set of events; $\leadsto \subseteq E \times E$ is an irreflexive disabling relation; $\mapsto \subseteq 2^E \times E$ is the causality relation such that $W \mapsto e \Rightarrow \forall e_1, e_2 \in W$ if $e_1 \neq e_2$ then $e_1 \leadsto e_2$ (Stability[4]); L is a set of labels; and $l : E \to L$ is a labeling function.*

Let $\mathbb{E}_L^{ab}$ denote the class of asymmetric bundle event structures over L.

The above definition allows an empty bundle, $\emptyset \mapsto e$, to be defined. The interpretation of such a bundle is that e can never happen, i.e. e is an impossible (self-conflicting) event. Notice that there are alternative ways to specify impossible events, for example, $\{e\} \mapsto e$ or $\{e'\} \mapsto e \leadsto e'$. All the bundles can always be eliminated while preserving the semantics. Notice that such impossible event can not be specified in asymmetric prime event structures.

---

[4] Stability ensures that two distinct events of a bundle set are in mutual disabling.

Fig. 2. An asymmetric bundle (l.h.s.) and an asymmetric dual (r.h.s.) event structure

In the graphical representation of an asymmetric bundle structure, bundles (W, e) are indicated by drawing an arrow from each element of W to e and connecting all the arrows by small arcs; pairs of the events included in a disabling relation are associated by squiggly arrows; and pairs of the events included in the symmetric conflict relation are marked by the symbol ♯.

Example 4: Figure 2(l.h.s.) depicts an asymmetric bundle structure $\mathcal{E}^{ab}$ over $L = \{a, b, c, d\}$ with $E_{\mathcal{E}^{ab}} = \{a, b, c, d\}$, $\leadsto_{\mathcal{E}^{ab}} = \{(a, b), (b, a), (a, d), (b, d)\}$, $\mapsto_{\mathcal{E}^{ab}} = \{(\{a, b\}, c)\}$, and the identity labeling function $l_{\mathcal{E}^{ab}}$.

Next, we present an extension of asymmetric bundle event structures, called asymmetric dual event structures [8,10]. Such structures are obtained by dropping the stability condition. This may lead to causal ambiguity, in the sense that, given a trace and one of its events, it is not always possible to determine what caused this event.

Definition 4. *An* asymmetric dual event structure *over L is a tuple $\mathcal{E} = (E, \leadsto, \mapsto, L, l)$, where E is a set of events; $\leadsto \subseteq E \times E$ is an irreflexive disabling relation; $\mapsto \subseteq 2^E \times E$ is the causality relation; L is a set of labels; and $l : E \to L$ is a labeling function.*

Let $\mathbb{E}_L^{ad}$ denote the class of asymmetric dual event structures over L. Asymmetric dual event structures are represented graphically in the same way as asymmetric bundle event structures.

Example 5: Figure 2(r.h.s) shows an asymmetric dual structure $\mathcal{E}^{ad}$ over $L = \{a, b, c, d\}$ with $E_{\mathcal{E}^{ad}} = \{a, b, c, d\}$, $\leadsto_{\mathcal{E}^{ad}} = \{(a, d), (c, d), (b, d), (d, b)\}$, $\mapsto_{\mathcal{E}^{ad}} = \{(\{a, b\}, c)\}$, and the identity labeling function $l_{\mathcal{E}^{ad}}$.

An asymmetric bundle/dual event structure $\mathcal{E}$ is called *with hereditary conflict* iff whenever $e \leadsto e'$ and $\exists W \mapsto e''$ such that $e \in W$, then $e'' \leadsto e'$.

A *trace* of an asymmetric bundle/dual event structure $\mathcal{E}$ is a sequence $t = e_1 \ldots e_n$ $(n \geq 0)$ of distinct events from E such that for all $1 \leq i, j \leq n$ if $e_i \leadsto e_j$, then $i < j$, and for all $1 \leq i \leq n$ if $W \mapsto e_i$, then $\overline{t_{i-1}} \cap W \neq \emptyset$. We use *Traces*$(\mathcal{E})$ to denote the set of traces of $\mathcal{E}$. Let $imp(\mathcal{E}) = \{e \in E \mid \nexists t' \in \textit{Traces}(\mathcal{E})$ s.t. $e \in \overline{t'}\}$ denote the set of impossible events of $\mathcal{E}$.

A set $X \subseteq E$ is a *configuration* of an asymmetric bundle/dual event structure $\mathcal{E}$ if there is a trace t such that $X = \overline{t}$. The set of the configurations of $\mathcal{E}$ is denoted as $Conf(\mathcal{E})$. For $X, X' \in Conf(\mathcal{E})$, we write $X \rightarrow X'$ iff there are $t, t' \in Traces(\mathcal{E})$ such that $X = \overline{t}$, $X' = \overline{t'}$, and $t \rightarrow t'$.

In an asymmetric bundle event structure $\mathcal{E}$, for a configuration $X \in Conf(\mathcal{E})$ and $d, e \in X$, we write $d \nearrow_X e$ iff $d \rightsquigarrow e$ or there is a set $W \subseteq E$ such that $d \in W$ and $W \mapsto e$. The causality relation on X, $\leq_X$, is defined as the reflexive and transitive closure of $\nearrow_X$. For a trace $t \in Traces(\mathcal{E})$ and $e \in \overline{t}$, we use the set $\lfloor e \rfloor_t = \{e' \in \overline{t} \mid e' \preceq_{\overline{t}} e\}$ to denote the *cause* of the event e in the trace t, where $\preceq_{\overline{t}}$ is the reflexive and transitive closure of $\{(d, e) \in \overline{t} \times \overline{t} \mid$ there is a set $W \subseteq E$ such that $d \in W$ and $W \mapsto e\}$. Let $\lfloor e \rfloor = \{\lfloor e \rfloor_{t'} \mid t' \in Traces(\mathcal{E})$ and $e \in \overline{t'}\}$ be the *cause* of e.

In (asymmetric) dual event structures, a configuration cannot be described by a single poset anymore, because of the causal ambiguity—a configuration may contain events whose causes are not determined uniquely. The authors of [10] defined five different interpretations of causality in a trace: liberal, bundle satisfaction, minimal, early and late posets. In all the interpretations, a cause of an event (the set of "causal predecessors" that enable the event) in a trace is not unique. Unlike [10], we are interested in maximal (w.r.t. $\mapsto$) causality being based on the idea that the cause of an event in a trace should be maximal, in the sense that the cause is not a subset of any other set which is also a cause of the event in the trace. This requirement guarantees the uniqueness of the cause of an event in a trace.

In an asymmetric dual event structure $\mathcal{E}$, let $t \in Traces(\mathcal{E})$ and $W_1 \mapsto e, \ldots,$ $W_m \mapsto e$ ($m \geq 0$) be all bundles pointing to $e \in \overline{t}$. The *0-cause* of e in t, $\lfloor e \rfloor_t^0$, is the singleton $\{e\}$. The *1-cause* of e in t, $\lfloor e \rfloor_t^1$, is a set satisfying the following conditions: (i) each $e' \in \lfloor e \rfloor_t^1$ occurs before e in t, (ii) $W_l \cap \lfloor e \rfloor_t^1 \neq \emptyset$, for all $1 \leq l \leq m$, and (iii) $\lfloor e \rfloor_t^1$ is a maximal (in set-theoretical sense) set satisfying (i) and (ii). Informally speaking, $\lfloor e \rfloor_t^1$ is the set of "immediate predecessors" of e in t. For $k > 0$, define the $k+1$-*cause* of e in t, $\lfloor e \rfloor_t^{k+1}$, as the set $\bigcup_{e' \in \lfloor e \rfloor_t^k} \lfloor e' \rfloor_t^1$. So, the $k + 1$-cause of e in t is a set containing the 1-causes of all the events from the k-cause of e in t. Let l be the first index such that $\lfloor e \rfloor_t^l = \emptyset$. Define the *cause* of the event e in the trace t as the set $\lfloor e \rfloor_t = \bigcup_{j=0}^{l-1} \lfloor e \rfloor_t^j$. Clearly, each event in a trace has a unique cause. Let $\lfloor e \rfloor = \{\lfloor e \rfloor_{t'} \mid t' \in Traces(\mathcal{E})$ and $e \in \overline{t'}\}$ be the *cause* of e.

Example 6: Consider the asymmetric dual event structure $\mathcal{E}_1^{ad}$ over $L = \{a, b,$ $c, d, e, f\}$ with $E_{\mathcal{E}_1^{ad}} = \{a, b, c, d, e, f\}$, $\rightsquigarrow_{\mathcal{E}_1^{ad}} = \emptyset$, $\mapsto_{\mathcal{E}_1^{ad}} = \{(\{b, c\}, a), (\{d\}, a),$ $(\{e\}, c), (\{f\}, b)\}$, and the identity labeling function $l_{\mathcal{E}_1^{ad}}$. The 1-cause of the event a in the trace $t = e f d b c a$ is the set $\lfloor a \rfloor_t^1 = \{b, c, d\}$ and 2-cause of a in t is $\lfloor a \rfloor_t^2 = \{e, f\}$. The cause of a in t is $\lfloor a \rfloor_t = \{a, b, c, d, e, f\}$.

For an asymmetric bundle/dual event structure $\mathcal{E}$ and $t \in Traces(\mathcal{E})$, define the sets:

$$\rightsquigarrow(t) = \{e \in E \backslash imp(\mathcal{E}) \backslash \overline{t} \mid e \rightsquigarrow e' \text{ for some } e' \in \overline{t}\} \quad \text{(strong syntactic conflict)}$$

$$\dagger(t) = \{e \in E \backslash imp(\mathcal{E}) \mid \forall \lfloor e \rfloor_{t'} \in \lfloor e \rfloor : \exists e' \in \lfloor e \rfloor_{t'} \text{ s.t. } e' \in \rightsquigarrow(t))\}$$
$$\text{(weak syntactic conflict)}$$

$$\ddagger(t) = \{e \in E \backslash imp(\mathcal{E}) \mid \nexists t' \in Traces(\mathcal{E}) \text{ s.t. } t \rightarrow t' \wedge e \in \overline{t'}\} \quad \text{(semantic conflict)}$$

We claim that the definitions properly extend those for asymmetric prime event structures:

Lemma 4. *Let $\mathcal{E}$ be an asymmetric bundle/dual event structure and $t \in Traces(\mathcal{E})$. Then $\rightsquigarrow(t) \subseteq \dagger(\sharp) = \ddagger(t)$; and $\rightsquigarrow(t) = \dagger(t) = \ddagger(t)$, if $\mathcal{E}$ is with hereditary conflict.*

Notes on the proof. The inclusion $\rightsquigarrow(t) \subseteq \dagger(t)$ follows directly from the definitions of $\rightsquigarrow(t)$ and $\dagger(t)$, whereas the reasoning, when proving the equality $\dagger(t) = \ddagger(t)$, is more involved and requires, in addition, the examination of the cause of an event in the trace t. The inclusion $\dagger(t) \subseteq \rightsquigarrow(t)$, i.e. if $e \in \dagger(t)$ then $e \in \rightsquigarrow(t)$, can be restated, using the definitions of $\dagger(t)$ and the cause of e, in such a way: if an event e' from the cause of e in some trace t' such that $e' \in \rightsquigarrow(t)$, then $e \in \rightsquigarrow(t)$; but this is possible only in event structures with hereditary conflict.

Let $\mathcal{E}$ be an asymmetric bundle/dual event structure. The equivalence class of $t \in Traces(\mathcal{E})$, $[t]$, is defined in an analogous way as for an asymmetric prime event structure. For $t \in Traces(\mathcal{E})$, determine a removal operator in the following way: $\mathcal{E} \backslash [t] = (E', \rightsquigarrow \cap(E' \times E'), \mapsto', L, l \mid_{E'})$, with $E' = E \backslash (\bar{t} \cup \dagger(t))$ and $\mapsto' = \{(W', e) \mid e \in E', \exists (W, e) \in \mapsto: W' = W \cap E' \text{ and } W \cap \bar{t} = \emptyset\}$. The intuitive interpretation of the above definition is as follows. First, all the events in t and events conflicting with some event in t (i.e. that cannot happen anymore) are removed. Second, each bundle $W \mapsto e$ such that some event in W has already happened in t is removed but each other bundle is retained with the bundle set containing only remaining events. Third, the conflicts between the remaining events are kept. We stress that in the above removal operator, semantic conflict can be used as well. The conflict sets are especially important for models without impossible events.[5] We write $\mathcal{E} \rightarrow_{\bar{t}} \mathcal{E}'$ iff there exists $t \in Traces(\mathcal{E})$ such that $\mathcal{E}' = \mathcal{E} \backslash [t]$.

The lemma below establishes correctness results for the removal operators in the setting of asymmetric prime, bundle and dual event structures. This seems identical to Lemma 2 but it should be stressed that the residuals obtained by the removal operators are, respectively, asymmetric prime, bundle and dual event structures, which do not allow traces that are disallowed by an original asymmetric structure.

---

[5] Notice that in [8], for asymmetric bundle/dual event structures the removal operator has been defined in a different way, without removing conflict sets. All the events in a trace t and bundles $W \mapsto e$ such that $W \cap \bar{t} \neq \emptyset$ are removed. However, the events conflicting with some event in t are retained simply making them impossible by adding empty bundles. There, the removal operator has been formally defined as follows: $\mathcal{E} \backslash [t] = (E', \mapsto', \rightsquigarrow \cap(E' \times E'), L, l \mid_{E'})$, where $E' = E \backslash \bar{t}$ and $\mapsto' = (\mapsto \backslash \{(W, e) \in \mapsto \mid W \cap \bar{t} \neq \emptyset\}) \cup \{(\emptyset, e) \mid e \in E', e \rightsquigarrow e', \text{ for some } e' \in \bar{t}\}$. We say in advance that the "residual" transition systems constructed on the base of the removal operator from [8] and our removal operator are isomorphic. This implies that all bisimilarity results obtained in our paper are valid for event structures treated within the process algebra PA in the work [8].

Lemma 5. *Let $\mathcal{E}$ be an asymmetric prime/bundle/dual event structure.*

(i) *For any $t \in Traces(\mathcal{E})$, $\mathcal{E}' = \mathcal{E}\backslash[t]$ is an asymmetric prime/bundle/dual event structure.*

(ii) *For any $\mathcal{E}' = \mathcal{E}\backslash[t]$ with $t \in Traces(\mathcal{E})$ and $\mathcal{E}'' = \mathcal{E}'\backslash[t']$ with $t' \in Traces(\mathcal{E}')$,*

    (o) *$imp(\mathcal{E}) \subseteq imp(\mathcal{E}')$, if $\mathcal{E}$ is an asymmetric bundle/dual event structure,*

    (a) *$t\,t' \in Traces(\mathcal{E})$,*

    (b) *if $t \to t''$ in $\mathcal{E}$, then $t''\backslash t \in Traces(\mathcal{E}')$,*

    (c) *$\dagger_{\mathcal{E}}(t\,t') = \dagger_{\mathcal{E}}(t) \cup \dagger_{\mathcal{E}'}(t')$,*

    (d) *$\mathcal{E}'' = \mathcal{E}\backslash[t\,t']$.*

Notes on the proof. Items (o) and (c) are auxiliary and needed for the validity of items (a) and (d), while (a), (b), and (d) are crucial for establishing bisimilarities between different kinds of transition systems from asymmetric prime/bundle/dual event structures (see Proposition 2 and Theorem 1).

3 Associating Transition Systems with Event Structures

In this section, we first give some basic definitions concerning labeled transition systems and then deal with two distinct kinds of transition systems associated with an event structure from the classes under consideration. The distinction appears in the choice of the states of the transition systems: either the configurations of the event structure or the residual event structures ("what remains of the event structure" after the computations of its configurations).

A transition system $T = (S, \to, i)$ over a set $\mathcal{L}$ of labels consists of a set of states S, a transition relation $\to \subseteq S \times \mathcal{L} \times S$, and an initial state $i \in S$. Two transition systems over $\mathcal{L}$ are isomorphic if their states can be mapped one-to-one to each other, preserving transitions and initial states.

We call a relation $R \subseteq S \times S'$ a *bisimulation* between transition systems T and T' over $\mathcal{L}$ iff $(i, i') \in R$, and for all $(s, s') \in R$ and $l \in L$: if $(s, l, s_1) \in \to$, then $(s', l, s'_1) \in \to$ and $(s_1, s'_1) \in R$, for some $s'_1 \in S'$; and if $(s', l, s'_1) \in \to$, then $(s, l, s_1) \in \to$ and $(s_1, s'_1) \in R$, for some $s_1 \in S$. A bisimulation R is *backward-forward* iff for all $(s_1, s'_1) \in R$ and $l \in L$: if $(s, l, s_1) \in \to$, then $(s', l, s'_1) \in \to$ and $(s, s') \in R$, for some $s' \in S'$, and if $(s', l, s'_1) \in \to$, then $(s, l, s_1) \in \to$ and $(s, s') \in R$, for some $s \in S$.

Conventions. From now on, we call an event structure $\mathcal{E} \in \mathbb{E}_L^p \cup \mathbb{E}_L^{ap} \cup \mathbb{E}_L^{ab} \cup \mathbb{E}_L^{ad}$ simply an event structure over L. We say that $\mathcal{E}$ is *conflict-free* if its disabling (conflict) relation is empty.

We introduce some auxiliary notation. Let $L_{int} := L$, and $L_{mset} := \mathbb{N}_0^L$ (the set of multisets over L, i.e. functions from L to the non-negative integers), and $L_{pom} := Pom_L$ (the set of isomorphic classes of partial orders labeled over L) be sets of labels.

For an event structure $\mathcal{E}$ over L and a set $X' \subseteq X \in Conf(\mathcal{E})$, we write:

- $l_{int}(X') = a \in L$ iff $X' = \{e\}$ and $l(e) = a$;
- $l_{mset}(X') = M \in \mathbb{N}_0^L$ iff $M(a) = |\{e \in X' \mid l(e) = a\}|$, for all $a \in L$,

− $l_{pom}(X') = \mathcal{Y} \in Pom_L$ iff $\leq_{X'}$ is defined and $\mathcal{Y} = [(X', \leq_{X'} \cap(X' \times X'), \emptyset, l \mid_{X'})]$.

We are ready to define TC-operators of an event structure over L.

Definition 5. *For an event structure* $\mathcal{E}$ *over* L *and* $* \in \{int, pom, mset\}$, $TC_*(\mathcal{E})$ *is the transition system* $(Conf(\mathcal{E}), \rightharpoonup_*, \emptyset)$ *over* L_*, *where* $X \xrightarrow{p}_* X'$ *for* $p \in L_*$ *iff* $X \rightarrow X'$ *and* $p = l_*(X' \backslash X)$, *with* $* \in \{int, mset\}$, *if* $\mathcal{E} \in \mathbb{E}_L^{ad}$, *and with* $* \in \{int, pom\}$, *otherwise.*

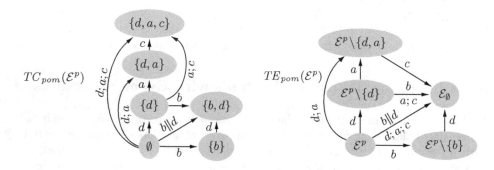

Fig. 3. The transition systems $TC_{pom}(\mathcal{E}^p)$ and $TE_{pom}(\mathcal{E}^p)$

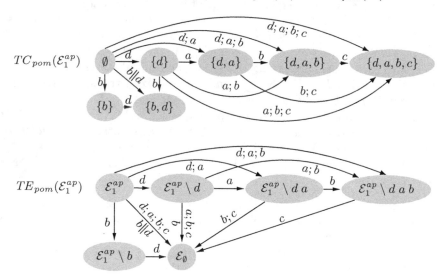

Fig. 4. The transition systems $TC_{pom}(\mathcal{E}_1^{ap})$ and $TE_{pom}(\mathcal{E}_1^{ap})$

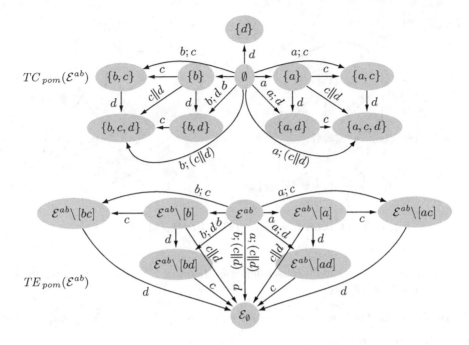

Fig. 5. The transition systems $TC_{pom}(\mathcal{E}^{ab})$ and $TE_{pom}(\mathcal{E}^{ab})$

Example 7: Figures 3, 4, and 5 (left hand sides or upper parts, respectively) show the transition systems $TC_{pom}(\cdot)$ of the event structures $\mathcal{E}^p$, $\mathcal{E}_1^{ap}$, and $\mathcal{E}^{ab}$, respectively, and Fig. 6(l.h.s.) depicts the transition system $TC_{mset}(\mathcal{E}^{ad})$.[6]

We move to the definition of *TE*-operators of an event structure over L.

Definition 6. *For an event structure $\mathcal{E}$ over L and $* \in \{int, pom, mset\}$,*

- $\mathcal{E} \xrightarrow{p}_* \mathcal{E}'$ *iff* $\mathcal{E} \rightarrow_X \mathcal{E}'$ *for some* $X \in Conf(\mathcal{E})$ *and* $p = l_*(X)$*, with* $* \in \{int, mset\}$*, if* $\mathcal{E} \in \mathbb{E}_L^{ad}$*, and with* $* \in \{int, pom\}$*, otherwise.*
- $Reach_*(\mathcal{E}) = \{\mathcal{F} \mid \exists \mathcal{E}_0, \ldots, \mathcal{E}_k \ (k \geq 0) \text{ such that } \mathcal{E}_0 = \mathcal{E}, \ \mathcal{E}_k = \mathcal{F} \text{ and } \mathcal{E}_i \xrightarrow{p}_* \mathcal{E}_{i+1}$ *for some* $p \in L_* \ (i < k)\}.$
- $TE_*(\mathcal{E})$ *is the transition system* $(Reach_*(\mathcal{E}), \rightarrow_*, \mathcal{E})$ *over* L_*.

Example 8: Figures 3, 4, and 5 (lower parts or right-hand sides, respectively) show the transition systems $TE_{pom}(\cdot)$ of the event structures $\mathcal{E}^p$, $\mathcal{E}_1^{ap}$, and $\mathcal{E}^{ab}$, respectively, and Fig. 6(r.h.s.)—the transition system $TE_{mset}(\mathcal{E}^{ad})$. It is easy to see that even $TC_{int}(\cdot)$ and $TE_{int}(\cdot)$, for all our example event structures, are not backward-forward bisimilar.

---

[6] We allow a single arrow between two states to denote multiple transitions. For instance, the arrow from $\mathcal{E}^p$ to $\mathcal{E}_\emptyset$ in $TE_{pom}(\mathcal{E}^p)$ (Fig. 3) denotes two transitions.

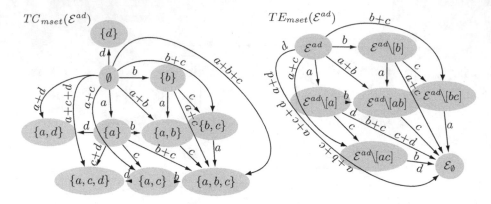

Fig. 6. The transition systems $TC_{mset}(\mathcal{E}^{ad})$ and $TE_{mset}(\mathcal{E}^{ad})$

The following is a direct consequence of Lemma 2 of this paper, together with Lemma 1 of [12].

Proposition 1. *Let $\mathcal{E}$ be a prime event structure, and let $* \in \{int, pom\}$.*

1. $Reach_{int}(\mathcal{E}) = Reach_{pom}(\mathcal{E})$.
2. *For any $X \in Conf(\mathcal{E})$, $\mathcal{E}\backslash X \in Reach_{int}(\mathcal{E})$.*
3. *For any $\mathcal{E}' \in Reach_{int}(\mathcal{E})$, there exists $X \in Conf(\mathcal{E})$ such that $\mathcal{E}' = \mathcal{E}\backslash X$.*
4. *For any $X', X'' \in Conf(\mathcal{E})$, if $X' \overset{P}{\to}_* X''$, then $\mathcal{E}\backslash X' \overset{P}{\to}_* \mathcal{E}\backslash X''$.*
5. *For any $\mathcal{E}', \mathcal{E}'' \in Reach_{int}(\mathcal{E})$, if $\mathcal{E}' \overset{P}{\to}_* \mathcal{E}''$, then there exist $X', X'' \in Conf(\mathcal{E})$ such that $\mathcal{E}' = \mathcal{E}\backslash X'$, $\mathcal{E}'' = \mathcal{E}\backslash X''$, and $X' \overset{P}{\to}_* X''$.*

Proposition 2. *Let $\mathcal{E}$ be an asymmetric prime/bundle/dual event structure, and let $* \in \{int, pom, mset\}$.*

1. $Reach_{int}(\mathcal{E}) = Reach_{mset}(\mathcal{E})$, *if $\mathcal{E} \in \mathbb{E}_L^{ad}$, and $Reach_{int}(\mathcal{E}) = Reach_{pom}(\mathcal{E})$, otherwise.*
2. *For any $t \in Traces(\mathcal{E})$, $\mathcal{E}\backslash[t] \in Reach_{int}(\mathcal{E})$.*
3. *For any $\mathcal{E}' \in Reach_{int}(\mathcal{E})$, there exists $t \in Traces(\mathcal{E})$ such that $\mathcal{E}' = \mathcal{E}\backslash[t]$.*
4. *For any $t', t'' \in Traces(\mathcal{E})$, if $\overline{t'} \overset{P}{\to}_* \overline{t''}$, then $\mathcal{E}\backslash[t'] \overset{P}{\to}_* \mathcal{E}\backslash[t'']$.*
5. *For any $\mathcal{E}', \mathcal{E}'' \in Reach_{int}(\mathcal{E})$, if $\mathcal{E}' \overset{P}{\to}_* \mathcal{E}''$, then there exist $t', t'' \in Traces(\mathcal{E})$ such that $\mathcal{E}' = \mathcal{E}\backslash[t']$, $\mathcal{E}'' = \mathcal{E}\backslash[t'']$, and $\overline{t'} \to_{P_*} \overline{t''}$.*

Notes on the proof. The validity of items (1)–(3) can be proved using Lemma 5ii(a, b, d); the validity of (4) requires Lemma 5ii(a, d); (5) can in turn be deduced from (1) and (3), using also Lemma 5ii(a, d).

More or less directly, Propositions 1 and 2 yield:

Theorem 1. *Given an event structure $\mathcal{E}$ over L and $* \in \{int, pom, mset\}$, $TC_*(\mathcal{E})$ and $TE_*(\mathcal{E})$ are bisimilar, with $* \in \{int, mset\}$, if $\mathcal{E} \in \mathbb{E}_L^{ad}$, and with $* \in \{int, pom\}$, otherwise.*

Corollary 1. *Given a conflict-free event structure $\mathcal{E}$ over L and $* \in \{int, pom, mset\}$, $TC_*(\mathcal{E})$ and $TE_*(\mathcal{E})$ are isomorphic, with $* \in \{int, mset\}$, if $\mathcal{E} \in \mathbb{E}_L^{ad}$, and with $* \in \{int, pom\}$, otherwise.*

Since in asymmetric dual event structures, several pomsets may correspond to a trace, our results in Proposition 2, Theorem 1, and Corollary 1 apply to multisets rather than pomsets.

4   Concluding Remarks

In this paper, we have demonstrated that for asymmetric versions of prime, bundle, and dual event structures, interleaving/pomset/multiset bisimilarity results can be obtained between configuration-based and residual-based transition system semantics. We have defined appropriate formal concepts underlying such results, both for removal operators (necessary for residual semantics), and for conflict sets of events in traces. Because of ambiguity of causality in asymmetric dual event structures, it was especially difficult to understand how to define the cause of an event in a trace needed in a weak syntactic conflict set, while this was more straightforward for asymmetric prime event structures, where causality is given as a partial order in their syntax, and for asymmetric bundle event structures, where partial order based causality can be defined in configurations.

Work on extending our approach to other types of event structures (from extended prime event structures [2] to configuration structures [5]) is under way and will be submitted elsewhere. It will be shown that the conflict set definition given in the present paper can actually be re-used. Our main goal will be to see how the results obtained in [3,5] for configuration-based transition systems can be interpreted in the context of residual-based ones. As shown in [17], the categories of occurrence nets (ONs) of safe Petri nets, prime event structures (PES) and finitary prime algebraic Scott domains are equivalent. Therefore, on the one hand, the results concerning different kinds of transitions systems for PES can be extended to ONs. On the other hand, it is unclear which kinds of domain correspond to residual-based transition systems, and it is worth noting that TE-operators on PES do not evolve into functors from PES to a category of transition systems [12], i.e., do not possess a categorical characterisation [18]. Also, it is a promising open question how our methods of constructing transition systems – even for asymmetric prime event structures – can be used in the context of occurrence contextual nets, because using a left adjoint functor, there is a coreflection (but not an equivalence) between the corresponding categories, as shown in [1].

References

1. Baldan, P., Corradini, A., Montanari, U.: Contextual petri nets, asymmetric event structures, and processes. Inf. Comput. **171**(1), 1–49 (2001)
2. Boudol, G., Castellani, I.: Concurrency and atomicity. Theor. Comput. Sci. **59**, 25–84 (1989)

3. van Glabbeek, R.J.: History preserving process graphs (1995). http://boole. stanford.edu/~rvg/pub/history.draft.dvi
4. van Glabbeek, R.J., Goltz, U.: Refinement of actions and equivalence notions for concurrent systems. Acta Informatica **37**, 229–327 (2001)
5. van Glabbeek, R.J., Plotkin, G.D.: Configuration structures, event structures and petri nets. Theor. Comput. Sci. **410**(41), 4111–4159 (2009)
6. van Glabbeek, R.J., Vaandrager, F.: Bundle event structures and CCSP. In: Amadio, R., Lugiez, D. (eds.) CONCUR 2003. LNCS, vol. 2761, pp. 57–71. Springer, Heidelberg (2003). doi:10.1007/978-3-540-45187-7_4
7. Gutierrez, J., Wooldridge, M.: Equilibria of concurrent games on event structures. In: Proceedings of CSL-LICS 2014, pp. 46:1–46:10 (2014)
8. Katoen, J.-P.: Quantitative and qualitative extensions of event structures. Ph.D. thesis. Twente University (1996)
9. Langerak, R.: Bundle event structures: a non-interleaving semantics for LOTOS. In: Formal Description Techniques V, IFIP Transactions, C-10 (1993)
10. Langerak, R., Brinksma, E., Katoen, J.-P.: Causal ambiguity and partial orders in event structures. In: Mazurkiewicz, A., Winkowski, J. (eds.) CONCUR 1997. LNCS, vol. 1243, pp. 317–331. Springer, Heidelberg (1997). doi:10.1007/3-540-63141-0_22
11. Loogen, R., Goltz, U.: Modelling nondeterministic concurrent processes with event structures. Fundamenta Informatica **XIV**, 39–74 (1991)
12. Majster-Cederbaum, M., Roggenbach, M.: Transition systems from event structures revisited. Inf. Process. Lett. **67**(3), 119–124 (1998)
13. Nielsen, M., Plotkin, G., Winskel, G.: Petri nets, event structures and domains. Theor. Comput. Sci. **13**(1), 85–108 (1981)
14. Nielsen, M., Thiagarajan, P.S.: Regular event structures and finite petri nets: the conflict-free case. In: Esparza, J., Lakos, C. (eds.) ICATPN 2002. LNCS, vol. 2360, pp. 335–351. Springer, Heidelberg (2002). doi:10.1007/3-540-48068-4_20
15. Pinna, G.M., Poigné, A.: On the nature of events: another perspectives in concurrency. Theor. Comput. Sci. **138**(2), 425–454 (1995)
16. Winskel, G.: Events in computation. Ph.D. thesis. University of Edinburgh (1980)
17. Winskel, G.: Event structures. In: Brauer, W., Reisig, W., Rozenberg, G. (eds.) ACPN 1986. LNCS, vol. 255, pp. 325–392. Springer, Heidelberg (1987). doi:10.1007/3-540-17906-2_31
18. Winskel, G., Nielsen, M.: Models for concurrency. In: Handbook of Logic in Computer Science, vol. 4 (1995)
19. Winskel, G.: Distributed probabilistic and quantum strategies. Electron. Notes Theor. Comput. Sci. **298**, 403–425 (2013)

Hardness of Deriving Invertible Sequences from Finite State Machines

Robert M. Hierons[1], Mohammad Reza Mousavi[2], Michael Kirkedal Thomsen[3], and Uraz Cengiz Türker[4(✉)]

[1] Department of Computer Science, Brunel University London, Uxbridge, UK
`rob.hierons@brunel.ac.uk`
[2] School of IT, Center for Research on Embedded Systems (CERES),
Halmstad University, Halmstad, Sweden
`m.r.mousavi@hh.se`
[3] Department of Computer Science, University of Copenhagen,
Copenhagen, Denmark
`m.kirkedal@di.ku.dk`
[4] Computer Engineering, Faculty of Engineering, Gebze Technical University,
Kocaeli, Turkey
`urazc@gtu.edu.tr`

Abstract. Many test generation algorithms use unique input/output sequences (UIOs) that identify states of the finite state machine specification M. However, it is known that UIO checking the existence of UIO sequences is PSPACE-complete. As a result, some UIO generation algorithms utilise what are called invertible sequences; these allow one to construct additional UIOs once a UIO has been found. We consider three optimisation problems associated with invertible sequences: deciding whether there is a (proper) invertible sequence of length at least K; deciding whether there is a set of invertible sequences for state set S' that contains at most K input sequences; and deciding whether there is a single input sequence that defines invertible sequences that take state set S'' to state set S'. We prove that the first two problems are NP-complete and the third is PSPACE-complete. These results imply that we should investigate heuristics for these problems.

1 Introduction

Software testing is an indispensable yet costly part of the development lifecycle and this has led to interest in test automation. Model based testing (MBT) is a high-profile approach to automation. It assumes the presence of a model that represents the abstraction of some aspect of the expected behaviour of the *system under test (SUT)*. The model is usually represented as an extended finite state machine, a finite state machine, or a labelled transition system.

In MBT, it is normal to generate test cases from a given model/specification M. A test case is then applied to M and the response (the expected behaviour) of M is recorded. The test case is then executed on the SUT N and the response

© Springer International Publishing AG 2017
B. Steffen et al. (Eds.): SOFSEM 2017, LNCS 10139, pp. 147–160, 2017.
DOI: 10.1007/978-3-319-51963-0_12

(observed behaviour) is recorded. If the expected behaviour and observed behaviour differ then the tester declares that the SUT failed the test. Otherwise, the tester declares that the SUT passed the test case.

A number of techniques have been developed for generating test cases from an FSM, with this line of research dating back to the seminal papers of Moore [1] and Hennie [2]. Although FSM-based test generation techniques vary, they typically aim to *test transitions*, where a transition is a tuple (s, x, y, s') specifying that if M receives input x when in state s then it moves to s' and outputs y. In order to test a transition τ of SUT N, it is necessary to bring N to a state from which τ can be executed, fire the transition, record its output and decide whether the resultant state of the SUT is the expected state. Most such techniques use *state identification sequences* for the last part of this procedure [2–8]. The most widely used state identification sequences are *distinguishing sequences* (DSs) [9], *unique input output sequences* (UIOs) [10] and *characterising sets* (CSs) [10].

There are two types of DSs. A *Preset Distinguishing Sequence (PDS)* and an *Adaptive Distinguishing Sequence (ADS)* (also known as a *Distinguishing Set* [11]). When applied, DSs lead to different output sequences from the different states of M. One important property of DSs is that it has been known that it is possible to construct test sequences in polynomial time [12].

However, it has been long known that an FSM need not have a DS and instead one might use a UIO for a state s': an input sequence that distinguishes s' from all other states of M but need not distinguish any other pairs of states of M. Although not all FSMs have a UIO for every state, it has been reported that in practice most FSMs do have such UIOs [3] and this has led to the development of many FSM-based test generation methods that use UIOs [3,13–20]. However, the problem of checking the existence of a UIO is PSPACE-hard [21].

A CS is a set of input sequences that distinguish all pairs of states and it has been shown that every minimum FSM has a CS [4,22]. Another appealing aspect of CSs is that one can compute a CS from a given FSM in polynomial time [4,22,23]. However, experiments suggest that the use of CSs can lead to relatively long tests [12].

1.1   Motivation and Problem Statement

When generating test cases from an FSM it is desirable to have techniques that reduce the time spent on deriving state identification sequences and there has thus been work on this problem [6,12,24–26]. One promising method is to use *invertible sequences*[1] [27,28]. Despite this, to our knowledge there is no work that investigates the problem of computing invertible sequences.

In this paper, we first extend the notion of invertibility to sets of states. Then we introduce optimisation problems related to invertible sequences, with

---

[1] An invertible sequence is a walk ρ with the property that if one determines the ending state of ρ then one also determines the starting state of ρ. In the following sections we formally define invertible sequences.

these being motivated by a desire to reduce the cost of generating state identification sequences. Finally, we determine the computational complexity of these problems.

1.2   Structure of the Paper

This paper is organised as follows. Section 2 defines FSMs and the corresponding notation, while Sect. 3 defines invertible sequences and the decision problems in which we are interested. In Sect. 4, we derive the bounds for the three decision problems considered. In Sect. 5, we draw conclusions and discuss possible lines of future work.

2   Preliminaries

In this section, we introduce some terminology related to finite state machines.

Definition 1. *A deterministic FSM is defined by a tuple* $M = (S, s_0, X, Y, \delta, \lambda)$, *where:* $S = \{s_1, s_2, \ldots, s_n\}$ *is the finite set of states;* $s_0 \in S$ *is the initial state;* $X = \{x_1, x_2, \ldots, x_r\}$ *is the finite set of inputs;* $Y = \{y_1, y_2, \ldots, y_v\}$ *is the finite set of outputs (X is disjoint from Y);* $\delta : S \times X \to S$ *is the transition function; and* $\lambda : S \times X \to Y$ *is the output function.*

Throughout this paper, $M = (S, s_0, X, Y, \delta, \lambda)$ denotes an FSM from which test sequences are to be generated. At any given time, M is in a state from S and accepts one input at a time. If an input $x \in X$ is applied when M is in state s then M changes its state to $\delta(s, x)$ and produces output $\lambda(s, x)$. We say that $\tau = (s, x, y, s')$ is a *transition* of M with *starting state* s, *ending state* s', and *label* x/y. The label x/y has *input portion* $(in(x/y))$ x and *output portion* y.

Given sequences $\bar{x}$ and $\bar{x}'$, $\bar{x}\bar{x}'$ denotes the concatenation of $\bar{x}$ and $\bar{x}'$. We use $pre(.)$ $(post(.))$ to denote the set of prefixes (suffixes). Given input/output pairs $x_1/y_1, \ldots, x_k/y_k$ we use $x_1/y_1 \ldots x_k/y_k$ and also $x_1x_2 \ldots x_k/y_1y_2 \ldots y_k$ to denote the corresponding input/output sequence. Further, we let $x_1 \ldots x_k$ and $y_1 \ldots y_k$ denote the *input portion* $(in(x_1/y_1 \ldots x_k/y_k))$ and the *output portion* $(out(x_1/y_1 \ldots x_k/y_k))$ of $x_1/y_1 \ldots x_k/y_k$ respectively.

The transition and output functions are extended to a sequence of inputs as follows, where ε denotes the empty sequence. For $\bar{x} \in X^\star$ and $x \in X$, $\delta(s, \varepsilon) = s$, $\delta(s, x\bar{x}) = \delta(\delta(s, x), \bar{x})$, $\lambda(s, \varepsilon) = \varepsilon$, $\lambda(s, x\bar{x}) = \lambda(s, x)\lambda(\delta(s, x), \bar{x})$.

An FSM can be represented by a directed graph. A vertex represents a state and a directed edge with label x/y that goes from a vertex with label s to a vertex with label s' represents the transition $\tau = (s, x, y, s')$.

Example 1. Figure 1 represents an FSM M_1 with state set $\{s_1, s_2, s_3, s_4\}$, inputs $\{x_1, x_2\}$, and outputs $\{y_1, y_2, y_3\}$.

The behaviour of an FSM M is defined in terms of the labels of walks that leave the initial state of M. A *walk* ω of M is a sequence of consecutive transitions

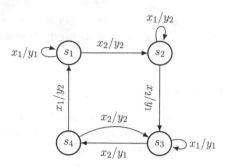

Fig. 1. An FSM M_1

$\omega = (s_1, x_1, y_1, s_2)(s_2, x_2, y_2, s_3) \ldots (s_{k-1}, x_{k-1}, y_{k-1}, s_k)(s_k, x_k, y_k, s_{k+1})$. Walk ω has *starting state* s_1, *ending state* s_{k+1}, and *label* $x_1/y_1 x_2/y_2 \ldots x_k/y_k$. Here $x_1/y_1 x_2/y_2 \ldots x_k/y_k$ is a *trace* of M.

Example 2. For example $\rho = (s_4, x_1, y_2, s_1)(s_1, x_1, y_1, s_1)(s_1, x_2, y_2, s_4)$ is a walk of M_1. The walk ρ has starting state s_4, ending state s_2, and label $x_1/y_2 x_1/y_1 x_2/y_2$. Here $x_1/y_2 x_1/y_1 x_2/y_2$ is a trace of M.

An FSM M defines the language L_M of labels of walks with starting state s_0 and we will use $L_M(s)$ to denote the language defined by making s the initial state of M. More formally, $L_M(s) = \{\bar{x}/\bar{y} | \bar{x} \in X^* \wedge \bar{y} = \lambda(s, \bar{x})\}$. Clearly, $L_M = L_M(s_0)$. Given $S' \subseteq S$, we let $L_M(S')$ denote the set of traces that can be produced if the initial state of M is in S', i.e., $L_M(S') = \cup_{s \in S'} L_M(s)$.

States s and s' of M are *equivalent* if $L_M(s) = L_M(s')$ and FSMs M and N are *equivalent* if $L_M = L_N$. FSM M is *minimal* if there is no equivalent FSM that has fewer states. FSM M is *strongly connected* if for every ordered pair (s, s') of states of M, there is a walk that has starting state s and ending state s'. Note that a strongly connected FSM M is minimal if and only if $L_M(s) \neq L_M(s')$ for all $s, s' \in S$ with $s \neq s'$. Throughout this paper we only consider minimal FSMs. This is not a significant restriction since one can convert an FSM into an equivalent minimal FSM in low order polynomial time [29].

Assumption 1. *We are testing from a minimal FSM $M = (S, s_0, X, Y, \delta, \lambda)$.*

Many test generation techniques use input sequences that identify states.

Definition 2. *An input sequence $\bar{x}$ defines a* unique input output sequence *for s if for all $s' \in S \backslash \{s\}$ we have that $\lambda(s, \bar{x}) \neq \lambda(s', \bar{x})$. Further, $\bar{x}$ defines a UIO for state set $S' \subseteq S$ if $\bar{x}$ defines a UIO for all $s \in S'$.*

3 Invertible Sequences

In this section, we first define invertible sequences. We then discuss optimisation problems with potential impact on MBT related to invertible sequences.

3.1 Definitions

Due to their potential role in test generation, we are interested in walks that are invertible. A walk ρ with input/output label $\bar{x}/\bar{y}$ that has ending state s is an *invertible sequence* for s if no other walk with ending state s has label $\bar{x}/\bar{y}$.

For testing purposes, we may want to find a set of invertible sequences with a common input portion. Given a set Γ, of invertible sequences we use Γ_i (respectively, Γ_o) to denote the set of input (respectively, output) portions of labels of the walks in Γ. We use Γ_{in} (respectively, Γ_{en}) to denote the sets of initial (ending) states of walks in Γ. Let us suppose that S' is a set of states of M. Then we say that Γ is an *invertible sequence for S'* if $\Gamma_i = \{\bar{x}\}$, $S' = \Gamma_{en}$, and all walks in Γ are invertible sequences. An *invertible transition* is an invertible sequence of length one.

Let us assume that we are given an input sequence $\bar{x}$ that defines an invertible sequence for a set of states S'. Consider any partitioning of $\bar{x}$ as $\bar{x} = \bar{x}'\bar{x}''\bar{x}'''$ where $\bar{x}, \bar{x}', \bar{x}'', \bar{x}''' \in X^+$. If $\bar{x}'\bar{x}'''$ also defines an invertible sequence for S' then $\bar{x}$ is called a *redundant invertible sequence* for S'. In this paper, we consider only irredundant invertible sequences. If an invertible sequence is redundant, then it can be replaced by a shorter irredundant invertible sequence.

It has been shown that a suffix of an invertible sequence might not be an invertible sequence but a prefix is; this fact is formally state in the following lemma [27].

Lemma 1. *If $\rho = \rho'\rho''$ is an invertible sequence, then ρ' is an invertible sequence but ρ'' might not be an invertible sequence.*

We now define what it means for an invertible sequence to be proper. We say that invertible sequence ρ is a *proper invertible sequence* for s, if every suffix ρ' of ρ is also an invertible sequence for s. An immediate consequence of the definition of an invertible and an proper invertible sequence is that every proper invertible sequence is an invertible sequence but an invertible sequence need not be proper.

3.2 Invertible Sequences in Test Generation

It has been shown that invertible sequences can be used to extend the set of UIOs [27].

Lemma 2 *(From [27]). If $\bar{x}/\bar{y}$ is a UIO for state s and $\rho = \bar{x}'/\bar{y}'$ is an invertible sequence for s starting from s' then $\bar{x}'\bar{x}/\bar{y}'\bar{y}$ is a UIO for s'.*

It should be noted that as every suffix of a proper invertible sequence ρ for s is a proper invertible sequence for s, a UIO for s can be used to compute a UIO for every state that a proper invertible sequence ρ visits.

Lemma 3. *Let $\bar{x}/\bar{y}$ be a UIO for state s, ρ be a proper invertible sequence for s and also let $\psi = \{(s', \rho')|s' \in S, \rho' \in post(\rho) \text{ and } s' \text{ is the initial state of } \rho'\}$ be the set of pairs of suffixes of ρ and states from which they originate, then for each pair (s', ρ') in ψ, $in(\rho')\bar{x}/out(\rho')\bar{y}$ is a UIO for s'.*

This result suggests that in computing UIOs, longer proper invertible sequences are desirable, because longer invertible sequence lead to the derivation of more UIOs.[2] Therefore we investigated the following problem.

Definition 3. *Longest proper invertible sequence (LPIS): Let M be an FSM and also let s be a state of M. The LPIS problem is to decide whether there is a proper invertible sequence ρ for s such that $|in(\rho)| \geq K$.*

In the next section, we show that the LPIS problem is NP-complete.

Assume that for a given set of states S', we have computed a state identifying sequence and this time our aim is to derive state identification sequences for a specific set of states S'' without actually computing them. Due to Lemma 3, this can be achieved by using invertible sequences. However in order to reduce the memory/test cost spend on the test sequences, we want to compute a *preset* input sequence that takes S'' to S'. These requirements lead us to the following problem definition.

Definition 4. *Preset reaching set invertible sequence (PRSIS): Let M be an FSM and also let S' and S'' be sets of states of M of cardinality K. The PRSIS problem is to decide whether there are invertible sequences with common input portion $\bar{x}$ for S' such that $\bar{x}$ takes S'' to S'.*

In the next section we show that the PRSIS problem is PSPACE-complete.

The following problem is also motivated by the fact that in some cases we want to derive as many state identification sequences as possible from those already computed. In other words, we would like to find a set of invertible sequences to derive state identification sequences. However, considering the similar motivation as PRSIS problem, we are looking for invertible sequences with a minimum number of input portions.[3]

Definition 5. *Minimum spanning invertible sequence (MINSIS): Let M be an FSM and also let S' be a set of states of M. The MINSIS problem is to decide whether there is a set Γ of invertible sequences for S' where $|\Gamma_i| \leq K$ such that for all $s \in S \setminus S'$ there exists an invertible sequence in Γ that takes s to a state $s' \in S'$.*

We show that the MINSIS problem is NP-complete.

4   Complexity Results

We show that the LPIS problem is NP-complete by providing a polynomial time reduction from the longest path problem (LPP) [30] to the LPIS problem. An instance of the LPP can be defined as follows, where a path[4] ($\mathcal{P}$) is said to *visit* a vertex v, if v is the starting vertex or the ending vertex of an edge in the path and the length of a path is the number of edges in the path.

---

[2] Recall that we restrict attention to invertible sequences that are not redundant.

[3] Recall that Γ_i is the set of input portions of labels of the walks in Γ.

[4] A path is a sequence of consecutive edges that, between them, do not visit any vertex more than once.

Definition 6. *Longest path problem (LPP):* *Consider a strongly connected directed graph $G = (V, E)$ with vertex set $V = \{v_1, v_2, \ldots, v_n\}$, edge set $E = \{e_1, e_2, \ldots, e_m\}$ and a positive integer $K < n$. The longest path problem for (G, K) is to decide whether there exists a path of G that visits at least K vertices.*

Let $out(v)$ be the number of outgoing edges of a vertex v. We let the *out-degree $(Out(G))$* of the graph G be the maximum value of $out(v)$ for G i.e., $Max(\{out(v) | v \in V\})$.

Given an instance of the LPP (G, K), we construct an FSM $M(G) = (S, s_0, X, Y, \delta, \lambda)$. Our aim is to arrange the transition structure of $M(G)$ in such a way that an invertible sequence of length K defines a solution to the LPP. We now show how we construct $M(G)$.

For each vertex of G we introduce a corresponding state of $M(G)$ and we copy over the edge structure; if there is an edge from vertex v, represented by state s, to vertex v', represented by state s', then there is a transition from s to s'. We also introduce an additional special state $s_\star$. Then for each transition, we assign a unique integer i in the range $[1, |E|]$ and use it as the output label (y_i) of the corresponding transition in $M(G)$. In other words, the label of each transition in $M(G)$ will have a unique output portion.

The cardinality of the input alphabet of $M(G)$ is $Out(G)$, i.e., $X = \{x_1, x_2, \ldots, x_{Out(G)}\}$, for some arbitrary, yet pairwise distinct, $x_1, x_2, \ldots, x_{Out(G)}$. If s is a state of FSM $M(G)$ and the number of outgoing transitions is ℓ, then for each transition leaving s, we pick a unique element from the first ℓ elements of X (i.e., we pick an element from $\{x_1, x_2, \ldots, x_\ell\}$) and assign this symbol as the input label of the corresponding transition. Note that different states may have different numbers of outgoing edges, therefore the constructed $M(G)$ could be partial. We complete the missing transitions of state s_i by adding transitions to $s_\star$ with output y_i. We introduce a distinct input symbol $\star$ such that from every state s_i of $M(G)$, there exists a transition to $s_\star$ with common output y_i (see Fig. 2). Finally, all transitions from $s_\star$ are self-loop transitions with output 0.

We now show how the longest path for a connected graph G relates to the LPIS problem for $M(G)$.

Proposition 1. *The longest path problem instance (G, K) has a solution if and only if state $s_\star$ of $M(G)$ has a proper invertible sequence ρ of length $K + 1$.*

Theorem 1. *The LPIS problem is* NP-complete.

We now show that MINSIS problem is NP-complete by a reduction from the minimum covering problem (MCP) [30].

Definition 7. *Minimum covering problem (MCP):* *Consider a set of elements $U = \{1, 2, \ldots, u\}$, a set of sets of elements $\mathcal{I} = \{I_1, I_2, \ldots, I_\mathcal{I}\}$ ($I_i \subseteq U$ for all $1 \leq i \leq \mathcal{I}$), and an integer K. The minimum covering problem is to decide whether there is a subset of $\mathcal{I}$ that contains at most K sets whose union is U.*

We show how FSM $M(U, \mathcal{I}, K)$ can be constructed such that the MCP problem for (U, I, K) corresponds to the MINSIS problem for $M(U, \mathcal{I}, K)$. For every

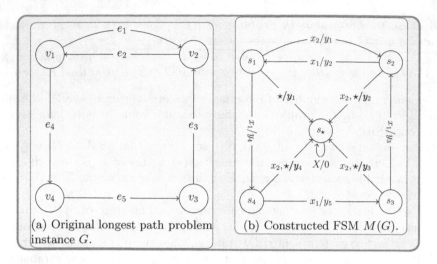

(a) Original longest path problem instance G.

(b) Constructed FSM $M(G)$.

Fig. 2. Construction of an FSM from a given longest path problem instance.

$I_i \in U$, we introduce a single state s_i and, in addition, we introduce a special state $s^\star$. For every set I_j in $\mathcal{I}$, we introduce an input symbol x_j and an output symbol y_j. We also introduce a distinct output 0. The transition and output functions of $M(U, \mathcal{I}, K)$ are then defined as follows:

$$\delta(s_i, x_j) = \begin{cases} s_\star, & \text{if } i \in I_j \\ s_i, & \text{otherwise} \end{cases}$$

$$\lambda(s_i, x_j) = \begin{cases} y_i, & \text{if } i \in I_j \\ 0, & \text{otherwise} \end{cases}$$

The construction ends by setting $S' = \{s_\star\}$. Please see Fig. 3 for an example.

Proposition 2. *The minimum covering problem instance $(G, \mathcal{I}, K)$ has a solution if and only if $S' = \{s_\star\}$ of $M(U, \mathcal{I}, K)$ has a minimum spanning invertible sequence Γ with $|\Gamma_i| \leq K$.*

Theorem 2. *The MINSIS problem is* NP-complete.

We show that the PRSIS problem is PSPACE-complete by a reduction from the finite automata intersection problem (FA INT), which was introduced by Kozen [31]. In the FA INT problem we are given a set of *regular* automata with a common alphabet and our aim is to decide whether the automata accept a common word. A regular automaton is defined as follows.

Definition 8. *A regular automaton is defined by 5-tuple $A = (Q, \Sigma, h, 0_A, F)$ where Q, Σ, h are a finite set of states, a finite set of inputs and a transition function, respectively. $0_A \in Q$ is the* initial state *and $F \subseteq Q$ is the set of* accepting *state. Automaton A accepts a word $w \in \Sigma^\star$ if $h(0_A, w) \in F$.*

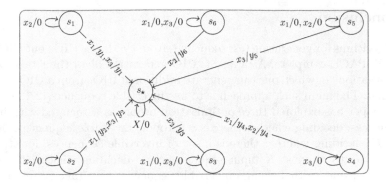

Fig. 3. Construction of a FSM $M(U, \mathcal{I}, K)$ from a given minimum covering problem instance $U = \{1, 2, 3, 4, 5, 6\}$, $\mathcal{I} = \{\{1, 2, 4\}, \{3, 4, 6\}, \{1, 2, 5\}\}$ and $K = 2$.

Definition 9. *Let $\mathbb{A} = \{A_1, A_2, \ldots, A_z\}$ be a set of regular automata with a common alphabet Σ. The FA INT problem is to determine whether there is a word w such that $w \in L(A_i)$ for all $1 \leq i \leq z$.*[5]

We show that the PRSIS problem is PSPACE-complete. We first show how we construct an FSM from a given instance of the FA INT problem.

Without loss of generality, we assume that the finite automata in $\mathbb{A}$ have disjoint sets of states. Given an instance of the FA INT problem defined by set $\mathbb{A} = \{A_1, A_2, \ldots, A_z\}$ of finite automata on common finite alphabet Σ ($A_i = (Q_i, \Sigma, h_i, 0_i, F_i)$), we construct an FSM $M(\mathbb{A}) = (S, s_0, X, Y, \delta, \lambda)$ as follows.

We copy the states of each automaton $A_i = (Q_i, \Sigma, \delta_i, 0_i, C_i)$ and given $q_j \in Q_i$ we let s_j denote the corresponding state in S. For each A_i we also introduce an additional state $\star_i$. The input alphabet of the FSM is given by $X = \Sigma \cup \{f, f'\}$ and the output alphabet of the FSM is given by $Y = \{0, 1, 2, \ldots, z\}$. The state transitions of the finite automata in $\mathbb{A}$ are inherited: if $a \in \Sigma$ and $q_j \in Q_i$ for $1 \leq i \leq z$ and $1 \leq j \leq |Q_i|$ then $\delta(s_j, a) = s_k$ if $h_i(q_j, a) = q_k$. In a state of the form $\star_i$, an input from Σ leads to no change in state and output 0.

Each transition with input $x \in \Sigma$ produces output 0. For each $\star_i$, we introduce a transition from $\star_i$ to 0_i with label f/i; all other transitions with input f have output 0. We also introduce states $s_1^F, s_2^F, \ldots, s_z^F$ and input f'; the input of f' in a state from F_i leads to state s_i^F and the input of f' when the FSM is in a state from some $Q_i \backslash F_i$ leads to state $\star_1$. The input of f' always leads to output 0.

Finally we set $S'' = \{\star_1, \star_2, \ldots, \star_z\}$ and $S' = \{s_1^F, s_2^F, \ldots, s_z^F\}$.

Theorem 3. *PRSIS problem is* PSPACE-complete.

---

[5] Note that in some cases the initial state of each automaton is an accepting state. Clearly, for such cases an empty input sequence defines a solution to the FA INT problem instance, hence we do not consider such cases.

5   Conclusion

Many algorithms for generating test sequences from FSMs use UIOs but UIO existence is PSPACE-complete. As a result, UIO generation algorithms take advantage of situations in which one can generate additional UIOs from a UIO that has been found. The main such approach is to use invertible sequences [27, 28].

This paper has explored three optimisation problems associated with invertible sequences: deciding whether there is a (proper) invertible sequence of length at least K; deciding whether there is a set of invertible sequences, for state set S', that contains at most K input sequences; and deciding whether there is a single input sequence that defines invertible sequences that take state set S'' to state set S'. We proved that the first two problems are NP-complete and the third is PSPACE-complete.

There are several lines of future work. First, in practice we might have an upper bound on the length of an invertible sequence that is of interest; there is the problem of deciding whether the complexity results change if one incorporates such an upper bound. It would also be interesting to use experiments to explore properties of invertible sequences and UIOs. Finally, there is potential to use invertible sequences in generating other types of tests that distinguish states of an FSM. One might, for example, consider problems associated with generating adaptive distinguishing sequences for an FSM or a given set of states of an FSM.

Acknowledgments. This work is supported by the COST Action under Grant #IC1405.

Appendix

Lemma 3. *Let $\bar{x}/\bar{y}$ be a UIO for state s, ρ be a proper invertible sequence for s and also let $\psi = \{(s', \rho')|s' \in S, \rho' \in post(\rho) \text{ and } s' \text{ is the initial state of } \rho'\}$ be the set of pairs of suffixes of ρ and states from which they originate, then for each pair (s', ρ') in ψ, $in(\rho')\bar{x}/out(\rho')\bar{y}$ is a UIO for s'.*

Proof. We use proof by contradiction. Let ψ be the set of pairs of suffixes and states of some invertible sequence ρ for state s. Consider a pair (s', ρ') and let us suppose that $in(\rho')\bar{x}/out(\rho')\bar{y}$ is not a UIO for s'. This implies that there exists a state $s'' \neq s'$ such that there exists a walk from s'' labeled with input/output sequence $in(\rho')\bar{x}/out(\rho')\bar{y}$. Now consider the state s''' reached from s'' with walk $in(\rho')/out(\rho')$. As the underlying FSM is deterministic we have two options:

– we have $s''' = s$,
– or we have $s''' \in S\backslash\{s\}$.

In the first case, ρ' cannot be an invertible sequence. Otherwise, if the second case holds, then $\bar{x}/\bar{y}$ cannot be a UIO for s. The result thus follows.   □

Proposition 1. *The longest path problem instance (G, K) has a solution if and only if state $s_\star$ of $M(G)$ has a proper invertible sequence ρ of length $K + 1$.*

Proof. First we prove that if G has a path $\mathcal{P} = e_1 e_2 \ldots e_K$ of length K, then $M(G)$ has a proper invertible sequence for $s_\star$ whose input portion has length $K + 1$. First note that for every vertex and edge of G there exists a state and a transition in $M(G)$ respectively. Let $\rho = x_1/y_1 x_2/y_2 \ldots x_K/y_K$ be the label of the walk corresponding to $\mathcal{P}$. Since every transition of $M(G)$ is labelled with unique input/output values, $\rho = x_1/y_1 x_2/y_2 \ldots x_K/y_K$ defines an invertible sequence for a state of $M(G)$. Finally, if we concatenate ρ with some $\rho' = \star/y_j$, which is the label of a walk that starts from the ending state of walk ρ, then $\rho'' = \rho\rho'$ defines an invertible sequence for $s_\star$.

Now assume that $s_\star$ has a proper invertible sequence $\rho = x_1/y_1 x_2/y_2 \ldots x_{K+1}/y_{K+1}$ of length $K + 1$ and we are required to prove that G has a path of length K. Note that since ρ is an invertible sequence for $s_\star$, the last input/output pair belongs to a transition that takes $M(G)$ to state $s_\star$. Besides, since ρ is a proper invertible sequence, the first K symbols of the input portion of ρ should visit $K+1$ different states of $M(G)$. Since for every state and transition of $M(G)$, there exists a corresponding vertex and edge in G, the first K inputs of ρ define a path of G with length K. Thus the result follows. $\qquad\square$

Theorem 1. *The LPIS problem is NP-complete.*

Proof. We first show that the LPIS problem is in NP. A non-deterministic Turing machine can guess an input sequence $\bar{x}$ of length K. It can then apply $\bar{x}$ to every state and record the resultant output sequence and state reached. Afterwards, it can compare the outputs to decide whether $\bar{x}$ defines an invertible sequence for a specific state s.

The problem is NP-hard due to Proposition 1 and the fact that the longest path problem with directed graphs is NP-hard. Therefore the result follows. $\qquad\square$

Proposition 2. *The minimum covering problem instance $(G, \mathcal{I}, K)$ has a solution if and only if $S' = \{s_\star\}$ of $M(U, \mathcal{I}, K)$ has a minimum spanning invertible sequence Γ with $|\Gamma_i| \leq K$.*

Proof. First we prove that if $U, \mathcal{I}, K$ has a minimum covering $\mathcal{I}' = \{I_1, I_2, \ldots, I_K\}$ then $M(U, \mathcal{I}, K)$ has a set of invertible sequences Γ for $S' = \{s_\star\}$ such that $\Gamma_i = \{x_1, x_2, \ldots, x_K\}$. Note that the transitions and output functions of the FSM $M(U, \mathcal{I}, K)$ dictates that for a given input x_i and output y_j pair, there exists at most one transition with ending state $s^\star$ and label x_i/y_j. Therefore, each transition with ending state $s_\star$ is an invertible transition and hence there is a set Γ of invertible sequences that take M from $S\backslash\{s_\star\}$ to $s_\star$. Further, for every set I_i in $\mathcal{I}$ there exists a single corresponding input symbol x_i and so $\Gamma_i = \{x_1, \ldots, x_K\}$. Thus, Γ defines a spanning invertible sequence for S' with $|\Gamma_i| = K$ as required.

Now we assume that $S' = \{s_\star\}$ has a maximum spanning invertible sequence Γ such that $|\Gamma_i| = K$ and we are required to prove that U has a minimum covering with at most K sets. First note that as we only consider invertible sequences that are not redundant, the length of each input sequence in set Γ_i is one. Let $\Gamma_i = \{\bar{x}_1, \bar{x}_2, \ldots, \bar{x}_K\}$. Therefore, there is a set $\mathcal{I}' = \{I_1, I_2, \ldots, I_K\}$ of sets derived from Γ_I. The result thus follows. $\qquad\square$

Theorem 2. *The MINSIS problem is* NP-complete.

Proof. The proof of being in NP is almost similar to that of Theorem 1. However this time Turing machine should guess at most K input sequences. The problem is NP-hard due to Proposition 2, thus the result follows.   □

Theorem 3. *PRSIS problem is* PSPACE-complete.

Proof. We first show that the PRSIS problem is in PSPACE. The working principle of the Turing machine for the PRSIS problem is as follows. First note that a non-deterministic Turing machine $\mathcal{T}$ can take S'' to S' input by input as follows: Let w be the sequences of inputs guessed by $\mathcal{T}$ so far, and $\mathcal{T}$ guesses an input x. After this point $\mathcal{T}$ applies x to states $\delta(S'', w)$. $\mathcal{T}$ should then check whether (a) $\delta(S'', wx) = S'$, and (b) For all $s \in S''$ and $s' \in S$, if $\delta(s, wx) = \delta(s', wx)$ then $\lambda(s, wx) \neq \lambda(s', wx)$ If these three conditions hold $\mathcal{T}$ returns at accepting state. Otherwise it returns at rejecting state.

To achieve this $\mathcal{T}$ maintains (and updates on each iteration) the following information (given input sequence w): (1) a partition D of S'' saying which pairs of states from S'' are not distinguished by w. (2) For each state $s \in S''$, the pair (s', S''') where: $s' = \delta(s, w)$ is the current state corresponding to s and S''' is the set of current states from states in $S \backslash S''$ that are not distinguished from s. Thus $S''' = \{\delta(s'', w) | s'' \in S \backslash S'' \wedge \lambda(s, w) = \lambda(s'', w)\}$

Clearly, it is straightforward to update this information if we extend w to wx (guessing x). It is also easy to spot when one should not extend further by x (either the current states reached from states of S'' not distinguished by w 'converge' or there is some (s', S''') such that s' and a state from S''' 'converge').

The above can clearly be stored in polynomial space. In addition to the terminating conditions mentioned above, $\mathcal{T}$ should terminate when the upper bound is reached. First note that the number of possible values for a pair (s', S''') is bounded above by $n.2^n$ and so the number of possible such pairs is bounded above by: $(n2^n)^K = n^K.2^{nK}$. Second, initially D contains K sets. The only way we can change D is by merging two or more sets, with this reducing the number of sets in D. Thus, the value of D can change at most $K - 1$ times.

Therefore the upper bound for the PRSIS is $(K-1).n^K.2^{(nK)}$. Note that this information can be stored in polynomial space, i.e. $O(log((K - 1).n^K.2^{(nK)})) = O(log(K - 1) + Klog(n) + nKlog(2))$ space and the Turing machine $\mathcal{T}$ can hold a counter and increment this by one after an input is guessed. Therefore when the value stored in the counter exceeds the upper bound value, $\mathcal{T}$ terminates.

Therefore, the entire search in this way can be performed in NPSPACE. Based on Savitch's Theorem [32], the PRSIS problem is in PSPACE as required.

Now we prove that if the automata accept a common word $w \in \Sigma$ then $M(\mathbb{A})$ has an invertible sequence that takes S'' to S'. Clearly the application of fwf' from a state of S'' brings $M(\mathbb{A})$ to one of states in S'. As the output produced as a response to input f is unique, fwf' is a PRSIS for S' as required.

Now we assume that there are invertible sequences with common input sequence $\bar{x}$ that take S'' to S' and we are required to prove that there is a common element for the automata in $\mathbb{A}$. Note since $\bar{x}$ takes S'' to S', the input sequence $\bar{x}$ should contain at least one f and must end with f'. Let $\bar{x}'f'$ be the suffix of $\bar{x}$ after the first input f. After the application of f, the FSM is in a state that corresponds to an initial state of the corresponding automaton. Since $\bar{x}$ takes S'' to S', $\bar{x}'f'$ must takes set $\delta(S'', f)$ to S' and so $\bar{x}$ must take initial states of the A_i to final states. The result thus follows setting $w = \bar{x}$. □

References

1. Moore, E.P.: Gedanken-experiments. In: Shannon, C., McCarthy, J. (eds.) Automata Studies. Princeton University Press (1956)
2. Hennie, F.C.: Fault-detecting experiments for sequential circuits. In: Proceedings of Fifth Annual Symposium on Switching Circuit Theory and Logical Design, Princeton, New Jersey, pp. 95–110, November 1964
3. Aho, A.V., Dahbura, A.T., Lee, D., Uyar, M.U.: An optimization technique for protocol conformance test generation based on UIO sequences and rural chinese postman tours. IEEE Trans. Commun. **39**(11), 1604–1615 (1991)
4. Chow, T.S.: Testing software design modelled by finite state machines. IEEE Trans. Soft. Eng. **4**, 178–187 (1978)
5. Hierons, R.M., Ural, H.: Generating a checking sequence with a minimum number of reset transitions. Autom. Softw. Eng. **17**(3), 217–250 (2010)
6. Ural, H., Zhu, K.: Optimal length test sequence generation using distinguishing sequences. IEEE/ACM Trans. Network. **1**(3), 358–371 (1993)
7. Luo, G.L., von Bochmann, G., Petrenko, A.: Test selection based on communicating nondeterministic finite-state machines using a generalized Wp-method. IEEE Trans. Softw. Eng. **20**(2), 149–161 (1994)
8. Petrenko, A., Yevtushenko, N., von Bochmann, G.: Testing deterministic implementations from nondeterministic FSM specifications. In: Baumgarten, B., Burkhardt, H.-J., Giessler, A. (eds.) IFIP TC6 9th International Workshop on Testing of Communicating Systems, Darmstadt, Germany, 9–11 September 1996, pp. 125–141. Chapman and Hall (1996)
9. Gill, A.: Introduction to The Theory of Finite State Machines. McGraw-Hill, New York (1962)
10. Kohavi, Z.: Switching and Finite State Automata Theory. McGraw-Hill, New York (1978)
11. Boute, R.T.: Distinguishing sets for optimal state identification in checking experiments. IEEE Trans. Comput. **23**, 874–877 (1974)
12. Ural, H., Wu, X., Zhang, F.: On minimizing the lengths of checking sequences. IEEE Trans. Comput. **46**(1), 93–99 (1997)
13. Aho, A.V., Dahbura, A.T., Lee, D., Uyar, M.U.: An optimization technique for protocol conformance test generation based on UIO sequences and rural chinese postman tours. In: Protocol Specification, Testing, and Verification VIII, pp. 75–86. Elsevier (North-Holland), Atlantic City (1988)
14. Chan, W.Y.L., Vuong, C.T., Otp, M.R.: An improved protocol test generation procedure based on UIOs. SIGCOMM Comput. Commun. Rev. **19**(4), 283–294 (1989)
15. Chen, W.-H., Ural, H.: Synchronizable test sequences based on multiple UIO sequence. IEEE/ACM Trans. Netw. **3**(2), 152–157 (1995)
16. Guyot, S., Ural, H.: Synchronizable checking sequences based on UIO sequences. In: Protocol Test Systems, VIII, Evry, France, September 1995, pp. 385–397. Chapman and Hall (1995)

17. Motteler, H., Chung, A., Sidhu, D.: Fault coverage of UIO-based methods for protocol testing. In: Proceedings of Protocol Test Systems VI, pp. 21–33 (1994)
18. Ramalingam, T., Thulasiraman, K., Das, A.: A generalization of the multiple UIO method of test sequence selection for protocols represented in FSM. In: The 7th International workshop on Protocol Test Systems, Japan, pp. 209–224. Chapman and Hall (1994)
19. Ural, H., Wang, Z.: Synchronizable test sequence generation using UIO sequences. Comput. Commun. **16**(10), 653–661 (1993)
20. Vuong, S.T., Chan, W.W.L., Ito, M.R.: The UIOv-method for protocol test sequence generation. In: The 2nd International Workshop on Protocol Test Systems, Berlin (1989)
21. Lee, D., Yannakakis, M.: Testing finite-state machines: state identification and verification. IEEE Trans. Comput. **43**(3), 306–320 (1994)
22. Vasilevskii, M.P.: Failure diagnosis of automata. Cybernetics **4**, 653–665 (1973)
23. Hierons, R.M., Türker, U.C.: Parallel algorithms for generating harmonised state identifiers, characterising sets (accepted). IEEE Trans. Softw. Eng. (2016)
24. Gonenc, G.: A method for the design of fault detection experiments. IEEE Trans. Comput. **19**, 551–558 (1970)
25. Hierons, R.M., Ural, H.: Optimizing the length of checking sequences. IEEE Trans. Comput. **55**, 618–629 (2006)
26. Hierons, R.M., Ural, H.: Reduced length checking sequences. IEEE Trans. Comput. **51**(9), 1111–1117 (2002)
27. Hierons, R.M.: Extending test sequence overlap by invertibility. Comput. J. **39**(4), 325–330 (1996)
28. Naik, K.: Efficient computation of unique input/output sequences in finite-state machines. IEEE/ACM Trans. Netw. **5**(4), 585–599 (1997)
29. Hopcroft, J.E.: An n log n algorithm for minimizing the states in a finite automaton. In: Kohavi, Z. (ed.) The Theory of Machines and Computation, pp. 189–196. Academic Press, New York (1971)
30. Garey, M.R., Johnson, D.S.: Computers and Intractability. W.H. Freeman and Company, New York (1979)
31. Kozen, D.: Lower bounds for natural proof systems. In: Proceedings of the 18th Annual Symposium on Foundations of Computer Science, SFCS 1977, pp. 254–266. IEEE Computer Society, Washington (1977)
32. Savitch, W.J.: Relationships between nondeterministic and deterministic tape complexities. J. Comput. Syst. Sci. **4**(2), 177–192 (1970)

Petri Nets, Games and Relaxed Data Structures

A Graph-Theoretical Characterisation
of State Separation

Eike Best[1], Raymond Devillers[2]([✉]), and Uli Schlachter[1]

[1] Department of Computing Science, Carl von Ossietzky Universität Oldenburg,
26111 Oldenburg, Germany
{eike.best,uli.schlachter}@informatik.uni-oldenburg.de
[2] Département d'Informatique, Université Libre de Bruxelles,
Boulevard du Triomphe - C.P. 212, 1050 Bruxelles, Belgium
rdevil@ulb.ac.be

Abstract. Region theory, as initiated by Ehrenfeucht and Rozenberg, allows the characterisation of the class of Petri net synthesisable finite labelled transition systems. Regions are substructures of a transition system which come in two varieties: ones solving event/state separation problems, and ones solving state separation problems. Linear inequation systems can be used in order to check the solvability of these separation problems. In the present paper, the class of finite labelled transition systems in which all state separation problems are solvable shall be characterised graph-theoretically, rather than linear-algebraically.

Keywords: Cyclic behaviour · Labelled transition systems · Persistent systems · System synthesis

1   Introduction

The linear algebra-based synthesis algorithm described in [1] allows to check whether a given edge-labelled transition system is isomorphic to the state graph of an unlabelled Petri net, and if so, to construct such a net. In this algorithm, the computational onus is on solving state separation problems, because their number is quadratic in the size of the state set, and the set of states tends to be very large, as compared with the set of edge labels.

It may therefore be interesting to characterise the solvability of state separation problems in a linear algebra-independent way. The present paper describes a purely graph-theoretical characterisation. Based on a generalised notion of paths and cycles, an exact condition for a transition system to have only solvable state separation problems shall be presented. We shall also investigate how such systems look like in the special, but interesting, case of persistent systems.

U. Schlachter—Supported by DFG (German Research Foundation) through grant Be 1267/15-1 ARS (Algorithms for Reengineering and Synthesis).

© Springer International Publishing AG 2017
B. Steffen et al. (Eds.): SOFSEM 2017, LNCS 10139, pp. 163–175, 2017.
DOI: 10.1007/978-3-319-51963-0_13

The structure of the paper is as follows: after recalling some notions about labelled transition systems and about regions in Sects. 2 and 3, Sect. 4 presents our graph-theoretical characterisation, and Sect. 5 develops the persistent case. Finally some concluding remarks are presented in Sect. 6.

2   Labelled Transition Systems

A labelled transition system can be understood as an edge-labelled directed graph. In this paper, we shall make use both of directed and of general (not necessarily directed) paths in such a graph. We shall call the latter *generalised* paths, and we shall employ the prefix "g-" (thus: g-paths, or g-cycles) in order to emphasise their use. If *directed* paths are meant, as a special case, we shall use the prefix "d-" (thus: d-paths, or d-cycles) explicitly.

Definition 1. LTS, PATHS, REACHABILITY
A labelled transition system with initial state, abbreviated lts, is a quadruple $TS = (S, \rightarrow, T, \imath)$ where S is a set of *states*, T is a set of *labels*, $\rightarrow \subseteq (S \times T \times S)$ is the *transition relation*, and $\imath \in S$ is an *initial state*. Let $\overleftarrow{T}$ be a copy of T:

$$\overleftarrow{T} = \{\overleftarrow{t} \mid t \in T\}, \text{ with } T \cap \overleftarrow{T} = \emptyset; \text{ and also define } \overleftarrow{\overleftarrow{t}} = t \text{ for all } t \in T$$

A *g-path* (*d-path*) is a sequence $\sigma \in (T \cup \overleftarrow{T})^*$ (respectively, $\sigma \in T^*$), where $*$ denotes the Kleene star. For $s, s' \in S$, a g-path $\sigma = a_1 \ldots a_m$ *leads from s to s'* (denoted by $s[\sigma\rangle s'$) if

$$\exists r_0, r_1, \ldots, r_m \in S: \ s = r_0 \ \wedge \ r_m = s' \ \wedge$$
$$\forall j \in \{1, \ldots, m\}: \begin{cases} (r_{j-1}, a_j, r_j) \in \rightarrow & \text{if } a_j \in T \\ (r_j, \overleftarrow{a_j}, r_{j-1}) \in \rightarrow & \text{if } a_j \in \overleftarrow{T} \end{cases}$$

That is, $s[\sigma\rangle s'$ contains all t-edges of σ ($t \in T$) in forward direction, and all $\overleftarrow{t}$-edges in backward direction. (Note that $s[\varepsilon\rangle s'$ is tantamount to $s = s'$.) We can extend the back-arrow notation to sequences in $(T \cup \overleftarrow{T})^*$ inductively as follows:

$$\overleftarrow{\varepsilon} = \varepsilon \text{ and } \overleftarrow{\sigma a} = \overleftarrow{a}\,\overleftarrow{\sigma}, \text{ for } a \in T \cup \overleftarrow{T} \text{ and } \sigma \in (T \cup \overleftarrow{T})^*$$

(Then $s[\sigma\rangle s'$ if and only if $s'[\overleftarrow{\sigma}\rangle s$.)
A d-path $\sigma \in T^*$ is called *enabled* in a state s, denoted by $s[\sigma\rangle$, if there is some state s' such that $s[\sigma\rangle s'$. A state s' is *reachable* from state s if $\exists \sigma \in T^*: s[\sigma\rangle s'$, also denoted $s' \in [s\rangle$.[1]   □

Definition 2. PARIKH VECTORS, CYCLES, AND LABEL-DISJOINTNESS
A *T-vector* is a function $\Phi: T \rightarrow \mathbb{Z}$; in linear algebra, it will usually be considered as a column-vector; its *support* is the set of indices corresponding to nonnull values.

---

[1] Note that enabledness and reachability refer to d-paths, rather than to g-paths.

For a g-path $\sigma \in (T \cup \overleftarrow{T})^*$, the *Parikh vector of* σ is a T-vector $\Psi(\sigma)$, defined inductively as follows:[2]

$$\Psi(\varepsilon) = \mathbf{0} \text{ (the null vector)}$$

$$(\Psi(\sigma a))(t) = \begin{cases} (\Psi(\sigma))(t) + 1 \text{ if } t = a \in T \\ (\Psi(\sigma))(t) - 1 \text{ if } \overleftarrow{t} = a \in \overleftarrow{T} \\ (\Psi(\sigma))(t) \quad\quad \text{ if } t \neq a \neq \overleftarrow{t} \end{cases}$$

Two finite sequences are *Parikh-equivalent* if they have the same Parikh vector. A g-path $s[\sigma\rangle s'$ is called a *g-cycle*, or more precisely a *g-cycle at (or around) state* s, if $s = s'$. Two d-paths $\sigma, \tau \in T^*$ are called *label-disjoint* if their Parikh vectors have disjoint supports. □

Definition 3. DETERMINISM, SPANNING TREE, EQUIVALENCES
TS is called *finite* if S and T (hence $\rightarrow$) are finite, *deterministic* if $\forall s, s', s'' \in S$, $t \in T$: $s[t\rangle s' \land s[t\rangle s'' \Rightarrow s' = s''$, and *totally reachable* if every state is reachable from $\imath$. An lts TS is called a *tree* (with *root* $\imath$) if it is totally reachable and $|\rightarrow| = |S| - 1$ (i.e., for each state, there is a single directed path from the root to it in the corresponding unlabelled graph). A tree $TS' = (S', \rightarrow', T', \imath')$ is called a *spanning tree* of TS if $S' = S$, $\rightarrow' \subseteq \rightarrow$, $T' \subseteq T$, and $\imath' = \imath$. The *language* of TS is the set $L(TS) = \{\sigma \in T^* \mid \imath[\sigma\rangle\}$.

Two lts $TS_1 = (S_1, \rightarrow_1, T, \imath_1)$ and $TS_2 = (S_2, \rightarrow_2, T, \imath_2)$ are *language-equivalent* if $L(TS_1) = L(TS_2)$, and *isomorphic* if there is a bijection $\zeta \colon S_1 \rightarrow S_2$ with $\zeta(\imath_1) = \imath_2$ and $(s, t, s') \in \rightarrow_1 \Leftrightarrow (\zeta(s), t, \zeta(s')) \in \rightarrow_2$, for all $s, s' \in S_1$. □

As an example, consider the labelled transition system TS_1 depicted in Fig. 1. The d-path aba emanating from state $\imath$ (more precisely, exhibiting all intermediate states, $\imath[a\rangle s_1[b\rangle \imath[a\rangle s_1$), has Parikh vector $(2, 1)$ (two a's, one b). The g-path $\overleftarrow{a}$ emanating from s_1 (i.e.: $s_1[\overleftarrow{a}\rangle \imath$) has Parikh vector $(-1, 0)$.

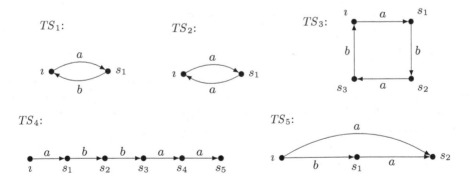

Fig. 1. Five illustrative transition systems.

---

[2] This definition generalises the classic notion of a Parikh vector to g-paths.

Here are a few simple observations about (generalised) paths and cycles.

(a) For any g-path $\sigma \in (T \cup \overleftarrow{T})^*$: $\Psi(\sigma) = -\Psi(\overleftarrow{\sigma})$.

(b) For any two g-paths $\sigma_1, \sigma_2 \in (T \cup \overleftarrow{T})^*$: $\Psi(\sigma_1\sigma_2) = \Psi(\sigma_1) + \Psi(\sigma_2)$.

(c) Let $r_0[\alpha_1\rangle r_1[\alpha_2\rangle r_2[\alpha_3\rangle r_0$ and $r_1[\beta_1\rangle r_3[\beta_2\rangle r_2$. Then, with $\kappa_1 = \alpha_1\alpha_2\alpha_3$, $\kappa_2 = \alpha_1\beta_1\beta_2\alpha_3$, and $\kappa_3 = \beta_1\beta_2\overleftarrow{\alpha_2}$, $r_0[\kappa_1\rangle r_0$, $r_0[\kappa_2\rangle r_0$, and $r_1[\kappa_3\rangle r_1$ are g-cycles, and $\Psi(\kappa_3) = \Psi(\kappa_2) - \Psi(\kappa_1)$. (Proof: simple calculation).

(d) If TS is a tree, then any g-cycle in TS has Parikh vector zero. (However, there may also be non-cycles with Parikh vector zero).

(e) Let $TS_0 = (S, \to_0, T_0, \iota)$ be a spanning tree of $TS = (S, \to, T, \iota)$. For any state s, let π_s denote the (unique) d-path from ι to s in TS_0 (it is thus also a d-path in TS). An edge $(s, t, s') \in (\to \setminus \to_0)$ is called a *chord*. Every chord (s, t, s') defines a g-cycle $\iota[\pi_s t \overleftarrow{\pi_{s'}}\rangle \iota$; let this g-cycle be called $\gamma_{(s,t,s')}$. Let

$$\Gamma_{TS,TS_0} = \{\gamma_{(s,t,s')} \mid (s, t, s') \text{ is a chord}\}$$

The set Γ_{TS,TS_0} is called a *g-cycle basis* (of TS, with regard to TS_0), as justified by the next point.

(f) The Parikh vector $\Psi(\kappa)$ of any g-cycle κ in TS can be written as

$$\Psi(\kappa) = \sum_{\gamma \in \Gamma_{TS,TS_0}} k_\gamma \cdot \Psi(\gamma)$$

for some coefficients $k_\gamma \in \mathbb{Z}$. (Proof: following the successive arcs $s[t\rangle s'$ of κ and the corresponding g-cycles $\iota[\pi_s t \overleftarrow{\pi_{s'}}\rangle \iota$, each π_s will be cancelled out by some $\overleftarrow{\pi_s}$, the arc yields a γ if it is a chord, a reverse γ if it is a reverse chord, and if the arc is not a chord (nor a reverse one), it is easy to see that $\Psi(\pi_s t \overleftarrow{\pi_{s'}}) = \mathbf{0}$).

In the remainder of this paper, we always assume that $TS = (S, \to, T, \iota)$ is a finite, totally reachable, labelled transition system. Note that by total reachability, TS has at least one spanning tree TS_0 [2]. We pick one of them and let $\Gamma = \Gamma_{TS,TS_0}$ denote the cycle basis defined by it.

3   Regions

Regions, to be defined next, mimick the properties of Petri net places at the transition system level. Our nomenclature accords with this idea, even though we shall not define Petri nets in the present paper: B and F assign backward and forward weights to labels t, so that these weights can serve as connecting arcs between a transition t (which realises the label t) and a place of a Petri net, while R assigns a token count in each marking to that place.

Definition 4. REGIONS OF AN LTS, AND THE EFFECT OF A LABEL
Let $TS = (S, \to, T, \iota)$ be an lts. A triple $\rho = (R, B, F) \in (S \to \mathbb{N}, T \to \mathbb{N}, T \to \mathbb{N})$ is a *region* of TS if for all $s, s' \in S$ and $t \in T$, $s[t\rangle s'$ implies $R(s) \geq B(t)$ and $R(s') = R(s) - B(t) + F(t)$. The derived function $E \colon T \to \mathbb{Z}$ defined by $E(t) = F(t) - B(t)$ is called the *effect* of t.   □

Definition 5. STATE AND EVENT/STATE SEPARATION PROPERTIES [1].
An lts $TS = (S, \rightarrow, T, \imath)$ satisfies SSP (state separation property) iff

$$\forall s, s' \in [\imath]: \quad s \neq s' \;\Rightarrow\; \exists \text{ region } \rho = (R, B, F) \text{ with } R(s) \neq R(s') \qquad (1)$$

meaning that if all regions agree on two states, then the latter are equal.
TS satisfies ESSP (event/state separation property) iff

$$\forall s \in [\imath\rangle \; \forall t \in T: \quad (\neg s[t\rangle) \;\Rightarrow\; \exists \text{ region } \rho = (R, B, F) \text{ with } R(s) < B(t)$$

meaning that if all regions satisfy $R(s) \geq B(t)$, then s enables t.   □

In usual parlance, two distinct (unordered) states $s, s' \in S$ yield a *state separation problem*, denoted by $\mathrm{SSP}(s, s')$, and if there is a region ρ as in (1), then ρ is said to *solve* $\mathrm{SSP}(s, s')$.[3] Intuitively, ρ differentiates between s and s'. Event/state separation problems are similarly defined, but in the remainder of this paper, we shall limit ourselves to state separation problems.

For example, in Fig. 1, TS_1 satisfies both SSP and ESSP. Indeed, if we represent the three functions of a region $\rho = (R, B, F)$ by their equivalent multisets, $\rho_1 = (\{s_1\}, \{b\}, \{a\})$ and $\rho_2 = (\{\imath\}, \{a\}, \{b\})$ are two regions such that ρ_1 solves the event/state separation problem $(\neg \imath[b\rangle)$ and ρ_2 solves the event/state separation problem $(\neg s_1[a\rangle)$. Either of them solves the state separation problem $\imath \neq s_1$. TS_2 and TS_3 (in Fig. 1) satisfy ESSP but not SSP, and TS_4 satisfies SSP but not ESSP. The significance of these properties is expressed by the following result [1]. (Place/transition Petri nets are defined, e.g., in [9]).

Theorem 1. BASIC REGION THEOREMS FOR PLACE/TRANSITION NETS.
A totally reachable, finite lts is isomorphic to the reachability graph of some place/transition Petri net if, and only if, it satisfies SSP∧ ESSP.
If a totally reachable, finite lts satisfies ESSP, then it is language-equivalent to the reachability graph of some Petri net.   □

For example, for TS_3 as shown in Fig. 1, even though there is no Petri net with an isomorphic reachability graph, there is still a Petri net with a language-equivalent reachability graph, for instance a net whose reachability graph is isomorphic to TS_1. Interestingly, a totally reachable, finite lts may be language-equivalent to some Petri net without satisfying ESSP. This is the case, for instance, for system TS_5 shown in Fig. 1: it is easy to build a Petri net with two transitions $\{a, b\}$ and the language $\{\varepsilon, a, b, ba\} = L(TS_5)$, but since $\imath[a\rangle s_2$ and $s_1[a\rangle s_2$, any region will assign the same token count to s_1 and $\imath$, so that it is not possible to allow b at $\imath$ and to exclude it from s_1; as a consequence, neither ESSP nor SSP are satisfied by this system.

Here are some observations about regions, g-paths and Parikh vectors. Let a finite, totally reachable lts $TS = (S, \rightarrow, T, \imath)$ be given and let TS_0 be any spanning tree of TS with root $\imath$.

---

[3] $\mathrm{SSP}(s, s')$ equals $\mathrm{SSP}(s', s)$, and thus, $\mathrm{SSP}(s, s')$ is solvable iff $\mathrm{SSP}(s', s)$ is solvable.

(g) Any T-vector $E \colon T \to \mathbb{Z}$ can be extended to g-paths in $(T \cup \overleftarrow{T})^*$ by defining

$$E(\sigma) = \sum_{t \in T} E(t) \cdot \Psi(\sigma)(t) = E^{\mathsf{T}} \cdot \Psi(\sigma), \quad \text{for any } \sigma \in (T \cup \overleftarrow{T})^*$$

(^{T} means 'transposed', $\cdot$ is scalar product)
If $\rho = (R, B, F)$ is a region with effect E, then for any g-path $s_1[\tau\rangle s_2$, we obtain: $R(s_2) = R(s_1) + E(\tau)$. (Proof: by easy induction on the length of τ.)

(h) In particular, by total reachability, for any state $s \in S$, we have $R(s) = R(\imath) + E(\pi_s)$. This implies that knowing $R(\imath)$ (and π_s) is sufficient for knowing $R(s)$, for every state s.

(j) Also, suppose that $s[\kappa\rangle s$ is a g-cycle in TS. By (g) again, we have $R(s) = R(s) + E(\kappa)$. This means that the effect is zero along g-cycles of TS, i.e., $E(\kappa) = 0$, for every g-cycle $s[\kappa\rangle s$ in TS.

4   State Separability

The synthesis task is to find, for any given separation problem, a region that solves it. The next definition describes a graph-theoretical property which will later turn out to characterise the solvability of state separation problems.

Definition 6. MILD [4] AND G-MILD CYCLE-CONSISTENCY
An lts $TS = (S, \to, T, \imath)$ is called *mildly cycle-consistent* (mcc) if for all d-cycles $r[\sigma\rangle r$ and d-paths $s[\sigma'\rangle s'$ where there is a $p \in \mathbb{N}\setminus\{0\}$ such that $\Psi(\sigma) = p \cdot \Psi(\sigma')$, then $s = s'$. It is called *g-mildly cycle-consistent* (g-mcc) if the same condition is satisfied for all g-cycles $r[\sigma\rangle r$ and g-paths $s[\sigma'\rangle s'$.   □

In other words, if there is at least one cycle $r[\sigma\rangle r$, then any σ' whose Parikh vector satisfies $\Psi(\sigma) = p \cdot \Psi(\sigma')$ for some integer number $p \neq 0$, also has a cyclic effect whenever it is realised. The relevance of the factor p is shown by TS_2 in Fig. 1, which does not enjoy property mcc, since, for example, $\imath[\sigma\rangle\imath$, $\imath[\sigma'\rangle s_1$, with $\sigma = aa$, $\sigma' = a$, $p = 2$, and $\imath \neq s_1$.

The two variants of cycle-consistency differ only in which kinds of paths are considered: d-paths in the plain version, and g-paths in the generalised version. The difference is illustrated by TS_6, as depicted in Fig. 2.

Proposition 1. A NECESSARY CONDITION FOR SSP SOLVABILITY.
Let $TS = (S, \to, T, \imath)$ be a totally reachable, finite lts.
If $SSP(s, s')$ is solvable for any two different states (s, s'), then TS is g-mcc.

Proof: By contraposition.
Suppose that TS is not g-mildly cycle-consistent. Then there are states r, s, s', a number $p \in \mathbb{N}\setminus\{0\}$ and g-paths σ, σ' such that $s \neq s'$, $r[\sigma\rangle r$, $s[\sigma'\rangle s'$, and $\Psi(\sigma) = p \cdot \Psi(\sigma')$. Let $\rho = (R, B, F)$ be any arbitrary region. Then

$$
\begin{aligned}
R(s') &= R(s) + E^{\mathsf{T}} \cdot \Psi(\sigma') &&\text{(by } s[\sigma'\rangle s' \text{ and Item (g) above)}\\
&= R(s) + E^{\mathsf{T}} \cdot (1/p) \cdot \Psi(\sigma) &&\text{(by } \Psi(\sigma) = p \cdot \Psi(\sigma'))\\
&= R(s) &&\text{(by } r[\sigma\rangle r, \text{ hence } E^{\mathsf{T}} \cdot \Psi(\sigma) = 0, \text{ by Item (j))}
\end{aligned}
$$

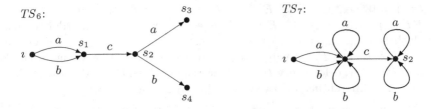

Fig. 2. TS_6 is mildly cycle-consistent but not g-mildly cycle-consistent, since there are a g-cycle $\imath[b\overleftarrow{a}\rangle\imath$ and a non-cyclic g-path $s_3[\overleftarrow{a}\,b\rangle s_4$ with the same Parikh vector $(-1, 1)$. TS_6 is deterministic, while TS_7 is deterministic, but not mcc.

It follows that $R(s') = R(s)$, and since ρ was arbitrary, no region solving $\mathrm{SSP}(s, s')$ exists. Hence the claim. $\square$

For the converse, we shall need a classical result of linear algebra (one of the many variants of the duality theorems):

Lemma 1. RATIONAL-INTEGER FREDHOLM ALTERNATIVE [7]
Let A, b be a rational (n, m)-matrix and a rational $(n, 1)$-vector, respectively. Exactly one of the following alternatives holds.
Either $A \cdot x = b$ has a rational solution x,
or $y^{\mathsf{T}} \cdot A = \mathbf{0}$, $y^{\mathsf{T}} \cdot b \neq 0$ has an integer solution y. $\square$

Proposition 2. A SUFFICIENT CONDITION FOR SSP SOLVABILITY.
Let $TS = (S, \rightarrow, T, \imath)$ be a totally reachable, finite lts.
If TS is g-mcc, then $\mathrm{SSP}(s, s')$ is solvable for any two different states s, s'.

Proof: By contraposition.
Assume that there are two states s, s' with $s \neq s'$ such that $\mathrm{SSP}(s, s')$ is not solvable. We shall construct a pattern in TS which shows that TS is not g-mcc, and we proceed in two steps.

Step 1: The non-solvability of $\mathrm{SSP}(s, s')$ can be characterised as follows: $\mathrm{SSP}(s, s')$ is not solvable if and only if there is no T-vector $E \colon T \to \mathbb{Z}$ satisfying

$$
\begin{array}{ll}
\text{(i)} & \forall \gamma \in \Gamma \colon E^{\mathsf{T}} \cdot \Psi(\gamma) = 0 \\
\text{(ii)} & E^{\mathsf{T}} \cdot \Psi(\pi_s) \neq E^{\mathsf{T}} \cdot \Psi(\pi_{s'})
\end{array}
\tag{2}
$$

where Γ is the cycle base defined before.

Proof: If $\mathrm{SSP}(s, s')$ is solvable by some region $\rho = (R, B, F)$, then the effect function $E \colon T \to \mathbb{Z}$ derivable from ρ clearly satisfies both (i) and (ii) of (2), from Items (j) and (h). Conversely, assume that (2) has a solution. Such a solution can easily be transformed into a region (R, B, F) solving $\mathrm{SSP}(s, s')$ by the following procedure. Let us choose some $R(\imath)$, and define for any $s \neq \imath$ $R(s) = R(\imath) + E(\pi_s)$ (this is compatible with the initial value since $\pi_\imath = \varepsilon$). For any arc $\tilde{s}[t\rangle \tilde{s}'$, the path $\imath[\pi_{\tilde{s}} t \overline{\pi_{\tilde{s}'}}\rangle \imath$ is a g-cycle; from Item (f) and point (i) of (2), we have that

$E(\pi_{\tilde{s}}t\overleftarrow{\pi_{\tilde{s}'}}) = 0$, i.e., $E(\pi_{\tilde{s}'}) = E(\pi_{\tilde{s}}) + E(t)$, so that $R(\tilde{s}') = R(\imath) + E(\pi_{\tilde{s}'}) = R(\imath) + E(\pi_{\tilde{s}}) + E(t) = R(\tilde{s}) + E(t)$, as requested for a region. In order to ensure that all those values are non-negative, one just has to choose a value high enough for $R(\imath)$. For B and F, we can choose minimal non-negative values such that $E(t) = F(t) - B(t)$, for every $t \in T$. The triple (R, B, F) so defined is then a region, and it differentiates between s and s' from point (ii) of (2).

Step 2: Now we show that the unsolvability of (2) implies that a pattern not conforming to g-mild cycle-consistency is hidden somewhere inside TS. Suppose that (2) is unsolvable. Let G be a matrix whose columns are all the Parikh vectors of cycles γ in Γ. The unsolvability of (2) is equivalent to the unsolvability (in the integer domain) of

$$
\begin{array}{lll}
\text{(i')} & E^{\mathsf{T}}{\cdot}G = \mathbf{0} & \text{(in fact, this is just a shorthand of (2(i)))} \\
\text{(ii')} & E^{\mathsf{T}}{\cdot}(\Psi(\pi_{s'}) - \Psi(\pi_s)) \neq 0 & \text{(just a rewriting of (2(ii)))}
\end{array} \tag{3}
$$

By Fredholm's duality result (Lemma 1), the unsolvability of (2) thus implies that the following system has a rational solution x:

$$
\text{(iii)} \quad G{\cdot}x = \Psi(\pi_{s'}) - \Psi(\pi_s) \tag{4}
$$

(4) just means that the T-vector $\Psi(\pi_{s'}) - \Psi(\pi_s)$ – so to speak, the "difference" between s' and s, with respect to $\imath$ – is a linear combination of cyclic Parikh vectors from Γ.

From x, we construct a counterexample to g-mild cycle-consistency as follows.

- First, note that for any $q \in S$ and g-cycle $q[\gamma\rangle q$, $\imath[\pi_q\gamma\overleftarrow{\pi_q}\rangle\imath$ is also a g-cycle, but around $\imath$, with $\Psi(\pi_q\gamma\overleftarrow{\pi_q}) = \Psi(\gamma)$.
- The g-path $\sigma' = \overleftarrow{\pi_s}\pi_{s'}$ leads from s to s', and $\Psi(\sigma') = \Psi(\pi_{s'}) - \Psi(\pi_s)$. Moreover, from (4), $\Psi(\sigma') = \sum_{\gamma \in \Gamma} x_\gamma{\cdot}\Psi(\gamma)$, where the x_γ can be (negative) rational numbers. By multiplying this with a suitable natural number $p > 0$, we get $p \cdot \Psi(\sigma') = \sum_{\gamma \in \Gamma} y_\gamma{\cdot}\Psi(\gamma)$, with integer numbers $p{\cdot}x_\gamma = y_\gamma \in \mathbb{Z}$.
- Using every γ exactly $|y_\gamma|$ times (backwards, if $y_\gamma < 0$), we can therefore realise a cycle $\imath[\sigma\rangle\imath$ with $\Psi(\sigma) = p \cdot \Psi(\sigma')$. Put $r = \imath$.

With the states r, s, s', number p, and g-paths σ, σ' just constructed, TS is not g-mildly cycle-consistent, since $s \neq s'$. This ends the proof.   □

For instance, consider TS_2 as shown in Fig. 1. The state separation problem $\mathrm{SSP}(s, s')$ with $s = \imath$ and $s' = s_1$ is not solvable. We obtain $G = (\Psi(aa)^{\mathsf{T}}) = 2$ (a single component since $T = \{a\}$) and $\Psi(\pi_{s'}) - \Psi(\pi_s) = 1$ (idem), because of $\imath[a\rangle s_1$; thus, $x = 1/2$ solves (4). Multiplying by $p = 2$ gives $y = 1$, and indeed, $\Psi(\sigma) = 2 \cdot \Psi(\sigma')$ with $\sigma = aa$ and $\sigma' = a$.

Theorem 2. G-MILD CYCLE-CONSISTENCY CHARACTERISES SSP
For a totally reachable, finite lts $TS = (S, \rightarrow, T, \imath)$, the following are equivalent:

- *TS is g-mcc.*
- *For any two different states $s \neq s'$, $\mathrm{SSP}(s, s')$ is solvable.*

Proof: By Propositions 1 and 2, considering also that all previous proofs hold for any chosen spanning tree of TS (since the choice of TS_0 was arbitrary).   □

5   Persistent Systems

In this section, we shall show that in case TS is persistent, there exist some useful variations of Theorem 2.

Definition 7. PERSISTENCE.
A labelled transition system $(S, \rightarrow, T, \imath)$ is called *persistent* if for all states $s, s', s'' \in S$, and labels $t, u \in T$ with $t \neq u$, if $s[t\rangle s'$ and $s[u\rangle s''$, then there is some state $r \in S$ such that both $s'[u\rangle r$ and $s''[t\rangle r$ (i.e., once two different labels are both enabled, neither can disable the other, and this leads to the same state, forming a characteristic diamond shape).   □

For example, TS_6, shown in Fig. 2, is not persistent, while TS_7 (also shown in that figure) is. Of course, g-mild cycle-consistency implies mild cycle-consistency. We will show that the converse is true for persistent lts. First, we recall Keller's theorem, which is useful for arguing concisely about persistent systems. For sequences $\tau, \sigma \in T^*$, the *residue* $\tau \stackrel{\bullet}{-} \sigma$ is defined inductively as follows:

if $\sigma = \varepsilon$: $\tau \stackrel{\bullet}{-} \varepsilon$ $= \tau$
if $\Psi(\tau)(t) = 0 : \tau \stackrel{\bullet}{-} t$ $= \tau$
if $\Psi(\tau)(t) \neq 0 :$ $\tau \stackrel{\bullet}{-} t$ $=$ the sequence obtained by erasing the leftmost t *in* τ
otherwise: $\tau \stackrel{\bullet}{-} (t\sigma) = (\tau \stackrel{\bullet}{-} t) \stackrel{\bullet}{-} \sigma$

Theorem 3. KELLER [8].
Let $(S, \rightarrow, T, \imath)$ be a *deterministic and persistent lts. Let $\tau \in T^*$ and $\sigma \in T^*$ be two d-paths activated at some state s. Then $\tau(\sigma \stackrel{\bullet}{-} \tau)$ and $\sigma(\tau \stackrel{\bullet}{-} \sigma)$ are also activated from s. Furthermore, $\sigma \stackrel{\bullet}{-} \tau$ and $\tau \stackrel{\bullet}{-} \sigma$ are label-disjoint, and the state reached after $\tau(\sigma \stackrel{\bullet}{-} \tau)$ equals the state reached after $\sigma(\tau \stackrel{\bullet}{-} \sigma)$.*   □

Lemma 2. G-PATHS AND SEMI-DIRECTED PATHS
In a deterministic and persistent lts, for any g-path $r[\alpha\rangle s$, there is a path $r[\beta_1 \overleftarrow{\beta_2}\rangle s$, where β_1 and β_2 are d-paths and $\Psi(\alpha) = \Psi(\beta_1) - \Psi(\beta_2)$.

Proof: Let us first assume that $r[\overleftarrow{\gamma_1}\rangle r'[\gamma_2\rangle s$ for two d-paths γ_1 and γ_2. From Keller's Theorem 3 and the definition of residues, since $r'[\gamma_1\rangle r$ and $r'[\gamma_2\rangle s$, we have $r[\gamma_2 \stackrel{\bullet}{-} \gamma_1\rangle r''$ and $s[\gamma_1 \stackrel{\bullet}{-} \gamma_2\rangle r''$ for some state r'', i.e., $r[(\gamma_2 \stackrel{\bullet}{-} \gamma_1)(\overleftarrow{\gamma_1 \stackrel{\bullet}{-} \gamma_2})\rangle s$; moreover $\Psi(\gamma_1(\gamma_2 \stackrel{\bullet}{-} \gamma_1)) = \max(\Psi(\gamma_1), \Psi(\gamma_2)) = \Psi(\gamma_2(\gamma_1 \stackrel{\bullet}{-} \gamma_2))$, so that $\Psi(\overleftarrow{\gamma_1}\gamma_2) = \Psi(\gamma_2) - \Psi(\gamma_1) = \Psi(\gamma_2 \stackrel{\bullet}{-} \gamma_1) - \Psi(\gamma_1 \stackrel{\bullet}{-} \gamma_2) = \Psi((\gamma_2 \stackrel{\bullet}{-} \gamma_1)(\overleftarrow{\gamma_1 \stackrel{\bullet}{-} \gamma_2}))$. (The max operation on Parikh vectors is meant componentwise, and we also use the fact that $\gamma_1 \stackrel{\bullet}{-} \gamma_2$ and $\gamma_2 \stackrel{\bullet}{-} \gamma_1$ are label-disjoint.) The claimed property then arises from an iterative application of this result, progressively pushing the backward paths to the right of forward ones while keeping the same Parikh vector.   □

A *home state* in an lts is a state $\tilde{s}$ such that, for any state $s \in S$, $\tilde{s} \in [s\rangle$. It is well known (see Corollary 4 of [3]) that, in a deterministic and persistent lts with a home state $\tilde{s}$, for any d-cycle $s[\alpha\rangle s$, there is a d-cycle $\tilde{s}[\beta\rangle\tilde{s}$ with $\Psi(\alpha) = \Psi(\beta)$ (i.e., cycles may be transported Parikh-equivalently to home states). Moreover (see Corollary 2 of [3]), any finite, totally reachable, deterministic and persistent lts has home states.

A non-empty d-cycle $s[\alpha\rangle s$ in an lts is called *small* if there is no Parikh-smaller non-empty d-cycle: $s'[\beta\rangle s'$ with $\Psi(\beta) \lneq \Psi(\alpha) \Rightarrow \beta = \varepsilon$ with $\alpha, \beta \in T^*$. An lts is said to satisfy the *disjoint small cycles property* if there is a set $\{\Upsilon_1, \ldots, \Upsilon_n\}$ of natural T-vectors with disjoint supports such that $\{\Upsilon_1, \ldots, \Upsilon_n\} = \{\Psi(\alpha)|$ there is a small cycle $s[\alpha\rangle s\}$.

Lemma 3. DISJOINT SMALL CYCLES BASIS
Let $TS = (S, \rightarrow, T, \imath)$ be a totally reachable, deterministic labelled transition system which is finite, mildly cycle-consistent and persistent. Then TS satisfies the disjoint small cycles property for some $\{\Upsilon_1, \ldots, \Upsilon_n\}$, and for any d-cycle $s[\alpha\rangle s$ we have the decomposition $\Psi(\alpha) = \sum_{i=1}^{n} k_i \cdot \Upsilon_i$ for some $k_1, \ldots, k_n \in \mathbb{N}$.

Proof: This follows from Theorem 2 of [3] and Theorem 2 of [4] (since finiteness, determinism, mild cycle-consistency and persistence easily imply the premises of the latter). □

Lemma 4. D-CYCLE BASE OF G-CYCLES
Let $TS = (S, \rightarrow, T, \imath)$ be a totally reachable, deterministic labelled transition system which is finite, mildly cycle-consistent and persistent. Then there is a set $\{\Upsilon_1, \ldots, \Upsilon_n\}$ of natural T-vectors with disjoint supports such that for any g-cycle $s[\alpha\rangle s$, there is a unique set of integers $k_1, \ldots, k_n \in \mathbb{Z}$ with $\Psi(\alpha) = \sum_{i=1}^{n} k_i \cdot \Upsilon_i$.

Proof: From Lemma 2, we know that, for some $s_1 \in S$, $s[\alpha_1\rangle s_1$ and $s[\alpha_2\rangle s_1$ with $\alpha_1, \alpha_2 \in T^*$ and $\Psi(\alpha) = \Psi(\alpha_1) - \Psi(\alpha_2)$. Applying Keller's theorem, we get $s_1[\beta_1\rangle s_2$ and $s_1[\beta_2\rangle s_2$ for some $s_2 \in S$, with $\beta_1 = \alpha_1 \overset{\bullet}{-} \alpha_2$, $\beta_2 = \alpha_2 \overset{\bullet}{-} \alpha_1$, $\Psi(\alpha_1) - \Psi(\alpha_2) = \Psi(\beta_1) - \Psi(\beta_2)$, β_1 and β_2 being label-disjoint. From the label-disjointness, we may then continue, and form a sequence $s_2[\beta_1\rangle s_3$, $s_2[\beta_2\rangle s_3$, ..., $s_n[\beta_1\rangle s_{n+1}$, $s_n[\beta_2\rangle s_{n+1}$, ..., but since S is finite, we must have $i < j$ such that $s_i = s_j$.

Thus, we have cycles $s_i[(\beta_1)^{j-i}\rangle s_i$, $s_i[(\beta_2)^{j-i}\rangle s_i$, but also $s_i[\beta_2(\beta_1)^{j-i-1}\rangle s_i$ and $s_i[\beta_1(\beta_2)^{j-i-1}\rangle s_i$. By Lemma 3, the Parikh vector of each of them is a linear combination of the Υ_i's, and from the label-disjointness of β_1 and β_2 on the one side, and of the Υ_i's on the other side, we must have $\Psi(\beta_1) = \sum_{l=1}^{n} k_{1,l} \cdot \Upsilon_l$ as well as $\Psi(\beta_2) = \sum_{l=1}^{n} k_{2,l} \cdot \Upsilon_l$, with $\forall l: k_{1,l} \geq 0, k_{2,l} \geq 0$ and $k_{1,l} \cdot k_{2,l} = 0$. As a consequence, $\Psi(\alpha) = \sum_{l=1}^{n} (k_{1,l} - k_{2,l}) \cdot \Upsilon_l$, and the claimed result is proved. □

Lemma 5. CYCLES MAY BE PUSHED TO HOME STATES [3]
Let $TS = (S, \rightarrow, T, \imath)$ be a totally reachable, deterministic labelled transition system which is finite and persistent. Then there exists a home state $\tilde{s} \in [\imath\rangle$ so that for any cycle $s[\alpha\rangle s$ there exists a cycle $\tilde{s}[\tilde{\alpha}\rangle \tilde{s}$ with $\Psi(\alpha) = \Psi(\tilde{\alpha})$.

Theorem 4. PERSISTENT LTS ARE G-MCC IFF THEY ARE MCC.
Let $TS = (S, \rightarrow, T, \imath)$ be a finite, totally reachable, deterministic, persistent labelled transition system. Then TS is g-mildly cycle-consistent iff it is mildly cycle-consistent.

Proof: It is clear that, if TS is g-mildly cycle-consistent, then it is mildly cycle-consistent.

For the other direction, note first that by Lemma 3, TS satisfies the disjoint small cycles property for some $\{\Upsilon_1, \ldots, \Upsilon_n\}$ if TS is mildly cycle-consistent.

Let us thus assume that $s[\alpha\rangle s$ is a g-cycle, $r[\beta\rangle r'$ is a g-path with $p \cdot \Psi(\beta) = \Psi(\alpha)$ for some $p \in \mathbb{Z}\backslash\{0\}$: we need to show that $r = r'$.

From Lemmas 3 and 5 we know that there is a home state $\tilde{s}$, with small cycles $\tilde{s}[\gamma_i\rangle\tilde{s}$, such that $\forall i \in \{1, \ldots, n\}$: $\Psi(\gamma_i) = \Upsilon_i$.

Lemma 4 implies that $\Psi(\alpha) = \sum_{i=1}^{n} k_i \cdot \Upsilon_i$, where each $k_i \in \mathbb{Z}$.

Since the lts is totally reachable, we have two d-paths $\imath[\delta_1\rangle r$ and $\imath[\delta_2\rangle r'$. By Keller's theorem, there is a state $\tilde{r}$ such that $r[\delta_2 \overset{\bullet}{-}\delta_1\rangle\tilde{r}$ and $r'[\delta_1 \overset{\bullet}{-}\delta_2\rangle\tilde{r}$, and $\delta_1 \overset{\bullet}{-}\delta_2$ and $\delta_2 \overset{\bullet}{-}\delta_1$ are label-disjoint.

Let us now consider the g-cycle $r[\beta(\delta_1 \overset{\bullet}{-}\delta_2)(\overleftarrow{\delta_2 \overset{\bullet}{-}\delta_1})\rangle r$. From Lemma 4 again, we know that $\Psi(\beta(\delta_1 \overset{\bullet}{-}\delta_2)(\overleftarrow{\delta_2 \overset{\bullet}{-}\delta_1})) = \Psi(\beta) + \Psi(\delta_1 \overset{\bullet}{-}\delta_2) - \Psi(\delta_2 \overset{\bullet}{-}\delta_1) = \sum_{i=1}^{n} h_i \cdot \Upsilon_i$, where each $h_i \in \mathbb{Z}$.

Gathering all these relations, we get:

$$p \cdot [\Psi(\delta_1 \overset{\bullet}{-}\delta_2) - \Psi(\delta_2 \overset{\bullet}{-}\delta_1)]$$

$$= \sum_{i=1}^{n} p \cdot h_i \cdot \Upsilon_i - p \cdot \Psi(\beta)$$

$$= \sum_{i=1}^{n} p \cdot h_i \cdot \Upsilon_i - \Psi(\alpha)$$

$$= \sum_{i=1}^{n} [p \cdot h_i - k_i] \cdot \Upsilon_i$$

From the label-disjointness of $\delta_1 \overset{\bullet}{-}\delta_2$ and $\delta_2 \overset{\bullet}{-}\delta_1$, as well as of the various Υ_i's, we may express $p \cdot \Psi(\delta_1 \overset{\bullet}{-}\delta_2) = \sum_{i=1}^{n} l_{1,i} \cdot \Upsilon_i$ and $p \cdot \Psi(\delta_2 \overset{\bullet}{-}\delta_1) = \sum_{i=1}^{n} l_{2,i} \cdot \Upsilon_i$ for some $l_{1,i}$'s and $l_{2,i}$'s in $\mathbb{N}$. As a consequence, since $p \cdot \Psi(\delta_1 \overset{\bullet}{-}\delta_2) = \Psi(\gamma_1^{l_{1,1}} \gamma_2^{l_{1,2}} \ldots \gamma_n^{l_{1,n}})$ and $\tilde{s}[\gamma_1^{l_{1,1}} \gamma_2^{l_{1,2}} \ldots \gamma_n^{l_{1,n}}\rangle\tilde{s}$, from mild cycle consistency we have $r = \tilde{r}$. Similarly, $r' = \tilde{r}$, and we get $r = r'$ as requested. $\square$

Theorem 4 can be understood intuitively by comparing TS_6 and TS_7, shown in Fig. 2. Any attempt to turn TS_6 into a persistent lts requires to extend the a/b forks at states $\imath$ and s_2 into persistent diamonds, which either yields an infinite result, or creates cycles such as the ones in TS_7, leading to a violation of mild cycle-consistency (not just of g-mild cycle-consistency, as in TS_6).

Finally, we use Theorems 2 and 4, together with previous results, in order to prove the following theorem.

Theorem 5. FOR PERSISTENT SYNTHESIS, SSP CAN LARGELY BE NEGLECTED
Let TS be a finite, totally reachable, deterministic labelled transition system which is mildly cycle-consistent and persistent. If TS satisfies ESSP, then it is isomorphic to the reachability graph of some place/transition Petri net.

Proof: By Theorem 4, *TS* is g-mildly cycle-consistent. By Theorem 2, it satisfies SSP. The claim then follows by Theorem 1 (first part, ($\Leftarrow$)).   □

For the reachability graphs of Petri nets, all premises of Theorem 5, except finiteness and persistence, are satisfied. (The proof of this is easy; see, e.g., [4].) For this reason, Theorem 5 can be paraphrased loosely as follows: "in the presence of persistence, SSP plays no role in finite Petri net synthesis". This complements Darondeau's theorem [5] which states (loosely speaking) that "in the presence of persistence, language equivalence is the same as isomorphism". Theorem 5 can also be viewed as a strengthened version of the second part of Theorem 1 (under the premise of persistence).

6   Conclusion

The main results of this paper can be summarised as follows:

- State separability, as defined in Petri net synthesis [1], has a graph-theoretical characterisation, using generalised – that is, not necessarily directed – paths and cycles (Theorem 2).
- In the presence of persistence, (i): this characterisation can be replaced by a simpler one, just using directed paths and cycles (Theorem 4); and (ii): state separation problems are generally solvable (Theorem 5).

It should be observed that the g-mcc characterisation given by Theorem 2 does not directly lead to a fast algorithm for checking the solvability of state separation problems. It remains to be found out (in future work) to what extent g-mild cycle-consistency lends itself to useful algorithmic treatment.

Finally, we would like to emphasise that, while there may be less event/state separation problems [1] in an lts than state separation problems, event/state problems are much harder to characterise purely graph-theoretically. This is true even for very simple (persistent, acyclic) transition systems [6].

Acknowledgments. We would like to thank the reviewers and Harro Wimmel for their very useful comments.

References

1. Badouel, É., Bernardinello, L., Darondeau, P.: Petri Net Synthesis. Texts in Theoretical Computer Science, 339 pages. Springer, Heidelberg (2015). ISBN 978-3-662-47967-4
2. Berge, C.: Graphs and Hypergraphs. North Holland Mathematical Library, Vol. 6, 528 pages. Elsevier, Oxford (1973)
3. Best, E., Darondeau, P.: A decomposition theorem for finite persistent transition systems. Acta Informatica **46**, 237–254 (2009)
4. Best, E., Devillers, R.: The power of prime cycles. In: Kordon, F., Moldt, D. (eds.) PETRI NETS 2016. LNCS, vol. 9698, pp. 59–78. Springer, Heidelberg (2016). doi:10.1007/978-3-319-39086-4_5

5. Darondeau, P.: Equality of languages coincides with isomorphism of reachable state graphs for bounded and persistent petri nets. Inf. Process. Lett. **94**, 241–245 (2005)
6. Erofeev, E., Barylska, K., Mikulski, L., Piątkowski, M.: Generating all minimal petri net unsolvable binary words. In: Proceedings of Stringology 2016. http://www.stringology.org/event/
7. Fredholm, I.: Sur une classe d'équations fonctionelles. Acta Math. **27**(1), 365–390 (1903)
8. Keller, R.M.: A fundamental theorem of asynchronous parallel computation. In: Feng, T. (ed.) Parallel Processing. LNCS, vol. 24, pp. 102–112. Springer, Heidelberg (1975). doi:10.1007/3-540-07135-0_113
9. Reisig, W.: Petri Nets. EATCS Monographs on Theoretical Computer Science, vol. 4. Springer, Heidelberg (1985)

Selfish Transportation Games

Dimitris Fotakis[1]([✉]), Laurent Gourvès[2], and Jérôme Monnot[2]

[1] National Technical University of Athens, 15780 Athens, Greece
fotakis@cs.ntua.gr
[2] Université Paris-Dauphine, PSL Research University, CNRS UMR [7243],
LAMSADE, 75016 Paris, France
{laurent.gourves,jerome.monnot}@dauphine.fr

Abstract. We study a natural strategic situation arising from the selection of shared means of transportation. Some clients (the players) are located on different nodes of a given graph and they want to be transported from their location to a common destination point (*e.g.* school, airport). A fixed number of resources (also called buses) is available and each client has to choose exactly one. Individual costs depend on the route chosen by the buses and the distance between the nodes. We investigate the case where each bus has a static permutation which prescribes the order by which the clients are visited. We identify the cases admitting a pure strategy equilibrium and consider the construction of an equilibrium, via a dedicated algorithm, or a dynamics. We also determine the price of anarchy and the price of stability for two natural social functions.

Keywords: Resource allocation game · Existence and computation of equilibria · Price of anarchy/stability

1 Introduction

In many applications some entities compete for the use of shared resources (*e.g.* processors, storage). These resources are typically rare enough to prevent the existence of an ideal situation where every entity is fully satisfied with the resources that it holds. Allocating scarce resources to a pool of agents is an important problem in the AGT community. An allocation can be found by a central planner who strives to optimize a prescribed social choice function. In practice, this approach is often too rigid as some users, who disregard the social cost and focus on their own individual cost, may not trust the planner's global solution. Therefore, one may prefer a more flexible mechanism, *i.e.* a decentralized way for constructing an allocation with which the agents can interact and be proactive. Unfortunately such a mechanism would fail if the agents were unable to commit in a feasible allocation of the resources, or if every allocation that the agents build has a high social cost. As a consequence, it is necessary to evaluate the worth of a mechanism with respect to at least two criteria: *(Stability)* Can

Supported by the project ANR CoCoRICo-CoDec.

the agents reach a stable state where no one is capable to acquire more revenue? *(Performance)* Are these stable states good from a social viewpoint?

We address these questions in a context where some agents, located on different places of a map, compete for the use of some public means of transportation (*e.g.* buses), so as to reach a common destination (*e.g.* an airport). Our work, motivated by services like *Dial-a-Ride*, *Lyft* or *Uber*, uses strategic games to model the situation. The models are called *selfish transportation games* because every agent (also called player) controls a part of the entire solution (*i.e.* which transportation means she decides to take) and this agent's choice is solely guided by her individual cost. Our study focuses on the existence of pure strategy equilibria, together with a worst-case analysis of the performance of the best (resp., worst) pure Nash equilibrium compared to configurations with minimum social cost. Two natural, yet different, notions of social cost are used. More importantly we concentrate on mechanisms where each bus visits and picks up the clients according to a fixed order (possibly different for each bus).

1.1 The Model

Let $G = (V, E)$ be an undirected graph with a source s and a destination t. The graph is also endowed with a distance function $d : V \times V \to \mathbb{R}_+$ which is possibly *metric*, i.e., symmetric and it obeys the triangle inequality. The *transportation game* has a set N of n players, and each one is located on a vertex of V. The goal of each player is to be transported from its location to the destination t at the lowest cost. There is a set M of $m \geq 2$ resources (also called buses). Each bus follows a path that starts from s, visits some players at their location, and finally reaches the destination t. We suppose that each bus j has its own algorithm $\mathcal{A}_j$ which, given $V' \subseteq V$, determines its route, *i.e.* an $s-t$ path whose set of intermediate nodes is V'. Every algorithm $\mathcal{A}_j$ is public. It is assumed that a bus always takes the direct link with distance $d(a, b)$ between two consecutive clients a and b and all links between two distinct clients are possible.

We consider a strategic game in which each player chooses by which bus it is picked. Thus, M is the strategy space of every player in N. There are different ways to define $c_i(\sigma)$, the individual cost of a player i under strategy profile σ. In this work $c_i(\sigma)$ is the distance travelled by σ_i (the bus selected by player i) between the original location of i (when player i is picked) and the destination t. We suppose that each $\mathcal{A}_j$, for $j \in M$, is based on a permutation $\pi_j : \{1, \ldots, n\} \to N$ (independent of the current strategy profile). Actually π_j indicates the reverse order by which the players are picked. This picking order is never violated, even if a bus visits a player's location more than once. The permutation is an expression of preferences, or priorities, that a resource has over the set of players (or their locations).

Example 1. Consider an instance with 4 players and 2 buses. The permutations of the buses are $(1\,2\,3\,4)$ and $(1\,4\,2\,3)$, respectively. Suppose player 1 chooses bus 1 whereas the others choose bus 2. Thus, bus 1 starts from s, visits 1 and goes to t. Bus 2 starts from s, visits players 3, 2, 4 and goes to t. Individual costs are $c_1(\sigma) = d(1, t)$, $c_4(\sigma) = d(4, t)$, $c_2(\sigma) = d(2, 4) + c_4(\sigma)$ and $c_3(\sigma) = d(3, 2) + c_2(\sigma)$.

In a totally equivalent model, every player is at t and wants to reach her location (*e.g.* airport to home). Each permutation π_j indicates by which order the players are dropped. In Example 1, bus 1 transports player 1 to his home. Bus 2 starts from t, drops player 4, then player 2, then player 3.

1.2   Motivation and Related Work

Transportation problems have a prominent place in operations research and combinatorial optimization (*e.g.* the *Traveling Salesman Problem* [2] or *Vehicle Routing Problems* [22]) because they present both practical and theoretical challenges to the researchers.

Ridesharing systems (see *e.g.*, [16,18]) are emerging transportation models and tools where car owners can share a ride with other persons via a dedicated application (*e.g.* avego, blablacar, carpoolworld, carticipate, etc.). Ridesharing systems, as public transportation systems, are valuable initiatives for the reduction of traffic congestion, CO_2 emissions and fuel expenditure.

In this article, we depart from the extensive literature dealing with centrally computed solutions (see *e.g.*, [20]) and focus on game theoretic approaches. Concerning transportation models, numerous articles on vehicle-routing games deal with cooperative games (see *e.g.*, [5,6,12]). However, noncooperative and competitive games are more closely related to our transportation game. For example, [13] study a competitive traveling salesmen problem in which two salespeople compete for visiting some clients earlier than their opponent. In this model, the players make their decisions in turn like in a game in perfect-information extensive form. A similar model, with possibly more than 2 salespersons, is considered in [17].

Our model of transportation differs from the aforementioned works since it is a strategic game. The literature on strategic games for routing problems can be divided in two parts, whether the players are *non-atomic* or *atomic*. In the mathematical models involving non-atomic players, there is traffic in a network and each infinitesimal portion of this traffic is associated with an autonomous agent (see *e.g.* [10] for the notion of *Wardrop equilibrium*). In this article, we assume that the players are atomic. In comparison, an atomic player represents a non-negligible portion of the traffic.

As resource selection games, transportation games are reminiscent of *scheduling games* with *coordination mechanisms* [9]. In coordination mechanisms we have a scheduling policy, which imposes a priority over players in each resource. The scheduling policy may be described by some simple rule, such as *shortest (resp., largest) job first*, or may be more sophisticated (see *e.g.*, [4]). Moreover, the same or different scheduling policies can be used for the resources. The goal is to find natural coordination mechanisms that can significantly improve the resulting *price of anarchy* (see *e.g.*, [4,7,9]) or can ensure the existence of an equilibrium in pure strategies or the fast convergence to it (see *e.g.*, [4]). Thus, coordination mechanisms modify (or enrich) the individual cost structure, aiming at improved efficiency (or equilibrium existence).

In transportation games, we employ a fixed player priority, possibly different in each bus, to simplify the individual cost structure and to allow for an efficient best response computation. Of course, one might think of more sophisticated player priorities and bus routes, which is somewhat reminiscent to more complex scheduling policies in coordination mechanisms. Such priorities may naturally depend on the set of players in the same bus and on their distances to each other and to the destination. But, if *e.g.*, we pick the players in each bus according to the shortest route starting from the source, going through all of them, and ending up to the destination, determining such a route and the corresponding individual costs requires the solution to an **NP**-hard optimization problem. Keeping the player priorities fixed and independent of their partition into buses, we simplify the individual cost structure so that transportation games are amenable to theoretical analysis.

Transportation games also bear some resemblance to (non-cooperative versions of) hedonic games (see *e.g.*, [8,11]), where the players are partitioned into coalitions and the individual cost of each player depends on the identities of other players in the same coalition (but not on the identity of the coalition). In transportation games, the players in each bus could be regarded as a coalition and the individual cost of each player depends on the identities of other players in the same bus (but in a more subtle way than in the hedonic games of *e.g.*, [14,15]). The special case of transportation games with the same player permutation for all buses could be regarded as a hedonic game, since the individual cost of each player depends on the locations of other players in the same bus (but not on the bus itself). However, to enrich the individual cost structure of transportation games, we allow for different player permutations in the buses, which makes the individual cost of each player also depend on the bus (in addition to the locations of the players to be picked up after him). This is a significant departure from variants of hedonic games studied in the literature and a source of difficulty in establishing the existence of pure Nash equilibria.

1.3   Contribution

We conduct a theoretical analysis of the transportation game by providing answers to the following questions. Which case admits an equilibrium? Can we compute an equilibrium in polynomial time? Do the players naturally converge to an equilibrium? How good is the best (or worst) equilibrium in comparison with a social optimum?

This work only deals with pure strategy profiles (each player's choice is deterministic). A *pure Nash equilibrium* (NE) is a strategy profile (also called *state*) σ such that no player can unilaterally change her strategy and benefit [21]. A *strong equilibrium* (SE) is a refinement of the NE to group deviations. In a SE, no group of players C can jointly deviate in such a way that every member of C benefits [3]. This article also deals with the dynamics of the transportation game. We say that the *dynamics converges* if, starting from *any* strategy profile, every series of improvement moves (better response) eventually reaches a stable state. Depending on the context (unilateral or group deviations), this stable state can be a NE or a SE.

Our results show that if all the resources have the same permutation then a SE exists and it can be computed in polynomial time (Theorem 1). But if the permutations are not identical, then there exists a simple 2-resource 3-player instance without any NE (Proposition 2). If there are 2 resources and if the distances is metric, then the dynamics converges to a NE (Theorem 2). Moreover, this equilibrium can be computed in linear time (Theorem 3).

Section 3 is devoted to a special metric case where distances can be 1 or 2. We provide an algorithm that computes a NE in $O(nm)$.

In Section 4, we analyse the *price of anarchy* and *stability* of the transportation game under two natural social cost functions namely *egalitarian* and *Vehicle Kilometers Travelled*. These notions are worst case comparisons of the worst and best NE with a social optimum, respectively. Without metric, the price of anarchy and stability of our transportation game are unbounded, but they are bounded for metric distances. Some possible extensions and future works are discussed in the last section.

2 Existence and Computation of an Equilibrium

At least two properties play an important role in the existence of an equilibrium: (*i*) whether the permutations of the buses are identical or not, (*ii*) whether the distances are metric or not.

2.1 Instances with Not Necessarily Metric Distances

Theorem 1. *If all the resources have the same permutation π, then the dynamics converges to a SE. Moreover, a SE can be built in $O(nm)$.*

Theorem 1 cannot be extended to show the existence of a *super strong equilibrium* (SSE), even with metric distances. A SSE is a refinement of the SE where no group of players C can jointly deviate in such a way that no member of C is worst off, while at least one member is better off.

Proposition 1. *There exists a metric instance of the transportation game with $m = 2$ resources having identical permutations which does not admit any SSE.*

Proposition 2. *There exists a non-metric instance of the transportation game with $m = 2$ resources and $n = 3$ players which does not admit any NE.*

Proof. Let the resources be 1 and 2 and let the players be α, β and γ. The permutations are (α, β, γ) for resource 1 and (γ, β, α) for resource 2. The distances are depicted in Fig. 1, on the left. Let us see that the instance has no pure Nash equilibrium. If β is alone on a resource (or she is the last to be picked before traveling to t) then she wants to move. In Fig. 1, on the right, the 4 remaining configurations are depicted. The player with a star on its right has incentive to switch. Hence, this instance does not admit any pure Nash equilibrium.   □

| states | | states | |

Fig. 1. A non-metric instance of the transportation game with $m = 2$ resources and $n = 3$ players that does not admit any pure Nash equilibrium (see also Proposition 2).

2.2 Instances with Metric Distances

Theorem 2. *For the transportation game with $m = 2$ resources and metric distances, better response dynamics converges to a NE.*

Proof. Suppose for the sake of contradiction that there exists a cycle in the Nash dynamics. Let $N_0 \subset N$ be the players who never change their strategy in the cycle, whereas $N_1 := N \setminus N_0 \neq \emptyset$. Note that there is some positive integer k_j, with $j \in \{1, 2\}$, such that the k_j first players in the permutation of resource j are in N_0 and they play j. Indeed, it is a dominant strategy for the first player in the permutation of resource j to play j, because metric distances, ie., the triangle inequality imposes that the cost of that player cannot be lower (namely her distance to t).

For $j \in \{1, 2\}$, let p_j denote the player of N_1 coming first in the permutation of resource j. Let d_j be the player of N_0 who is just before p_j in the permutation of resource j. Let c_{d_j} denote the cost of d_j in the cycle which is invariant. In the cycle, if p_j plays resource j then her cost is equal to $d(p_j, d_j) + c_{d_j}$, whatever the players of $N_1 \setminus \{p_j\}$ play. It must be $p_1 \neq p_2$, otherwise we get a contradiction with $p_1 \in N_1$ because the cost of p_1 does not depend on the strategy adopted by $N_1 \setminus \{p_1\}$. Since the players do unilateral deviations in the cycle, there must be a state of the cycle in which p_1 and p_2 play the same strategy. Suppose wlog. that at some point p_2 profitably moves from resource 2 to resource 1, where p_1 is. The new cost of p_2 is at least her distance to p_1 plus the cost of p_1. Hence, $d(p_2, d_2) + c_{d_2} > d(p_2, p_1) + d(p_1, d_1) + c_{d_1}$. At some point in the cycle p_1 profitably moves to resource 2 where its cost is at least its distance to d_2 plus the cost of d_2. Thus, $d(p_1, d_1) + c_{d_1} > d(p_1, d_2) + c_{d_2}$. Combine previous inequalities to get that $d(p_2, d_2) > d(p_2, p_1) + d(p_1, d_2)$, which is a violation of the triangle inequality. $\square$

From this proof, we know that a potential function exists. Providing an explicit potential function for metric transportation games with two resources is an open question. Another open question asks whether the Nash dynamics converges in polynomial time. We next show how to efficiently compute one equilibrium with some central coordination (2 buses).

Theorem 3. *For $m = 2$ resources and metric distances, the transportation game has a NE that can be computed in $O(n)$.*

Algorithm 1. Greedy algorithm for computing a NE

Input: set N of n players, set M of m resources, permutations π_j for all $j \in M$ (each
    π_j ends with $\lhd$),
    distance function d (we assume that $d(u, \lhd) = \infty$).
Output: assignment $\sigma : N \to R$ that is a PNE
    for all $j \in M$ **do**
        $\text{cost}(j) \leftarrow 0$; $p_j \leftarrow t$; $n_j \leftarrow$ the first player in π_j;
    for all $v \in N$ **do**
        $\text{cost}(v) \leftarrow \infty$; $\sigma(v) \leftarrow \lhd$;
    while $\exists j$ with $n_j \neq \lhd$ **do**
        $k = \arg\min_j\{\text{cost}(j) + d(p_j, n_j)\}$; $u \leftarrow n_k$;
        in case of ties, select resource k with minimum $\text{cost}(k)$
        if $\sigma(u) = \lhd$ **then**
            assign u to resource k and set $\sigma(u) \leftarrow k$ and $c(u) \leftarrow \text{cost}(k) + d(p_k, u)$;
        if $\sigma(u) \neq \lhd$ and $c(u) > \text{cost}(k) + d(p_k, u)$ **then**
            restore $\text{cost}(\sigma(u))$ and $p_{\sigma(u)}$ to their values before u's assignment to $\sigma(u)$;
            $n_{\sigma(u)}$ becomes the first player v after u in $\pi_{\sigma(u)}$ with $c(v) > \text{cost}(\sigma(u)) +$
$d(p_{\sigma(u)}, v)$;
            reassign u from $\sigma(u)$ to k and set $\sigma(u) \leftarrow k$ and $c(u) \leftarrow \text{cost}(k) + d(p_k, u)$;
        let n_k be the next player after u in π_k (n_k becomes $\lhd$ if u is the last player);
        if $\sigma(u) = k$ **then** $p_k \leftarrow u$
    return assignment σ

---

3   Computing a Pure Nash Equilibrium for Distances 1 and 2

For the simplest case of metric distances i.e., corresponding to the case that all distances are either 1 or 2, a NE exists for any number of resources and can be computed in linear time by a natural greedy algorithm.In Algorithm 1, a player is available for assignment to a resource if she is currently the first player in the resource's permutation. Among all available players, Greedy picks the player u that can be assigned to a resource k at a minimum cost. Ties are broken in favor of resources with minimum cost. If player u is not assigned to any resource, she is assigned to k. Otherwise, if u prefers k to her current resource, she is reassigned to k. In both cases, u is removed from the permutation of resource k and Greedy continues. We next show that Greedy terminates with a pure NE assignment if the distances are either 1 or 2.

Example 2. Consider an instance with 8 players, $p_0, \ldots, p_7$, and 3 resources r_1, r_2 and r_3. The permutations are $(p_7\, p_6\, p_5\, p_4\, p_3\, p_2\, p_1\, p_0)$, $(p_0\, p_1\, p_2\, p_3\, p_4\, p_5\, p_6\, p_7)$ and $(p_3\, p_2\, p_6\, p_7\, p_0\, p_5\, p_4\, p_1)$ for r_1, r_2 and r_3, respectively. The nodes are partitioned in three sets: $\{t, p_0, p_1\}$, $\{p_2, p_3, p_4\}$ and $\{p_5, p_6, p_7\}$. The nodes in the same set are within distance 1 to each other. All other distances are 2. In Algorithm 1, at the beginning, players p_7, p_0 and p_3 are available for assignment to r_1, r_2 and r_3, respectively. In the first iteration, p_0 is assigned to r_2 and p_1 becomes available for r_2. In the subsequent iterations, p_7 is assigned to r_1, p_3 to r_3, and p_1 to r_2

(this takes place last due to the tie breaking rule). At this point, we have that $n_1 = p_6$ and $n_2 = n_3 = p_2$. Next, p_6 is assigned to r_1, p_2 to r_3, p_2 and p_3 are considered for and not assigned to r_2, p_4 is assigned to r_2, and p_5 is assigned to r_1. From that point on, p_6, p_7, p_0, p_5, p_4 and p_1 are considered for and not assigned to r_3, p_4, p_3, p_2, p_1 and p_0 are considered for and not assigned to r_1, and p_5, p_6 and p_7 are not assigned to r_2. The final assignment is $(p_7 \, p_6 \, p_5)$ to r_1, $(p_0 \, p_1 \, p_4)$ to r_2, and $(p_3 \, p_2)$ to r_3, which is a NE.

Theorem 4. *Algorithm 1 computes a NE in $O(nm)$ time if the distances are either 1 or 2. Moreover, each player is reassigned at most once through the execution of the algorithm.*

Proof. We refer to a player u as a *candidate* for resource j if either $n_j = u$ or u appears in π_j after n_j (so u will be considered for assignment or reassignment to j in a subsequent iteration). For convenience, we let $\text{cost}^{\text{max}} = \max_j \text{cost}(j)$ and $\text{cost}^{\text{min}} = \min_j \text{cost}(j)$. We use induction on the number of iterations and show that at the end of the current iteration: (i) no assigned player wants to deviate to any resource j, unless she is a candidate for j; (ii) $\text{cost}^{\text{max}} - \text{cost}^{\text{min}} \leq 2$; (iii) cost^{min} does not decrease from one iteration to the next; and (iv) if player u is reassigned from resource $\sigma(u)$ to resource k, her cost at $\sigma(u)$ is $\text{cost}^{\text{max}} = \text{cost}^{\text{min}} + 2$ and her cost at k is $\text{cost}^{\text{min}} + 1$. At the end of the algorithm, no player is a candidate for any resource. Hence, (i) implies that if Greedy terminates, the assignment σ is a pure NE.

Claims (i)-(iv) are true before the first iteration. We inductively assume that (i)-(iv) hold at the end of any iteration. To establish (i)-(iv) hold at the end of the next iteration, we distinguish between three cases: whether u is assigned for the first time to k, whether u is reassigned to k, and whether u stays with $\sigma(u)$. If u stays with $\sigma(u)$, nothing changes and (i)-(iv) remain true at the end of the current iteration.

If u is assigned or reassigned to k, u does not want to deviate at the end of the current iteration, because k minimizes u's cost among all resources j with $n_j = u$. If u is assigned to k, other resources and assigned players are not affected, and claim (i) remains true. If u is reassigned to k, the cost of resource $\sigma(u)$ decreases. To maintain (i), we let $n_{\sigma(u)}$ be the first player after u in $\pi_{\sigma(u)}$ that wants to be assigned to $\sigma(u)$ (this may involve some backtracking in $\pi_{\sigma(u)}$). Then, if an assigned player wants to deviate to $\sigma(u)$, so as to take advantage of u's move out of $\sigma(u)$, she has become a candidate for $\sigma(u)$. So, claim (i) holds at the end of the current iteration.

As for claims (ii)-(iv), since all distances are either 1 and 2, and due to the greedy choice of resource k and to the tie-breaking rule, k's cost is equal to cost^{min}. Hence, if u is assigned for the first time to k, u's cost becomes at most $\text{cost}^{\text{min}} + 2$. Moreover, cost^{min} does not decrease and cost^{max} either does not change or becomes $c(u) \leq \text{cost}^{\text{min}} + 2$. Therefore, (ii)-(iv) hold after u's assignment.

If u is reassigned from $\sigma(u)$ to k, the cost of u at $\sigma(u)$ is $c(u) = \text{cost}^{\text{max}} = \text{cost}^{\text{min}} + 2$. Furthermore, $\text{cost}(k) = \text{cost}^{\text{min}}$ (just before u's reassignment) and the cost of u at k (after u's reassignment) is $\text{cost}^{min} + 1$. These follow from the facts that $\text{cost}^{max} - \text{cost}^{min} \leq 2$ at the end of the previous iteration, that $c(u) > \text{cost}(k) + d(p_k, u)$ and that all distances are 1 and 2. So, after u's reassignment, $\text{cost}(k)$ is at most cost^{max} and $\text{cost}(\sigma(u))$ decreases by 2 and becomes cost^{min}. These imply that (ii)-(iv) remain true after u's reassignment.

Claims (iii) and (iv) imply that any player is reassigned at most once. Due to (iv), if a player u is reassigned from resource $\sigma(u)$ to resource k, $\text{cost}(\sigma(u))$ decreases from cost^{max} to $\text{cost}^{min} = \text{cost}^{max} - 2$ and the new cost of u at k is $\text{cost}^{min} + 1$. Thus, if u is reassigned from resource k later on, the new cost^{min} would be $\text{cost}^{min} - 1$, which contradicts (iii). Hence, Greedy terminates after n assignments and at most n reassignments.

Each reassignment causes a backtrack of at most n players in $\pi_{\sigma(u)}$. But only assigned players with cost $\text{cost}^{min} + 2$ can be reassigned to $\sigma(u)$ after u moves out. So, after u is reassigned to k, we need to insert at the beginning of $\pi_{\sigma(u)}$ only assigned players that appear after u in $\pi_{\sigma(u)}$ and have cost equal to $\text{cost}^{min} + 2$. Since there are at most m such players, the additional running time due to each reassignment is $O(m)$. So the running time of Greedy is $O(nm)$, i.e., linear in the size of the input. $\qquad\square$

4   The Price of Anarchy and the Price of Stability

We consider two different social functions. For a strategy profile σ, $\mathsf{D}(\sigma)$ is the total distance travelled by the buses when they transport at least one client (for each bus we neglect the distance between s and the first client). This function reflects the environmental impact of the solution and it corresponds to the objective *Vehicle Kilometers Travelled* considered in [18]. The second function is the classical *egalitarian* social cost function $\mathsf{E}(\sigma)$ defined as $\max_{i \in N} c_i(\sigma)$, which is also the maximum distance travelled by a single bus if the distance between s and the first client is neglected.

For every $f \in \{\mathsf{D}, \mathsf{E}\}$ and any given instance, σ^* denotes a state for which $f(\sigma^*)$ is minimum. The (pure) *price of anarchy* (PoA for short) is the largest ratio $f(\sigma)/f(\sigma^*)$, over all instances of the game, where σ is a pure NE [19]. The (pure) price of stability (PoS for short) is the largest ratio $f(\sigma)/f(\sigma^*)$, over all instances of the game, where σ is the best NE with respect to f [1]. Therefore $\text{PoA} \geq \text{PoS}$.

Proposition 3. *For every $n \geq 3$, the PoS is unbounded for D or E if the distance is not metric, even if all the permutations are identical.*

4.1   Function D with Metric Distances

Due to Proposition 3, from now on, we assume that the distances are metric.

Lemma 1. *If d is metric, $d(x, y) \leq \mathsf{D}(\sigma^*)$ holds for all nodes $x, y \in N \cup \{t\}$.*

Proof. If x and y are covered by the same bus in σ^*, then suppose wlog. that the bus visits x before y. Therefore, $D(\sigma^*)$ is at least the distance covered by the bus between x and y, while the latter is at least $d(x,y)$, by the triangle inequality. Hence, suppose x and y are covered by two different buses in σ^*, and denote them by b_x and b_y, respectively. Therefore, $D(\sigma^*)$ is at least the distance covered by b_x between x and t plus the distance covered by b_y between y and t. The latter is at least $d(x,y)$, by the triangle inequality. $\square$

Proposition 4. *If d is metric, then $D(\sigma) \leq nD(\sigma^*)$ holds for every state σ.*

Corollary 1. *The PoA with respect to D of the transportation game on n players with metric distances and $m \geq 2$ resources is upper bounded by n.*

Proposition 5. *For any $n \geq 2$, there are metric instances of the transportation game on n players and $m \geq 2$ resources where the PoS is asymptotically n, even if all the resources have the same permutation.*

4.2   Function E Without Metric

Lemma 2. *$d(x,y) \leq 2E(\sigma^*)$ holds for every pair of nodes $(x,y) \in N$, and $d(x,t) \leq E(\sigma^*)$ holds for every node $x \in N$.*

Lemma 3. *In any pure Nash equilibrium, the cost of a player is at most $\left(2\lceil\frac{n}{m}\rceil - 1\right) E(\sigma^*)$.*

Proof. By contradiction, suppose there is a pure NE σ and a player i such that $c_i(\sigma) > (2\lceil\frac{n}{m}\rceil - 1)E(\sigma^*)$. Let k denote the number of players that the bus selected by i picks between i and t (this includes i). Using Lemma 2 we have $c_i(\sigma) \leq (2k - 1)E(\sigma^*)$. These bounds on $c_i(\sigma)$ give $k > \lceil\frac{n}{m}\rceil$. But if more than $\lceil\frac{n}{m}\rceil$ players use the same bus, then there must be another bus, say b, selected by less than $\frac{n}{m}$ players. Even if player i appears last in the permutation of b, her cost if she moves to b would be less than $(2\frac{n}{m} - 1)E(\sigma^*)$ (Lemma 2). We get a contradiction with the fact that σ is a NE. $\square$

Corollary 2. *The PoS with respect to E of the transportation game is $O(\frac{n}{m})$.*

Proposition 6. *For the transportation game, PoA$= 2\lceil\frac{n}{m}\rceil - 1$ if $n > m$ and PoA$= 1$ if $n \leq m$.*

We can also bound the PoA according to the parameters $d_{\min} = \min_{x \neq y} d(x,y)$ and $d_{\max} = \max d(x,y)$. As an immediate corollary, we obtain that PoS $=$ PoA $= 2$ for distances 1 and 2.

Proposition 7. *PoS $=$ PoA $= d_{\max}/d_{\min}$ for the transportation game.*

5   Future Directions

In this work we supposed that the route of the buses are prescribed by a permutation that is independent of the current state. There is an interesting challenge of proposing different ways to define the route of the buses. This modification would induce a different structure of the individual costs and possibly provide better PoA and PoS, under the constraint that a pure equilibrium exists. This challenge is similar to the search of coordination mechanisms in scheduling games.

In transportation problems, it is important to predict the situation so it would be interesting to identify the cases where the equilibrium is unique. In the future, the model of transportation can be extended in several natural aspects. Each bus may have a capacity, its own speed and dedicated roads. The players may have different sizes (*e.g.* a player is a group of persons).

References

1. Anshelevich, E., Dasgupta, A., Kleinberg, J.M., Tardos, É., Wexler, T., Roughgarden, T.: The price of stability for network design with fair cost allocation. In: 45th Symposium on Foundations of Computer Science (FOCS 2004), 17–19 , Rome, Italy, Proceedings, pp. 295–304. IEEE Computer Society, October 2004
2. Applegate, D.L., Bixby, R.E., Chvatal, V., Cook, W.J.: The Traveling Salesman Problem: A Computational Study. Princeton Series in Applied Mathematics. Princeton University Press, Princeton (2007)
3. Aumann, R.J.: Acceptable points in general cooperative n-person games. In: Tucker, A.W., Luce, R.D. (eds.) Contribution to the Theory of Games. Annals of Mathematics Studies, 40 volume IV, pp. 287–324. Princeton University Press (1959)
4. Azar, Y., Jain, K., Mirrokni, V.S.: (Almost) optimal coordination mechanisms for unrelated machine scheduling. In: Shang-Hua Teng, (ed.) Proceedings of the Nineteenth Annual ACM-SIAM Symposium on Discrete Algorithms, SODA, San Francisco, California, USA, January 20–22, pp. 323–332. SIAM (2008)
5. Bistaffa, F., Farinelli, A., Ramchurn, S.D.: Sharing rides with friends: a coalition formation algorithm for ridesharing. In: Bonet, B., Koenig, S. (eds.) Proceedings of the Twenty-Ninth AAAI Conference on Artificial Intelligence, January 25–30, Austin, Texas, USA, pp. 608–614. AAAI Press (2015)
6. Borm, P., Hamers, H., Hendrickx, R.: Operations research games: a survey. Top **9**(2), 139–199 (2001)
7. Caragiannis, I.: Efficient coordination mechanisms for unrelated machine scheduling. Algorithmica **66**(3), 512–540 (2013)
8. Cechlárová, K.: Stable partition problem. In: Kao, M.-Y. (ed.) Encyclopedia of Algorithms, pp. 1–99. Springer, New York (2008). doi:10.1007/978-0-387-30162-4_397
9. Christodoulou, G., Koutsoupias, E., Nanavati, A.: Coordination mechanisms. Theor. Comput. Sci. **410**(36), 3327–3336 (2009)
10. Correa, J.R., Stier-Moses, N.E.: Wardrop equilibria. Wiley Encyclopedia of Operations Research and Management Science (2011)
11. Drèze, J.H., Greenberg, J.: Hedonic coalitions: optimality and stability. Econometrica **48**(4), 987–1003 (1980)

12. Engevall, S., Lundgren, M., Värbrand, P.: The heterogeneous vehicle - routing game. Transp. Sci. **38**(1), 71–85 (2004)
13. Fekete, S.P., Fleischer, R., Fraenkel, A., Schmitt, M.: Traveling salesmen in the presence of competition. Theor. Comput. Sci. **313**(3), 377–392 (2004). Algorithmic Combinatorial Game Theory
14. Feldman, M., Lewin-Eytan, L., Naor, J.: Hedonic clustering games. In: Blelloch, G.E., Herlihy, M. (eds.) 24th ACM Symposium on Parallelism in Algorithms and Architectures, SPAA 2012, Pittsburgh, PA, USA, June 25–27, pp. 267–276. ACM (2012)
15. Gairing, M., Savani, R.: Computing stable outcomes in hedonic games. In: Kontogiannis, S., Koutsoupias, E., Spirakis, P.G. (eds.) SAGT 2010. LNCS, vol. 6386, pp. 174–185. Springer, Heidelberg (2010). doi:10.1007/978-3-642-16170-4_16
16. Kamar, E., Horvitz, E.: Collaboration, shared plans in the open world: studies of ridesharing. In: Boutilier, C. (ed.) Proceedings of the 21st International Joint Conference on Artificial Intelligence, IJCAI, Pasadena, California, USA, July 11–17, p. 187 (2009)
17. Kendall, G., Li, J.: Competitive travelling salesmen problem: a hyper-heuristic approach. J. Oper. Res. Soc. **64**, 208–216 (2013)
18. Kleiner, A., Nebel, B., Ziparo, V.A.: A mechanism for dynamic ride sharing based on parallel auctions. In: Walsh, T. (ed.) Proceedings of the 22nd International Joint Conference on Artificial Intelligence, IJCAI, Barcelona, Catalonia, Spain, July 16–22, pp. 266–272. IJCAI/AAAI (2011)
19. Koutsoupias, E., Papadimitriou, C.: Worst-case equilibria. In: Meinel, C., Tison, S. (eds.) STACS 1999. LNCS, vol. 1563, pp. 404–413. Springer, Heidelberg (1999). doi:10.1007/3-540-49116-3_38
20. Lau, H.C., Agussurja, L., Cheng, S.-F., Tan, P.J.: A multi-objective memetic algorithm for vehicle resource allocation in sustainable transportation planning. In: Rossi, F. (ed.) Proceedings of the 23rd International Joint Conference on Artificial Intelligence, IJCAI, Beijing, China, August 3–9. IJCAI/AAAI (2013)
21. Nash, J.: Non-cooperative games. Ann. Math. **54**(2), 286–295 (1951)
22. Toth, P., Vigo, D. (eds.): The Vehicle Routing Problem. Society for Industrial and Applied Mathematics, Philadelphia (2001)

Decomposable Relaxation for Concurrent Data Structures

Chao Wang[1,2]([⊠]), Yi Lv[1,2], and Peng Wu[1,2]

[1] State Key Laboratory of Computer Science,
Institute of Software, CAS, Beijing, China
{wangch,lvyi,wp}@ios.ac.cn
[2] University of Chinese Academy of Sciences, Beijing, China

Abstract. We propose a relaxation scheme for defining specifications of relaxed data structures. It can produce a relaxed specification parameterized with a specification of a standard data structure, a transition cost function and a relaxation strategy represented by a finite automaton. We show that this relaxation scheme can cover the known specifications of typical relaxed queues and stacks.

   We then propose a method to reduce a relaxed specification defined under the relaxation scheme into a finite number of finite automata called witness automata. By applying this method we prove that the specifications of typical relaxed queues and stacks can be equivalently characterized by a finite number of witness automata. Thus, the problem whether a relaxed queue or stack is linearizable with respect to its relaxed specification can be efficiently checked through automata-theoretic approaches. Moreover, all these witness automata can be generated automatically. In this way, our relaxation scheme can well balance the expressiveness of relaxation strategies with the complexity of verification.

1   Introduction

Developing concurrent data structures often requires subtle synchronization mechanisms, e.g., non-blocking or fine-grained synchronization, to support for concurrency. Hence, concurrent data structures are often error-prone and notoriously hard to verify. Recent developments of concurrent data structures even relax their correctness requirements for better performance and scalability [3,6,7,10,11].

   However, the correctness requirements of relaxed data structures have been far less studied. Recently, quantitative relaxation frameworks have been proposed in [3,7] for relaxed data structures. These frameworks can characterize relaxation strategies for typical relaxed data structures, but inevitably raise the complexity of verification.

This work is partially supported by the National Natural Science Foundation of China under Grants No. 60721061, No. 60833001, No. 61672504, No. 61572478, No. 61672503, No. 61100069, and No. 61161130530.

B. Steffen et al. (Eds.): SOFSEM 2017, LNCS 10139, pp. 188–202, 2017.
DOI: 10.1007/978-3-319-51963-0_15

We observe that there have been two classes of relaxation strategies for specifications of typical relaxed data structures in the literature: one concerns the bounded cost of an individual operation; while the other concerns the bounded costs of a bounded number of certain operations. A cost of an operation is the *distance* of the operation from a "normal" one. For instance, a *deq* operation of cost k for a queue removes from the queue an element that is k elements away from the head of the queue. Such bounded relaxation strategies can be equivalently characterized by specific finite automata.

Based on this observation, we propose a relaxation scheme to define specifications of relaxed data structures (or *relaxed specifications* for short). A relaxed specification is parameterized with a *quantitative specification* [7] and a relaxation strategy represented by a *specification automaton*. A quantitative specification is a labeled transition system (LTS) obtained from a sequential specification by determining the cost of each transition. A specification automaton is a finite automaton that uses predicates over the costs as parts of its transition labels to represent the permitted costs of the transitions in the quantitative specification. Herein, we pre-assume that relaxed data structures have been instrumented with linearization points. Under this assumption, the linearizability problem of such a relaxed specification, i.e., the problem of whether a relaxed data structure is linearizable with respect to the relaxed specification, can be characterized as the inclusion problem between the set of the operation sequences derived by executing the relaxed data structure and the relaxed specification itself. Our relaxation scheme can cover typical relaxed queue specifications [3,6,7,10,11] and relaxed stack specifications [7].

The advantage of our relaxation scheme is that many relaxed specifications defined under the relaxation scheme can be reduced into a finite number of finite automata, called *witness automata*. Moreover, these witness automata can be generated automatically. Thus, although such a relaxed specification and its violations may be far beyond the scope of a regular language, its corresponding witness automata can be exploited for linearizability checking through automata-theoretic approaches.

The reduction of such a relaxed specification can be achieved in two steps. Firstly, we reduce the violations of the relaxed specification into either *ill-formed operation sequences*, or several violations languages. An ill-formed operation sequence is an operation sequence that contains some operation with ∞ cost, such as dequeuing (*deq*) an element from a queue that is not in the queue at the moment. A violation language is a regular language on predicates over operations and their costs. Second, we devise witness automata for checking ill-formed operation sequences, and for checking whether there is a differentiated operation sequence that satisfies some violation language. A differentiated operation sequence is an operation sequence in which each value is added at most once. The correctness of both steps need to be proved case-by-case for individual relaxed data structures and their relaxed specifications.

We then demonstrate the applicability of our relaxation scheme with two typical relaxed queue specifications [3,6,7,10,11]. We adopt the notion of data-independence [16] to handle the operations with an unbounded data domain, over which any value can be safely renamed. Although a relaxed queue specification and its violations may not be regular, the first reduction step essentially partitions the violations of the relaxed queue specification into different classes: ill-formed operation sequences, or operation sequences that satisfies a violation language. This reduction is feasible due to the *non-increasing condition*, a common feature of specification automata of relaxed queue specifications. A consequence of the non-increasing condition is that a bounded number of *deq* operations with bounded costs are enough for capturing the violations. These violation scenarios are represented by violation languages. Then, the second reduction step requires to devise witness automata for the violation languages. Given an operation sequence that satisfies a violation language, we can effectively find a *witness sequence*, which is a minimal sequence that contains the same number of *deq* operations with their costs satisfying the corresponding predicates in the violation language. Due to the data-independence of relaxed queue specifications, from a witness sequence we can generate a witness automaton by safely assuming that other operations use fresh arguments and return values. Since witness sequences have a bounded number of operations, these witness automata can be automatically generated by enumeration.

Related Work. Quasi-linearizability [3] was the first relaxation scheme for sequential specifications of concurrent data structures. A quantitative relaxation framework [7] was then proposed. As preliminary attempts, verification tools have been adapted to model checking relaxed data structures [2, 17]. However, the motivations of the quantitative relaxation frameworks in [3, 7] are to characterize as many relaxed data structures as possible, while our relaxed scheme aims to balance the expressiveness of relaxation strategies with the complexity of verification.

The idea of reducing a linearizability problem with the aids of specific finite automata or simple properties has been studied in [1, 4, 8] for the standard queue and stack specifications (i.e., the specifications with cost 0). Specifically, [1] requires linearization points to be instrumented à *priori*, while [4, 8] do not. All these work do not consider relaxed data structures, and the construction and correctness proofs of the finite automata or simple properties have to be carried out manually. On the contrast, our approach applies to relaxed queue and stack specifications with the aids of witness automata, which can be generated automatically. When applying our approach to standard queue and stack specifications, the finite automata in [1] can be essentially obtained. [4] uses more complicated finite automata, and hence can deal with the cases where linearization points are not instrumented.

2   Notations and Terminologies

For sequences l and l', let $l \cdot l'$ denote their concatenation. Let $l \uparrow_\Sigma$ denote the projection of l onto Σ. Let _ denote an item, of which the value is irrelevant, and ϵ denote the empty sequence. A *labelled transition system* (LTS) is a tuple

$\mathcal{A} = (Q, \Sigma, \rightarrow, q_0)$, where Q is a set of states, Σ is an alphabet of transition labels, $\rightarrow \subseteq Q \times \Sigma \times Q$ is a transition relation and q_0 is the initial state. A path of $\mathcal{A}$ is a finite transition sequence $q_0 \xrightarrow{\alpha_1} q_1 \xrightarrow{\alpha_2} \ldots \xrightarrow{\alpha_k} q_k$ with $k \geq 0$. A finite sequence $t = \alpha_1 \cdot \alpha_2 \cdot \ldots \cdot \alpha_k$ with $k \geq 0$ is a trace of $\mathcal{A}$ if there exists a path $q_0 \xrightarrow{\alpha_1} q_1 \xrightarrow{\alpha_2} \ldots \xrightarrow{\alpha_k} q_k$ of $\mathcal{A}$.

2.1   Concurrent Data Structures and Their Specifications

A concurrent data structure (implementation) encapsulates a collection of methods for accessing a possibly shared instance of the concurrent data structure. We presume a potential infinite data domain $\mathcal{D}$ and a finite set $\mathcal{M}$ of methods. We identify a set of input methods that takes one input argument, such as the typical *enq* method of queue and *push* method of stack. Let $\mathcal{M}_{inp}$ be the set of input methods in $\mathcal{M}$ and $\mathcal{M}_{oth} = \mathcal{M} - \mathcal{M}_{inp}$. Each method declares its local variables and method body, which is built from atomic commands (e.g., write, read, assignment, compare-and-swap, malloc and free) using the standard control-flow constructs (including the sequential composition, selection and loop constructs). The execution of a method is started by an invocation with arguments in $\mathcal{D}$ and terminated by executing a return command, which may return values in $\mathcal{D}$. For simplicity, we assume that each method has only one parameter and one return value (if it returns).

An operation $m(a, b)$ represents that method m is called with argument a and returns value b. A (sequential) specification of a concurrent data structure is defined as a prefix-closed set of sequences over $\{m(a, b) | m \in \mathcal{M}, a, b \in \mathcal{D}\}$.

2.2   Linearizability with Linearization Points

Linearizability [9] is the *de facto* standard correctness condition for concurrent data structures. In this paper we consider a concurrent system that consists of an unbounded number of concurrent processes, each of which may at any time invoke any method in $\mathcal{M}$ with any argument in $\mathcal{D}$. An execution of the concurrent system is modeled by a history, which is a finite sequence of call and return actions. A call action happens when a method is called by a process. A return action happens when a called method returns to the calling process.

Intuitively, a history is linearizable with respect to its sequential specification, if every method of the history appears to take effect instantaneously at some point between the call and the return action of the method, and the sequence of taking effect belongs to its sequential specification. A concurrent data structure is linearizable with respect to its sequential specification, if each of its history is. The time point when a method takes effect is called a linearization point, and locating linearization points is an intuitive approach for proving linearizability.

In this paper, we assume that the linearization points of each method have already been instrumented. When a command, which is introduced as the linearization point between a call action of method m with argument a and the corresponding return action with value b, is being executed, it will generate an operation $m(a, b)$. Such instrumentation process may not be that straightforward, since for some concurrent data structures, the linearization points of one method may vary and depend on future interleaving of a history, which is unpredictable, or locate in other methods [12]. Thus, each execution of the concurrent system can generate a sequence of such operations. Let $OpSeq(\mathcal{L})$ be the set of all the sequences of the operations generated by the concurrent system with concurrent data structure $\mathcal{L}$. Then, the notion of linearizability with linearization points is defined as follows:

Definition 1 (linearizability with linearization points). *A concurrent data structure $\mathcal{L}$, which has been instrumented with linearization points, is linearizable with respect to a specification Spec for an unbounded number of processes, if $OpSeq(\mathcal{L}) \subseteq Spec$.*

3   Specifications of Relaxed Data Structures

In this section we propose our relaxation scheme for defining specifications of relaxed data structures. We use the k-FIFO queues [10] as the running example to intuitively introduce relaxed data structures, and then instantiate the relaxation scheme to define the relaxed queue specification for k-FIFO queues.

3.1 k-FIFO Queues

k-FIFO [10] queues are a typical relaxation of FIFO queues. A k-FIFO queue maintains a linked list of segments, each of which is an array of k cells. Each enq operation attempts to put an element into an empty cell of the tail segment, while each deq operation attempts to remove an element from the head segment. k-FIFO

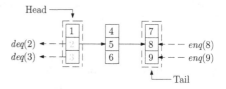

Fig. 1. 3-FIFO queue

queues scatter the contention for both enq and deq operations, and hence exhibit better performance than Michael-Scott queue [13] at the expense of relaxing correctness. Figure 1 shows a 3-FIFO queue, which contains three 3-cell segments. k-FIFO queues may exhibit behaviors that violate the FIFO order, because the values in the same segments may be removed in an arbitrary order. For example, suppose in Fig. 1 values are enqueued in the increasing order. Then, 1, 2 and 3 may be dequeued in an arbitrary order. However, a k-FIFO queue additionally requires that a $deq(null)$ operation happens only when the queue is empty. Here $null$ is the special value denoting that a data structure contains no data item.

3.2   Relaxation Strategies

An operation has cost r, if it has *distance* r from a corresponding "normal" operation, such as dequeuing an element from a queue that is r elements away from the head of the queue. According to [3,7], the specifications of relaxed data structures are obtained by relaxing the specifications of standard data structures (where each operation has cost 0). We observe that there have been two relaxation strategies for specifications of typical relaxed data structures. Take queue specifications for example. Given sequence $s = (o_1, r_1) \cdots (o_l, r_l)$, where o_i is an *enq* or *deq* operation with cost r_i for $1 \leq i \leq l$. Roughly speaking, s can be accepted under either of the following relaxation strategies (conditions):

– Each *enq* operation has cost 0, while each *deq* operation has cost no greater than some constant $k \in \mathbb{N}$, or is *well-formed*, i.e., having cost in $\mathbb{N}$.
– s must adhere to the segment mechanism as in k-FIFO queues. Specially, as in [3,7], we use an "over-approximation" of this sort of relaxation strategies, i.e., (1) the maximal length of successive but not necessarily adjacent *deq* operations that do not return *null* and have non-0 costs is *k-1*, where k is the length of a segment, and (2) the maximal permitted cost of the *i-th* successive *deq* operation is *k-i*.

The first and second relaxation strategies capture the specifications of the relaxed data structures defined in [3,6,11] and in [3,7,10], respectively.

3.3 Relaxed Specifications

The above relaxation strategies consider only costs of individual operations or a bounded number of certain operations, which subject to simple conditions such as "no greater than some constant k", "in $\mathbb{N}$" and "equal to 0". By representing these conditions as predicates, these relaxation strategies can be equivalently captured by finite automata. Based on this intuition, in this subsection we propose a relaxation scheme for defining specifications of relaxed data structures (or relaxed specifications for short).

A relaxed specification is obtained by relaxing a specification of a standard data structure with a relaxation strategy specified in the form of a finite automaton, called a *specification automaton*. The relaxation scheme is divided into two steps. Similar to [7], the first step is to semantically point out the costs of each operation in the specification of the standard data structure. This results in a *quantitative specification*. In the second step, the relaxed specification is obtained by filtering the quantitative specification with the specification automaton.

Quantitative Specifications: Given a specification *Spec*, we semantically represent it as an *LTS LTS(Spec)* $= (Q, \Sigma, \rightarrow, q_0)$, with the only requirement that the set of traces of *LTS(Spec)* must be *Spec*. A quantitative specification is a tuple *QLTS(Spec, f)* $= (Q, \Sigma, Q \times \Sigma \times Q, q_0, f)$, which makes transitions between all the pairs of the states of *LTS(Spec)* with all the operations as labels. $f : Q \times \Sigma \times Q \mapsto \mathbb{N} \cup \{\infty\}$ is a transition cost function, where ∞ is the special number that is greater than any natural number. It is used to determine the costs of the transitions between every pair of states of *LTS(Spec)*. Specially, f maps only the transitions of *LTS(Spec)* to 0. This process of determining costs for transitions is same as that in [7].

Specification Automata: The operations with methods in $\mathcal{M}_{inp}$ are referred to as $\mathcal{M}_{inp}$ operations, while the operations with methods in $\mathcal{M}_{oth}$ that do not return *null* (respectively, that return *null*) are referred to as $\mathcal{M}_{oth}^v$ (respectively, $\mathcal{M}_{oth}^n$) operations.

Given $k \in \mathbb{N}$, let *Nat*, $E(k)$, $N(k)$, $LE(k)$ and $G(k)$ represent predicate "is a natural number (not ∞)", "equal to k", "not equal to k", "less than or equal to k" and "greater than k", respectively. Let M_{inp}^p, M_{oth}^{p-v} and M_{oth}^{p-n} represent the predicate that identifies $\mathcal{M}_{inp}$ operations, $\mathcal{M}_{oth}^v$ operations and $\mathcal{M}_{oth}^n$ operations, respectively. Then, a specification automaton is a finite automaton $\mathcal{A} = (Q_{\mathcal{A}}, F_{\mathcal{A}}, \Sigma_{\mathcal{A}}, \rightarrow_{\mathcal{A}}, q_{init})$, where

- $Q_{\mathcal{A}}$ is the finite set of states; $q_{init} \in Q_{\mathcal{A}}$ is the initial state, and $F_{\mathcal{A}} \subseteq Q_{\mathcal{A}}$ is the set of final states.
- $\Sigma_{\mathcal{A}}$ is a finite set of transition labels, each of which is represented as a pair (po, pc) of predicates. $po \in \{M_{inp}^p, M_{oth}^{p-v}, M_{oth}^{p-n}\}$ is used to select certain operations; while $pc \in \{Nat, N(0), E(0)\} \cup \{LE(i), LE(i) \wedge N(0), G(i) | i \in \mathbb{N}\}$ is used to select certain costs.
- $\rightarrow_{\mathcal{A}} \subseteq Q_{\mathcal{A}} \times \Sigma_{\mathcal{A}} \times Q_{\mathcal{A}}$ is the transition relation.

Relaxed Specifications: A sequence $(o_1, r_1) \cdot \ldots \cdot (o_l, r_l)$ is said to be accepted by $QLTS(Spec, f)$ and $\mathcal{A}$, if it is a trace of $QLTS(Spec, f)$, and there exist transitions $q_1 \xrightarrow{(po_1, pc_1)}_{\mathcal{A}} q_2, \ldots, q_l \xrightarrow{(po_l, pc_l)}_{\mathcal{A}} q_{l+1}$ of $\mathcal{A}$ from the initial state $q_{init} \equiv q_1$ to a final state q_{l+1} in $F_{\mathcal{A}}$, such that for each $1 \leq i \leq l$, o_i satisfies po_i, $r_i \in \mathbb{N}$ satisfies pc_i. Then, the relaxed specification $Spec_{\mathcal{A},f}$ is obtained by filtering the traces of $QLTS(Spec, f)$ with $\mathcal{A}$, as defined below:

Definition 2 (relaxed specification). *Given specification Spec, transition cost function f and specification automaton $\mathcal{A}$, the relaxed specification $Spec_{\mathcal{A},f}$ is defined such that an operation sequence $s = o_1 \cdot \ldots \cdot o_l$ is in $Spec_{\mathcal{A},f}$, if there exist costs $r_1, \ldots, r_l$, such that $(o_1, r_1) \cdot \ldots \cdot (o_l, r_l)$ is accepted by $QLTS(Spec, f)$ and $\mathcal{A}$.*

Since an operation with ∞ cost often means an ill-formed operation, we do not consider operations with ∞ cost in Definition 2.

3.4 Relaxed Queue Specifications

In this subsection we instantiate the above relaxation scheme for defining specifications of relaxed queues. The definition of a relaxed stack specification is rather similar and can be found in the technical report version of this paper [14].

Specification of FIFO Queues as an LTS: An FIFO queue has typically two methods: *enq* and *deq*, among which *enq* is the input method. Since *enq* has no return value and *deq* has no input argument, we abbreviate operation $enq(a, \_)$ and $deq(\_, b)$ as $enq(a)$ and $deq(b)$, respectively. The set of operations for an FIFO queue is $\{enq(d) | d \in \mathcal{D}\} \cup \{deq(d') | d' \in \mathcal{D} \cup \{null\}\}$. Let *Queue* be the specification of an FIFO queue, whose definition is obvious and hence omitted here. $LTS(Queue)$ is constructed as follows as in [7]:

– Each state is a sequence over $\{enq(d)|d \in \mathcal{D}\}$; specially, the initial state is ϵ; each transition label is an enq or deq operation;
– $s \xrightarrow{enq(d)} s \cdot enq(d)$ for each state s; $s \xrightarrow{deq(d)} s'$ if $s = enq(d) \cdot s'$; and $s \xrightarrow{deq(null)} s$ if $s = \epsilon$.

Quantitative Specification of FIFO Queues: A quantitative specification $QLTS(Queue, f_{seg})$ can be constructed by using the segment cost function f_{seg} in [7] as the transition cost function. f_{seg} maps a transition between s and s' with label o to cost r, if r is the length of a minimum sequence v such that

– $s = u \cdot v \cdot w$, $s' = u' \cdot v \cdot w$ and $u \cdot w \xrightarrow{o} u' \cdot w$ is a transition of $LTS(Queue)$, or
– $s = u \cdot v \cdot w$, $s' = u \cdot v \cdot w'$ and $u \cdot w \xrightarrow{o} u \cdot w'$ is a transition of $LTS(Queue)$;

or $r = \infty$ if such v does not exist. Intuitively, the segment cost of a transition is the length of the shortest word v whose removal enables a transition.

Specification Automata for k-FIFO Queues: We abbreviate sets $\{enq\}$, $\{deq\}^v$, $\{deq\}^n$, and predicates $\{enq\}^p$, $\{deq\}^{p-v}$ and $\{deq\}^{p-n}$ as enq, deq^v, deq^n, enq^p, deq^{p-v} and deq^{p-n}, respectively. We require each enq operation to have cost 0. Let K_n represent the maximal permitted cost of a deq^n operation, and k be the length of a segment. Figure 2 shows the specification automaton $\mathcal{A}^q_{seg-(3,0)}$ for the second relaxation strategy with $k = 3$ and $K_n = 0$ (which is the case of 3-FIFO queues). Here $c_1 = (enq^p, E(0)), (deq^{p-v}, E(0)), (deq^{p-n}, E(0))$, $c_2 = (enq^p, E(0)), (deq^{p-n}, E(0))$, and q_{trap} is the trap state which is not a state in $F_\mathcal{A}$ and has no outgoing transitions.

$\mathcal{A}^q_{seg-(3,0)}$ requires that deq^v operations is relaxed according to the segment mechanism, while enq and deq^n operations have cost 0. It also requires that the maximal length of successive but not necessarily adjacent deq^v operations with non-0 cost is 2, and the maximal permitted cost of the first (respectively, second) successive deq^v operation is 2 (respectively, 1). This represents a "shrinking window" of size up to 3, while the values in a shrinking window can be removed in an arbitrary order.

Please refer to the technical report version of this paper [14] for a detailed definition of the specification automaton $\mathcal{A}^q_{seg-(k,K_n)}$ for the second relaxation strategy. In [14] we also define the specification automaton $\mathcal{A}^q_{max-(K_v,K_n)}$ for the first relaxation strategy, where K_v represents the maximal permitted cost

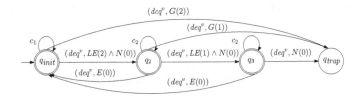

Fig. 2. Specification automaton $\mathcal{A}^q_{seg-(3,0)}$

of a deq^v operation. In the rest of this paper, let $Queue_{\mathcal{A}_{max}}$ (respectively, $Queue_{\mathcal{A}_{seg}}$) denote the relaxed specification generated from $QLTS(Queue, f_{seg})$ and $\mathcal{A}^q_{max-(K_v,K_n)}$ (respectively, $\mathcal{A}^q_{seg-(k,K_n)}$).

4   Reducing Relaxed Specifications into Witness Automata

In this section, we present our method for reducing a relaxed specification into a finite number of finite automata. We would need the following notions to capture counterexamples of a relaxed specification. An operation sequence s is *differentiated*, if for all $m \in M_{inp}$ and all $a \in \mathcal{D}$, $|s \uparrow_{\{m(a,b)|b \in \mathcal{D}\}}| \leq 1$. A set of operation sequences is *differentiated* if each of the operation sequences is. For a quantitative specification $QLTS(Spec, f)$, an operation sequence $s = o_1 \cdot \ldots \cdot o_l$ is well-formed, if there exist costs $r_1, \ldots, r_l \in \mathbb{N}$, such that $(o_1, r_1) \cdot \ldots \cdot (o_l, r_l)$ is a trace of $QLTS(Spec, f)$; otherwise, s is ill-formed. Obviously, each sequence in $Spec_{\mathcal{A},f}$ is well-formed. Then, our reduction method proceeds in the following two steps.

Step 1: In the first step, we construct a finite number of regular languages $VioLang(\mathcal{A})$ from the specification automaton $\mathcal{A}$. Each regular language in $VioLang(\mathcal{A})$ is called a *violation language*, of which the alphabet is $\{(po, pc)|po \in \{\mathcal{M}^p_{inp}, \mathcal{M}^{p-v}_{oth}, \mathcal{M}^{p-n}_{oth}\}, pc \in \{Nat, N(0)\} \cup \{G(k)|k \in \mathbb{N}\}\}$. Each violation language represents a category of executions that carries cost and can cause violations to the relaxed specification. An operation sequence $s = o_1 \cdot \ldots \cdot o_l$ satisfies a violation language lan, if there exist costs $r_1, \ldots, r_l \in \mathbb{N}$ and sequence $(po_1, pc_1) \cdot \ldots \cdot (po_l, pc_l) \in lan$, such that $(o_1, r_1) \cdot \ldots \cdot (o_l, r_l)$ is a trace of $QLTS(Spec, f)$, and for each $1 \leq i \leq l$, o_i satisfies po_i and r_i satisfies pc_i. Then, this step needs to ensure the following condition:

Condition 1: Given concurrent data structure $\mathcal{L}$, $OpSeq(\mathcal{L}) \nsubseteq Spec_{\mathcal{A},f}$, if and only if there exists an ill-formed sequence $s \in OpSeq(\mathcal{L})$, or a well-formed differentiated sequence $s \in OpSeq(\mathcal{L})$, such that s satisfies some violation language $lang \in VioLang(\mathcal{A})$.

Step 2: In the second step, we construct a finite set $IllAut$ of finite automata for capturing ill-formed sequences, and a finite set $Aut(lang)$ of finite automata for each violation language $lang$ in $VioLan(\mathcal{A})$. Let $Aut(\mathcal{A})$ be the union of the finite automata constructed for each violation language in $VioLan(\mathcal{A})$. We call each automaton in $Aut(\mathcal{A}) \cup IllAut$ a *witness automaton*. Furthermore, this step needs to ensure the following condition:

Condition 2: There exists an ill-formed sequence $s \in OpSeq(\mathcal{L})$, or a well-formed differentaited $s \in OpSeq(\mathcal{L})$, such that s satisfies some violation language $lang \in VioLang(\mathcal{A})$, if and only if there exists a sequence $s' \in OpSeq(\mathcal{L})$, such that s' is accepted by some automaton in $Aut(\mathcal{A}) \cup IllAut$.

Conditions 1 and 2 need to be proved case-by-case for individual concurrent data structures and their relaxed specifications. Once the above two steps are accomplished with the corresponding conditions established, it can be seen that $Spec_{\mathcal{A},f}$ is equivalently characterized by $Aut(\mathcal{A}) \cup IllAut$, as indicated by the following theorem:

Theorem 1. *If Condition 1 and Condition 2 hold, then $OpSeq(\mathcal{L}) \subseteq Spec_{\mathcal{A},f}$, if and only if no sequence in $OpSeq(\mathcal{L})$ is accepted by any automaton in $Aut(\mathcal{A}) \cup IllAut$.*

By Definition 1 the linearizability problem of a relaxed data structure with respect to its relaxed specification can be considered as the sequence inclusion problem between the set of the operation sequences derived by executing the relaxed data structure and the relaxed specification itself. However, relaxed specifications are often far beyond the scope of regular languages. By Theorem 1 checking the linearizability of a relaxed data structure can be reduced to the emptiness problem of the intersection between the set of the operation sequences derived by executing the relaxed data structure and the languages of a finite number of witness automata. This renders the possibility of using automata-theoretic approaches for linearizability checking based on witness automata, as shown in [1] for standard queue and stack specifications.

5 Equivalent Characterizations of Relaxed Queues

In this section, we use the relaxed specifications $Queue_{\mathcal{A}_{seg}}$ of 3-FIFO queues as the running examples to demonstrate the process of reducing typical relaxed queue specifications into a finite number of witness automata, according to the reduction method introduced in Sect. 4. Along this process, it can be seen that these witness automata can be generated automatically. The case for relaxed stack specifications is rather similar, and hence omitted here. The detailed definitions and proofs can be found in the technical report version of this paper [14].

5.1 Data-Independence

Data-independence [16] is a practical feature in many real-life data structures. Each value added into a data-independent data structure can be considered as a unique one and can be safely renamed. A renaming function $\sigma : \mathcal{D} \rightarrow \mathcal{D}$ can be applied to an operation sequence s, resulting in the sequence $\sigma(s)$, where each value d in s is replaced with $\sigma(d)$. A set S of operation sequences is *data-independent*, if for each $s \in S$,

- There exists a differentiated operation sequence $s' \in S$ with $s = \sigma(s')$ for some renaming function σ.
- $\sigma(s) \in S$ for any renaming function σ.

A concurrent data structure $\mathcal{L}$ is data-independent, if $OpSeq(\mathcal{L})$ is. We prove in [14] that the relaxed queue specifications $Queue_{\mathcal{A}_{max}}$ and $Queue_{\mathcal{A}_{seg}}$ are data-independent. Herein, we rely on the notion of data-independence (1) to generate differentiated operation sequences by renaming operation sequences, and (2) to generate operation sequences with a finite data domain by renaming differentiated operation sequences that potentially uses an unbounded data domain.

5.2   Violation Languages of Relaxed Queue Specifications

In this subsection we define the violation languages for the relaxed specification $Queue_{A_{seg}}$ with $K_n = 0$ and $k = 3$, and prove that these violation languages satisfy Condition 1.

Let $\top = (\mathcal{M}_{oth}^{p\text{-}v} + \mathcal{M}_{oth}^{p\text{-}n}, Nat) + (\mathcal{M}_{inp}^{p}, E(0))$ represent a placeholder for enq and deq operations. Let $\top' = (\mathcal{M}_{oth}^{p\text{-}n}, Nat) + (\mathcal{M}_{inp}^{p}, E(0))$ represent a placeholder for enq and deq^n operations. The violation languages of $\mathcal{A}_{seg-(3,0)}^{q}$ include the following two languages: the first language is $\top^* \cdot ((deq^{p\text{-}n}, N(0)) \cdot \top^*$, and is used to capture deq^n operations that have non-0 cost; while the second language contains $vl_{seg-(3,i)}$ $(1 \le i \le 3)$ and is used to capture deq^v operations that violate the segment mechanism. Here $vl_{seg-(k,i)}$ denotes the violation language $\top^* \cdot ((deq^{p\text{-}v}, N(0)) \cdot \top'^*)^{i\text{-}1} \cdot (deq^{p\text{-}v}, G(k\text{-}i)) \cdot \top^*$.

We now explain why the above violation languages satisfy Condition 1. Note that in $\mathcal{A}_{seg-(3,0)}^{q}$, the maximal permitted costs of deq^v transitions from q_{init} to q_2, from q_2 to q_3, and from q_3 to q_{init} are in the decreasing order. This feature is called *the non-increasing property*. Due to the non-increasing property, a bounded number of deq^v operations with certain costs are enough for capturing violations to the relaxed specification, while costs of any other operations are not relevant any more. For example, if a deq^v operation with cost 2 is captured in a differentiated operation sequence, then this operation sequence violates the relaxed specification for sure. In [14] we show in details how to generate violation languages for the relaxed queue specifications. The following lemma states that such violation languages satisfy Condition 1:

Lemma 1. *Assume that $\mathcal{L}$ is data-independent. $OpSeq(\mathcal{L}) \nsubseteq Queue_{A_{max}}$ (respectively, $Queue_{A_{seg}}$), if and only if there exists an ill-formed sequence $s \in OpSeq(\mathcal{L})$, or a well-formed differentiated sequence $s \in OpSeq(\mathcal{L})$, such that s satisfies some violation language $lang \in VioLang(\mathcal{A}_{max-(K_v,K_n)}^{q})$ (respectively, $VioLang(\mathcal{A}_{seg-(k,K_n)}^{q}))$.*

5.3   Witness Automata for Ill-Formed Sequences

In this subsection, we present witness automata $\mathcal{A}_{cre}^{q}$ and $\mathcal{A}_{dup}^{q}$ to detect the existence of an ill-formed sequence. Let $d_1, d_2, \ldots,$ be distinct constants in $\mathcal{D}$, and if $\mathcal{D} = \mathbb{N}$, then $d_1, d_2, \ldots$ can just be $1, 2, \ldots$, respectively. $\mathcal{A}_{cre}^{q}$ and $\mathcal{A}_{dup}^{q}$ are shown in Fig. 3(a) and (b), respectively, where $c = enq(d_1), deq(d_1), deq(null)$.

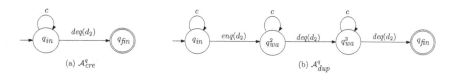

(a) $\mathcal{A}_{cre}^{q}$

(b) $\mathcal{A}_{dup}^{q}$

Fig. 3. Witness automaton $\mathcal{A}_{cre}^{q}$ and $\mathcal{A}_{dup}^{q}$.

For any state s of $QLTS(Queue)$ and a enq or deq^n operation o, we can always find state s' and cost $r \in \mathbb{N}$, such that the operation o from s to s' has cost r. But this does not hold for deq^v operations. Therefore, $\mathcal{A}_{cre}^q$ and $\mathcal{A}_{dup}^q$ only focus on deq^v operations. $\mathcal{A}_{cre}^q$ monitors whether a deq^v transition returns a value d_2 that has never been enqueued before, while $\mathcal{A}_{dup}^q$ monitors whether a value d_2 has been enqueued only once but is dequeued twice. Similar automata have been used in [1,4] for FIFO queues. The following lemma states that the set $IllAut^q = \{\mathcal{A}_{cre}^q, \mathcal{A}_{dup}^q\}$ captures exactly ill-formed sequences in accessing a data-independent relaxed data structure.

Lemma 2. *Assume that $\mathcal{L}$ is data-independent. There exists an ill-formed sequence in $OpSeq(\mathcal{L})$, if and only if some sequence of $OpSeq(\mathcal{L})$ is accepted by automata in $IllAut^q$.*

5.4 Witness Automata for Violation Languages

A *well-formed* sequence ws is a witness sequence of a violation language $vl_{seg-(3,j)}$, if (1) ws contains j deq^v operations but no deq^n operations; (2) the first j-1 deq^v operation have non-0 cost, while the last deq^v operation has cost greater than 3-j; (3) ws is a minimal sequence having the above two conditions, i.e., ws contains the minimum number of enq operations for the above two conditions to hold. Additionally, the i-th enq operation in ws uses distinct d_i for each $i > 0$. Each witness sequence is well-formed and differentiated. It can be seen that the number of enq operations in a witness sequence is bounded with respect to segment length k. For example, for violation language $vl_{seg-(3,2)}$, its witness sequence contains two deq^v operations, the maximal number of enq operations before the first (or second) deq operation is 4, and after the second deq operation there is no enq operation.

Given witness sequence ws, a witness automaton $\mathcal{A}_{ws}$ can be constructed as follows: a chain of nodes from q_{in} to q_{fin} is created through connections labeled with operations in ws one by one; q_{in} is then connected to itself with multiple labels, including a deq^n operation, and an enq and a deq^v operation with the fresh value that is distinct from values in $\mathcal{A}_{ws}$; each intermediate node is also connected to itself with multiple labels, including a deq^n operation and an enq operation with the fresh value. For example, $ws = enq(d_1) \cdot enq(d_2) \cdot enq(d_3) \cdot enq(d_4) \cdot deq(d_2) \cdot deq(d_4)$ is a witness sequence of violation language $vl_{seg-(3,2)}$, and Fig. 4 shows the witness automaton for ws, where $c_1 = enq(d_5), deq(d_5), deq(null)$, $c_2 = enq(d_5), deq(null)$ and d_5 is the fresh value.

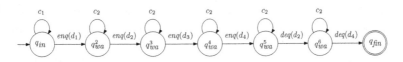

Fig. 4. Witness automaton for $enq(d_1) \cdot enq(d_2) \cdot enq(d_3) \cdot enq(d_4) \cdot deq(d_2) \cdot deq(d_4)$

Similarly, we can construct a witness automaton from violation language $\top^* \cdot ((deq^{p-n}, N(0)) \cdot \top^*$. We prove that these witness automata are able to capture well-formed differentiated sequences that satisfy the violation languages defined in Sect. 5.2, as indicated by the following lemma:

Lemma 3. *Assume $OpSeq(\mathcal{L})$ is data-independent. There exists a well-formed differentiated $s \in OpSeq(\mathcal{L})$, such that s satisfies some violation language lang $\in VioLang(\mathcal{A}^q_{max-(K_v,K_n)})$ (or $VioLang(\mathcal{A}^q_{seg-(k,K_n)})$), if and only if there exists a sequence $s' \in OpSeq(\mathcal{L})$, such that s' is accepted by some automaton in $Aut(lang)$.*

Lemmas 2 and 3 make Condition 2 hold. Therefore, $Aut(\mathcal{A}^q_{max-(K_v,K_n)}) \cup IllAut^q$ (respectively, $Aut(\mathcal{A}^q_{seg-(k,K_n)}) \cup IllAut^q$) constitutes an equivalent characterization of the relaxed queue specification $Queue_{\mathcal{A}_{max}}$ (respectively, $Queue_{\mathcal{A}_{seg}}$).

Theorem 2. *Assume $OpSeq(\mathcal{L})$ is data-independent. $OpSeq(\mathcal{L}) \nsubseteq Queue_{\mathcal{A}_{max}}$ (respectively, $Queue_{\mathcal{A}_{seg}}$), if and only if some sequence in $OpSeq(\mathcal{L})$ is accepted by some automaton in $Aut(\mathcal{A}^q_{max-(K_v,K_n)}) \cup IllAut^q$ (respectively, $Aut(\mathcal{A}^q_{seg-(k,K_n)}) \cup IllAut^q$).*

It can be seen that a witness sequence has bounded length, because the number of deq^v and deq^n operations in a witness sequence is fixed, while the number of enq operations in a witness sequence is bounded. Thus, we can automatically generate witness sequences by enumeration. In [14] we show that the number of witness automata for $Queue_{\mathcal{A}_{seg}}$ is at least exponential to the length of a segment. Take violation language $vl_{seg-(k,k)}$ as an example. We get a subset of 2^k witness sequences of $vl_{seg-(k,k)}$. The i-th $(1 \le i \le k)$ deq^v operation in each of these witness sequences can have either cost 1 or cost 2. This implies the lower bound of the number of witness sequences (and hence the number of witness automata) is at least exponential. The number of witness automata for $Queue_{\mathcal{A}_{max}}$ is four: two for ill-formed operation sequences, one for deq^v operations with non-0 costs and one for deq^n operations with non-0 costs. The standard FIFO queue specification is a special case of $Queue_{\mathcal{A}_{max}}$ with $K_v = K_n = 0$, and the number of witness automata for it is exactly four.

6   Conclusion and Future Work

Many relaxed data structures have been implemented for the sake of performance and scalability, while their verification problems were often left untouched or less concerned. Quasi-linearizability [3] and the quantitative relaxation framework [7] can characterize many of these relaxed implementations. However, we proved in [15] that quasi-linearizability is undecidable. The quantitative relaxation framework [7] indeed subsumes quasi-linearizability and can be proved undecidable. On the contrast, our relaxation scheme can be proved decidable, and equivalently characterized by a finite number of witness automata.

Our relaxation scheme achieves a balance between the expressiveness of quantitative relaxation and the complexity in verifying the correctness of relaxed data structures. We have shown that our relaxation scheme is expressive enough to cover typical relaxed queues and stacks. We also have proposed the methodology of reducing a relaxed specification defined under our relaxation scheme into a finite number of witness automata, and applied it to relaxed queues and stacks. We conjecture that the state-of-the-art safety verification tools, such as [1], can then be applied to verify the linearizability of relaxed data structures through automata-theoretic approaches. Note that the number of witness automata for $Queue_{\mathcal{A}_{seg}}$ is exponential to the length of a segment while the number of witness automata for FIFO queues is constant. This reveals the inherent complexity of verifying relaxed specifications.

It is interesting for future work to further investigate automata-theoretic approaches for non-data-independent concurrent data structures. We would also like to study the linearizability problem of relaxed data structures without instrumenting their linearization points explicitly, as in [4,8].

References

1. Abdulla, P.A., Haziza, F., Holík, L., Jonsson, B., Rezine, A.: An integrated specification and verification technique for highly concurrent data structures. In: Piterman, N., Smolka, S.A. (eds.) TACAS 2013. LNCS, vol. 7795, pp. 324–338. Springer, Heidelberg (2013). doi:10.1007/978-3-642-36742-7_23
2. Adhikari, K., Street, J., Wang, C., Liu, Y., Zhang, S.J.: Verifying a quantitative relaxation of linearizability via refinement. In: Bartocci, E., Ramakrishnan, C.R. (eds.) SPIN 2013. LNCS, vol. 7976, pp. 24–42. Springer, Heidelberg (2013). doi:10.1007/978-3-642-39176-7_3
3. Afek, Y., Korland, G., Yanovsky, E.: Quasi-linearizability: relaxed consistency for improved concurrency. In: Lu, C., Masuzawa, T., Mosbah, M. (eds.) OPODIS 2010. LNCS, vol. 6490, pp. 395–410. Springer, Heidelberg (2010). doi:10.1007/978-3-642-17653-1_29
4. Bouajjani, A., Emmi, M., Enea, C., Hamza, J.: On reducing linearizability to state reachability. In: Halldórsson, M.M., Iwama, K., Kobayashi, N., Speckmann, B. (eds.) ICALP 2015. LNCS, vol. 9135, pp. 95–107. Springer, Heidelberg (2015). doi:10.1007/978-3-662-47666-6_8
5. Bouajjani, A., Emmi, M., Enea, C., Hamza, J.: Verifying concurrent programs against sequential specifications. In: Felleisen, M., Gardner, P. (eds.) ESOP 2013. LNCS, vol. 7792, pp. 290–309. Springer, Heidelberg (2013). doi:10.1007/978-3-642-37036-6_17
6. Haas, A., Lippautz, M., Henzinger, T.A., Payer, H., Sokolova, A., Kirsch, C.M., Sezgin, A.: Distributed queues in shared memory: multicore performance and scalability through quantitative relaxation. In: CF 2013, p. 17: 1–17: 9 (2013)
7. Henzinger, T.A., Kirsch, C.M., Payer, H., Sezgin, A., Sokolova, A.: Quantitative relaxation of concurrent data structures. POPL **2013**, 317–328 (2013)
8. Henzinger, T.A., Sezgin, A., Vafeiadis, V.: Aspect-Oriented Linearizability Proofs. In: D'Argenio, P.R., Melgratti, H. (eds.) CONCUR 2013. LNCS, vol. 8052, pp. 242–256. Springer, Heidelberg (2013). doi:10.1007/978-3-642-40184-8_18

9. Herlihy, M.P., Wing, J.M.: Linearizability: a correctness condition for concurrent objects. ACM Trans. Program. Lang. Syst. **12**(3), 463–492 (1990)
10. Kirsch, C.M., Lippautz, M., Payer, H.: Fast and scalable, lock-free k-FIFO queues. In: Malyshkin, V. (ed.) PaCT 2013. LNCS, vol. 7979, pp. 208–223. Springer, Heidelberg (2013). doi:10.1007/978-3-642-39958-9_18
11. Kirsch, C.M., Payer, H., Röck, H., Sokolova, A.: Performance, scalability, and semantics of concurrent FIFO queues. In: ICA3p. 2012, Part I, pp. 273–287 (2012)
12. Liang, H., Feng, X.: Modular verification of linearizability with non-fixed linearization points. PLDI **2013**, 459–470 (2013)
13. Michael, M.M., Scott, M.L.: Simple, fast, and practical non-blocking and blocking concurrent queue algorithms. PODC **1996**, 267–275 (1996)
14. Wang, C., Lv, Y., Wu, P.: Decomposable relaxation for concurrent data structures. Technical report ISCAS-SKLCS-16-01, State Key Laboratory of Computer Science, ISCAS, CAS (2016). http://lcs.ios.ac.cn/lvyi/files/ISCAS-SKLCS-16-01.pdf
15. Wang, C., Lv, Y., Liu, G., Wu, P.: Quasi-linearizability is undecidable. In: Feng, X., Park, S. (eds.) APLAS 2015. LNCS, vol. 9458, pp. 369–386. Springer, Heidelberg (2015). doi:10.1007/978-3-319-26529-2_20
16. Wolper, P.: Expressing interesting properties of programs in propositional temporal logic. POPL **18986**, 184–193 (1986)
17. Zhang, L., Chattopadhyay, A., Wang, C.: Round-up: runtime checking quasi linearizability of concurrent data structures. ASE **2013**, 4–14 (2013)

Graph Theory and Scheduling Algorithms

Sufficient Conditions for a Connected Graph to Have a Hamiltonian Path

Benjamin Momège[✉]

Inria, University of Lille, Villeneuve-d'Ascq, France
benjamin.momege@inria.fr

Abstract. Let G be a connected graph on n vertices. Let $\sigma_k(G)$ be the least possible value that is obtained as the sum of the degrees of k pairwise distinct and non-adjacent vertices. We show that if one of the following conditions is satisfied:

- $\sigma_3(G) \geq n$ and there is a longest cycle in G which is not a dominating cycle,
- $\sigma_2(G) \geq \frac{2}{3}n$ and G is $K_{1,4}$-free (i.e. without induced $K_{1,4}$),
- each triple of pairwise non-adjacent vertices contains two vertices u and v such that $deg_G(u) + deg_G(v) \geq n - 1$,

then G contains a Hamiltonian path.

Keywords: Combinatorial problems · Connected graphs · Hamiltonian path · Degree

1 Introduction

The Hamiltonian problem: determining conditions under which a graph contains a spanning path or cycle, has long been fundamental in graph theory. Named after Sir William Rowan Hamilton (and his Icosian game), this problem traces its origins to the 1850s. Today, however, the constant stream of results in this area continues to supply us with new and interesting theorems and still further questions.

There are three fundamental results that we feel deserve special attention here; both for their contribution to the overall theory and for their effect on the development of the area. In many ways, these three results are the foundation of much of today's work.

Let G be an undirected and simple graph. For $1 \leq k \leq |V_G|$ we define

$$\sigma_k(G) = \min\left\{\sum_{v \in H} deg_G(v) \ : \ H \subseteq V_G \text{ stable set in } G \text{ with } |H| = k\right\},$$

with the convention $\min \emptyset = +\infty$, where a *stable set* is a set of vertices all pairwise non-adjacent.

Theorem 1 (Dirac - 1952 - [6]). *A graph G on $n \geq 3$ vertices in which $\sigma_1(G) \geq \frac{n}{2}$ contains a Hamiltonian cycle.*

© Springer International Publishing AG 2017
B. Steffen et al. (Eds.): SOFSEM 2017, LNCS 10139, pp. 205–216, 2017.
DOI: 10.1007/978-3-319-51963-0_16

Theorem 2 (Ore - 1960 - [15]). *A graph G on $n \geq 3$ vertices in which $\sigma_2(G) \geq n$ contains a Hamiltonian cycle.*

Theorem 3 (Bondy-Chvátal -1976 - [2]). *A graph G on n vertices contains a Hamiltonian cycle if and only if the graph uniquely constructed from G by repeatedly adding a new edge connecting a pair of non-adjacent vertices with sum of their degrees at least n until no more pairs with this property can be found, contains a Hamiltonian cycle.*

These original results started a new approach to develop sufficient conditions on degrees for a graph to have a Hamiltonian path or cycle. A lot of effort has been made by various people in obtaining generalizations of these theorems and this area is one of the core subjects in Hamiltonian graph theory and extremal graph theory. For more results, see [10–13].

It is natural to ask if strengthening the connectivity conditions would allow us to lower the degree conditions. We shall not attempt to survey paths and cycles in k-connected graphs (graph who has more than k vertices and remains connected whenever fewer than k vertices are removed) with $k \geq 1$ (most of the results are in the texts cited above and in [9]) but we can see that Dirac's and Ore's general results (Theorems 1 and 2) may be strengthened when conditions are added.

An *induced subgraph* of a graph G is a subset of V_G together with any edges both of whose endpoints are in this subset. For a graph F, we say that G is *F-free* if it does not contain an induced subgraph isomorphic to F.

Theorem 4 (Zhang - *1988* - [16]). *Let $k \geq 2$ and G be a k-connected, $K_{1,3}$-free graph on n vertices with $\sigma_{k+1}(G) \geq n - k$. Then G contains a Hamiltonian cycle.*

Theorem 5 (Markus - 1993 - [14]). *Let G be a 2-connected, $K_{1,4}$-free graph on n vertices with $\sigma_1(G) \geq \frac{n+2}{3}$. Then G contains a Hamiltonian cycle.*

Theorem 6 (Chen-Schelp - 1995 - [4]). *Let $k \geq 2$ and G be a k-connected, $K_{1,4}$-free graph on $n \geq 3$ vertices such that $\sigma_{k+1}(G) \geq n + k$. Then G contains a Hamiltonian cycle.*

We will concentrate our efforts on problems and results dealing with spanning paths in connected graphs. For this problem, the only result we know is the following:

Theorem 7 (Duffus-Jacobson-Gould - 1982 - [7] or [11]). *A connected, $\{K_{1,3}, N\}$-free graph contains a Hamiltonian path.*

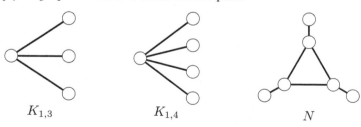

$K_{1,3}$ $K_{1,4}$ N

In this paper, we show that if a connected graph G on n vertices satisfies one of the following conditions:

- $\sigma_3(G) \geq n$ and there is a longest cycle in G which is not a dominating cycle (A cycle C in a graph G is called *dominating* if every edge of G has at least one vertex on C.),
- $\sigma_2(G) \geq \frac{2}{3}n$ and G is $K_{1,4}$-free,
- each triple of pairwise non-adjacent vertices contains two vertices u and v such that $deg_G(u) + deg_G(v) \geq n - 1$,

then G contains a Hamiltonian path.

2   Preliminary Definitions

We refer to [3] or [5] for undefined notations. The graphs $G = (V_G, E_G)$ considered in this paper are undirected and simple. The *size* of a graph is its number of vertices. For a graph $G = (V_G, E_G)$ and $u, v \in V_G$ we define

$$G + uv = (V_G, E_G \cup \{uv\}) \text{ and } G - uv = (V_G, E_G \setminus \{uv\}).$$

A *path* $P = (V_P, E_P)$ in G is a nonempty subgraph P of the form

$$V_P = \{v_1, \ldots, v_k\} \subseteq V_G \text{ and } E_P = \{v_i v_{i+1} : i \in \{1, \ldots, k-1\}\} \subseteq E_G$$

where the vertices v_i are all distinct. A *cycle* C in G is a subgraph of the form $P + v_1 v_k$ where P is a path. We often use the notations $P = v_1, v_2, \ldots, v_k$ and $C = v_1, v_2, \ldots, v_k, v_1$. A path or a cycle is *Hamiltonian* if $k = |V_G|$. The *neighbourhood* of a vertex v in a graph G is $N_G(v) = \{u : uv \in E_G\}$. The degree of v is $deg_G(v) = |N_G(v)|$.

For a path $P = v_1, \ldots, v_k$ in G we define

$$L_P(v_1) = \{v_{i-1} \in V_P \mid v_i \in N_G(v_1)\}$$

and

$$R_P(v_k) = \{v_{i+1} \in V_P \mid v_i \in N_G(v_k)\}.$$

3   Some Lemmas and the Proof That, if $\sigma_3(G) \geq n$ and There is a Longest Cycle in G Which Is Not a Dominating Cycle, Then G Contains a Hamiltonian Path

The proof of the following result is straightforward.

Lemma 1. *Let G be a connected graph on n vertices and $k \leq n-1$. If G contains a cycle of size k, then it contains a path of size $k + 1$.*

Lemma 2. *Let G be a graph on n vertices and $1 \leq k \leq n - 1$. We have*

$$\sigma_{k+1}(G) \geq \frac{k+1}{k} \sigma_k(G).$$

Proof. If $\sigma_{k+1}(G) = +\infty$ the result is true. Else, let $v_1, \ldots, v_{k+1}$ be pairwise non-adjacent vertices of G. We have

$$k \sum_{i=1}^{k+1} deg_G(v_i) = \sum_{\substack{I \subset \{1,\ldots,k+1\} \\ |I| = k}} \sum_{i \in I} deg_G(v_i) \geq \binom{k+1}{k} \sigma_k(G) = (k+1)\sigma_k(G),$$

and by dividing by k

$$\sum_{i=1}^{k+1} deg_G(v_i) = \frac{k+1}{k} \sigma_k(G).$$

Finally, as this is true for all pairwise non-adjacent vertices $v_1, \ldots, v_{k+1}$, we have

$$\sigma_{k+1}(G) \geq \frac{k+1}{k} \sigma_k(G).$$

This concludes the proof.   □

Lemma 3. *Let $P = v_1, \ldots, v_k$ be a longest path in a graph G without Hamiltonian path and $v \in V_G \setminus V_P$. Then*

$$N_G(v) \cap (L_P(v_1) \cup R_P(v_k)) = \emptyset.$$

Proof. Indeed, if there is $v_i \in N_G(v) \cap L_P(v_1)$, then $P + vv_i + v_1v_{i+1} - v_iv_{i+1}$ ($P + vv_1$ if $i = 1$) is a path of size $k + 1$ in G, which contradicts the maximality of k.

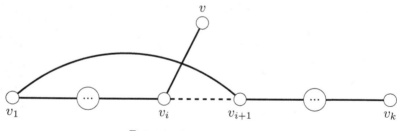

$$P + vv_i + v_1v_{i+1} - v_iv_{i+1}$$

Symmetrically, we show that $N_G(v) \cup R_P(v_k)$. This concludes the proof.   □

For a graph G, let $p(G)$ be the size of a longest path in G and $c(G)$ the size of a longest cycle in G. Enomoto et al. [8] prove the following result.

Theorem 8 (Enomoto - van den Heuvel - Kaneko - Saito - 1995 -[8]).
Let G be a connected graph on n vertices with $\sigma_3(G) \geq n$. Then G satisfies $c(G) \geq p(G) - 1$ or G is in one of six families of exceptional graphs.

For the case $p(G) \leq n - 1$, the converse of Lemma 1 is also true when $\sigma_3(G) \geq n$, and we have this interesting result:

Lemma 4. *Let G be a connected graph on n vertices with $\sigma_3(G) \geq n$ and such that $p(G) \leq n - 1$. Then:*

1. $c(G) = p(G) - 1$
2. *If C is a longest cycle of G, then for all v in $V_G \setminus V_C$ we have $N_G(v) \subset V_C$.*

Proof. 1. Let $P = v_1 \ldots, v_k$ be a longest path in G. As G is connected and $k \leq n - 1$ we have $n \geq 4$ and $k \geq 3$.

Suppose that there is a cycle of size at least k in G. If the cycle is Hamiltonian, then we have a path of size $n > k$ in G. Else, by Lemma 1 we have a path of size $k + 1$ in G. In the two cases, the maximality of k is contradicted. So we have $c(G) \leq p(G) - 1$ and $v_1 v_k \notin E_G$. Let $v \in V_G \setminus V_P$. As P is a longest path, we have $vv_1 \notin E_G$ and $vv_k \notin E_G$. So, as $\sigma_3(G) \geq n$ and $v_1 v_k, vv_1, vv_k \notin E_G$ we have

$$deg_G(v) + deg_G(v_1) + deg_G(v_k) \geq n. \tag{1}$$

By Lemma 3 we have $N_G(v) \cap (L_P(v_1) \cup R_P(v_k)) = \emptyset$ and therefore

$$deg_G(v) \leq n - 1 - |L_P(v_1) \cup R_P(v_k)|$$
$$\leq n - 1 - |L_P(v_1)| - |R_P(v_k)| + |L_P(v_1) \cap R_P(v_k)|.$$

Since $|L_P(v_1)| = deg_G(v_1)$ and $|R_P(v_k)| = deg_G(v_k)$ we have

$$deg_G(v) + deg_G(v_1) + deg_G(v_k) - n + 1 \leq |L_P(v_1) \cap R_P(v_k)|,$$

and with Eq. (1) we obtain

$$|L_P(v_1) \cap R_P(v_k)| \geq 1.$$

Let $v_j \in L_P(v_1) \cap R_P(v_k)$. The subgraph $P + v_1 v_{j+1} + v_{j-1} v_k - v_{j-1} v_j - v_j v_{j+1}$ is a cycle of size $k - 1$ in G, and therefore as $c(G) \leq p(G) - 1$, we have $c(G) = p(G) - 1$.

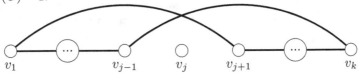

$$P + v_1 v_{j+1} + v_{j-1} v_k - v_{j-1} v_j - v_j v_{j+1}$$

2. If there is a vertex $v \in V_G \setminus V_C$ such that $N_G(v) \cap (V_G \setminus V_C) \neq \emptyset$, then there is a path of size at least 2 in the subgraph of G induced by $V_G \setminus V_C$. By connectivity there is a path P of size 2 in $V_G \setminus V_C$ with an edge e between V_C and V_P. By removing an edge e' adjacent to e of C, we obtain a path $C + P + e - e'$ of size at least $k + 1$ in G which contradicts the maximality of k.

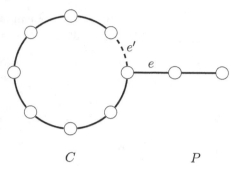

$$C \qquad\qquad\qquad P$$

This concludes the proof. □

Theorem 9 (Bondy - 1981 - [1]). *Let G be a 2-connected graph on n vertices with $\sigma_3(G) \geq n + 2$. Then each longest cycle of G is a dominating cycle.*

In line with this result, we consider the case of connected graphs. We easily derive from Lemma 4 the following result.

Theorem 10. *Let G be a connected graph on n vertices with $\sigma_3(G) \geq n$. Then either there is a Hamiltonian path in G or each longest cycle of G is a dominating cycle.*

4   If $\sigma_2(G) \geq \frac{2}{3}n$ and G is $K_{1,4}$-free, then G Contains a Hamiltonian Path

From the result of Ore (Theorem 2) we can easily deduce:

Corollary 1. *If G is a graph on n vertices with $\sigma_2(G) \geq n - 1$, then it contains a Hamiltonian path.*

In line with this result, we consider the case of connected graphs. Let G be a connected graph on n vertices with $\sigma_2(G) \geq \frac{2}{3}n$ and without Hamiltonian path. See Remark 13 for an example of such a graph.

By Lemma 2 we have $\sigma_3(G) \geq n$, and by Lemma 4 there is a longest cycle $C = c_1, \ldots, c_k, c_1$ of size $k \leq n - 2$ in G and two vertices u and v in $V_G \setminus V_C$ such that

$$N_G(u) \subset V_C \text{ and } N_G(v) \subset V_C,$$

and therefore

$$uv \notin E_G.$$

We often use the identifications $c_0 = c_k$ and $c_{k+1} = c_1$. As $deg_G(u) + deg_G(v) \geq \frac{2}{3}n$, by symmetry we can suppose that $deg_G(v) \geq \frac{n}{3}$. We define:

$$S_C(u) = \{c_{i+1} \mid c_i \in N_G(u)\}.$$

Let

$$\{c_{\alpha(1)}, c_{\alpha(2)}, \ldots, c_{\alpha(|V_C \setminus S_C(u)|)}\} = V_C \setminus S_C(u)$$

and assume $\alpha_{(i)} \leq \alpha_{(i+1)}$ for $1 \leq i \leq |V_C \setminus S_C(u)| - 1$ and

$$\alpha_{(|V_C \setminus S_C(u)|+1)} = \alpha_{(1)}.$$

Lemma 5. *There is $j \in \{1, \ldots, |V_C \setminus S_C(u)|\}$ such that $vc_{\alpha_{(j)}} \in E_G$ and $vc_{\alpha_{(j+1)}} \in E_G$.*

Proof. Firstly, we have

$$N_G(v) \subset V_C \setminus S_C(u). \tag{2}$$

Indeed, if there is

$$c_{l+1} \in N_G(v) \cap S_C(u)$$

then

$$C + uc_l + vc_{l+1} - c_l c_{l+1}$$

is a path of size at least $k + 2$ in G which contradicts the maximality of k.

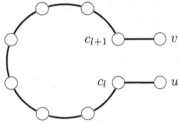

$$C + uc_l + vc_{l+1} - c_l c_{l+1}$$

Secondly, we have

$$|N_G(v)| \geq \frac{|V_C \setminus S_C(u)|}{2} + 1. \tag{3}$$

Indeed, as $|S_C(u)| = |N_G(u)|$ we have

$$|V_C \setminus S_C(u)| \leq n - 2 - |S_C(u)| = n - 2 - |N_G(u)|.$$

Using $deg_G(u) + deg_G(v) \geq \frac{2}{3}n$ we obtain

$$|V_C \setminus S_C(u)| \leq n - 2 - \frac{2}{3}n + |N_G(v)| = \frac{n}{3} + |N_G(v)| - 2.$$

Now, with $deg_G(v) \geq \frac{n}{3}$ we find

$$|V_C \setminus S_C(u)| \leq 2|N_G(v)| - 2.$$

Inequality (3) is obtained by dividing by 2.

Now, if for all $j \in \{1, \ldots, |V_C \setminus S_C(u)|\}$ we have

$$vc_{\alpha_{(j)}} \in E_G \Rightarrow vc_{\alpha_{(j+1)}} \notin E_G,$$

then by Inclusion (2)

$$|N_G(v)| \leq |V_C \setminus S_C(u)| - |N_G(v)|$$

i.e.

$$|N_G(v)| \leq \frac{|V_C \setminus S_C(u)|}{2}$$

which contradicts Inequality (3). Finally, there is $j \in \{1, \ldots, |V_C \setminus S_C(u)|\}$ such that $vc_{\alpha_{(j)}} \in E_G$ and $vc_{\alpha_{(j+1)}} \in E_G$. This concludes the proof. □

Lemma 6. *We have $\alpha_{(j+1)} - \alpha_{(j)} = 2$.*

Proof. - If $\alpha_{(j+1)} - \alpha_{(j)} = 1$, then $C + vc_{\alpha_{(j)}} + vc_{\alpha_{(j+1)}} - c_{\alpha_{(j)}}c_{\alpha_{(j+1)}}$ is a cycle of size $k + 1$ in G which contradicts the maximality of k.

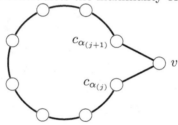

$$C + vc_{\alpha_{(j)}} + vc_{\alpha_{(j+1)}} - c_{\alpha_{(j)}}c_{\alpha_{(j+1)}}$$

- If $\alpha_{(j+1)} - \alpha_{(j)} \geq 3$, then as $c_{\alpha_{(j)}+1} \in S_C(u)$, $c_{\alpha_{(j)}+2} \in S_C(u)$, we have $c_{\alpha_{(j)}} \in N_G(u)$, $c_{\alpha_{(j)}+1} \in N_G(u)$ and $C + uc_{\alpha_{(j)}} + uc_{\alpha_{(j)}+1} - c_{\alpha_{(j)}}c_{\alpha_{(j)}+1}$ is a cycle of size $k + 1$ in G which contradicts the maximality of k.

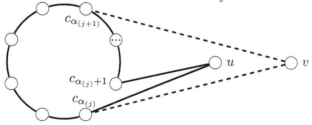

$$C + uc_{\alpha_{(j)}} + uc_{\alpha_{(j)}+1} - c_{\alpha_{(j)}}c_{\alpha_{(j)}+1}$$

This concludes the proof. □

Lemma 7. *The graph G contains $K_{1,4}$.*

Proof. By Lemma 5, there is a $j \geq 1$ such that $vc_{\alpha(j)} \in E_G$ and $vc_{\alpha(j+1)} \in E_G$. By Lemma 6, $\alpha_{(j+1)} - \alpha_{(j)} = 2$. So we have $c_{\alpha(j)+1} \in S_C(u)$ and therefore $uc_{\alpha(j)} \in E_G$. See the following figure.

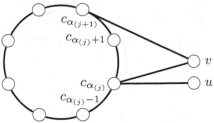

We consider the subgraph H induced by $u, v, c_{\alpha(j)-1}, c_{\alpha(j)}$ and $c_{\alpha(j)+1}$. We have $uc_{\alpha(j)} \in E_G$, $vc_{\alpha(j)} \in E_G$, $c_{\alpha(j)-1}c_{\alpha(j)} \in E_G$ and $c_{\alpha(j)+1}c_{\alpha(j)} \in E_G$. If there is no other edge between the vertices of H, then $H \cong K_{1,4}$.

- As $N_G(u) \subseteq V_C$, we have $uv \notin E_G$.
- As $c_{\alpha(j)} \notin S_C(u)$, we have $uc_{\alpha(j)-1} \notin E_G$.
- As $c_{\alpha(j+1)} \notin S_C(u)$ and $\alpha_{(j+1)} - \alpha_{(j)} = 2$, we have $uc_{\alpha(j)+1} \notin E_G$.
- If $vc_{\alpha(j)-1} \in E_G$, then $C + vc_{\alpha(j)-1} + vc_{\alpha(j)} - c_{\alpha(j)-1}c_{\alpha(j)}$ is a cycle of size $k+1$ in G, which contradicts the maximality of k.

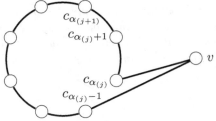

$$C + vc_{\alpha(j)-1} + vc_{\alpha(j)} - c_{\alpha(j)-1}c_{\alpha(j)}$$

- If $vc_{\alpha(j)+1} \in E_G$, then $C + vc_{\alpha(j)} + vc_{\alpha(j)+1} - c_{\alpha(j)}c_{\alpha(j)+1}$ is a cycle of size $k+1$ in G, which contradicts the maximality of k.

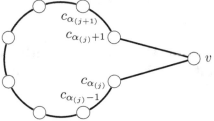

$$C + vc_{\alpha(j)} + vc_{\alpha(j)+1} - c_{\alpha(j)}c_{\alpha(j)+1}$$

- If $c_{\alpha(j)-1}c_{\alpha(j)+1} \in E_G$, then $C + vc_{\alpha(j)} + vc_{\alpha(j+1)} + c_{\alpha(j)-1}c_{\alpha(j)+1} - c_{\alpha(j)-1}c_{\alpha(j)} - c_{\alpha(j)+1}c_{\alpha(j+1)}$ is a cycle of size $k+1$ in G, which contradicts the maximality of k.

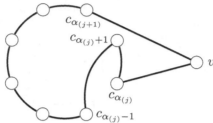

$$C + vc_{\alpha(j)} + vc_{\alpha(j+1)} + c_{\alpha(j)-1}c_{\alpha(j)+1} - c_{\alpha(j)-1}c_{\alpha(j)} - c_{\alpha(j)+1}c_{\alpha(j+1)}$$

Finally, we have $H \cong K_{1,4}$. This concludes the proof. $\square$

Theorem 11. *If G is a $K_{1,4}$-free connected graph on n vertices with $\sigma_2(G) \geq \frac{2}{3}n$, then G contains a Hamiltonian path.*

Remark 12. *The bound from Theorem 11 is sharp for the class of $K_{1,4}$-free graphs, as seen by $K_{1,3}$.*

Remark 13. *There are connected graphs G on n vertices with $\sigma_2(G) \geq \frac{2}{3}n$ and without Hamiltonian path. For example, for $p \geq 2$ the graph $G = K_{p,p+2}$ contains $K_{1,4}$ and is a connected graph on $n = 2p+2$ vertices with $\sigma_2(G) \geq \frac{2}{3}n$ and without Hamiltonian paths. The largest value of $\sigma_2(G)$ compared to $|V_G|$ in this family is achieved for $p = 2$, and it is $\frac{2}{3}$.*

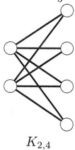

$K_{2,4}$

5   If Each Triple of Pairwise Non-adjacent Vertices Contains Two Vertices u and v s.t. $deg_G(u) + deg_G(v) \geq n - 1$, Then G Contains a Hamiltonian Path

Theorem 14. *If G is a connected graph on n vertices such that each triple of pairwise non-adjacent vertices contains two vertices u and v satisfying $deg_G(u) + deg_G(v) \geq n - 1$, then G contains a Hamiltonian path.*

Proof. For $n = 1, 2$ or 3 the result is true. If $n \geq 4$, let $P = v_1 \ldots, v_k$ be a longest path in G. We want to prove that $k = n$. As G is connected we have $k \geq 3$. Suppose that $k < n$ and take $v \in V_G \setminus V_P$.

If $v_1 v_k \in E_G$, then by Lemma 1 we have a path of size $k + 1$ in G, which contradicts the maximality of k.

If $v v_1 \in E_G$ or $v v_k \in E_G$, then there is a path of size $k + 1$ in G, which contradicts the maximality of $k + 1$.

So v_1, v_k and v are pairwise non-adjacent vertices.

By Lemma 3, we have $N_G(v) \subseteq V_G \setminus (L_P(v_1) \cup \{v, v_k\})$ and therefore

$$deg_G(v) \leq n - 2 - |L_P(v_1)| = n - 2 - deg_G(v_1),$$

i.e

$$deg_G(v) + deg_G(v_1) \leq n - 2. \tag{4}$$

Similarly, by Lemma 3, we have $N_G(v) \subseteq V_G \setminus (R_P(v_k) \cup \{v, v_1\})$ and therefore

$$deg_G(v) \leq n - 2 - |R_P(v_k)| = n - 2 - deg_G(v_k),$$

i.e.

$$deg_G(v) + deg_G(v_k) \leq n - 2. \tag{5}$$

If there are two vertices v_i and v_{i+1} of P such that $v_1 v_{i+1} \in E_G$ and $v_k v_i \in E_G$, then $P + v_1 v_{i+1} + v_i v_k - v_i v_{i+1}$ is a cycle of length k in G. By Lemma 1 there is a path of length $k + 1$ in G, which contradicts the maximality of k.

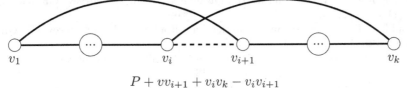

$$P + v v_{i+1} + v_i v_k - v_i v_{i+1}$$

So we have $N_G(v_1) \subseteq V_P \setminus (R_P(v_k) \cup \{v_1\})$, hence

$$deg_G(v_1) \leq |V_P| - |R_P(v_k) \cup \{v_1\}| = n - 2 - deg_G(v_k),$$

i.e.

$$deg_G(v_1) + deg_G(v_k) \leq n - 2. \tag{6}$$

Finally, (4), (5) and (6) contradict the hypothesis that for each triple of pairwise non-adjacent vertices contains two vertices u and v such that $deg_G(u) + deg_G(v) \geq n - 1$. Thus $k = n$. This concludes the proof. $\square$

Remark 15. *The bound from Theorem 14 is sharp as seen by $K_{p,p+2}$ with $p \geq 1$.*

References

1. Bondy, J.A.: Integrity in graph theory. In: Chartrand, G., Alavi, Y., Goldsmith, D.L., Lesniak-Foster, L., Lick, D.R. (eds.) The Theory and Applications of Graphs: Proceedings of the 4th International Graph Theory Conference, pp. 117–125. Wiley, New York (1981)
2. Bondy, J.A., Chvátal, V.: A method in graph theory. Discrete Math. **15**(2), 111–135 (1976)
3. Bondy, J.A., Siva, U., Murty, R.: Graph Theory. Springer, London Ltd. (2010)
4. Chen, G., Schelp, R.H.: Hamiltonicity for $K_{1,r}$-free graphs. J. Graph Theory **20**(4), 423–439 (1995)
5. Diestel, R.: Graph Theory. Graduate Texts in Mathematics, 4th edn., vol. 173. Springer, New York (2012)
6. Dirac, G.A.: Some theorems on abstract graphs. Proc. London Math. Soc. **2**, 69–81 (1952)
7. Duffus, D., Gould, R.J., Jacobson, M.S.: Forbidden subgraphs and the Hamiltonian theme. In: The Theory and Applications of Graphs, 4th International Conference, Kalamazoo, Mich., pp. 297–316. Wiley, New York (1981)
8. Enomoto, H., van den Heuvel, J., Kaneko, A., Saito, A.: Relative length of long paths and cycles in graphs with large degree sums. J. Graph Theory **20**(2), 213–225 (1995)
9. Faudree, R.J., Flandrin, E., Ryjáček, Z.: Claw-free graphs - a survey. Discrete Math. **164**(1–3), 87–147 (1997)
10. Gould, R.J.: Updating the Hamiltonian problem - a survey. J. Graph Theory **15**(2), 121–157 (1991)
11. Gould, R.J.: Advances on the Hamiltonian problem - a survey. Graphs Comb. **19**(1), 7–52 (2003)
12. Gould, R.J.: Recent advances on the Hamiltonian problem: survey III. Graphs Comb. **30**(1), 1–46 (2014)
13. Li, H.: Generalizations of Dirac's theorem in Hamiltonian graph theory - a survey. Discrete Math. **313**(19), 2034–2053 (2013)
14. Markus, L.R.: Hamiltonian results in $K_{1,r}$-free graphs. Congr. Numer. **98**, 143–149 (1993)
15. Ore, Ø.: Note on Hamiltonian circuits. Am. Math. **67**, 55 (1960)
16. Zhang, C.-Q.: Hamilton cycles in claw-free graphs. J. Graph Theory **12**(2), 209–216 (1988)

Enumerating Minimal Tropical Connected Sets

Dieter Kratsch[1]([⊠]), Mathieu Liedloff[2], and Mohamed Yosri Sayadi[1]

[1] Université de Lorraine, LITA, Metz, France
{dieter.kratsch,yosri.sayadi}@univ-lorraine.fr
[2] INSA Centre Val de Loire, LIFO EA 4022, Université d'Orléans,
45067 Orléans, France
mathieu.liedloff@univ-orleans.fr

Abstract. Enumerating objects of a specified type is one of the principal tasks in algorithmics. In graph algorithms one often enumerates vertex subsets satisfying a certain property. The optimization problem *Tropical Connected Set* is strongly related to the *Graph Motif* problem which deals with vertex-colored graphs and has various applications in metabolic networks and biology. A tropical connected set of a vertex-colored graph is a subset of the vertices which induces a connected subgraph in which all colors of the input graph appear at least once; among others this generalizes steiner trees. We investigate the enumeration of the inclusion-minimal tropical connected sets of a given vertex-colored graph. We present algorithms to enumerate all minimal tropical connected sets on colored graphs of the following graph classes: on split graphs in running in time $O^*(1.6402^n)$, on interval graphs in $O^*(1.8613^n)$ time, on cobipartite graphs and block graphs in $O^*(3^{n/3})$. Our algorithms imply corresponding upper bounds on the number of minimal tropical connected sets in graphs on n vertices for each of these graph classes. We also provide various new lower bound constructions thereby obtaining matching lower bounds for cobipartite and block graphs.

1 Introduction

Algorithmic enumeration deals with the construction and analysis of algorithms to enumerate, generate or list all objects of specified type and property. It has important applications in various domains of computer science, such as data mining, machine learning, and artificial intelligence, as well as in biology. The classical approach in algorithmic enumeration (also called output-sensitive) measures the running time of an enumeration algorithm in dependence of the length of its input and output. The (most) efficient algorithms of this approach are algorithms of polynomial delay. Recently an approach via exact exponential algorithms, sometimes called input-sensitive, constructing enumeration algorithms whose running time is measured in the length of the input only, has attracted a lot of attention. The reason for this is two-fold. Firstly, many exact exponential-time algorithms for the solution of NP-hard problems rely on such enumeration

This work is supported by the French National Research Agency (ANR project GraphEn / ANR-15-CE40-0009).

B. Steffen et al. (Eds.): SOFSEM 2017, LNCS 10139, pp. 217–228, 2017.
DOI: 10.1007/978-3-319-51963-0_17

algorithms. Sometimes the fastest known algorithm to solve an optimization problem is by simply enumerating all minimal or maximal feasible solutions (e.g., for subset feedback vertex sets [12]), whereas other times the enumeration of some objects is useful for algorithms solving completely different problems (e.g., enumeration of maximal independent sets in triangle-free graphs for computing graph homomorphisms [11]). Secondly, the running times of such exponential-time enumeration algorithms imply an upper bound on the maximum number of enumerated objects a graph can have. This may help to establish results of combinatorial nature in a new way. Various classical examples exist in this direction; a well-known example was achieved by Moon and Moser [23] who showed that the maximum number of maximal independent sets in a graph on n vertices is exactly $3^{n/3}$.

Unfortunately, for many graph properties such matching lower and upper bounds are not known, and hence for the maximum number of such objects there is a sometimes large gap between the currently best known lower and upper bounds in general n-vertex graphs. This motivates the study of enumeration of objects in graphs restricted to belong to a certain graph classes. For example, due to a cornerstone result by Fomin et al. the maximum number of minimal dominating sets in graphs is at most 1.7159^n [10], however no graph having more than 1.5704^n minimal dominating sets is known. On the other hand, matching lower and upper bounds have been established for the maximum number of minimal dominating sets on many graph classes [4,6]. As a consequence, there has been extensive research in this direction recently, both on general graphs and on graph classes. Algorithms for the enumeration and combinatorial lower and upper bounds on graph classes for various objects in graphs have been established in the last years, among them minimal feedback vertex sets, minimal dominating sets, minimal separators, minimal transversals, minimal connected vertex covers and minimal steiner trees [4–6,8,9,12,14–18,25].

Problems on vertex-colored graphs have been widely studied in the last 20 years, notably the *Graph Motif* problem which was introduced in 1994 by McMorris et al. [22] and motivated by applications in biology and metabolic networks [21,24]. We revisit the *Tropical Connected Set* problem which takes as input a vertex-colored graph $G = (V, E)$ and asks to find a tropical connected set, i.e. a connected subset $S \subseteq V$ such that each color of G appears in S, and is of minimum cardinality. The notion 'tropical' is due to Manoussakis et al., see [1] which shows various NP-completeness results for the problem, even when restricted to colored trees. In [3] an $O(1.2721^n)$ time algorithm for trees is provided as well as an $O(1.5359^n)$ time algorithm for general graphs. It is also not hard to see that *Tropical Connected Set* generalizes the well-known NP-complete *Steiner Tree* problem with unit edge weights.

In this paper we initiate the study of input-sensitive enumeration and the maximum number of minimal tropical connected sets (abbreviated mtcs) in n-vertex colored graphs. Interestingly, the best known upper bound for the maximum number of mtcs in an arbitrary graph and even for chordal graphs is the trivial one which is 2^n. The best lower bound we achieve in this paper is 1.4916^n, and thus the gap between the known lower and upper bounds is huge on chordal and arbitrary graphs. Our results are summarized in the following table, where n is the number of vertices of an input graph belonging to the given class.

Graph class	Lower bound	Upper bound	Enumeration
Chordal graphs	1.4961^n	2^n	$O^*(2^n)$
Split graphs	1.4766^n	1.6042^n	$O(1.6042^n)$
Cobipartite graphs	$3^{n/3}$	$n^2 \cdot 3^{n/3} + n^2$	$O^*(3^{n/3})$
Interval graphs	$3^{n/3}$	1.8613^n	$O(1.8613^n)$
Block graphs	$3^{n/3}$	$3^{n/3}$	$O^*(3^{n/3})$

2   Preliminaries

For graph-theoretic notions not defined in the paper we refer to the monograph of Diestel [7]. Throughout this paper, we denote by $G = (V, E)$ an undirected graph with $n = |V|$ and $m = |E|$. The *(open) neighborhood* of a vertex v is denoted by $N(v)$ and its *closed neighborhood* $N(v) \cup \{v\}$ is denoted by $N[v]$. For a given vertex subset X, we define $N_X(v) = N(v) \cap X$ and $N_X[v] = N[v] \cap X$. The *degree* of a vertex v is denoted by $d(v)$ and we define $d(v) = |N_X(v)|$. Finally $X \subseteq V$ is a *clique* (respectively, an *independent set*) of $G = (V, E)$ if all vertices of X are pairwise adjacent (respectively, non adjacent).

Let $G = (V, E)$ be a (not necessarily properly) vertex-colored graph. We denote by c, the function assigning to each vertex a color. For any color, we call the set of all vertices of G having this color a *color class*. Given a subset of vertices X, we define $\mathcal{C}(X) = \{c(v) : v \in X\}$ as the set of different colors assigned to the vertices of X. The set $\mathcal{C}(V)$ is simply denoted by $\mathcal{C}$. A *tropical set* of a graph G is a subset X of its vertices such that $\mathcal{C}(X) = \mathcal{C}$; such a set is a *tropical connected set* (abbreviated *tcs*) if additionally, the graph induced by X, denoted by $G[X]$, is connected. A tcs X is a *minimal* (abbreviated *mtcs*) if there is no proper subset of X being tropical connected.

For an introduction and further reading on branching algorithms we refer the reader to the book "Exact exponential algorithms" [13] (Chaps. 1, 2 and 6). We mention a few important notations. The O^* hides polynomials, i.e. we write $f(n) = O^*(g(n))$ if $f(n) = O(p(n) \cdot g(n))$ where p is a polynomial in n. Branching vectors and branching numbers are crucial for the time analysis of branching algorithms. We denote the branching number of a branching vector $(t_1, t_2, \ldots, t_r)$ by $\alpha(t_1, t_2, \ldots, t_r)$.

Informations on the studied graph classes will given in the corresponding sections. For further informations on structural and algorithmic properties of graph classes we refer to the monographs [2,19].

Finally we mention an observation which implies a lower bound of $3^{n/3}$ applying to all graph classes in this paper.

Lemma 1. *Complete graphs on n vertices in which each color appears exactly three times have $3^{n/3}$ minimal tropical connected sets. Hence, for all graph classes containing all complete graphs there is a graph having $3^{n/3}$ mtcs.*

To see this note that in a complete graph each set containing exactly one vertex of each color is an mtcs, and hence one out of three vertices is chosen for each color class.

3   Split Graphs

Split graphs are those graphs for which their vertex set V can be partitioned into a clique C and an independent set I. We denote such a split graph by $G = (C, I, E)$. Note that all split graphs are chordal graphs. In this section we construct a branching algorithm to enumerate all mtcs of a given split graph. Its running time analysis uses Measure & Conquer. Upper and lower bounds on the maximum number of mtcs in split graphs are given. A correctness proof is postponed to the full paper.

3.1   An Enumeration Algorithm

We consider a recursive branching algorithm called ENUMTCS(K, S, F, X) that enumerates all mtcs T of G such that $X \subseteq T$, where $K \subseteq C$ is a clique, $\{S \cup F\} \subseteq I$ is an independent set and initial call $K = C$, $S = I$ and $F = \emptyset$. The basic idea is that when we select $x \in K$, we add it immediately to X; however when we select $y \in S$, we move it first to F, and only when at least one of its neighbors is selected we add it to X. This way we guarantee that $G[X]$ is always connected. In our algorithm $X, K, S, F \subseteq V(G)$ are disjoint such that a) $X \subseteq T$ and b) $T \setminus X \subseteq K \cup S \cup F$, and c) $F \subseteq T \cap I$. We denote by $H = G[K \cup S \cup F]$. In each step of the algorithm, we either reduce the considered instance or branch and call in each branch the corresponding subroutine. We denote by $nc(x, H')$ the number of vertices of color $c(x)$ in the induced subgraph H' of G.

ENUMTCS(K, S, F, X)

1. If $K = \emptyset$, then check whether X is a minimal tropical connected sets of G and output it if it holds; then stop.
2. If there is $y \in F$ such that $d_K(y) = 0$, then discard X and stop.
3. If there is $x \in K$ such that $d(x) = |K| - 1$ and $nc(x, X) \geq 1$, then call ENUMTCS($K \setminus \{x\}, S, F, X$).
4. If there is $x \in S$:
   If $nc(x, H) = 1$, then call ENUMTCS($K, S \setminus \{x\}, F \cup \{x\}, X$).
   If $nc(x, H) = 2$, then let y be the other vertex such that $c(x) = c(y)$:
   – If $y \in S$, then branch:
   (i) call ENUMTCS($K, S \setminus \{x, y\}, F \cup \{x\}, X$)
   (ii) call ENUMTCS($K, S \setminus \{x, y\}, F \cup \{y\}, X$)
   – If $y \in K$, then branch:
   (i) call ENUMTCS($K \setminus \{y\}, S \setminus \{x\}, F, X \cup \{y\}$)
   (ii) call ENUMTCS($K \setminus \{y\}, S \setminus \{x\}, F \cup \{x\}, X$)

If $nc(x, H) \geq 3$, then branch:

  (i) call ENUMTCS($K \setminus \{v : c(v) = c(x)\}, S \setminus \{v : c(v) = c(x)\}, F \cup \{x\}, X$)

  (ii) call ENUMTCS($K, S \setminus \{x\}, F, X$)

5. If there is $x \in K$ such that $d_F(x) \geq 2$, then branch:

  (i) call ENUMTCS($K \setminus \{x\}, S, F \setminus N_F(x), X \cup \{x\} \cup N_F(x)$)

  (ii) call ENUMTCS($K \setminus \{x\}, S, F, X$)

6. If there is $y \in F$ such that $d_K(y) = 1$ and x is the unique neighbor of y in K, then call ENUMTCS($K \setminus \{x\}, S, F \setminus \{y\}, X \cup \{x, y\}$).

7. If there is $x \in K$ such that $d_F(x) = 1$ and $nc(x, X) \geq 1$, then let $\{y\} = N_F(x)$ and branch:

  (i) call ENUMTCS($K \setminus N_k(y), S, F \setminus \{y\}, X \cup \{x, y\}$)

  (ii) call ENUMTCS($K \setminus \{x\}, S, F, X$)

8. If there is $x \in K$ such that $nc(x, H) = 1$:

  If $d_F(x) = 0$, then call ENUMTCS($K \setminus \{x\}, S, F, X \cup \{x\}$).

  If $d_F(x) = 1$, then let $\{y\} = N_F(x)$ and call ENUMTCS($K \setminus \{x\}, S, F \setminus \{y\}, X \cup \{x, y\}$).

9. If there is $y \in F$ and $x_1, x_2 \in N_K(y)$ such that $c(x_1) = c(x_2)$: If $d_K(y) = 2$, then branch:

  (i) call ENUMTCS($K \setminus \{x_1, x_2\}, S, F \setminus \{y\}, X \cup \{x_1, y\}$)

  (ii) call ENUMTCS($K \setminus \{x_1, x_2\}, S, F \setminus \{y\}, X \cup \{x_2, y\}$)

  If $d_K(y) \geq 3$, then branch:

  (i) call ENUMTCS($K \setminus \{x_1, x_2\}, S, F \setminus \{y\}, X \cup \{x_1, y\}$)

  (ii) call ENUMTCS($K \setminus \{x_1, x_2\}, S, F \setminus \{y\}, X \cup \{x_2, y\}$)

  (iii) call ENUMTCS($K \setminus \{x_1, x_2\}, S, F, X$)

10. If there is $y \in F$ such that $d_K(y) = 2$, then let $N(y) = \{x_1, x_2\}$ and branch:

  (i) call ENUMTCS($K \setminus (\{u : c(u) = c(x_1)\} \cup \{v : c(v) = c(x_2)\}), S, F \setminus \{y\}, X \cup \{x_1, x_2, y\}$)

  (ii) call ENUMTCS($K \setminus \{x_1, x_2\}, S, F \setminus \{y\}, X \cup \{x_1, y\}$)

  (iii) call ENUMTCS($K \setminus \{x_1, x_2\}, S, F \setminus \{y\}, X \cup \{x_2, y\}$)

11. If there is $y \in F$ such that $d_K(y) = 3$, then let $N(y) = \{x_1, x_2, x_3\}$ and branch:

  (i) call ENUMTCS($K \setminus \{x_1\}, S, F \setminus \{y\}, X \cup \{x_1, y\}$)

  (ii) call ENUMTCS($K \setminus \{x_1, x_2\}, S, F \setminus \{y\}, X \cup \{x_2, y\}$)

  (iii) call ENUMTCS($K \setminus \{x_1, x_2, x_3\}, S, F \setminus \{y\}, X \cup \{x_3, y\}$)

12. If there is $y \in F$ such that $d_K(y) = 4$, then let $N(y) = \{x_1, x_2, x_3, x_4\}$ and branch:

  (i) call ENUMTCS($K \setminus N_K(y), S, F \setminus \{y\}, X \cup \{x_1, y\}$)

  (ii) call ENUMTCS($K \setminus (\{u : c(u) = c(x_1)\} \cup \{v : c(v) = c(x_2)\}), S, F \setminus \{y\}, X \cup \{x_1, x_2, y\}$)

  (iii) call ENUMTCS($K \setminus (\{u : c(u) = c(x_1)\} \cup \{v : c(v) = c(x_3)\} \cup \{x_2\}), S, F \setminus \{y\}, X \cup \{x_1, x_3, y\}$)

  (iv) call ENUMTCS($K \setminus (\{u : c(u) = c(x_1)\} \cup \{v : c(v) = c(x_4)\} \cup \{x_2, x_3\}), S, F \setminus \{y\}, X \cup \{x_1, x_4, y\}$)

  (v) call ENUMTCS($K \setminus \{x_1\}, S, F, X$)

13. If there is $x_1, x_2, \in K$ such that $d_F(x_1) = 1$, $d_F(x_2) = 1$ and $c(x_1) = c(x_2)$, then let $\{y_1\} = N_F(x_1)$, $\{y_2\} = N_F(x_2)$ and branch:
    (i) call ENUMTCS($K \setminus (N_K(y_1) \cup N_K(y_2)), S, F \setminus \{y_1, y_2\}, X \cup \{x_1, x_2, y_1, y_2\}$)
    (ii) call ENUMTCS($K \setminus \{x_1, x_2\}, S, F \setminus \{y_1\}, X \cup \{x_1, y_1\}$)
    (iii) call ENUMTCS($K \setminus \{x_1, x_2\}, S, F \setminus \{y_2\}, X \cup \{x_2, y_2\}$)
    (iv) call ENUMTCS($K \setminus \{x_1, x_2\}, S, F, X$)
14. If there is $x \in K$ such that $d_F(x) = 1$, then let $\{y\} = N_F(x)$ and branch:
    (i) call ENUMTCS($K \setminus \{u : c(u) = c(x)\}, S, F \setminus \{y\}, X \cup \{x, y\}$)
    (ii) for each $v \in \{u : c(u) = c(x)\} \setminus \{x\}$, call ENUMTCS($K \setminus \{u : c(u) = c(x)\}, S, F, X \cup \{v\}$)
15. If there is $x \in K$, then branch:
    (i) for each $v \in \{u : c(u) = c(x)\}$, call ENUMTCS($K \setminus \{u : c(u) = c(x)\}, S, F, X \cup \{v\}$)

To analyze the running time of the algorithm, we compute the branching vectors for all branching steps of the algorithm. We set the measure of an instance (K, S, F, X) to $|K| + |S| + |F|w$ where $w = 0.533244$. Notice that in Steps 1–3,6,8 we reduce an input without branching (reduction rules). Hence, to analyze the time, we only have to analyze Steps 4,5,7,9–15 (branching rules)

Step 4. By moving a vertex from S to F, we gain $1 - w = 0.466756$. So the three branching vectors in Step 4 are $(2-w, 2-w)$, $(2, 2-w)$ and $(3-w, 1)$ respectively. The maximum value of the branching numbers is achieved for $(2-w, 2-w)$ and thus $\alpha_4 < 1.6042$.

Step 5. The branching vector is $(1 + 2w, 1)$ and thus $\alpha_5 < 1.6042$.

Step 7. Due to Step 6 we have $d_K(y) \geq 2$, thus we the branching vector is $(2 + w, 1)$ and thus $\alpha_7 < 1.5241$.

Step 9. For its two subcases, we have the branching vectors $(2 + w, 2 + w)$ and $(2 + w, 2 + w, 2)$. The maximum value of the branching numbers is achieved for the second vector and thus $\alpha_9 < 1.5991$.

Step 10. Notice that $|\{u : c(u) = c(x_1)\}| \geq 2$, $|\{v : c(v) = c(x_2)\}| \geq 2$, and $c(x_1) \neq c(x_2)$ because Step 8 and 9 do not apply. Thus the branching vector is $(4 + w, 2 + w, 2 + w)$ and $\alpha_{10} < 1.4329$.

Step 11. We have the branching vector $(1 + w, 2 + w, 3 + w)$ and thus $\alpha_{11} < 1.5860$.

Step 12. Notice that for all $i \in \{1, \ldots, 4\}$ we have $|\{u : c(u) = c(x_i)\}| \geq 2$ and that for all $i \neq j$, $c(x_i) \neq c(x_j)$ because Step 8 and 9 do not apply. Thus the branching vector is $(4 + w, 4 + w, 5 + w, 6 + w, 1)$ and $\alpha_{12} < 1.5891$.

Step 13. For all $i \in \{1, 2\}$ we have $d_K(y_i) \geq 5$. Thus the branching vector is $(10 + 2w, 2 + w, 2 + w, 2)$ and $\alpha_{13} < 1.6029$.

Step 14. Let $t = nc(x, K) - 1$. Notice that $t \geq 1$ because Step 8 does not apply. Thus the branching vector is $(t + 1 + w, \underbrace{t + 1, \ldots, t + 1}_{t})$. The maximum value of their branching numbers is achieved for $t = 2$ and thus $\alpha_{14} < 1.4147$.

Step 15. Let $t = nc(x, K)$ with $t \geq 2$. We obtain the vector $(\underbrace{t, \ldots, t}_{t})$. The maximum value of the branching number is achieved for $t = 3$ and thus $\alpha_{15} = 3^{1/3} < 1.4423$.

The largest branching number is (majorized by) 1.6042 (attained by Steps 4 and 5). Thus we may conclude with the following theorem.

Theorem 1. *A split graph has at most 1.6042^n minimal tropical connected sets, and these can be enumerated in time $O(1.6042^n)$.*

3.2 A Lower Bound

Since all complete graphs are split graphs by Lemma 1 there is a lower bound of $3^{n/3}$. To improve upon it, first consider a split graph $\tilde{G} = (C, I, E)$ where the clique is $C = \{v_i, 1 \leq i \leq 5\}$ and the independent set is $I = \{x_j, y_j, z_j, 1 \leq j \leq 5\}$. In addition to the edges implied by the clique, the set E also contains all possible edges between v_i and x_j, y_j, z_j, for any $i, j \in \{1, \ldots, 5\}$ except for $i = j$. Note that the graph $\tilde{G}$ has 20 vertices. Suppose that each vertex v_i has color 0 ($1 \leq i \leq 5$) and for each j ($1 \leq j \leq 5$) the three vertices x_j, y_j, z_j have color j. Observe that by the construction of $\tilde{G}$, any of its mtcs S is obtained by choosing precisely one vertex of $\{x_j, y_j, z_j\}$ for all j ($1 \leq j \leq 5$) and, to make S connected, two vertices of C. Thus the total number of mtcs of $\tilde{G}$ is $3^5 \cdot \binom{5}{2} = 2430$. Consider now a split graph over n vertices, where $n = 20 \cdot k$ for some integer k. The graph is constructed by taking k disjoint copies of $\tilde{G}$, where each copy has distinct colors, and by then making one (big) clique of all the vertices of cliques in the copies of $\tilde{G}$. Such a graph has at least $2430^{n/20}$ mtcs, and thus at least 1.4766^n mtcs.

Theorem 2. *There exist split graphs with at least 1.4766^n minimal tropical connected sets.*

4   Cobipartite Graphs

A graph G is a cobipartite graph if its vertex set can be partitioned into two cliques X_1 and X_2 and we denote such a graph by $G = (X_1, X_2, E)$. Suppose that $S \subseteq X_1 \cup X_2$ is a minimal tropical connected set of G. Observe that one of the following cases occurs : Either $S \subseteq X_i$ for some $i \in \{1, 2\}$ (type 1), or $S \cap X_i \neq \emptyset$ for any $i \in \{1, 2\}$ (type 2). The algorithm we present first enumerates all mtcs of type 1 and then those of type 2.

Type 1. For $i \in \{1, 2\}$ all mtcs S of type 1 are obtained by choosing exactly one vertex v of each color in X_i.

Type 2. For each edge $\{v_1, v_2\}$ such that $v_1 \in X_1$ and $v_2 \in X_2$, let S be the set consisting of v_1, v_2 and exactly one vertex of each color different from $c(v_1)$ and $c(v_2)$. If S is minimal then S is a mtcs of type 2.

Our algorithm simply enumerates all possible mtcs of either type 1 or type 2. Clearly, for any mtcs of type 1, as X_i is a clique, it is sufficient to pick exactly one vertex per color class. As any tcs of type 2 is connected, there should be a pair of adjacent vertices v_1, v_2 such that $v_i \in X_i$ (for $i \in \{1, 2\}$). To enumerate all tcs of type 2 our algorithm generates all sets S consisting of such a pair v_1, v_2 and one vertex of each color different from $c(v_1)$ and $c(v_2)$. Such a tcs S might not be minimal only if $c(v_1) = c(v_2)$ and $S - \{v_1\}$ or $S - \{v_2\}$ is a tcs and for any S this can be checked in time $O(n + m)$.

We now provide an upper bound on the number of mtcs. Let $T(n)$ be the maximum number of mtcs in a cobipartite graph. Consider a color class having d vertices. As exactly one vertex of the class has to be chosen, whenever a vertex is picked, the other vertices of the color class can be removed from the graph. Thus, we obtain the recurrence : $T(n) = d \cdot T(n - d)$. Standard computations (see e.g. [13]) show that $T(n) = O(3^{n/3})$ (the maximum is reached for $d = 3$, when d is an integer). As a consequence, there are at most $3^{n/3}$ mtcs of Type 1 and at most $n^2 \cdot 3^{n/3}$ of Type 2 (where a pair v_1, v_2 has first to be selected) which implies an upper bound of $n^2 \cdot 3^{n/3}$. Since all complete graphs are cobipartite a lower bound of $3^{n/3}$ follows from Lemma 1.

Theorem 3. *The number of minimal tropical connected sets in a cobipartite graph is at most $n^2 \cdot 3^{n/3}$ and all mtcs can be enumerated in time $O^*(3^{n/3})$. Moreover there exist cobipartite graphs with $3^{n/3}$ mtcs.*

5 Interval Graphs

An interval graph is an intersection graph of intervals on the real line. Let G be an interval graph and let S be any mtcs of G. Suppose that $\mathcal{I}$ is an interval model of G (see e.g. [2,19]) such that the interval assigned to a vertex v has left endpoint $l(v)$ and right endpoint $r(v)$. Let $v_{\min} = \operatorname{argmin}_{v \in S} l(v)$ and $v_{\max} = \operatorname{argmax}_{v \in S} r(v)$. As $G[S]$ is connected, there exists a path P between $v_{\min}$ and $v_{\max}$ in $G[S]$ and, by definition of $v_{\min}$ and $v_{\max}$, each vertex of S has at least one neighbor in P.

To enumerate all mtcs of G, our algorithm proceeds as follows: it first guesses a pair $v_{\min}, v_{\max}$ and then computes all possible induced paths P between these two vertices (Step 1). Then for each color class with no vertices in P, one vertex is chosen (Step 2). To analyse the running time of our algorithm and thus to achieve an upper bound on the number of mtcs, the Measure &Conquer technique is used with a single weight (see e.g. Chapter 6 in [13]). Formally, given an interval graph $G = (V, E)$ with B and R disjoint subsets of V, we define its measure $\mu = \mu(G) = |B| + w|R|$ where w is a weight later to be chosen in $[0, 1]$. Note that $\mu \leq |V|$. Let $T(\mu)$ be the maximum number of mtcs in an interval graph of measure at most μ. We are now ready to describe our algorithm and its running time analysis.

Consider algorithm **mintcs** on the next page. For each pair of vertices $v_{\min}$, $v_{\max} \in V$ such that $\mathcal{C} = \mathcal{C}(B)$, call **mintcs**$(G, B, \emptyset, [v_{\min}], v_{\min}, v_{\max})$, where $B := \{v : l(v_{\min}) \leq l(v) \leq r(v) \leq r(v_{\max})\}$. The output of this call are all mtcs S in $G[B]$ containing both $v_{\min}$ and $v_{\max}$. Hence the algorithm produces all mtcs of G when called for all the $O(n^2)$ vertex pairs $v_{\min}, v_{\max}$.

To analyze the running time, note that initially R is empty and B contains at most n vertices; thus $\mu \leq n$. First, consider Step 1 in the algorithm. As long

---

Algorithm mintcs($G, B, R, P, v_{\min}, v_{\max}$)

   if $v_{\max} \notin P$ **then**   /*   **Step 1**   */

      Let v_{last} be the last vertex added to P

      if $v_{\max} \in N_B(v_{\text{last}})$ **then**

         mintcs($G, B \setminus N_B(v_{\text{last}}), R \cup (N_B(v_{\text{last}}) \setminus \{v_{\max}\}), P \cup \{v_{\max}\}, v_{\min}, v_{\max}$)

      else

         foreach $v \in N_B(v_{\text{last}})$ **do**

           mintcs($G, B \setminus N_B(v_{\text{last}}), R \cup (N_B(v_{\text{last}}) \setminus \{v\}), P \cup \{v\}, v_{\min}, v_{\max}$)

   else   /*   **Step 2**   */

      if $\mathcal{C}(R) \setminus \mathcal{C}(P)$ *is non empty* **then**

         Let *col* be a color in $\mathcal{C}(R) \setminus \mathcal{C}(P)$

         $T \leftarrow \{v \in R \text{ s.t. } c(v) = col\}$

         foreach $v \in T$ **do**

           mintcs($G, B, R \setminus T, P \cup \{v\}, v_{\min}, v_{\max}$)

      else if P *is a mtcs* **then**

         output "P is a mtcs."

---

as P is not an induced path between $v_{\min}$ and $v_{\max}$, the last vertex added to P, named v_{last}, is considered. Exactly one vertex v from $N_B(v_{\text{last}})$ is added to P and removed from B, and the other ones are moved from B to R. Note that $t = |N_B(v_{\text{last}})|$, thus we obtain the following recurrence for the running time on **Step 1**: $T(\mu) \leq t \cdot T(\mu - (1 + (t-1)(1-w)))$. Note that if $v_{\max}$ belongs to the neighborhood of v_{last}, the algorithm add $v_{\max}$ to P and only one recursive call is made in such a case. Consider **Step 2**. For each color class whose color does not yet appear in P, exactly one vertex of that color is added to P and all the vertices of the color class are removed from R. Thus, if we denote by s the size of the color class, the recurrence $T(\mu) \leq s \cdot T(\mu - s \cdot w)$ for the running time of **Step 2** is obtained.

Choosing $w = 0.5895$, the solutions of both recurrences are bounded by 1.8613^{μ}. (The maximum is reached for $t = 4$ in the recurrence of **Step 1** and for $s = 3$ in the recurrence of **Step 2**.) This establishes the following theorem.

Theorem 4. *The number of minimal tropical connected sets in an interval graph is at most $n^2 \cdot 1.8613^n$ and they can be enumerated in time $O(1.8613^n)$.*

6   Block Graphs

A graph $G = (V, E)$ is a *block graph* if it is connected and every maximal 2-connected subgraph (called a *block*) is a clique [20]. One useful characterization of connected block graphs is that they are precisely graphs in which there is a unique induced path between any pair of vertices; an immediate consequence of the definition. This suggests a simple algorithm to enumerate all mtcs in block graphs. Pick one vertex in each color class to obtain a set S of vertices, and then make S connected. As there is a unique induced path between each two vertices of S, it is sufficient to add to S all vertices of each of these induced paths. Clearly S is a tcs and it finally remains to check that S is indeed minimal. In this way, it is possible to enumerate all at most $3^{n/3}$ mtcs of the block graph. The upper bound of $3^{n/3}$ is then established by an analysis similar to the one of Sect. 4. The upper bound is sharp by Lemma 1.

Theorem 5. *A block graph has at most $3^{n/3}$ minimal tropical connected sets, and they can be enumerated in $O^*(3^{n/3})$ time. There exist block graph with $3^{n/3}$ mtcs.*

7   A Lower Bound for Chordal Graphs

We prove a lower bound of 1.4916^n on the maximum number of mtcs in chordal graphs. To show this bound, we describe a graphs which achieve such a number of mtcs. Our construction might be viewed as a full rooted tree $\mathcal{T}$ of height h, where the root is of degree 5, and each node has 4 children.

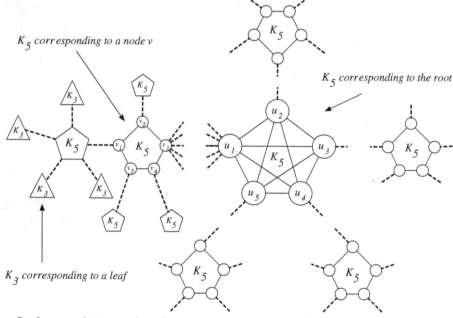

In fact, each internal node v is replaced by a K_5 (denoted K_5^v) and each leaf is replaced by a K_3. For each K_5^v, there is a one-to-one correspondence between the vertices of the corresponding K_5 and the 5 neighbors of v in the tree $\mathcal{T}$. Let v be an internal node of $\mathcal{T}$ and u its parent. Let K_5^v (resp. K_5^u) be the K_5 associated to v (resp. to u). Let x_u be the vertex of K_5^v mapped to the parent u of v and let x_v be the vertex of K_5^u mapped to the child v of u in $\mathcal{T}$. We add an edge between any pair of vertices (y, z) such that $y \in K_5^v$, $z \in K_5^u$, $y \neq x_u$ and

$z \neq x_v$. (See the figure below.) Given a leaf v and its parent u in $\mathcal{T}$, we denote by K_3^v the K_3 associated to v and by K_5^u the K_5 associated to u. We add to the graph all possible edges (y, z) such that $y \in K_5^u$, $z \in K_3^v$ and $y \neq x_v$, where x_v is the vertex of K_5^u mapped to the child v of u in $\mathcal{T}$.

Regarding the colors, all five vertices of any K_5 as well as all three vertices of any K_3 obtain the same color which is unique to the K_5 respectively K_3. This implies that any tcs of the resulting graph must contain at least one vertex of each K_5 and of each K_3. Observe that for each K_5 precisely two vertices are necessary to ensure the connectivity of the tcs. Indeed, since each x of a tcs belonging to a K_5 is non-adjacent to either one child or to the parent, at least one other vertex y of the K_5 must belongs to this tcs. In fact one additional vertex suffices as x and y are then connected to all children and to the parent in this tcs. Regarding the K_3 leaves, it is sufficient to take only one vertex. It is not hard to verify that the graph constructed is chordal.

Let us consider the number of mtcs in such a chordal graph. Recall that the tree $\mathcal{T}$ is of height h. At level $i = 0$, there is only one K_5 (corresponding to the root), and two vertices have to be picked from that set. For each i, $1 \leq i \leq h$, the number of K_5 or K_3 at level i is $5 \cdot 4^{i-1}$. Thus the number of mtcs and the number of vertices of the graph are

$$\#TCS(h) = \binom{5}{2} \cdot \binom{5}{2}^{\sum_{i=1}^{h-1} 5 \cdot 4^{i-1}} \cdot 3^{5 \cdot 4^{h-1}} \text{ and } n(h) = 5 + \sum_{i=1}^{h-1} 5^2 \cdot 4^{i-1} + 5 \cdot 4^{h-1} \cdot 3.$$

For $h = 9$, computations show that $\#TCS(h)^{1/n(h)} \approx 1.4916...$ Since disjoint copies of chordal graphs result in a chordal graph, the maximum number of mtcs of a chordal graph is at least 1.4916^n. (Note that choosing a larger value for h gives a larger chordal graph with at least 1.4916^n mtcs.)

Theorem 6. *There exist chordal graphs with at least 1.4916^n minimal tropical connected sets.*

References

1. Angles d'Auriac, J.-A., Cohen, N., El Maftouhi, A., Harutyunyan, A., Legay, S., Manoussakis, Y.: Connected tropical subgraphs in vertex-colored graphs. Discrete Math. Theor. Comput. Sci. **17**(3), 327–348 (2016). http://dmtcs.episciences.org/2151
2. Brandstädt, A., Le, V.B., Spinrad, J.P.: Graph classes: a survey. society for industrial and applied mathematics (SIAM), Philadelphia, PA, SIAM Monographs on Discrete Mathematics and Applications (1999)
3. Chapelle, M., Cochefert, M., Kratsch, D., Letourneur, R., Liedloff, M.: Exact exponential algorithms to find a tropical connected set of minimum size. In: Cygan, M., Heggernes, P. (eds.) IPEC 2014. LNCS, vol. 8894, pp. 147–158. Springer, Heidelberg (2014)
4. Couturier, J., Heggernes, P., van't Hof, P., Kratsch, D.: Minimal dominating sets in graph classes, combinatorial bounds and enumeration. Theor. Comput. Sci. **487**, 82–94 (2013)

5. Couturier, J.-F., Heggernes, P., van't Hof, P., Villanger, Y.: Maximum number of minimal feedback vertex sets in chordal graphs and cographs. In: Gudmundsson, J., Mestre, J., Viglas, T. (eds.) COCOON 2012. LNCS, vol. 7434, pp. 133–144. Springer, Heidelberg (2012)

6. Couturier, J., Letourneur, R., Liedloff, M.: On the number of minimal dominating sets on some graph classes. Theor. Comput. Sci. **562**, 634–642 (2015)

7. Diestel, R.: Graph Theory. Graduate Texts in Mathematics, vol. 173. Springer, Heidelberg (2012)

8. Fomin, F.V., Gaspers, S., Pyatkin, A.V., Razgon, I.: On the minimum feedback vertex set problem: exact and enumeration algorithms. Algorithmica **52**(2), 293–307 (2008)

9. Fomin, F.V., Gaspers, S., Lokshtanov, D., Saurabh, S.: Exact algorithms via monotone local search. In: Proceedings of STOC, pp. 764–775 (2016)

10. Fomin, F.V., Grandoni, F., Pyatkin, A.V., Stepanov, A.A.: Combinatorial bounds via measure, conquer: bounding minimal dominating sets and applications. ACM Trans. Algorithms **5**(1), 9 (2008)

11. Fomin, F.V., Heggernes, P., Kratsch, D.: Exact algorithms for graph homomorphisms. Theor. Comp. Sys. **41**(2), 381–393 (2007)

12. Fomin, F.V., Heggernes, P., Kratsch, D., Papadopoulos, C., Villanger, Y.: Enumerating minimal subset feedback vertex sets. Algorithmica **69**(1), 216–231 (2014)

13. Fomin, F.V., Kratsch, D.: Exact Exponential Algorithms. Texts in Theoretical Computer Science. An EATCS Series. Springer, Heidelberg (2010)

14. Fomin, F.V., Villanger, Y.: Finding induced subgraphs via minimal triangulations. In: Proceedings STACS 2010, Dagstuhl, LIPIcs, vol. 43, pp. 383–394 (2010)

15. Gaspers, S., Mackenzie, S.: On the number of minimal separators in graphs, CoRR abs/1503.01203 (2015)

16. Gaspers, S., Mnich, M.: Feedback vertex sets in tournaments. J. Graph Theor. **72**(1), 72–89 (2013)

17. Golovach, P.A., Heggernes, P., Kratsch, D.: Enumeration and maximum number of minimal connected vertex covers in graphs. In: Lipták, Z., Smyth, W.F. (eds.) IWOCA 2015. LNCS, vol. 9538, pp. 235–247. Springer, Heidelberg (2016)

18. Golovach, P.A., Heggernes, P., Kratsch, D., Saei, R.: Subset feedback vertex sets in chordal graphs. J. Discr. Algorithms **26**, 7–15 (2014)

19. Golumbic, M.C.: Algorithmic Graph Theory and Perfect Graphs. Annals of Discrete Mathematics, vol. 57, 2nd edn. Elsevier Science B.V., Amsterdam (2004)

20. Kay, D.C., Chartrand, G.: A characterization of certain Ptolemaic graphs. Can. J. Math. **17**, 342–346 (1965)

21. Lacroix, V., Fernandes, C.G., Sagot, M.-F.: Motif search in graphs: application to metabolic networks. IEEE/ACM Trans. Comput. Biol. Bioinform. **3**(4), 360–368 (2006)

22. McMorris, F., Warnow, T., Wimer, T.: Triangulating vertex-colored graphs. SIAM J. Discr. Math. **7**, 296–306 (1994)

23. Moon, J.W., Moser, L.: On cliques in graphs. Israel J. Math. **3**, 23–28 (1965)

24. Scott, J., Ideker, T., Karp, R.M., Sharan, R.: Efficient algorithms for detecting signaling pathways in protein interaction networks. J. Comput. Biol. **13**, 133–144 (2006)

25. Telle, J.A., Villanger, Y.: Connecting terminals and 2-disjoint connected subgraphs. In: Brandstädt, A., Jansen, K., Reischuk, R. (eds.) WG 2013. LNCS, vol. 8165, pp. 418–428. Springer, Heidelberg (2013)

Bamboo Garden Trimming Problem
(Perpetual Maintenance of Machines with Different Attendance Urgency Factors)

Leszek Gąsieniec[1], Ralf Klasing[2]([✉]), Christos Levcopoulos[3], Andrzej Lingas[3], Jie Min[1], and Tomasz Radzik[4]

[1] Department of Computer Science, University of Liverpool, Liverpool, UK
{l.a.gasieniec,J.Min2}@liverpool.ac.uk
[2] CNRS, LaBRI, Université de Bordeaux, Talence, France
ralf.klasing@labri.fr
[3] Department of Computer Science, Lund University, Lund, Sweden
{christos.levcopoulos,andrzej.lingas}@cs.lth.se
[4] Department of Informatics, King's College London, London, UK
tomasz.radzik@kcl.ac.uk

Abstract. A garden G is populated by $n \geq 1$ bamboos $b_1, b_2, ..., b_n$ with the respective daily growth rates $h_1 \geq h_2 \geq \cdots \geq h_n$. It is assumed that the initial heights of bamboos are zero. The robotic gardener or simply a robot maintaining the bamboo garden is attending bamboos and trimming them to height zero according to some schedule. The *Bamboo Garden Trimming Problem*, or simply BGT, is to design a perpetual schedule of cuts to maintain the elevation of bamboo garden as low as possible. The bamboo garden is a metaphor for a collection of machines which have to be serviced with different frequencies, by a robot which can service only one machine during a visit. The objective is to design a perpetual schedule of servicing the machines which minimizes the maximum (weighted) waiting time for servicing.

We consider two variants of BGT. In *discrete* BGT the robot is allowed to trim only one bamboo at the end of each day. In *continuous* BGT the bamboos can be cut at any time, however, the robot needs time to move from one bamboo to the next one and this time is defined by a weighted network of connections.

For discrete BGT, we show a simple 4-approximation algorithm and, by exploiting relationship between BGT and the classical Pinwheel scheduling problem, we obtain also a 2-approximation and even a closer approximation for more balanced growth rates. For continuous BGT, we propose approximation algorithms which achieve approximation ratios $O(\log(h_1/h_n))$ and $O(\log n)$.

L. Gąsieniec and J. Min's work was partially supported by Network Sciences and Technologies (NeST) at University of Liverpool.

R. Klasing's work was partially funded by the ANR project DISPLEXITY (ANR-11-BS02-014). This study has been carried out in the frame of "the Investments for the future" Programme IdEx Bordeaux – CPU (ANR-10-IDEX-03-02).

T. Radzik's work was supported in part by EPSRC grant EP/M005038/1, "Randomized algorithms for computer networks."

B. Steffen et al. (Eds.): SOFSEM 2017, LNCS 10139, pp. 229–240, 2017.
DOI: 10.1007/978-3-319-51963-0_18

1   Introduction

In this paper we consider a perpetual scheduling problem in which a collection of (possibly virtual) machines need to be attended with very often *known* but possibly different frequencies, i.e., some machines need to be attended more often than others. We model such scheduling problems as *Bamboo Garden Trimming (BGT) Problem*. A collection (garden) G of n bamboos $b_1, b_2, \ldots, b_n$ with known respective daily growth rates $h_1 \geq h_2 \geq \cdots \geq h_n > 0$ is given. Initially the height of each bamboo is set to zero. The robotic gardener maintaining the garden trims bamboos to height zero according to some schedule. The height of a bamboo b_i after $t \geq 0$ days is equal to $(t - t')h_i$, where t' is the last time when this bamboo was trimmed, or $t' = 0$, if it has never been trimmed by time t. The main task in BGT is to design a perpetual schedule of cuts to keep the highest bamboo in the garden as low as possible, while complying with some specified constraints on the timing of cutting. The basic constraints considered in this paper are that the gardener can cut only one (arbitrary) bamboo at the end of each day and is not allowed to attend the garden at any other times. Once the gardener has decided which bamboo to trim in the current round (at the end of the current day), the action of actual trimming is instantaneous. The problem, while of inherent combinatorial interest, originates from perpetual testing of virtual machines in cloud systems [1]. In such systems frequency in which virtual machines are tested for undesirable symptoms vary depending on importance of dedicated cloud operational mechanisms.

BGT is also a natural extension of several classical algorithmic problems with the focus on *monitoring* and *mobility*, including the *Art Gallery Problem* [17] and its dynamic extension called the *k-Watchmen Problem* [20]. In a more recent work on *fence patrolling* [9,10] the studies focus on monitoring vital (possibly disconnected) parts of a linear environment where each point is expected to be attended with the same frequency. The authors of [11] study monitoring linear environments by robots prone to faults. Our paper focuses on the case where each vital part of the environment has its own, possibly unique urgency factor, which makes it related to *periodic scheduling* [19], a series of papers on the *Pinwheel* problems [6,7,13] including the *periodic Pinwheel* problem [14,16] and the *Pinwheel scheduling* problem [18], as well as the concept of *P-fairness* in sharing multiple copies of some resource among various tasks [2,3].

We consider two variants of the BGT problem. The constraints that only one bamboo is cut at the end of each day define *discrete* BGT. In the second variant, *continuous* BGT, we assume that for any two bamboos b_i and b_j, we know the time $t_{i,j} > 0$ that the robot needs to relocate from b_i to b_j. In this variant the time when the next bamboo is trimmed depends on how far that bamboo is from the bamboo which has just been trimmed. As in discrete BGT, when the robot arrives at the bamboo which is to be trimmed, the actual action of trimming is instantaneous. We assume that the travel times are symmetric, that is, $t_{i,j} = t_{j,i}$, and can be fractional. Previous work on problems of similar nature as the continuous BGT includes recent work on patrolling [9–11,15].

In related research on minimizing the maximum occupancy of a buffer in a system of n buffers, the usual setting is a game between the player and the adversary [4,5,8]. The adversary decides how the fixed total increase of data in each round is distributed among the buffers and tries to maximize the maximum occupancy of a buffer. The player decides which buffer (or buffers, depending on the variant of the problem) should be emptied next and tries to minimize the maximum buffer size. The upper bounds developed in this more general context can be translated into upper bounds for our BGT problems, but our aim is to derive tighter bounds for the case when the rates of growth of bamboos are fixed and known.

Probably the most natural strategy to keep the elevation of the bamboo garden low is the greedy approach of always cutting next the highest bamboo. This approach, called *Reduce-Max*, was considered recently in the context of periodic testing of virtual machines in cloud systems [1], and was also studied in the adversarial setting of the buffer minimization problems mentioned above. The results presented in [5] imply a tight bound of $H(H_{n-1} + 1) = \Theta(H \log n)$ on the performance of Reduce-Max for discrete BGT when the adversary keeps changing the growth rates of bamboos, where H is the sum of the daily growth rates (the adversary cannot change this sum) and $H_k = \sum_{i=1}^{k} \frac{1}{k} = \Theta(\log k)$ is the k-th harmonic number. While the $O(H \log n)$ upper bound applies obviously also to our setting of the discrete BGT, when the growth rates are fixed, it is not clear whether there are instances which force Reduce-Max to leave bamboos of height $\Omega(H \log n)$. On the contrary, the experimental work presented in [1] indicates possibility that Reduce-Max keeps the maximum bamboo height within $O(H)$. The upper bound of $O(H \log n)$ on Reduce-Max for discrete BGT implies an $O(DH \log n)$ upper bound on the same approach for continuous BGT, where D is the diameter of the set of bamboos (the largest travel time between any pair of bamboos), but again this upper bound from the adversarial setting does not help us in analyzing how well we can do for given growth rates.

In both cases, discrete and continuous, we consider algorithms $\mathcal{A}$ which for an input instance I (of the form $\langle h_i : 1 \leq i \leq n \rangle$ in the discrete case and $[\langle h_i : 1 \leq i \leq n \rangle, \langle t_{i,j} : 1 \leq i, j \leq n \rangle]$ in the continuous case) produce a perpetual (trimming) schedule $\mathcal{A}(I)$, that is, a sequence of indices of bamboos $(i_1, i_2, \dots)$ which defines the order in which the bamboos are trimmed. We are mainly interested in the *approximation ratios* of such algorithms, which are defined in the usual way. For an input instance I and a trimming schedule $\mathcal{S}$ for I, let $MH(\mathcal{S})$ denote the supremum of the heights of bamboos over all times $t \geq 0$ when the trimming proceeds according to schedule $\mathcal{S}$, and let $OPT(I)$ denote the infimum of $MH(\mathcal{S})$ over all schedules $\mathcal{S}$ for I. The upper bounds on Reduce-Max imply that $OPT(I)$ is finite. The approximation ratio of a schedule $\mathcal{S}$ is defined as $MH(\mathcal{S})/OPT(I)$ and the approximation ratio of an algorithm $\mathcal{A}$ is the supremum of $MH(\mathcal{A}(I))/OPT(I)$ over all input instances I. While our main goal is a low approximation ratio, we are also interested in the time complexity of BGT algorithms and try to keep low both the time of any preprocessing and the time needed to compute the index of the next bamboo in the schedule.

For each instance of discrete BGT with the sum of the growth rates $H = h_1 + h_2 + \cdots + h_n$, $OPT(I) \geq H$, as shown below. Thus the approximation ratio of Reduce-Max is $O(\log n)$ but it remains an open questions whether this upper bound is tight. In Sect. 2, we show that a simple modification of Reduce-Max has the approximation ratio at most 4. We also show more complicated algorithms, which are based on the relation between discrete BGT and the Pinwheel problem and have approximation ratios of 2, for any growth rate sequence, and $(1 + \delta)$, for a constant $0 < \delta < 1$ and "balanced" growth rate sequences.

In Sect. 3, we show algorithms for continuous BGT with approximation ratios $O(\log(h_1/h_n))$ and $O(\log n)$. In the full version of our paper, we show also some hard instances of the continuous BGT problem such that for any schedule the maximum bamboo height is greater than our lower bounds by a $\Theta(\log n)$ factor. Thus for these input instances our $O(\log n)$-approximation algorithm computes in fact constant-approximation schedules. We also leave to the full version of the paper a $O(1)$-approximation algorithm for continuous BGT for the case when $h_1 = \Theta(H)$.

Lower Bound on Discrete BGT. We note a natural lower bound of $H = h_1 + h_2 + \cdots + h_n$ on the maximum height of a bamboo in the discrete BGT problem. Thus neither Reduce-Max nor any other algorithm for the discrete BGT problem can keep the bamboos within the height H, that is, $\max\{MH(\mathcal{A}(I)) : \text{sum of growth rates in } I \text{ is } H\}/H$ is an upper bound on the approximation ratio of an algorithm $\mathcal{A}$. This bound can be proved by contradiction. Assume there exists a perpetual schedule that keeps the heights of all bamboos below $H_{MAX} < H$. During each day the *total height* T of the bamboos, that is, the sum of the current heights of all bamboos, increases at least by $H - H_{MAX} > 0$. Thus after $\lfloor nH_{MAX}/(H - H_{MAX}) \rfloor + 1$ days the height of at least one bamboo is greater than H_{MAX} – a contradiction. A similar lower bound argument can be obtained via density restrictions in *Pinwheel* problem, discussed later in Sect. 2.2.

2 Discrete BGT

We consider two types of algorithms for the discrete variant of BGT. An *online* algorithm is based on simple queries of type "what is the tallest bamboo?" (as in Reduce-Max), or "what is the fastest growing bamboo with the height above some threshold?" (as below in Reduce-Fastest). Such queries can be answered without knowing the whole distribution of growth rates. Online scheduling is more flexible since its performance can adapt, if the growth rates change. On the downside, the performance analysis of online scheduling is more complex and the approximation bounds tend to be weaker. In contrast, an *offline* algorithm determines which bamboo is to be trimmed during a particular round by producing, based on the knowledge of the whole distribution of growth rates, the full perpetual schedule during preprocessing. This reduces the flexibility of the solution, but leads to stronger approximation bounds. We note that our online-offline characterization is to indicate only a general nature of possible BGT algorithms.

2.1 Constant Approximation of BGT by Online Scheduling

We obtain our first constant-approximation algorithm by the following simple modification of Reduce-Max. We cut next the fastest growing bamboo among those with the current heights at least $x \cdot H$, for some constant $x > 1$. We call this algorithm Reduce-Fastest(x) and show the following approximation bound.

Theorem 1. Reduce-Fastest(2) *is a 4-approximation algorithm for discrete BGT.*

Proof. Without loss of generality, we assume that if there are two or more bamboos with the same fastest growth rate among the bamboos with the current height at least $x \cdot H$, then Reduce-Fastest chooses for trimming the bamboo with the smallest index. Thus the largest height of bamboo b_1 is at most $xH + h_1 \le (x+1)H$.

We consider now a bamboo b_i, for some arbitrary $2 \le i \le n$, and assume that it reaches the height at least $C \cdot H$ for some constant $C \ge x+1$. At any time the heights of bamboos belong to two disjoint regions: the lower region $[0, x \cdot H)$ and the upper region $[x \cdot H, \infty)$. At some point bamboo b_i must stay in the upper region for at least $\lfloor \frac{(C-x) \cdot H}{h_i} \rfloor$ consecutive rounds to reach the height $C \cdot H$.

We consider a period of $t = \lfloor \frac{(C-x) \cdot H}{h_i} \rfloor$ consecutive rounds when bamboo b_i remains in the upper region. At each of these rounds, trimming of bamboo b_i "is blocked" by trimming of another bamboo b_j for some $j < i$. The number of times when bamboo b_j can block bamboo b_i during this period is at most $t_j = 1 + \lfloor \frac{t}{f_j} \rfloor$, where $f_j = \lceil \frac{x \cdot H}{h_j} \rceil$ is the number of rounds needed by bamboo b_j to climb back to the upper region after trimming. Thus the number of rounds when bamboo b_i is blocked is at most

$$\sum_{j=1}^{i-1} t_j = \sum_{j=1}^{i-1} \left(1 + \left\lfloor \frac{\lfloor \frac{(C-x)H}{h_i} \rfloor}{\lceil \frac{xH}{h_j} \rceil} \right\rfloor \right) \le \left\lfloor \frac{(C-x) \cdot H}{h_i} \right\rfloor \left(\frac{i-1}{\lfloor \frac{(C-x) \cdot H}{h_i} \rfloor} + \sum_{j=1}^{i-1} \frac{1}{\lceil \frac{x \cdot H}{h_j} \rceil} \right)$$

Using $h_i \le H/i$ and $\sum_{j=1}^{i-1} h_j < H$, we obtain

$$\frac{i-1}{\lfloor \frac{(C-x) \cdot H}{h_i} \rfloor} + \sum_{j=1}^{i-1} \frac{1}{\lceil \frac{x \cdot H}{h_j} \rceil} < \frac{1}{C-x} + \frac{1}{x}.$$

Bamboo b_i is blocked in all $\lfloor \frac{(C-x) \cdot H}{h_i} \rfloor$ rounds, so

$$\sum_{j=1}^{i-1} t_j \ge \left\lfloor \frac{(C-x) \cdot H}{h_i} \right\rfloor,$$

implying that

$$\frac{1}{C-x} + \frac{1}{x} > 1.$$

The above inequality is equivalent to $C < 2 + (x-1) + 1/(x-1)$. This bound is minimized for $x = 2$, giving $C < 4$. Thus the approximation ratio of Reduce-Fastest(2) is at most 4. $\qquad\square$

2.2   Offline Scheduling

In this section we focus on off-line scheduling which permits tighter approximation results. We recall first classical *Pinwheel* scheduling problem which is
closely related to BGT. This is followed by the presentation of a 2-approximation
algorithm for any distribution of the growth rates and a $(1 + \delta)$-approximation
algorithm for instances with more balanced growth rates in BGT.

Pinwheel. The Pinwheel problem [13] is defined as follows. Given a set $V = f_1, f_2, \ldots, f_n$ of positive integers called Pinwheel frequencies. One is asked to
create an infinite sequence S of indices drawn from the set $1, 2, \ldots, n$, s.t., any
sub-sequence of $f_i \in V$ consecutive elements in S includes at least one index
i. The density of set V is defined as $D = \sum_{i=1}^{n} \frac{1}{f_i}$. It has been coined in [13]
that Pinwheel is NP-hard assuming succinct representation of the problem. It is
also known [13] that all instances of Pinwheel with the density exceeding value
1 cannot be scheduled. On the other hand any instance of Pinwheel with the
density at most $\frac{3}{4}$ can be scheduled, however, finding such a schedule may require
a substantial time [12].

In order to determine the relationship between BGT and Pinwheel problems
we show first how to relate the daily growth rates in BGT with the frequencies in
Pinwheel. We define the set of frequencies $f_i = H/h_i$, for $i = 1, 2, \ldots, n$, which
form a *pseudo-instance* of Pinwheel with frequencies as real numbers (rather
than integers) and with the density

$$D = \sum_{i=1}^{n} \frac{1}{f_i} = \sum_{i=1}^{n} \frac{h_i}{H} = 1.$$

Note that one can replace H by $H' = (1 + \delta)H$, for any $\delta > 0$ to reduce the
density of the respective pseudo-instance to

$$D' = \sum_{i=1}^{n} \frac{1}{f_i'} = \sum_{i=1}^{n} \frac{h_i}{(1 + \delta)H} = \frac{1}{(1 + \delta)} \sum_{i=1}^{n} \frac{1}{f_i} = \frac{1}{(1 + \delta)} D.$$

In other words, by manipulating δ one can obtain another pseudo-instance $I'(\delta)$
of Pinwheel with the density $\frac{1}{(1+\delta)}$ lower than one. For example, by adopting
$\delta = \frac{1}{3}$ one can obtain a pseudo-instance $I'(\frac{1}{3})$ of Pinwheel with the density $\frac{3}{4}$.

Furthermore, having a pseudo-instance $I'(\delta)$ with sufficiently low density
$\frac{1}{(1+\delta)}$, for $\delta > 0$, enables replacement of non-integral frequencies by their floors
to create a proper instance $I(\delta)$ of Pinwheel with the density below one.

Lemma 1. *A solution (if feasible) to the proper instance $I(\delta)$ of Pinwheel results
in a $(1 + \delta)$-approximation schedule for the original BGT problem.*

Proof. In $I(\delta)$ the frequence $f_i \leq \frac{H(1+\delta)}{h_i}$ is an upper bound on the number of
rounds between two consecutive visits to b_i in BGT. And since the height of b_i
is limited to $h_i \cdot f_i$ we get the upper bound $H(1 + \delta)$ on the height of each b_i. □

A 2-approximation algorithm. According to Lemma 1 the main challenge in BGT, i.e., keeping all bamboos as low as possible can be reduced to finding the smallest value of δ for which the relevant proper instance of Pinwheel problem can be scheduled. The main idea behind our solution refers to the result from [13] indicating that any instance of Pinwheel with frequencies being powers of 2 and the density at most 1 can be scheduled efficiently. By adopting $H' = 2H$ one can first translate any instance of BGT to a pseudo-instance of Pinwheel with the density $\frac{1}{2}$, and later by reducing each frequency to the nearest power of 2 produce a proper instance of Pinwheel with the density at most 1.

Corollary 1. *The algorithm described above provides a 2-approximation for the BGT problem.*

A $(1 + \delta)$-approximation algorithm for more balanced growth rates. In search for more tight approximation one cannot reduce frequencies to just the closest power of 2. Instead, to obtain greater granularity we start with reduction of frequencies (in the respective pseudo-instance of Pinwheel) to the closest values of the form $2^k(1 + \frac{j}{C})$, where $C = 2^a$, for some integer constant $a \geq 0$, and $j \in [0, C)$. We make the following two observations.

Observation 1. Any two frequencies of the form $2^k(1 + \frac{j}{C})$ can be combined via their equidistant superposition into a shorter frequency $2^{k-1}(1 + \frac{j}{C})$. For example, for $k = 4, C = 4$ and $j = 3$ we obtain two frequencies f_1, f_2 of size $2^k(1 + \frac{j}{C}) = 2^4(1 + \frac{3}{4}) = 28$ which can be combined into a shorter frequency $2^{k-1}(1 + \frac{j}{C}) = 2^3(1 + \frac{3}{4}) = 14$ by alternating f_1 and f_2 in a round robin fashion.

Observation 2. One can combine $m_j = C + j$ frequencies $2^k(1 + \frac{j}{C})$ into one frequency $2^k/C$ which is also a power of 2, since $2^k(1 + \frac{j}{C})/m_j = 2^k/C$.

We say that an instance of BGT is α-balanced, if $h_1 \leq \alpha \cdot H$, for some constant $\alpha < 1$.

The Main Algorithm. Given an α-balanced instance of BGT with growth rates $h_1, h_2, \ldots, h_n$.

1. Adopt $H' = (1 + \delta)H$, and form the respective pseudo-instance of Pinwheel with the frequencies $f_1, f_2, \ldots, f_n > 2^{min}$, for the largest possible integer min, and the density $\frac{1}{1+\delta}$.
2. Reduce each frequency f_i to the closest value of the form $2^k(1 + \frac{j}{C})$, for some $k \geq min$ and $j \in [0, C)$.
   [*This increases the density by a factor of* $1 + \frac{1}{C}$ *to the value* $(1 + \frac{1}{C})/(1 + \delta)$.]
3. Use Observation 1 for as long as possible to combine pairs of the same frequencies pushing them down towards the range $[2^{min}, 2^{min+1})$.
   [*On the conclusion of this step there is at most one frequency* $2^k(1 + \frac{j}{C})$, *for* $k > min$ *and* $j \in [0, C)$.]
4. Apply the transformation from Observation 2 in the range $[2^{min}, 2^{min+1})$ until there are at most $C + j - 1$ frequencies $2^k(1 + \frac{j}{C})$ left, for any $j \in (0, C)$.
   [*After this step, there are at most* $C+j-1$ *frequencies in each group* j *in the range* $[2^{min}, 2^{min+1})$.]

5. In each range reduce all remaining frequencies (different to powers of two) group by group starting from the top group $j = C - 1$ and apply the transformation from Observation 2 whenever possible.

[*We gain an extra density ΔD. We must ensure that $\frac{1+\frac{1}{C}}{1+\delta} + \Delta D \leq 1$. This can be done by the appropriate selection of parameters C and δ, see below.*]

The following theorem about the approximation of the above algorithm is proven in the full version of the paper.

Theorem 2. *For any $\delta > 0$, the Main Algorithm produces $(1+\delta)$-approximation BGT schedules for α-balance instances, if $\alpha \leq \frac{\delta^2(1+\delta)}{(2+\delta)^2}$.*

3   Continuous BGT

We consider now the continuous variant of the BGT problem. Since this variant models scenarios when bamboos are spread over some geographical area, we will now refer not only to bamboos $b_1, b_2, \ldots, b_n$ but also to the points $v_1, v_2, \ldots, v_n$ (in the implicit underlying space) where these bamboos are located. We will denote by V the set of these points.

Recall that input I for the continuous BGT problem consists of the rates of growth of bamboos ($h_i : 1 \leq i \leq n$) and the travel times between bamboos ($t_{i,j} : 1 \leq i, j \leq n$). We assume that $h_1 \geq h_2 \geq \ldots \geq h_n$, as before, and normalize these rates, for convenience, so that $h_1 + h_2 + \ldots + h_n = 1$ (this is done without loss of generality, since the exact unit of the heights of bamboos is irrelevant). We assume that the travel distances are symmetric and form a metric on V. (In the scenarios which we model, if $t_{i,j}$ was greater than $t_{i,k} + t_{k,j}$, then the robot would travel between points v_i and v_j via the point v_k.)

For any $V' \subseteq V$, the minimum growth rate among all points in V' is denoted by $h_{\min}(V')$, and the maximum growth rate among all points in V' is denoted by $h_{\max}(V')$. Let $h_{\min} = h_{\min}(V) = h_n$, and $h_{\max} = h_{\max}(V) = h_1$.

The diameter of the set V is denoted by $D = D(V) = \max\{t_{i,j} : 1 \leq i, j \leq n\}$. For any $V' \subseteq V$, $MST(V')$ denotes the minimum weight of a Steiner tree on V'. Recall that for an algorithm $\mathcal{A}$ and input I, $MH(\mathcal{A}(I))$ denotes the maximum height that any bamboo ever reaches, if trimming is done according to the schedule computed by $\mathcal{A}$, and $OPT(I)$ is the optimal (minimal) maximum height of a bamboo over all schedules.

3.1   Lower Bounds

We first show some simple lower bounds on the maximum height of a bamboo. For notational brevity, we omit the explicit reference to the input I. For example, the inequality $MH(\mathcal{A}) \geq Dh_{\max}$ in the lemma below is to be understood as $MH(\mathcal{A}(I)) \geq D(V(I)) \cdot h_{\max}(V(I))$, for each input instance I.

Lemma 2. $MH(\mathcal{A}) \geq Dh_{\max}$, *for any algorithm $\mathcal{A}$.*

Algorithm 1. An $O(h_{\max}/h_{\min})$-approximation algorithm for continuous BGT.

1. Calculate a minimum spanning tree T of the point set V.
2. Repeatedly perform an Euler-tour traversal of T.

Proof. The robot must visit another point x in V at distance at least $D/2$ from v_1. When the robot comes back to v_1 after visiting x (possibly via a number of points in V), the bamboo at v_1 has grown at least to the height of Dh_1.   □

Lemma 3. $MH(\mathcal{A}) = \Omega(h_{\min}(V') \cdot MST(V'))$, *for any algorithm* $\mathcal{A}$ *and* $V' \subseteq V$.

Proof. Let v be the point in V' visited last: all points in $V' \backslash \{v\}$ have been visited at least once before the first visit to v. The distance traveled until the first visit to v is at least $MST(V')$, so the bamboo at v has grown to the height at least $h_v \cdot MST(V')$.   □

3.2 Approximation Algorithms

We describe our Algorithms 1, 2 and 3 for the continuous BGT problem in pseudocode and give their approximation ratio in the theorems below.

Theorem 3. *Algorithm 1 is an* $O(h_{\max}/h_{\min})$-*approximation algorithm for the continuous BGT problem.*

Proof. Let $\mathcal{A}_1$ denote Algorithm 1. Every point $v_i \in V$ is visited by $\mathcal{A}_1$ at least every $2 \cdot MST(V)$ time units. Hence,

$$MH(\mathcal{A}_1) = O(h_{\max}(V) \cdot MST(V)). \tag{1}$$

According to Lemma 3,

$$OPT = \Omega(h_{\min}(V) \cdot MST(V)). \tag{2}$$

Combining the two bounds (1) and (2), it follows that Algorithm 1 is an $O(h_{\max}/h_{\min})$-approximation algorithm for BGT.   □

Theorem 4. *Algorithm 2 is an* $O(\log(h_{\max}/h_{\min}))$-*approximation algorithm for the continuous BGT problem.*

Proof. Consider any point $v \in V_i$, for any $i \in \{1, 2, \ldots, s\}$. The distance traveled between two consecutive visits to v is at most

$$O\left(D \cdot \log\left(\frac{h_{\max}}{h_{\min}}\right) \cdot \left\lceil \frac{MST(V_i)}{D} \right\rceil \right) = O\left(\log\left(\frac{h_{\max}}{h_{\min}}\right) \cdot \max\{D, MST(V_i)\} \right).$$

Hence, the height of the bamboo at v is never larger than

$$O\left(h_{\max}(V_i) \cdot \log\left(\frac{h_{\max}}{h_{\min}}\right) \cdot \max\{D, MST(V_i)\} \right). \tag{3}$$

Algorithm 2. An $O(\log(h_{\max}/h_{\min}))$-approximation algorithm for continuous BGT.

1. Let $s = \lceil \log_2(h_{\max}/h_{\min}) \rceil$.
2. For $i \in \{1, 2 \ldots, s\}$, let $V_i = \{v_j \in V \mid 2^{i-1} \cdot h_{\min} \leq h_j < 2^i \cdot h_{\min}\}$, let T_i be an $O(1)$-approximation of the minimum Steiner tree on V_i, and let C_i be an Euler-tour traversal of T_i.
3. For $i \in \{2, \ldots, s\}$, define an arbitrary point on C_i as the last visited point on C_i.
4. Start at an arbitrary point on C_1.
5. **repeat forever**
6.   **for** $i = 1$ **to** $s - 1$ **do**
7.   Walk distance D on C_i in clockwise direction.
8.   Walk to the last visited point on C_{i+1}.
9.   **for** $i = s$ **to** 2 **do**
10.   Walk distance D on C_i in clockwise direction.
11.   Walk to the last visited point on C_{i-1}.

On the other hand, using Lemmas 2 and 3, we obtain

$$OPT = \Omega(h_{\min}(V_i) \cdot \max\{D, MST(V_i)\}). \tag{4}$$

Combining the two bounds (3) and (4), and observing that $h_{\max}(V_i) \leq 2 \cdot h_{\min}(V_i)$, we see that Algorithm 2 is an $O(\log(h_{\max}/h_{\min}))$-approximation algorithm for BGT.   □

Theorem 5. *Algorithm 3 is an $O(\log n)$-approximation algorithm for the continuous BGT problem.*

Proof. Consider any point $v \in V_i$, for any $i \in \{1, 2, \ldots, s\}$. Then, the distance traveled between two consecutive visits of v is at most

$$O(D \cdot \log n \cdot \left\lceil \frac{MST(V_i)}{D} \right\rceil) = O(\log n \cdot \max\{D, MST(V_i)\}).$$

Hence, the height of the bamboo at v is never larger than

$$O(h_{\max}(V_i) \cdot \log n \cdot \max\{D, MST(V_i)\}). \tag{5}$$

On the other hand, using Lemmas 2 and 3, we obtain

$$OPT = \Omega(h_{\min}(V_i) \cdot \max\{D, MST(V_i)\}). \tag{6}$$

Since $h_{\max}(V_i) \leq 2h_{\min}(V_i)$, then the height of the bamboo at v is always $O(OPT \cdot \log n)$.

Consider a point $v \in V_0$. Then, the distance traveled between two consecutive visits of v is at most

$$O(|V_0| \cdot D \cdot \log n) = O(n \cdot D \cdot \log n).$$

Algorithm 3. An $O(\log n)$-approximation algorithm for continuous BGT.

1. Let $s = \lceil 2 \cdot \log_2 n \rceil$.
2. Let $V_0 = \{v_i \in V \mid h_i \leq n^{-2}\}$.
   For $i \in \{1, 2, \ldots, s\}$, let $V_i = \{v_j \in V \mid 2^{i-1} \cdot n^{-2} < h_j \leq 2^i \cdot n^{-2}\}$.
   For $i \in \{1, 2, \ldots, s\}$, let T_i be an $O(1)$-approximation of the minimum Steiner tree on V_i, and let C_i be an Euler-tour traversal of T_i.
3. For $i \in \{2, 3, \ldots, s\}$, define an arbitrary point on C_i as the last visited point on C_i. Let $V_0 = \{v'_0, v'_1, \ldots, v'_{\ell-1}\}$.
4. Start at an arbitrary point on C_1.
5. $j = 0$.
6. **repeat forever**
7.   **for** $i = 1$ **to** $s - 1$ **do**
8.   Walk distance D on C_i in clockwise direction.
9.   Walk to the last visited point on C_{i+1}.
10.   **for** $i = s$ **to** 2 **do**
11.   Walk distance D on C_i in clockwise direction.
12.   Walk to the last visited point on C_{i-1}.
13.   Walk to $v'_{j \bmod \ell}$ and back.
14. $j = j + 1$.

Hence, the height of the bamboo at v is never larger than

$$O(n \cdot h_{\max}(V_0) \cdot D \cdot \log n) = O(n \cdot n^{-2} \cdot D \cdot \log n) = O(h_{\max} \cdot D \cdot \log n). \quad (7)$$

On the other hand, using Lemma 2, we obtain

$$OPT = \Omega(h_{\max} \cdot D), \quad (8)$$

so the height of the bamboo at a point in V_0 is also always $O(OPT \cdot \log n)$. Thus Algorithm 3 is an $O(\log n)$-approximation algorithm for BGT. $\quad\square$

4 Open Problems

There are several interesting open questions about approximation algorithms for the BGT problems, including better understanding of the approximation ratio of Reduce-Max for discrete BGT. For continuous BGT, we do not know whether our Algorithm 3 or any other algorithm achieves an approximation ratio $o(\log n)$. There are also questions about efficient implementation of BGT algorithms. For example, how can we select the highest bamboo in Reduce-Max faster than in linear time per round, if the growth rates are known to the gardener?

References

1. Alshamrani, S., Kowalski, D.R., Gąsieniec, L.: How reduce max algorithm behaves with symptoms appearance on virtual machines in clouds. In: Proceedings of IEEE International Conference CIT/IUCC/DASC/PICOM, pp. 1703–1710 (2015)

2. Baruah, S.K., Cohen, N.K., Plaxton, C.G., Varvel, D.A.: Proportionate progress: a notion of fairness in resource allocation. Algorithmica 15(6), 600–625 (1996)
3. Baruah, S.K., Lin, S.-S.: Pfair scheduling of generalized pinwheel task systems. IEEE Trans. Comput. 47(7), 812–816 (1998)
4. Bender, M.A., Fekete, S.P., Kröller, A., Mitchell, J.S.B., Liberatore, V., Polishchuk, V., Suomela, J.: The minimum backlog problem. Theor. Comput. Sci. 605, 51–61 (2015)
5. Bodlaender, M.H.L., Hurkens, C.A.J., Kusters, V.J.J., Staals, F., Woeginger, G.J., Zantema, H.: Cinderella versus the Wicked Stepmother. In: Baeten, J.C.M., Ball, T., Boer, F.S. (eds.) TCS 2012. LNCS, vol. 7604, pp. 57–71. Springer, Heidelberg (2012). doi:10.1007/978-3-642-33475-7_5
6. Chan, M.Y., Chin, F.Y.L.: General schedulers for the pinwheel problem based on double-integer reduction. IEEE Trans. Comput. 41(6), 755–768 (1992)
7. Chan, M.Y., Chin, F.: Schedulers for larger classes of pinwheel instances. Algorithmica 9(5), 425–462, May 1993
8. Chrobak, M., Csirik, J., Imreh, C., Noga, J., Sgall, J., Woeginger, G.J.: The buffer minimization problem for multiprocessor scheduling with conflicts. In: Orejas, F., Spirakis, P.G., Leeuwen, J. (eds.) ICALP 2001. LNCS, vol. 2076, pp. 862–874. Springer, Berlin (2001). doi:10.1007/3-540-48224-5_70
9. Collins, A., Czyzowicz, J., Gąsieniec, L., Kosowski, A., Kranakis, E., Krizanc, D., Martin, R., Ponce, O.M.: Optimal patrolling of fragmented boundaries. In: Proceedings of the Twenty-fifth Annual ACM Symposium on Parallelism in Algorithms and Architectures, SPAA 2013, New York, USA, pp. 241–250 (2013)
10. Czyzowicz, J., Gąsieniec, L., Kosowski, A., Kranakis, E.: Boundary patrolling by mobile agents with distinct maximal speeds. In: Demetrescu, C., Halldórsson, M.M. (eds.) ESA 2011. LNCS, vol. 6942, pp. 701–712. Springer, Heidelberg (2011). doi:10.1007/978-3-642-23719-5_59
11. Czyzowicz, J., Gasieniec, L., Kosowski, A., Kranakis, E., Krizanc, D., Taleb, N.: When Patrolmen Become Corrupted: Monitoring a Graph Using Faulty Mobile Robots. In: Elbassioni, K., Makino, K. (eds.) ISAAC 2015. LNCS, vol. 9472, pp. 343–354. Springer, Heidelberg (2015). doi:10.1007/978-3-662-48971-0_30
12. Fishburn, P.C., Lagarias, J.C.: Pinwheel scheduling: achievable densities. Algorithmica 34(1), 14–38, September 2002
13. Holte, R., Mok, A., Rosier, L., Tulchinsky, I., Varvel, D.: The pinwheel: a real-time scheduling problem. In: II: Software Track, Proceedings of the Twenty-Second Annual Hawaii International Conference on System Sciences, vol. 2, pp. 693–702, January 1989
14. Holte, R., Rosier, L., Tulchinsky, I., Varvel, D.: Pinwheel scheduling with two distinct numbers. Theor. Comput. Sci. 100(1), 105–135 (1992)
15. Kawamura, A., Kobayashi, Y.: Fence patrolling by mobile agents with distinct speeds. Distrib. Comput. 28(2), 147–154 (2015)
16. Lin, S.-S., Lin, K.-J.: A pinwheel scheduler for three distinct numbers with a tight schedulability bound. Algorithmica 19(4), 411–426, December 1997
17. Ntafos, S.: On gallery watchmen in grids. Inf. Process. Lett. 23(2), 99–102 (1986)
18. Romer, T.H., Rosier, L.E.: An algorithm reminiscent of euclidean-gcd for computing a function related to pinwheel scheduling. Algorithmica 17(1), 1–10 (1997)
19. Serafini, P., Ukovich, W.: A mathematical model for periodic scheduling problems. SIAM J. Discrete Math. 2(4), 550–581 (1989)
20. Urrutia, J.: Art gallery and illumination problems. In: Handbook of Computational Geometry, vol. 1, no. 1, pp. 973–1027 (2000)

Quantum and Matrix Algorithms

Exact Quantum Query Complexity of EXACT$_{k,l}^n$

Andris Ambainis[1], Jānis Iraids[1(✉)], and Daniel Nagaj[2]

[1] Faculty of Computing, University of Latvia, Raiņa bulvāris 19, Riga 1586, Latvia
janis.iraids@gmail.com
[2] Institute of Physics, Slovak Academy of Sciences, Dúbravská cesta 9,
845 11 Bratislava, Slovakia

Abstract. In the exact quantum query model a successful algorithm must always output the correct function value. We investigate the function that is true if exactly k or l of the n input bits given by an oracle are 1. We find an optimal algorithm (for some cases), and a nontrivial general lower and upper bound on the minimum number of queries to the black box.

1 Introduction

In this paper we study the computational complexity of Boolean functions in the quantum black box model. It is a generalization of the decision tree model, where we are computing an n-bit function $f : \{0,1\}^n \rightarrow \{0,1\}$ on an input $x \in \{0,1\}^n$ that can only be accessed through a black box by querying some bit x_i of the input. In the quantum black box model the state of the computation is described by a quantum state from the Hilbert space $\mathcal{H}_Q \otimes \mathcal{H}_W \otimes \mathcal{H}_O$ where $\mathcal{H}_Q = \{|0\rangle, |1\rangle, \ldots, |n\rangle\}$ is the query subspace, $\mathcal{H}_W$ is the working memory and $\mathcal{H}_O = \{|0\rangle, |1\rangle\}$ is the output subspace. A computation using t queries consists of a sequence of unitary transformations $U_t \cdot O_x \cdot U_{t-1} \cdot O_x \cdot \ldots \cdot O_x \cdot U_0$ followed by a measurement, where the U_i's are independent of the input and $O_x = O_{Q,x} \otimes I \otimes I$ with

$$O_{Q,x}|i\rangle = \begin{cases} (-1)^{x_i}|i\rangle = \hat{x}_i|i\rangle, \text{ if } i \in [n], \\ |0\rangle, \text{ if } i = 0, \end{cases}$$

is the query transformation, where $x_i \in \{0,1\}$ or equivalently, $\hat{x}_i \in \{-1,1\}$. The final measurement is a complete projective measurement in the computational basis and the output of the algorithm is the result of the last register, $\mathcal{H}_O$. We say that a quantum algorithm computes f exactly if for all inputs x the output of the algorithm always equals $f(x)$. Let us denote by $Q_E(f)$ the minimum number of queries over all quantum algorithms that compute f exactly.

For quite a long time the largest known separation between the classical decision tree complexity $D(f)$ and $Q_E(f)$ was only by a factor of two — the XOR of two bits can be computed exactly using only 1 quantum query [7–9]. However, in 2012 Ambainis gave the first asymptotic separation that achieved

© Springer International Publishing AG 2017
B. Steffen et al. (Eds.): SOFSEM 2017, LNCS 10139, pp. 243–255, 2017.
DOI: 10.1007/978-3-319-51963-0_19

$Q_E(f) = O(D(f)^{0.8675})$ for a class of functions f [1]. Next, in 2015 Ambainis et al. used pointer functions to show a near-quadratic separation between these two measures: $Q_E(f) = \tilde{O}(\sqrt{D(f)})$ [2]. On the other hand Midrijānis has proved that the maximum possible separation between $Q_E(f)$ and $D(f)$ is at most cubic [12].

However, the techniques for designing exact quantum algorithms are rudimentary compared to the bounded error setting. Other than the well known XOR *trick* — constructing a quantum algorithm from a classical decision tree that is allowed to "query" the XOR of any two bits — there are few alternate approaches. In addition to the asymptotic separations of [1,2], Montanaro et al. [13] gave a 2-query quantum algorithm for the symmetric 4-bit function

$$\text{EXACT}_2^4(x) = \begin{cases} 1, & \text{if } x_1 + x_2 + x_3 + x_4 = 2, \\ 0, & \text{otherwise,} \end{cases}$$

and showed that it could not be computed optimally using the XOR trick. Afterwards Ambainis et al. gave an algorithm [4] for two classes of symmetric functions:

$$\text{EXACT}_k^n(x) = \begin{cases} 1, & \text{if } |x| = k, \\ 0, & \text{otherwise} \end{cases}; \quad Q_E(\text{EXACT}_k^n) \leq \max\{k, n-k\},$$

and the threshold function

$$\text{TH}_k^n(x) = \begin{cases} 1, & \text{if } |x| \geq k, \\ 0, & \text{otherwise} \end{cases}; \quad Q_E(\text{TH}_k^n) \leq \max\{k, n-k+1\}.$$

For partial functions quantum algorithms with superpolynomial speedup are known [6,8]. Our work is somewhat connected to the results of Qiu and Zheng on partial functions based on the Deutsch-Jozsa problem [14], in particular, our algorithm from Sect. 3.1 also achieves claim (3) from [14].

1.1 Our Results

We consider exact quantum algorithms for symmetric total Boolean functions, i.e., functions for which permuting the input bits does not change its value. For symmetric functions, the largest known separation remains a factor of 2. We know from von zur Gathen's and Roche's work on polynomials [10] and quantum lower bounds using polynomials [5] that for symmetric f : $Q_E(f) \geq \frac{n}{2} - O(n^{0.548})$, thus the largest known separation is either optimal or close to being optimal.

However, many of the known exact algorithms are for symmetric functions (for example, XOR, EXACT and TH functions mentioned in the previous section). Because of that, we think that symmetric functions may be an interesting ground to explore new methods for developing more exact quantum algorithms.

In Sect. 3.1 we present an algorithm achieving up to $D(f) = 2Q_E(f)$ for a certain class of symmetric functions.

Definition 1. *Let* EXACT$^n_{k,l}$ *for* $0 \leq k \leq l \leq n$, *be an n-argument symmetric Boolean function that returns 1 if and only if the input contains exactly k ones or exactly l ones.*

$$\text{EXACT}^n_{k,l}(x) = \begin{cases} 1, & \text{if } |x| \in \{k, l\}; \\ 0, & \text{otherwise.} \end{cases}$$

Let us denote by d the separation between l and k: $d = l - k$. In general a symmetric Boolean function SYM_a on n input bits can be defined by a list $a = (a_0, \ldots, a_n) \in \{0,1\}^{n+1}$ such that $\text{SYM}_a(x) = a_{|x|}$. When $d > 0$ it may be convenient to think of EXACT$^n_{k,l}$ in this way. In this representation EXACT$^n_{k,l}$ corresponds to lists a of length $n+1$ with two 1s and the number of zeroes before the first, after the last 1, and distance between 1s correspond to parameters k, $n - l$, and d respectively.

The boundary cases, $d = 0$ and $d = n$, have been solved previously. When $d = n$, the function is usually referred to as EQUALITY$_n$. It can be solved with $n - 1$ quantum queries using the well-known XOR trick. The case $d = 0$ is also known as the EXACT^n_k function which has been analyzed in [4] where it was shown that $Q_E(\text{EXACT}^n_k) = \max\{k, n - k\}$. In this paper, we completely solve the $d \in \{2, 3\}$ cases and partially solve the $d = 1$ case and $d \geq 4$ case.

The first of our results is

Theorem 1. *If* $d = 1$, $l = n-k$ *and* $k > 0$, *then for* EXACT$^n_{k,l}$ = EXACT$^{2k+1}_{k,k+1}$

$$Q_E(\text{EXACT}^{2k+1}_{k,k+1}) = k + 1.$$

The algorithm we provide in the proof works also when $l \neq n - k$ by padding the function. Unfortunately, the algorithm is then only an upper bound on $Q_E(\text{EXACT}^n_{k,k+1})$. For example, $Q_E(\text{EXACT}^3_{2,3}) = 2$ because EXACT$^3_{2,3}$ is the MAJORITY function on 3 bits. Instead, our algorithm uses 3 queries for the padded version of the function (if we pad the input with two zeroes, we end up computing EXACT$^5_{2,3}$). Furthermore, the computations by Montanaro et al. [13] suggest that $Q_E(\text{EXACT}^3_{3,4}) = 3$ and $Q_E(\text{EXACT}^6_{4,5}) = 4$. There, unlike the EXACT$^3_{2,3}$ case, we don't know what the optimal algorithm looks like.

Next, we have a complete understanding of the $d \in \{2, 3\}$ case,

Theorem 2. *If* $d \in \{2, 3\}$, *then*

$$Q_E(\text{EXACT}^n_{k,l}) = \max\{n - k, l\} - 1.$$

In particular, when $d = 2$ and $l = n-k$, we have $l = k+2$ and $n = 2k+2$, meaning $l = \frac{n}{2} + 1$, giving us $Q_E(\text{EXACT}^n_{k,l}) = \frac{n}{2}$ whereas the deterministic query complexity is $D(\text{EXACT}^n_{k,l}) = n$, hence we exhibit a factor of 2 gap between $Q_E(f)$ and $D(f)$ which is the largest known gap for a symmetric Boolean function.

For larger values of d, we provide an exact quantum algorithm and a lower bound that is 2 queries less than the complexity of the algorithm:

Theorem 3. *If $d \geq 4$, then*

$$\max\{n - k, l\} - 1 \leq Q_E(\text{EXACT}_{k,l}^n) \leq \max\{n - k, l\} + 1,$$

We conjecture that our lower bound is tight, i.e., that

Conjecture 1. If $d \geq 2$, then

$$Q_E(\text{EXACT}_{k,l}^n) = \max\{n - k, l\} - 1.$$

The lower bound of Theorem 3 combined with Theorem 1 implies that

$$Q_E(\text{EXACT}_{k,l}^n) \geq \frac{n}{2}.$$

Interestingly, the algorithm of Theorem 3 can be used to compute a wide variety of symmetric functions with asymptotically optimal number of queries. Namely, in the extended version of the paper [3] we show

Theorem 4. *Let $a \in \{0,1\}^{n+1}$ be a binary string with no 1-s far from its center, i.e. there exists some $g(n) \in o(n)$ such that $|i - \frac{n}{2}| > g(n) \implies a_i = 0$. Then,*

$$Q_E(\text{SYM}_a) = \frac{n}{2} + o(n).$$

Since $D(\text{SYM}_a) = n$ for any such non-constant function SYM_a, we obtain a factor-$(2 - o(1))$ advantage for exact quantum algorithms for any such SYM_a.

The outline for the rest of the paper is as follows. We describe the lower bound parts of Theorems 1, 2 and 3 in Sect. 2 and the algorithms for these theorems in Sect. 3.

2   The Lower Bounds

2.1   Proofs of the Lower Bound Theorems

Theorem 5. *If $d \geq 1$, then*

$$Q_E(\text{EXACT}_{k,l}^n) \geq \max\{n - k, l\} - 1.$$

This theorem provides the lower bound part for Theorems 2 and 3.

Proof (of Theorem 5). Consider the function $\text{EXACT}_{k,l}^n$ with $l \leq n-k$ ($l \geq n-k$ is symmetric and gives the $l - 1$ result in the theorem). If the first k input bits are ones, a quantum algorithm computing $\text{EXACT}_{k,l}^n$ must be computing $\text{EXACT}_{0,l-k}^{n-k}$ on the remaining $n - k$ input bits. Next we proceed similarly as in the lower bound via polynomials for OR_n function [5]. There must exist a state $|\psi(x)\rangle \in \mathcal{H}_Q \otimes \mathcal{H}_W \otimes |1\rangle$ which for $x = (0, \ldots, 0)$ is non-zero at the end of the computation. If the algorithm performs t queries, then the amplitude of the state $|\psi(x)\rangle$ can be expressed as a degree $\leq t$ multilinear polynomial in $\hat{x}$:

$$p(\hat{x}_1, \dots, \hat{x}_n) = \sum_{\substack{S:S\subseteq[n]\\|S|\leq t}} \alpha_S \prod_{i\in S} \hat{x}_i.$$

Let $p_{sym}(\hat{x}_1, \dots, \hat{x}_n) = \sum_{\pi\in S_n} \frac{p(\hat{x}_{\pi(1)}, \dots, \hat{x}_{\pi(n)})}{n!}$. Crucially, for the inputs $x \in \{(0,\dots,0)\} \cup \{x | \text{EXACT}_{0,l-k}^{n-k}(x) = 0\}$: $p_{sym}(\hat{x}_1, \dots, \hat{x}_n) = p(\hat{x}_1, \dots, \hat{x}_n)$. Following [5, Lemma 3.2] we can obtain a polynomial $q(s)$ with $\deg q \leq \deg p_{sym}$ that for all $\hat{x} \in \{-1,1\}^n$: $q\left(\frac{n-(\hat{x}_1+\dots+\hat{x}_n)}{2}\right) = p_{sym}(\hat{x}_1, \dots, \hat{x}_n)$. The polynomial q is therefore non-zero on $s = 0$ and zero on $s \in \{0,1,\dots,n-k\}\setminus\{0,l-k\}$. Thus $\deg q \geq n - k - 1$. On the other hand the degree of q is at most the number of queries t. Thus $n - k - 1 \leq \deg q \leq t$.   □

This lower bound is not tight when $d = 1$ and $l = n - k$. In this case we use a more sophisticated approach and give a different proof.

Theorem 6. *If $d = 1$, $n > 1$ and $l = n-k$, then for $EXACT_{k,l}^n = EXACT_{k,k+1}^{2k+1}$*

$$Q_E(\text{EXACT}_{k,k+1}^{2k+1}) \geq k + 1.$$

Theorem 6 yields a lower bound that is better by one query than Theorem 5, which yields a lower bound of k.

To show Theorem 6, we use an unpublished result by Blekherman.

Theorem 7 (Blekherman). *Let $q(\hat{x})$ be the symmetrization of a polynomial $p^2(\hat{x}_1, \dots, \hat{x}_n)$ where $p(\hat{x})$ is a polynomial of degree $t \leq \frac{n}{2}$. Then, over the Boolean hypercube $\hat{x} \in \{-1,1\}^n$,*

$$q(\hat{x}) = \sum_{j=0}^{t} p_{t-j}(|x|) \left(\prod_{0\leq i<j} (|x| - i)(n - |x| - i) \right)$$

where p_{t-j} is a univariate polynomial that is a sum of squares of polynomials of degree at most $t - j$ and $|x|$ denotes the number of variables $i : \hat{x}_i = -1$.

See [11] for a proof of Blekherman's theorem. Furthermore, we provide a considerably shorter proof in the extended version of this paper [3].

Proof (of Theorem 6). Let NOT-EXACT$_{k,k+1}^{2k+1}$ denote the negation of the function. Assume, towards a contradiction, that there exists a quantum algorithm computing the function with k queries. Then there exists a sum of squares representation of NOT-EXACT$_{k,k+1}^{2k+1}$: NOT-EXACT$_{k,k+1}^{2k+1}(x) = \sum_i r_i^2(\hat{x})$, such that $\deg r_i \leq k$. Since the function is symmetric, the symmetrization is also a valid representation. Since $Sym(\sum_i r_i^2(\hat{x})) = \sum_i Sym(r_i^2(\hat{x}))$, it follows from Blekherman's theorem that there is a univariate polynomial of the form

$$q(|x|) = \sum_{j=0}^{k} p_{k-j}(|x|) \left(\prod_{i=0}^{j-1} (|x| - i)(n - |x| - i) \right), \tag{1}$$

where $q(|x|) = \text{NOT-EXACT}_{k,k+1}^{2k+1}(x)$ on the Boolean hypercube and p_{k-j} are sum of squares polynomials with $\deg p_{k-j} \leq 2k - 2j$. The polynomial $q(|x|)$ is non-negative in the interval $|x| \in [k - 1, k + 2]$. Since the polynomial is 0 at $|x| = k$ and $|x| = k + 1$, it must have at least 3 local extrema in the interval $|x| \in [k, k + 1]$. Additionally, it is 1 when $|x| \in \{0, 1, \dots, 2k + 1\} \backslash \{k, k + 1\}$, hence it has $2k - 2$ more extrema — at least one in each of the intervals $(0, 1)$, $(1, 2), \dots, (k - 2, k - 1)$ and $(k + 2, k + 3)$, $(k + 3, k + 4), \dots, (2k, 2k + 1)$. In total the polynomial has at least $2k + 1$ local extrema, therefore its degree is at least $2k + 2$. On the other hand by our assumption $\deg q \leq 2k$ which is a contradiction.   . $\square$

3   The Algorithms

In Sect. 3.1 we now provide the algorithm for $d \leq 3$ (the algorithm part of Theorems 1 and 2) which we know to be optimal for $d = 1$ with $l = n - k$, and for $d = 2, 3$ and any k, l. Next, in Sect. 3.4 we present the sub-optimal algorithm that works for all d, resulting in a general upper bound on $Q_E(\text{EXACT}_{k,l}^n)$ (the algorithm part of Theorem 3). Throughout Sect. 3 we will refer to $\hat{x}_1 + \dots + \hat{x}_n$ as the unbalance of the input or simply unbalance, in other words, the unbalance increases as the difference between ones and zeroes in the input increases. When $l = n - k$, the condition $\text{EXACT}_{k,n-k}^n(x) = 1$ is equivalent to the requirement that the unbalance is $\pm d$, i.e., $|\hat{x}_1 + \dots + \hat{x}_n| = n - 2k = d$. Hence we will refer to $\text{EXACT}_{k,n-k}^n$ as testing for unbalance $d = n - 2k$.

3.1   The Algorithm for Unbalance $d \leq 3$

For the upper bound, we now provide a quantum algorithm for the $l = n - k$ case which can be extended to the $l \neq n - k$ case. Let us introduce the function $\text{UNBALANCE}_d^n = \text{EXACT}_{\frac{n-d}{2}, \frac{n+d}{2}}^n$. When $l = n - k$ then $d = n - 2k$ and so n and d have the same parity.

Theorem 8

$$Q_E(\text{UNBALANCE}_d^n) \leq \begin{cases} \frac{n+d}{2} \: if \: d = 1, \\ \frac{n+d}{2} - 1 \: if \: d \in \{2, 3\}. \end{cases}$$

We can compute $\text{EXACT}_{k,l}^n$ for $l \neq n-k$ by reducing it to $\text{UNBALANCE}_{d'}^{n'}$:

Lemma 1

$$Q_E(\text{EXACT}_{k,l}^n) \leq Q_E\left(\text{UNBALANCE}_{l-k}^{n+\max\{n-l-k, l+k-n\}}\right)$$

Proof. For the $l < n - k$ case ($l > n - k$, respectively) simply pad the input bits with $n - l - k$ ones ($l + k - n$ zeroes, resp.) and run $\text{UNBALANCE}_d^{n+|n-l-k|}$ on the padded input. The complexity of the algorithm on the padded problem will be $Q_E(\text{EXACT}_{k,l}^n) \leq Q_E\left(\text{UNBALANCE}_d^{n+|n-l-k|}\right)$. $\square$

From Lemma 1 and Theorem 8, the upper bounds of Theorems 1 and 2 follow:

$$Q_E(\text{EXACT}_{k,l}^n) \leq \begin{cases} \max\{n-k,l\}, \text{ if } d=1, \\ \max\{n-k,l\}-1, \text{ if } d \in \{2,3\}. \end{cases}$$

3.2   The Structure of the Algorithm

The algorithm of Theorem 8 will use two kinds of subroutines to calculate the function:

- The main routine UNB$_d^n$ will start in a quantum state independent of the input and compute a UNBALANCE$_d^n$ instance;
- The subroutine UNB-R$_d^n$ will require a precomputed state in the form

$$\sum_{i \in [n]} \hat{x}_i \, |\mathcal{S}\rangle + \sqrt{\gamma} \sum_{\substack{i,j \in [n] \\ i<j}} (\hat{x}_i - \hat{x}_j) \, |i,j\rangle. \tag{2}$$

$\mathcal{S}$ in the basis state $|\mathcal{S}\rangle$ refers to the amplitude being a sum of $\hat{x}_i$'s.

Let us denote by $\gamma(\text{UNB-R}_d^n)$ the constant coefficient γ of the algorithm UNB-R$_d^n$. Let us denote by $T(\mathsf{S})$ the number of queries performed by algorithm S.

Lemma 2 (Recursive step for UNB-R$_d^n$). *If $d < n$, $n \geq 3$, and there exists a quantum algorithm UNB-R$_d^{n-2}$ computing the function UNBALANCE$_d^{n-2}$ starting in an unnormalized quantum state of the form (2) on $n-2$ inputs with $\gamma(\text{UNB-R}_d^{n-2}) < 1$ then there exists an algorithm UNB-R$_d^n$ using UNB-R$_d^{n-2}$ as a subroutine, and computing UNBALANCE$_d^n$, starting in the state (2) where*

$$\gamma(\text{UNB-R}_d^n) = \frac{1}{(n^2-d^2)^2} \left(n^2(n-2)^2 \frac{\gamma(\text{UNB-R}_d^{n-2})}{1-\gamma(\text{UNB-R}_d^{n-2})} + d^4 \right) \tag{3}$$

and using one more query, i.e., $T(\text{UNB-R}_d^n) = T(\text{UNB-R}_d^{n-2}) + 1$.

For a sketch of the proof of Lemma 2 see Sect. 3.3 and the full proof is in the extended version [3, Sect. 3.2].

The main routine UNB$_d^n$ will also be recursive and make use of UNB-R$_d^n$.

Lemma 3 (Recursive step for UNB-R$_d^n$). *If there exists UNB$_d^{n-2}$ and UNB-R$_d^n$ with $\gamma(\text{UNB-R}_d^n) \leq 1$, then there exists UNB$_d^n$ such that*

$$T(\text{UNB}_d^n) = 1 + \max\{T(\text{UNB}_d^{n-2}), T(\text{UNB-R}_d^n)\}.$$

See extended version for the proof of Lemma 3 [3, Sect. 3.3].

Now we are ready to prove Theorem 8:

Proof (of Theorem 8). We can draw the subroutine dependency graph like so:

$$\text{UNB}_d^d \;\leftarrow\; \text{UNB}_d^{d+2} \;\leftarrow\; \text{UNB}_d^{d+4} \;\leftarrow\; \cdots \leftarrow\; \text{UNB}_d^{d+2k}$$
$$\downarrow \qquad\qquad \downarrow \qquad\qquad \downarrow \qquad\qquad\qquad \downarrow$$
$$\text{UNB-R}_d^d \leftarrow \text{UNB-R}_d^{d+2} \leftarrow \text{UNB-R}_d^{d+4} \leftarrow \cdots \leftarrow \text{UNB-R}_d^{d+2k}$$

Each subroutine performs one query and calls one of the subroutines in the dependency graph based on the result of the measurement. Using Lemma 2 starting with an algorithm $\text{UNB-R}_d^{d+2k_0}$ we can build chains of algorithms $\text{UNB-R}_d^{d+2k_0}$, $\text{UNB-R}_d^{d+2(k_0+1)}, \ldots, \text{UNB-R}_d^{d+2k}$ as long as $\gamma(\text{UNB-R}_d^{d+2k_i}) < 1$. Notice that we may use multiple chains to cover all $k > 0$. Fortunately, as we will show for $d \in \{1,2,3\}$, a single infinite chain will suffice.

Then, using Lemma 3 we can build algorithms UNB_d^{d+2k} for all $k > 0$ if we additionally have an initial base algorithm for UNB_d^d. The query complexity of UNB_d^{d+2k} built in this way on a chain of UNB-R_d^{d+2k} starting at $k_0 \in \{0,1\}$ will have

$$T(\text{UNB}_d^{d+2k}) = \max\{k + T(\text{UNB}_d^d), T(\text{UNB-R}_d^{d+2k_0}) + k - k_0 + 1\}.$$

Since UNB_d^d is computing EQUALITY_d, it uses $d-1$ queries, so we can disregard $k + T(\text{UNB}_d^d)$, since $k = \frac{n-d}{2}$ and therefore $k + T(\text{UNB}_d^d) \leq \frac{n+d}{2} - 1$. To finish the proof we now need to show that there exists a chain of UNB-R_d^{d+2k} starting at k_0 with $\gamma(\text{UNB-R}_d^n) < 1$ and

$$T(\text{UNB-R}_d^{d+2k_0}) + k - k_0 + 1 \leq \begin{cases} n - k, & \text{if } d = 1, \\ n - k - 1, & \text{if } d \in \{2,3\}. \end{cases}$$

When $d = 1$, we will have $k_0 = 0$ and show that $T(\text{UNB-R}_d^d) \leq n - 2k + k_0 - 1 = d + k_0 - 1 = 0$. Since the function UNBALANCE_1^1 does not depend on input variables, there exists UNB-R_1^1 with $\gamma(\text{UNB-R}_1^1) = 0$ using 0 queries.

When $d = 2$ we will again have $k_0 = 0$ and $T(\text{UNB-R}_d^d) \leq d + k_0 - 2 = 0$. The subroutine UNB-R_2^2 is essentially required to compute $XOR(x_1, x_2)$ starting in a non-normalized state $(\hat{x}_1 + \hat{x}_2)|\mathcal{S}\rangle + \sqrt{\gamma} \cdot (\hat{x}_1 - \hat{x}_2)|1,2\rangle$. If $\gamma = 0$ we can only measure $|\mathcal{S}\rangle$ if $XOR = 0$ and no queries are necessary.

When $d = 3$ a single infinite chain starting at $k_0 = 0$ does not exist. It does exist starting at $k_0 = 1$ and $T(\text{UNB-R}_d^{d+2}) \leq d + k_0 - 2 = 2$. We give an algorithm for UNB-R_3^5 in the extended version of the paper [3, Abstract A]:

Lemma 4. *There exists a 2-query subroutine UNB-R_3^5 with $\gamma(\text{UNB-R}_3^5) = \frac{1}{112}$.*

To show that the chains of algorithms UNB-R_d^{d+2k} obtained by repeated applications of Lemma 2 never have $\gamma(\text{UNB-R}_d^{d+2k}) \geq 1$, we use the recursive identity (3). It would be sufficient to show that $\exists n_{init} \forall n \geq n_{init} : \gamma(\text{UNB-R}_d^n) \leq \frac{1}{n}$. For small n the condition $\gamma(\text{UNB-R}_d^n) \leq \frac{1}{n}$ can be verified through explicit computation. To establish the condition for all sufficiently large n it would be sufficient

to show that $\exists n_{init} : \gamma(\text{UNB-R}_d^{n_{init}}) \leq \frac{1}{n_{init}} \wedge \forall n > n_{init} : \gamma(\text{UNB-R}_d^{n-2}) \leq \frac{1}{n-2} \rightarrow$
$\gamma(\text{UNB-R}_d^n) \leq \frac{1}{n}$. The implication holds whenever

$$\frac{\frac{n^2(n-2)^2}{n-3} + d^4}{(n^2 - d^2)^2} \leq \frac{1}{n},$$

or equivalently, $n^4 + (-2d^2 - 4)n^3 + (6d^2 - d^4)n^2 + 4d^4n - 3d^4 \geq 0$. When $d = 1$ the inequality holds for $n \geq 5$. We can then numerically verify that $\gamma(\text{UNB-R}_1^5) \approx 0.008 \leq \frac{1}{5}$. When $d = 2$ the inequality holds onwards from $n \geq 12$. For our base case $\gamma(\text{UNB-R}_2^{12}) \approx 0.039 \leq \frac{1}{12}$. When $d = 3$ the inequality holds onwards from $n \geq 23$. For our chain $\gamma(\text{UNB-R}_3^{23}) \approx 0.030 \leq \frac{1}{23}$. $\qquad\square$

3.3 Proof Sketch of Lemma 2

Proof. Our algorithm will utilize the following two unitaries and their inverses:

- R_α works on basis vectors $|0\rangle$, $|\mathcal{L}\rangle$, and $|\mathcal{R}\rangle$. It is a unitary completion of the following transformation:

$$R_\alpha |0\rangle = \sqrt{\alpha} |\mathcal{L}\rangle + \sqrt{1 - \alpha} |\mathcal{R}\rangle, \quad \forall \alpha : 0 \leq \alpha \leq 1.$$

- U_n works on basis vectors $\{|1\rangle, |2\rangle, \ldots, |n\rangle, |\mathcal{S}\rangle, |1,2\rangle, |1,3\rangle, \ldots, |n-1,n\rangle\}$. It is a unitary completion of the following transformation:

$$U_n |i\rangle = \frac{1}{\sqrt{n}} \left(|\mathcal{S}\rangle - \sum_{j=1}^{i-1} |j,i\rangle + \sum_{j=i+1}^{n} |i,j\rangle \right). \tag{4}$$

Note that on a superposition of input vectors U_n acts as:

$$U_n \sum_{i \in [n]} \alpha_i |i\rangle = \frac{1}{\sqrt{n}} \left(\sum_{i \in [n]} \alpha_i |\mathcal{S}\rangle + \sum_{\substack{i,j \in [n] \\ i<j}} (\alpha_i - \alpha_j) |i,j\rangle \right).$$

Let $\gamma = \gamma(\text{UNB-R}_d^n)$ and $\gamma' = \gamma(\text{UNB-R}_d^{n-2})$. The algorithm starts in the state:

$$\sum_{i \in [n]} \hat{x}_i |\mathcal{S}\rangle + \sqrt{\gamma} \sum_{\substack{i,j \in [n] \\ i<j}} (\hat{x}_i - \hat{x}_j) |i,j\rangle.$$

Through certain applications of U_n and R_α, their inverses and one query, it is possible to transform it into state

$$c_1 \left(\sum_{i,j \in [n]} \hat{x}_i \hat{x}_j - d^2 \right) |\mathcal{S}\rangle$$

$$+ c_2 \sum_{\substack{i,j \in [n] \\ i<j}} (\hat{x}_i - \hat{x}_j) |i,j\rangle \left(\sum_{\substack{l \in [n] \\ l \notin \{i,j\}}} \hat{x}_l |\mathcal{S}\rangle + \sqrt{\gamma'} \sum_{\substack{u,v \in [n] \\ u,v \notin \{i,j\} \\ u<v}} (\hat{x}_u - \hat{x}_v) |u,v\rangle \right) \tag{5}$$

for some non-negative constants c_1, c_2, provided that γ, n, d and γ' satisfy the relationship (3) in the statement of the lemma. See the extended version for how to achieve this [3].

Finally, we measure whether the state of (5) is in subspace $\{|\mathcal{S}\rangle\}$. Whenever $\mathrm{UNBALANCE}_d^n(x) = 1$ or equivalently $\hat{x}_1 + \ldots + \hat{x}_n = \pm d$, the amplitude of $|\mathcal{S}\rangle$ is zero. If on the other hand the state is not in subspace $|\mathcal{S}\rangle$, we end up measuring $|i, j\rangle$ in the first register. Without loss of generality we may assume that the result is $\{n-1, n\}$. Thus we have learned that $\{\hat{x}_{n-1}, \hat{x}_n\} = \{-1, 1\}$ is a balanced pair that can be removed from consideration. Furthermore, we ended up in a useful (unnormalized) state

$$\sum_{i \in [n-2]} \hat{x}_i \, |\mathcal{S}\rangle + \sqrt{\gamma'} \sum_{\substack{i,j \in [n-2] \\ i < j}} (\hat{x}_i - \hat{x}_j) \, |i, j\rangle.$$

Therefore, we can call $\mathrm{UNB\text{-}R}_d^{n-2}$ recursively, since

$$\mathrm{UNBALANCE}_d^n(x_1, \ldots, x_n) = \mathrm{UNBALANCE}_d^{n-2}(x_1, \ldots, x_{n-2}). \qquad \square$$

3.4   The General Upper Bound

We now present a general upper bound to $Q(\mathrm{EXACT}_{k,l}^n)$. The algorithm we present is worse (by at most 2 queries) than the one in Sect. 3.1 when $l - k = d \leq 3$. However, it works for any k, l and thus also for any d.

First, for the special case $l = n - k$, we claim

Theorem 9

$$Q_E(\mathrm{EXACT}_{k,n-k}^n) \leq n - k + 1.$$

Second, for the general case $l \neq n-k$, we obtain the upper bound of Theorem 3 using the reduction of Lemma 1:

$$Q_E(\mathrm{EXACT}_{k,l}^n) \leq \max\{n - k, l\} + 1.$$

Proof (of Theorem 9: an algorithm for unbalance $\pm d$)
Our goal is to find an algorithm deciding whether the number of 1's in the function values is k or $n - k$. Equivalently, this problem can be also called $\mathrm{UNBALANCE}_d^n$ with $d = l - k = n - 2k$: does the input x have "unbalance" $\sum_i \hat{x}_i = \pm d$ or not?

We start our algorithm with two registers prepared in the unnormalized state

$$\left(\frac{d}{n} |0\rangle + |1\rangle \right) |\mathcal{S}\rangle,$$

with d the unbalance we test for. Conditioned on the first register being $|1\rangle$, we transform the second register to a uniform superposition of states $\frac{1}{\sqrt{n}} \sum_{i=1}^n |i\rangle$. We then query the oracle. This gives us

$$\frac{d}{n} |0\rangle \, |\mathcal{S}\rangle + \frac{1}{\sqrt{n}} |1\rangle \sum_i \hat{x}_i \, |i\rangle.$$

Controlled by the first register, we apply the operation U_n from (4) to the second register (this is where another factor of $\frac{1}{\sqrt{n}}$ comes from), producing

$$\frac{d}{n}|0\rangle|\mathcal{S}\rangle + \frac{1}{n}|1\rangle\sum_i\hat{x}_i|\mathcal{S}\rangle + \frac{1}{n}|1\rangle\sum_{i,j\in[n],i<j}(\hat{x}_i-\hat{x}_j)|i,j\rangle.$$

As we are looking at unnormalized states, we can now omit the common prefactor $\frac{1}{n}$. Finally, we apply a Hadamard to the first (ancilla) register and get the unnormalized state

$$\left(\left(d+\sum_i\hat{x}_i\right)|0\rangle + \left(d-\sum_i\hat{x}_i\right)|1\rangle\right)|\mathcal{S}\rangle + (|0\rangle - |1\rangle)\sum_{i,j\in[n],i<j}(\hat{x}_i-\hat{x}_j)|i,j\rangle.$$

Finally, we measure the second register. Whenever we get a pair $|i,j\rangle$, we know that it is an unbalanced one, with $\hat{x}_i = -\hat{x}_j$. We can get rid of it, and continue solving a smaller problem with $n' = n - 2$. On the other hand, if we get $|\mathcal{S}\rangle$ in the second register, we need to look at the ancilla (first) register as well. If the ancilla is $|0\rangle$, we learn that the overall unbalance is not $-d$. On the other hand, if the ancilla is $|1\rangle$, we learn that the overall unbalance is not d. Thus, by using a single query, our problem changes from UNBALANCE^n_d to EXACT^n_k or EXACT$^n_{n-k}$. Switching to the optimal algorithm for EXACT^n_k, this reduced problem can be solved in $\leq n - k$, i.e. $\leq \frac{n+d}{2}$ queries.

Therefore, by iterating the above steps, we reduce the problem size by 2 several times, and then at some point reduce the problem to EXACT$^{n'}_{k'}$ or EXACT$^{n'}_{n'-k'}$. The worst option in terms of the number of queries is when we never reduce the problem size, and use the very first query just to rule out one of the options d or $-d$ for the unbalance. We then end up having to solve EXACT^n_k or EXACT$^n_{n-k}$, that each can use another $n - k$ queries. Altogether, we require $Q_E(\text{EXACT}^n_{k,n-k}) \leq n - k + 1$ queries.   □

4 Conclusion

We have shown that the exact quantum query complexity for EXACT$^n_{k,l}$ is

$$Q_E(\text{EXACT}^n_{k,l}) = \begin{cases} \max\{n-k,l\}, & \text{if } d = 1 \text{ and } l = n-k, \\ \max\{n-k,l\} - 1, & \text{if } d \in \{2,3\}. \end{cases}$$

where $d = l - k$. When $d = 2$ and $l = n - k$, this provides another example of a symmetric function with $D(f) = 2Q_E(f)$ which is the largest known gap between $D(f)$ and $Q_E(f)$ for symmetric functions f. To show that $Q_E(\text{EXACT}^{2k+1}_{k,k+1}) > k$ we use an approach based on representation theory. We do not know if this lower bound method is sufficient to prove $Q_E(f) \geq \frac{n}{2}$ for all symmetric f. In particular, it seems difficult to apply it for the symmetric function SYM$_a$ that has, for example, $a = 0^51^50^51^50^5$.

We also give a general algorithm and a lower bound, for all l, k, showing that:

$$\max\{n - k, l\} - 1 \leq Q_E(\text{EXACT}_{k,l}^n) \leq \max\{n - k, l\} + 1.$$

Previously known quantum algorithms for symmetric functions (e.g., the well known algorithm for PARITY and the algorithms for EXACT_k^n [4]) typically measure the quantum state after each query. In contrast, our algorithm for $d \in \{1, 2, 3\}$ does not have this structure. Moreover, our numerical simulations suggest that there is no algorithm for $\text{EXACT}_{k,l}^n$ that uses an optimal number of queries and measures the state completely after each query. We think that it is an interesting problem to study the power of quantum algorithms with the restriction that after each query the state must be measured completely and the limits of what can be achieved with such algorithms.

Acknowledgements. This research was supported by the ERC Advanced Grant MQC, Latvian State Research Programme NexIT Project No. 1, EU FP7 project QALGO, the People Programme (Marie Curie Actions) EU's 7th Framework Programme under REA grant agreement No. 609427, Slovak Academy of Sciences, and the Slovak Research and Development Agency grant APVV-14-0878 QETWORK.

References

1. Ambainis, A.: Superlinear advantage for exact quantum algorithms. In: Proceedings of the 45th Annual ACM Symposium on Theory of Computing, pp. 891–900. ACM (2013). http://dl.acm.org/citation.cfm?id=2488721
2. Ambainis, A., Balodis, K., Belovs, A., Lee, T., Santha, M., Smotrovs, J.: Separations in query complexity based on pointer functions. In: Proceedings of the 48th Annual ACM Symposium on Theory of Computing, pp. 800–813. ACM (2016)
3. Ambainis, A., Iraids, J., Nagaj, D.: Exact quantum query complexity of $\text{EXACT}_{k,l}^n$. arXiv preprint abs/1608.02374 (2016). http://arxiv.org/abs/1608.02374
4. Ambainis, A., Iraids, J., Smotrovs, J.: Exact quantum query complexity of EXACT and THRESHOLD. In: TQC, pp. 263–269 (2013)
5. Beals, R., Buhrman, H., Cleve, R., Mosca, M., de Wolf, R.: Quantum lower bounds by polynomials. J. ACM **48**(4), 778–797 (2001)
6. Brassard, G., Høyer, P.: An exact quantum polynomial-time algorithm for Simon's problem. In: 1997 Proceedings of the Fifth Israeli Symposium on Theory of Computing and Systems, pp. 12–23, June 1997
7. Cleve, R., Ekert, A., Macchiavello, C., Mosca, M.: Quantum algorithms revisited. Proc. R. Soc. Lond. Ser. A Math. Phys. Eng. Sci. **454**(1969), 339–354 (1998)
8. Deutsch, D., Jozsa, R.: Rapid solution of problems by quantum computation. Proc. R. Soc. Lond. A Math. Phys. Eng. Sci. **439**(1907), 553–558 (1992)
9. Farhi, E., Goldstone, J., Gutmann, S., Sipser, M.: Limit on the speed of quantum computation in determining parity. Phys. Rev. Lett. **81**, 5442–5444 (1998). doi:10.1103/PhysRevLett.81.5442
10. von Zur Gathen, J., Roche, J.R.: Polynomials with two values. Combinatorica **17**(3), 345–362 (1997). doi:10.1007/BF01215917

11. Lee, T., Prakash, A., de Wolf, R., Yuen, H.: On the sum-of-squares degree of symmetric quadratic functions. In: Raz, R. (ed.) 31st Conference on Computational Complexity (CCC 2016), Leibniz International Proceedings in Informatics (LIPIcs), vol. 50, pp. 17:1–17:31. Schloss Dagstuhl-Leibniz-Zentrum fuer Informatik, Dagstuhl, Germany (2016). http://drops.dagstuhl.de/opus/volltexte/2016/5838

12. Midrijānis, G.: Exact quantum query complexity for total boolean functions. arXiv preprint quant-ph/0403168 (2004). http://arxiv.org/abs/quant-ph/0403168

13. Montanaro, A., Jozsa, R., Mitchison, G.: On exact quantum query complexity. Algorithmica **71**(4), 775–796 (2015). doi:10.1007/s00453-013-9826-8

14. Qiu, D., Zheng, S.: Characterizations of symmetrically partial boolean functions with exact quantum query complexity. arXiv preprint abs/1603.06505 (2016). http://arxiv.org/abs/1603.06505

Adjacent Vertices Can Be Hard to Find by Quantum Walks

Nikolajs Nahimovs and Raqueline A.M. Santos$^{(\boxtimes)}$

Faculty of Computing, University of Latvia, Raina bulv. 19, Riga 1586, Latvia
{nikolajs.nahimovs,rsantos}@lu.lv

Abstract. Quantum walks have been useful for designing quantum algorithms that outperform their classical versions for a variety of search problems. Most of the papers, however, consider a search space containing a single marked element only. We show that if the search space contains more than one marked element, their placement may drastically affect the performance of the search. More specifically, we study search by quantum walks on general graphs and show a wide class of configurations of marked vertices, for which search by quantum walk needs $\Omega(N)$ steps, that is, it has no speed-up over the classical exhaustive search. The demonstrated configurations occur for certain placements of two or more adjacent marked vertices. The analysis is done for the two-dimensional grid and hypercube, and then is generalized for any graph.

Keywords: Quantum walks · Stationary states · Multiple marked vertices · Quantum search · Exceptional configurations · General graphs · Hypercube · Two-dimensional grid

1 Introduction

Quantum walks are quantum counterparts of classical random walks [1]. Similarly to classical random walks, there are two types of quantum walks: discrete-time quantum walks, first introduced by Aharonov *et al.* [2], and continuous-time quantum walks, introduced by Farhi *et al.* [3]. For the discrete-time version, the step of the quantum walk is usually given by coin and shift operators, which are applied repeatedly. The coin operator acts on the internal state of the walker and rearranges the amplitudes of going to adjacent vertices. The shift operator moves the walker between the adjacent vertices.

Quantum walks have been useful for designing algorithms for a variety of search problems [4–6]. To solve a search problem using quantum walks, we introduce the notion of marked elements (vertices), corresponding to elements of the search space that we want to find. We perform a quantum walk on the search

This work was supported by the European Union Seventh Framework Programme (FP7/2007-2013) under the QALGO (Grant Agreement No. 600700) project and the RAQUEL (Grant Agreement No. 323970) project, the Latvian State Research Programme NeXIT project No. 1 and the ERC Advanced Grant MQC.

© Springer International Publishing AG 2017
B. Steffen et al. (Eds.): SOFSEM 2017, LNCS 10139, pp. 256–267, 2017.
DOI: 10.1007/978-3-319-51963-0_20

space with one transition rule at the unmarked vertices, and another transition rule at the marked vertices. If this process is set up properly, it leads to a quantum state in which marked vertices have higher probability than the unmarked ones. This method of search using quantum walks was first introduced in [7], which describes a quantum search in the hypercube, and has been used many times since then.

Not many papers in the literature consider search by quantum walks with multiple marked vertices. Wong [8] analyzed the spatial search problem solved by continuous-time quantum walk on the simplex of complete graphs and showed that the location of marked vertices can dramatically influence the required jumping rate of the quantum walk. Wong and Ambainis [9] analysed the discrete-time quantum walk on the simplex of complete graphs and showed that if one of the complete graphs is fully marked then there is no speed-up over classical exhaustive search. Nahimovs and Rivosh [10] studied the dependence of the running time of the AKR algorithm [4] on the number and the placement of marked locations. They found some "exceptional configurations" of marked vertices, for which the probability of finding any of the marked vertices does not grow over time. Another previously known exceptional configuration for the two-dimensional grid is the "diagonal construction" by Ambainis and Rivosh [11].

In this paper, we extend the work of Nahimovs and Rivosh [12]. We study search by quantum walks on general graphs with multiple marked vertices and show a wide class of configurations of marked vertices, for which the probability of finding any of the marked vertices does not grow over time. These configurations occur for certain placements of two and more adjacent marked vertices. We prove that for such configurations the state of the algorithm is close to a stationary state.

We start by reviewing the simple example of the two-dimensional grid from [12] by showing that any pair of adjacent marked vertices forms an exceptional configuration. The same construction is valid for the hypercube. We extend the proof to general graphs by showing that any pair of adjacent marked vertices having the same degree d forms an exceptional configuration, for which the probability of finding a marked vertex is limited by const $\cdot\, d^2/N$. Then, we prove that any k-clique of marked vertices forms an exceptional configuration. Additionally, we formulate general conditions for a state to be stationary given a configuration of marked vertices. Our results greatly extend the class of known exceptional configurations.

2 Two-Dimensional Grid

2.1 Quantum Walk on the Two-Dimensional Grid

Consider a two-dimensional grid of size $\sqrt{N} \times \sqrt{N}$ with periodic (torus-like) boundary conditions. Let us denote $n = \sqrt{N}$. The locations of the grid define a set of state vectors, $|x, y\rangle$, which span the Hilbert space, $\mathcal{H}_\mathcal{P}$, associated to the position. Additionally, we define a 4-dimensional Hilbert space with the set of states $\{|c\rangle : c \in \{\leftarrow, \rightarrow, \uparrow, \downarrow\}\}$, $\mathcal{H}_\mathcal{C}$, associated with the direction. We refer to it as the direction or the coin subspace. The quantum walk has associated Hilbert space $\mathcal{H}_P \otimes \mathcal{H}_C$ with basis states $|x, y, c\rangle$ for $x, y \in \{0, \ldots, n-1\}$ and $c \in \{\uparrow, \downarrow, \leftarrow, \rightarrow\}$.

The evolution of a state of the walk is driven by the unitary operator $U = S \cdot (I \otimes C)$, where S is the flip-flop shift operator

$$S|i, j, \uparrow\rangle = |i, j+1, \downarrow\rangle \tag{1}$$

$$S|i, j, \downarrow\rangle = |i, j-1, \uparrow\rangle \tag{2}$$

$$S|i, j, \leftarrow\rangle = |i-1, j, \rightarrow\rangle \tag{3}$$

$$S|i, j, \rightarrow\rangle = |i+1, j, \leftarrow\rangle, \tag{4}$$

and the coin operator is given by the Grover's diffusion transformation $C = 2|s\rangle\langle s| - I$, where $|s\rangle$ is the uniform superposition of the basis states in the coin subspace.

The spatial search algorithm uses the unitary operator $U' = S \cdot (I \otimes C) \cdot (Q \otimes I)$, where Q is the query transformation which flips the sign of marked vertices, that is, $Q|x, y\rangle = -|x, y\rangle$, if (x, y) is marked and $Q|x, y\rangle = |x, y\rangle$, otherwise. The initial state of the algorithm is

$$|\psi(0)\rangle = \frac{1}{\sqrt{4N}} \sum_{i,j=0}^{n-1} (|i, j, \uparrow\rangle + |i, j, \downarrow\rangle + |i, j, \leftarrow\rangle + |i, j, \rightarrow\rangle). \tag{5}$$

Note that $|\psi(0)\rangle$ is a 1-eigenvector of U but not of U'. If there are marked vertices, the state of the algorithm starts to deviate from $|\psi(0)\rangle$. In case of one marked vertex, after $O(\sqrt{N \log N})$ steps the inner product $\langle\psi(t)|\psi(0)\rangle$ becomes close to 0. If we measure the state at this moment, we will find the marked vertex with $O(1/\log N)$ probability [4]. This gives the total running time of $O(\sqrt{N} \log N)$ steps with amplitude amplification.

By analyzing the quantum search algorithm for a group of marked vertices of size $\sqrt{k} \times \sqrt{k}$, Ref. [12] identified that the algorithm does not work as expected when k is even, meaning that the overlap of the initial state with the state at time t, $\langle\psi(0)|\psi(t)\rangle$, stays close to 1. Moreover, the same effect holds for any block of size $2k \times l$ or $k \times 2l$, with l and k being positive integers. The reason for such behavior is that blocks of marked vertices form stationary states, as we are going to see below.

2.2   Stationary States for the Two-Dimensional Grid

Consider a two-dimensional grid with two marked vertices (i, j) and $(i+1, j)$. Let $|\phi_{stat}^a\rangle$ be a state having amplitudes of all basis states equal to a except for $|i, j, \rightarrow\rangle$ and $|i+1, j, \leftarrow\rangle$, which have amplitudes equal to $-3a$ (see Fig. 1), that is,

$$|\phi_{stat}^a\rangle = \sum_{x,y=0}^{n-1} \sum_c a|x, y, c\rangle - 4a|i, j, \rightarrow\rangle - 4a|i+1, j, \leftarrow\rangle. \tag{6}$$

Then, this state is not changed by a step of the algorithm.

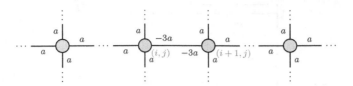

Fig. 1. The amplitudes of the state $|\phi_{stat}^a\rangle$. The vertices (i,j) and $(i+1,j)$ are marked.

Lemma 1. *Consider a grid of size $\sqrt{N} \times \sqrt{N}$ with two adjacent marked vertices (i,j) and $(i+1,j)$. Then the state $|\phi_{stat}^a\rangle$, given by Eq. (6), is not changed by the step of the algorithm, that is, $U'|\phi_{stat}^a\rangle = |\phi_{stat}^a\rangle$.*

Proof. Consider the effect of a step of the algorithm on $|\phi_{stat}^a\rangle$. The query transformation changes the signs of all the amplitudes of the marked vertices. The coin transformation performs an inversion about the average: for unmarked vertices, it does nothing, as all amplitudes are equal to a; for marked vertices, the average is 0, so applying the coin results in sign flip. Thus, $(I \otimes C)(Q \otimes I)$ does nothing for the amplitudes of the non-marked vertices and twice flips the sign of the amplitudes of the marked vertices. Therefore, we have $(I \otimes C)(Q \otimes I)|\phi_{stat}^a\rangle = |\phi_{stat}^a\rangle$. The shift transformation swaps the amplitudes of near-by vertices. For $|\phi_{stat}^a\rangle$, it swaps a with a and $-3a$ with $-3a$. Thus, we have $S(I \otimes C)(Q \otimes I)|\phi_{stat}^a\rangle = |\phi_{stat}^a\rangle$. □

The initial state of the algorithm, given by Eq. (5), can be written as

$$|\psi(0)\rangle = |\phi_{stat}^a\rangle + 4a(|i,j,\rightarrow\rangle + |i+1,j,\leftarrow\rangle), \tag{7}$$

for $a = 1/\sqrt{4N}$. Therefore, the only part of the initial state which is changed by the step of the algorithm is $\frac{2}{\sqrt{N}}(|i,j,\rightarrow\rangle + |i+1,j,\leftarrow\rangle)$.

Let us establish an upper bound on the probability of finding a marked vertex,

$$p_M = \langle\psi(t)| \left(\sum_{v \in M} |v\rangle\langle v| \otimes I \right) |\psi(t)\rangle, \tag{8}$$

where M is the set of marked vertices.

Lemma 2. *Consider a grid of size $\sqrt{N} \times \sqrt{N}$ with two adjacent marked vertices (i,j) and $(i,j+1)$. Then for any number of steps, the probability of finding a marked vertex p_M is $O\left(\frac{1}{N}\right)$.*

Proof. Follows from the proof of Theorem 2 by substituting $d = 4$ and $m = 2N$. □

Figure 2 shows the absolute value of the overlap, $|\langle\psi(0)|\psi(t)\rangle|$, and the probability of finding a marked vertex, p_M, during the first 100 steps of the walk for a grid of size 50×50 and two different sets of marked vertices. In the first case

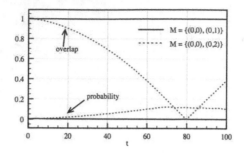

Fig. 2. Probability of finding a marked vertex, p_M, and absolute value of the overlap, $|\langle\psi(0)|\psi(t)\rangle|$, for the first 100 steps of the quantum walk on a grid of size 50×50. (Solid line) We have two adjacent marked vertices, $(0,0)$ and $(0,1)$. (Dashed line) We have two non-adjacent marked vertices, $(0,0)$ and $(0,2)$.

(solid line), we have two adjacent marked vertices, $M = \{(0,0),(0,1)\}$ and in the second case (dashed line), we have $M = \{(0,0),(0,2)\}$. Clearly, one can see the effect of the stationary state on the evolution. If the two marked vertices are adjacent, the overlap stays closes to 1 and the probability of finding a marked vertex stays close to the probability in the initial state. If the two marked vertices are not adjacent, the quantum walk behaves as expected (as in the single marked vertex case).

Note that if we have a block of marked vertices of size $k \times m$, we can construct a stationary state as long as we can tile it by blocks of size 1×2 and 2×1. For example, consider $M = \{(0,0),(0,1),(2,0),(3,0)\}$ for $n \geq 3$. Then the stationary state is given by

$$|\phi_{stat}^a\rangle = \sum_{x,y=0}^{n-1}\sum_c a|x,y,c\rangle - 4a|0,0,\rightarrow\rangle - 4a|0,1,\leftarrow\rangle - 4a|2,0,\uparrow\rangle - 4a|3,0,\downarrow\rangle. \quad (9)$$

More details on alternative constructions of stationary states for blocks of marked vertices on the two-dimensional grid can be found in [12].

3   Hypercube

3.1   Quantum Walk on the Hypercube

The n-dimensional hypercube is a graph with $N = 2^n$ vertices where each vertex has degree n. The discrete-time quantum walk has associated Hilbert space $\mathcal{H}^{2^n} \otimes \mathcal{H}^n$. The evolution operator is given by $U = S \cdot (I \otimes C)$, where the shift operator, S, acts as $S|v\rangle|c\rangle = |v \oplus e_c\rangle|c\rangle$, with v being the binary representation of v and e_c being the binary vector with 1 in the c-th position. Note, that vertices are connected to each other if their binary representations have Hamming distance 1 (differ in only one position). The coin transformation is the Grover coin $C = 2|s\rangle\langle s| - I$, where $|s\rangle = \frac{1}{\sqrt{n}}\sum_{i=0}^{n-1}|i\rangle$.

Searching for marked vertices in the hypercube is done by using the unitary operator $U' = S \cdot (I \otimes C) \cdot (Q \otimes I)$, where Q is the query transformation, which flips the sign of marked vertices. The initial state of the algorithm is given by

$$|\psi(0)\rangle = \frac{1}{\sqrt{nN}} \sum_{v=0}^{N-1} \sum_{c=0}^{n-1} |v\rangle |c\rangle. \tag{10}$$

In case of algorithm with one marked vertex [7], if we measure the state of the quantum walk after $O(\sqrt{N})$ time steps, we will find the marked vertex with probability $1/2 - O(1/n)$. Hence, we expect to repeat the algorithm a constant number of times, which gives the total running time of $O(\sqrt{N})$ steps.

3.2   Stationary States for the Hypercube

Consider a hypercube with two adjacent marked vertices i and j. Without loss of generality, suppose i and j differ in the first bit. Let $|\phi_{stat}^a\rangle$ be a state having amplitudes of all basis states equal to a except for $|i, 0\rangle$ and $|j, 0\rangle$ which have amplitudes equal to $-(n-1)a$ (see Fig. 3), that is,

$$|\phi_{stat}^a\rangle = a \sum_{v=0}^{N-1} \sum_{c=0}^{n-1} |v, c\rangle - an \left(|i, 0\rangle + |j, 0\rangle\right). \tag{11}$$

Lemma 3. *Consider an n-dimensional hypercube with two adjacent marked vertices i and j. Then $|\phi_{stat}^a\rangle$, given by Eq. (11), is not changed by a step of the algorithm, that is, $U'|\phi_{stat}^a\rangle = |\phi_{stat}^a\rangle$.*

Proof. Similar to proof of Lemma 1.   □

The probability of finding a marked vertex is bounded as follows.

Lemma 4. *Consider an n-dimensional hypercube with two adjacent marked vertices i and j. Then for any number of steps, the probability of finding a marked vertex p_M is $O\left(\frac{n^2}{N}\right)$.*

Proof. Follows from the proof of Theorem 2 by substituting $d = n$ and $m = (nN)/2$.   □

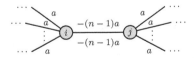

Fig. 3. Amplitudes of the stationary state in an n-dimensional hypercube with two adjacent marked vertices i and j.

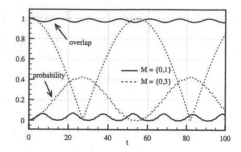

Fig. 4. Probability of finding a marked vertex, p_M, and absolute value of the overlap, $|\langle\psi(0)|\psi(t)\rangle|$, for 100 steps of the quantum walk on hypercube with $N = 2^{10}$ vertices. (Solid line) We have two adjacent marked vertices, 0 and 1. (Dashed line) We have two non-adjacent marked vertices, 0 and 3.

Figure 4 shows the probability of finding a marked vertex and the absolute value of the overlap, $|\langle\psi(0)|\psi(t)\rangle|$, for a hypercube of dimension $n = 10$ for the first 100 steps of the algorithm. We consider two different sets of marked vertices. In the first case (solid line), we have two adjacent marked vertices $M = \{0, 1\}$. In this case, the overlap stays close to 1 and the probability stays close to the probability in the initial state, because the quantum walk has a stationary state. In the second case (dashed line), we have two non-adjacent marked vertices $M = \{0, 3\}$. As one can see, the behavior in the second case is very different from the behavior in the first case.

4   General Graphs

4.1   Quantum Walks on General Graphs

Consider a graph $G = (V, E)$ with a set of vertices V and a set of edges E. Let $n = |V|$ and $m = |E|$. The discrete-time quantum walk on G has associated Hilbert space $\mathcal{H}^{2m}$ with the set of basis states $\{|v, c\rangle : v \in V, 0 \leq c < d_v\}$, where d_v is the degree of vertex v. Note, that the state $|v, c\rangle$ cannot be written as $|v\rangle \otimes |c\rangle$ unless G is regular.

The evolution operator is given by $U = SC$. The coin transformation C is the direct sum of coin transformations for individual vertices, i.e. $C = C_{d_1} \oplus \cdots \oplus C_{d_n}$ with C_{d_i} being the Grover diffusion transformation of dimension d_i. The shift operator S acts in the following way: $S|v, c\rangle = |v', c'\rangle$, where v and v' are adjacent, c and c' represent the directions that points v to v' and v' to v, respectively.

Searching for marked vertices is done by using the unitary operator $U' = SCQ$, where Q is the query transformation, which flips the signs of the amplitudes at the marked vertices, that is,

$$Q = I - 2 \sum_{w \in M} \sum_{c=0}^{d_w - 1} |w, c\rangle\langle w, c|, \tag{12}$$

with M being the set of marked vertices. The initial state of the algorithm is the equal superposition over all vertex-direction pairs:

$$|\psi(0)\rangle = \frac{1}{\sqrt{2m}} \sum_{v=0}^{n-1} \sum_{c=0}^{d_v-1} |v,c\rangle. \tag{13}$$

It can be easily verified that the initial state stays unchanged by the evolution operator U, regardless of the number of steps.

The running time of the algorithm depends on both the structure of the graph as well as the placement of marked vertices.

4.2   Stationary States for General Graphs

Two Adjacent Marked Vertices. Consider a graph $G = (V, E)$ with two adjacent marked vertices i and j with the same degree, that is, $d_i = d_j = d$. Let $|\phi_{stat}^a\rangle$ be a state having all amplitudes equal to a except of the amplitude of vertex i pointing to vertex j and amplitude of vertex j pointing to vertex i, which are equal to $-(d-1)a$. Figure 5 shows the configuration of the amplitudes in the marked vertices. Then, this state is not changed by a step of the algorithm.

Theorem 1. *Let $G = (V, E)$ be a graph with two adjacent marked vertices i and j with $d_i = d_j = d$, and let*

$$|\phi_{i,j}^a\rangle = -ad \left(|i, c_{(i,j)}\rangle + |j, c_{(j,i)}\rangle \right), \tag{14}$$

where $c_{(i,j)}$ represents the direction which points vertex i to vertex j. Then,

$$|\phi_{stat}^a\rangle = a \sum_{v=0}^{n-1} \sum_{c=0}^{d_v-1} |v,c\rangle + |\phi_{i,j}^a\rangle, \tag{15}$$

is not affected by a step of the algorithm, that is, $U'|\phi_{stat}^a\rangle = |\phi_{stat}^a\rangle$.

Proof. Consider the effect of a step of the algorithm. The query transformation changes the sign of all amplitudes of the marked vertices. The coin flip performs an inversion about the average of these amplitudes: for unmarked vertices, it does nothing as all amplitudes are equal to a; for marked vertices, the average is 0, so it results in sign flip. Thus, CQ does nothing for the amplitudes of the unmarked vertices and twice flips the sign of amplitudes of the marked vertices. Therefore, we have $CQ|\phi_{stat}^a\rangle = |\phi_{stat}^a\rangle$. The shift transformation swaps amplitudes of adjacent vertices. For $|\phi_{stat}^a\rangle$, it swaps a with a and $-(d-1)a$ with $-(d-1)a$. Thus, we have $SCQ|\phi_{stat}^a\rangle = |\phi_{stat}^a\rangle$. $\square$

The initial state of the algorithm $|\psi(0)\rangle$, given by Eq. (13), can be written as $|\psi(0)\rangle = |\phi_{stat}^a\rangle - |\phi_{i,j}^a\rangle$, for $a = 1/\sqrt{2m}$. Therefore, the only part of the initial state which is changed by a step of the algorithm is $|\phi_{i,j}^a\rangle$. From this fact, we can establish an upper bound for the probability of finding a marked vertex.

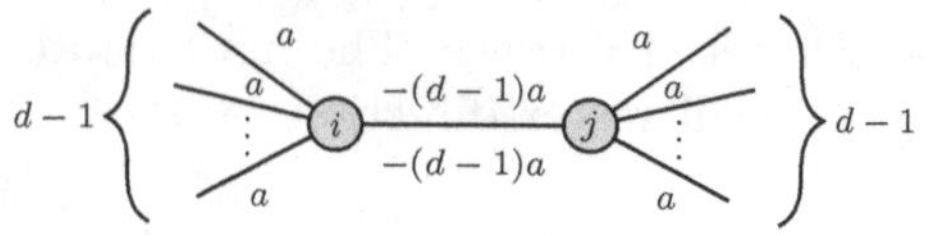

Fig. 5. The amplitudes for the stationary state with two adjacent marked vertices i and j.

Theorem 2. *Let $G = (V, E)$ be a graph with two adjacent marked vertices i and j with $d_i = d_j = d$, and let the probability of finding a marked vertex be given by*

$$p_M = \langle \psi(t) | \left(\sum_{v \in M} \sum_{c=0}^{d_v - 1} |v, c\rangle \langle v, c| \right) |\psi(t)\rangle, \qquad (16)$$

where $|\psi(t)\rangle = U^t |\psi(0)\rangle$. Then, $p_M = O\left(\frac{d^2}{m}\right)$, where m is the number of edges of the graph.

Proof. The only part of the initial state $|\psi(0)\rangle$ which is changed by the step of the algorithm is $|\phi_{i,j}^a\rangle = -ad\left(|i, c_{(i,j)}\rangle + |j, c_{(j,i)}\rangle\right)$, for $a = 1/\sqrt{2m}$. Since the evolution is unitary, this part will keep its norm unchanged. In this way, we want to find how big amplitudes can get in order to maximize the value of p_M. This means we want to maximize the function

$$2(d-1)(a+x_1)^2 + 2(-(d-1)a - x_2)^2, \qquad (17)$$

subject to $2(d-1)x_1^2 + 2x_2^2 = |||\phi_{i,j}^a\rangle||^2 = 2a^2d^2$. Note that x_1 represents the amplitudes going from the marked vertices to unmarked vertices and x_2 represents the amplitudes going from one marked vertex to the other. Then, we obtain

$$p_M \leq 2a^2(2\sqrt{(d-1)d^3} + d(2d-1)) = O\left(\frac{d^2}{m}\right). \qquad (18)$$

$\square$

One of corollaries of Theorem 2 is that if the degree of the marked vertices is constant or if it does not grow as a function of n, then for large n, the probability of finding a marked vertex will stay close to the initial probability.

Three Adjacent Marked Vertices. Now, consider a graph $G = (V, E)$ with three adjacent marked vertices i, j and k, that is, a marked triangle. The stationary state for this case will have the amplitudes in the marked vertices as depicted in Fig. 6. Note that in order to have a stationary state the sum of amplitudes of each marked vertex should be 0, so the action of the coin operator will be a sign flip. By solving the following system of equations:

$$\begin{cases} l_{ij} + l_{ik} = d_i - 2 \\ l_{ij} + l_{jk} = d_j - 2 \\ l_{ik} + l_{jk} = d_k - 2 \end{cases} \qquad (19)$$

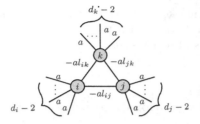

Fig. 6. Sketch of amplitudes for the stationary state with three adjacent marked vertices i, j and k.

we obtain,

$$l_{ij} = \frac{d_i + d_j - d_k}{2} - 1, \quad l_{ik} = \frac{d_i + d_k - d_j}{2} - 1 \quad \text{and} \quad l_{jk} = \frac{d_j + d_k - d_i}{2} - 1.$$
$$(20)$$

Theorem 3. *Let $G = (V, E)$ be a graph with three adjacent marked vertices i, j and k; and let*

$$|\phi^a_{i,j,k}\rangle = -a(l_{ij} + 1)\left(|i, c_{(i,j)}\rangle + |j, c_{(j,i)}\rangle\right) - a(l_{ik} + 1)\left(|i, c_{(i,k)}\rangle + |k, c_{(k,i)}\rangle\right)$$
$$- a(l_{jk} + 1)\left(|i, c_{(j,k)}\rangle + |k, c_{(k,j)}\rangle\right),$$
$$(21)$$

where $l_{ij}, l_{ik},$ and l_{jk} are defined in (20). Then,

$$|\phi^a_{stat}\rangle = a \sum_{v=0}^{n-1} \sum_{c=0}^{d_v-1} |v, c\rangle + |\phi^a_{i,j,k}\rangle,$$
$$(22)$$

is not affected by a step of the quantum walk on G.

Proof. Similar to Theorem 1.   □

k-clique of Marked Vertices. Next, we generalize the previous result for any complete subgraph of marked vertices.

Theorem 4. *Let $G = (V, E)$ be a graph with k marked vertices $v_1, \ldots, v_k$ forming a k-clique. Then it forms an exceptional configuration.*

Proof. Let $d_{v_j} = (k - 1) + d'_j$, where d'_j is the number of edges of v_j outside the clique. To construct a stationary state, we need to assign amplitudes to internal edges of the clique, so that the amplitudes in vertex v_j sum up to d'_j. Without a loss of generality let $d'_1 < d'_2 < \cdots < d'_k$. We set the amplitude of the edge (v_1, v_2) to $-ad'_1$ and amplitudes of other edges within the clique outgoing from v_1 to 0. By this, we have satisfied the condition for the vertex v_1 and reduced the problem from size k to $k - 1$. I.e. now we have a $(k - 1)$-clique with degrees $(d'_2 - d'_1), d'_3, \ldots, d'_k$. Next, we recursively repeat the previous step until we get a 3-clique, which always have an assignment. In this way, we have constructed a stationary state for a k-clique of marked vertices.   □

Note that any set of marked vertices which can be divided into unique blocks of two adjacent marked vertices with the same degree and/or k-clique marked vertices will result in a stationary state.

General Conditions

Theorem 5 (General conditions). *Let $|\psi\rangle$ be a state with the following properties:*

1 *All amplitudes of the unmarked vertices are equal;*
2 *The sum of the amplitudes of any marked vertex is 0;*
3 *The amplitudes of two adjacent vertices pointing to each other are equal.*

Then, $|\psi\rangle$ is not changed by a step of the quantum walk, that is, $U|\psi\rangle = |\psi\rangle$.

Proof. Item 1 is required in order for the coin transformation to have no effect on the unmarked vertices. It is easy to see that $C_n|u\rangle = |u\rangle$, where $|u\rangle = a\sum_{i=0}^{n-1}|i\rangle$ for some constant a. Item 2 is necessary so the coin transformation can flip the signs of the amplitudes in the marked vertices. Note that previously the sign of these amplitudes were inverted by the query transformation. Item 3 is necessary for the shift transformation to have no effect on the state.   □

Note, that the aforementioned conditions are established for the case $CQ|\psi\rangle = |\psi\rangle$ and $S|\psi\rangle = |\psi\rangle$. There might be even more general conditions for the case $SCQ|\psi\rangle = |\psi\rangle$.

5   Conclusions

In this paper, we have demonstrated a wide class of exceptional configurations of marked vertices for the quantum walk based search on various graphs. The above phenomenon is purely quantum. Classically, additional marked vertices result in the decrease of the number of steps of the algorithm and the increase of the probability of finding a marked location. Quantumly, the addition of a marked vertex can drastically drop the probability of finding a marked location.

An open question is whether the found phenomenon has analogs for other models of quantum walks (continuous time quantum walks [3], Szegedy's quantum walk [13], staggered quantum walks [14], etc.) as well as for alternative coin operators.

Another open question is algorithmic applications of the found effect. For example, in case of two-dimensional grid the search algorithm can "distinguish" between odd-times-odd and even-times-even groups of marked locations. Moreover, if there are multiple odd-times-odd and even-times-even groups of marked locations, the algorithm will find only odd-times-odd groups and will "ignore" even-times-even groups. Nothing like this is possible for classical random walks without adding additional memory resources and complicating the algorithm. Another example is the general graphs where the algorithm "ignores" complete subgraphs of marked vertices.

Acknowledgements. The authors thank Andris Ambainis for helpful ideas and suggestions, which was a great help during this research, and Tom Wong for useful comments and careful revision of the manuscript.

References

1. Portugal, R.: Quantum Walks and Search Algorithms. Springer, New York (2013)
2. Aharonov, Y., Davidovich, L., Zagury, N.: Quantum random walks. Phys. Rev. A **48**(2), 1687–1690 (1993)
3. Farhi, E., Gutmann, S.: Quantum computation and decision trees. Phys. Rev. A **58**, 915–928 (1998)
4. Ambainis, A., Kempe, J., Rivosh, A.: Coins make quantum walks faster. In: Proceedings of the 16th ACM-SIAM Symposium on Discrete Algorithms, pp. 1099–1108 (2005)
5. Magniez, F., Santha, M., Szegedy, M.: An $o(n^{1.3})$ quantum algorithm for the triangle problem. In: Proceedings of SODA, pp. 413–424 (2005)
6. Ambainis, A.: Quantum walk algorithm for element distinctness. In: Proceedings of the 45th Annual IEEE Symposium on Foundations of Computer Science (2004)
7. Shenvi, N., Kempe, J., Whaley, K.B.: A quantum random walk search algorithm. Phys. Rev. A **67**(052307), 1–11 (2003)
8. Wong, T.G.: Spatial search by continuous-time quantum walk with multiple marked vertices. Quantum Inf. Process. **15**(4), 1411–1443 (2016)
9. Wong, T.G., Ambainis, A.: Quantum search with multiple walk steps per oracle query. Phys. Rev. A **92**, 022338 (2015)
10. Nahimovs, N., Rivosh, A.: Quantum walks on two-dimensional grids with multiple marked locations arXiv:quant-ph/150703788 (2015)
11. Ambainis, A., Rivosh, A.: Quantum walks with multiple or moving marked locations. In: Geffert, V., Karhumäki, J., Bertoni, A., Preneel, B., Návrat, P., Bieliková, M. (eds.) SOFSEM 2008. LNCS, vol. 4910, pp. 485–496. Springer, Heidelberg (2008). doi:10.1007/978-3-540-77566-9_42
12. Nahimovs, N., Rivosh, A.: Exceptional configurations of quantum walks with Grover's coin. In: Kofroň, J., Vojnar, T. (eds.) MEMICS 2015. LNCS, vol. 9548, pp. 79–92. Springer, Cham (2016). doi:10.1007/978-3-319-29817-7_8
13. Szegedy, M.: Quantum speed-up of Markov chain based algorithms. In: Proceedings of the 45th Symposium on Foundations of Computer Science, pp. 32–41 (2004)
14. Portugal, R., Santos, R.A.M., Fernandes, T.D., Gonçalves, D.N.: The staggered quantum walk model. Quantum Inf. Process. **15**(1), 85–101 (2015)

Matrix Semigroup Freeness Problems in SL(2, ℤ)

Sang-Ki Ko$^{(\boxtimes)}$ and Igor Potapov

Department of Computer Science, University of Liverpool,
Ashton Street, Liverpool L69 3BX, UK
{sangkiko,potapov}@liverpool.ac.uk

Abstract. In this paper we study decidability and complexity of decision problems on matrices from the special linear group SL(2, ℤ). In particular, we study the freeness problem: given a finite set of matrices G generating a multiplicative semigroup S, decide whether each element of S has at most one factorization over G. In other words, is G a code? We show that the problem of deciding whether a matrix semigroup in SL(2, ℤ) is non-free is NP-hard. Then, we study questions about the number of factorizations of matrices in the matrix semigroup such as the finite freeness problem, the recurrent matrix problem, the unique factorizability problem, etc. Finally, we show that some factorization problems could be even harder in SL(2, ℤ), for example we show that to decide whether every prime matrix has at most k factorizations is PSPACE-hard.

Keywords: Matrix semigroups · Freeness · Decision problems · Decidability · Computational complexity

1   Introduction

In general, many computational problems for matrix semigroups are proven to be undecidable starting from dimension three or four [3,5,8,16,25]. One of the central decision problems for matrix semigroups is the membership problem. Let $S = \langle G \rangle$ be a matrix semigroup generated by a generating set G. The *membership problem* is to decide whether or not a given matrix M belongs to the matrix semigroup S. In other words the question is whether a matrix M can be factorized over the generating set G or not.

Another fundamental problem for matrix semigroups is the *freeness problem*, where we want to know whether every matrix in the matrix semigroup has a unique factorization over G. Mandel and Simon [22] showed that the freeness problem is decidable in polynomial time for matrix semigroups with a single generator for any dimension over rational numbers. Indeed, the freeness problem for matrix semigroups with a single generator is the complementary problem of the *matrix torsion problem* which asks whether there exist two integers $p, q \geq 1$ such that $M^p = M^{q+p}$. Klarner et al. [17] proved that the freeness problem in dimension three over natural numbers is undecidable.

This research was supported by EPSRC grant EP/M00077X/1.

B. Steffen et al. (Eds.): SOFSEM 2017, LNCS 10139, pp. 268–279, 2017.
DOI: 10.1007/978-3-319-51963-0_21

Decidability of the freeness problem in dimension two has been already an open problem for a long time [7,8]. However the solutions for some special cases exist. For example Charlier and Honkala [10] showed that the freeness problem is decidable for upper-triangular matrices in dimension two over rationals when the products are restricted to certain bounded languages. Bell and Potapov [4] showed that the freeness problem is undecidable in dimension two for matrices over quaternions.

The study in [8] revealed a class of matrix semigroups formed by two 2×2 matrices over natural numbers for which the freeness in unknown, highlighting a particular pair:

$$\begin{pmatrix} 2 & 0 \\ 0 & 3 \end{pmatrix} \text{ and } \begin{pmatrix} 3 & 5 \\ 0 & 5 \end{pmatrix}.$$

The above case was simultaneously solved in two papers [9,14], where authors were providing new algorithms for checking freeness at some subclasses.

However the status of the freeness problem for natural, integer and complex numbers is still unknown. The decidability of the freeness problem for SL(2, $\mathbb{Z}$) was shown in [9] following the idea of solving the membership problem in SL(2, $\mathbb{Z}$) shown in [11].

The effective symbolic representation of matrices in SL(2, $\mathbb{Z}$) leads recently to several decidability and complexity results. The mortality, identity and vector reachability problems were shown to be NP-hard for SL(2, $\mathbb{Z}$) in [1,6]. For the modular group, the membership problem was shown to be decidable in polynomial time by Gurevich and Schupp [15]. Decidability of the membership problem in matrix semigroups in SL(2, $\mathbb{Z}$) and the *identity problem* in $\mathbb{Z}^{2 \times 2}$ was shown to be decidable in [11] in 2005. Later in 2016, Semukhin and Potapov showed that the *vector reachability problem* is also decidable in SL(2, $\mathbb{Z}$) [27].

In this paper we study decidability and complexity questions related to freeness and various other factorization problems in SL(2, $\mathbb{Z}$). The new hardness results are interesting in the context of understanding complexity in matrix semigroups in general and the decidability results on factorizations in SL(2, $\mathbb{Z}$) can be important in other areas and fields. In particular, the special linear group SL(2, $\mathbb{Z}$) has been extensively exploited in hyperbolic geometry [12,32], dynamical systems [24], Lorenz/modular knots [21], braid groups [26], high energy physics [30], M/en theories [13], music theory [23], and so on.

In this paper, we show that the question about non-freeness for matrix semigroups in SL(2, $\mathbb{Z}$) is NP-hard by finding a different reduction than the one used in [1,6]. Then we show both decidability and hardness results for the *finite freeness problem*: decide whether or not every matrix in the matrix semigroup has a finite number of factorizations. Also we prove NP-hardness of the problem whether a given matrix has more than one factorization in SL(2, $\mathbb{Z}$) and undecidability of this problem in $\mathbb{Z}^{4 \times 4}$, or more specifically in SL(4, $\mathbb{Z}$). Then it is shown that both problems whether a particular matrix has an infinite number factorizations or it has more than k factorizations are decidable and NP-hard in SL(2, $\mathbb{Z}$) while they are undecidable in $\mathbb{Z}^{4 \times 4}$. Finally we show that some of the factorizations problems could be even harder in SL(2, $\mathbb{Z}$), for example we show that to decide whether every prime matrix has at most k-factorizations is PSPACE-hard.

2   Preliminaries

In this section we formulate several problems, provide important definitions and notation as well as several technical lemmas used throughout the paper.

Basic Definitions. A *semigroup* is a set equipped with an associative binary operation. Let S be a semigroup and X be a subset of S. We say that a semigroup S is *generated* by a subset X of S if each element of S can be expressed as a composition of elements of X. Then, we call X the *generating set* of S. Then, X is a *code* if and only if every element of S has a unique factorization over X. A semigroup S is *free* if there exists a subset $X \subseteq S$ which is a code and $S = X^+$.

Given an alphabet $\Sigma = \{1, 2, \ldots, m\}$, a word w is an element of Σ^*. For a letter $a \in \Sigma$, we denote by $\bar{a}$ the inverse letter of a such that $a\bar{a} = \varepsilon$ where ε is the empty word.

A *nondeterministic finite automaton* (NFA) is a tuple $A = (\Sigma, Q, \delta, q_0, F)$ where Σ is the input alphabet, Q is the finite set of states, $\delta \colon Q \times \Sigma \to 2^Q$ is the multivalued transition function, $q_0 \in Q$ is the initial state and $F \subseteq Q$ is the set of final states. In the usual way δ is extended as a function $Q \times \Sigma^* \to 2^Q$ and the language accepted by A is $L(A) = \{w \in \Sigma^* \mid \delta(q_0, w) \cap F \neq \emptyset\}$. The automaton A is a deterministic finite automaton (DFA) if δ is a single valued function $Q \times \Sigma \to Q$. It is well known that the deterministic and nondeterministic finite automata recognize the class of *regular languages* [29].

Factorization and Freeness Problems. Let S be a matrix semigroup generated by a finite set G of matrices. Then we define a matrix M is *k-factorizable* for $k \in \mathbb{N}$ if there are at most k different factorizations of M over G. In the matrix semigroup freeness problem, we check whether every matrix in S is 1-factorizable.

Problem 1. Given a finite set G of $n \times n$ matrices generating a matrix semigroup S, is S free? (i.e., does every element $M \in S$ have a unique factorization over G?)

The above problem is well-known as the *freeness problem*. Clearly, the *non-freeness problem* is to decide whether the matrix semigroup S is not free.

For a matrix M, if there exists $k < \infty$ where M is k-factorizable, then we say that M is *finitely factorizable*. In other words, a finitely factorizable matrix M has finitely many different factorizations over G. We define a matrix semigroup S is *finitely free* if every matrix in S is finitely factorizable and define the *finite freeness problem* as follows:

Problem 2. Given a finite set G of $n \times n$ matrices generating a matrix semigroup S, does every element $M \in S$ have a finite number of factorizations over G?

Freeness and finite freeness problems are asking about factorization properties for all matrices in the semigroup. In case where a semigroup is not free or not finitely free, instead of asking whether the semigroup is free or finitely free, it is possible to define problems for a given particular matrix in the semigroup as follows:

Problem 3. Given a finite set G of $n \times n$ matrices generating a matrix semi-group S and a matrix M in S, does M have

a. a unique factorization over G? (matrix unique factorizability problem)
b. at most k factorizations over G? (matrix k-factorizability problem)
c. an infinite number of factorizations over G? (recurrent matrix problem)

Group Alphabet Encodings. Let us introduce several technical lemmas that will be used in encodings for NP-hardness and undecidability results. Our original encodings require the use of group alphabet and the following lemmas for showing the transformation from an arbitrary group alphabet into a binary group alphabet and later into matrix form that is computable in polynomial time.

Lemma 4. *Let $\Sigma = \{z_1, z_2, \ldots, z_l\}$ be a group alphabet and $\Sigma_2 = \{a, b, \bar{a}, \bar{b}\}$ be a binary group alphabet. Define the mapping $\alpha : \Sigma \to \Sigma_2^*$ by:*

$$\alpha(z_i) = a^i b \bar{a}^i, \quad \alpha(\bar{z}_i) = a^i \bar{b} \bar{a}^i,$$

where $1 \leq i \leq l$. Then α is a monomorphism. Note that α can be extended to domain Σ^* in the usual way.

Lemma 5 (Lyndon and Schupp [20]). *Let $\Sigma_2 = \{a, b, \bar{a}, \bar{b}\}$ be a binary group alphabet and define $f : \Sigma_2^* \to \mathbb{Z}^{2 \times 2}$ by:*

$$f(a) = \begin{pmatrix} 1 & 2 \\ 0 & 1 \end{pmatrix}, \ f(\bar{a}) = \begin{pmatrix} 1 & -2 \\ 0 & 1 \end{pmatrix}, \ f(b) = \begin{pmatrix} 1 & 0 \\ 2 & 1 \end{pmatrix}, \ f(\bar{b}) = \begin{pmatrix} 1 & 0 \\ -2 & 1 \end{pmatrix}.$$

Then f is a monomorphism.

The composition of Lemmas 4 and 5 gives us the following lemma that ensures that encoding the *subset sum problem* (SSP) and the *equal subset sum problem* (ESSP) instances into matrix semigroups can be completed in polynomial time.

Lemma 6 (Bell and Potapov [6]). *Let z_j be in Σ and α, f be mappings as defined in Lemmas 4 and 5, then, for any $i \in \mathbb{N}$,*

$$f(\alpha(z_j^i)) = f((a^j b \bar{a}^j)^i) = \begin{pmatrix} 1 + 4ij & -8ij^2 \\ 2i & 1 - 4ij \end{pmatrix}.$$

Symbolic Representation of Matrices from SL(2, $\mathbb{Z}$). Here we provide another technical details about the representation of SL(2, $\mathbb{Z}$) and their properties [2, 28]. It is known that SL(2, $\mathbb{Z}$) is generated by two matrices

$$\mathbf{S} = \begin{pmatrix} 0 & -1 \\ 1 & 0 \end{pmatrix} \text{ and } \mathbf{R} = \begin{pmatrix} 0 & -1 \\ 1 & 1 \end{pmatrix},$$

which have respective orders 4 and 6. This implies that every matrix in $\mathrm{SL}(2,\mathbb{Z})$ is a product of $\mathbf{S}$ and $\mathbf{R}$. Since $\mathbf{S}^2 = \mathbf{R}^3 = -\mathbf{I}$, every matrix in $\mathrm{SL}(2,\mathbb{Z})$ can be uniquely brought to the following form:

$$(-\mathbf{I})^{i_0}\mathbf{R}^{i_1}\mathbf{SR}^{i_2}\mathbf{S}\cdots\mathbf{SR}^{i_{n-1}}\mathbf{SR}^{i_n}, \tag{1}$$

where $i_0 \in \{0,1\}$, $i_1, i_n \in \{0,1,2\}$, and $i_j \neq 0 \mod 3$ for $1 < j < n$.

The representation (1) for a given matrix in $\mathrm{SL}(2,\mathbb{Z})$ is unique, but it is very common to present this result ignoring the sign, i.e. considering the projective special linear group. Let $\Sigma_{SR} = \{s,r\}$ be a binary alphabet. We define a mapping $\varphi : \Sigma_{SR} \rightarrow \mathrm{SL}(2,\mathbb{Z})$ as follows: $\varphi(s) = \mathbf{S}$ and $\varphi(r) = \mathbf{R}$. Naturally, we can extend the mapping φ to the morphism $\varphi : \Sigma_{SR}^* \rightarrow \mathrm{SL}(2,\mathbb{Z})$. We call a word $w \in \Sigma_{SR}^*$ *reduced* if there is no occurrence of subwords ss or rrr in w. Then, we have the following fact.

Theorem 7 (Lyndon and Schupp [20]). *For every matrix $M \in \mathrm{SL}(2,\mathbb{Z})$, there exists a unique reduced word $w \in \Sigma_{SR}^*$ in form of (1) such that either $M = \varphi(w)$ or $M = -\varphi(w)$.*

Following Theorem 7, all word representations of a particular matrix M in $\mathrm{SL}(2,\mathbb{Z})$ over the alphabet Σ_{SR} can be expressed as a context-free language.

Lemma 8. *Let M be a matrix in $SL(2,\mathbb{Z})$. Then, there exists a context-free language over Σ_{SR} which contains all representations $w \in \Sigma_{SR}^*$ such that $\varphi(w) = M$.*

3   Matrix Semigroup Freeness

The matrix semigroup freeness problem is to determine whether every matrix in the semigroup has a unique factorization. Note that the decidability of the matrix semigroup freeness in $\mathrm{SL}(2,\mathbb{Z})$ has been shown by Cassaigne and Nicolas [9] but the complexity of the problem has not been resolved yet despite various NP-hardness results on other matrix problems [1,6]. Here we show that the problem of deciding whether the matrix semigroup in $\mathrm{SL}(2,\mathbb{Z})$ is not free is NP-hard by encoding different NP-hard problem comparing to the one used in [1,6].

Theorem 9. *Given a matrix semigroup S in $SL(2,\mathbb{Z})$ generated by the set G of matrices, the problem of deciding whether S is not free is NP-hard.*

Proof. We use an encoding of the *equal subset sum problem* (ESSP), which is proven to be NP-hard, into a set of two-dimensional integral matrices [31]. The ESSP is, given a set $U = \{s_1, s_2, \ldots, s_k\}$ of k integers, to decide whether or not there exist two disjoint nonempty subsets $U_1, U_2 \subseteq U$ whose elements sum up to the same value. Namely, $\sum_{s_1 \in U_1} s_1 = \sum_{s_2 \in U_2} s_2$.

Define an alphabet $\Sigma = \{0, 1, \ldots, k-1, \overline{1}, \overline{2}, \ldots, \overline{(k-2)}, \overline{(k-1)}, \overline{k}, a\}$. We define a set W of words which encodes the ESSP instance.

$$W = \{i \cdot a^{i+1} \cdot \overline{(i+1)}, \ i \cdot \varepsilon \cdot \overline{(i+1)} \mid 0 \leq i \leq k-1\} \subseteq \Sigma^*.$$

Fig. 1. Structure of the matrix semigroup encoded by the set W. Each matrix in the generating set of the matrix semigroup corresponds to each transition of the automaton structure.

We define 'border letters' as letters from $\Sigma \setminus \{a\}$ and the inner border letters of a word as all border letters excluding the first and last. We call a word a 'partial cycle' if all inner border letters in that word are inverse to a consecutive inner border letter. Moreover, we note that for any partial cycle $u \in W^+$ the first border letter of u is strictly smaller than the last border letter if we compare them as integers. Figure 1 shows the structure of our encoding of the ESSP instance.

First we prove that if there is a solution to the ESSP instance, then the matrix semigroup generated by matrices encoded from the set W is not free. Let us assume that there exists a solution to the ESSP instance, which is two sequences of integers where each of two sequences sums up to the same integer x. Then, the solution can be represented by the following pair of sequences:

$$Y = (y_1, y_2, \ldots, y_{k-1}, y_k) \text{ and } Z = (z_1, z_2, \ldots, z_{k-1}, z_k),$$

where $y_i, z_i \in \{0, s_i\}, 1 \le i \le k$ and $\sum_{i=1}^{k} y_i = \sum_{i=1}^{k} z_i = x$. Note that $y_i \ne z_i$ in at least one index i for $1 \le i \le k$.

For a sequence Y, there exists a word $w_Y = w_1 w_2 \cdots w_k \in W^+$ such that $w_i = (i-1) \cdot a^{y_i} \cdot \overline{i}$. Since $\sum_{i=1}^{k} y_i = x$, the reduced representation of w_Y is $r(w_Y) = 0 \cdot s^x \cdot \overline{k}$ as all inner border letters are cancelled. Analogously, we have a word w_Z for a sequence Z and its reduced representation $r(w_Z)$ is equal to $r(w_Y)$ as the sum of integers in the sequence Z is equal to the sum of integers in Y. As we have two words in W^+ whose reduced representations are equal, the semigroup generated by matrices encoded from the set W is not free.

Now we prove the opposite direction: if there is no solution to the ESSP instance, then the matrix semigroup is free. Assume that there is no solution to the ESSP instance and the matrix semigroup is not free. Since the matrix semigroup is not free, we have two different words $w, w' \in W^+$ whose reduced representations are equal, namely, $r(w) = r(w')$.

For a word w, we decompose w into subwords $w = u_1 u_2 \cdots u_m$ such that each $u_i \in W^+, 1 \le i \le m$ is a partial cycle of maximal size. Similarly, we decompose w' into subwords of maximal partial cycles as follows: $w' = u'_1 u'_2 \cdots u'_n$. Since $r(w) = r(w')$, it follows that $r(u_i) = r(u'_i)$ should hold for $1 \le i \le m$ and $m = n$. On the other hand, since $w \ne w'$, there exists $i, 1 \le i \le m$ where $u_i \ne u'_i$. Note that the maximal partial cycles u_i and u'_i should have the same number of a's since $r(u_i) = r(u'_i)$ and the letter a cannot be cancelled by the reduction of words. As we mentioned earlier, the first border letter and last border letter of a partial cycle are integers where the first border letter is strictly smaller than the last border letter. Let us say that i_1 is the first border letter and i_2 is the last border letter of u_i and u_i'. Then, the number of a's in u_i and u_i' is the sum of subset of integers from the set $\{s_{i_1+1}, s_{i_1+2}, \ldots, s_{i_2}\}$. It follows from the fact that $u_i \neq u_i'$ that we have two distinct subsets of the set $\{s_{i_1+1}, s_{i_1+2}, \ldots, s_{i_2}\}$ whose sums are the same. This contradicts our assumption since we have two disjoint subsets of equal subset sum.   □

Recently, Bell et al. proved that the problem of deciding whether the identity matrix is in S, where S is an arbitrary regular subset of $SL(2,\mathbb{Z})$, is in NP [2]. Since we can show that the matrix semigroup S is not free by showing that the equation $M_1 M M_2 = M_3 M' M_4$ is satisfied where $M_1 \neq M_3$, $M_2 \neq M_4$, and $M_i, M, M' \in S$ for $1 \leq i \leq 4$. We can show that S is not free by showing that the matrix $M_1 M M_2 M_4^{-1} M'^{-1} M_3^{-1}$ is the identity matrix.

Let $M_1 M^* M_2 M_4^{-1} (M^{-1})^* M_3^{-1}$ be a regular subset of $SL(2,\mathbb{Z})$ subject to $M_1 \neq M_3$, $M_2 \neq M_4$ and $M \in S$. Then, we can decide whether or not S is free by deciding whether or not a regular subset of $SL(2,\mathbb{Z})$ contains the identity matrix. Therefore, we can conclude as follows:

Corollary 10. *Given a matrix semigroup S in $SL(2,\mathbb{Z})$ generated by the set G of matrices, the problem of deciding whether S is not free is NP-complete.*

If the matrix semigroup is not free (not every matrix have unique factorization) we still have a question whether each matrix in a given semigroup has only a finite number of factorizations. Next we show that the problem of checking whether there exists a matrix in the semigroup which has an infinite number of factorizations is decidable and NP-hard in $SL(2,\mathbb{Z})$.

Theorem 11. *Given a matrix semigroup S in $SL(2,\mathbb{Z})$ generated by the set G of matrices, the problem of deciding whether S contains a matrix with an infinite number of factorizations is decidable and NP-hard.*

Proof. Let us consider a matrix semigroup S which is generated by the set $G = \{M_1, M_2, \ldots, M_n\}$ of matrices. Let $w_1, w_2, \ldots, w_n \in \Sigma_{SR}^*$ be words encoding the generators, such that $\varphi(w_i) = M_i$ for $1 \leq i \leq n$. Then, we can define a regular language L_S corresponding to S as $L_S = \{w_1, w_2, \ldots, w_n\}^+$. Let $A = (Q, \Sigma, \delta, Q_0, F)$ be an NFA accepting L_S constructed based on S. For states q and p, where the state p is reachable from q by reading ss or rrr, we add an ε-transition from q to p. We repeat this process until there is no such pair of states following to the procedure proposed in [11].

If there exists a matrix M which can be represented by infinitely many factorizations over G, then there is an infinite number of accepting runs for the matrix M in A. It is easy to see that we have an infinite number of accepting runs for some matrix $M \in S$ if and only if there is a cycle only consisting of ε-transitions. As we can compute the ε-closure of states in A, the problem of deciding whether there exists a matrix with an infinite number of factorizations is decidable.

For the NP-hardness of the problem, we modify and adapt the NP-hardness proof of the identity problem in $SL(2,\mathbb{Z})$ [6]. We use an encoding of the *subset*

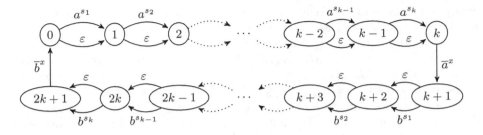

Fig. 2. Structure of the matrix semigroup encoded by the set W.

sum problem (SSP), which is, given a set $U = \{s_1, s_2, \ldots, s_k\}$ of k integers, to decide whether or not there exists a subset $U' \subseteq U$ whose elements sum up to the given integer x. Namely, $\sum_{s \in U'} s = x$.

Define an alphabet $\Sigma = \{0, 1, \ldots, 2k + 1, \overline{1}, \overline{2}, \ldots, \overline{(2k+1)}, a, b, \overline{a}, \overline{b}\}$. We define a set W of words which encodes the SSP instance.

$$
\begin{aligned}
W = &\{i \cdot a^{i+1} \cdot \overline{(i+1)}, \ \ i \cdot \varepsilon \cdot \overline{(i+1)} \mid 0 \le i \le k - 1\} \ \cup \\
&\{i \cdot b^{i+1} \cdot \overline{(i+1)}, \ \ i \cdot \varepsilon \cdot \overline{(i+1)} \mid k + 1 \le i \le 2k\} \ \cup \qquad (2) \\
&\{k \cdot \overline{a}^x \cdot \overline{(k+1)}\} \cup \{(2k+1) \cdot \overline{b}^x \cdot \overline{0}\} \subseteq \Sigma^*.
\end{aligned}
$$

Figure 2 shows the structure of the word encoding of the SSP instance. The full proof for showing that the matrix semigroup S corresponding to W^+ has a matrix with an infinite number of factorizations if and only if the SSP instance has a solution can be found in the archive version [18] of the paper. □

4   Matrix Factorizability Problems

In the matrix semigroup freeness problem, we ask whether every matrix in the semigroup has a unique factorization. Instead of considering a question about every matrix in the semigroup, we restrict our question to a given particular matrix, which may have a unique factorization, a finite number of unique factorizations or even an infinite number of unique factorizations.

4.1   Unique Factorizability Problem

In the *matrix unique factorizability problem*, we consider the problem of deciding whether or not a particular matrix M in S has a unique factorization over G. We first establish the decidability and NP-hardness of the problem.

Theorem 12. *Given a matrix semigroup S in $SL(2, \mathbb{Z})$ generated by the set G of matrices and a particular matrix M in S, the problem of deciding whether the matrix M has more than one factorization over G is decidable and NP-hard.*

Proof. From Lemma 8, we can represent a set of all unreduced representations for M over $\Sigma_{SR} = \{s, r\}$ as a context-free language L_M.

We can also obtain a regular language that corresponds to the matrix semi-group S. Let $G = \{M_1, M_2, \ldots, M_n\}$ be the generating set of S. Namely, $S = \langle M_1, M_2, \ldots, M_n \rangle$. Let $w_1, w_2, \ldots, w_n \in \Sigma_{SR}^*$ be words encoding the generators, such that $\varphi(w_i) = M_i$ for $1 \leq i \leq n$. Then, we can define a regular language L_S corresponding to S as $L_S = \{w_1, w_2, \ldots, w_n\}^+$. Then, the intersection of $L_M \cap L_S$ contains all words that correspond to the matrix M in the semi-group S. If the cardinality of $L_M \cap L_S$ is larger than one, we immediately have two different factorizations for the matrix M over G. Therefore, let us assume that $|L_M \cap L_S| = 1$ and w be the only word in $L_M \cap L_S$. Clearly, $\varphi(w) = M$ and M can be generated by the set G. Note that each accepting path of w in L_S corresponds to a unique factorization of M over G. Now we can decide whether or not M has a unique factorization over G by counting the number of accepting paths of words in $L_M \cap L_S$ from an NFA accepting L_S.

The NP-hardness can be proven by the reduction from the SSP in a similar manner to the proof of Theorem 11. See Eq. (2) for the word encoding of the SSP instance. Let us pick the word $w = 0 \cdot \varepsilon \cdot \overline{1}$ in W and notice that the matrix $M = f(\alpha(w))$ which is encoded from w is in the matrix semigroup S. We will show that the matrix M in S has at least two factorizations over the generating set $\{f(\alpha(w)) \mid w \in W\}$ of S if and only if the SSP instance has a solution. The full proof can be found in the archive version [18].   □

We reduce the *fixed element PCP* (FEPCP) [3] which is proven to be unde-cidable to the unique factorizability problem over $\mathbb{Z}^{4 \times 4}$ for the following unde-cidability result.

Theorem 13. *Given a matrix semigroup S over $\mathbb{Z}^{4 \times 4}$ generated by the set G of matrices and a particular matrix M in S, the problem of deciding whether the matrix M has more than one factorization over G is undecidable.*

4.2 Recurrent Matrix Problem

We first tackle the problem of deciding whether or not a particular matrix in the semigroup has an infinite number of factorizations. Note that we call this decision problem the *recurrent matrix problem* instead of the *matrix finite factorizabil-ity problem* as we named for the other variants. The recurrent matrix problem has been introduced by Bell and Potapov [3] and proven to be undecidable for matrices over $\mathbb{Z}^{4 \times 4}$ based on the reduction from FEPCP.

We show that the recurrent matrix problem is decidable and NP-hard for matrix semigroups in $SL(2, \mathbb{Z})$. We first mention that the recurrent matrix prob-lem is different with the identity problem. One may think that the recurrent matrix problem is equivalent to the identity problem since it is obvious that if the identity matrix exists then every matrix in the semigroup has an infinite number of factorizations. However, the opposite does not hold as follows:

Proposition 14. *Let S be a matrix semigroup generated by the generating set G and M be a matrix in S. Then, the matrix M has an infinite number of factorizations over G if the identity matrix exists in S. However, the opposite does not hold in general.*

Now we establish the results for the recurrent matrix problem in SL(2, $\mathbb{Z}$).

Theorem 15. *The recurrent matrix problem in SL(2, $\mathbb{Z}$) is decidable and in fact, NP-hard.*

We also consider the matrix k-factorizability problem which is to decide whether a particular matrix M in the semigroup has at most k factorizations over the generating set G.

Lemma 16. *Given a matrix semigroup S in SL(2, $\mathbb{Z}$) generated by the set G of matrices, a particular matrix $M \in S$, and a positive integer $k \in \mathbb{N}$, the problem of deciding whether the matrix M has more than k factorizations over G is decidable and NP-hard.*

We mention that the matrix k-factorizability problem is also undecidable over $\mathbb{Z}^{4 \times 4}$ following Theorem 13.

5   On the Finite Number of Factorizations

Recall that the matrix semigroup freeness problem examines whether or not there exists a matrix in the semigroup has more than one factorization. The finite freeness problem asks whether there exists a matrix in the semigroup which has an infinite number of factorizations. In that sense, we may interpret these problems as the problems asking whether the number of factorizations in the semigroup is bounded by one (the freeness problem) or unbounded (the finite freeness problem).

In this section, we are interested in finding a number $k \in \mathbb{N}$ by which the number of factorizations of matrices in the matrix semigroup is bounded. In other words, we check whether every matrix in the semigroup is k-factorizable. However, it is not easy to define the k-freeness problem as we define the general freeness problem by the following observation.

Let S be a matrix semigroup generated by the set G of matrices and M be a k-factorizable matrix over G. Let us denote the number of factorizations of M by $\mathrm{dec}(M)$. Thus, we can write $\mathrm{dec}(M) = k$. It is easy to see that S is free if for every matrix M in S, $\mathrm{dec}(M) = 1$. Let us assume that $\mathrm{dec}(M_1) = m$ and $\mathrm{dec}(M_2) = n$ for $m, n \in \mathbb{N}$. Then, $\mathrm{dec}(M_1 M_2) = k$ where $k \geq mn$. This means that if S is not free, then there is no finite value k such that every matrix in S is k-factorizable.

In that reason, we define the following notion which prevents the multiplicative property of the number of factorizations. We say that a matrix M is *prime* if it is impossible to decompose M into $M = M_1 M_2$ such that $\mathrm{dec}(M) = \mathrm{dec}(M_1) \times \mathrm{dec}(M_2)$, $\mathrm{dec}(M_1) \neq 1$, and $\mathrm{dec}(M_2) \neq 1$. We define a matrix semigroup S to be *k-free* if every prime matrix M in S has at most k different factorizations over G. Formally, a matrix semigroup S is k-free if and only if $\max\{\operatorname{dec}(M) \mid M \in S, M \text{ is prime}\} \leq k$.

This definition gives rise to the following problem which is a generalized version of the matrix semigroup freeness problem.

Problem 17. Given a finite set G of $n \times n$ matrices generating a matrix semigroup S, does every prime element $M \in S$ have at most k factorizations over G?

In this paper, we leave the decidability of the k-freeness problem open but establish the PSPACE-hardness result as a lower bound of the problem, which is interesting compared to the NP-hardness of the other freeness problems.

Theorem 18. *Given a matrix semigroup S in $SL(2, \mathbb{Z})$ generated by the set G of matrices and a positive integer $k \in \mathbb{N}$, the problem of deciding whether or not every prime matrix in S has at most k factorizations is PSPACE-hard.*

Proof. For the PSPACE-hardness of the problem, we reduce the DFA intersection emptiness problem [19] to the k-freeness problem. Note that given k DFAs, the DFA intersection emptiness problem asks whether the intersection of k DFAs is empty. The full proof can be found in the archive version [18].   □

References

1. Bell, P.C., Hirvensalo, M., Potapov, I.: Mortality for 2×2 matrices is NP-hard. In: Proceedings of the 37th International Symposium on Mathematical Foundations of Computer Science, pp. 148–159 (2012)
2. Bell, P.C., Hirvensalo, M., Potapov, I.: The identity problem for matrix semigroups in $SL(2, \mathbb{Z})$ is NP-complete (2016). To appear in SODA 17
3. Bell, P.C., Potapov, I.: Periodic and infinite traces in matrix semigroups. In: Proceedings of the 34th Conference on Current Trends in Theory and Practice of Computer Science, pp. 148–161 (2008)
4. Bell, P.C., Potapov, I.: Reachability problems in quaternion matrix and rotation semigroups. Inf. Comput. **206**(11), 1353–1361 (2008)
5. Bell, P.C., Potapov, I.: On the undecidability of the identity correspondence problem and its applications for word and matrix semigroups. Int. J. Found. Comput. Sci. **21**(6), 963–978 (2010)
6. Bell, P.C., Potapov, I.: On the computational complexity of matrix semigroup problems. Fundamenta Infomaticae **116**(1–4), 1–13 (2012)
7. Blondel, V.D., Cassaigne, J., Karhumäki, J.: Problem 10.3: freeness of multiplicative matrix semigroups. In: Unsolved Problems in Mathematical Systems and Control Theory, pp. 309–314. Princeton University Press (2004)
8. Cassaigne, J., Harju, T., Karhumäki, J.: On the undecidability of freeness of matrix semigroups. Int. J. Algebra Comput. **09**(03–04), 295–305 (1999)
9. Cassaigne, J., Nicolas, F.: On the decidability of semigroup freeness. RAIRO - Theor. Inf. Appl. **46**(3), 355–399 (2012)
10. Charlier, E., Honkala, J.: The freeness problem over matrix semigroups and bounded languages. Inf. Comput. **237**, 243–256 (2014)

11. Choffrut, C., Karhumäki, J.: Some decision problems on integer matrices. RAIRO - Theor. Inf. Appl. **39**(1), 125–131 (2010)
12. Elstrodt, J., Grunewald, F., Mennicke, J.: Arithmetic applications of the hyperbolic lattice point theorem. Proc. Lond. Math. Soc. **s3–57**(2), 239–283 (1988)
13. García del Moral, M.P., Martín, I., Peña, J.M., Restuccia, A.: SL(2, ℤ) symmetries, supermembranes and symplectic torus bundles. J. High Energy Phys. **9**, 1–12 (2011)
14. Gawrychowski, P., Gutan, M., Kisielewicz, A.: On the problem of freeness of multiplicative matrix semigroups. Theor. Comput. Sci. **411**(7–9), 1115–1120 (2010)
15. Gurevich, Y., Schupp, P.: Membership problem for the modular group. SIAM J. Comput. **37**(2), 425–459 (2007)
16. Halava, V., Harju, T., Hirvensalo, M.: Undecidability bounds for integer matrices using claus instances. Int. J. Found. Comput. Sci. **18**(05), 931–948 (2007)
17. Klarner, D.A., Birget, J.-C., Satterfield, W.: On the undecidability of the freeness of integer matrix semigroups. Int. J. Algebra Comput. **01**(02), 223–226 (1991)
18. Ko, S.-K., Potapov, I.: Matrix semigroup freeness problems in SL(2, ℤ) (2016). CoRR, abs/1610.09834
19. Kozen, D.: Lower bounds for natural proof systems. In: Proceedings of the 18th Annual Symposium on Foundations of Computer Science, pp. 254–266 (1977)
20. Lyndon, R.C., Schupp, P.E.: Combinatorial Group Theory. Springer, Heidelberg (1977)
21. Mackenzie, D.: A New Twist in Knot Theory, vol. 7 (2009)
22. Mandel, A., Simon, I.: On finite semigroups of matrices. Theor. Comput. Sci. **5**(2), 101–111 (1977)
23. Noll, T.: Musical intervals and special linear transformations. J. Math. Music **1**(2), 121–137 (2007)
24. Polterovich, L., Rudnick, Z.: Stable mixing for cat maps and quasi-morphisms of the modular group. Ergodic Theor. Dyn. Syst. **24**, 609–619 (2004)
25. Potapov, I.: From post systems to the reachability problems for matrix semigroups and multicounter automata. In: Calude, C.S., Calude, E., Dinneen, M.J. (eds.) DLT 2004. LNCS, vol. 3340, pp. 345–356. Springer, Heidelberg (2004). doi:10.1007/978-3-540-30550-7_29
26. Potapov, I.: Composition problems for braids. In: IARCS Annual Conference on Foundations of Software Technology and Theoretical Computer Science, vol. 24, pp. 175–187 (2013)
27. Potapov, I., Semukhin, P.: Vector reachability problem in SL(2, ℤ). In: 41st International Symposium on Mathematical Foundations of Computer Science, pp. 84:1–84:14 (2016)
28. Rankin, R.: Modular Forms and Functions. Cambridge University Press, Cambridge (1977)
29. Shallit, J.: A Second Course in Formal Languages and Automata Theory, 1st edn. Cambridge University Press, New York (2008)
30. Witten, E.: SL(2, ℤ) action on three-dimensional conformal field theories with abelian symmetry, vol. 2, pp. 1173–1200 (2005)
31. Woeginger, G.J., Yu, Z.: On the equal-subset-sum problem. Inf. Process. Lett. **42**(6), 299–302 (1992)
32. Zagier, D.: Elliptic Modular Forms and Their Applications, pp. 1–103 (2008)

Planar and Molecular Graphs

Order-Preserving 1-String Representations
of Planar Graphs

Therese Biedl and Martin Derka[✉]

David R. Cheriton School of Computer Science, University of Waterloo,
Waterloo, ON, Canada
{biedl,mderka}@uwaterloo.ca

Abstract. This paper considers 1-string representations of planar graphs that are *order-preserving* in the sense that the order of crossings along the curve representing vertex v is the same as the order of edges in the clockwise order around v in the planar embedding. We show that this does not exist for all planar graphs (not even for all planar 3-trees), but show existence for some subclasses of planar partial 3-trees. In particular, for outer-planar graphs it can be order-preserving and *outer-string* in the sense that all ends of strings are on the outside of the representation.

1 Introduction

String representations recently received a lot of attention, especially for planar graphs. Scheinerman [21] had asked in 1984 whether every planar graph can be represented as the intersection graph of segments in the plane. This was settled partially by Chalopin, Gonçalves and Ochem [7], who showed that every planar graph has a 1-string representation, i.e., a representation as an intersection graph of strings such that any two strings may cross at most once. Extending their result, in 2009 Chalopin and Gonçalves finally settled Scheinerman's conjecture in the positive [6]. We later showed that 1-string representations of planar graphs can be achieved even with orthogonal curves with at most 2 bends [3]. A number of other papers gave string representations for subclasses of planar graphs that are simpler to build and/or have other useful properties, see for example [2,9,10, 12,15]. Testing whether a graph has a string representation is NP-hard [16,19] and in NP [20]; the latter is not obvious because string representations may require exponentially many bends for non-planar graphs [17].

Our Results: In this paper, we study the following question: Does every planar graph have a 1-string representation where the order of crossings along curves *preserves* the planar embedding in the sense that the order of crossings along the curve of v corresponds to the cyclic order of edges around v in some planar embedding? This is motivated by that we found string representations quite hard to read; during our work on [3] we struggled to verify correctness in some

---

T. Biedl—Research supported by NSERC.

M. Derka—was supported by the Vanier CGS.

B. Steffen et al. (Eds.): SOFSEM 2017, LNCS 10139, pp. 283–294, 2017.
DOI: 10.1007/978-3-319-51963-0_22

cases because the crossing of curves for an edge occurred at unexpected places. Furthermore, having an order-preserving string representation could make it easier to create such representations by using the typical incremental approach that adds one vertex on the outer-face at a time; for this it would be especially helpful if such representations were also *outer-string* in the sense that ends of strings are on the infinite region defined by the representation. We show the following:

- Not all planar graphs have order-preserving 1-string representations. In fact, we can construct a planar 3-tree that has no such representation.
- For some subclasses of planar partial 3-trees, we construct order-preserving 1-string representations. For outer-planar graphs, these are additionally outer-string (and use segments), while for the other graph classes we show that order-preserving outer-1-string representations do not always exist.

We are not aware of any previous results on order-preserving 1-string representations. (On the other hand, string-representations of planar graphs obtained from contact representations are usually order-preserving, but strings then intersect twice, at least for some edges.) The closest related results are on the *abstract graph realizability problem* [16,19], which asks to draw a graph such that only a given set of edge-pairs are allowed to cross.

2   Definitions

A *string representation* $\mathcal{R}$ assigns a curve $\mathbf{v}$ in the plane to every vertex v in a graph in such a way that (v, w) is an edge if and only if $\mathbf{v}$ intersects $\mathbf{w}$. (Throughout the paper, bold-face $\mathbf{x}$ always denotes the curve assigned to vertex x.) We demand that $\mathbf{u}$ and $\mathbf{v}$ intersect only if there is a proper crossing, i.e., any sufficiently small circle centered at an intersection-point crosses $\mathbf{u}, \mathbf{v}, \mathbf{u}, \mathbf{v}$ in that order. (In particular no curve $\mathbf{u}$ should end on another curve $\mathbf{v}$, though such a touching-point could always be resolved into a proper crossing by extending $\mathbf{u}$ a bit.) We also do not allow three curves to share a point. A *1-string representation* is a string representation such that any two curves cross at most once. A *segment representation* uses straight-line segments in place of strings. A B_k-*VPG-representation* uses orthogonal curves with at most k bends as strings.

A string representation $\mathcal{R}$ divides the plane into connected regions. The *contour* is the infinite region of $\mathbb{R}^2 - \mathcal{R}$. A string representation is called *weakly outer-string* if all vertex curves are incident to the contour. It is called *outer-string* if all vertex curves have an end incident to the contour.[1] A weakly outer-string representation can be made outer-string by "doubling back" along the curve of each vertex, but this does not work for an outer-1-string representation, because

---

[1] One could distinguish this further by whether both ends must be on the contour or whether one end suffices. All our outer-string constructions have both ends on the contour, while all our impossibility-results hold even if only one end is required to be on the contour, so the distinction does not matter for the results in our paper.

doubling back along the curve would make some curves cross twice. See [5,14] and the references therein for more on outer-string representations.

In this paper, we only consider connected graphs. A graph is called *planar* if it can be drawn in the plane without crossing. Such a planar drawing Γ defines, by enumerating edges around vertices in clockwise order, a *rotation scheme*, i.e., an assignment of a cyclic order of edges at each vertex. From the rotation scheme, one can read the *faces*, i.e., the vertices and edges that are incident to each connected piece of $\mathbb{R}^2 - \Gamma$. A *plane graph* is a planar graph with a fixed rotation scheme. An *outer-planar graph* is a planar graph that has a rotation scheme such that all vertices are incident to one face. An *outer-plane graph* is a plane graph with the rotation system that describes such an embedding. A *k-tree* (used here only for $k = 2, 3$) is a graph that has a vertex order $v_1, \ldots, v_n$ such that $v_1, \ldots, v_k$ is a clique, and each v_i for $i > k$ has exactly k neighbours in $v_1, \ldots, v_{i-1}$, and they form a clique. A *partial k-tree* is a subgraph of a k-tree. Every outer-planar graph is a partial 2-tree.

Fix a rotation scheme of a graph. We say that a 1-string representation is *order-preserving* with respect to the rotation scheme if for any vertex v, we can walk along curve **v** from one end to the other and encounter the crossings with $\mathbf{w_1}, \ldots, \mathbf{w_k}$ in the same order in which the neighbours $w_1, \ldots, w_k$ of v appear in the cyclic order of edges around v. This leaves open the choice which neighbour of v should be w_1, since the order at v is cyclic while the order along **v** is not.[2]

3 Graphs with No Order-Preserving Representations

In this section, we show that there exist planar graphs that have no 1-string representation that preserves the order of any planar embedding. To define them, we need the following graph operation: Given a plane graph G, the *stellation* of G is obtained by inserting a new vertex into every face of G, and making it adjacent to all vertices incident to that face. The *triple-stellation* of G is obtained by stellating G to get G', stellating G' to get G'', and finally stellating G''.

Lemma 1. *Let G be a plane graph with minimum degree 3 and at least $|V(G)| + 1$ faces that are triangles. Then the triple-stellation G''' of G has no order-preserving 1-string representation with respect to this rotation scheme.*

Proof. Assume for contradiction we had such a 1-string representation $\mathcal{R}$, and let $\mathcal{R}_G$ be the induced 1-string representation of G, which is also order-preserving. The following notation will be helpful: If a, c are neighbours of b, then let $\mathbf{b}[a, c]$ be the stretch of **b** between the intersection with **a** and **c**.

Consider a face-vertex-incidence in G, which can be described by giving a vertex b and two neighbours a, c of b that are consecutive in the clockwise order

---

[2] Once we fix how to break up the cyclic order at all vertices, there is a construction that describes the order-preserving 1-string representation as a graph H and so that it can be realized if and only if H is planar. Hence the problem is interesting only if we keep this choice.

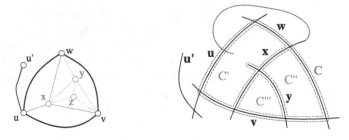

Fig. 1. For the proof of Lemma 1.

at b. We call such a face-vertex-incidence *unbroken* if (in $\mathcal{R}_G$) $b[a, c]$ contains no other crossing, else we call it *broken*. Since $\mathcal{R}_G$ is order-preserving, for every vertex b in G only one face-vertex-incidence at b is broken. Since G has at least $|V(G)| + 1$ triangular faces, there exists a face $T = \{u, v, w\}$ of G such that all face-vertex-incidences at T are unbroken. We will find a contradiction at the stellation vertices that were placed in T. See also Fig. 1.

Let x be the vertex that (during the stellation of G to get G') was placed in face T. We claim that $\mathbf{x}$ must intersect $\mathbf{u}$ in $\mathbf{u}[v, w]$. To see this, recall that $\deg_G(u) \geq 3$, hence u has at least one other neighbour u' in G. Since the face-incidence at u is unbroken, $\mathbf{u}[v, w]$ contains no other crossing of $\mathcal{R}_G$, so $\mathbf{u}'$ intersects $\mathbf{u}$ outside this stretch. Since T is a face in G, the (clockwise or counter-clockwise) order of neighbours at u in G' contains u', v, x, w. To maintain this order in the string representation, the intersection between $\mathbf{x}$ and $\mathbf{u}$ (in $\mathcal{R}$) must be on $\mathbf{u}[v, w]$. Similarly one argues that $\mathbf{x}$ intersects $\mathbf{v}[u, w]$ and $\mathbf{w}[u, v]$.

Let C be the region bounded by $\mathbf{u}[v, w] \cup \mathbf{w}[u, v] \cup \mathbf{v}[w, u]$. Curve $\mathbf{x}$ intersects δC three times, and no more since curves intersect at most once in a 1-string representation. So $\mathbf{x}$ starts (say) inside C, crosses δC to go outside, crosses δC to go inside, and then crosses δC again to end outside. Between the second and third crossing, $\mathbf{x}$ contains a stretch that is inside C; after possible renaming of $\{u, v, w\}$ we assume that this is $\mathbf{x}[v, w]$. This stretch splits C into two parts, say C' (incident to parts of $\mathbf{u}$) and C^r (incident to the crossing of $\mathbf{v}$ and $\mathbf{w}$).

Let y be the vertex that (during the stellation of G' to get G'') was placed in the face $\{v, w, x\}$ of G'. Since v, w, x all have degree 3 or more in G', as before one argues that $\mathbf{y}$ must intersect $\mathbf{x}[v, w]$, $\mathbf{w}[x, v]$ and $\mathbf{v}[w, x]$. Curve $\mathbf{y}$ intersects $\delta C'$ (in $\mathbf{x}[v, w]$), but cannot intersect $\delta C'$ a second time, else it would cross $\mathbf{u}$ (but $(u, y) \notin E$) or would cross one of $\mathbf{x}, \mathbf{v}, \mathbf{w}$ twice (which is not allowed). Hence $\mathbf{y}$ starts inside C', then crosses $\mathbf{x}$, and then crosses one of $\mathbf{v}$ and $\mathbf{w}$. Up to renaming of $\{v, w\}$ we may assume that $\mathbf{y}$ crosses $\mathbf{v}$ first. Hence $\mathbf{y}[x, v]$ splits C^r into two parts, say C'' (incident to parts of $\mathbf{w}$) and C''' (incident to the crossing of $\mathbf{v}$ and $\mathbf{x}$).

Now finally consider the vertex z that was placed in $\{x, y, v\}$ when stellating G'' to obtain G'''. As before one argues that $\mathbf{z}$ has an end inside C', because it crosses $\mathbf{x}$ in stretch $\mathbf{x}[v, y] \subset \mathbf{x}[v, w]$, and it cannot cross C' again. But we can also see that $\mathbf{z}$ has an end inside C'', since it crosses $\mathbf{y}[x, v]$ and crosses no other curve on the boundary of C''. But this means that **z** has both ends outside C''', contradicting that it must intersect the boundary of C''' three times to respect the edge-orders at x, y, v. Contradiction, so G''' does not have an order-preserving 1-string representation.   □

Theorem 1. *There exists a planar 3-tree that has no order-preserving 1-string representation.*

Proof. Start with an arbitrary planar 3-tree G with $n \geq 6$ vertices; this has minimum degree 3 and $2n-4 \geq n+2$ triangular faces in its (unique) rotation scheme. Stellating a 3-tree gives again a 3-tree, so by Lemma 1 the triple-stellation of G is a 3-tree that has no order-preserving 1-string representation.   □

4 Order-Preserving Outer-1-String Representations

Now we turn towards positive results and show that every outer-plane graph has an order-preserving outer-1-string representation. We first discuss one existing result that does not quite achieve this. It is easy to show that every outer-planar graph can be represented as touching-graph of line segments (see e.g. [15] for much broader results). The standard way to do this (see also Fig. 2) results, after extending the segments a bit, in a segment-representation that is order-preserving and weakly outer-string. However, this does not quite achieve our goal, because the ends of segments are not necessarily on the outer-face.

We instead give two other constructions. The first one uses that any outer-planar graph is a *circle graph*, i.e., the intersection graph of chords of a circle [22]. This obviously gives an end-outer-segment representation, but it need not be order-preserving (see Fig. 2). Our first construction hence re-proves this result and maintains invariants to ensure that the representation is indeed order-preserving.

The resolution in this representation could be very bad, and we therefore give a second construction where the curves are orthogonal instead. We use one bend for each vertex curve here, and so obtain a B_1-VPG-representation. Since there are n vertices and at most n bends, the representation can be embedded into a grid of size $O(n) \times O(n)$.

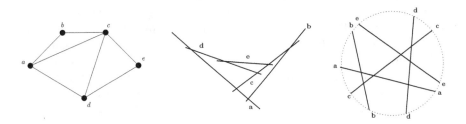

Fig. 2. An outer-planar graph, a weakly segment-representation that is not outer-segment at **e**, and a representation as circle graph that is not order-preserving at **c**.

In our proofs, we use that any 2-connected outer-planar graph G can be built up as follows [13, Lemma 3]: Fix an edge (u, v). Now repeatedly add an *ear*, i.e., a path $P = u_0, u_1, \ldots, u_k, u_{k+1}$ with $k \geq 1$ where (u_0, u_{k+1}) is an edge on the outer-face of the current graph G', and $u_1, \ldots, u_k$ are new vertices that induce a path and have no edges to G' other than (u_0, u_1) and (u_k, u_{k+1}).

A crucial requirement of the constructed representation $\mathcal{R}$ of such a subgraph is the following *order-condition*: If w and w' are the counterclockwise and clockwise neighbours of v on the outer-face, then we encounter the neighbours of v in order, starting with w and ending with w', while walking along $\mathbf{v}$. Put differently, the broken face-vertex-incidence is the one with the outer-face. We consider $\mathbf{v}$ to be directed so that it intersects first $\mathbf{w}$ and last $\mathbf{w}'$.

The second crucial ingredient for both proofs is to reserve for edges (somewhat similar as was done for faces in [2,3,7,10]) a region that can be used to attach subgraphs. Thus define a *private region* S_{uv} of edge (u, v) to be a region that contains an end of $\mathbf{u}$ and an end of $\mathbf{v}$ and does not intersect any other curve or private regions of $\mathcal{R}$. Both constructions maintain such a private region S_{uv} for every outer-face edge (u, v). Moreover, if v is the clockwise neighbour of u, then S_{uv} contains the tail of $\mathbf{u}$ and the head of $\mathbf{v}$.

4.1   Circle-Chord Representation

We now re-prove that outer-planar graphs are circle graphs, and show that furthermore the order can be preserved.

Theorem 2. *Every outer-plane graph has an order-preserving representation as intersection graph of chords of a circle C.*

Proof. It suffices to prove the claim for a 2-connected outer-planar graph G since every outer-planar graph G' is an induced subgraph of a 2-connected outer-planar graph G, and therefore a string representation for G also yields one for G' by deleting curves of vertices in $G - G'$.

We create a representation $\mathcal{R}$ while building up the graph via adding ears, and maintain curve directions and private regions as explained before. Each private region S_{uv} is bounded by parts of circle C and a chord of C and does not contain the crossing of $\mathbf{u}$ and $\mathbf{v}$. Further, the tail of $\mathbf{u}$ and the head of $\mathbf{v}$ are in the interior of the circular arc that bounds S_{uv}.

In the base case, G is an edge (u, v) which can be represented by two chords through the center of C. See Fig. 3. We reserve two private regions for (u, v), because the outer-face of a single-edge graph should be viewed as containing this edge twice (we can add ears twice at it). All conditions are easily verified.

For the induction step, let us assume that G was obtained by adding an ear $P = u, x_1, \ldots, x_k, v$ at some edge (u, v), with u the counter-clockwise neighbour of v on the outer-face. Let $C[u, v]$ be the arc of C between the tail of $\mathbf{u}$ and the head of $\mathbf{v}$ that lies inside S_{uv}. Let u' and v' be two points on C just outside $C[u, v]$ but still within S_{uv}. If $k = 1$, then we add x_1 by using chord $\overline{u'v'}$ for $\mathbf{x_1}$. If $k > 1$, then we insert $2k - 2$ points on the interior of $C[u, v]$ and create

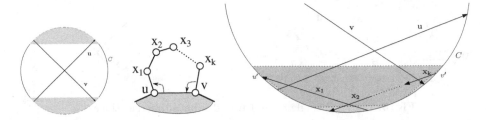

Fig. 3. The base case, and adding chords for an ear for $k = 2$.

chords for $x_1, \dots, x_k$ so that everyone intersects as required. See Fig. 3, which also shows the private regions that we define for the new outer-face edges.

Since S_{uv} was convex, all new curves are inside it and do not intersect any other curves. The orientation of these new curves is determined by the order-condition: x_i should be oriented so that it intersects first x_{i+1} (where $x_0 := u$) and then x_{i-1} (where $x_{k+1} := v$). In particular this means that the private region $S_{x_i x_{i+1}}$ contains the tail of x_i and the head of x_{i+1}, and hence satisfies the condition on private regions.

It remains to check that the order-condition is satisfied for u. Since S_{uv} contained the tail of u, this means that x_1 becomes the first curve to be intersected by u, which is correct since x_1 is the clockwise neighbour of u on the outer-face. Likewise one argues that the order-condition holds for v. Hence all conditions hold, and after repeating for all ears we obtain an order-preserving representation as intersection graph of chords of a circle.   □

4.2 B_1-VPG Representation

Now we create, for any outer-planar graph, a B_1-VPG representation that is order-preserving and outer-string. However, the ends will not be on a circle; instead they will lie on a closed curve S that we maintain throughout the construction and that surrounds the entire representation $\mathcal{R}$ without truly intersecting any curve. All vertices are 1-bend poly-lines with slopes ± 1 (after rotating by $45°$ this gives the B_1-VPG representation); this allows us to use an orthogonal curve for S. Figure 4 illustrates types of private regions that we will use for this construction: S_{uv} contains no bend of u or v, and it is an isosceles right triangle whose hypotenuse lies on S.

Fig. 4. Three types of private regions (three more can be obtained by flipping horizontally), and the base case.

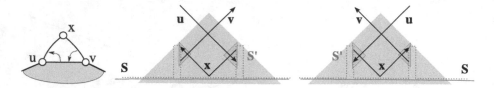

Fig. 5. Adding a single node if **u** and **v** have different slopes.

Theorem 3. *Every outer-planar graph G has an order-preserving outer-1-string B_1-VPG-representation $\mathcal{R}$.*

Proof. As before it suffices to prove the claim for 2-connected outer-planar graphs G. We proceed by induction on the number of vertices, building $\mathcal{R}$ while adding ears. In the base case, G is an edge (u, v) which can be represented by two 1-bend curves positioned and oriented as shown in Fig. 4, which also shows the private region. We use a horizontal segment for S (this can be expanded into a closed curve surrounding $\mathcal{R}$ arbitrarily).

For the induction step, let us assume that G was obtained by adding an ear $P = u, x_1, \ldots, x_k, v$ at some edge (u, v), with u the counter-clockwise neighbour of v on the outer-face. After possible rotation the hypotenuse of the private region S_{uv} is horizontal with S_{uv} above it. We distinguish cases:

1. **u** *and* **v** *have different slopes in* S_{uv} *and* $k = 1$ *(i.e. we add one vertex x).* We add a 1-bend curve **x** with the bend pointing downwards. See Fig. 5, which also shows the private regions that we define for (u, x) and (x, v). Curve **x** fits entirely inside S_{uv} by placing the bend in the interior of S_{uv} and shortening **u** and **v** appropriately so that the ends of **x** are vertically aligned with those of **u** and **v**. We can now easily find a new curve S' by adding "detours" to S that reach the hypotenuses of the new private regions. These detours are inside S_{uv} and hence intersect no other curves (since we shortened **u** and **v**). So the new curve S' is a closed curve that surround the new representation as desired.

   The orientation of **x** is again determined by the order-condition, and exactly as in Theorem 2 one argues that this respects the order-condition at **u** and **v**, since our choice of curve for **x** ensures that it crosses **u** *after* the crossing of **u** with **v**.

2. **u** *and* **v** *have different slopes in* S_{uv} *and* $k > 1$ *(i.e. we add at least two vertices $x_1, \ldots, x_k$.)* We add a path of 1-bend curves $x_1, x_2, \ldots, x_k$ with their bends at the top, and define private regions as illustrated in Fig. 6. Each curve x_i is oriented as required by the order-condition, and again one verifies the order-condition for **u** and **v**. We can re-use the same S.

3. **u** *and* **v** *have the same slope inside* S_{uv}. We add a path of 1-bend curves $x_1, x_2, \ldots, x_k$ (possibly $k = 1$) with their bends at the top, and define private regions as illustrated in Fig. 7. Each curve x_i is oriented as required by the order-condition, and one verifies all conditions using the same S.

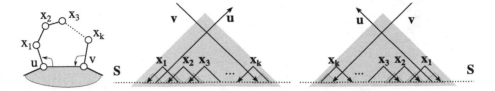

Fig. 6. Adding 2 or more nodes if **u** and **v** have different slopes.

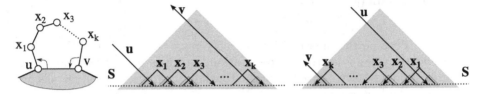

Fig. 7. Adding one or more vertices if **u** and **v** have the same slope. We only show two of the four possible configurations.

After having represented the entire graph in this way, we are order-preserving due to the order-condition, outer-string due to poly-line S, and B_1-VPG (after a 45°-rotation) since every curve has one bend.   □

In our B_1-VPG-representation, every vertex-curve is an ∟ in one of the four possible rotations ∟, ⌐, Г, ⌐. (All four may be used, since private regions get rotated in Case 1.) We would have preferred a representation that uses ∟ (or the two shapes ∟ and ⌐), because then the stretching-techniques by Middendorf and Pfeiffer [18] could have been applied to obtain another segment-representation. It is easy to create a representations with ∟ only if we need not be order-preserving (use ⌃ in Case 1) or need not be outer-string (see also Lemma 2), but finding an outer-string order-preserving representation using only ∟s remains open.

5   Beyond Outer-Planar Graphs?

One wonders what other graph classes might have order-preserving 1-string representations, preferably outer-string ones. We study this here for some graph classes. We start with the *series-parallel graphs*, which are the same as the partial 2-trees, and hence generalize outer-planar graphs.

Lemma 2. *Every series-parallel graph G has a 1-string representation with ∟s that is order-preserving for some planar embedding of G.*

Proof. It is easy to show that every 2-tree has a representation by touching true ∟s, i.e., each vertex is assigned an ∟ (not rotated and not degenerated into a line segment), curves are disjoint except at ends, and (u, v) is an edge if and only if

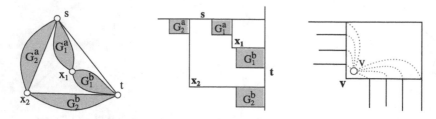

Fig. 8. Representing series-parallel graphs by touching ⌐s, and converting this into a planar drawing with the same order.

the end of **u** lies on the interior of **v** or vice versa.[3] See also Fig. 8. Extending the ⌐s slightly gives a 1-string representation, and it is order-preserving for a planar embedding easily derived from the touching ⌐ representation. Details are provided in the long version [4].   □

It would be interesting to know whether this result can be extended to the so-called *planar Laman-graphs*, which have a representation by touching ⌐s [15], but not all ⌐s are necessarily in the same rotation and so it is not clear whether this is order-preserving. Of particular interest would be planar bipartite graphs, which can even be represented by horizontal and vertical touching line segments [12], but again it is not clear how to make this order-preserving.

As for having strings additionally end at the contour for series-parallel graphs: this is not always possible. Let H be the graph obtained by subdividing every edge in a $K_{2,3}$; one verifies that H is series-parallel. It is easy to see (see also [5]) that H cannot be outer-string, since $K_{2,3}$ is not outer-planar. So H has no outer-string representation, much less one that is 1-string and order-preserving.

Now we turn to partial 3-trees. We showed in Theorem 1 that there exist planar 3-trees (hence partial 3-trees) that do not have an order-preserving 1-string representation. We now study some subclasses of partial 3-trees that are superclasses of outer-planar graphs.

An *IO-graph* is a planar graph G that has an independent set I such that $G - I$ is a 2-connected outer-planar graph O for which all vertices in I are inside inner faces of O. A *Halin*-graph is a graph that consists of a tree T and a cycle C that connects all leaves of T. Both types of graphs are well-known to be partial 3-trees. In [2], we gave 1-string representations for both Halin graphs and IO-graphs; the latter uses only unrotated ⌐s. Independently, Francis and Lahiri also constructed 1-string representations of Halin-graphs, using only unrotated ⌐s [11]. Inspection of both constructions shows that these respect the standard planar embedding (where O respectively C is one face). We hence have:

Theorem 4 (based on [2,11]). *Every IO-graph and every Halin-graph has an order-preserving 1-string representation in which every vertex is an* ⌐.

---

[3] We have not been able to find a direct reference for this, but it follows for example from the works of Chaplick et al. [8] or with an iterative approach similar to the 6-sided contact representations in [1].

In these constructions, the ends of the strings are not on the outer-face, and we now show that this is unavoidable. This is obvious for Halin-graphs, since the subdivided $K_{2,3}$ is an induced subgraph of a Halin-graph. As for IO-graphs, define the *wheel* W_n to be the graph that consists of a cycle $C = \{v_1, \ldots, v_n\}$ with n vertices and one universal vertex c connected to all of them. Let the *extended wheel-graph* W_n^+ be the wheel-graph W_n with additionally a vertex w_i incident to v_i and v_{i+1} for $i = 1, \ldots, n$ (and $w_{n+1} := w_1$). Notice that W_n^+ is an IO-graph. The proof of the following is presented in the long version [4].

Theorem 5. *For $n \geq 7$, the IO-graph W_n^+ has no order-preserving outer-1-string representation.*

6 Final Remarks

In this paper, we studied 1-string representations that respect a planar embedding. As for open problems, what other graph classes have order-preserving 1-string representations? A natural candidate to investigate would be the 2-outer-planar graphs, for which Lemma 1 cannot be applied since a triple-stellation is never 2-outer-planar. Other interesting candidates would be planar bipartite graphs (or more generally planar Laman-graphs), or planar 4-connected graphs.

Secondly, what is the complexity of testing whether an order-preserving 1-string representation exists? Given the NP-hardness of the abstract graph realization problem [16,19], this is very likely NP-hard if we are allowed to prescribe an arbitrary rotation scheme (not from a planar drawing). But is it NP-hard for plane graphs?

One unsatisfactory aspect of our definition of "order-preserving" is that graphs with an end-contact representation (i.e., with disjoint strings where for every edge one string ends on the other string) do not automatically have an order-preserving 1-string representation: We can obtain a 1-string representation by extending the strings slightly, but it does not need to be order-preserving. A reviewer hence suggested to us the following alternate model: Thicken each string slightly, and consider the cyclic order of intersections while walking around the thickened string. Let now "order-preserving" mean that the cyclic order of neighbours around a vertex forms a subsequence of the intersections encountered while walking "around" its string. With this, any end-contact representation becomes an order-preserving 1-string representation after extending the curves a bit. This includes for example planar bipartite graphs and Laman graphs. Since this model's restriction is weaker, all our positive results transfer, but the proofs of the negative results no longer hold. Are there plane graphs that do not have an order-preserving 1-string representation in this new model?

References

1. Alam, M.J., Biedl, T., Felsner, S., Gerasch, A., Kaufmann, M., Kobourov, S.G.: Linear-time algorithms for hole-free rectilinear proportional contact graph representations. Algorithmica **67**(1), 3–22 (2013)

2. Biedl, T., Derka, M.: 1-string B_1-VPG-representations of planar partial 3-trees and some subclasses. In: Canadian Conference on Computational Geometry (CCCG 2015), pp. 37–42 (2015)
3. Biedl, T., Derka, M.: 1-string B_2-VPG representations of planar graphs. J. Comput. Geom. **7**(2), 191–215 (2016)
4. Biedl, T., Derka, M.: Order-preserving 1-string representations of planar graphs (2016). CoRR abs/1609.08132
5. Cabello, S., Jejčič, M.: Refining the hierarchies of classes of geometric intersection graphs (2016). CoRR abs/1603.08974
6. Chalopin, J., Gonçalves, D.: Every planar graph is the intersection graph of segments in the plane: extended abstract. In: ACM Symposium on Theory of Computing (STOC 2009), pp. 631–638 (2009)
7. Chalopin, J., Gonçalves, D., Ochem, P.: Planar graphs have 1-string representations. Discrete Comput. Geom. **43**(3), 626–647 (2010)
8. Chaplick, S., Kobourov, S.G., Ueckerdt, T.: Equilateral L-contact graphs. In: Brandstädt, A., Jansen, K., Reischuk, R. (eds.) WG 2013. LNCS, vol. 8165, pp. 139–151. Springer, Heidelberg (2013). doi:10.1007/978-3-642-45043-3_13
9. Chaplick, S., Ueckerdt, T.: Planar graphs as VPG-graphs. J. Graph Algorithms Appl. **17**(4), 475–494 (2013)
10. Felsner, S., Knauer, K.B., Mertzios, G.B., Ueckerdt, T.: Intersection graphs of L-shapes and segments in the plane. Discrete Appl. Math. **206**, 48–55 (2016)
11. Francis, M.C., Lahiri, A.: VPG and EPG bend-numbers of Halin graphs (2015). CoRR abs/1505.06036
12. de Fraysseix, H., de Mendez, P.O., Pach, J.: Representation of planar graphs by segments. Intuitive Geom. **63**, 109–117 (1991)
13. Govindan, R., Langston, M.A., Yan, X.: Approximating the pathwidth of outer-planar graphs. Inf. Process. Lett. **68**(1), 17–23 (1998)
14. Keil, J.M., Mitchell, J.S., Pradhan, D., Vatshelle, M.: An algorithm for the maximum weight independent set problem on outerstring graphs. Comput. Geom. **60**, 19–25 (2016)
15. Kobourov, S.G., Ueckerdt, T., Verbeek, K.: Combinatorial and geometric properties of planar Laman graphs. In: SIAM Symposium on Discrete Algorithms (SODA 2013), pp. 1668–1678 (2013)
16. Kratochvíl, J.: String graphs II recognizing string graphs is NP-hard. J. Comb. Theor. Ser. B **52**(1), 67–78 (1991)
17. Kratochvíl, J., Matoušek, J.: Intersection graphs of segments. J. Comb. Theor. Ser. B **62**(2), 289–315 (1994)
18. Middendorf, M., Pfeiffer, F.: The max clique problem in classes of string-graphs. Discrete Math. **108**, 365–372 (1992)
19. Middendorf, M., Pfeiffer, F.: Weakly transitive orientations, hasse diagrams and string graphs. Discrete Math. **111**, 393–400 (1993)
20. Schaefer, M., Sedgwick, E., Štefankovič, D.: Recognizing string graphs is in NP. J. Comput. Syst. Sci. **67**(2), 365–380 (2003)
21. Scheinerman, E.R.: Intersection classes and multiple intersection parameters of graphs. Ph.D. thesis, Princeton University (1984)
22. Wessel, W., Pöschel, R.: On circle graphs. In: Sachs, H. (ed.) Graphs, Hypergraphs and Applications, pp. 207–210. Teubner, Leipzig (1985)

How to Draw a Planarization

Thomas Bläsius[1,2], Marcel Radermacher[1(✉)], and Ignaz Rutter[1]

[1] Faculty of Informatics, Karlsruhe Institute of Technology (KIT),
Karlsruhe, Germany
{radermacher,rutter}@kit.edu
[2] Research Group Algorithm Engineering, Hasso Plattner Institute,
Potsdam, Germany
thomas.blaesius@hpi.de

Abstract. We study the problem of computing straight-line drawings of non-planar graphs with few crossings. We assume that a crossing-minimization algorithm is applied first, yielding a *planarization*, i.e., a planar graph with a dummy vertex for each crossing, that fixes the topology of the resulting drawing. We present and evaluate two different approaches for drawing a planarization in such a way that the edges of the input graph are as straight as possible. The first approach is based on the planarity-preserving force-directed algorithm IMPRED [18], the second approach, which we call *Geometric Planarization Drawing*, iteratively moves vertices to their locally optimal positions in the given initial drawing.

1   Introduction

In his seminal paper "How to Draw a Graph" [20], Tutte showed that every planar graph admits a planar straight-line drawing. His result has been strengthened in various ways, e.g., improving the running time and the required area [3]. In practice, however, many graphs are non-planar and we are interested in finding straight-line drawings with few crossings. Unfortunately, crossing minimization for straight-line drawings (rectilinear crossing number) is $\exists\mathbb{R}$-complete, i.e., as hard as the existential theory of the reals [16]. We thus need to relax either the condition of minimizing the number of crossings or the requirement of straight edges. Approximating the rectilinear crossing number seems difficult, and for complete graphs K_n, it is only known for $n \leq 27$ [1]. We thus follow the second approach, i.e., we insist on a small (though not necessarily minimal) number of crossings and optimize the straightness of the edges in the drawing.

In contrast to the geometric setting, the crossing number for topological drawings has received considerable attention and there is a plethora of results on crossing minimization; see [2] for a survey. The output of these algorithms

This work was initiated within the FYS *Heuristische Verfahren zur Visualisierung von dynamischen Netzwerken*, financially supported by the "Concept for the Future" of KIT within the framework of the German Excellence Initiative. Work was partially supported by grant WA 654/21-1 of the German Research Foundation (DFG).

© Springer International Publishing AG 2017
B. Steffen et al. (Eds.): SOFSEM 2017, LNCS 10139, pp. 295–308, 2017.
DOI: 10.1007/978-3-319-51963-0_23

typically is a planarization G_p of the input graph G together with a planar embedding. To profit from the results in this area, we focus on the problem of drawing G_p such that for each edge of G the corresponding *planarization path* in the drawing of G_p is as straight as possible.

This type of problem is prototypical for several fundamental problems in graph drawing that ask for a geometric realization of a given combinatorial description of a drawing. The most prominent examples are the topology-shape-metrics framework for orthogonal graph drawing [19] and the fundamental ($\exists\mathbb{R}$-complete) problem STRETCHABILITY, which asks whether a given arrangement of pseudo-lines can be realized by geometric lines [14]. There have been several other works that consider the problem of realizing a given combinatorial description of a drawing geometrically. Hong et al. [9] give a characterization and testing algorithm for 1-planar graphs that admit a straight-line drawing. Grilli et al. [7] study the problem of realizing a given simultaneous planar embedding of two (or more) graphs with few bends per edge. Feng et al. [6] study trade-offs between straightness and area of drawings of clustered graphs where clusters are represented by convex drawings. The algorithm of Dwyer et al. [5] minimizes the stress of a layout while preserving the topology of the drawing. Didimo et al. [4] present an algorithm that is able to preserve the topology unless changing the topology improves the number of crossings. Simonetto et al. [18] improve a known force-directed layout algorithm for planar graphs that preserves the combinatorial embedding of the input drawing.

Contribution and Outline. We study the problem of finding a drawing of a given planarization G_p of a graph G such that the planarization paths corresponding to the edges of G are drawn as straight as possible. Throughout, we assume without loss of generality that G_p is biconnected; see Appendix. We present two approaches, one is based on an adaption of IMPRED that includes additional forces to facilitate straightening the planarization paths (Appendix). The second is a geometric framework that iteratively moves the vertices of a given drawing one by one to locally optimal positions such that (i) the planarization and its planar embedding are preserved and (ii) the angles on planarization paths influenced by that vertex are optimized (Sect. 3). This framework has several degrees of freedom, such as the vertex processing order and the exact placement strategy for vertices. We experimentally evaluate the modified IMPRED algorithm (IMPRED++) and several configurations of the Geometric Planarization Drawing approach in a quantitative study (Sect. 4). We show that all our methods significantly increase the straightness compared to the initial drawing and that the geometric algorithms typically outperform IMPRED++ in terms of quality. Statistical tests are used to show that these results are significant with 95% confidence.

2   Preliminaries

Intuitively, a planarization of a graph G is the graph resulting from placing dummy vertices at the intersections of edges in a drawing of G. More formally,

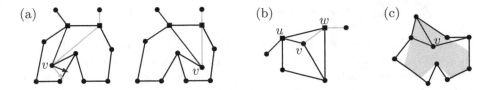

Fig. 1. (a) An initial drawing (left) that is difficult to repair using the force-directed algorithm although v could be moved to an optimal position without violating planarity (right). (b) The closer v lies to the edge uw, the better are the v-active angles. (c) The (green) planarity region of v. (Color figure online)

let $G = (V, E)$ be a graph and let $G_p = (V \dot\cup V_p, E' \dot\cup E_p)$ be a planar graph such that every edge in E_p is incident to at least one vertex in V_p. The vertices in V_p are *dummy vertices*. Then G_p is a *planarization* of G if the following conditions hold. (i) Dummy vertices have degree 4, (ii) $E' \subseteq E$, (iii) for every edge $e = uw \in E \backslash E'$, G_p contains a *planarization path* from u to w whose edges are in E_p and whose internal vertices are in V_p, (iv) for any two distinct edges $e, e' \in E \backslash E'$ the paths p_e and $p_{e'}$ are edge-disjoint, and (v) the paths p_e, $e \in E \backslash E'$ cover all edges in E_p. We call the planarization G_p k-*planar* if the longest planarization path has k dummy vertices.

A *dissected pair* (u, v, w) is a pair $uv, vw \in E_p$ of edges that belong to the same planarization path. The *crossing angle* cr-$\alpha(u, v, w)$ of (u, v, w) is the angle cr-$\alpha(u, v, w) = \pi - \angle(u, v, w)$; A crossing angle is *active* with respect to v (also called v-*active*) if moving v can alter that angle. For a dissected pair (u, v, w), v is a dummy vertex and u and w are *tail* vertices. A dummy that is not a tail is called *pure dummy* and a tail that is not a dummy is called *pure tail*. Vertices that are both, tail and dummy, are called *hybrid*. A vertex that is neither a dummy nor a tail vertex is called *independent*.

Let P be a polygon and let v be a vertex of P. A point p in the interior of P is *visible* from v if the straight line connecting p with v does not intersect an edge of P. The *visibility region* is the set of all points in P that are visible from v. The *size* of a polygon P is the number of its vertices.

A *shrinked* polygon P' of a polygon P is the result of moving the vertices towards the interior of a polygon P with constant speed along the *straight skeleton* of P [10]. A *geometric center* of a polygon P is obtained by shrinking P to a single point.

3   Geometric Planarization Drawing

The spring embedder described in the appendix restricts the movement of each vertex in a very conservative manner, i.e., the restrictions ensure a preservation of the given planar embedding. This may waste a lot of potential; see Fig. 1a. The approach presented in this section aims to tap the full potential by making each movement locally optimal. As the simultaneous movement of multiple vertices leads to non-trivial and non-local dependencies, we move only a single vertex in each step.

To make this precise, we need to answer two questions. First, to which points can a vertex v be moved such that the planar embedding is preserved? Second, which of these points is the best position for v? Concerning the first question, we call the set of points satisfying this property the *planarity region* of v and denote it by $\mathcal{PR}(v)$. The (non-convex) planarity region is independent of the geometric position of v within it surrounding. We show in Sect. 3.1 how to compute $\mathcal{PR}(v)$ efficiently. Concerning the second question, we define the *cost* of a point $p \in \mathcal{PR}(v)$ to be the maximum of all v-active crossing angles when placing v to p. A point in $\mathcal{PR}(v)$ is a *locally optimal* position for v if $\mathcal{PR}(v)$ contains no other point with strictly smaller cost. In Sect. 3.2, we show how to compute an arbitrarily exact approximation of the locally optimal position.

The overall algorithm can be described as follows. We iterate over all vertices of the graph. In each step, the current vertex is moved to its locally optimal position. We repeat until we reach a drawing that is stable or up to a limited number of iterations.

One important degree of freedom in this algorithm is the order in which we iterate over the vertices. Another choice we have not fixed so far is the placement of independent vertices. As an independent vertex has no active angle, each point in its planarity region is equally good. We propose and evaluate different ways of filling these degrees of freedom in Sect. 4.

For a tail or dummy vertex v, it can happen that there exists no locally optimal position due to the fact that $\mathcal{PR}(v)$ is an open set. The cost may for example go down, the closer we place v to an edge connecting two other vertices; see Fig. 1b. We therefore shrink $\mathcal{PR}(v)$ slightly and consider it to be a closed set; see Sect. 4 for more details.

3.1 Planarity Region

Let G_p be a planarization with a given drawing and let v be a vertex of G_p. Let $N(v)$ be the neighbors of v and let f_v be the face of $G_p - v$ that contains the current position of v. Assume for now that f_v is bounded by a simple polygon $\mathrm{surr}(v)$, which we call the *surrounding* of v. Consider a point p in the interior of f_v and assume that we use p as the new position for v. Clearly, the resulting drawing is planar if and only if p is visible from each of v's neighbors; see Fig. 1c. Thus, the planarity region $\mathcal{PR}(v)$ is the intersection of all visibility regions in $\mathrm{surr}(v)$ with respect to the neighbors of v. It follows that the planarity region can be obtained by first computing the visibility polygons of v's neighbors in $\mathrm{surr}(v)$, and then intersecting these visibility polygons. Let n_v be the number of vertices of the surrounding polygon $\mathrm{surr}(v)$ and let d_v be the degree of v. Computing the d_v visibility polygons takes $O(d_v n_v)$ time [12]. To intersect these d_v visibility polygons (each having size $O(n_v)$), one can use a sweep-line algorithm [15] consuming $O((k + d_v n_v) \log n_v)$ time, where k is the number of intersections between segments of the visibility polygons. As there are at most $d_v n_v$ segments, $k \in O(d_v^2 n_v^2)$ holds, yielding the running time $O(d_v^2 n_v^2 \log n_v)$ for computing the planarity region. We can improve this running time as stated in the following theorem; see Appendix for a proof.

Theorem 1. $\mathcal{PR}(v)$ *has size* $O(n_v)$ *and can be computed in* $O(d_v n_v \log n_v)$ *time.*

Now assume surr(v) is not a simple polygon. As we assume G_p to be biconnected, surr(v) has a single connected component. It may, however, have cutvertices with multiple incidences to the interior of surr(v). We eliminate this issue by slightly shrinking surr(v), yielding a simple polygon. Another special case is the outer face. However, we can treat it like an interior face by basically placing the whole drawing in a box.

3.2   Finding a Locally Optimal Position

In this section, we are given a vertex v together with its planarity region $\mathcal{PR}(v)$ and we want to compute a locally optimal position. We consider the two cases where v is a pure tail-vertex and the one where v is a pure dummy-vertex. These two cases can be combined to also handle hybrid vertices. For both cases, our approach is the following. For a given angle α, we show how to test whether $\mathcal{PR}(v)$ contains a point with cost less or equal to α. For any $\varepsilon > 0$ we can then apply $O(\log(1/\varepsilon))$ steps of a binary search over the domain $\alpha \in [0, 2\Pi)$ to find a position in $\mathcal{PR}(v)$ whose cost is at most ε larger than the cost of a locally optimal position.

Placing a Pure Tail Vertex. Let v be a pure tail vertex and let $D(v) \subseteq N(v)$ be the set of dummy neighbors of v; see Fig. 2a. For each dummy neighbor $q \in D(v)$ there is a dissected pair (w_q, q, v) whose angle is active. Note that these are the only active angles of a pure tail vertex. Consider the (oriented) line $\ell(t) = q + t \cdot d_q$ with the direction vector $d_q = q - w_q$. Clearly, placing v onto $\ell(t)$

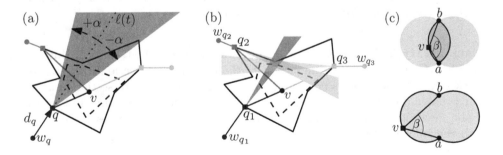

Fig. 2. (a) A cone with respect to one neighbor q of v. (b) The intersection of all cones with the planarity region (dashed) includes possible positions for the vertex v. (c) The angle $\angle avb$ is at least β for $\beta > 90°$ ($\beta < 90°$) if and only if v lies in the intersection (union) of two discs (including its boundary, but excluding a and b).

(for $t > 0$) results in the crossing angle cr-$\alpha(w_q, q, v) = 0$. Moreover, all points in the plane that yield cr-$\alpha(w_q, q, v) \leq \alpha$ lie in a *cone*, i.e., in the intersection (union if $\alpha \geq \pi/2$) of two appropriately chosen half planes.

It follows, that v can be moved to a position with cost α if and only if the intersection of all cones has a non-empty intersection with the planarity region $\mathcal{PR}(v)$; see for example Fig. 2b. As v has at most d_v dummy neighbors (recall that d_v is the degree of v), the intersections of all cones can be computed in $O(d_v^2 \log d_v)$ time using a sweep-line algorithm [15]. Let $\mathcal{C}$ be the resulting intersection of the cones. Testing whether $\mathcal{C}$ and $\mathcal{PR}(v)$ have non-empty intersection can be done in $O((n_v + d_v^2) \log n_v)$ time.

Lemma 1. *Let v be a pure tail vertex and assume $\mathcal{PR}(v)$ has already been computed. For any $\epsilon > 0$, an absolute ϵ-approximation of the locally optimal position can be computed in time $O(\log(1/\epsilon)(n_v + d_v^2) \log n_v)$.*

Placing a Pure Dummy Vertex. A pure dummy vertex v has only two active crossing angles. Let $N(v) = \{a, p, b, q\}$ be the neighbors of v so that (a, v, b) and (p, v, q) are dissected pairs. Consider the angle $\beta = \angle avb$. By a generalization of *Thales' Theorem*, β does not change when moving v on a circular arc with endpoints a and b. Thus, to make sure that β is at least $\pi - \alpha$ (i.e., to ensure that cr-$\alpha(a, v, b) \leq \alpha$), one has to place v in the intersection of two discs (union if $\alpha > \pi/2$); see Fig. 2c. These two disks must have a and b on their boundary and basic geometry shows that their radii has to be $|ab|/(2\sin(\pi - \alpha))$ (which uniquely defines the two disks).

The same applies for $\angle pvq$. Thus, requiring both active crossing angles cr-$\alpha(a, v, b)$ and cr-$\alpha(p, v, q)$ to be at most α restricts the possible positions of the dummy vertex v either to the intersection of four disks, or to the intersection of the union of two disks with the union of two other disks. The check whether this intersection is empty requires time linear in the size of the planarity region.

Lemma 2. *Let v be a pure dummy vertex and assume $\mathcal{PR}(v)$ has already been computed. For any $\epsilon > 0$, an absolute ϵ-approximation of the locally optimal position can be computed in time $O(\log(1/\epsilon)n_v)$.*

Placing a Hybrid Vertex. Let v be a dummy vertex with at least one dummy neighbor. Combining the techniques from the two previous sections, we have to check whether $\mathcal{PR}(v)$ has a non-empty intersection with the intersection of up to four cones and up to four disks. This can again be done in linear time in the size of the planarity region. We can thus conclude (for all three types of vertices) with the following theorem.

Theorem 2. *Let v be a vertex and assume $\mathcal{PR}(v)$ has already been computed. For any $\epsilon > 0$, an absolute ϵ-approximation of the locally optimal position can be computed in time $O(\log(1/\epsilon)(n_v + d_v^2) \log n_v)$.*

Overall Running Time. We have seen that the planarity region for a vertex v can be computed in $O(d_v n_v \log n_v)$ time (Theorem 1) and that a locally optimal position can be approximated in $O(\log(1/\varepsilon)(n_v + d_v^2) \log n_v)$ time. In the following, we assume that ε is a small constant and omit it from the running time.

As the degree d_v of a vertex v is a lower bound for the size n_v of its surounding, the running time of computing the planarity region dominates the time for computing the locally optimal position. Each iteration thus needs $O(\sum_{v \in V} d_v n_v \log n_v)$ time. Bounding vertex face degrees improve the running time; see appendix.

Theorem 3. *One iteration of Geometric Planarization Drawing takes* $O(n^3 \log n)$ *time.*

4   Evaluation

We present an empirical evaluation of our planarization drawing methods. We first discuss the remaining degrees of freedom in our Geometric Planarization Drawing framework. Afterwards, we describe our experimental setup and the statistical tests we use for the evaluation. The first part of our evaluation focuses on the quality of different configurations of our Geometric Planarization Drawing approach. The second set of experiments focuses on the running time. The first set of experiments has a limited time contingent and the second runs until convergence limited by 100 iterations.

4.1   Degrees of Freedom in the Geometric Framework

As pointed out above, our algorithmic framework offers quite a number of degrees of freedom and possibilities for tweaking the outcome of the algorithm.

Initial Drawing. Both, our geometric approach and our implementation of IMPRED, improve an initial drawing of a planarization. While in principle an arbitrary planar straight-line drawing may be used for creating the initial drawing, we restrict ourselves to algorithms implemented within OGDF[1], which offers two algorithms: TUTTELAYOUT [20] and PLANARSTRAIGHTLAYOUT [13]. The former may generate drawings with exponentially bad resolution (creating problems with the floating point arithmetic). Hence, we cannot use these layouts as initial drawing. To gain a broader set of initial drawings we applied 100 iterations of the following two algorithms to the PLANARSTRAIGHTLAYOUT: (i) IMPRED without the forces to optimize the planarization, (ii) the GEOMETRIC CENTER heuristic places every vertex in the geometric center of its planarity region. Due to space constraints we only present the results with IMPRED as initial drawing. For these drawings we observe the worst initial crossing-angles but result in the potentially best overall quality. The results for the other initial drawings.

---

[1] The Open Graph Drawing Framework: ogdf.net.

Vertex Orders. We propose different orders for processing the vertices. An OUTER SHELL is obtained by iteratively removing the vertices of the outer face. An INNER SHELL order is the reverse of an OUTER SHELL, and an ALTERNATING SHELL order is obtained by alternating between the two orders.

Placement of Independent Vertices. For independent vertices, every position in the planarity region is equally good since all crossing angles are inactive. To reduce the restrictions imposed by independent vertices on their neighbors, we suggest two placement strategies for them: RANDOMIZED PLACEMENT, which puts v at a random position in $\mathcal{PR}(v)$, and GEOMETRIC CENTER, where v is placed in the geometric center of $\mathcal{PR}(v)$.

Shrinking the Planarity Region. As mentioned before, a locally optimal position for a vertex v may not exists as $\mathcal{PR}(v)$ is an open set; see Fig. 1b. Moreover, it is visually unpleasant when vertices are placed too close to non-incident edges. We thus shrink $\mathcal{PR}(v)$ as follows. Let D_B be the length of the smallest side of the planarity region's bounding box and let D_v be the distance of v from the boundary of $\mathcal{PR}(v)$. We offset by the minimum of μD_B and D_v, where μ is a parameter. In our experiments we used $\mu = 0.1$. Note that shrinking by at most D_v ensures that the previous position of v remains valid. Thus, we do not have to move v to a worse position due to the shrinking.

Angle Relaxation. While the placement of the tail and hybrid vertices introduced in Sect. 3.2 works independently from the vertex order, it is natural to require that *unplaced* vertices (i.e., vertices that will be moved later in the same iteration) should have a smaller influence on positioning decisions. When performing the binary search in the cone construction, we replace the opening angle α of the cones of unplaced vertices by $(1 - \gamma)\alpha + \gamma\pi$, where $\gamma \in [0, 1]$ is the *angle relaxation weight*, thus widening their cone depending on the value of γ.

Configurations. The presented degrees of freedom allow for many different configurations of our algorithm. Due to space constraints, we focus on the three configurations shown in Table 1 (see Appendix for additional configurations).

Table 1. Configurations for our geometric graph drawing approach.

Configuration	Vertex order	Angle relax. weight
ALTERNATING SHELL	ALTERNATING-SHELL	0.0
SHELL	OUTER-SHELL	0.0
RELAX-1	ALTERNATING-SHELL	0.1

The drawing area is always limited by a box that is twice as large as the bounding box of the initial drawing and use the GEOMETRIC CENTER heuristic for independent vertices.

To allow a fair comparison between all algorithms, each algorithm gets exactly $5n$ s to optimize the drawings. For experiments regarding the running

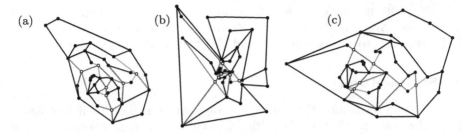

Fig. 3. (a): Initial drawing, (b): Final drawing computed with the SHELL configuration (c) Drawing with the optional post processing step; see Appendix. Unfilled disks represent dummies.

time, we measure the time until convergence limited by 100 iterations. Figure 3 shows an example, where our geometric algorithm finds a nearly optimal solution; also see Appendix.

4.2 Experimental Setup

For a set of graphs $\mathcal{G}$ we want to compare the quality of two sets of drawings Γ_1, Γ_2 of these graphs. We use the crossing-angles to measure the quality of a drawing. Aggregating the crossing-angles per graph yields a loss of information, thus we compare the crossing-angles directly. Let D be the set of all dissected-pairs in $\mathcal{G}$ and $\{\text{cr-}\alpha_i(u, v, w) \mid (u, v, w) \in D\}$ the set of all crossing-angles in drawing $\Gamma_i, i = 1, 2$. The drawings Γ_1 have an *advantage* of $\Delta \in \mathbb{N}_0$ over the drawing Γ_2 if for more then 50% of the dissected pairs (u, v, w) the inequality $\text{cr-}\alpha_1(u, v, w) + \Delta < \text{cr-}\alpha_2(u, v, w)$ holds.

Further, we are interested in the smallest angle $\delta \in \mathbb{N}_0$ such that the angles in our drawings of a graph G_p are smaller then δ. We define a hypothetical drawing called δ-*drawing* where each crossing angle is δ. For each algorithm, we seek the smallest angle δ such that the resulting drawing has an advantage over the δ-drawing.

To take the lengths of the planarization paths into account, we a priori define three classes of instances: LOW($\mathcal{L}$), MEDIUM($\mathcal{M}$) and HIGH($\mathcal{H}$). A planarization belongs to $\mathcal{L}$ and to $\mathcal{H}$ if it is at most 4- and at least 9-planar, respectively. Instances in the class $\mathcal{M}$ are k-planar with $4 < k < 9$.

We ran the algorithms on 100 randomly selected non-planar Rome graphs[2]. For each of them, we used the (single) non-planar biconnected component. There are 68 graphs with in total 604 dummy vertices in $\mathcal{L}$, 26 graphs with in total 959 dummy vertices in $\mathcal{M}$, and 6 graphs with in total 443 dummy vertices in $\mathcal{H}$. We compare the crossing angles directly and do not aggregate them per graph. Thus, we have 4012 samples in total (twice the number of dummy vertices). We partitioned the set of samples into a training set, containing 20% of the samples, and a verification set containing the remaining 80%.

---

[2] graphdrawing.org/data.html.

We use OGDF[3] to planarize the graphs [8] and to compute the initial drawing [13]. We use the libraries CGAL[4] to compute line arrangements, STALGO [10,11] to shrink polygons, and GMP[5] to represent coordinates.

4.3 Statistical Test

Our evaluation focuses on the comparison of crossing angles in different drawings of the same graph, e.g., the initial drawing vs. the final drawing of some algorithm. Since the underlying distribution of the angles is unknown and not likely to be, e.g., normal, the median and quantiles are not useful to compare two drawings. Instead we use a binomial test, which compares two dependent samples and is independent of the underlying distribution [17].

For each dissected pair (u, v, w) we compare the crossing angles cr-$\alpha_1(u, v, w)$ and cr-$\alpha_2(u, v, w)$ generated by two different algorithms. The comparison cr-$\alpha_1(u, v, w) + \Delta <$ cr-$\alpha_2(u, v, w)$ yields a sequence of 0 s and 1 s. With the binomial test we check whether 1 s occur significantly more often than 0 s at a significance level of $\alpha = 0.05$.

In order to formulate our hypothesis we compute the maximum Δ such that the binomial test shows significance on the training set. In order to get a robust and likely hypothesis we choose $3/4 \cdot \Delta$ as the conjectured value. Hypothesis regarding the δ drawings conjecture that the angles are smaller then $4/3 \cdot \delta$, where δ was computed on the training set.

4.4 Quality of the Drawings

In this Section we discuss the quality of our drawings. The evaluation is guided by the following hypotheses.

- (I) Geometric Planarization Drawing approach and IMPRED++ advantage of at least 4° over the initial drawing.
- (II) Geometric Planarization Drawing has an advantage of at least 6° over IMPRED++.
- (III) In class $\mathcal{H}$, RELAX-1 has an advantage over ALTERNATING-SHELL (due to the weakened influence of unplaced vertices).

We use Figs. 4 and 5a to show whether or not the binomial tests support our hypotheses. A value Δ in a cell in Fig. 4 shows that the algorithm on the x-axis has an hypothetical advantage of Δ over the algorithm on the y-axis. These values are computed on the training set. A green cell means that we can accept the hypothesis with a confidence of 95%. On the contrary, with a red cell we have to reject the hypothesis. An empty cell, indicates that the algorithm did not have an advantage on the training set.

---

[3] ogdf.net.

[4] cgal.org.

[5] gmplib.org.

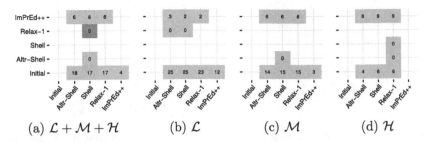

Fig. 4. Advantage of each configuration (x-axis) compared to each configuration (y-axis), factored by the classes $\mathcal{L}$, $\mathcal{M}$, and $\mathcal{H}$.

For example, in the class $\mathcal{H}$ (see Fig. 4d), we conjecture, based on the observation in the training set, that the drawings of the SHELL configuration have an advantage of 9° over the drawings of IMPRED++. Recall, that having an advantage means that 50% of the crossing angles, plus an additional buffer of 9°, of the first drawings are smaller then the crossing angles of the second. Since the cell is green, the binomial test on the verification set says that we can accept the hypothesis with a confidence of 95%.

By Fig. 5a, for class $\mathcal{L}$ we can say with 95% confidence that 50% of the crossing angles of the SHELL configuration are smaller then the crossing-angles of a drawing where each crossing angle is 2°. We now discuss our hypotheses.

Hypothesis (I) Advantage over the INITIAL *drawing.* The binomial tests support this hypothesis for every configuration and for IMPRED++; see Fig. 4. Note that the advantage over the INITIAL drawing decreases with the length of the longest planarization path in a drawing. The Figure indicates, that IMPRED++ does not have an advantage over the INITIAL drawing on long planarization paths. Figure 4a indicates that there is support for the hypothesis when considering all instances (not separated into classes).

Hypothesis (II) Advantage over IMPRED++. Figure 4 shows that for $\Delta = 6$ we have can accept the hypothesis with high confidence for every configuration and class.

Hypothesis (III) Angle relaxation helps with long planarization paths. Figure 4d shows for instances of the class $\mathcal{H}$ that the RELAX-1 configurations has a (small) advantage. Figure 5a further shows that this configuration tends to produce smaller crossing angle in instances of $\mathcal{H}$ in comparison to the other configurations.

4.5   Running Time

We conclude the Section with a running time analysis. Table 2 shows a descriptive evaluation of the running time of our Geometric Planarization Drawing approach.

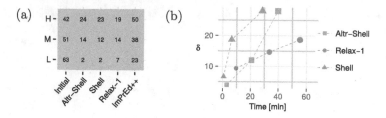

Fig. 5. (a) The minimum δ for each configuration (x-axis) such that it has an advantage over a δ-drawing, factored by the classes $\mathcal{L}$, $\mathcal{M}$, and $\mathcal{H}$ (y-axis). (b) Time until convergence versus the δ-value. Symbol sizes indicate the classes $\mathcal{L}$, $\mathcal{M}$, and $\mathcal{H}$. Note: the δ-values of both figures are not coincident due to different experimental setups. The setup for the quality assessment does not allow a running time analysis.

Table 2. Running time measurements for each configuration.

Configuration	Time per iteration			# iterations			Total time		
	$\mathcal{L}$	$\mathcal{M}$	$\mathcal{H}$	$\mathcal{L}$	$\mathcal{M}$	$\mathcal{H}$	$\mathcal{L}$	$\mathcal{M}$	$\mathcal{H}$
ALTERNATING SHELL	8.3 s	15.0 s	24.8 s	20.2	82.4	93.0	2.9 min	20.6 min	39.6 min
SHELL	8.1 s	18.0 s	25.1 s	5.5	22.4	66.6	0.7 min	6.4 min	28.4 min
RELAX-1	8.2 s	20.3 s	33.5 s	59.8	100.0	100.0	9.5 min	33.6 min	55.3 min

Running Time vs. Quality. We use the δ-values to compare the quality of the drawings with respect to the running time. Each point in Fig. 5b represents final drawings of a different configuration, divided into the introduced classes. The figure compares the average running time required to compute the final drawing against the smallest δ computed with the introduced methodology; all δ-value can be accepted with high confidence. For class $\mathcal{L}$ the configuration the (ALTERNATING) SHELL configurations have small angles and require only few minutes to finish. With increasing complexity of the drawings the relevance of the angle relaxation increases. For class $\mathcal{M}$ the ALTERNATING SHELL configuration has the smallest δ-value but is slower then the SHELL configuration. For drawings of class $\mathcal{H}$, there is no clear dominance. In class $\mathcal{H}$ the RELAX-1 configuration yields the best results but the SHELL configuration requires less time. We suggest to use the SHELL configuration for less complex drawings and when computing time is relevant and for drawings with increasing complexity the RELAX-1 configuration.

5   Conclusion

We presented two approaches for drawing planarizations such that the edges of the original (non-planar) graph are as straight as possible. Our experiments show that the Geometric Planarization Drawing approach has an significant advantage over our adaption of the force-directed algorithm IMPRED. For instances with short planarization paths, we get very good crossing angles. Even though the crossing angles are worse for instances with longer planarization paths, our Geometric Planarization Drawing approach still significantly improves the angles of the initial drawing. Concerning future research, it would be interesting to investigate the effect of different initial drawings and to see how our geometric approach in Sect. 3 performs when additional optimization criteria such as the angular resolution are incorporated.

References

1. Ábrego, B.M., Fernández-Merchant, S., Leaños, J., Salazar, G.: The maximum number of halving lines and the rectilinear crossing number of kn for n ≤ 27. Electron. Notes Discrete Math. **30**, 261–266 (2008)
2. Buchheim, C., Chimani, M., Gutwenger, C., Jünger, M., Mutzel, P.: Crossings and planarization. In: Handbook of Graph Drawing and Visualization, pp. 43–85. Chapman and Hall/CRC (2013)
3. Chambers, E.W., Eppstein, D., Goodrich, M.T., Löffler, M.: Drawing graphs in the plane with a prescribed outer face and polynomial area. J. Graph Alg. Appl. **16**(2), 243–259 (2012)
4. Didimo, W., Liotta, G., Romeo, S.A.: Topology-driven force-directed algorithms. In: Brandes, U., Cornelsen, S. (eds.) GD 2010. LNCS, vol. 6502, pp. 165–176. Springer, Heidelberg (2011). doi:10.1007/978-3-642-18469-7_15
5. Dwyer, T., Marriott, K., Wybrow, M.: Topology preserving constrained graph layout. In: Tollis, I.G., Patrignani, M. (eds.) GD 2008. LNCS, vol. 5417, pp. 230–241. Springer, Heidelberg (2009). doi:10.1007/978-3-642-00219-9_22
6. Feng, Q.-W., Cohen, R.F., Eades, P.: How to draw a planar clustered graph. In: Du, D.-Z., Li, M. (eds.) COCOON 1995. LNCS, vol. 959, pp. 21–30. Springer, Heidelberg (1995). doi:10.1007/BFb0030816
7. Grilli, L., Hong, S.-H., Kratochvíl, J., Rutter, I.: Drawing simultaneously embedded graphs with few bends. In: Duncan, C., Symvonis, A. (eds.) GD 2014. LNCS, vol. 8871, pp. 40–51. Springer, Heidelberg (2014). doi:10.1007/978-3-662-45803-7_4
8. Gutwenger, C., Mutzel, P., Weiskircher, R.: Inserting an edge into a planar graph. Algorithmica **41**(4), 289–308 (2005)
9. Hong, S.-H., Eades, P., Liotta, G., Poon, S.-H.: Fáry's theorem for 1-planar graphs. In: Gudmundsson, J., Mestre, J., Viglas, T. (eds.) COCOON 2012. LNCS, vol. 7434, pp. 335–346. Springer, Heidelberg (2012). doi:10.1007/978-3-642-32241-9_29
10. Huber, S., Held, M.: Motorcycle graphs: stochastic properties motivate an efficient yet simple implementation. J. Exper. Algo. **16**, 1–3 (2011)
11. Huber, S., Held, M.: A fast straight-skeleton algorithm based on generalized motorcycle graphs. Int. J. Comput. Geom. Appl. **22**(05), 471–498 (2012)
12. Joe, B., Simpson, R.B.: Corrections to Lee's visibility polygon algorithm. BIT Num. Math. **27**(4), 458–473 (1987)
13. Kant, G.: Drawing planar graphs using the canonical ordering. Algorithmica **16**(1), 4–32 (1996)
14. Mnev, N.E.: The universality theorems on the classification problem of configuration varieties and convex polytopes varieties. In: Viro, O.Y., Vershik, A.M. (eds.) Topology and Geometry — Rohlin Seminar. LNM, vol. 1346, pp. 527–543. Springer, Heidelberg (1988). doi:10.1007/BFb0082792

15. Nievergelt, J., Preparata, F.P.: Plane-sweep algorithms for intersecting geometric figures. Commun. ACM **25**(10), 739–747 (1982)
16. Schaefer, M.: Complexity of some geometric and topological problems. In: Eppstein, D., Gansner, E.R. (eds.) GD 2009. LNCS, vol. 5849, pp. 334–344. Springer, Heidelberg (2010). doi:10.1007/978-3-642-11805-0_32
17. Sheskin, D.J.: Handbook of Parametric and Nonparametric Statistical Procedures. Chapman and Hall/CRC (2003)
18. Simonetto, P., Archambault, D., Auber, D., Bourqui, R.: ImPrEd: an improved force-directed algorithm that prevents nodes from crossing edges. Comput. Graph. Forum (EuroVis 2011) **30**(3), 1071–1080 (2011)
19. Tamassia, R.: On embedding a graph in the grid with the minimum number of bends. SIAM J. Comput. **16**(3), 421–444 (1987)
20. Tutte, W.T.: How to draw a graph. Proc. Lond. Math. Soc. **s3–13**(1), 743–767 (1963)

Finding Largest Common Substructures of Molecules in Quadratic Time

Andre Droschinsky, Nils Kriege$^{(\boxtimes)}$, and Petra Mutzel

Department of Computer Science, Technische Universität Dortmund,
Dortmund, Germany
{andre.droschinsky,nils.kriege,petra.mutzel}@tu-dortmund.de

Abstract. Finding the common structural features of two molecules is a fundamental task in cheminformatics. Most drugs are small molecules, which can naturally be interpreted as graphs. Hence, the task is formalized as maximum common subgraph problem. Albeit the vast majority of molecules yields outerplanar graphs this problem remains NP-hard.

We consider a variation of the problem of high practical relevance, where the rings of molecules must not be broken, i.e., the block and bridge structure of the input graphs must be retained by the common subgraph. We present an algorithm for finding a maximum common connected induced subgraph of two given outerplanar graphs subject to this constraint. Our approach runs in time $\mathcal{O}(\Delta n^2)$ in outerplanar graphs on n vertices with maximum degree Δ. This leads to a quadratic time complexity in molecular graphs, which have bounded degree. The experimental comparison on synthetic and real-world datasets shows that our approach is highly efficient in practice and outperforms comparable state-of-the-art algorithms.

1 Introduction

The maximum common subgraph problem arises in many application domains, where it is necessary to elucidate common structural features of objects represented as graphs. In cheminformatics this problem has been extensively studied [5,12,13] and is often referred to as maximum or *largest common substructure problem*. Two variants of the problem can be distinguished: The maximum common induced subgraph problem (MCIS) is to find isomorphic induced subgraphs of two given graphs with the largest possible number of vertices. The maximum common edge subgraph problem (MCES) does not require that common subgraphs are induced and aims at maximizing the number of edges. Both variants can be reduced to a maximum clique problem in the product graph of the two input graphs [12]. In cheminformatics MCES is used more frequently since it (i) reflects the notion of chemical similarity more adequately [12], and (ii) can reduce the running time of product graph based algorithms [11]. Although such algorithms still have exponential running time in the worst case, they are commonly applied to molecular graphs in practice [12].

This work was supported by the German Research Foundation (DFG), priority programme "Algorithms for Big Data" (SPP 1736).

© Springer International Publishing AG 2017
B. Steffen et al. (Eds.): SOFSEM 2017, LNCS 10139, pp. 309–321, 2017.
DOI: 10.1007/978-3-319-51963-0_24

However, there are several restricted graph classes which render polynomial time algorithms possible [1,2,15]. The seminal work in this direction is attributed to J. Edmonds [10], who proposed a polynomial time algorithm for the maximum common subtree problem. Here, the given graphs and the desired common subgraph must be trees. Recently, it was shown that this problem can be solved in time $\mathcal{O}(\Delta n^2)$ for (unrooted) trees on n vertices with maximum degree Δ [3]. The (induced) subgraph isomorphism problem (SI) is to decide if a pattern graph is isomorphic to an (induced) subgraph of another graph and is generalized by MCIS and MCES, respectively. Both variants of SI are NP-complete, even when the pattern is a forest and the other graph a tree [6]; just as when the pattern is a tree and the other is outerplanar [14]. On the other hand, when both graphs are biconnected and outerplanar, induced SI can be solved in time $\mathcal{O}(n^2)$ [14] and SI in $\mathcal{O}(n^3)$ [9]. These complexity results and the demand in cheminformatics lead to the consideration of MCES under the so-called *block and bridge preserving* (BBP) constraint [13], which requires the common subgraph to retain the local connectivity of the input graphs. BBP-MCES is not only computable in polynomial-time, but also yields meaningful results for cheminformatics. A polynomial-time algorithm was recently proposed for BBP-MCIS, which requires time $\mathcal{O}(n^6)$ in series-parallel and $\mathcal{O}(n^5)$ in outerplanar graphs [7].

Most of the above mentioned polynomial time algorithms are either not applicable to molecular graphs or impractical due to high constants. A positive exception is the BBP-MCES approach of [13], which has been shown to outperform state-of-the-art algorithms on molecular graphs in practice. This algorithm is stated to have a running time of $\mathcal{O}(n^{2.5})$, but in fact leads to a running time of $\Omega(n^4)$ in the worst case [3].

Our Contribution. We take up the concept of BBP and propose a novel BBP-MCIS algorithm with running time $\mathcal{O}(\Delta n^2)$ in outerplanar graphs with n vertices and maximum degree Δ. We obtain this result by combining ideas of [3] for the maximum common subtree problem with a new algorithm for biconnected MCIS in biconnected outerplanar graphs. For this subproblem we develop a quadratic time algorithm, which exploits the fact that the outerplanar embedding of a biconnected outerplanar graph is unique. Moreover, the algorithm allows to list all solutions in quadratic total time. Our approach supports to solve BBP-MCIS w.r.t. a weight function on the mapped vertices and edges. The experiments show that BBP-MCIS in almost all cases yields the same results as BBP-MCES for molecular graphs under an adequate weight function. Our method outperforms in terms of efficiency the BBP-MCES approach of [13] by orders magnitude.

2   Preliminaries

We consider simple undirected graphs. Let $G = (V, E)$ be a graph, we refer to the set of *vertices* V by $V(G)$ or V_G and to the set of *edges* by $E(G)$ or E_G. An edge connecting two vertices $u, v \in V$ is denoted by uv or vu. The *order* $|G|$ of a graph G is its number of vertices. Let $V' \subseteq V$, then the graph $G[V'] = (V', E')$ with

$E' = \{uv \in E \mid u, v \in V'\}$ is called *induced* subgraph. For $U \subseteq V$ we write $G \backslash U$ for $G[V \backslash U]$. A graph is *connected* if there is a path between any two vertices. A *connected component* of a graph G is a maximal connected subgraph of G. A graph $G = (V, E)$ with $|V| \geq 3$ is called *biconnected* if $G \backslash \{v\}$ is connected for any $v \in V$. A maximal biconnected subgraph of a graph G is called *block*. If an edge uv is not contained in any block, the subgraph $(\{u, v\}, \{uv\})$ is called a *bridge*. A vertex v of G is called *cutvertex*, if $G \backslash \{v\}$ consists of more connected components than G. A graph is *planar* if it admits a drawing on the plane such that no two edges cross. The connected regions of the drawing enclosed by the edges are called *faces*, the unbounded region is referred to as *outer face*. An edge and a face are said to be *incident* if the edge touches the face. Two faces are *adjacent* if they are incident with a common edge. A graph is called *outerplanar* if it admits a drawing on the plane without crossings, in which every vertex lies on the boundary of the outer face. A *matching* in a graph $G = (V, E)$ is a set of edges $M \subseteq E$, such that no two edges share a vertex. A matching M is *maximal* if there is no other matching $M' \supsetneq M$ and *perfect*, if $2|M| = |V|$. A *weighted graph* is a graph endowed with a function $w : E \to \mathbb{R}$. A matching M in a weighted graph has weight by $W(M) := \sum_{e \in M} w(e)$; it is a *maximum weight matching* (MWM) if there is no matching M' of G with $W(M') > W(M)$.

An *isomorphism* between two graphs G and H is a bijection $\phi : V(G) \to V(H)$ such that $uv \in E(G) \Leftrightarrow \phi(u)\phi(v) \in E(H)$. A *common (induced) subgraph isomorphism* is an isomorphism between (induced) subgraphs $G' \subseteq G$ and $H' \subseteq H$. A subgraph $G' \subseteq G$ is *block and bridge preserving* (BBP) if (i) each bridge in G' is a bridge in G, (ii) any two edges in different blocks in G' are in different blocks in G. A common subgraph isomorphism ϕ is BBP if both subgraphs are BBP, it is *maximal* if it cannot be extended. Molecular graphs are typically annotated with atom and bond types, which should be preserved under isomorphisms. More general, we allow for a weight function $\omega : (V_G \times V_H) \cup (E_G \times E_H) \to \mathbb{R}^{\geq 0} \cup \{-\infty\}$. The weight $\mathcal{W}(\phi)$ of an isomorphism ϕ between G and H under ω is the sum of the weights $\omega(v, \phi(v))$ and $\omega(uv, \phi(v)\phi(v))$ for all vertices v and edges uv mapped by ϕ. A common subgraph isomorphism ϕ is *maximum* if its weight $\mathcal{W}(\phi)$ is maximum. A maximum isomorphism does not map any vertices or edges contributing weight $-\infty$ and we call these pairs *forbidden*. We further define $[1..k] := \{1, \ldots, k\}$ for $k \in \mathbb{N}$.

3   Biconnected MCIS in Outerplanar Graphs

In this section we present an algorithm to determine the weight of a maximum common biconnected induced subgraph isomorphism (2-MCIS) of two biconnected outerplanar graphs. First we show how to compute the maximal common biconnected subgraph isomorphisms. Since these may contain forbidden vertex and edge pairs, we then describe how to obtain the weight of a maximum solution from them. Finally we show how to output one or all maximum solutions.

Outerplanar graphs are well-studied and have several characteristic properties, see [14] for further information. In particular, our algorithm exploits the fact that biconnected outerplanar graphs have a unique outerplanar embedding in the plane (up to the mirror image). In these embeddings, every edge is incident to exactly two faces that are uniquely defined. We observe that the mapping is determined by starting parameters, i.e., an edge of both input graphs together with the mapping of their endpoints and incident faces.

We say a face is mapped by an isomorphism ϕ if all the vertices bordering the face are mapped by ϕ. We distinguish four cases to describe the mapping of an edge $uv \in E(G)$ to an edge $u'v' \in E(H)$ by an isomorphism ϕ between biconnected induced subgraphs. Assume the edge uv is incident to the faces A and B in G and $u'v'$ is incident to A' and B' in H, see Fig. 1(a). At least one face incident to uv must be mapped by ϕ, since the common subgraph must be biconnected. For the sake of simplicity of the case distinction, we also associate the two other faces, regardless of whether they are mapped or not. The isomorphism may map the endpoints of the edges in two different ways—just as the two incident faces. We can distinguish the following four cases: (1) $u \mapsto u'$, $v \mapsto v'$, $A \mapsto A'$, $B \mapsto B'$, (2) $u \mapsto v'$, $v \mapsto u'$, $A \mapsto A'$, $B \mapsto B'$, (3) $u \mapsto u'$, $v \mapsto v'$, $A \mapsto B'$, $B \mapsto A'$, (4) $u \mapsto v'$, $v \mapsto u'$, $A \mapsto B'$, $B \mapsto A'$.

Given an isomorphism ϕ between biconnected common induced subgraphs that maps the two endpoints of an edge e, let the function $\text{type}(e, \phi) \in [1..4]$ determine the type of the mapping as above. The following result is the key to obtain our efficient algorithm.

Lemma 1. *Let ϕ and ϕ' be maximal isomorphisms between biconnected common induced subgraphs of the biconnected outerplanar graphs G and H. Assume $e \in E(G)$ is mapped to the same edge $e' \in E(H)$ by ϕ and ϕ', then*

$$\text{type}(e, \phi) = \text{type}(e, \phi') \iff \phi' = \phi.$$

Proof. It is obvious that the direction $\impliedby$ is correct. We prove the implication $\implies$. Since the common subgraph is required to be biconnected, the isomorphisms ϕ and ϕ' both must map at least one face of G incident to the edge e to a face of H incident to e'. The two faces as well as the mapping of endpoints of the two edges are uniquely determined by the type of the mapping. We consider the mapping of the vertices on the cyclic border of these faces. Since the mapping of the endpoints of e are fixed, the mapping of all vertices on the border of the face is unambiguously determined. Since the common subgraph is required to be biconnected, every extension of the mapping must include all the vertices of a neighboring face. For this face, again, the mapping of the endpoints of the shared edge implicates the mapping of all vertices on the cyclic border and the extension is unambiguous. Therefore, the mapping can be successively extended to an unmapped face. Consequently $\phi(u) = \phi'(u)$ holds for all $u \in \text{dom}(\phi) \cap \text{dom}(\phi')$. Since ϕ and ϕ' are maximal it is not possible that one of them can be extended and, hence, we must have $\text{dom}(\phi) = \text{dom}(\phi')$ and the result follows. $\square$

The proof of Lemma 1 constructively shows how to obtain a maximal solution given two edges $uv \in E(G)$, $u'v' \in E(H)$ and a type parameter $t \in [1..4]$. We assume that this approach is realized by the procedure MAXIMALISO($uv, u'v', t$), which returns the unique maximal isomorphism that maps the two given edges according to the specified type. The algorithm can be implemented by means of a tree structure that encodes the neighboring relation between inner faces, e.g., SP-trees as in [7,8] or weak dual graphs similar to the approach of [14]. The running time to compute a maximal solution ϕ then is $\mathcal{O}(|\phi|) \subseteq \mathcal{O}(n)$. Note that for some edge pairs not all four types of mappings are possible. The type $t \in [1..4]$ is *valid* for a pair of edges if at least one incident face can be mapped according to type t, i.e., the edges are incident to faces that are bordered by the same number of vertices.

A maximal solution ϕ may map vertex and edge pairs that are forbidden according to the weight function. In order to obtain the maximum weight, we split ϕ into *split isomorphisms* $\phi_1, \ldots, \phi_k$ such that each (i) has non-negative weight and (ii) again is an isomorphism between biconnected induced common subgraphs. The split isomorphisms can be obtained in time $\mathcal{O}(|\phi|)$ as follows. We consider the graph $G' = G[\mathrm{dom}(\phi)]$. For every forbidden edge uv that is incident to two inner faces in G', we split the graph into $G'_i[V(C_i) \cup \{u, v\}]$, where C_i is a connected component of $G' \setminus \{u, v\}$, $i \in [1..2]$. In these graphs we delete the forbidden vertices and edges and determine the blocks $B_1, \ldots, B_k$. Then ϕ, restricted to the vertices $V(B_i)$ of a block B_i, yields the split isomorphism ϕ_i for $i \in [1..k]$. This approach is realized by the function SPLITISO(ϕ) used in the following. Every edge $e \in E(G)$ is mapped by at most one of the resulting isomorphisms, referred to by ϕ_e. Every 2-MCIS is a split isomorphism obtained from some maximal solution.

Algorithm 1 uses a table $D(e, f, t)$, $e \in E(G)$, $f \in E(H)$, $t \in [1..4]$ storing the weight of a 2-MCIS under the constraint that it maps e to f according to type t. The size of the table is $4|E(G)||E(H)| \in \mathcal{O}(nm)$, where $n = |V(G)|$ and $m = |V(H)|$. The algorithm starts with all pairs of edges and all valid types of mappings between them. For each, the maximal isomorphism between biconnected common induced subgraphs is computed by extending this initial mapping. By splitting the maximal solution, multiple valid isomorphisms with non-negative weight are obtained. These weights are then stored in D for all pairs of edges contained in ϕ considering the type of the mapping. This includes the $-\infty$ weights occurring if there are forbidden vertices or edges. Keeping these values allows to avoid generating the same isomorphism multiple times. The main procedure loops over all pairs of edges and the four possible mappings for each pair. Note that a mapping ϕ and its split isomorphisms are computed in time $\mathcal{O}(|\phi|) \subseteq \mathcal{O}(n)$. Improved analysis gives the following result.

Theorem 1. *Algorithm 1 computes the weight of a 2-MCIS between biconnected outerplanar graphs G and H in time $\mathcal{O}(|G||H|)$.*

Proof. We allocate the costs for a call of MAXIMALISO followed by SPLITISO to cells of the table D. A mapping ϕ containing k edges is computed in time $\mathcal{O}(k)$ and as a result exactly k cells of the table D are filled with a value. The value of a cell is computed at most once: Line 2 assures that an edge mapping of a specific type is not used as initial mapping when the corresponding cell is

---

Algorithm 1. 2-MCIS in outerplanar graphs

Input   : Biconnected outerplanar graphs G and H.
Output : Weight of a maximum common biconnected subgraph isomorphism.
Data   : Table $D(e, f, t)$, $e \in E(G)$, $f \in E(H)$, $t \in [1..4]$ storing the weight of
             a 2-MCIS ϕ mapping e to f with type$(e, \phi) = t$.

1 **forall the** $uv \in E(G)$, $u'v' \in E(H)$ and $t \in [1..4]$ **do**
2   **if** *type* t *valid for* uv *and* $u'v'$ **and** $D(uv, u'v', t)$ *undefined* **then**
3          $\phi \leftarrow$ MAXIMALISO$(uv, u'v', t)$
4          $(\phi_1, \ldots, \phi_k) \leftarrow$ SPLITISO(ϕ)
5   **forall the** *edges* $e \in E(G)$ *mapped to* $f \in E(H)$ *by* ϕ **do**
6              $D(e, f, \text{type}(e, \phi)) \leftarrow \begin{cases} W(\phi_e) & \text{if } e \text{ is mapped by the split iso. } \phi_e \\ -\infty & \text{otherwise.} \end{cases}$

7 **return** maximum entry in D

---

already filled. Every initial mapping that is extended must lead to an isomorphism containing only edge mappings associated with undefined cells according to Lemma 1. Therefore the total costs of the algorithm can be allocated to cells of D, such that each cell pays a constant amount. This proves that the total running time is bounded by the size of the table, which is $\mathcal{O}(|G||H|)$. □

We can easily modify the algorithm to enumerate all maximum isomorphisms without affecting the total running time. First we run Algorithm 1 once to obtain the maximum weight $W_{\max}$. Then we run a modified version of Algorithm 1 that outputs every split isomorphism ϕ_i of size $W(\phi_i) = W_{\max}$ as soon as it is found, right after SPLITISO(ϕ) is called in line 4.

4   Solving BBP-MCIS in Outerplanar Graphs

In the previous section we have presented an algorithm to compute a 2-MCIS between two biconnected outerplanar graphs. In this section we will generalize it to compute a BBP-MCIS between two outerplanar graphs G and H. In the following we assume the isomorphisms to be BBP. We require the input graphs to be connected. Otherwise we compute a BBP-MCIS for all pairs of connected components and select an isomorphism of maximum weight.

We proceed as follows. First, we give insight into the *BC-tree* data structure, which helps to partition the set S of all BBP common subgraph isomorphisms between G and H into subsets w.r.t. certain conditions. Then we compute an isomorphism of maximum weight in each of the subsets using a dynamic programming approach similar to the one used in [3] to solve the maximum common subtree problem. Among the computed isomorphisms we output one with maximum weight, thus a BBP-MCIS.

The BC-tree Data Structure. Given a BBP-MCIS, we can observe that bridges of G are mapped to bridges of H and that edges in one block of G can

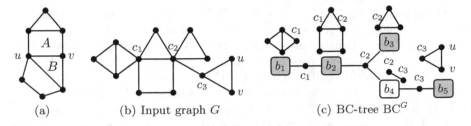

Fig. 1. A biconnected outerplanar graph (a) with an edge uv incident to the faces A and B; a connected outerplanar graph (b) and its BC-tree (c). Block nodes have a gray background, while bridge nodes are not filled. The solid black nodes are the cutvertices. The corresponding subgraphs of G are shown above the block and bridge nodes.

only be mapped to edges contained in exactly one block of H, such that the mapped edges form a biconnected common subgraph. For a connected graph G let C^G denote the set of cutvertices, Bl^G the set of blocks and Br^G the set of bridges and $B^G := Bl^G \cup Br^G$. The *BC-tree* BC^G of G is the tree with nodes $B^G \cup C^G$ and edges between nodes $b \in B^G$ and $c \in C^G$ iff $c \in V(b)$. We refer to the vertices of the BC-tree as B- and C-nodes and distinguish block nodes from bridge nodes. An example of a graph G and its BC-tree BC^G is shown in Fig. 1. For any graph G, we define $CC(V', U)$ as the connected component of $G[V']$ that includes at least one vertex of U. We allow only such sets U, where the component is unambiguous. For example, in Fig. 1, $CC(V_G \backslash V_{b_2}, V_{b_4})$ is the graph $G[\{c_3, u, v\}]$.

Partitioning of all BBP Isomorphisms $\mathcal{S}$ into $\mathcal{S} = \bigcup_x \mathcal{S}_x$. First, we define $\mathcal{S}_1$ and $\mathcal{S}_2$. Let $b \in B^G$ be an arbitrary block or bridge in G. We define $\mathcal{S}_1$ to contain all isomorphisms ϕ where at least one edge in b is mapped by the isomorphisms, i.e., $|\mathrm{dom}(\phi) \cap V(b)| \geq 2$. $\mathcal{S}_2$ is defined to contain all isomorphisms where exactly one vertex in b is mapped by the isomorphism. We can observe that $\mathcal{S}_1$ and $\mathcal{S}_2$ are disjoint and all other isomorphisms between G and H do not contain any vertices of b. Let $N = \{b_1, \ldots, b_k\} \subseteq B^G$ be the blocks and bridges that share a cutvertex with b, i.e., $b_i \in N$ iff there is a node $c \in C^G$ with bc and cb_i edges in the BC-tree BC^G. Any isomorphism ϕ that maps no vertex of b, maps vertices of at most one node b_i, because $G[\mathrm{dom}(\phi)]$ is connected by definition. For every b_i we recursively define sets $\mathcal{S}_x$ of isomorphisms as described above that map only vertices of $CC(V_G \backslash V_b, V_{b_i})$.

As example consider Fig. 1(c) and let $b := b_2$. $\mathcal{S}_1$ consist of isomorphisms which map at least one edge of b_2 to an edge in H. The isomorphisms in $\mathcal{S}_2$ map exactly one vertex of $V(b)$ to H. The recursion continues on $N = \{b_1, b_3, b_4\}$. Three additional sets consist of isomorphisms which map at least one edge (and three more for exactly one vertex) of $V(b_i)$, $i \in \{1, 3, 4\}$, but no vertex of $V(b_2)$, operating on $CC(V_G \backslash V_{b_2}, V_{b_i})$. The recursion for $b := b_4$ continues with $N = \{b_5\}$ and two additional sets. Some of the sets $\mathcal{S}_x$ are empty.

Partitioning of $\mathcal{S}_x$ into $\mathcal{S}_x = \bigcup_y \mathcal{P}_{xy}$. Before computing an isomorphism of maximum weight in a set $\mathcal{S}_x$, we partition $\mathcal{S}_x$ into subsets $\mathcal{P}_{x1}, \mathcal{P}_{x2}, \ldots$. The focus for the separation now is on the graph H. We distinguish two cases. If $\mathcal{S}_x$ is a set, where at least one edge of a certain block (bridge) b is mapped, then $\mathcal{S}_x$ is partitioned into $|\mathrm{Bl}^H|$ ($|\mathrm{Br}^H|$) subsets. The meaning is that for each B-node $\bar{b} \in Bl^H$ ($\bar{b} \in \mathrm{Br}^H$) the mapped vertices of the B-node $b \in B^G$ are mapped only to $V(\bar{b})$. In terms of BBP this is block (bridge) preserving between b and $\bar{b}$, as intended. If $\mathcal{S}_x$ is a set, where exactly one vertex of b is mapped, the subsets are defined as follows. For each $(v, \bar{v}) \in V(b) \times V(H)$, where $\omega(v\bar{v}) \neq -\infty$ and v is in the CC we operate on, we define a subset with the restriction $\phi(v) = \bar{v}$.

Computing a Maximum Isomorphism in a Subset $\mathcal{P}_{xy}$. We now describe how to compute an isomorphism ϕ of maximum weight in a subset $\mathcal{P}_{xy} \subseteq \mathcal{S}_x$. The idea is to recursively extend mappings between some vertices of two single bridges or two single blocks along all pairs of mapped cutvertices into other B-nodes determined by MWMs, while preserving bridges and blocks. Between the computed isomorphisms we select one of maximum weight.

First, let $\mathcal{P}_{xy}$ be a subset, where at least one edge of a B-node $b \in B^G$ has to be mapped to an edge of a B-node $\bar{b} \in B^H$. If b and $\bar{b}$ are bridges, the two possible mappings $V(b) \to V(\bar{b})$ are considered. If both are blocks, all maximal common biconnected subgraph isomorphisms between the blocks are considered (cf. Algorithm 1). We may have given a fixed mapping $v \mapsto \bar{v}$ (cf. (i) below). We call a considered isomorphism valid, if it respects the possible fixed mapping and contains only vertices of the CC we are operating on. We extend all the valid isomorphisms ϕ along all pairs $\phi(c) = \bar{c}, c \neq v$ of mapped cutvertices as follows. Let $B_c := \{b_1, \ldots b_k\}$, be the B-nodes of B^G, where bcb_i is a path, and $\bar{B}_c := \{\bar{b}_1, \ldots \bar{b}_l\}$, be the B-nodes of B^H, where $\bar{b}\bar{c}\bar{b}_j$ is a path, $i \in [1..k], j \in [1..l]$. For each pair $(b_i, \bar{b}_j) \in B_c \times \bar{B}_c$ we recursively calculate a BBP-MCIS φ_{ij} under the following restrictions: (i) The cutvertices must be mapped: $c \mapsto \bar{c}$. (ii) b_i and $\bar{b}_j$ are both bridges or both blocks. (iii) At least one other vertex in the block (bridge) b_i must be mapped, but only to $V(\bar{b}_j)$. Restriction (iii) assures that at least one vertex is added to the isomorphism. Therefore, the recursion to compute φ_{ij} is the method described in this paragraph. After computing φ_{ij} for each pair $(b_i, \bar{b}_j)$, we construct a weighted bipartite graph with vertices $B_c \uplus \bar{B}_c$ for each pair of mapped cutvertices. The weight of each edge $b_i\bar{b}_j$ is determined by the weight of a BBP-MCIS under the above restrictions, subtracted by $\omega(c, \bar{c})$ for the appropriate cutvertices c and $\bar{c}$. If there in no such restricted BBP-MCIS, there is no edge. Computing a MWM on each of the bipartite graphs determines the extension of ϕ. For each matching edge the corresponding computed isomorphisms are merged with ϕ. After extending all valid isomorphisms, we select one of maximum weight.

Second, let $\mathcal{P}_{xy}$ be a subset, where exactly one vertex v of $V(b)$ is mapped, and let $\phi(v) = \bar{v}$. If v is no cutvertex, the only possible expansion is within $V(b)$, which is not allowed in this subset. Therefore this subset contains exactly one isomorphism, $v \mapsto \bar{v}$. Next, assume v is a cutvertex. If $\bar{v}$ is a cutvertex, we may extend ϕ similar to the previous paragraph. In doing so, $c := v, \bar{c} := \bar{v}$ and B_c

as before. The only difference is $\bar{B}_c$, which is defined by all B-nodes containing $\bar{v} = \bar{c}$. The reason is that we have not mapped any other vertices yet, therefore we may expand in all directions in H. If $\bar{v}$ is no cutvertex, then $\bar{v}$ is contained in exactly one $\bar{b} \in B^H$. We are interested in BBP isomorphisms only. This means, all vertices that are mapped to $V(\bar{b})$ must be in the same block or bridge $b' \in B^G$. Therefore, for each $b' \in B^G$, where bvb' is a path and b' and $\bar{b}$ are of the same type (bridge/block), we compute an isomorphism with fixed mapping $v \mapsto \bar{v}$, where at least one edge of b' is mapped to $\bar{b}$. This falls back to the method of the above paragraph as well. Among the computed isomorphisms we select one of maximum weight. The pseudocode of the method described above is available in the extended version of this paper [4].

Time Complexity. The time to compute a BBP-MCIS essentially depends on the time to compute the BC-trees, the biconnected isomorphisms between the blocks of G and H, and the time to compute all the MWMs. The time to compute a BC-tree is linear in the number of edges and vertices. Considering all pairs of blocks and Theorem 1 we can bound the time for computing all the biconnected isomorphisms by $\mathcal{O}(\sum_b \sum_{\bar{b}} |V_b||V_{\bar{b}}|) \subseteq \mathcal{O}(|G||H|)$. We only need to compute MWMs for the pairs of cutvertices of the two graphs. It follows from the result of [3, Theorem 7] for the maximum common subtree problem, that the total time for this is $\mathcal{O}(|G||H|(\min\{\Delta^G, \Delta^H\} + \log\max\{\Delta^G, \Delta^H\}))$, where $\Delta^{\mathcal{G}}$ is the maximum degree of a C-node in $BC^{\mathcal{G}}$. This proves the following theorem.

Theorem 2. *BBP-MCIS between two outerplanar graphs G and H can be solved in time $\mathcal{O}(|G||H|\Delta(G, H))$, where $\Delta(G, H) = 1$ iff G or H is biconnected or both are of bounded degree; otherwise $\Delta(G, H) = \min\{\Delta^G, \Delta^H\} + \log\max\{\Delta^G, \Delta^H\}$.*

5   Experimental Evaluation

In this section we evaluate our BBP-MCIS algorithm experimentally and compare to the BBP-MCES approach of [13].[1] Both algorithms were implemented in C++ and compiled with GCC v.4.8.4 as 64-bit application. Running times were measured on an Intel Core i7-3770 CPU using a single core. The available memory of 16 GB was sufficient for all the computations.

We are interested in answering the following questions:

(H1) To what extent differs BBP-MCIS from BBP-MCES on molecular graphs?
(H2) How large is the difference in terms of running time on molecular graphs?
(H3) How is the running time affected by specific properties of the input graphs?

To answer **(H1)** and **(H2)** we extracted 29000 randomly chosen pairs of outerplanar molecular graphs from a large chemical database.[2] The molecules in the database contain up to 104 vertices and 22 vertices on an average.

---

[1] We are grateful to Leander Schietgat for providing the implementation used in [13].
[2] NCI Open Database, GI50, http://cactus.nci.nih.gov.

The weight function ω was set to 1 for each pair of vertices and edges with the same label and $-\infty$ otherwise. This matches the setting in [13].

To answer **(H3)** we compared the algorithms on randomly generated connected outerplanar graphs. Our graph generator takes several parameters as input. With them we evaluated three different properties: the graph size, the average ratio $|E|/|V|$ of edges to vertices, and the average block size. For any outerplanar graphs the ratio of edges to vertices is less than 2. While evaluating the effect of one property, we preserved the other two. This procedure allows to verify whether our theoretical findings are consistent with the running times observed in practice. We set the weight function ω to 1 for each pair of vertices and edges, which corresponds to uniformly labeled graphs.

(H1). While comparing the weight of the isomorphisms computed by the two algorithms we observed a difference for only 0.40 % of the 29 000 tested molecule pairs. This suggests that BBP-MCIS yields a valid notion of similarity for outerplanar molecular graphs as it was shown for BBP-MCES [13].

(H2). Our algorithm computed the solutions on average 84 times faster. The dots in Fig. 2 represent the computation times of the two algorithms. The results are summarized in Table 1. Schietgat et al. [13] compared their BBP-MCES algorithm to a state-of-the-art algorithm for general MCIS. Their algorithm had

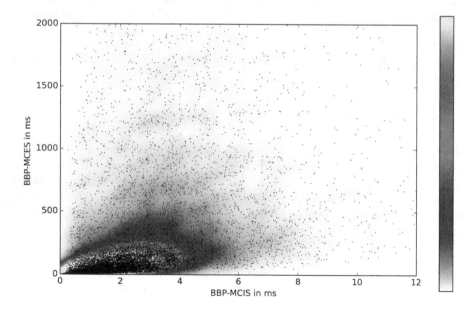

Fig. 2. Running times in ms for 28 399 BBP-MCIS computations. Each black dot represents a BBP-MCIS computation on two randomly chosen outerplanar molecular graphs. It directly compares the running time of our algorithm (MCIS, x-axis) and the implementation from [13] (MCES, y-axis). The running times of another 601 BBP-MCIS computations did not fit into the borders.

Table 1. Upper half: running times for our implementation (MCIS) and the implementation from [13] (MCES). Lower half: relative differences in computation times.

Algorithm	Average time	Median time	95 % less than	Maximum time
MCIS	1.97 ms	1.51 ms	5.28 ms	40.35 ms
MCES	207.08 ms	41.43 ms	871.48 ms	26 353.68 ms
Comparison	Average factor	Median factor	Minimum factor	Maximum factor
MCES/MCIS	83.8	25.6	1.8	28912.5

Table 2. Average time ± SD over 100 BBP-MCIS computations on random outerplanar graphs, varying one property (graph size, ratio of edges to vertices, block size BS). Note the units of measurement; timeout—total time exceeds 3 days.

Size	10	20	40	80	160
MCIS	0.7 ± 0.3 ms	2.3 ± 0.8 ms	8.2 ± 1.6 ms	33.5 ± 3.6 ms	133.2 ± 10.1 ms
MCES	207 ± 118 ms	3.4 ± 6.0 s	38.6 ± 90.6 s	234.2 ± 420.9 s	Timeout
$|E|/|V|$	0.98	1.10	1.24	1.46	1.78
MCIS	3.8 ± 0.3 ms	4.0 ± 1.1 ms	8.2 ± 1.6 ms	30.8 ± 4.0 ms	110.3 ± 11.6 ms
MCES	223 ± 16 ms	2.2 ± 2.6 s	38.6 ± 90.6 s	111.0 ± 213.8 s	216.1 ± 288.3 s
BS	3	5	10	20	40
MCIS	27 ± 6.4 ms	13.3 ± 2.4 ms	8.4 ± 1.7 ms	5.5 ± 1.4 ms	4.5 ± 0.9 ms
MCES	132 ± 14 ms	689 ± 548 ms	83.7 ± 118.7 s	30.4 ± 27.8 min	Timeout

similar computation times on small graphs and was much faster on large graphs. The maximum time of the general MCIS algorithm was more than 24 h. In contrast, our computation time never exceeded 41 ms. This clearly indicates that our algorithm is orders of magnitude faster than the general approach.

(H3). We first varied the size of the input graphs, while preserving an average ratio of edges to vertices of 1.24 and an average block size of 8. Based on Theorem 2 we expected the average time to increase by a factor of a bit more than 4, if we double the size. The results in Table 2 closely match this expectation.

Next, we evaluated different ratios of edges to vertices. The graph size was set to 40 and the average block size to 8. A higher ratio results in a higher number of faces in the blocks and consequently affects the time required by Algorithm 7. In particular, the table size and, thus, the running time is expected to show a quadratic growth. The increase in running time exceeds our expectation. This might be explained by the increasing size of the data structure used to represent the faces of the blocks.

Finally, we evaluated different average block sizes. The graph size was set to 40 and the average ratio of edges to vertices to 1.24. Higher block sizes mean less MWMs to compute, which are the most costly part in the BBP-MCIS computation. Therefore we expected the running time to decrease. The results shown in Table 2 support this.

6   Conclusion

We have developed an algorithm, which computes a well-defined, chemical mean-ingful largest common substructure of outerplanar molecular graphs in a fraction of a second. Hence, our method makes the graph-based comparison in large mole-cular datasets possible. As future work, we would like to extend our approach to more general graph classes with a focus on efficiency in practice.

References

1. Akutsu, T.: A polynomial time algorithm for finding a largest common subgraph of almost trees of bounded degree. IEICE Trans. Fundam. Electron. Commun. Comput. Sci. **E76–A**(9), 1488–1493 (1993)
2. Akutsu, T., Tamura, T.: A polynomial-time algorithm for computing the maxi-mum common connected edge subgraph of outerplanar graphs of bounded degree. Algorithms **6**(1), 119–135 (2013)
3. Droschinsky, A., Kriege, N., Mutzel, P.: Faster algorithms for the maximum com-mon subtree isomorphism problem. MFCS 2016. LIPIcs, **58**, 34:1–34:14 (2016). arXiv:1602.07210
4. Droschinsky, A., Kriege, N., Mutzel, P.: Finding largest common substructures of molecules in quadratic time (2016). CoRR arXiv:1610.08739
5. Ehrlich, H.C., Rarey, M.: Maximum common subgraph isomorphism algorithms and their applications in molecular science: a review. Wiley Interdiscip. Rev. Com-put. Mol. Sci. **1**(1), 68–79 (2011)
6. Garey, M.R., Johnson, D.S.: Computers and Intractability: A Guide to the Theory of NP-Completeness. W.H. Freeman, New York (1979)
7. Kriege, N., Kurpicz, F., Mutzel, P.: On maximum common subgraph problems in series-parallel graphs. In: Kratochvíl, J., Miller, M., Froncek, D. (eds.) IWOCA 2014. LNCS, vol. 8986, pp. 200–212. Springer, Heidelberg (2015). doi:10.1007/978-3-319-19315-1_18
8. Kriege, N., Mutzel, P.: Finding maximum common biconnected subgraphs in series-parallel graphs. In: Csuhaj-Varjú, E., Dietzfelbinger, M., Ésik, Z. (eds.) MFCS 2014. LNCS, vol. 8635, pp. 505–516. Springer, Heidelberg (2014). doi:10.1007/978-3-662-44465-8_43
9. Lingas, A.: Subgraph isomorphism for biconnected outerplanar graphs in cubic time. Theor. Comput. Sci. **63**(3), 295–302 (1989)
10. Matula, D.W.: Subtree isomorphism in $O(n^{5/2})$. In: Alspach, B., P.H., Miller, D. (eds.) Algorithmic Aspects of Combinatorics, Annals of Discrete Mathematics, vol. 2, pp. 91–106. Elsevier (1978)
11. Nicholson, V., Tsai, C.C., Johnson, M., Naim, M.: A subgraph isomorphism theo-rem for molecular graphs. In: Graph Theory and Topology in Chemistry. Studies in Physical and Theoretical Chemistry, no. 51, pp. 226–230. Elsevier (1987)
12. Raymond, J.W., Willett, P.: Maximum common subgraph isomorphism algorithms for the matching of chemical structures. J. Comput. Aided Mol. Des. **16**(7), 521–533 (2002)
13. Schietgat, L., Ramon, J., Bruynooghe, M.: A polynomial-time maximum common subgraph algorithm for outerplanar graphs and its application to chemoinformatics. Ann. Math. Artif. Intell. **69**(4), 343–376 (2013)

14. Sysło, M.M.: The subgraph isomorphism problem for outerplanar graphs. Theor. Comput. Sci. **17**(1), 91–97 (1982)
15. Yamaguchi, A., Aoki, K.F., Mamitsuka, H.: Finding the maximum common subgraph of a partial k-tree and a graph with a polynomially bounded number of spanning trees. Inf. Process. Lett. **92**(2), 57–63 (2004)

Coloring and Vertex Covers

Lower Bounds for On-line Interval Coloring with Vector and Cardinality Constraints

Grzegorz Gutowski$^{(\boxtimes)}$ and Patryk Mikos

Theoretical Computer Science Department, Faculty of Mathematics
and Computer Science, Jagiellonian University, Kraków, Poland
{gutowski,mikos}@tcs.uj.edu.pl

Abstract. We propose two strategies for Presenter in the on-line interval graph coloring games. Specifically, we consider a setting in which each interval is associated with a d-dimensional vector of weights and the coloring needs to satisfy the d-dimensional bandwidth constraint, and the k-cardinality constraint. Such a variant was first introduced by Epstein and Levy and it is a natural model for resource-aware task scheduling with d different shared resources where at most k tasks can be scheduled simultaneously on a single machine.

The first strategy forces any on-line interval coloring algorithm to use at least $(5m - 3)\frac{d}{\log d + 3}$ different colors on an $m\left(\frac{d}{k} + \log d + 3\right)$-colorable set of intervals. The second strategy forces any on-line interval coloring algorithm to use at least $\lfloor \frac{5m}{2} \rfloor \frac{d}{\log d + 3}$ different colors on an $m\left(\frac{d}{k} + \log d + 3\right)$-colorable set of unit intervals.

Keywords: On-line coloring · Interval graphs · Unit interval graphs

1 Introduction

A *proper coloring* of a graph G is an assignment of colors to the vertices of the graph such that adjacent vertices receive distinct colors. A *k-bounded coloring* of G is a proper coloring of G such that the number of vertices that receive any single color is at most k. For a graph G, let $\chi(G)$ denote the *chromatic number* of G, that is the minimum number of colors in a proper coloring of G, and let $\omega(G)$ denote the *clique number* of G, that is, the maximum size of a subset of vertices such that any two vertices in the subset are adjacent.

An *on-line graph coloring game* is a two-person game, played by Presenter and Algorithm. In each round Presenter introduces a new vertex of a graph with its adjacency status to all vertices presented earlier. Algorithm assigns a color to the incoming vertex in such a way that the coloring of the presented graph is proper. The color of the new vertex is assigned before Presenter introduces the next vertex and the assignment is irrevocable. The goal of Algorithm is to minimize the number of different colors used during the game. In the *k-bounded* variant of the game, the coloring constructed by Algorithm needs to be a k-bounded coloring of the presented graph.

Research partially supported by NCN grant number 2014/14/A/ST6/00138.

B. Steffen et al. (Eds.): SOFSEM 2017, LNCS 10139, pp. 325–335, 2017.
DOI: 10.1007/978-3-319-51963-0_25

For an interval $I = [l, r]$ on the real line, we say that l is the left endpoint, and r is the right endpoint of I. The *length* of interval I is the difference between its right endpoint and its left endpoint. A set of intervals on the real line represents a graph in the following way. Each interval represents a vertex and any two vertices are joined by an edge whenever the corresponding intervals intersect. A graph which admits such a representation is an *interval graph*.

An *on-line interval coloring game* is a two-person game, again played by Presenter and Algorithm. In each round Presenter introduces a new interval on the real line. Algorithm assigns a color to the incoming interval in such a way that the coloring of the presented interval graph is proper, i.e. all intervals of the same color are pairwise disjoint. The color of the new interval is assigned before Presenter introduces the next interval and the assignment is irrevocable. The goal of Algorithm is to minimize the number of different colors used during the game.

We consider a few variants of the on-line interval coloring game. In the *unit* variant of the game, all intervals presented by Presenter are of length exactly 1. In the *d-dimensional* variant of the game, Presenter associates a d-dimensional vector of weights from $[0, 1]$ with each presented interval. Moreover, the coloring constructed by Algorithm needs to satisfy a different condition. The condition is that for each color γ and any point p on the real line, the sum of weights of intervals containing p and colored γ does not exceed 1 in any of the coordinates. In the *k-cardinality* variant of the game, the coloring constructed by Algorithm needs to satisfy that for each color γ and any point p on the real line, the number of intervals containing p and colored γ does not exceed k.

We are most interested in the *on-line (k, d) interval coloring*, a variant in which each interval has a d-dimensional vector of weights and the coloring must satisfy constraints of both d-dimensional and k-cardinality variant. That is, for each color γ and any point p, the number of intervals containing p and colored γ does not exceed k, and the sum of weights of those intervals does not exceed 1 in any coordinate.

In the context of various on-line coloring games, the measure of the quality of a strategy for Algorithm is given by competitive analysis. A coloring strategy for Algorithm is *r-competitive* if it uses at most $r \cdot c$ colors for any c-colorable graph, or set of intervals, presented by Presenter. The *competitive ratio* for a problem is the infimum of all values r such that there exists an r-competitive strategy for Algorithm for this problem. In this paper we give lower bounds on competitive ratios for different problems. We obtain these results by presenting explicit strategies for Presenter that force any Algorithm strategy to use many colors while the presented graph, or set of intervals, is colorable with a smaller number of colors.

We say that a strategy for Presenter in an on-line coloring problem is *transparent* if after each time Algorithm assigns a color to a vertex, or interval, Presenter colors the vertex with his own color and reveals that color to Algorithm. The coloring constructed by Presenter must satisfy the same conditions as the coloring constructed by Algorithm. The number of colors used by a transparent strategy for Presenter gives an upper bound on the minimum number of colors that can be used in a coloring.

1.1 Previous Work

There is a simple strategy for Presenter in on-line graph coloring game that forces Algorithm to use any number of colors while the constructed graph is 2-colorable. Thus, the competitive ratio for this problem is unbounded. Nevertheless, it is an interesting question what is the competitive ratio when the on-line game is played only for at most n rounds. Halldórsson and Szegedy [4] presented a transparent strategy for Presenter that forces Algorithm to use at least $2\frac{n}{\log n}(1 + o(1))$ different colors in n rounds of the game while the constructed graph is $\log n(1 + o(1))$-colorable. The best known upper bound of $O\left(\frac{n}{\log^* n}\right)$ on the competitive ratio for the n-round on-line graph coloring problem was given by Lovasz, Saks and Trotter [6].

The competitive ratio for the on-line interval coloring problem was established by Kierstead and Trotter [5]. They constructed a strategy for Algorithm that uses at most $3\omega - 2$ colors while the clique size of the constructed graph is ω. They also presented a matching lower bound – a strategy for Presenter that forces Algorithm to use at least $3\omega - 2$ colors. Unit variant of the on-line interval coloring problem was studied by Epstein and Levy [2]. They presented a strategy for Presenter that forces Algorithm to use at least $\lfloor \frac{3\omega}{2} \rfloor$ colors while the clique size of the constructed graph is ω. Moreover, they showed that First-Fit algorithm uses at most $2\omega - 1$ colors. Epstein and Levy [3] introduced many variants of the on-line interval coloring problem. The best known lower bound on the competitive ratio for the on-line (k, d) interval coloring is 3 for small k and $\frac{24}{7}$ for large k. For unit variant of this problem the best known lower bound is $\frac{3}{2}$.

Halldórsson and Szegedy ideas were adopted by Azar et al. [1] to show lower bounds on competitive ratio for *on-line d-vector bin packing*. This problem is equivalent to a variant of d-dimensional on-line interval coloring where all presented intervals are the interval $[0, 1]$ with different vectors of weights. Their strategy for Presenter shows that the competitive ratio for the on-line d-dimensional unit interval coloring problem is at least $2\frac{d}{\log^2 d}(1 + o(1))$.

1.2 Our Results

We generalize Halldórsson and Szegedy [4] strategy into the setting of the k-bounded coloring, and using the technique similar to the one by Azar et al. [1] we adopt it to the on-line (k, d) interval coloring problem. We present how to combine this technique with classical results by Kierstead and Trotter [5], and by Epstein and Levy [2,3] to obtain a new lower bound of $5\frac{d}{\log d\left(\frac{d}{k}+\log d\right)}(1 + o(1))$ on the competitive ratio for the on-line (k, d) interval coloring, and a lower bound of $\frac{5}{2}\frac{d}{\log d\left(\frac{d}{k}+\log d\right)}(1 + o(1))$ for unit variant of this problem.

2 Graph Coloring

Theorem 1. *For every $n \geqslant 2$ and $k \in \mathbb{N}_+$, there is a transparent strategy for Presenter that forces Algorithm to use at least $2\frac{n}{\log n + 3}$ different colors in the n-round, k-bounded on-line graph coloring game and uses $\frac{n}{k} + \log n + 3$ colors.*

Proof. Let $b = \lfloor \log n \rfloor + 3$. The state of a k-bounded on-line graph coloring game is represented by a *progress matrix* M. Each cell $M[i, j]$ is either empty or it contains exactly one vertex. At the beginning of the game, all cells are empty. A vertex in $M[i, j]$ is colored by Algorithm with color j and by Presenter with color i. Each player can use a single color γ to color at most k vertices, so there are at most k vertices in any column, and in any row of the progress matrix. We say that a row with k vertices is *depleted*. Presenter can no longer use colors corresponding to depleted rows. Presenter maintains a set of exactly b *active* rows, denoted $\mathcal{A}$, that contains all nonempty non-depleted rows and additionally some empty rows ($\{i : 1 \leqslant |\cup_j M[i, j]| < k\} \subset \mathcal{A}$ and $|\mathcal{A}| = b$). At the beginning of the game there are no depleted rows and $\mathcal{A} = \{1, \ldots, b\}$. When some row becomes depleted then it is removed from $\mathcal{A}$ and a new empty row is added to $\mathcal{A}$. A *pattern* is a subset of rows. We say that a pattern p *represents* a column j if $\forall i : i \in p \iff M[i, j] \neq \emptyset$. A pattern p is *active* if it is a nonempty subset of $\mathcal{A}$ such that $|p| \leqslant \lfloor \frac{b}{2} \rfloor$. An active pattern p is *present* in M if at least one column of M is represented by p.

Table 1 shows a possible state of the progress matrix M after 15 rounds of the 4-bounded on-line graph coloring game with $n = 4$ and $b = 4$. In this example, the last introduced vertex v_{15} is colored by Algorithm with color 2 and by Presenter with color 3. Rows 1 and 3 are depleted and the set of active rows is $\mathcal{A} = \{2, 4, 5, 6\}$. There are 10 different active patterns, but only 2 of them are present in M: pattern $\{2, 5\}$ in column 6, and pattern $\{5\}$ in column 9.

The transparent strategy for Presenter for round t is as follows:

1. Choose an active pattern p_t that is not present in M.
2. Introduce a new vertex v_t that is adjacent to all vertices colored by Presenter with colors not in p_t.

Table 1. Example of a progress matrix after 15 rounds

	1	2	3	4	5	6	7	8	9	10	...
1	v_1		v_3	v_5	v_7						
2*		v_2				v_{10}		v_{12}			
3		v_{15}	v_4				v_9	v_{13}			
4*	v_6					v_{11}					
5*						v_8			v_{14}		
6*											
7											
...											

3. Algorithm colors v_t with color γ.
4. Color v_t with any color ϱ such that $\varrho \in p_t$ and $M[\varrho, \gamma] = \emptyset$.

We claim that Presenter can follow this strategy as long as there is an active pattern not present in the progress matrix. To prove that, we need to show that in step (4) Presenter always can choose an appropriate color ϱ, and that the coloring constructed by Presenter is a k-bounded coloring of the constructed graph.

Let q be a pattern that represents column $M[*, \gamma]$ of the progress matrix before round t. We claim that $q \subsetneq p_t$. Assume to the contrary that $i \in q \smallsetminus p_t$. It follows, that there is a vertex v in cell $M[i, \gamma]$ and by rule (2) v is adjacent to v_t. Thus, Algorithm cannot color vertex v_t with color γ. Pattern q is present in M before round t and by rule (1) pattern p_t is not present in M before round t. It follows that q is a strict subset of p_t and Presenter has at least one choice for color ϱ in step (4).

When Presenter assigns color ϱ to vertex v_t, we have that $\varrho \in p_t$; p_t is an active pattern; ϱ is an active row, and there are less than k vertices colored by Presenter with ϱ. Rule (2) asserts that none of the vertices adjacent to v_t is colored with any of the colors in p_t. Thus, we have that Presenter can follow the strategy as long as there is a choice of an appropriate pattern in step (1).

We claim that the game can be played for at least n rounds. Indeed, there are $\binom{b}{x}$ different patterns of size x and each one of them must represent a column of the progress matrix with exactly x vertices. Thus, when all active patterns represent some column of the progress matrix, the game has been played for at least $\sum_{1 \leqslant x \leqslant \lfloor \frac{b}{2} \rfloor} x \binom{b}{x} \geqslant n$ rounds.

After n rounds, Presenter used colors corresponding to depleted and active rows. There are at most $\lfloor \frac{n}{k} \rfloor$ depleted rows and exactly $\lfloor \log n \rfloor + 3$ active rows. Thus, Presenter uses at most $\frac{n}{k} + \log n + 3$ colors in the first n rounds.

Let q_j be a pattern representing column $M[*, j]$ after n rounds. Let t be the last round when a vertex was added to column j. We have that q_j is a subset of pattern p_t which was an active pattern before round t, and the size of q_j is at most $\lfloor \frac{b}{2} \rfloor$. Thus, there are at least $2\frac{n}{\log n + 3}$ nonempty columns after n rounds. $\square$

For fixed parameters n and k, denote a generalized Halldórsson and Szegedy strategy by $HS_{k,n}$. Note that for $k = +\infty$, there are no depleted rows in matrix M and k-bounded coloring is simply a proper coloring. In this case we get the original Halldórsson and Szegedy result for the on-line graph coloring problem.

Theorem 2 (Halldórsson, Szegedy [4]). *For every integer $n \geqslant 2$, there is a transparent strategy for Presenter that forces Algorithm to use at least $2\frac{n}{\log n + 3}$ colors in the n-round on-line graph coloring game and uses $\log n + 3$ colors.*

3   Interval Coloring

In the proof of the following theorem, we use strategy $HS_{k,d}$ to show a lower bound on the competitive ratio for the on-line (k, d) interval coloring problem.

Theorem 3. *For every $d \geqslant 2$ and $k, m \in \mathbb{N}_+$, there is a strategy for Presenter that forces Algorithm to use at least $(5m - 3)\frac{d}{\log d + 3}$ different colors in the on-line (k, d) interval coloring game while the constructed set of intervals is $m\left(\frac{d}{k} + \log d + 3\right)$-colorable.*

Proof. For any fixed parameters $k \in \mathbb{N}_+, d \geqslant 2, L < R, \varepsilon \in (0, \frac{1}{d})$ we describe an auxiliary strategy $HS_{k,d}(\varepsilon, L, R)$. Let $\alpha = 1 - \frac{1}{2}\varepsilon, \delta = \frac{1}{2d}\varepsilon$. In the t-th round of the on-line (k, d) interval coloring game, Presenter uses $HS_{k,d}$ strategy to get a new vertex v_t. Then, presents an interval $[L, R]$ with weights w_t, where $w_t = (x_1, \ldots, x_d)$ is a d-dimensional vector with $x_t = \alpha$, $x_i = \varepsilon$ for all $i < t$ such that v_i is adjacent to v_t, and $x_i = \delta$ in every other coordinate. Figure 1 shows an example of w_6 for a vertex v_6 that is adjacent to v_2 and v_5.

$([L, R], w_t)$ is colored by Algorithm with color γ_t. Then, γ_t is forwarded to $HS_{k,d}$ as the color of v_t. $HS_{k,d}$ colors v_t with ϱ_t, but Presenter discards that information. See Fig. 2 for a diagram of the strategy $HS_{k,d}(\varepsilon, L, R)$, and Fig. 3 for an example encoding of a graph.

We claim that the encoding strategy ensures that any intervals I_i and I_j can get the same color iff vertices v_i and v_j are not adjacent. First, assume that $i < j$ and v_i is adjacent to v_j. Vector w_i has α in the i-th coordinate, vector w_j has ε in the i-th coordinate, and $\alpha + \varepsilon > 1$. Thus, intervals I_i and I_j must be colored with different colors. Let $\mathcal{J} \subset \{I_1, \ldots, I_{t-1}\}$ be the set of intervals colored with

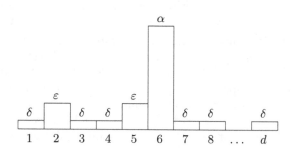

Fig. 1. Encoding of v_6 in a d-dimensional vector of weights

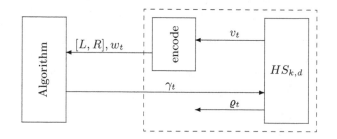

Fig. 2. Encoding of $HS_{k,d}$ strategy

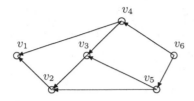

w_1	α	δ	δ	δ	δ	δ
w_2	ε	α	δ	δ	δ	δ
w_3	δ	ε	α	δ	δ	δ
w_4	ε	δ	ε	α	δ	δ
w_5	δ	ε	ε	δ	α	δ
w_6	δ	δ	δ	ε	ε	α

Fig. 3. Example of a graph and vectors of weights corresponding to the vertices

γ before round $t \leqslant d$. Assume that v_t is not adjacent to any of the vertices in $\mathcal{J}$. Denote the l-th coordinate of the sum of vectors of weights of intervals in $\mathcal{J}$ by W_l. For any $1 \leqslant l \leqslant d$, if $I_l \in \mathcal{J}$ then $W_l = \alpha + \delta(|\mathcal{J}| - 1) < 1 - \delta$. In this case we have that v_t is not adjacent to v_l, and that the l-th coordinate of the vector of weights of v_t is δ. If $I_l \notin \mathcal{J}$ then $W_l \leqslant \varepsilon|\mathcal{J}| < 1 - \varepsilon$. For $l = t$, we have $W_l \leqslant \delta|\mathcal{J}| \leqslant 1 - \alpha$. Thus, the sum of vector of weights of the intervals in the set $\mathcal{J} \cup \{I_t\}$ does not exceed 1 in any coordinate and I_t can be colored with γ.

Consider a sequence of parameters $\{\varepsilon_i\}_{i \in \mathbb{N}_+}$ defined as $\varepsilon_i := \left(\frac{1}{2d}\right)^i$. See that for every $i \in \mathbb{N}_+$ we have $\varepsilon_i \in (0, \frac{1}{d})$ and we can use $HS_{k,d}(\varepsilon_i, L, R)$ strategy. Let $\alpha_i = 1 - \frac{1}{2}\varepsilon_i$ and $\delta_i = \frac{1}{2d}\varepsilon_i = \varepsilon_{i+1}$.

Let $\mathcal{J}_i$ be a set of intervals constructed by $HS_{k,d}(\varepsilon_i, L_i, R_i)$ strategy and $\mathcal{J}_j$ be a set of intervals constructed by $HS_{k,d}(\varepsilon_j, L_j, R_j)$ strategy. Assume that $i < j$, $[L_i, R_i] \cap [L_j, R_j] \neq \emptyset$ and that the construction of $\mathcal{J}_i$ is finished before the construction of $\mathcal{J}_j$ starts. Any interval $I \in \mathcal{J}_j$ has weight α_j in one of the coordinates and every interval in $\mathcal{J}_i$ has weight either α_i, ε_i or δ_i in that coordinate. In any case, sum of those weights exceeds 1 and no two intervals, one in $\mathcal{J}_i$, other in $\mathcal{J}_j$ can be colored with the same color.

The rest of the proof uses a technique similar to the one by Kierstead and Trotter [5]. For $m \in \mathbb{N}_+$, let $c_m = (5m - 3)\frac{d}{\log d + 3}$, and $o_m = m\left(\frac{d}{k} + \log d + 3\right)$. By induction on m, we show a strategy S_m for Presenter such that: all introduced intervals are contained in a fixed region $[A, B]$; all intervals come from calls of strategies $HS_{k,d}(\varepsilon, L, R)$ with ε in $\{\varepsilon_1, \ldots, \varepsilon_{3m}\}$; Algorithm uses at least c_m different colors; constructed set of intervals is o_m-colorable. For $m = 1$ and a fixed region $[A, B]$, Presenter uses strategy $HS_{k,d}(\varepsilon_1, A, B)$. This strategy forces Algorithm to use at least c_1 different colors, and the constructed set of intervals is o_1-colorable. Thus, in this case we are done.

Let $\bar{c} = 3\binom{c_{m+1}}{c_m} + 1$. Presenter splits the fixed region $[A, B]$ into $\bar{c}$ disjoint regions $[l_1, r_1], \ldots, [l_{\bar{c}}, r_{\bar{c}}]$. By induction, in each region Presenter can use strategy S_m independently. As a result, in each region $[l_i, r_i]$, we get a set of intervals $\mathcal{J}_i$. If during the construction Algorithm uses at least c_{m+1} colors, we are done. Otherwise, let C_i be a c_m-element subset of colors used by Algorithm to color $\mathcal{J}_i$. Some c_m-element set of colors C^* appears on the list $(C_1, \ldots, C_{\bar{c}})$ at least 4 times. Let $a, b, c, d \in \{1, \ldots, \bar{c}\}$, $a < b < c < d$ be indices such that $C_a = C_b = C_c = C_d = C^*$. Define $p_i = \frac{1}{2}(r_i + l_{i+1})$ for $i = a, b, c$.

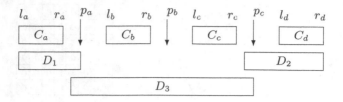

Fig. 4. Construction in case $|D_1 \cap D_2| \leqslant \frac{1}{2}c_1$

Presenter uses strategy $HS_{k,d}(\varepsilon_{3m+1}, l_a, p_a)$ to get a set of intervals $\mathcal{K}_1$ and then strategy $HS_{k,d}(\varepsilon_{3m+1}, \frac{r_c+p_c}{2}, r_d)$ to get a set of intervals $\mathcal{K}_2$. Let D_1 be a c_1-element subset of colors used by Algorithm to color $\mathcal{K}_1$, and D_2 be a c_1-element subset of colors used to color $\mathcal{K}_2$. The construction of $\mathcal{J}_a$ and $\mathcal{J}_d$ is finished before the construction of $\mathcal{K}_1$ and $\mathcal{K}_2$ started and region $[l_a, p_a]$ covers $[l_a, r_a]$, and region $\left[\frac{r_c+p_c}{2}, r_d\right]$ covers $[l_d, r_d]$. Thus, none of the colors in C^* can be used to color any interval in $\mathcal{K}_1$ or $\mathcal{K}_2$. Now, the strategy splits into two cases: we either have $|D_1 \cap D_2| \leqslant \frac{1}{2}c_1$ or $|D_1 \cap D_2| > \frac{1}{2}c_1$.

Case 1. $|D_1 \cap D_2| \leqslant \frac{1}{2}c_1$. Presenter uses strategy $HS_{k,d}(\varepsilon_{3m+2}, \frac{r_a+p_a}{2}, p_c)$ to get a set of intervals $\mathcal{K}_3$. Let D_3 be the set of colors used to color $\mathcal{K}_3$. See Fig. 4 for a diagram of the construction. Region $\left[\frac{r_a+p_a}{2}, p_c\right]$ covers $[l_b, r_b]$ and we get $C^* \cap D_3 = \emptyset$. Moreover, any interval in $\mathcal{K}_3$ intersects any interval in $\mathcal{K}_1$, and any interval in $\mathcal{K}_2$. Thus, $D_3 \cap D_1 = \emptyset$, $D_3 \cap D_2 = \emptyset$, and Algorithm uses at least $|C^* \cup D_1 \cup D_2 \cup D_3| \geqslant c_m + c_1 + \frac{1}{2}c_1 + c_1 = c_{m+1}$ colors. Each set of intervals $\mathcal{J}_1, \ldots, \mathcal{J}_{\bar{c}}$ intersects with intervals in at most one of the sets $\mathcal{K}_1$, $\mathcal{K}_2$, or $\mathcal{K}_3$. Thus, all presented intervals can be colored with $\max\{2, m+1\}(\frac{d}{k} + \log d + 3) = o_{m+1}$ colors and in this case we are done.

Case 2. $|D_1 \cap D_2| > \frac{1}{2}c_1$. Presenter uses strategy $HS_{k,d}(\varepsilon_{3m+2}, \frac{r_b+p_b}{2}, p_c)$ to get a set of intervals $\mathcal{K}_4$ and then strategy $HS_{k,d}(\varepsilon_{3m+3}, \frac{r_a+p_a}{2}, p_b)$ to get $\mathcal{K}_5$. Let D_4 be a c_1-element subset of colors used by Algorithm to color $\mathcal{K}_4$, and D_5 be the set of colors used to color $\mathcal{K}_5$. See Fig. 5 for a diagram of the construction. Similar argument as in the previous case gives $C^* \cap D_4 = \emptyset$, $C^* \cap D_5 = \emptyset$, $D_2 \cap D_4 = \emptyset$, $D_1 \cap D_5 = \emptyset$, and $D_4 \cap D_5 = \emptyset$. Set D_2 contains at least $\frac{1}{2}c_1$

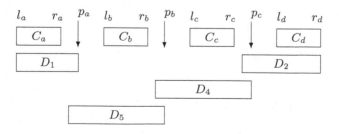

Fig. 5. Construction in case $|D_1 \cap D_2| \geq \frac{1}{2}c_1$

elements from the set D_1. Thus, we have $|D_4 \cap D_1| \leqslant \frac{1}{2}c_1$. Algorithm uses at least $|C^* \cup D_1 \cup D_4 \cup D_5| \geqslant c_m + c_1 + \frac{1}{2}c_1 + c_1 = c_{m+1}$ colors. Each set of intervals $\mathcal{J}_1, \ldots, \mathcal{J}_{\bar{c}}$ intersects with intervals in at most one of the sets $\mathcal{K}_1, \mathcal{K}_2, \mathcal{K}_4,$ or $\mathcal{K}_5$. Thus, all intervals can be colored with $\max\{2, m+1\}(\frac{d}{k} + \log d + 3) = o_{m+1}$ colors.   □

4   Unit Interval Coloring

Theorem 4. *For every $d \geqslant 2$ and $k, m \in \mathbb{N}_+$, there is a strategy for Presenter that forces Algorithm to use at least $\lfloor \frac{5m}{2} \rfloor \frac{d}{\log d+3}$ different colors in the on-line (k, d) unit interval coloring game while the constructed set of intervals is $m(\frac{d}{k} + \log d + 3)$-colorable.*

Proof. The proof combines strategy $HS_{k,d}(\varepsilon, L, R)$ introduced in the proof of Theorem 3 with technique similar to the one by Epstein and Levy [2,3]. Assume that the sequence of encoding parameters $\{\varepsilon_i\}_{i \in \mathbb{N}_+}$ is defined the same way as in the proof of Theorem 3.

The strategy consists of 3 phases. In the *initial phase* Presenter uses strategy $HS_{k,d}(\varepsilon_i, 0, 1)$ for $i = 1, \ldots, \lfloor \frac{m}{2} \rfloor$ sequentially. There is a coloring of all intervals introduced in the initial phase using $\lfloor \frac{m}{2} \rfloor (\frac{d}{k} + \log d + 3)$ colors, but Algorithm uses at least $\lfloor \frac{m}{2} \rfloor \frac{2d}{\log d+3}$ colors. Let C_{init} be a $\lfloor \frac{m}{2} \rfloor \frac{2d}{\log d+3}$-element subset of colors used by Algorithm in the initial phase.

For $L < R < L+1$, let $Sep(L, R)$ be the *separation strategy* that introduces d unit intervals in the following way. Initialize $l = L$, and $r = R$. To get next interval, calculate $p = \frac{1}{2}(l+r)$ and introduce interval $I = [p, p+1]$. If Algorithm colors I with color in C_{init}, then update $r = p$. Otherwise, *mark* interval I and update $l = p$. Observe that to the left of p there are only left endpoints of marked intervals. Moreover, all introduced intervals have nonempty intersection.

The *separation phase* consists of $2\lfloor \frac{m}{2} \rfloor$ subphases. We fix $L_1 = \frac{3}{2}$ and $R_1 = 2$. For $i = 2, \ldots, 2\lfloor \frac{m}{2} \rfloor$, points L_i and R_i are established after the $(i-1)$-th subphase. Denote by Sub_i, the strategy for the i-th subphase being a combination of the $HS_{k,d}(\varepsilon_i, 0, 1)$ strategy and the $Sep(L_i, R_i)$ strategy. Strategy Sub_i introduces d intervals. The position of each interval is determined using $Sep(L_i, R_i)$ strategy, and the d-dimensional vector of weights associated with each interval is determined according to $HS_{k,d}(\varepsilon_i, 0, 1)$. See Fig. 6 for a diagram of the strategy Sub_i.

At the end of each subphase, Presenter decides whether the subphase is *marked* or not. The set of marked subphases is denoted by $\mathcal{M}$. Let C_i be the set of colors used by Algorithm in the i-th subphase and not present in the set C_{init}. Subphase i is marked if and only if one of the following conditions holds:

1. the number of remaining subphases including the i-th is $\lfloor \frac{m}{2} \rfloor - |\mathcal{M}|$.
2. $|C_i| \geqslant \frac{d}{\log d+3}$ and $|\mathcal{M}| < \lfloor \frac{m}{2} \rfloor$,

Observe that at the end of the separation phase we have exactly $\lfloor \frac{m}{2} \rfloor$ marked subphases.

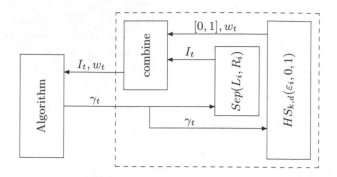

Fig. 6. Strategy Sub_i for a single subphase

Let L^* be the left endpoint of the leftmost interval introduced in the i-th subphase. Let L be the left endpoint of the rightmost interval introduced in the i-th subphase and colored by Algorithm with a color $c \notin C_{init}$. Set $L = L_i$ if such an interval does not exist. Let R be the left endpoint of the leftmost interval introduced in the i-th subphase and colored by Algorithm with a color $c \in C_{init}$. Set $R = R_i$ if such an interval does not exist. If subphase i is marked then $L_{i+1} = L$ and $R_{i+1} = R$. Otherwise, $L_{i+1} = L_i$ and $R_{i+1} = L^*$. This completes the definition of the separation phase.

Let $m' = 2\lfloor \frac{m}{2} \rfloor$ and $P = \frac{1}{2}(L_{m'+1} + R_{m'+1})$. Observe that every interval introduced in the separation phase with the left endpoint to the left of P belongs to a marked subphase and is colored with a color $c \notin C_{init}$. Let C_{sep} be the set of colors used in the separation phase to color intervals with the left endpoint to the left of P.

In each subphase Algorithm uses at least $\frac{2d}{\log d + 3}$ different colors, so in the separation phase Algorithm uses at least $2\lfloor \frac{m}{2} \rfloor \frac{2d}{\log d + 3}$ colors in total. Because $|C_{init}| = \lfloor \frac{m}{2} \rfloor \frac{2d}{\log d + 3}$, Algorithm, in the separation phase, uses at least $\lfloor \frac{m}{2} \rfloor \frac{2d}{\log d + 3}$ colors not in C_{init}. The set of marked subphases $\mathcal{M}$ contains x subphases in which Algorithm used at least $\frac{d}{\log d + 3}$ such colors and $\lfloor \frac{m}{2} \rfloor - x$ last subphases. From the first $\lfloor \frac{m}{2} \rfloor + x$ subphases only x subphases are marked. By the definition, in an unmarked subphase i for $i \leqslant \lfloor \frac{m}{2} \rfloor + x$, Algorithm uses less than $\frac{d}{\log d + 3}$ colors not in C_{init}. Thus, at most $\lfloor \frac{m}{2} \rfloor \frac{d}{\log d + 3}$ such colors from subphases 1 up to $\lfloor \frac{m}{2} \rfloor + x$ are not in the set C_{sep}. All colors not in C_{init} used in the subphase i for $i > \lfloor \frac{m}{2} \rfloor + x$ are in the set C_{sep}. Thus, $|C_{sep}| \geqslant \lfloor \frac{m}{2} \rfloor \frac{d}{\log d + 3}$.

In the *final phase*, Presenter uses strategy $HS_{k,d}(\varepsilon_i, P - 1, P)$ for $i = m + 1, \ldots, m + \lceil \frac{m}{2} \rceil$ sequentially. Every interval introduced in the final phase intersects with every interval from the initial phase and every interval from the separation phase with the left endpoint to the left of P. Thus, each color used in the final phase belongs neither to C_{init} nor to C_{sep}. In the final phase, Algorithm uses at least $\lceil \frac{m}{2} \rceil \frac{2d}{\log d + 3}$ colors.

In total, Algorithm uses at least $\left(2\left\lfloor\frac{m}{2}\right\rfloor + \left\lfloor\frac{m}{2}\right\rfloor + 2\left\lceil\frac{m}{2}\right\rceil\right)\frac{d}{\log d+3} = \left\lfloor\frac{5m}{2}\right\rfloor\frac{d}{\log d+3}$ different colors. On the other hand, the presented set of intervals can be easily colored using $\left(\left\lfloor\frac{m}{2}\right\rfloor + \left\lceil\frac{m}{2}\right\rceil\right)\left(\left\lfloor\frac{d}{k}\right\rfloor + \log d + 3\right) = m\left(\left\lfloor\frac{d}{k}\right\rfloor + \log d + 3\right)$ colors.   □

Note that for $k = +\infty$, the strategy $HS_{\infty,d}$ becomes independent of k-cardinality constraint. This gives two new bounds on the competitive ratio for on-line d-dimensional interval coloring problems.

Theorem 5. *For every $d \geqslant 2$ and $n \in \mathbb{N}_+$, there is a strategy for Presenter that forces Algorithm to use at least $(5m - 3)\frac{d}{\log d+3}$ different colors in the on-line d-dimensional interval coloring game while the constructed set of intervals is $m(\log d + 3)$-colorable.*

Theorem 6. *For every $d \geqslant 2$ and $n \in \mathbb{N}_+$, there is a strategy for Presenter that forces Algorithm to use at least $\left\lfloor\frac{5m}{2}\right\rfloor\frac{d}{\log d+3}$ different colors in the on-line d-dimensional unit interval coloring game while the constructed set of intervals is $m(\log d + 3)$-colorable.*

References

1. Azar, Y., Cohen, I.R., Kamara, S., Shepherd, B.: Tight bounds for online vector bin packing. In: Proceedings of the 45th Annual ACM Symposium on Theory of Computing, STOC 2013, Palo Alto, CA, USA, June 2013, pp. 961–970 (2013)
2. Epstein, L., Levy, M.: Online interval coloring and variants. In: Caires, L., Italiano, G.F., Monteiro, L., Palamidessi, C., Yung, M. (eds.) ICALP 2005. LNCS, vol. 3580, pp. 602–613. Springer, Heidelberg (2005). doi:10.1007/11523468_49
3. Epstein, L., Levy, M.: Online interval coloring with packing constraints. In: Jędrzejowicz, J., Szepietowski, A. (eds.) MFCS 2005. LNCS, vol. 3618, pp. 295–307. Springer, Berlin (2005). doi:10.1007/11549345_26
4. Halldórsson, M.M., Szegedy, M.: Lower bounds for on-line graph coloring. Theoret. Comput. Sci. **130**(1), 163–174 (1994)
5. Kierstead, H.A., Trotter, W.T.: An extremal problem in recursive combinatorics. In: Proceedings of the 12th Southeastern Conference on Combinatorics, Graph Theory and Computing, vol. II. Congressus Numerantium, vol. 33, Baton Rouge, LA, USA, March 1981, pp. 143–153 (1981)
6. Lovasz, L., Saks, M., Trotter, W.: An on-line graph coloring algorithm with sublinear performance ratio. Discrete Math. **75**(1), 319–325 (1989)

Parameterized and Exact Algorithms for Class Domination Coloring

R. Krithika[1], Ashutosh Rai[1], Saket Saurabh[1,2], and Prafullkumar Tale[1(✉)]

[1] The Institute of Mathematical Sciences, HBNI, Chennai, India
{rkrithika,ashutosh,saket,pptale}@imsc.res.in
[2] University of Bergen, Bergen, Norway

Abstract. A class domination coloring (also called as cd-coloring) of a graph is a proper coloring such that for every color class, there is a vertex that dominates it. The minimum number of colors required for a cd-coloring of the graph G, denoted by $\chi_{cd}(G)$, is called the class domination chromatic number (cd-chromatic number) of G. In this work, we consider two problems associated with the cd-coloring of a graph in the context of exact exponential-time algorithms and parameterized complexity. (1) Given a graph G on n vertices, find its cd-chromatic number. (2) Given a graph G and integers k and q, can we delete at most k vertices such that the cd-chromatic number of the resulting graph is at most q? For the first problem, we give an exact algorithm with running time $\mathcal{O}(2^n n^4 \log n)$. Also, we show that the problem is FPT with respect to the number of colors q as the parameter on chordal graphs. On graphs of girth at least 5, we show that the problem also admits a kernel with $\mathcal{O}(q^3)$ vertices. For the second (deletion) problem, we show NP-hardness for each $q \geq 2$. Further, on split graphs, we show that the problem is NP-hard if q is a part of the input and FPT with respect to k and q. As recognizing graphs with cd-chromatic number at most q is NP-hard in general for $q \geq 4$, the deletion problem is unlikely to be FPT when parameterized by the size of deletion set on general graphs. We show fixed parameter tractability for $q \in \{2,3\}$ using the known algorithms for finding a vertex cover and an odd cycle transversal as subroutines.

1   Introduction

A *dominating set* is a set of vertices whose closed neighbourhood contains the vertex set of the graph. A *proper coloring* of a graph is a partition of its vertex set into independent sets. That is, the graph induced by all the vertices of any partition is an independent set. The minimum number of colors in any proper coloring is called as the *chromatic number* of the graph. Given a graph G, the DOMINATING SET problem is to find a minimum dominating set of G and the GRAPH COLORING or CHROMATIC NUMBER problem is to compute a coloring

S. Saurabh—The research leading to these results has received funding from the European Research Council under the European Union's Seventh Framework Programme (FP7/2007-2013)/ERC grant agreement no. 306992.

B. Steffen et al. (Eds.): SOFSEM 2017, LNCS 10139, pp. 336–349, 2017.
DOI: 10.1007/978-3-319-51963-0_26

that uses the minimum number of colors. DOMINATING SET and GRAPH COL-ORING are two classical problems in the field of combinatorics and combinatorial algorithms. Being notoriously hard problems, they have been studied extensively in algorithmic realms like exact algorithms [3,17,18,23,24,32], approximation algorithms [4,21,22,25], and parameterized algorithms [1,2,5,14]. Further, the complexity of variants of these two problems like EDGE-CHROMATIC NUMBER, ACHROMATIC NUMBER, b-CHROMATIC NUMBER, INDEPENDENT DOMINATING SET and CONNECTED DOMINATING SET have also been widely investigated in the literature.

DOMINATOR COLORING and CLASS DOMINATION COLORING are two problems that have the flavour of both DOMINATING SET and CHROMATIC NUMBER. The former problem, introduced in [20], is the task of determining a minimum proper coloring of the graph such that every vertex contains at least one color class in its neighbourhood. The latter problem, also known as CD-COLORING, is to obtain a minimum proper coloring such that every color class is contained in the neighbourhood of some vertex. The decision versions of both the problems are known to be NP-complete when the number of colors is at least four and polynomial-time solvable otherwise [19,35]. Characterization of graphs that admit such colorings using at most 3 colors are also known [6,35]. In this paper, we study CLASS DOMINATION COLORING which is formally defined as follows.

CD-COLORING
Input: A graph G, an integer q.
Question: Can G be properly colored using at most q colors such that every color class is contained in the neighbourhood of some vertex?

The minimum number of colors needed in any cd-coloring of G is called the *class domination chromatic number (cd-chromatic number)* and is denoted by $\chi_{cd}(G)$. Also, G is said to be q-cd-colorable if $\chi_{cd}(G) \leq q$. The problem has also been studied on many restricted graph classes like split graphs, P_4-free graphs [35] and middle and central graphs of $K_{1,n}$, C_n and P_n [36]. We study this problem in the context of exact exponential-time algorithms and parameterized complexity. The field of exact algorithms typically deal with designing algorithms for NP-hard problems that are faster than brute-force search while the goal in parameterized complexity is to provide efficient algorithms for NP-complete problems by switching from the classical view of single-variate measure of the running time to a multi-variate one. In parameterized complexity, we consider instances (I, k) of parameterized a problem $\Pi \subseteq \Sigma^* \times \mathbb{N}$, where Σ is a finite alphabet. Algorithms in this area have running times of the form $f(k)|I|^{\mathcal{O}(1)}$, where k is an integer measuring some part of the problem. This integer k is called the *parameter*, and a problem that admits such an algorithm is said to be *fixed-parameter tractable* (FPT). The running time $f(k)|I|^{\mathcal{O}(1)}$ where f is an exponential function is also specified as $\mathcal{O}^*(f(k))$ suppressing the polynomial factors. In most of the cases, the solution size is taken to be the parameter, which means that this approach results in efficient (polynomial-time) algorithms when the solution is of small size. A *kernelization* algorithm for a parameterized problem Π is a polynomial time procedure which takes as input an instance (x, k) of Π and returns an instance (x', k') such that $(x, k) \in \Pi$ if and only if $(x', k') \in \Pi$ and $|x'| \leq h(k)$ and $k' \leq g(k)$, for some computable functions h, g. The returned instance is called as the *kernel* for Π and $h(k) + g(k)$ is said to be the *size of the kernel*. We say that Π admits a *polynomial kernel* if h and g are polynomial. For more background on parameterized complexity, we refer the reader to the monographs [11, 13, 15, 29].

We first observe that parameterizing CD-COLORING by the solution size (which is the number of colors) does not help in designing efficient algorithms as the problem is para-NP-hard (NP-hard even for constant values of the parameter). Hence, this problem is unlikely to be FPT when parameterized by the solution size. Then, we describe an $\mathcal{O}(2^n n^4 \log n)$-time algorithm for finding the cd-chromatic number of a graph using polynomial method. Next, we show that CD-COLORING is FPT when parameterized by the number of colors and the treewidth of the input graph. Further, we show that the problem is FPT when parameterized by the number of colors on chordal graphs. Kaminski and Lozin [28] showed that determining if a graph of girth at least g admits a proper coloring with at most q colors or not is NP-complete for any fixed $q \geq 3$ and $g \geq 3$. In particular, CHROMATIC NUMBER is para-NP-hard for graphs of girth at least 5. In contrast, we show that CD-COLORING is FPT on this graph class and admits a kernel with $\mathcal{O}(q^3)$ vertices.

On a graph G that is not q-cd-colorable, a natural optimization question is to check if we can delete at most k vertices from G such that the cd-chromatic number of the resultant graph is at most q? We define this problem as follows.

CD-PARTIZATION
Input: Graph G, integers k and q
Question: Does there exist $S \subseteq V(G)$, $|S| \leq k$, such that $\chi_{cd}(G - S) \leq q$?

If q is fixed, then we refer to the problem as q-CD-PARTIZATION. Once again, from parameterized complexity point of view, this question is not interesting on general graphs for values of q greater than three, as in those cases, an FPT algorithm with deletion set (solution) size as the parameter is a polynomial-time recognition algorithm for q-cd-colorable graphs. Hence, the deletion question is interesting only on graphs where the recognition problem is polynomial-time solvable. We show that q-CD-PARTIZATION is NP-complete for each $q \geq 2$, and that for $q \in \{2, 3\}$, the problem is FPT with respect to the solution size as the parameter. Our algorithms use the known parameterized algorithms for finding a vertex cover and an odd cycle transversal as subroutines. We also show that CD-PARTIZATION remains NP-complete on split graphs and is FPT when parameterized by the number of colors and solution size. Due to space constraints, proofs of results marked † have been omitted. They will appear in the full version of the paper.

2 Preliminaries

The set of integers $\{1, 2, \ldots, k\}$ is denoted by $[k]$. All graphs considered in this paper are finite, undirected and simple. For the terms which are not explicitly defined here, we use standard notations from [12]. For a graph G, its vertex set is denoted by $V(G)$ and its edge set is denoted by $E(G)$. For a vertex $v \in V(G)$, its (open) *neighbourhood* $N_G(v)$ is the set of all vertices adjacent to it and its *closed neighborhood* is the set $N_G(v) \cup \{v\}$. We omit the subscript in the notation for neighbourhood if the graph under consideration is implicitly clear. The degree of a vertex v is the size of its open neighborhood.

For a set $S \subseteq V(G)$, the *subgraph of G induced by S*, denoted by $G[S]$, is defined as the subgraph of G with vertex set S and edge set $\{(u, v) \in E(G) : u, v \in S\}$. The subgraph of G obtained after deleting S (and the edges incident on it) is denoted as $G - S$. The *girth* of a graph is the length of a smallest cycle. A set $D \subseteq V(G)$ is said to be a *dominating set* of G if every vertex in $V(G) \backslash D$ is adjacent to some vertex in D. A dominating set is called *total dominating set* if every vertex in $V(G)$ is adjacent to some vertex in it.

A *proper coloring* of G with q colors is a function $f : V(G) \to [q]$ such that for all $(u, v) \in E(G)$, $f(u) \neq f(v)$. For a proper coloring f of G with q colors and $i \in [q]$, $f^{-1}(i) \subseteq V(G)$ is called a *color class* in the coloring f. The *chromatic number* $\chi(G)$ of G is the minimum number of colors required in a proper coloring of G. A *clique* is a graph which has an edge between every pair of vertices. The *clique number* $\omega(G)$ of G is the size of a largest clique which is a subgraph of G. A *vertex cover* is a set of vertices that contains at least one endpoint of every edge in the graph. An *independent set* is a set of pairwise nonadjacent vertices. A graph is said to be a *bipartite graph* if its vertex set can be partitioned into 2 independent sets. An *odd cycle transversal* is a set of vertices whose deletion results in a bipartite graph. A *tree-decomposition* of a graph G is a pair $(\mathbb{T}, \mathcal{X} = \{X_t\}_{t \in V(\mathbb{T})})$ such that

- $\bigcup_{t \in V(\mathbb{T})} X_t = V(G)$,
- for every edge $(x, y) \in E(G)$ there is a $t \in V(\mathbb{T})$ such that $\{x, y\} \subseteq X_t$, and
- for every vertex $v \in V(G)$ the subgraph of $\mathbb{T}$ induced by the set $\{t \mid v \in X_t\}$ is connected.

The *width* of a tree decomposition is $\max_{t \in V(\mathbb{T})} |X_t| - 1$ and the *treewidth* of G, denoted by $\mathbf{tw}(G)$, is the minimum width over all tree decompositions of G. The syntax of *Monadic Second Order Logic (MSO)* of graphs includes the logical connectives $\vee$, $\wedge$, $\neg$, $\Rightarrow$, $\Leftrightarrow$, variables for vertices, edges, sets of vertices, sets of edges, the quantifiers $\forall$, $\exists$ that can be applied to these variables and the following five binary relations.

- $u \in U$ where u is a vertex variable and U is a vertex set variable;
- $e \in F$ where e is an edge variable and F is an edge set variable;
- $\mathbf{inc}(e, u)$, where e is an edge variable, u is a vertex variable, and the interpretation is that the edge e is incident with the vertex u;

– **adj**(u, v), where u and v are vertex variables and the interpretation is that u and v are adjacent;
– equality of variables representing vertices, edges, sets of vertices, and sets of edges.

For a MSO formula ϕ, $||\phi||$ denotes the length of its encoding as a string.

Theorem 1 (Courcelle's theorem, [9,10]). *Let ϕ be a graph property that is expressible in MSO. Suppose G is a graph on n vertices with treewidth tw equipped with the evaluation of all the free variables of ϕ. Then, there is an algorithm that verifies whether ϕ is satisfied in G in $f(||\phi||, tw) \cdot n$ time for some computable function f.*

We end the preliminaries section with following simple observations.

Observation 1. *If $G_1, \ldots, G_l$ are the connected components of G, then $\chi_{cd}(G) = \sum_{i=1}^{l} \chi_{cd}(G_i)$.*

Observation 2. *If G is q-cd-colorable, then G has a dominating set of size at most q.*

3   Exact Algorithm for cd-Chromatic Number

Let G denote the input graph on n vertices. Given a coloring of $V(G)$, we can check in polynomial time whether it is a cd-coloring or not. Therefore, to compute $\chi_{cd}(G)$, we can iterate over all possible colorings of $V(G)$ with at most n colors and return the valid cd-coloring that uses the minimum number of colors. This brute force algorithm runs in $2^{\mathcal{O}(n \log n)}$ time. In this section we present an algorithm which runs in $\mathcal{O}(2^n n^4 \log(n))$ time. The idea for this algorithm is inspired by an exact algorithm for b-CHROMATIC NUMBER presented in [30]. We first list some preliminaries on polynomials and Fast Fourier Transform following the framework of [30].

A binary vector ϕ is a finite sequence of bits and $val(\phi)$ denotes the integer d of which ϕ is the binary representation. All vectors considered here are binary vectors and are synonymous to binary numbers. Further, they are the binary representations of integers less than 2^n and are assumed to consist of n bits. $\phi_1 + \phi_2$ denotes the vector obtained by the bitwise addition of the binary numbers (vectors) ϕ_1 and ϕ_2. Let $U = \{u_1, u_2, \ldots, u_n\}$ denote a universe with a fixed ordering on its elements. The *characteristic vector* of a set $S \subseteq U$, denoted by $\psi(S)$, is the vector of length $|U|$ whose j^{th} bit is 1 if $u_j \in S$ and 0 otherwise. The *Hamming weight* of a vector ϕ is the number of 1s in ϕ and it is denoted by $\mathcal{H}(\phi)$. Observe that $\mathcal{H}(\psi(S)) = |S|$. The Hamming weight of an integer is define as hamming weight of its binary representation. To obtain the claimed running time bound for our exponential-time algorithm, we make use of the algorithm for multiplying polynomials based on the Fast Fourier Transform.

Lemma 1 [33]. *Two polynomials of degree at most d over any commutative ring $\mathcal{R}$ can be multiplied using $\mathcal{O}(d \cdot \log d \cdot \log \log d)$ additions and multiplications in $\mathcal{R}$.*

Let z denote an indeterminate variable. We use the monomial $z^{val(\psi(S))}$ to represent the set $S \subseteq U$ and as a natural extension, we use univariate polynomials to represent a family of sets.

Definition 1 (Characteristic Polynomial of a Family of Sets). *For a family $\mathcal{F} = \{S_1, S_2, \ldots, S_q\}$ of subsets of U, the characteristic polynomial of $\mathcal{F}$ is defined as $p_\psi(\mathcal{F}) = \sum_{i=1}^{q} z^{val(\psi(S_i))}$.*

Definition 2 (Representative Polynomial). *For a polynomial $p(z) = \sum_{i=1}^{q} a_i \cdot z^i$, we define its representative polynomial as $\sum_{i=1}^{q} b_i \cdot z^i$ where $b_i = 1$ if $a_i \neq 0$ and $b_i = 0$ if $a_i = 0$.*

Definition 3 (Hamming Projection). *The Hamming projection of the polynomial $p(z) = \sum_{i=1}^{q} a_i \cdot z^i$ to the integer h is defined as $\mathcal{H}_h(p(z)) := \sum_{i=1}^{q} b_i \cdot z^i$ where $b_i = a_i$ if $\mathcal{H}(i) = h$ and $b_i = 0$ otherwise.*

Next, for two sets $S_1, S_2 \subseteq U$, we define a modified multiplication operation ($\star$) of the monomials $z^{\psi(S_1)}$ and $z^{\psi(S_2)}$ in the following way.

$$z^{val(\psi(S_1))} \star z^{val(\psi(S_2))} = \begin{cases} z^{val(\psi(S_1)) + val(\psi(S_2))} & \text{if } S_1 \cap S_2 = \emptyset \\ 0 & \text{otherwise} \end{cases}$$

For a polynomial function $p(z)$ of z and a positive integer $\ell \geq 2$, we inductively define the polynomial $p(z)^\ell$ as $p(z)^\ell := p(z)^{\ell-1} \star p(z)$. Here, coefficients of monomials follow addition and multiplications defined over underlying field. We now describe an algorithm for implementing the $\star$ operation using the standard multiplication operation and the notion of Hamming weights of bit strings associated with exponents.

Algorithm 3.1. Compute ($\star$) product of two polynomials

Input: Two polynomials $q(z), r(z)$ of degree at most 2^n
Output: $q(z) \star r(z)$
1 Initialize polynomials $t(z)$ and $t'(z)$ to 0
2 **for** *each ordered pair (i, j) such that $i + j \leq n$* **do**
3 | Compute $s_i(z) = \mathcal{H}_i(q(z))$ and $s_j(z) = \mathcal{H}_j(r(z))$
4 | Compute $s_{ij}(z) = s_i(z) \star s_j(z)$ using Lemma 1
5 | $t'(z) = t(z) + \mathcal{H}_{i+j}(s_{ij}(z))$
6 | Set $t(z)$ as the representative polynomial of $t'(z)$
7 **return** $t(z)$

Lemma 2 (†). *Let $\mathcal{F}_1$ and $\mathcal{F}_2$ be two families of subsets of U. Let $\mathcal{F}$ denote the collection $\{S_1 \cup S_2 \mid S_1 \in \mathcal{F}_1, S_2 \in \mathcal{F}_2 \text{ and } S_1 \cap S_2 = \emptyset\}$. Then, $p_\psi(\mathcal{F}_1) \star p_\psi(\mathcal{F}_2)$ computed by Algorithm 3.1 is $p_\psi(\mathcal{F})$.*

Corollary 1 (†). *Given a polynomial $p(z)$ of degree at most 2^n, there is an algorithm that computes $p(z)^\ell$ in $\mathcal{O}(2^n n^3 \log n \cdot l)$ time.*

We now prove a result which correlates the existence of a partition of a set with the presence of a monomial in a polynomial associated with it.

Lemma 3. *Consider a universe U and a family $\mathcal{F}$ of its subsets with characteristic polynomial $p(z)$. For any $W \subseteq U$, W is the disjoint union of ℓ sets from $\mathcal{F}$ if and only if there exists a monomial $z^{val(\psi(W))}$ in $p(z)^\ell$.*

Proof. Let W be the disjoint union of $S_1, S_2, \ldots, S_\ell$ such that $S_i \in \mathcal{F}$ for all $i \in [\ell]$. For any $j \in [n]$, the jth bit of $\psi(W)$ is 1 if and only if there is exactly one S_i such that j^{th} bit of $\psi(S_i)$ is 1. Thus, $val(\psi(W)) = val(\psi(S_1)) + val(\psi(S_2)) + \cdots + val(\psi(S_\ell))$. Now, for every S_i there is a term $z^{val(\psi(S_i))}$ in $p(z)$. Further, as the S_i's are pairwise disjoint, the monomial $z^{val(\psi(S_1))} \star z^{val(\psi(S_2))} \star \cdots \star z^{val(\psi(S_\ell))}$ which is equal to $z^{val(\psi(W))}$ is present in $p(z)^\ell$. We prove the converse by induction on ℓ. For $\ell = 1$, the statement is vacuously true and for $\ell = 2$, the claim holds from the proof of Lemma 2. Assume that the claim holds for all the integers which are smaller than ℓ, i.e. if there exists a monomial $z^{val(\psi(W))}$ in $p(z)^{\ell-1}$ then W can be partitioned into $\ell - 1$ disjoint sets from $\mathcal{F}$.

If there exists a monomial $z^{val(\psi(W))}$ in $p(z)^\ell = p(z)^{\ell-1} \star p(z)$ then it is the product of two monomials, say $z^{val(\psi(W_1))}$ in $p(z)^{\ell-1}$ and $z^{val(\psi(W_2))}$ in $p(z)$ respectively with $W_1 \cap W_2 = \emptyset$. By induction hypothesis, W_1 is the disjoint union of $S_1, S_2, \ldots, S_{\ell-1}$ such that $S_i \in \mathcal{F}$ for all $i \in [\ell-1]$. Also, W_2 is in $\mathcal{F}$ and since $W_1 \cap W_2 = \emptyset$, $S_i \cap W_2 = \emptyset$ for each i. Therefore, W can be partitioned into sets $S_1, S_2, \ldots, S_{\ell-1}, W_2$ each of which belong to $\mathcal{F}$. □

We now are in a position to state the main theorem of this section.

Theorem 2. *Given a graph G on n vertices, there is an algorithm which finds its cd-chromatic number in $\mathcal{O}(2^n n^4 \log n)$ time.*

Proof. Fix an arbitrary ordering on $V(G)$. With $V(G)$ as the universe, we define the family $\mathcal{F}$ as $\{X \subseteq V(G) | X$ is an independent set and $\exists\, y \in V(G)$ s.t. $X \subseteq N(y)\}$. Every set in $\mathcal{F}$ is an independent set and there exists a vertex which dominates it. That is, $\mathcal{F}$ is the collection of the possible color classes in any cd-coloring of G. Let $p(z)$ be the characteristic polynomial of $\mathcal{F}$. By Lemma 3, if there exists a monomial $z^{val(\psi(V(G)))}$ in $p(z)^\ell$ then $V(G)$ can be partitioned into ℓ sets each belonging to $\mathcal{F}$. Hence the smallest integer ℓ for which there exists a monomial $z^{val(\psi(V(G)))}$ in $p(z)^\ell$ is $\chi_{cd}(G)$. By Corollary 1, $p(z)^\ell$ can be computed in $\mathcal{O}(2^n n^3 \log n \cdot l)$ time. As the cd-chromatic number of a graph is upper bounded by n, the claimed running time bound follows. □

4   FPT Algorithms for cd-Chromatic Number

Determining whether a graph G has cd-chromatic number at most q is NP-hard on general graphs for $q \geq 4$. This implies that the CD-COLORING problem parameterized by the number of colors is para-NP-hard on general graphs. Thus this necessitates the search for special classes of graphs where CD-COLORING is FPT. In this section we give FPT algorithms for CD-COLORING on chordal graphs and graphs of girth at least 5.

We start by proving that CD-COLORING parameterized by the number of colors and treewidth of graph is FPT. Towards this, we will use Courcelle's powerful theorem which interlinks the fixed parameter tractability of a certain graph property with its expressibility as an MSO formula. We can write many graph theoretical properties as an MSO formula. Following are three examples which we will use in writing an MSO formula to check whether a graph has cd-chromatic number at most q.

- To check whether $V_1, V_2, \ldots, V_q$ is a partition of $V(G)$.

$$\mathsf{Part}(V_1, V_2, \ldots, V_q) \equiv \forall u \in V(G)[\exists i \in [q][(u \in V_i) \wedge (\forall j \in [q][i \neq j \Rightarrow u \notin V_j)]]]$$

- To check whether a given vertex set V_i is an independent set or not.

$$\mathsf{IndSet}(V_i) \equiv \forall u \in V_i[\forall v \in V_i[\neg adj(u, v)]]$$

- To check whether given vertex set V_i is dominated by some vertex or not.

$$\mathsf{Dom}(V_i) \equiv \exists u \in V(G)[\forall v \in V_i[adj(u, v)]]$$

We use $\phi(G, q)$ to denote the MSO formula which states that G has cd-chromatic number at most q. We use the formulas defined above as macros in $\phi(G, q)$.

$$\phi(G, q) \equiv \exists V_1, V_2, \ldots, V_q \subseteq V(G)[\mathsf{Part}(V_1, V_2, \ldots, V_q) \wedge$$
$$\mathsf{IndSet}(V_1) \wedge \cdots \wedge \mathsf{IndSet}(V_q) \wedge \mathsf{Dom}(V_1) \wedge \cdots \wedge \mathsf{Dom}(V_q)]$$

It is easy to see that the length of $\phi(G, q)$ is upper bounded by a linear function of q. By applying Theorem 1 we obtain the following result.

Theorem 3. CD-COLORING *parameterized by the number of colors and the treewidth of the input graph is* FPT.

4.1 Chordal Graphs

As the graph gets more structured, we expect many NP-hard problems to get *easier* in some sense on the restricted class of graphs having that structure. For example, CHROMATIC-COLORING is NP-hard on general graphs but it is polynomial time solvable on chordal graphs. However, CD-COLORING is NP-hard even on the chordal graphs [34] and we show that it is FPT when parameterized by the number of colors.

Theorem 4. CD-COLORING *parameterized by the number of colors is* FPT *on chordal graphs.*

4.2   Graphs with Girth at Least 5

In this section, we show that CD-COLORING on graphs of girth at least 5 is FPT with respect to the solution size as the parameter. By Observation 1, we can assume that the input graph G is connected. We can define cd-coloring of a connected graph as a proper coloring such that every color class is contained in the open neighbourhood of some vertex. In other words, we do not allow a vertex to dominate itself. One can verify that the two definitions of cd-coloring are identical on connected graphs. We now define the notion of a *total-dominating set* of a graph G. A set $S \subseteq V(G)$ is called a *total-dominating set* if $V(G) = \bigcup_{v \in S} N(v)$. That is, for every vertex $v \in V(G)$, there exists a vertex $u \in S$, $u \neq v$, such that $v \in N(u)$. Our interest in total-dominating set is because of its relation to cd-coloring in graphs that do not contain triangles, that is, graphs of girth at least 4. In particular, we show the following lemma.

Lemma 4. *If $g(G) \geq 4$, then the size of a minimum total dominating set is equal $\chi_{cd}(G)$.*

Lemma 4 shows that to prove that CD-COLORING is FPT on graphs of $g(G) \geq 4$ it suffices to show that finding a total dominating set of size at most k is FPT on these graphs. This leads to the TOTAL DOMINATING SET problem. Given a graph G and an integer k, the TOTAL DOMINATING SET problem asks whether there exists a total dominating set of size at most k. Observe that we can test whether G has a total dominating set of size at most k by enumerating all subsets S of $V(G)$ of size at most k and checking whether it forms a total-dominating set in polynomial time. This immediately gives an algorithm with running time $n^{\mathcal{O}(k)}$ for CD-COLORING on graphs with girth at least 4. It is not hard to modify the reduction given in [31] to show that TOTAL DOMINATING SET is $W[2]$ hard on bipartite graphs. Thus, Lemma 4 implies that even CD-COLORING is $W[2]$ hard on bipartite graphs. Hence, if we need to show that CD-COLORING is FPT, we must assume that the girth of the input graph is at least 4. In the rest of the section, we show that CD-COLORING is FPT on graphs with girth at least 5 by showing that TOTAL DOMINATING SET is FPT on those graphs. Before proceeding further, we note some simple properties of graphs with girth at least 5.

Observation 3. *For a graph G, if $g(G) \geq 5$ then for any v in $V(G)$, $N(v)$ is an independent set and for any u, v in $V(G)$, $|N(v) \cap N(u)| \leq 1$.*

Raman and Saurabh [31] defined a variation of SET COVER problem, namely, BOUNDED INTERSECTION SET COVER. An input to the problem consists of a universe $\mathcal{U}$, a collection $\mathcal{F}$ of subsets of $\mathcal{U}$ and a positive integer k with the property that for any two S_i, S_j in $\mathcal{F}$, $|S_i \cap S_j| \leq c$ for some constant c and the objective is to check whether there exists a sub-collection $\mathcal{F}_0$ of $\mathcal{F}$ of size at most k such that $\bigcup_{S \in \mathcal{F}_0} = \mathcal{U}$. In the same paper, the authors proved that the BOUNDED INTERSECTION SET COVER is FPT when parameterized by the solution size. TOTAL DOMINATING SET on (G, k) where G has girth at least 5 can be reduced to BOUNDED INTERSECTION SET COVER with $\mathcal{U} = V(G)$ and $\mathcal{F} = \{N(v)| \ \forall v \in V(G)\}$. By Observation 3, we can fix the constant c to be 1. Hence we have the following lemma.

Lemma 5. *On graphs with girth at least 5,* TOTAL DOMINATING SET *is* FPT *when parameterized by the solution size.*

We now prove that the problem has a polynomial kernel and use it to design another FPT algorithm.

Lemma 6. TOTAL DOMINATING SET *admits a kernel of* $\mathcal{O}(k^3)$ *vertices on the class of graphs with girth at least 5.*

Proof. Let G be a graph with girth at least 5. We first show that every vertex of degree at least $k + 1$ should be included in any total dominating set of size at most k. Suppose there exists a total dominating set X of G of size at most k which does not contain such a vertex u. Since $N(u)$ (having size at least $k + 1$) is dominated by X and no vertex can dominate itself, by the Pigeon Hole Principle, there exists a vertex, say w, in X which is adjacent to at least two vertices, say, v_1, v_2 in $N(u)$. This implies that w, v_1, v_2, u forms a cycle of length 4, contradicting the fact that girth of G is at least 5.

Suppose G has a total dominating set of size at most k. Construct a tri-partition of $V(G)$ as follows:

$$H = \{u \in V(G) \mid |N(u)| \geq k + 1\};$$
$$J = \{v \in V(G) \mid v \notin H, \ \exists u \in H \text{ such that } (u,v) \in E(G)\};$$
$$R = V(G) \backslash (H \cup J)$$

By the above claim, H is contained in every total dominating set of size at most k. Hence, the size of H is upper bounded by k. Note that there is no edge between a vertex in H and a vertex in R. Thus, R has to be dominated by at most k vertices from $J \cup R$. However, the degree of vertices in $J \cup R$ is at most k and hence $|R| \leq \mathcal{O}(k^2)$ and $|J \cap N(R)|$ is upper bounded by $\mathcal{O}(k^3)$. We will now bound the size of $J^\star = J \backslash N(R)$. For that, we first apply the following reduction rule on the vertices in $J^\star$.

Reduction Rule 1. *For* $u, v \in J^\star$, *if* $N(u) \cap H \subseteq N(v) \cap H$ *then delete* u.

The correctness of this reduction follows from the observation that all the vertices in J have been dominated by the vertices in H. The only reason any vertex in $J^\star$ is part of a total dominating set is because that vertex is used to dominate some vertex in H. If this is the case then the vertex u in the solution can be replaced by the vertex v. In the reverse direction, if X is a total dominating set of $G - \{u\}$ and $|X| \leq k$, then $H \subseteq X$. Hence u is dominated by $x \in X \cap H$ in G too. That is, X is a total dominating set of G.

All that remains is to bound the size of $J^\star$. We partition $J^\star$ into two sets namely J_1 and J_2. The set J_1 is the set of vertices which are adjacent to exactly one vertex in H whereas each vertex in J_2 is adjacent to at least two vertices in H. After exhaustive application of Reduction Rule 1, no two vertices in J_1 can be adjacent to one vertex in H and hence $|J_1| \leq |H| \leq k$. Any vertex in J_2 is adjacent to at least two vertices in H. For every vertex u in J_2, we assign a pair of vertices in H to which u is adjacent. By Observation 3, no two vertices in J_2 can be assigned to the same pair and hence the size of J_2 is upper bounded by $\binom{k}{2} \leq k^2$. Combining all the bounds, we get a kernel with $\mathcal{O}(k^3)$ number of vertices. $\square$

Combining Lemmas 4 and 6 we obtain the following theorem.

Theorem 5. *On graphs with girth at least 5, CD-COLORING admits an algorithm running in $\mathcal{O}(2^{\mathcal{O}(q^3)} q^{12} \log q^3)$ time and an $\mathcal{O}(q^3)$ sized vertex kernel, where q is number of colors.*

5 Complexity of CD-Partization

In this section, we study the complexity of CD-PARTIZATION. As recognizing graphs with cd-chromatic number at most q is NP-hard on general graphs for $q \geq 4$, the deletion problem is also NP-hard on general graphs for such values of q. For $q = 1$, the problem is trivial as $\chi_{cd}(G) = 1$ if and only if G is the graph on one vertex. In this section, we show NP-hardness for $q \in \{2, 3\}$. We remark that $\mathcal{G} = \{G \mid \chi_{cd}(G) \leq q\}$ is not a hereditary graph class and so the generic result of Lewis and Yannakakis [26] does not imply the claimed NP-hardness.

5.1 Para-NP-Hardness in General Graphs

Given a graph G, integers k and q, the PARTIZATION problem is the task of determining whether there exists $S \subseteq V(G)$, $|S| \leq k$, such that $\chi(G - S) \leq q$ or not. Once again if q is fixed, we refer to the problem as q-PARTIZATION. Observe that the classical NP-complete problems VERTEX COVER [16] and ODD CYCLE TRANSVERSAL [16] are 1-PARTIZATION and 2-PARTIZATION, respectively. Now, we proceed to show the claimed hardness.

Theorem 6 (†). *q-CD-PARTIZATION is NP-complete for $q \in \{2, 3\}$.*

5.2 NP-Hardness and Fixed-Parameter Tractability in Split Graphs

A graph is a *split graph* if its vertex set can be partitioned into a clique and an independent set. As split graphs are perfect (clique number is equal to the chromatic number for every induced subgraph), it follows that a split graph G is r-colorable if and only if $\omega(G) \leq r$. From [8,37], PARTIZATION ON SPLIT GRAPHS is known to be NP-complete. This hardness was shown by a reduction from SET COVER [16]. We modify this reduction to show that CD-PARTIZATION is NP-complete on split graphs. The problem is in NP as the cd-chromatic coloring of a split graph can be verified in polynomial time [35].

Theorem 7 (†). CD-PARTIZATION *on split graphs is* NP-*hard.*

Further, as SET COVER parameterized by solution size is W[2]-hard [11], we have the following result.

Corollary 2. CD-PARTIZATION *on split graphs parameterized by q is* W[2]-*hard.*

Now, we show that the problem is FPT with respect to q and k.

Theorem 8 (†). CD-PARTIZATION *on split graphs is* FPT *with respect to parameters q and k. Furthermore, the problem does not admit a polynomial kernel unless* NP $\subseteq$ coNP/*poly.*

6   Deletion to 3-cd-Colorable Graphs

We use the characterization of 3-cd-colorable graphs known from [35] and the following well-known results on VERTEX COVER and ODD CYCLE TRANSVERSAL to show the main result of this section. Given a graph G and a positive integer k, there is an algorithm running in $\mathcal{O}^*(1.2738^k)$ time that determines if G has a vertex cover of size at most k or not [7] and there is an algorithm running in $\mathcal{O}^*(2.3146^k)$ time that determines if G has an odd cycle transversal of size at most k or not [27].

As we would subsequently show, our algorithms reduce the problem of finding an optimum deletion set into finding appropriate vertex covers and constrained odd cycle transversals. The current best parameterized algorithm for finding a vertex cover can straightaway be used as a subroutine in our algorithm while the one for finding an odd cycle transversal requires the following results. Consider a graph G and let v be a vertex in G. Define the graph G' to be the graph obtained from G by deleting v and adding a new vertex v_{ij} for each pair v_i, v_j of neighbors of v; further v_{ij} is adjacent to v_i and v_j.

Lemma 7 (†). *G has a minimal odd cycle transversal of size at most k that excludes vertex v if and only if G′ has a minimal odd cycle transversal of size at most k.*

Let $P, Q \subseteq V(G)$ be two disjoint sets. Let G'' be the graph constructed from G by adding an independent set I_P of $k+1$ new vertices each of which is adjacent to every vertex in P and an independent set I_Q of $k+1$ new vertices each of which is adjacent to every vertex in Q. Further, every vertex in I_P is adjacent to every vertex in I_Q.

Lemma 8 (†). *G has a minimal odd cycle transversal O of size at most k such that G − O has a bipartition (X,Y) with $P \subseteq X$ and $Q \subseteq Y$ if and only if G″ has a minimal odd cycle transversal of size at most k.*

This leads to the following result.

Theorem 9 (†). *Given a graph G and an integer k, there is an algorithm that determines if there is a set S of size k whose deletion results in a graph H with $\chi_{cd}(H) \leq 3$ in $\mathcal{O}^*(2.3146^k)$ time.*

7   Concluding Remarks

In this work, we described exact and FPT algorithms for problems associated with cd-coloring. We also explored the complexity of finding the cd-chromatic number in graphs of girth at least 5 and chordal graphs. On the former graph class, we described a polynomial kernel. The kernelization complexity on other graph classes and whether the problem is FPT parameterized by only treewidth are natural directions for further study.

References

1. Alber, J., Bodlaender, H.L., Fernau, H., Kloks, T., Niedermeier, R.: Fixed parameter algorithms for dominating set and related problems on planar graphs. Algorithmica **33**(4), 461–493 (2002)
2. Alon, N., Gutner, S.: Linear time algorithms for finding a dominating set of fixed size in degenerated graphs. Algorithmica **54**(4), 544–556 (2009)
3. Björklund, A., Husfeldt, T., Koivisto, M.: Set partitioning via inclusion-exclusion. SIAM J. Comput. **39**(2), 546–563 (2009)
4. Blum, A., Karger, D.R.: An $\tilde{\mathcal{O}}(n^{3/14})$-coloring algorithm for 3-colorable graphs. Inf. Process. Lett. **61**(1), 49–53 (1997)
5. Cai, L.: Parameterized complexity of vertex colouring. Discrete Appl. Math. **127**(3), 415–429 (2003)
6. Chellali, M., Maffray, F.: Dominator Colorings in Some Classes of Graphs. Graph. Comb. **28**(1), 97–107 (2012)
7. Chen, J., Kanj, I., Xia, G.: Improved upper bounds for vertex cover. Theor. Comput. Sci. **411**(40–42), 3736–3756 (2010)
8. Corneil, D.G., Fonlupt, J.: The complexity of generalized clique covering. Discrete Appl. Math. **22**(2), 109–118 (1989)
9. Courcelle, B.: The monadic second-order logic of graphs. I. Recognizable sets of finite graphs. Inf. Comput. **85**(1), 12–75 (1990)
10. Courcelle, B.: The monadic second-order logic of graphs III: tree-decompositions. Minor Complex. Issues **ITA 26**, 257–286 (1992)
11. Cygan, M., Fomin, F.V., Kowalik, L., Lokshtanov, D., Marx, D., Pilipczuk, M., Pilipczuk, M., Saurabh, S.: Parameterized Algorithms. Springer, Cham (2015)
12. Diestel, R.: Graph Theory. Springer, Heidelberg (2006)
13. Downey, R.G., Fellows, M.R.: Fundamentals of Parameterized Complexity. Springer, London (2013)
14. Downey, R.G., Fellows, M.R., McCartin, C., Rosamond, F.A.: Parameterized approximation of dominating set problems. Inf. Process. Lett. **109**(1), 68–70 (2008)
15. Flum, J., Grohe, M.: Parameterized Complexity Theory. Springer, Heidelberg (2006)
16. Garey, M.R., Johnson, D.S.: Computers and Intractability: A Guide to the Theory of NP-Completeness. W.H. Freeman and Company, New York (1979)
17. Gaspers, S., Kratsch, D., Liedloff, M., Todinca, I.: Exponential time algorithms for the minimum dominating set problem on some graph classes. ACM Trans. Algorithms **6**(1), 9:1–21 (2009)
18. Gaspers, S., Liedloff, M.: A branch-and-reduce algorithm for finding a minimum independent dominating set. Discrete Math. Theor. Comput. Sci. **14**(1), 29–42 (2012)

19. Gera, R.: On dominator colorings in graphs. In: Graph Theory Notes of New York LII, pp. 25–30 (2007)
20. Gera, R., Rasmussen, C., Horton, S.: Dominator colorings and safe clique partitions. Congressus Numerantium **181**(7–9), 1932 (2006)
21. Guha, S., Khuller, S.: Improved methods for approximating node weighted steiner trees and connected dominating sets. Inf. Comput. **150**(1), 57–74 (1999)
22. Kim, D., Zhang, Z., Li, X., Wang, W., Wu, W., Du, D.Z.: A better approximation algorithm for computing connected dominating sets in unit ball graphs. IEEE Trans. Mob. Comput. **9**(8), 1108–1118 (2010)
23. Kratsch, D.: Exact algorithms for dominating set. In: Kao, M.-Y. (ed.) Encyclopedia of Algorithms, pp. 284–286. Springer, New York (2008)
24. Lawler, E.: A note on the complexity of the chromatic number problem. Inf. Process. Lett. **5**(3), 66–67 (1976)
25. Lenzen, C., Wattenhofer, R.: Minimum dominating set approximation in graphs of bounded arboricity. In: Lynch, N.A., Shvartsman, A.A. (eds.) DISC 2010. LNCS, vol. 6343, pp. 510–524. Springer, Heidelberg (2010). doi:10.1007/978-3-642-15763-9_48
26. Lewis, J.M., Yannakakis, M.: The node-deletion problem for hereditary properties is NP-complete. J. Comput. Syst. Sci. **20**(2), 219–230 (1980)
27. Lokshtanov, D., Narayanaswamy, N.S., Raman, V., Ramanujan, M.S., Saurabh, S.: Faster parameterized algorithms using linear programming. ACM Trans. Algorithms **11**(2), 15:1–15:31 (2014)
28. Lozin, V.V., Kaminski, M.: Coloring edges and vertices of graphs without short or long cycles. Contrib. Discrete Math. **2**(1), 61–66 (2007)
29. Niedermeier, R.: Invitation to Fixed Parameter Algorithms. Oxford University Press, Oxford (2006)
30. Panolan, F., Philip, G., Saurabh, S.: B-Chromatic number: beyond NP-hardness. In: 10th International Symposium on Parameterized and Exact Computation, IPEC 2015, pp. 389–401 (2015)
31. Raman, V., Saurabh, S.: Short cycles make w-hard problems hard: FPT algorithms for W-hard problems in graphs with no short cycles. Algorithmica **52**(2), 203–225 (2008)
32. van Rooij, J.M.M., Bodlaender, H.L.: Exact algorithms for dominating set. Discrete Appl. Math. **159**(17), 2147–2164 (2011)
33. Schönhage, A., Strassen, V.: Schnelle Multiplikation grosser Zahlen. Computing **7**(3–4), 281–292 (1971)
34. Shalu, M.A., Sandhya, T.P.: Personal communication (2016)
35. Shalu, M.A., Sandhya, T.P.: The cd-coloring of graphs. In: Govindarajan, S., Maheshwari, A. (eds.) CALDAM 2016. LNCS, vol. 9602, pp. 337–348. Springer, Heidelberg (2016). doi:10.1007/978-3-319-29221-2_29
36. Venkatakrishnan, Y.B., Swaminathan, V.: Color class domination number of middle graph and center graph of $K_{1,n}$, C_n, P_n. Adv. Model. Optim. **12**, 233–237 (2010)
37. Yannakakis, M., Gavril, F.: The maximum k-colorable subgraph problem for chordal graphs. Inf. Process. Lett. **24**(2), 133–137 (1987)

The Approximability
of Partial Vertex Covers in Trees

Vahan Mkrtchyan[1]([⊠]), Ojas Parekh[2], Danny Segev[3], and K. Subramani[1]

[1] LDCSEE, West Virginia University, Morgantown, WV, USA
vahanmkrtchyan2002@ysu.am, ksmani@csee.wvu.edu
[2] Sandia National Laboratories, Albuquerque, NM, USA
odparek@sandia.gov
[3] Department of Statistics, University of Haifa, 31905 Haifa, Israel
segevd@stat.haifa.ac.il

Abstract. Motivated by applications in risk management of computational systems, we focus our attention on a special case of the partial vertex cover problem, where the underlying graph is assumed to be a tree. Here, we consider four possible versions of this setting, depending on whether vertices and edges are weighted or not. Two of these versions, where edges are assumed to be unweighted, are known to be polynomial-time solvable. However, the computational complexity of this problem with weighted edges, and possibly with weighted vertices, has not been determined yet. The main contribution of this paper is to resolve these questions by fully characterizing which variants of partial vertex cover remain intractable in trees, and which can be efficiently solved. In particular, we propose a pseudo-polynomial DP-based algorithm for the most general case of having weights on both edges and vertices, which is proven to be **NP-hard**. This algorithm provides a polynomial-time solution method when weights are limited to edges, and combined with additional scaling ideas, leads to an **FPTAS** for the general case. A secondary contribution of this work is to propose a novel way of using centroid decompositions in trees, which could be useful in other settings as well.

1 Introduction

The General Setting. In the partial vertex cover problem we are given an undirected graph $G = (V, E)$ on n vertices, as well as a coverage requirement

---

V. Mkrtchyan—This research has been supported in part by the Air Force of Scientific Research through Award FA9550-12-1-0199.

K. Subramani—Supported by the National Science Foundation through Award CCF-1305054 and also supported by the Air Force of Scientific Research through Award FA9550-12-1-0199.

Sandia National Laboratories is a multi-program laboratory managed and operated by Sandia Corporation, a wholly owned subsidiary of Lockheed Martin Corporation, for the U.S. Department of Energys National Nuclear Security Administration under contract DE-AC04-94AL85000.

© Springer International Publishing AG 2017
B. Steffen et al. (Eds.): SOFSEM 2017, LNCS 10139, pp. 350–360, 2017.
DOI: 10.1007/978-3-319-51963-0_27

$P \geq 0$, standing for the number of edges to be covered. In this context, a feasible solution corresponds to a vertex set $U \subseteq V$ that covers at least P edges, where an edge (u, v) is said to be covered by U when the latter contains at least one of the vertices u and v. The objective is to compute a minimum cardinality vertex set that covers at least P edges.

The above-mentioned setting is a well-studied generalization of the classical vertex cover problem, where we wish to cover all edges. The latter is known to be **APX-complete** [18], and moreover, cannot be approximated within a factor smaller than 1.3606 unless **P = NP** [6]. In addition, assuming the unique games conjecture, the vertex cover problem cannot be approximated within factor $2 - \epsilon$, for any fixed $\epsilon > 0$ [14]. These hardness results apply to partial vertex cover as well since it is a generalization of vertex cover. On the positive side, however, several polynomial-time algorithms have been devised for computing approximate partial vertex covers in general graphs. These algorithms attain a performance guarantee of 2 [2,15], or slightly improve on this constant by lower order terms [1,3,12]. Other results on the topic can be found in [11,19].

The Case of Tree Networks. In this paper, we focus our attention on a special case of the partial vertex cover problem where the underlying graph is assumed to be a tree. We consider four possible versions of this setting, depending on whether vertices and edges are weighted or not. Specifically, in the most general version, to which we refer as weighted partial vertex cover on trees (WPVCT), each vertex is associated with a cost, specified by an integer-valued function $c : V \rightarrow \mathbb{N}$. Similarly, each edge is associated with a coverage profit, given by $p : E \rightarrow \mathbb{N}$. With these definitions, our goal is to compute a vertex set of minimum cost, such that the collective profit of all edges covered is at least P. The three additional versions are obtained by restricting all edges to take unit profits (VPVCT), all vertices to take unit costs (EPVCT), and having both restrictions at the same time (PVCT).

In contrast to the intractability of computing partial vertex covers in general graphs, on tree networks the simplest version (i.e., PVCT) can be solved to optimality by means of dynamic programming. It turns out that a result similar to this holds for VPVCT, meaning that VPVCT is polynomial-time solvable. In fact, Gandhi, Khuller, and Srinivasan [8] showed that this problem can be solved in linear time even on graphs of bounded treewidth, with arbitrary vertex costs and with unit-profit edges, meaning in particular that VPVCT is polynomial-time solvable. However, to our knowledge, the computational complexity of WPVCT and EPVCT has not been determined yet and cannot be directly inferred from existing work in this direction.

Finally, let us note that in [5], the partial vertex cover problem is solved for bipartite graphs that satisfy the MNC property. In [5], a graph G is said to be MNC, if for each $k \geq 1$, $OPT_G(k+2) - OPT_G(k+1) \leq OPT_G(k+1) - OPT_G(k)$. Here $OPT_G(k)$ denotes the maximum number of edges of G that can be covered by a subset of k vertices of G. In [5], it is claimed that PVCT can be solved in polynomial time since all trees are MNC. However, the latter statement is incorrect: for example, the tree T from Fig. 1 is not MNC.

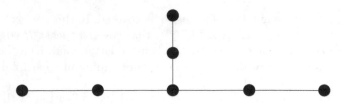

Fig. 1. In this example $OPT_T(1) = 3$, $OPT_T(2) = 4$ and $OPT_T(3) = 6$, hence $OPT_T(3) - OPT_T(2) \not\leq OPT_T(2) - OPT_T(1)$.

1.1   Our Results

The main contribution of this paper is to resolve the above-mentioned questions by fully characterizing which variants of partial vertex cover remain intractable in trees and which can be efficiently solved. Our findings can be briefly summarized as follows:

1. We propose an exact algorithm for EPVCT, showing that this problem can be solved to optimality in polynomial time.
2. We observe that WPVCT is **NP-hard** and design a fully polynomial-time approximation scheme (**FPTAS**) for this problem.

From a technical perspective, a secondary contribution of this work is to propose a novel way of using centroid decompositions in trees. At first glance, it appears as if our approach leads to a dynamic-programming algorithm running in quasi-polynomial time[1]. However, additional insight allows us to argue that there are only polynomially-many states to be evaluated throughout the overall computation, while all other states are actually irrelevant for our particular purposes. We believe that ideas in this spirit could be useful in additional settings.

1.2   Practical Motivation

Our interest towards partial vertex covers is motivated by recent applications in risk management of computational systems or devices [17]. Consider internet-accessible devices, such as servers, personal computers, or smartphones, routinely facing a large number of attacks on stored data, on their operating system, or on a specific software. In such scenarios, it is impossible to expect a manual response to each and every attack. Instead, such devices need to be configured in a way that enables automated response to potential attacks, which is a major technological challenge.

From a conceptual perspective, the risk to most devices of this nature depends on three factors: threats and their occurrence probabilities, existing weaknesses of the system, and the undesirable effects experienced after a successful attack. While threats cannot be controlled by system designers, the other two factors

---

[1] That is, having an exponent of poly-logarithmic order (in the input size).

can typically be handled by decreasing functionality. Therefore, there is constant tension between the desired levels of security and functionality, and the main approach is to allow users to have maximum functionality, subject to a predefined level of risk.

Such problems were modeled by Caskurlu et al. [4] as network flows in tri-partite graphs $G = (T \cup V \cup A, E)$, whose vertex partition represented threats (T), vulnerabilities (V), and the system assets (A). An edge joining two vertices represents a contribution to the overall risk, as shown in Fig. 2. In this model, the objective is to reduce the system risk, measured as the total flow between T and A, below a given threshold level by either restricting user permissions, or encapsulating the system assets. In graph-theoretic terms, these strategies correspond to deleting a minimum weight subset of $V \cup A$, so that the flow between T and A reduces beyond some predefined level. As shown by Caskurlu et al. [4], the vertex set T can be merged into V by scaling each vulnerability weight appropriately. Their transformation establishes the equivalence between the above-mentioned risk management problem and the partial vertex cover problem on bipartite graphs, arguing in particular that trees form an important special case for real-life instances. We refer the reader to an additional paper in this context [10] for further discussion on risk management models in this spirit.

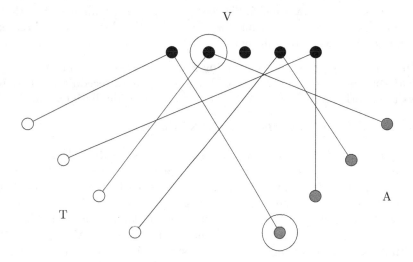

Fig. 2. The tripartite graph of threats (T), vulnerabilities (V), and system assets (A). In this example, each edge has unit capacity. It is easy to notice that the initial (maximum) flow from T to A is of value 4; removing the two circled vertices decreases this value to 2.

2   Preliminaries

In what follows, we define a closely-related variant of WPVCT, which lends itself better to the divide-and-conquer approach proposed in Sect. 3. We explain how algorithms for this variant can be converted into ones for WPVCT and vice versa, and we prove that both problems are **NP-hard**.

The BMVCT Problem. An instance of budgeted maximum vertex cover on trees (BMVCT, for short) consists of an undirected graph $G = (V, E)$, where each vertex is associated with a cost given by $c : V \rightarrow \mathbb{N}$, and each edge has a coverage profit specified by $p : E \rightarrow \mathbb{N}$. Given a budget $B \geq 0$, the objective is to compute a vertex set of cost at most B such that the combined profit of all covered edges is maximized.

It is not difficult to verify that an exact algorithm $\mathcal{A}$ for BMVCT can be utilized as a subroutine, in order to obtain an exact algorithm for WPVCT. For this purpose, it is sufficient to identify the minimal budget $B(P)$ needed to meet the coverage requirement P. This task can be accomplished by making use of $\mathcal{A}$ in a binary search for $B(P)$ over the interval $[C_{\max}, n \cdot C_{\max}]$. Here, $C_{\max}$ is the maximum cost of a vertex belonging to the optimal vertex set that attains the coverage requirement. This quantity is not known in advance, but can be found by trying all vertex costs as potential values for $C_{\max}$. Overall, we perform $O(n \cdot \log n)$ subroutine calls for $\mathcal{A}$. Similarly, analogous arguments show that, in order to obtain an exact algorithm for BMVCT, $O(n \cdot \log n)$ calls to an exact algorithm for WPVCT are sufficient.

NP-hardness. We proceed by describing a polynomial-time reduction from the classical knapsack problem to BMVCT. Based on the preceding discussion, it follows that both BMVCT and WPVCT are computationally intractable.

Theorem 1. *WPVCT and BMVCT are* **NP-hard***.*

Proof. In the knapsack problem, we are given n items, each of which has a value v_i and a weight w_i, both are assumed to be positive integers. Given a weight bound of W, we wish to find a maximum-value subset of items I whose total weight is at most W. In other words, the goal is to maximize $\sum_{i \in I} v_i$ subject to the packing constraint $\sum_{i \in I} w_i \leq W$. This problem is **NP-hard** [9,13].

Given a knapsack instance, we construct an instance of BMVCT as follows. We initially set up a matching M that consists of n edges, $(x_1, y_1), \ldots, (x_n, y_n)$, corresponding to the items $1, \ldots, n$, respectively. For every i, the profit of (x_i, y_i) is v_i, while the vertex costs of the endpoints x_i and y_i are w_i. The matching M is now augmented into a tree by adding an auxiliary vertex z, which is joined by edges to each of the vertices $y_1, \ldots, y_n$. This vertex has a zero cost, while all edges of the form (z, y_i) have zero profits. Finally, the total budget for picking vertices is W. This construction is sketched in Fig. 3.

Notice that, if I is a subset of items with total weight at most W, then the subset of vertices $U_I = \{y_i : i \in I\}$ has exactly the same weight (cost). Therefore, U_I meets the budget constraint, and covers edges with identical value (profit).

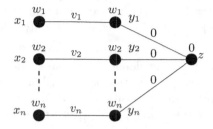

Fig. 3. The tree obtained in the reduction.

Conversely, suppose that U is a subset of vertices with total cost at most W. Then, by defining the subset of items $\{i : \{x_i, y_i\} \cap U \neq \emptyset\}$, we can only decrease the combined cost (weight), while preserving the total profit (value).

3   DP-Based Algorithm

In this section, we devise a divide-and-conquer method for computing an exact solution to BMVCT in pseudo-polynomial time. By converting the suggested method into a dynamic programming algorithm, we will argue that the resulting running time is $O(B^2 \cdot n^{O(1)})$. Based on the discussion in Sect. 2, we immediately obtain a pseudo-polynomial algorithm for WPVCT whose running time is $O(C^2 \cdot n^{O(1)})$, where $C = \sum_{v \in V} c(v)$. This claim follows by observing that each subroutine call to BMVCT is testing a candidate budget in $[C_{\max}, n \cdot C_{\max}]$, and $C_{\max} \leq C$.

3.1   Divide-and-Conquer Algorithm

Our method makes use of a well-known result regarding nearly-balanced decompositions of tree networks, stating that any tree can be partitioned into two edge-disjoint subtrees with roughly the same number of edges.

Definition 1. *Let $T = (V, E)$ be a tree. A centroid decomposition of T is a partition of T into two edge-disjoint subtrees (sharing an intersection vertex) such that each subtree contains between $\frac{|E|}{3}$ and $\frac{2|E|}{3}$ edges.*

Theorem 2 *([7]). Let $T = (V, E)$ be a tree with $|E| \geq 2$. A centroid decomposition of T exists and can be found in linear time.*

Now suppose we are given an instance of BMVCT, consisting of a tree $T = (V, E)$ with integer vertex costs and edge profits, as well as an integer budget $B \geq 0$. For purposes of analysis, we focus attention on a fixed optimal solution U^*, i.e., a vertex set that satisfies the budget constraint $\sum_{v \in U^*} c(v) \leq B$ and maximizes the combined profit of all covered edges. Our algorithm proceeds as follows.

Trivial Scenario: $|E| = 1$. In this case, we simply compute an optimal solution by trying all 4 possible subsets of vertices as candidate solutions.

General Scenario: $|E| \geq 2$. By employing Theorem 2, we compute a centroid decomposition (T_1, T_2) of T, and denote by r the single intersection vertex of these subtrees. We proceed by guessing two attributes of the optimal vertex set U^*, as it relates to the decomposition (T_1, T_2), in order to break the current instance into two mutually independent instances, $\mathcal{I}_1$ and $\mathcal{I}_2$, one for each subtree:

- We first guess whether the intersection vertex r belongs to the optimal solution U^* or not.
- We then guess, by means of exhaustive enumeration, how much of the budget B is spent on picking vertices (for U^*) in the subtree T_1, other than r. In other words, by trying all $B + 1$ possible options, we assume that $B_1^* = \sum_{v \in U^* \setminus T_2} c(v)$ is known.

Note that the overall number of guesses is $O(B)$. Having this information at hand, we create two independent instances as follows:

- Case 1: When $r \notin U^*$, in the instance $\mathcal{I}_1$ we would have T_1 as the underlying tree, with budget B_1^*. Similarly, in $\mathcal{I}_2$ the tree is T_2, with budget $B - B_1^*$. Furthermore, from this point on, we will keep an additional piece of information for each of these instances, stating that the vertex r has not been picked. This means, in particular, that the edges adjacent to r have not been covered yet.
- Case 2: When $r \in U^*$, in the instance $\mathcal{I}_1$ we would have T_1 as the underlying tree, with budget B_1^*, similar to the previous case. For the instance $\mathcal{I}_2$ we need a small modification: While the tree is still T_2, since r has to be paid for, the budget is now $B - B_1^* - c(r)$. The additional piece of information for each instance would be that the vertex r has been picked. So, in particular, the edges adjacent to r have already been covered.

As an immediate consequence of the above discussion, it follows that in order to compute an optimal solution, it remains to recursively solve the instances $\mathcal{I}_1$ and $\mathcal{I}_2$. From a running-time perspective, we make $O(B)$ guesses in each step, and recurse (for every possible guess) into two subproblems, each with an underlying tree consisting of at most $\frac{2|E|}{3}$ edges. This corresponds to a recursion tree with node degree $O(B)$ and depth $O(\log n)$, implying that our algorithm runs in $O((n \cdot B)^{O(\log n)})$ time.

3.2 Dynamic Programming Implementation

We now explain how to efficiently implement the divide-and-conquer algorithm suggested above by means of dynamic programming. To this end, we will first solve all instances corresponding to single-edge subtrees, which constitute the leaves of the recursion tree. These will be utilized in turn to solve instances located one level up the recursion tree, consisting of two edges, which will then be recombined into subtrees with three or four edges, so forth and so on. Formally, each of these instances is a state of the dynamic program, characterized by the following properties[2]:

1. Subtree $S \subseteq T$, created during our recursive application of centroid decompositions.
2. Remaining budget $B_S \geq 0$, for picking vertices in S.
3. Two subsets of vertices, U^+ and U^-, summarizing the additional information accumulated in higher levels of the recursion. That is, U^+ are the vertices in S that have already been picked (Case 2), and similarly, U^- are the vertices that should not be picked (Case 1).

To bound the relevant number of states, note that the number of subtrees that result from recursively breaking the original tree T via centroid decompositions is $O(n)$. Furthermore, the remaining budget B_S is clearly restricted to take integer values in $[0, B]$. Now, as far as the vertex sets U^+ and U^- are concerned, one can naively argue that $|U^+| + |U^-| = O(\log n)$, since in each step of the recursion a single vertex is added, either to U^+ or to U^-. Therefore, without additional insight, the number of possible subsets could be as large as $O(n^{O(\log n)})$.

However, the important observation is that the collection of vertices for which a decision has been made in the divide-and-conquer algorithm has a special structure. Letting T_1 be the subtree considered one level above S in the recursion, we know that the intersection vertex r_1 in the centroid decomposition of T_1 (into S and some other subtree) is the one added to either U^+ or U^-. Similarly, letting T_2 be the subtree considered one level above T_1, we know that the intersection vertex r_2 in the centroid decomposition of T_2 (into T_1 and some other subtree) is added to either U^+ or U^-, so on and so forth. For this reason, focusing on the subtree S, our recursive decomposition determines a unique sequence of intersection vertices $r_1, r_2, \ldots$ which comprises U^+ and U^-. Consequently, we can equivalently represent these two subsets as a binary sequence of length $O(\log n)$, corresponding to whether each of the vertices $r_1, r_2, \ldots$ is picked or not. The number of such sequences is only $O(2^{O(\log n)}) = O(n^{O(1)})$.

In summary, it follows that the overall number of states is $B \cdot n^{O(1)}$, and since each one can be evaluated in $O(n \cdot B)$ time, we obtain an improved running time of $O(B^2 \cdot n^{O(1)})$. Based on the relation between BMVCT and WPVCT, discussed at the beginning of this section, we have just proven the following.

Theorem 3. *The WPVCT problem can be solved to optimality in $O(C^2 \cdot n^{O(1)})$ time, where $C = \sum_{v \in V} c(v)$.*

As an immediate corollary, note that when all vertices are associated with unit costs, we obtain the EPVCT problem, where $C = n$. Therefore, Theorem 3 allows us to resolve the open question regarding the tractability of this variant (see Sect. 1).

Theorem 4. *The EPVCT problem can be solved to optimality in polynomial time.*

---

[2] In addition to vertex costs and edge profits, which are common to all states.

4   Fully Polynomial-Time Approximation Scheme

In what follows, we show that standard scaling arguments can be used to ensure that the sum of vertex costs C becomes polynomial in the number of vertices n, with only negligible loss in optimality. Specifically, given an error parameter $\epsilon > 0$, we define a rounded cost function $\tilde{c} : V \to \mathbb{N}$ satisfying the next two properties:

1. $\tilde{C} = \sum_{v \in V} \tilde{c}(v) = O(\frac{n^3}{\epsilon})$.
2. The optimal vertex set U w.r.t. $\tilde{c}$ has a near-optimal cost w.r.t. c, that is,

$$\sum_{v \in U} c(v) \leq (1 + \epsilon) \cdot \mathrm{OPT}_c.$$

Combined with the pseudo-polynomial algorithm given in Theorem 3, we complement the **NP-hardness** proof of WPVCT (see Theorem 1) with a fully polynomial-time approximation scheme.

Theorem 5. *The WPVCT problem admits an* **FPTAS***, with a running time of* $O(\frac{1}{\epsilon^2} \cdot n^{O(1)})$.

Defining $\tilde{c}$. To construct the rounded cost function $\tilde{c}$, as before, let $C_{\max}$ be the maximum cost of a vertex belonging to the optimal vertex set that attains the coverage requirement. This parameter can be assumed to be known in advance, by trying all vertex costs as potential values for $C_{\max}$. Now, for each vertex v, its rounded cost is determined according to two cases:

- If $c(v) > C_{\max}$, then $\tilde{c}(v) = \lceil \frac{n^2}{\epsilon} \rceil + 1$.
- Otherwise, $\tilde{c}(v) = \lceil \frac{n}{\epsilon} \cdot \frac{c(v)}{C_{\max}} \rceil$.

Note that this definition indeed satisfies property 1, since

$$\tilde{C} = \sum_{v \in V} \tilde{c}(v) \leq n \cdot \left(\left\lceil \frac{n^2}{\epsilon} \right\rceil + 1 \right) = O\left(\frac{n^3}{\epsilon} \right).$$

In addition, to establish property 2, we can upper bound the cost of the optimal vertex set U w.r.t. $\tilde{c}$ by relating it to that of the optimal set U^* w.r.t. c as follows:

$$\sum_{v \in U} c(v) \leq \frac{\epsilon \cdot C_{\max}}{n} \cdot \sum_{v \in U} \tilde{c}(v)$$

$$\leq \frac{\epsilon \cdot C_{\max}}{n} \cdot \sum_{v \in U^*} \tilde{c}(v)$$

$$\leq \sum_{v \in U^*} \left(c(v) + \frac{\epsilon \cdot C_{\max}}{n} \right)$$

$$= \sum_{v \in U^*} c(v) + \frac{|U^*|}{n} \cdot \epsilon \cdot C_{\max}$$

$$\leq (1 + \epsilon) \cdot \mathrm{OPT}_c.$$

Here, the first and third inequalities are implied by the definition of $\tilde{c}$, and by the observation that U cannot contain any vertex v with $c(v) > C_{\max}$. The second inequality is implied by the optimality of U w.r.t. $\tilde{c}$. The final inequality holds since $C_{\max} \leq \mathrm{OPT}_c$.

5 Conclusion

In this paper, we considered four variants of the partial vertex cover problem restricted to trees. We have fully characterized which variants of partial vertex cover remain intractable in trees, and which can be efficiently solved. In particular, we proposed a pseudo-polynomial DP-based algorithm for the most general case of having weights on both edges and vertices, which we observed to be **NP-hard**. This algorithm provided a polynomial-time solution method when weights were limited to edges, and combined with additional scaling ideas, led to an **FPTAS** for the general case. A secondary contribution of this work was the novel way of using centroid decompositions in trees, which could be useful in other settings as well.

The following directions of research appear worth pursuing:

- The extension of the algorithm of Sect. 3.1 from trees to graphs of bounded treewidth.
- Comparing the performance of our pseudo-polynomial DP-based algorithm with performances of alternative (DP-based) algorithms for the partial vertex cover problem restricted to trees.

References

1. Bar-Yehuda, R.: Using homogeneous weights for approximating the partial cover problem. J. Algorithms **39**(2), 137–144 (2001)
2. Bar-Yehuda, R., Flysher, G., Mestre, J., Rawitz, D.: Approximation of partial capacitated vertex cover. SIAM J. Discrete Math. **24**(4), 1441–1469 (2010)
3. Bshouty, N.H., Burroughs, L.: Massaging a linear programming solution to give a 2-approximation for a generalization of the vertex cover problem. In: Proceedings of the 15th Annual Symposium on Theoretical Aspects of Computer Science, pp. 298–308 (1998)

4. Caskurlu, B., Gehani, A., Bilgin, C.Ç., Subramani, K.: Analytical models for risk-based intrusion response. Comput. Netw. **57**(10), 2181–2192 (2013)
5. Caskurlu, B., Subramani, K.: On partial vertex cover on bipartite graphs and trees (2013). arXiv: 1304.5934
6. Dinur, I., Safra, S.: On the hardness of approximating minimum vertex cover. Ann. Math. **162**(1), 439–485 (2005)
7. Frederickson, G.N., Johnson, D.B.: Finding k-th paths and p-centers by generating and searching good data structures. J. Algorithms **4**(1), 61–80 (1983)
8. Gandhi, R., Khuller, S., Srinivasan, A.: Approximation algorithms for partial covering problems. J. Algorithms **53**(1), 55–84 (2004)
9. Garey, M.R., Johnson, D.S.: Computers and Intractability: A Guide to the Theory of NP-Completeness. W. H. Freeman and Co., New York (1979)
10. Gehani, A.: Performance-sensitive real-time risk management is NP-hard. In: Workshop on Foundations of Computer Security, Affiliated with the 19th IEEE Symposium on Logic in Computer Science (2004)
11. Halperin, E., Srinivasan, A.: Improved approximation algorithms for the partial vertex cover problem. In: Jansen, K., Leonardi, S., Vazirani, V. (eds.) APPROX 2002. LNCS, vol. 2462, pp. 161–174. Springer, Heidelberg (2002). doi:10.1007/3-540-45753-4_15
12. Hochbaum, D.S.: The t-vertex cover problem: extending the half integrality framework with budget constraints. In: Proceedings of the 1st International Workshop on Approximation Algorithms for Combinatorial Optimization, pp. 111–122 (1998)
13. Karp, R.M.: Reducibility among combinatorial problems. In: Miller, R.E., Thatcher, J.W., Bohlinger, J.D. (eds.) Complexity of Computer Computations. The IBM Research Symposia Series, pp. 85–103. Springer, USA (1972)
14. Khot, S., Regev, O.: Vertex cover might be hard to approximate to within $2 - \epsilon$. J. Comput. Syst. Sci. **74**(3), 335–349 (2008)
15. Mestre, J.: A primal-dual approximation algorithm for partial vertex cover: making educated guesses. Algorithmica **55**(1), 227–239 (2009)
16. Moser, H.: Exact algorithms for generalizations of vertex cover. Master thesis, Jena University (2005)
17. N.B. of standards. In: 4th Computer Security Risk Management Model Builders Workshop, University of Maryland, College Park, Maryland, August 1991
18. Papadimitriou, C.H., Yannakakis, M.: Optimization, approximation, and complexity classes. J. Comput. Syst. Sci. **43**(3), 425–440 (1991)
19. Srinivasan, A.: Distributions on level-sets with applications to approximation algorithms. In: Proceedings of the 42nd Annual Symposium on Foundations of Computer Science, pp. 588–597 (2001)

Algorithms for Strings and Formal Languages

Longest Common Subsequence in at Least k Length Order-Isomorphic Substrings

Yohei Ueki[1][✉], Diptarama[1], Masatoshi Kurihara[1], Yoshiaki Matsuoka[2],
Kazuyuki Narisawa[1], Ryo Yoshinaka[1], Hideo Bannai[2], Shunsuke Inenaga[2],
and Ayumi Shinohara[1]

[1] Graduate School of Information Sciences, Tohoku University, Sendai, Japan
{yohei_ueki,diptarama,masatoshi_kurihara}@shino.ecei.tohoku.ac.jp,
{narisawa,ry,ayumi}@ecei.tohoku.ac.jp
[2] Department of Informatics, Kyushu University, Fukuoka, Japan
{yoshiaki.matsuoka,bannai,inenaga}@inf.kyushu-u.ac.jp

Abstract. We consider the longest common subsequence (LCS) problem with the restriction that the common subsequence is required to consist of at least k length substrings. First, we show an $O(mn)$ time algorithm for the problem which gives a better worst-case running time than existing algorithms, where m and n are lengths of the input strings. Furthermore, we mainly consider the LCS in at least k length order-isomorphic substrings problem. We show that the problem can also be solved in $O(mn)$ worst-case time by an easy-to-implement algorithm.

Keywords: Longest common subsequence · Dynamic programming · Order-isomorphism · Order-preserving matching

1 Introduction

The *longest common subsequence (LCS)* problem is fundamental and well studied in computer science. The most common application of the LCS problem is measuring similarity between strings, which can be used in many applications such as the `diff` tool, the time series data analysis [12], and in bioinformatics.

One of the major disadvantages of LCS as a measure of similarity is that LCS cannot consider consecutively matching characters effectively. For example, for strings $X = $ ATGG, $Y = $ ATCGGC and $Z = $ ACCCTCCCGCCCG, ATGG is the LCS of X and Y, which is also the LCS of X and Z. Benson *et al.* [2] introduced the *longest common subsequence in k length substrings (LCS_k)* problem, where the subsequence needs to be a concatenation of k length substrings of given strings. For example, for strings $X = $ ATCTATAT and $Y = $ TAATATCC, TAAT is an LCS_2 since $X[4:5] = Y[1:2] = $ TA and $X[7:8] = Y[5:7] = $ AT, and no longer one exists. They showed a quadratic time algorithm for it, and Deorowicz and Grabowski [7] proposed several algorithms, such as a quadratic worst-case time algorithm for unbounded k and a fast algorithm on average.

Pavetić *et al.* [15] considered the *longest common subsequence in at least k length substrings (LCS_{k+})* problem, where the subsequence needs to be a

© Springer International Publishing AG 2017
B. Steffen et al. (Eds.): SOFSEM 2017, LNCS 10139, pp. 363–374, 2017.
DOI: 10.1007/978-3-319-51963-0_28

concatenation of *at least* k length substrings of given strings. They argued that LCS_{k+} would be more appropriate than LCS_k as a similarity measure of strings. For strings $X = $ ATTCGTATCG, $Y = $ ATTGCTATGC, and $Z = $ AATCCCTCAA, $LCS_2(X, Y) = LCS_2(X, Z) = 4$, where $LCS_2(A, B)$ denotes the length of an LCS_2 between A and B. However, it seems that X and Y are more similar than X and Z. Instead, if we consider LCS_{2+}, we have $LCS_{2+}(X, Y) = 6 > 4 = LCS_{2+}(X, Z)$, that better fits our intuition. The notion of LCS_{k+} is applied to bioinformatics [16].

Pavetić *et al.* showed that LCS_{k+} can be computed in $O(m + n + r \log r + r \log n)$ time, where m, n are lengths of the input strings and r is the total number of matching k length substring pairs between the input strings. Their algorithm is fast on average, but in the worst case, the running time is $O(mn \log(mn))$. Independently, Benson *et al.* [2] proposed an $O(kmn)$ worst-case time algorithm for the LCS_{k+} problem.

In this paper, we first propose an algorithm to compute LCS_{k+} in $O(mn)$ worst-case time by a simple dynamic programming. Secondly, we introduce the *longest common subsequence in at least k length order-isomorphic substrings (op-LCS_{k+})* problem. Order-isomorphism is a notion of equality of two numerical strings, intensively studied in the *order-preserving matching* problem[1] [13,14]. op-LCS_{k+} is a natural definition of similarity between numerical strings, and can be used in time series data analysis. The op-LCS_{k+} problem cannot be solved as simply as the LCS_{k+} problem due to the properties of the order-isomorphism. However, we will show that the op-LCS_{k+} problem can also be solved in $O(mn)$ worst-case time by an easy-to-implement algorithm, which is one of the main contributions of this paper. Finally, we report experimental results.

2   Preliminaries

We assume that all strings are over an *alphabet* Σ. The length of a string $X = (X[1], X[2], \cdots, X[n])$ is denoted by $|X| = n$. A *substring* of X beginning at i and ending at j is denoted by $X[i : j] = (X[i], X[i+1], \cdots, X[j-1], X[j])$. We denote $X\langle i, +l \rangle = X[i : i + l - 1]$ and $X\langle j, -l \rangle = X[j - l + 1 : j]$. Thus $X\langle i, +l \rangle = X\langle i + l - 1, -l \rangle$. We write $X[: i]$ and $X[j :]$ to denote the *prefix* $X[1 : i]$ and the *suffix* $X[j : n]$ of X, respectively. Note that $X[: 0]$ is the empty string. The reverse of a string X is denoted by X^{R}, and the operator $\cdot$ denotes the concatenation. We simply denote a string $X = (X[1], X[2], \cdots, X[n])$ as $X = X[1]X[2] \cdots X[n]$ when clear from the context.

We formally define the LCS_{k+} problem as follows.

Definition 1 ($\mathbf{LCS}_{k+}$ problem [2,15][2]). *Given two strings X and Y of length m and n, respectively, and an integer $k \geq 1$, we say that Z is a* common

---

[1] Since the problem is motivated by the order-preserving matching problem, we abbreviate it to the op-LCS_{k+} problem.

[2] The formal definition given by Pavetić *et al.* [15] contains a minor error, i.e., they do not require that each chunk is identical, while Benson *et al.* [2] and we do (confirmed by F. Pavetić, personal communication, October 2016).

subsequence in at least k length substrings *of X and Y, if there exist $i_1, \cdots, i_t$ and $j_1, \cdots, j_t$ such that $X\langle i_s, +l_s \rangle = Y\langle j_s, +l_s \rangle = Z\langle p_s, +l_s \rangle$ and $l_s \geq k$ for $1 \leq s \leq t$, and $i_s + l_s \leq i_{s+1}$, $j_s + l_s \leq j_{s+1}$ and $p_{s+1} = p_s + l_s$ for $1 \leq s < t$, $p_1 = 1$ and $|Z| = p_t + l_t - 1$. The* longest common subsequence in at least k length substrings (LCS_{k+}) *problem asks for the length of an LCS_{k+} of X and Y.*

Remark that the LCS_{1+} problem is equivalent to the standard LCS problem. Without loss of generality, we assume that $n \geq m$ through the paper.

Example 1. For strings $X = \mathtt{acdbacbc}$ and $Y = \mathtt{aacdabca}$, $Z = \mathtt{acdbc}$ is the LCS_{2+} of X and Y, since $X\langle 1, +3 \rangle = Y\langle 2, +3 \rangle = \mathtt{acd} = Z\langle 1, +3 \rangle$ and $X\langle 7, +2 \rangle = Y\langle 6, +2 \rangle = \mathtt{bc} = Z\langle 4, +2 \rangle$. Note that the standard LCS of X and Y is $\mathtt{acdabc}$.

The main topic of this paper is to give an efficient algorithm for computing the longest common subsequence *under order-isomorphism*, defined below.

Definition 2 (Order-isomorphism[13,14]). *Two strings S and T of the same length l over an ordered alphabet are* order-isomorphic *if $S[i] \leq S[j] \iff T[i] \leq T[j]$ for any $1 \leq i, j \leq l$. We write $S \approx T$ if S is order-isomorphic to T, and $S \not\approx T$ otherwise.*

Example 2. For strings $S = (32, 40, 4, 16, 27)$, $T = (28, 32, 12, 20, 25)$ and $U = (33, 51, 10, 22, 42)$, we have $S \approx T$, $S \not\approx U$, and $T \not\approx U$.

Definition 3 (op-LCS_{k+} problem). *The* op-LCS_{k+} *problem is defined as the problem obtained from Definition 1 by replacing the matching relation $X\langle i_s, +l_s \rangle = Y\langle j_s, +l_s \rangle = Z\langle p_s, +l_s \rangle$ with order-isomorphism $X\langle i_s, +l_s \rangle \approx Y\langle j_s, +l_s \rangle \approx Z\langle p_s, +l_s \rangle$.*

Example 3. For strings $X = (14, 84, 82, 31, 74, 68, 87, 11, 20, 32)$ and $Y = (21, 64, 2, 83, 73, 51, 5, 29, 7, 71)$, $Z = (1, 3, 2, 31, 74, 68, 87)$ is an op-LCS_{3+} of X and Y since $X\langle 1, +3 \rangle \approx Y\langle 3, +3 \rangle \approx Z\langle 1, +3 \rangle$ and $X\langle 4, +4 \rangle \approx Y\langle 7, +4 \rangle \approx Z\langle 4, +4 \rangle$.

The op-LCS_{k+} problem does not require that $(X\langle i_1, +l_1 \rangle \cdot X\langle i_2, +l_2 \rangle \cdot \cdots \cdot X\langle i_t, +l_t \rangle) \approx (Y\langle j_1, +l_1 \rangle \cdot Y\langle j_2, +l_2 \rangle \cdot \cdots \cdot Y\langle j_t, +l_t \rangle)$. Therefore, the op-$\mathrm{LCS}_{1+}$ problem makes no sense. Note that the op-LCS_{k+} problem with this restriction is **NP**-hard already for $k = 1$ [3].

3   The LCS_{k+} Problem

In this section, we show that the LCS_{k+} problem can be solved in $O(mn)$ time by dynamic programming. We define $Match(i, j, l) = 1$ if $X\langle i, -l \rangle = Y\langle j, -l \rangle$, and 0 otherwise. Let $C[i, j]$ be the length of an LCS_{k+} of $X[: i]$ and $Y[: j]$, and $A_{i,j} = \{C[i - l, j - l] + l \cdot Match(i, j, l) : k \leq l \leq \min\{i, j\}\}$. Our algorithm is based on the following lemma.

Lemma 1 ([2]). *For any $k \leq i \leq m$ and $k \leq j \leq n$,*

$$C[i,j] = \max\left(\{C[i,j-1], C[i-1,j]\} \cup A_{i,j}\right), \tag{1}$$

and $C[i,j] = 0$ otherwise.

The naive dynamic programming algorithm based on Eq. (1) takes $O(m^2 n)$ time, because for each i and j, the naive algorithm for computing $\max A_{i,j}$ takes $O(m)$ time assuming $n \geq m$. Therefore, we focus on how to compute $\max A_{i,j}$ in constant time for each i and j in order to solve the problem in $O(mn)$ time. It is clear that if $Match(i,j,l_1) = 0$ then $Match(i,j,l_2) = 0$ for all valid $l_2 \geq l_1$, and $C[i',j'] \geq C[i'-l',j'-l']$ for all valid i', j' and $l' > 0$. Therefore, in order to compute $\max A_{i,j}$, it suffices to compute $\max_{k \leq l \leq L[i,j]}\{C[i-l, j-l]+l\}$, where $L[i,j] = \max\{l : X\langle i, -l\rangle = Y\langle j, -l\rangle\}$.

We can compute $L[i,j]$ for all $0 \leq i \leq m$ and $0 \leq j \leq n$ in $O(mn)$ time by dynamic programming because the following equation clearly holds:

$$L[i,j] = \begin{cases} L[i-1,j-1]+1 & (\text{if } i,j > 0 \text{ and } X[i] = Y[j]) \\ 0 & (\text{otherwise}). \end{cases} \tag{2}$$

Next, we show how to compute $\max_{k \leq l \leq L[i,j]}\{C[i-l,j-l]+l\}$ in constant time for each i and j. Assume that the table L has already been computed. Let $M[i,j] = \max_{k \leq l \leq L[i,j]}\{C[i-l,j-l]+l\}$ if $L[i,j] \geq k$, and -1 otherwise.

Lemma 2. *For any $0 \leq i \leq m$ and $0 \leq j \leq n$, if $L[i,j] > k$ then $M[i,j] = \max\{M[i-1,j-1]+1, C[i-k,j-k]+k\}$.*

Proof. Let $l = L[i,j]$. Since $L[i,j] > k$, we have $L[i-1,j-1] = l-1 \geq k$, and $M[i-1,j-1] \neq -1$. Therefore, $M[i-1,j-1] = \max_{k \leq l' \leq l-1}\{C[i-1-l', j-1-l']+l'\} = \max_{k+1 \leq l' \leq l}\{C[i-l',j-l']+l'\} - 1$. Hence, $M[i,j] = \max_{k \leq l' \leq l}\{C[i-l',i-l']+l'\} = \max\{M[i-1,j-1]+1, C[i-k,j-k]+k\}$. $\square$

By Lemma 2 and the definition of $M[i,j]$, we have

$$M[i,j] = \begin{cases} \max\{M[i-1,j-1]+1, C[i-k,j-k]+k\} & (\text{if } L[i,j] > k) \\ C[i-k,j-k]+k & (\text{if } L[i,j] = k) \\ -1 & (\text{otherwise}). \end{cases} \tag{3}$$

Equation (3) shows that each $M[i,j]$ can be computed in constant time if $L[i,j]$, $M[i-1,j-1]$, and $C[i-k,j-k]$ have already been computed.

We can fill in tables C, L and M of size $(m+1) \times (n+1)$ based on Eqs. (1), (2) and (3) in $O(mn)$ time by dynamic programming. An example of computing LCS_{3+} is shown in Fig. 1(a). We note that LCS_{k+} itself (not only its length) can be extracted from the table C in $O(m+n)$ time, by tracing back in the same way as the standard dynamic programming algorithm for the standard LCS problem. Our algorithm requires $O(mn)$ space since we use three tables of size $(m+1) \times (n+1)$. Note that if we want to compute only the length of an LCS_{k+}, the space complexity can be easily reduced to $O(km)$. Hence, we get the following theorem.

		a	b	c	b	c	d	e	f
	0	1	2	3	4	5	6	7	8
0	0	0	0	0	0	0	0	0	0
a 1	0	0	0	0	0	0	0	0	0
b 2	0	0	0	0	0	0	0	0	0
c 3	0	0	0	3	3	3	3	3	3
d 4	0	0	0	3	3	3	3	3	3
e 5	0	0	0	3	3	3	3	4	4
f 6	0	0	0	3	3	3	3	4	6

(a) Table C for the LCS$_{3+}$ problem

		4	0	9	6	2	0	3	1
	0	1	2	3	4	5	6	7	8
0	0	0	0	0	0	0	0	0	0
5 1	0	0	0	0	0	0	0	0	0
1 2	0	0	2	2	2	2	2	2	2
3 3	0	0	2	2	2	2	2	2	2
8 4	0	0	2	2	2	2	2	4	4
7 5	0	0	2	2	4	4	4	4	5
2 6	0	0	2	2	4	5	5	5	5

(b) Table C for the op-LCS$_{2+}$ problem

Fig. 1. Examples of computing LCS$_{3+}$ and op-LCS$_{2+}$

Theorem 1. *The LCS$_{k+}$ problem can be solved in $O(mn)$ time and $O(km)$ space.*

4 The op-LCS$_{k+}$ Problem

In this section, we show that the op-LCS$_{k+}$ problem can be solved in $O(mn)$ time as well as the LCS$_{k+}$ problem. We redefine $C[i,j]$ to be the length of an op-LCS$_{k+}$ of $X[:\,i]$ and $Y[:\,j]$, and $Match(i,j,l) = 1$ if $X\langle i,-l\rangle \approx Y\langle j,-l\rangle$, and 0 otherwise. It is easy to prove that Eq. (1) also holds with respect to the order-isomorphism. However, the op-LCS$_{k+}$ problem cannot be solved as simply as the LCS$_{k+}$ problem because Eqs. (2) and (3) do not hold with respect to the order-isomorphism, as follows. For two strings A, B of length l such that $A \approx B$, and two characters a, b such that $A \cdot a \not\approx B \cdot b$, the statement "$(A \cdot a)[i\,:]\not\approx (B \cdot b)[i\,:]$ for all $1 \le i \le l + 1$" is not always true. For example, for strings $A = (32, 40, 4, 16, 27)$, $B = (28, 32, 12, 20, 25)$, $A' = A \cdot (41)$ and $B' = B \cdot (26)$, we have $A \approx B$, $A' \not\approx B'$, and $A'[3\,:]\approx B'[3\,:]$. Moreover, for $A'' = A \cdot (15)$ and $B'' = B \cdot (22)$, we have $A''[5\,:]\approx B''[5\,:]$. These examples show that Eqs. (2) and (3) do not hold with respect to the order-isomorphism. Therefore, we must find another way to compute $\max_{k \le l' \le l}\{C[i - l', j - l'] + l'\}$, where $l = \max\{l' : X\langle i,-l'\rangle \approx Y\langle j,-l'\rangle\}$ in constant time.

First, we consider how to find $\max\{l : X\langle i,-l\rangle \approx Y\langle j,-l\rangle\}$ in constant time. We define the *order-preserving longest common extension (op-LCE)* query on strings S_1 and S_2 as follows.

Definition 4 (op-LCE query). *Given a pair (S_1, S_2) of strings, an op-LCE query is a pair of indices i_1 and i_2 of S_1 and S_2, respectively, which asks $opLCE_{S_1,S_2}[i_1, i_2] = \max\{l : S_1\langle i_1, +l\rangle \approx S_2\langle i_2, +l\rangle\}$.*

Since $\max\{l : X\langle i,-l\rangle \approx Y\langle j,-l\rangle\} = opLCE_{X^{\mathrm{R}}, Y^{\mathrm{R}}}[m - i + 1, n - j + 1]$, we can find $\max\{l : X\langle i,-l\rangle \approx Y\langle j,-l\rangle\}$ by using op-LCE queries on X^{R} and Y^{R}. Therefore, we focus on how to answer op-LCE queries on S_1 and S_2 in constant time with at most $O(|S_1||S_2|)$ time preprocessing. Hereafter we write $opLCE[i_1, i_2]$ for $opLCE_{S_1,S_2}[i_1, i_2]$ fixing two strings S_1 and S_2.

If S_1 and S_2 are strings over a polynomially-bounded integer alphabet $\{1, \cdots, (|S_1| + |S_2|)^c\}$ for an integer constant c, op-LCE queries can be answered in $O(1)$ time and $O(|S_1| + |S_2|)$ space with $O((|S_1| + |S_2|) \log^2 \log(|S_1| + |S_2|)/\log\log\log(|S_1| + |S_2|))$ time preprocessing, by using the *incomplete generalized op-suffix-tree* [6] of S_1 and S_2 and finding the *lowest common ancestor (LCA)* [1] in the op-suffix-tree. The proof is similar to that for LCE queries in the standard setting [10].

However, implementing the incomplete generalized op-suffix-tree is quite difficult. Therefore, we introduce another much simpler method to answer op-LCE queries in $O(1)$ time with $O(|S_1||S_2|)$ time preprocessing. In a preprocessing step, our algorithm fills in the table $opLCE[i_1, i_2]$ for all $1 \leq i_1 \leq |S_1|$ and $1 \leq i_2 \leq |S_2|$ in $O(|S_1||S_2|)$ time. Then, we can answer op-LCE queries in constant time.

In the preprocessing step, we use the *Z-algorithm* [10,11] that calculates the following table efficiently.

Definition 5 (Z-table). *The Z-table Z_S of a string S is defined by $Z_S[i] = \max\{l : S\langle 1, +l\rangle \approx S\langle i, +l\rangle\}$ for each $1 \leq i \leq |S|$.*

By definition, we have

$$opLCE[i_1, i_2] = \min\{Z_{(S_1 \cdot S_2)i_1}[|S_1| - i_1 + i_2 + 1], |S_1| - i_1 + 1\}. \qquad (4)$$

If we use the Z-algorithm and Eq. (4) naively, it takes $O((|S_1| + |S_2|)^2 \log(|S_1| + |S_2|))$ time to compute $opLCE[i_1, i_2]$ for all $1 \leq i_1 \leq |S_1|$ and $1 \leq i_2 \leq |S_2|$, because the Z-algorithm requires $O(|S| \log |S|)$ time to compute Z_S for a string S. We extend the Z-algorithm to compute Z_{Si} for *all* $1 \leq i \leq |S|$ totally in $O(|S|^2)$ time.

In order to verify the order-isomorphism in constant time with preprocessing, Hasan *et al.* [11] used tables called $Prev_S$ and $Next_S$. For a string S where all the characters are distinct[3], $Prev_S$ and $Next_S$ are defined as

$$Prev_S[i] = j \text{ if there exists } j = \underset{1 \leq k < i}{\operatorname{argmax}}\{S[k] : S[k] < S[i]\}, \text{ and } \quad -\infty \text{ otherwise}$$

$$Next_S[i] = j \text{ if there exists } j = \underset{1 \leq k < i}{\operatorname{argmin}}\{S[k] : S[k] > S[i]\}, \text{ and } \quad \infty \text{ otherwise}$$

for all $1 \leq i \leq |S|$. Their algorithm requires $O(|S| \log |S|)$ time to compute the tables $Prev_S$ and $Next_S$, and all operations except computing the tables take only $O(|S|)$ time. Therefore, if we can compute tables $Prev_{Si}$ and $Next_{Si}$ for each $1 \leq i \leq |S|$ in $O(|S|)$ time with $O(|S| \log |S|)$ time preprocessing, Z_{Si} for

---

[3] Hasan *et al.* [11] assume that characters in a string are distinct. If the assumption is false, use Lemma 4 in [4] in order to verify the order-isomorphism, that is, modify line 10 of Algorithm 4 in [11] and line 7 and 12 in Algorithm 1. Note that *Prev* and *Next* are denoted as *LMax* and *LMin* in [4], respectively, with slight differences.

Algorithm 1. The algorithm for computing op-LCE queries

---

1 **Function** preprocess(S, i, S', S'')
2   Let s and t be empty stacks that support **push**, **top**, and **pop** operations;
3   Let $Prev$ and $Next$ be tables of size $|S| - i + 1$;
4   **for** $j \leftarrow 1$ **to** $|S|$ **do**
5   **if** $S'[j] \geq i$ **then**
6   **while** $s \neq \emptyset$ *and* $s.\text{top}() > S'[j]$ **do** $s.\text{pop}()$;
7   **if** $s = \emptyset$ **then** $Prev[S'[j] - i + 1] \leftarrow -\infty$;
8   **else** $Prev[S'[j] - i + 1] \leftarrow s.\text{top}() - i + 1$;
9             $s.\text{push}(S'[j])$;
10   **if** $S''[j] \geq i$ **then**
11   **while** $t \neq \emptyset$ *and* $t.\text{top}() > S''[j]$ **do** $t.\text{pop}()$;
12   **if** $t = \emptyset$ **then** $Next[S''[j] - i + 1] \leftarrow \infty$;
13   **else** $Next[S''[j] - i + 1] \leftarrow t.\text{top}() - i + 1$;
14            $t.\text{push}(S''[j])$;
15   **return** $(Prev, Next)$;

16 **Function** Z-function(S, i_1, S', S'')
17     $(Prev, Next) \leftarrow$ preprocess(S, i_1, S', S''); $S \leftarrow S[i_1 :]$;
18   Do the same operations described in line 3-17 of Algorithm 4 in [11];
19   **return** Z;

20 **Function** preprocess-opLCE(S_1, S_2)
21   Let $opLCE$ be a table of size $|S_1| \times |S_2|$; $S \leftarrow S_1 \cdot S_2$;
22   Let S' and S'' be stably sorted positions of S with respect to their elements
        in ascending and descending order, respectively;
23   **for** $i_1 \leftarrow 1$ **to** $|S_1|$ **do**
24         $Z \leftarrow$ Z-function(S, i_1, S', S'');
25   **for** $i_2 \leftarrow 1$ **to** $|S_2|$ **do**
26             $opLCE[i_1, i_2] \leftarrow \min\left\{ Z[|S_1| - i_1 + i_2 + 1], |S_1| - i_1 + 1 \right\}$;
27   **return** $opLCE$;

---

all $1 \leq i \leq |S|$ can be computed in $O(|S|^2)$ time. We also assume that all the characters in S are distinct (see footnote 3).

In order to compute the tables $Prev_{Si}$ and $Next_{Si}$, we modify a sort-based algorithm presented in Lemma 1 in [14] instead of the algorithm in [11] that uses a balanced binary search tree. First, for computing $Prev_S$ (resp. $Next_S$), we stably sort positions of S with respect to their elements in ascending (resp. descending) order. We can compute $Prev_{Si}$ and $Next_{Si}$ for each $1 \leq i \leq |S|$ in $O(|S|)$ time by using the sorted tables and the stack-based algorithm presented in [14], ignoring all elements of the sorted tables less than i.

Algorithm 1 shows the pseudocode of the op-LCE algorithm based on the Z-algorithm. The push(x) operation inserts x on the top of the stack, top() returns the top element in the stack, and pop() removes it. Algorithm 1 takes $O(|S_1||S_2|)$ time as discussed above. The total space complexity is $O(|S_1||S_2|)$

Algorithm 2. The algorithm for the op-LCS$_{k+}$ problem

Input: A string X of length m, a string Y of length n, and an integer k
Output: The length of an op-LCS$_{k+}$ between X and Y

1 Let C be a table of size $(m+1) \times (n+1)$ initialized by 0;
2 Let R_i for $-n+k \le i \le m-k$ be semi-dynamic RMQ data structures;
3 $opLCE \leftarrow$ preprocess-opLCE$(X^{\mathrm{R}}, Y^{\mathrm{R}})$;
4 **for** $i \leftarrow 0$ **to** $m-k$ **do**
5   **if** $i < k$ **then** $n' \leftarrow n-k$;
6   **else** $n' \leftarrow k-1$;
7   **for** $j \leftarrow 0$ **to** n' **do** R_{i-j}.prepend$(C[i,j] - \min\{i,j\})$;

8 **for** $i \leftarrow k$ **to** m **do**
9   **for** $j \leftarrow k$ **to** n **do**
10         $l \leftarrow opLCE[m-i+1, n-j+1]$;
11   **if** $l \ge k$ **then** $M \leftarrow R_{i-j}$.rmq$(k,l) + \min\{i,j\}$;
12   **else** $M \leftarrow 0$;
13         $C[i,j] \leftarrow \max\{C[i,j-1], C[i-1,j], M\}$;
14   R_{i-j}.prepend$(C[i,j] - \min\{i,j\})$;

15 **return** $C[m,n]$;

---

because the Z-algorithm requires linear space [11], and the table $opLCE$ needs $O(|S_1||S_2|)$ space. Hence, we have the following lemma.

Lemma 3. *op-LCE queries on S_1 and S_2 can be answered in $O(1)$ time and $O(|S_1||S_2|)$ space with $O(|S_1||S_2|)$ time preprocessing.*

Let opLCE(i,j) be the answer to the op-LCE query on X^{R} and Y^{R} with respect to the index pair (i,j). We consider how to find the maximum value of $C[i-l, j-l] + l$ for $k \le l \le$ opLCE$(m-i+1, n-j+1)$ in constant time. We use a *semi-dynamic range maximum query (RMQ)* data structure that maintains a table A and supports the following two operations:

- prepend(x): add x to the beginning of A in $O(1)$ amortized time.
- rmq(i_1, i_2): return the maximum value of $A[i_1 : i_2]$ in $O(1)$ time.

The details of the semi-dynamic RMQ data structure will be given in Sect. 5.
    By using the semi-dynamic RMQ data structures and the following obvious lemma, we can find $\max_{k \le l \le \mathrm{opLCE}(m-i+1, n-j+1)} \{C[i-l, j-l] + l\}$ for all $1 \le i \le m$ and $1 \le j \le n$ in totally $O(mn)$ time.

Lemma 4. *We may assume that $i \ge j$ without loss of generality. Let $A[l] = C[i-l, j-l] + l$ and $A'[l] = C[i-l, j-l] - j + l$ for each $1 \le l \le j$. For any $1 \le i_1, i_2 \le |A|$, we have $\max_{i_1 \le l \le i_2} A[l] = (\max_{i_1 \le l \le i_2} A'[l]) + j$ and $\mathrm{argmax}_{i_1 \le l \le i_2} A[l] = \mathrm{argmax}_{i_1 \le l \le i_2} A'[l]$.*

Algorithm 2 shows our algorithm to compute op-LCS$_{k+}$. An example of computing op-LCS$_{2+}$ is shown in Fig. 1(b). As discussed above, the algorithm runs

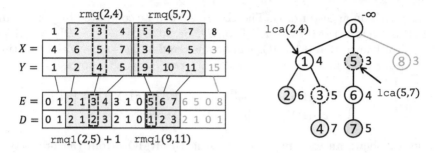

Fig. 2. An example of searching for the RMQ by using a 2d-Min-Heap and the $\pm$1RMQ algorithm [1]. The tree shows the 2d-Min-Heap of $X = (4, 6, 5, 7, 3, 4, 5, 3)$ represented by arrays E and D. The gray node 8 in the tree and gray numbers in the table are added when the last character $X[8] = 3$ is processed. The boxes with the dashed lines show the answers of RMQs $\mathtt{rmq}(2, 4)$ and $\mathtt{rmq}(5, 7)$.

in $O(mn)$ time. Each semi-dynamic RMQ data structure requires linear space and a total of $O(mn)$ elements are maintained by the semi-dynamic RMQ data structures. Therefore, the total space of semi-dynamic RMQ data structures is $O(mn)$. Consequently, the total space complexity is $O(mn)$. Hence, we have the following theorem.

Theorem 2. *The op-LCS_{k+} problem can be solved in $O(mn)$ time and space.*

5   The Semi-dynamic Range Minimum/Maximum Query

In this section we will describe the algorithm that solves the semi-dynamic RMQ problem with $O(1)$ query time and amortized $O(1)$ prepend time. To simplify the algorithm, we consider the prepend operation as appending a character into the end of array. In order to solve this problem, Fischer [8] proposed an algorithm that uses a 2d-Min-Heap [9] and dynamic LCAs [5]. However, the algorithm for dynamic LCAs is very complex to implement. Therefore, we propose a simple semi-dynamic RMQ algorithm that can be implemented easily if the number of characters to be appended is known beforehand. This algorithm uses a 2d-Min-Heap and the $\pm$1RMQ algorithm proposed by Bender and Farach-Colton [1].

Let X be a string of length n and let $X[0] = -\infty$. The 2d-Min-Heap H of X is an ordered tree of $n + 1$ nodes $\{0, 1, \cdots, n\}$, where 0 is the root node, and the parent node of node $i > 0$ is $\max\{j < i : X[j] < X[i]\}$. Moreover, the order of the children is chosen so that they increase from left to right (see Fig. 2 for instance). Note that the vertices are inevitably aligned in preorder. Actually, the tree H is represented by arrays E and D that store the sequences of nodes and their depths visited in an Euler tour of H, respectively. In addition, let Y be an array defined as $Y[i] = \min\{j : E[j] = i\}$ for each $1 \leq i \leq n$.

For two positions $1 \leq i_1 \leq i_2 \leq n$ in X, $\mathtt{rmq}(i_1, i_2)$ can be calculated by finding $\mathtt{lca}(i_1, i_2)$, the LCA of the nodes i_1 and i_2 in H. If $\mathtt{lca}(i_1, i_2) = i_1$, then $\mathtt{rmq}(i_1, i_2) = i_1$. Otherwise, $\mathtt{rmq}(i_1, i_2) = i_3$ such that i_3 is a child of

$lca(i_1, i_2)$ and an ancestor of i_2. The $lca(i_1, i_2)$ can be computed by performing the ± 1RMQ query $rmq1(Y[i_1], Y[i_2])$ on D, because $D[j+1] - D[j] = \pm 1$ for every j. It is known that ± 1RMQs can be answered in $O(1)$ time with $O(n)$ time preprocessing [1]. Therefore, we can calculate $rmq(i_1, i_2)$ as follows,

$$rmq(i_1, i_2) = \begin{cases} E[rmq1(Y[i_1], Y[i_2])] & (\text{if } E[rmq1(Y[i_1], Y[i_2])] = i_1) \\ E[rmq1(Y[i_1], Y[i_2]) + 1] & (\text{otherwise}). \end{cases}$$

Figure 2 shows an example of calculating the RMQ. From the property of a 2d-Min-Heap, arrays E and D are always extended to the end when a new character is appended. Moreover, the ± 1RMQ algorithm can be performed semi dynamically if the size of sequences is known beforehand, or by increasing the arrays size exponentially. Therefore, this algorithm can be performed online and can solve the semi-dynamic RMQ problem, as we intended.

6   Experimental Results

In this section, we present experimental results. We compare the running time of the proposed algorithm in Sect. 3 to the existing algorithms [2,15]. Furthermore, we show the running time of Algorithm 2. We used a machine running Ubuntu 14.04 with Core i7 4820 K and 64 GB RAM. We implemented all algorithms in C++ and compiled with gcc 4.8.4 with -O2 optimization. We used an implementation of the algorithm proposed by Pavetić et al., available at github.com/fpavetic/lcskpp. We denote the algorithm proposed by Pavetić et al. [15] and the algorithm proposed by Benson et al. [2] as PŽŠ and BLMNS, respectively.

We tested the proposed algorithm in Sect. 3, PŽŠ, and BLMNS in the following three conditions: (1) random strings over an alphabet of size $|\Sigma| = 4$ with $n = m = 1000, 2000, \cdots, 10000$ and $k = 1, 2, 3, 4$ (2) random strings over alphabets of size $|\Sigma| = 1, 2, 4, 8$ with $n = m = 1000, 2000, \cdots, 10000$ and $k = 3$ (3) DNA sequences that are available at www.ncbi.nlm.nih.gov/nuccore/346214858 and www.ncbi.nlm.nih.gov/nuccore/U38845.1, with $k = 1, 2, 3, 4, 5$. The experimental results under the conditions (1), (2) and (3) are shown in Fig. 3(a), (b), and (c), respectively.

The proposed algorithm in Sect. 3 runs faster than PŽŠ for small k or small alphabets. This is due to that PŽŠ strongly depends on the total number of matching k length substring pairs between input strings, and for small k or small alphabets there are many matching pairs. In general BLMNS runs faster than ours. The proposed algorithm runs a little faster for small k or small alphabets, except $|\Sigma| = 1$. We think that this is because for small k or small alphabets the probability that $L[i, j] \geq k$ is high, and this implies that we need more operations to compute $M[i, j]$ by definition. In Fig. 3(b), it is observed that the proposed algorithm with $|\Sigma| = 1$ runs faster than with $|\Sigma| = 2$. Since $|\Sigma| = 1$ implies that $X = Y$ if X and Y have the same length, $L[i, j] > k$ almost always holds, which leads to reduce branch mispredictions and speed up execution.

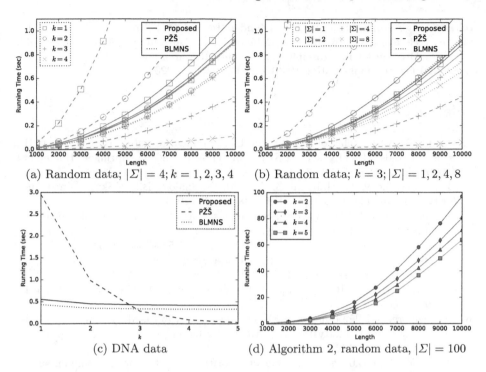

(a) Random data; $|\Sigma| = 4; k = 1, 2, 3, 4$ (b) Random data; $k = 3; |\Sigma| = 1, 2, 4, 8$

(c) DNA data   (d) Algorithm 2, random data, $|\Sigma| = 100$

Fig. 3. Running times of the proposed algorithm in Sect. 3, PŽŠ, and BLMNS (Fig. 3(a), (b) and (c)), and Algorithm 2 (Fig. 3(d)). In Fig. 3(a), (b), and (c), the line styles denote algorithms. The line markers in Fig. 3(a) and (b) represent the parameter k and the alphabet size, respectively.

We show the running time of Algorithm 2 in Fig. 3(d). We tested Algorithm 2 on random strings over $\Sigma = \{1, 2, \cdots, 100\}$ with $n = m = 1000, 2000, \cdots, 10000$ and $k = 2, 3, 4, 5$. It is observed that the algorithm runs faster as the parameter k is smaller. We suppose that the hidden constant of the RMQ data structure described in Sect. 5 is large. Therefore, the running time of Algorithm 2 depends on the number of times the rmq operation is called, and for small k the number of them increases since the probability that $l \geq k$ is high.

7 Conclusion

We showed that both the LCS_{k+} problem and the op-LCS_{k+} problem can be solved in $O(mn)$ time. Our result on the LCS_{k+} problem gives a better worst-case running time than previous algorithms [2, 15], while the experimental results showed that the previous algorithms run faster than ours on average. Although the op-LCS_{k+} problem looks much more challenging than the LCS_{k+}, since the former cannot be solved by a simple dynamic programming due to the properties of order-isomorphisms, the proposed algorithm achieves the same time complexity as the one for the LCS_{k+}.

Acknowledgements. This work was funded by ImPACT Program of Council for Science, Technology and Innovation (Cabinet Office, Government of Japan), Tohoku University Division for Interdisciplinary Advance Research and Education, and JSPS KAKENHI Grant Numbers JP24106010, JP16H02783, JP26280003.

References

1. Bender, M.A., Farach-Colton, M.: The LCA problem revisited. In: Gonnet, G.H., Viola, A. (eds.) LATIN 2000. LNCS, vol. 1776, pp. 88–94. Springer, Heidelberg (2000). doi:10.1007/10719839_9
2. Benson, G., Levy, A., Maimoni, S., Noifeld, D., Shalom, B.: LCSk: a refined similarity measure. Theor. Comput. Sci. **638**, 11–26 (2016)
3. Bouvel, M., Rossin, D., Vialette, S.: Longest common separable pattern among permutations. In: Ma, B., Zhang, K. (eds.) CPM 2007. LNCS, vol. 4580, pp. 316–327. Springer, Heidelberg (2007). doi:10.1007/978-3-540-73437-6_32
4. Cho, S., Na, J.C., Park, K., Sim, J.S.: A fast algorithm for order-preserving pattern matching. Inf. Process. Lett. **115**(2), 397–402 (2015)
5. Cole, R., Hariharan, R.: Dynamic LCA queries on trees. SIAM J. Comput. **34**(4), 894–923 (2005)
6. Crochemore, M., Iliopoulos, C.S., Kociumaka, T., Kubica, M., Langiu, A., Pissis, S.P., Radoszewski, J., Rytter, W., Waleń, T.: Order-preserving indexing. Theor. Comput. Sci. **638**, 122–135 (2016)
7. Deorowicz, S., Grabowski, S.: Efficient algorithms for the longest common subsequence in k-length substrings. Inf. Process. Lett. **114**(11), 634–638 (2014)
8. Fischer, J.: Inducing the LCP-array. In: Dehne, F., Iacono, J., Sack, J.-R. (eds.) WADS 2011. LNCS, vol. 6844, pp. 374–385. Springer, Heidelberg (2011). doi:10.1007/978-3-642-22300-6_32
9. Fischer, J., Heun, V.: Space-efficient preprocessing schemes for range minimum queries on static arrays. SIAM J. Comput. **40**(2), 465–492 (2011)
10. Gusfield, D.: Algorithms on Strings, Trees, and Sequences: Computer Science and Computational Biology. Cambridge University Press, New York (1997)
11. Hasan, M.M., Islam, A., Rahman, M.S., Rahman, M.: Order preserving pattern matching revisited. Pattern Recogn. Lett. **55**, 15–21 (2015)
12. Khan, R., Ahmad, M., Zakarya, M.: Longest common subsequence based algorithm for measuring similarity between time series: a new approach. World Appl. Sci. J. **24**(9), 1192–1198 (2013)
13. Kim, J., Eades, P., Fleischer, R., Hong, S.H., Iliopoulos, C.S., Park, K., Puglisi, S.J., Tokuyama, T.: Order-preserving matching. Theor. Comput. Sci. **525**(13), 68–79 (2014)
14. Kubica, M., Kulczynski, T., Radoszewski, J., Rytter, W., Walen, T.: A linear time algorithm for consecutive permutation pattern matching. Inf. Process. Lett. **113**(12), 430–433 (2013)
15. Pavetić, F., Žužić, G., Šikić, M.: *LCSk++*: practical similarity metric for long strings (2014). CoRR 1407.2407
16. Sović, I., Šikić, M., Wilm, A., Fenlon, S.N., Chen, S., Nagarajan, N.: Fast and sensitive mapping of nanopore sequencing reads with GraphMap. Nat. Commun. **7**, Article No. 11307 (2016). doi:10.1038/ncomms11307

Computing Longest Single-arm-gapped Palindromes in a String

Shintaro Narisada[1($\boxtimes$)], Diptarama[1], Kazuyuki Narisawa[1], Shunsuke Inenaga[2], and Ayumi Shinohara[1]

[1] Graduate School of Information Sciences, Tohoku University, Sendai, Japan
{shintaro_narisada,diptarama}@shino.ecei.tohoku.ac.jp,
{narisawa,ayumi}@ecei.tohoku.ac.jp
[2] Department of Informatics, Kyushu University, Fukuoka, Japan
inenaga@inf.kyushu-u.ac.jp

Abstract. We introduce new types of approximate palindromes called *single-arm-gapped palindromes* (*SAGPs*). A SAGP contains a gap in either its left or right arm, which is in the form of either $wgucu^Rw^R$ or $wucu^Rgw^R$, where w and u are non-empty strings, w^R and u^R are their reversed strings respectively, g is a gap, and c is either a single character or the empty string. We classify SAGPs into two groups: those which have ucu^R as a maximal palindrome (type-1), and the others (type-2). We propose several algorithms to compute all type-1 SAGPs with longest arms occurring in a given string using suffix arrays, and them a linear-time algorithm based on suffix trees. We also show how to compute type-2 SAGPs with longest arms in linear time. We perform some preliminary experiments to evaluate practical performances of the proposed methods.

1 Introduction

A palindrome is a string that reads the same forward and backward. Discovering palindromic structures in strings is a classical, yet important task in combinatorics on words and string algorithmics (e.g., see [1,3,8,14]). A natural extension to palindromes is to allow for a *gap* between the left and right arms of palindromes. Namely, a string x is called a gapped palindrome if $x = wgw^R$ for some strings w, g with $|w| \geq 1$ and $|g| \geq 0$. Finding gapped palindromes has applications in bioinformatics, such as finding secondary structures of RNA sequences called *hairpins* [9]. If we further allow for another gap *inside either arm*, then such a palindrome can be written as $wg_2ug_1u^Rw^R$ or $wug_1u^Rg_2w^R$ for some strings w, g_1, g_2, u with $|u| \geq 1$, $|g_1| \geq 0$, $|g_2| \geq 0$, and $|w| \geq 1$. These types of palindromes characterize *hairpins with bulges* in RNA sequences, known to occur frequently in the secondary structures of RNA sequences [16]. Notice that the special case where $|g_1| \leq 1$ and $|g_2| = 0$ corresponds to usual palindromes, and the special case where $|g_1| \geq 2$ and $|g_2| = 0$ corresponds to gapped palindromes.

In this paper, we consider a new class of generalized palindromes where $|g_1| \leq 1$ and $|g_2| \geq 1$, i.e., palindromes with gaps *inside* one of its arms. We call such palindromes as *single-arm-gapped palindromes* (*SAGPs*). For instance,

© Springer International Publishing AG 2017
B. Steffen et al. (Eds.): SOFSEM 2017, LNCS 10139, pp. 375–386, 2017.
DOI: 10.1007/978-3-319-51963-0_29

string abb|ca|cb|bc|bba is an SAGP of this kind, taking $w =$ abb, $g_1 = \varepsilon$ (the empty string), $g_2 =$ ca, and $u =$ cb.

We are interested in occurrences of SAGPs as substrings of a given string T. For simplicity, we will concentrate on SAGPs with $|g_1| = 0$ containing a gap in their left arms. However, slight modification of all the results proposed in this paper can easily be applied to all the other cases. For any occurrence of an SAGP $wguu^R w^R$ beginning at position b in T, the position $b + |wgu| - 1$ is called the *pivot* of the occurrence of this SAGP. This paper proposes various algorithms to solve the problem of computing longest SAGPs for every pivot in a given string T of length n. We classify longest SAGPs into two groups: those which have uu^R as a maximal palindrome (*type-1*), and the others (*type-2*). Firstly, we show a naïve $O(n^2)$-time algorithm for computing type-1 longest SAGPs. Secondly, we present a simple but practical $O(n^2)$-time algorithm for computing type-1 longest SAGPs based on simple scans over the suffix array [15]. We also show that the running time of this algorithm can be improved by using a dynamic predecessor/successor data structure. If we employ the van Emde Boas tree [4], we achieve $O((n + occ_1) \log \log n)$-time solution, where occ_1 is the number of type-1 longest SAGPs to output. Finally, we present an $O(n + occ_1)$-time solution based on the suffix tree [17]. For type-2 longest SAGPs, we show an $O(n + occ_2)$-time algorithm, where occ_2 is the number of type-2 longest SAGPs to output. Combining the last two results, we obtain an optimal $O(n + occ)$-time algorithm for computing all longest SAGPs, where occ is the number of outputs. We performed preliminary experiments to compare practical performances of our algorithms for finding type-1 longest SAGPs. All proofs are omitted due to lack of space. A full version of this paper is available at arXiv:1609.03000.

Related work. For a *fixed* gap length d, one can find all gapped palindromes wgw^R with $|g| = d$ in the input string T of length n in $O(n)$ time [9]. Kolpakov and Kucherov [13] showed an $O(n + L)$-time algorithm to compute *long-armed palindromes* in T, which are gapped palindromes wgw^R such that $|w| \geq |g|$. Here, L denotes the number of outputs. They also showed how to compute, in $O(n + L)$ time, *length-constrained palindromes* which are gapped palindromes wgw^R such that the gap length $|g|$ is in a predefined range. Recently, Fujishige et al. [6] proposed online algorithms to compute long-armed palindromes and length-constrained palindromes from a given string. A gapped palindrome wgw^R is an α-*gapped palindrome*, if $|wg| \leq \alpha|w|$ for $\alpha \geq 1$. Gawrychowski et al. [7] showed that the maximum number of α-gapped palindromes occurring in a string of length n is at most $28\alpha n + 7n$. Since long-armed palindromes are 2-gapped palindromes for $\alpha = 2$, $L = O(n)$ and thus Kolpakov and Kucherov's algorithm runs in $O(n)$ time. Gawrychowski et al. [7] also proposed an $O(\alpha n)$-time algorithm to compute all α-gapped palindromes in a given string for any predefined $\alpha \geq 1$. Hsu et al. [10] showed an $O(kn)$ time algorithm that finds all maximal approximate palindromes uvw in a given string such that $|v| = q$ and the Levenshtein distance between u and w^R is at most k, for any $q \geq 0$ and $k > 0$. We emphasize that none of the above algorithms can directly be applied to computing SAGPs.

2 Preliminaries

Let $\Sigma = \{1, \ldots, \sigma\}$ be an integer alphabet of size σ. An element of Σ^* is called a *string*. For any string w, $|w|$ denotes the length of w. The empty string is denoted by ε. Let $\Sigma^+ = \Sigma^* - \{\varepsilon\}$. For any $1 \leq i \leq |w|$, $w[i]$ denotes the i-th symbol of w. For a string $w = xyz$, strings x, y, and z are called a *prefix*, *substring*, and *suffix* of w, respectively. The substring of w that begins at position i and ends at position j is denoted by $w[i..j]$ for $1 \leq i \leq j \leq |w|$, i.e., $w[i..j] = w[i] \cdots w[j]$. For $j > i$, let $w[i..j] = \varepsilon$ for convenience. For two strings X and Y, let $lcp(X, Y)$ denote the length of the longest common prefix of X and Y.

For any string x, let x^R denote the reversed string of x, i.e. $x^R = x[|x|] \cdots x[1]$. A string p is called a *palindrome* if $p = p^R$. Let T be any string of length n. Let $p = T[b..e]$ be a palindromic substring of T. The position $i = \lfloor \frac{b+e}{2} \rfloor$ is called the *center* of this palindromic substring p. The palindromic substring p is said to be the *maximal palindrome* centered at i iff there are no longer palindromes than p centered at i, namely, $T[b-1] \neq T[e+1]$, $b = 1$, or $e = n$.

A string x is called a *single-arm-gapped palindrome* (SAGP) if x is in the form of either $wgucu^R w^R$ or $wucu^R gw^R$, with some non-empty strings $w, g, u \in \Sigma^+$ and $c \in \Sigma \cup \{\varepsilon\}$. For simplicity and ease of explanations, in what follows we consider only SAGPs whose left arms contain gaps and $c = \varepsilon$, namely, those of form $wguu^R w^R$. But our algorithms to follow can easily be modified to compute other forms of SAGPs occurring in a string as well.

Let b be the beginning position of an occurrence of a SAGP $wguu^R w^R$ in T, namely, $T[b..b + 2|wu| + |g| - 1] = wguu^R w^R$. The position $i = b + |wgu| - 1$ is called the *pivot* of this occurrence of the SAGP. This position i is also the center of the palindrome uu^R. An SAGP $wguu^R w^R$ for pivot i in string T is represented by a quadruple $(i, |w|, |g|, |u|)$ of integers. In what follows, we will identify the quadruple $(i, |w|, |g|, |u|)$ with the corresponding SAGP $wguu^R w^R$ for pivot i.

For any SAGP $x = wguu^R w^R$, let $armlen(x)$ denote the length of the arm of x, namely, $armlen(x) = |wu|$. A substring SAGP $y = wguu^R w^R$ for pivot i in a string T is said to be a *longest* SAGP for pivot i, if for any SAGP y' for pivot i in T, $armlen(y) \geq armlen(y')$.

Notice that there can be different choices of u and w for the longest SAGPs at the same pivot. For instance, consider string ccabcabbace. Then, $(7, 1, 3, 2) = $ c|abc|ab|ba|c and $(7, 2, 3, 1) = $ ca|bca|b|b|ac are both longest SAGPs (with arm length $|wu| = 3$) for the same pivot 7, where the underlines represent the gaps. Of all longest SAGPs for each pivot i, we regard those that have longest palindromes uu^R centered at i as *canonical* longest SAGPs for pivot i. In the above example, $(7, 1, 3, 2) = $ c|abc|ab|ba|c is a canonical longest SAGP for pivot 7, while $(7, 2, 3, 1) = $ ca|bca|b|b|ac is not. Let $SAGP(T)$ be the set of canonical longest SAGPs for all pivots in T. In this paper, we present several algorithms to compute $SAGP(T)$.

For an input string T of length n over an integer alphabet of size $\sigma = n^{O(1)}$, we perform standard preprocessing which replaces all characters in T with integers from range $[1, n]$. Namely, we radix sort the original characters in T, and replace each original character by its rank in the sorted order. Since the original integer alphabet is of size $n^{O(1)}$, the radix sort can be implemented with $O(1)$ number of bucket sorts, taking $O(n)$ total time. Thus, whenever we speak of a string T over an integer alphabet of size $n^{O(1)}$, one can regard T as a string over an integer alphabet of size n.

Tools: Suppose a string T ends with a unique character that does not appear elsewhere in T. The *suffix tree* [17] of a string T, denoted by $STree(T)$, is a path-compressed trie which represents all suffixes of T. Then, $STree(T)$ can be defined as an edge-labelled rooted tree such that (1) Every internal node is branching; (2) The out-going edges of every internal node begin with mutually distinct characters; (3) Each edge is labelled by a non-empty substring of T; (4) For each suffix s of T, there is a unique leaf such that the path from the root to the leaf spells out s. It follows from the above definition of $STree(T)$ that if $n = |T|$ then the number of nodes and edges in $STree(T)$ is $O(n)$. By representing every edge label X by a pair (i, j) of integers such that $X = T[i..j]$, $STree(T)$ can be represented with $O(n)$ space. For a given string T of length n over an integer alphabet of size $\sigma = n^{O(1)}$, $STree(T)$ can be constructed in $O(n)$ time [5]. For each node v in $STree(T)$, let $str(v)$ denote the string spelled out from the root to v. According to Property (4), we sometimes identify each position i in string T with the leaf which represents the corresponding suffix $T[i..n]$.

Suppose the unique character at the end of string T is the lexicographically smallest in Σ. The *suffix array* [15] of string T of length n, denoted SA_T, is an array of size n such that $SA_T[i] = j$ iff $T[j..n]$ is the ith lexicographically smallest suffix of T for $1 \leq i \leq n$. The *reversed suffix array* of T, denoted SA_T^{-1}, is an array of size n such that $SA_T^{-1}[SA_T[i]] = i$ for $1 \leq i \leq n$. The *longest common prefix array* of T, denoted LCP_T, is an array of size n such that $LCP_T[1] = -1$ and $LCP_T[i] = lcp(T[SA_T[i-1]..n], T[SA_T[i]..n])$ for $2 \leq i \leq n$. The arrays SA_T, SA_T^{-1}, and LCP_T for a given string T of length n over an integer alphabet of size $\sigma = n^{O(1)}$ can be constructed in $O(n)$ time [11,12].

For a rooted tree $\mathcal{T}$, the lowest common ancestor $LCA_{\mathcal{T}}(u, v)$ of two nodes u and v in $\mathcal{T}$ is the deepest node in $\mathcal{T}$ which has u and v as its descendants. It is known that after a linear-time preprocessing on the input tree, querying $LCA_{\mathcal{T}}(u, v)$ for any two nodes u, v can be answered in constant time [2].

Consider a rooted tree $\mathcal{T}$ where each node is either marked or unmarked. For any node v in $\mathcal{T}$, let $NMA_{\mathcal{T}}(v)$ denote the deepest marked ancestor of v. There exists a linear-space algorithm which marks any unmarked node and returns $NMA_{\mathcal{T}}(v)$ for any node v in amortized $O(1)$ time [18].

Let A be an integer array of size n. A range minimum query $RMQ_A(i, j)$ of a given pair (i, j) of indices $(1 \leq i \leq j \leq n)$ asks an index k in range $[i, j]$ which stores the minimum value in $A[i..j]$. After $O(n)$-time preprocessing on A, $RMQ_A(i, j)$ can be answered in $O(1)$ time for any given pair (i, j) of indices [2].

Let S be a set of m integers from universe $[1, n]$, where n fits in a single machine word. A predecessor (resp. successor) query for a given integer x to S asks the largest (resp. smallest) value in S that is smaller (resp. larger) than x. Let $u(m, n)$, $q(m, n)$ and $s(m, n)$ denote the time for updates (insertion/deletion) of elements, the time for predecessor/successor queries, and the space of a dynamic predecessor/successor data structure. Using a standard balanced binary search tree, we have $u(m,n) = q(m,n) = O(\log m)$ time and $s(n,m) = O(m)$ space. The Y-fast trie [19] achieves $u(m,n) = q(m,n) = O(\log\log n)$ *expected* time and $s(n,m) = O(m)$ space, while the van Emde Boas tree [4] does $u(m,n) = q(m,n) = O(\log\log n)$ *worst-case* time and $s(n,m) = O(n)$ space.

3   Algorithms for Computing Canonical Longest SAGPs

In this section, we present several algorithms to compute the set $SAGP(T)$ of canonical longest SAGPs for all pivots in a given string T.

A position i in string T is said to be of *type-1* if there exists a SAGP $wguu^R w^R$ such that uu^R is the maximal palindrome centered at position i, and is said to be of *type-2* otherwise. For example, consider $T =$ baaabaabaacbaabaabac of length 20. Position 13 of T is of type-1, since there are canonical longest SAGPs $(13, 4, 4, 2) =$ abaa|baac|ba|ab|aaba and $(13, 4, 1, 2) =$ abaa|c|ba|ab|aaba for pivot 13, where ba|ab is the maximal palindrome centered at position 13. On the other hand, Position 6 of T is of type-2; the maximal palindrome centered at position 6 is aaba|abaa but there are no SAGPs in the form of $w$gaaba|abaaw^R for pivot 6. The canonical longest SAGPs for pivot 6 is $(6, 1, 1, 3) =$ a|a|aba|aba|a.

Let $Pos_1(T)$ and $Pos_2(T)$ be the sets of type-1 and type-2 positions in T, respectively. Let $SAGP(T,i)$ be the subset of $SAGP(T)$ whose elements are canonical longest SAGPs for pivot i. Let $SAGP_1(T) = \bigcup_{i\in Pos_1(T)} SAGP(T,i)$ and $SAGP_2(T) = \bigcup_{i\in Pos_2(T)} SAGP(T,i)$. Clearly $SAGP_1(T) \cup SAGP_2(T) = SAGP(T)$ and $SAGP_1(T) \cap SAGP_2(T) = \emptyset$. The following lemma gives an useful property to characterize the type-1 positions of T.

Lemma 1. *Let i be any type-1 position of a string T of length n. Then, a SAGP $wguu^R w^R$ is a canonical longest SAGP for pivot i iff uu^R is the maximal palindrome centered at i and w^R is the longest non-empty prefix of $T[i + |u^R| + 1..n]$ such that w occurs at least once in $T[1..i - |u| - 1]$.*

We define two arrays *Pals* and *LMost* as follows:

$$Pals[i] = \{r \mid T[i - r + 1..i + r] \text{ is a maximal palindrome in } T \text{ for pivot } i\}.$$
$$LMost[c] = \min\{i \mid T[i] = c\} \text{ for } c \in \Sigma.$$

By Lemma 1, a position i in T is of type-1 iff $LMost[i + Pals[i] + 1] < i - Pals[i]$.

Lemma 2. *Given a string T of length n over an integer alphabet of size $n^{O(1)}$, we can determine whether each position i of T is of type-1 or type-2 in a total of $O(n)$ time and space.*

By Lemmas 1 and 2, we can consider an algorithm to compute $SAGP(T)$ by computing $SAGP_1(T)$ and $SAGP_2(T)$ separately, as shown in Algorithm 1.

Algorithm 1. computing $SAGP(T)$

    Input: string T of length n
    Output: $SAGP(T)$
1 compute $Pals$;
2 **for** $i = n$ **downto** 1 **do**
3 $c = T[i]$; $NextPos[i] = LMost[c]$; $LMost[c] = i$;

4 **for** $i = 1$ **to** n **do**
5   **if** $LMost[i + Pals[i] + 1] < i - Pals[i]$ **then**
6 $Pos_1(T) = Pos_1(T) \cup \{i\}$;   /* position i is of type-1 */
7   **else**
8 $Pos_2(T) = Pos_2(T) \cup \{i\}$;   /* position i is of type-2 */

9 compute $SAGP_1(T)$;   /* Sect. 3.1 */
10 compute $SAGP_2(T)$;   /* Sect. 3.2 */

In this algorithm, we also construct an auxiliary array $NextPos$ defined by $NextPos[i] = \min\{j \mid i < j,\ T[i] = T[j]\}$ for each $1 \le i \le n$, which will be used in Sect. 3.2.

Lemma 3. *Algorithm 1 correctly computes $SAGP(T)$.*

In the following subsections, we present algorithms to compute $SAGP_1(T)$ and $SAGP_2(T)$ respectively, assuming that the arrays $Pals$, $LMost$ and $NextPos$ have already been computed.

3.1 Computing $SAGP_1(T)$ for Type-1 Positions

In what follows, we present several algorithms corresponding to the line 9 in Algorithm 1. Lemma 1 allows us greedy strategies to compute the longest prefix w^R of $T[i + Pals[i] + 1..n]$ such that w occurs in $T[1..i - Pals[i] - 1]$.

Naïve Quadratic-Time Algorithm with RMQs. Let $T' = T\$T^R\#$. We construct the suffix array $SA_{T'}$, the reversed suffix array $SA_{T'}^{-1}$, the LCP array $LCP_{T'}$ for T', and the array $RMQ_{LCP_{T'}}$ to support RMQ on $LCP_{T'}$.

For each $Pals[i]$ in T, for each gap size $G = 1, \ldots, i - Pals[i] - 1$, we compute $W = lcp(T[1..i - Pals[i] - G]^R, T[i + Pals[i] + 1..n])$ in $O(1)$ time by $RMQ_{LCP_{T'}}$. Then, the gap sizes G with largest values of W give all longest SAGPs for pivot i. Since we test $O(n)$ gap sizes for every pivot i, it takes a total of $O(n^2)$ time to compute $SAGP_1(T)$. The working space of this method is $O(n)$.

Simple Quadratic-Time Algorithm Based on Suffix Array. Given a string T, we construct $SA_{T'}$, $SA_{T'}^{-1}$, and $LCP_{T'}$ for string $T' = T\$T^R\#$ as in the previous subsection. Further, for each position $n + 2 \le j \le 2n + 1$ in the reversed part T^R of $T' = T\$T^R\#$, let $op(j)$ denote its "original" position in the string T, namely, let $op(j) = 2n - j + 2$. Let e be any entry of $SA_{T'}$ such that $SA_{T'}[e] \geq n + 2$. We associate each such entry of $SA_{T'}$ with $op(SA_{T'}[e])$.

Let $SA_{T'}[k] = i + Pals[i] + 1$, namely, the kth entry of $SA_{T'}$ corresponds to the suffix $T[i + Pals[i] + 1..n]$ of T. Now, the task is to find the longest prefix w^R of $T[i + Pals[i] + 1..n]$ such that w occurs completely inside $T[1..i - Pals[i] - 1]$. Let $b = i - Pals[i] + 1$, namely, b is the beginning position of the maximal palindrome uu^R centered at i. We can find w for any maximal SAGP $wguu^Rw^R$ for pivot i by traversing $SA_{T'}$ from the kth entry forward and backward, until we encounter the nearest entries $p < k$ and $q > k$ on $SA_{T'}$ such that $op(SA_{T'}[p]) < b - 1$ and $op(SA_{T'}[q]) < b - 1$, if they exist. The size W of w is equal to

$$\max\{\min\{LCP_{T'}[p+1], \ldots, LCP_{T'}[k]\}, \min\{LCP_{T'}[k+1], \ldots, LCP_{T'}[q]\}\}. \tag{1}$$

Assume w.l.o.g. that p gives a larger lcp value with k, i.e. $W = \min\{LCP_{T'}[p + 1], \ldots, LCP_{T'}[k]\}$. Let s be the largest entry of $SA_{T'}$ such that $s < p$ and $LCP_{T'}[s + 1] < W$. Then, any entry t of $SA_{T'}$ such that $s < t \leq p + 1$ and $op(SA_{T'}[t]) < b - 1$ corresponds to an occurrence of a longest SAGP for pivot i, with gap size $b - op(SA_{T'}[t]) - 1$. We output longest SAGP $(i, W, b - op(SA_{T'}[t]) - 1, |u|)$ for each such t. The case where q gives a larger lcp value with k, or p and q give the same lcp values with k can be treated similarly.

We find p and s by simply traversing $SA_{T'}$ from k. Since the distance from k to s is $O(n)$, the above algorithm takes $O(n^2)$ time. The working space is $O(n)$.

Algorithm Based on Suffix Array and Predecessor/Successor Queries. Let $occ_1 = |SAGP_1(T)|$. For any position r in T, we say that the entry j of $SA_{T'}$ is *active* w.r.t. r iff $op(SA_{T'}[j]) < r - 1$. Let $Active(r)$ denote the set of active entries of $SA_{T'}$ for position r, namely, $Active(r) = \{j \mid op(SA_{T'}[j]) < r - 1\}$.

Let $t_1 = p$, and let $t_2, \ldots, t_h$ be the decreasing sequence of entries of $SA_{T'}$ which correspond to the occurrences of longest SAGPs for pivot i. Notice that for all $1 \leq \ell \leq h$ we have $op(SA_{T'}[t_\ell]) < b - 1$ and hence $t_\ell \in Active(b)$, where $b = i - |u| + 1$. Then, finding t_1 reduces to a predecessor query for k in $Active(b)$. Also, finding t_ℓ for $2 \leq \ell \leq h$ reduces to a predecessor query for $t_{\ell-1}$ in $Active(b)$.

To effectively use the above observation, we compute an array U of size n from $Pals$ such that $U[b]$ stores a list of all maximal palindromes in T which begin at position b if they exist, and $U[b]$ is nil otherwise. U can be computed in $O(n)$ time e.g., by bucket sort. After computing U, we process $b = 1, \ldots, n$ in increasing order. Assume that when we process a certain value of b, we have maintained a dynamic predecessor/successor query data structure for $Active(b)$. The key is that the same set $Active(b)$ can be used to compute the longest SAGPs for every element in $U[b]$, and hence we can use the same predecessor/successor data structure for all of them. After processing all elements in $U[b]$, we insert all elements of $Active(b+1) \setminus Active(b)$ to the predecessor/successor data structure. Each element to insert can be easily found in constant time.

Since we perform $O(n + occ_1)$ predecessor/successor queries and $O(n)$ insertion operations in total, we obtain the following theorem.

Theorem 1. *Given a string T of size n over an integer alphabet of size $\sigma = n^{O(1)}$, we can compute $SAGP_1(T)$ in $O(n(u(n,n)+q(n,n))+occ_1 \cdot q(n,n))$ time with $O(n+s(n,n))$ space by using the suffix array and a predecessor/successor data structure, where $occ_1 = |SAGP_1(T)|$.*

Since every element of $Active(b)$ for any b is in range $[1, 2n+2]$, we can employ the van Emde Boas tree [4] as the dynamic predecessor/successor data structure using $O(n)$ total space. Thus we obtain the following theorem.

Theorem 2. *Given a string T of size n over an integer alphabet of size $\sigma = n^{O(1)}$, we can compute $SAGP_1(T)$ in $O((n+occ_1) \log \log n)$ time and $O(n)$ space by using the suffix array and the van Emde Boas tree, where $occ_1 = |SAGP_1(T)|$.*

Optimal-Time Algorithm Based on Suffix Tree. In this subsection, we show that the problem can be solved in *optimal* time and space, using the following three suffix trees regarding the input string T. Let $\mathcal{T}_1 = STree(T\$T^R\#)$ for string $T\$T^R\#$ of length $2n+2$, and $\mathcal{T}_2 = STree(T^R\#)$ of length $n+1$. These suffix trees $\mathcal{T}_1$ and $\mathcal{T}_2$ are static, and thus can be constructed offline, in $O(n)$ time for an integer alphabet. We also maintain a growing suffix tree $\mathcal{T}_2' = STree(T^R[k..n])\#)$ for decreasing $k = n, \dots, 1$.

Lemma 4. *Given $\mathcal{T}_2 = STree(T^R\#)$, we can maintain $\mathcal{T}_2' = STree(T^R[k..n]\#)$ for decreasing $k = n, \dots, 1$ incrementally, in $O(n)$ total time for an integer alphabet of size $n^{O(1)}$.*

Theorem 3. *Given a string T of length n over an integer alphabet of size $\sigma = n^{O(1)}$, we can compute $SAGP_1(T)$ in optimal $O(n+occ_1)$ time and $O(n)$ space by using suffix trees, where $occ_1 = |SAGP_1(T)|$.*

Proof. We first compute the array U. Consider an arbitrary fixed b, and let uu^R be a maximal palindrome stored in $U[b]$ whose center is $i = b + |u| - 1$. Assume that we have a growing suffix tree $\mathcal{T}_2'$ for string $T^R[n-b+1..n]\#$ which corresponds to the prefix $T[1..b]$ of T of size b. We use a similar strategy as the suffix array based algorithms. For each position $2n - b + 2 \leq j \leq 2n + 1$ in string $T' = T\$T^R\#$, $1 \leq op(j) \leq b - 2$. We maintain the NMA data structure over the suffix tree $\mathcal{T}_1$ for string T' so that all the ancestors of the leaves whose corresponding suffixes start at positions $2n - b + 2 \leq j \leq 2n + 1$ are marked, and any other nodes in $\mathcal{T}_1$ remain unmarked at this step.

As in the suffix-array based algorithms, the task is to find the longest prefix w^R of $T[i + |u^R| + 1..n]$ such that w occurs completely inside $T[1..b-2] = T[1..i-|u|-1]$. In so doing, we perform an NMA query from the leaf $i + |u^R| + 1$ of $\mathcal{T}_1$, and let v be the answer to the NMA query. By the way how we have maintained the NMA data structure, it follows that $str(v) = w^R$.

To obtain the occurrences of w in $T[1..b-2]$, we switch to $\mathcal{T}_2'$, and traverse the subtree rooted at v. Then, for any leaf ℓ in the subtree, $(i, |str(v)|, b - op(\ell), |u|)$ is a canonical longest SAGP for pivot i.

After processing all the maximal palindromes in $U[b]$, we mark all unmarked ancestors of the leaf $2n - b$ of T_1 in a bottom-up manner, until we encounter the lowest ancestor that is already marked. This operation is a preprocessing for the maximal palindromes in $U[b+1]$, as we will be interested in the positions between 1 and $op(2n-b) = b-1$ in T. In this preprocessing, each unmarked node is marked at most once, and each marked node will remain marked. In addition, we update the growing suffix tree T_2' by inserting the new leaf for $T^R[n-b..n]\#$.

We analyze the time complexity of this algorithm. Since all maximal palindromes in $U[b]$ begin at position b in T, we can use the same set of marked nodes on T_1 for all of those in $U[b]$. Thus, the total cost to update the NMA data structure for all b's is linear in the number of unmarked nodes that later become marked, which is $O(n)$ overall. The cost for traversing the subtree of T_2' to find the occurrences of w can be charged to the number of canonical longest SAGPs to output for each pivot, thus it takes $O(occ_1)$ time for all pivots. Updating the growing suffix tree T_2' takes overall $O(n)$ time by Lemma 4. What remains is how to efficiently link the new internal node introduced in the growing suffix tree T_2', to its corresponding node in the static suffix tree T_1 for string T'. This can be done in $O(1)$ time using a similar technique based on LCA queries on T_1, as in the proof of Lemma 4. Summing up all the above costs, we obtain $O(n + occ_1)$ optimal running time and $O(n)$ working space.   □

3.2 Computing $SAGP_2(T)$ for Type-2 Positions

In this subsection, we present an algorithm to compute $SAGP_2(T)$ in a given string T, corresponding to the line 10 in Algorithm 1.

Lemma 5. *For any type-2 position i in string T, every (not necessarily longest) SAGP for i must end at one of the positions between $i+2$ and $i + Pals[i]$.*

Lemma 6. *For any type-2 position i in string T, if $wguu^Rw^R$ is a canonical longest SAGP for pivot i, then $|w| = 1$.*

For every type-2 position i in T, let $u = T[i..i + Pals[i]]$. By Lemma 6, any canonical longest SAGP is of the form $cguu^Rc$ for $c \in \Sigma$. For each $2 \leq k \leq Pals[i]$, let $c_k = u^R[k]$, and let u_k^R be the proper prefix of u^R of length $k - 1$. Now, observe that the largest value of k for which $LMost[c_k] \leq i - |u_k| - 1$ corresponds to a canonical longest SAGP for pivot i, namely, $c_k g_k u_k u_k^R c_k$ is a canonical longest SAGP for pivot i, where $g_k = T[LMost[c_k] + 1..i - |u_k|]$. In order to efficiently find the largest value of such, we consider a function $findR(t, i)$ defined by

$$findR(t, i) = \min\{r \mid t \leq r < i \text{ and } T[l] = T[r] \text{ for some } 1 \leq l < r\} \cup \{+\infty\}.$$

Lemma 7. *For any type-2 position i in T, quadruple $(i, 1, r - LMost[T[r]], i - r)$ represents a canonical longest SAGP for pivot i, where $r = findR(i - Pals[i] + 1, i) \neq \infty$. Moreover, its gap is the longest among all the canonical longest SAGPs for pivot i.*

Algorithm 2. constructing the array *FindR*

Input: string T of length n

Output: array *FindR* of size n

1 Let Occ_1 and Occ_2 be arrays of size Σ_T initialized by $+\infty$;

2 Let *FindR* be an arrays of size n, and let *Stack* be an empty stack;

3 $min_{in} = +\infty$;

4 **for** $i = n$ **downto** 1 **do**

5 $\quad$ $c = T[i]$; $Occ_2[c] = Occ_1[c]$; $Occ_1[c] = i$;

6 $\quad$ $min_{in} = \min\{min_{in}, Occ_2[c]\}$;

7 $\quad$ $Stack.push(i)$;

8 $\quad$ **while** *Stack is not empty* **and** $LMost[T[Stack.top]] \geq i$ **do** $Stack.pop()$;

9 $\quad$ $min_{out} = Stack.top$ **if** *Stack is not empty* **else** $+\infty$;

10 $\quad$ $FindR[i] = \min\{min_{in}, min_{out}\}$

By Lemma 7, we can compute a canonical longest SAGP for any type-2 pivot i in $O(1)$ time, assuming that the function $findR(t, i)$ returns a value in $O(1)$ time. We define an array *FindR* of size n by

$$FindR[t] = \min\{r \mid t \leq r \text{ and } T[l] = T[r] \text{ for some } 1 \leq l < r\} \cup \{+\infty\}, \quad (2)$$

for $1 \leq t \leq n$. If the array *FindR* has already been computed, then $findR(t, i)$ can be obtained in $O(1)$ time by $findR(t, i) = FindR[t]$ if $FindR[t] < i$, and $+\infty$ otherwise. Algorithm 2 shows a pseudo-code to compute *FindR*.

Lemma 8. *Algorithm 2 correctly computes FindR in $O(n)$ time and space.*

By Lemma 8, we can compute $SAGP_2(T)$ for type-2 positions as follows.

Theorem 4. *Given a string T of length n over an integer alphabet of size $n^{O(1)}$, we can compute $SAGP_2(T)$ in $O(n + occ_2)$ time and $O(n)$ space, where $occ_2 = |SAGP_2(T)|$.*

Proof. For a given T, we first compute the array *FindR* by Algorithm 2. By Lemma 7, we can get a canonical longest SAGP $x_1 = (i, 1, |g_1|, Pals[i])$ if any, in $O(1)$ time by referring to *LMost* and *FindR*. Note that x_1 is the one whose gap $|g_1|$ is the longest. Let $b_1 = i - Pals[i] - |g_1|$ be the beginning position of x_1 in T. Then the next shorter canonical longest SAGP for the same pivot i begins at position $b_2 = NextPos[b_1]$. By repeating this process $b_{j+1} = NextPos[b_j]$ while the gap size $|g_j| = i - Pals[i] - |b_j|$ is positive, we obtain all the canonical longest SAGPs for pivot i. Overall, we can compute all canonical longest SAGPs for all pivots in T in $O(n + occ_2)$ time. The space requirement is clearly $O(n)$. $\square$

We now have the main theorem from Theorems 3, 4 and Lemmas 2, 3 as follows.

Theorem 5. *Given a string T of length n over an integer alphabet of size $n^{O(1)}$, Algorithm 1 can compute $SAGP(T)$ in optimal $O(n + occ)$ time and $O(n)$ space, where $occ = |SAGP(T)|$.*

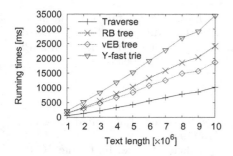

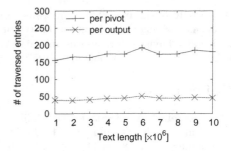

Fig. 1. Running times on random strings of length from 10^6 to 10^7 with $|\Sigma| = 10$.

Fig. 2. Average numbers of traversed entries of suffix array per pivot/output.

4   Experiments

In this section, we show some experimental results which compare performance of our algorithms for computing $SAGP_1(T)$. We implemented the naïve quadratic-time algorithm (Naïve), the simple quadratic-time algorithm which traverses suffix arrays (Traverse), and three versions of the algorithm based on suffix array and predecessor/successor data structure, each employing red-black trees (RB tree), Y-fast tries (Y-fast trie), and van Emde Boas trees[1] (vEB tree), as the predecessor/successor data structure. We implemented all these algorithms with Visual C++ 12.0 (2013), and performed all experiments on a PC (Xeon W3565, 12 GB of memory) running on Windows 7.

We tested these programs on randomly generated strings of lengths from 10^6 to 10^7 with $|\Sigma| = 10$. Figure 1 shows the average running times of 10 executions, where Naïve is exculded because it was too slow. As one can see, Traverse was the fastest for all lengths. We also conducted the same experiments varying alphabet sizes as 2, 4, and 20, and obtained similar results as the case of alphabet size 10.

To verify why Traverse runs fastest, we measured the average numbers of suffix array entries which are traversed, per pivot and output (i.e., canonical longest SAGP). Figure 2 shows the result. We can observe that although in theory $O(n)$ entries can be traversed per pivot and output for a string of length n, in both cases the actual number is far less than $O(n)$ and grows very slowly as n increases. This seems to be the main reason why Traverse is faster than RB tree, vEB tree, and Y-fast trie which use sophisticated but also complicated predecessor/successor data structures.

We also tested Traverse, RB tree, vEB tree, and Y-fast trie on a genome of *M.tuberculosis* H37Rv (size: 4411529 bp, GenBank accession: NC_000962). The running times were Traverse: 4304.8, RB tree: 12126.7, vEB tree: 9729.8, Y-fast trie: 17862.6, all in milli-seconds. Here again, Traverse was the fastest.

---

[1] We modified a van Emde Boas tree implementation from https://code.google.com/archive/p/libveb/ so that it works with Visual C++.

Acknowledgements. This work was funded by ImPACT Program of Council for Science, Technology and Innovation (Cabinet Office, Government of Japan), Tohoku University Division for Interdisciplinary Advance Research and Education, and JSPS KAKENHI Grant Numbers JP15H05706, JP24106010, JP26280003.

References

1. Apostolico, A., Breslauer, D., Galil, Z.: Parallel detection of all palindromes in a string. Theor. Comput. Sci. **141**(1&2), 163–173 (1995)
2. Bender, M.A., Farach-Colton, M.: The LCA problem revisited. In: Gonnet, G.H., Viola, A. (eds.) LATIN 2000. LNCS, vol. 1776, pp. 88–94. Springer, Heidelberg (2000). doi:10.1007/10719839_9
3. Droubay, X., Pirillo, G.: Palindromes and sturmian words. Theor. Comput. Sci. **223**(1–2), 73–85 (1999)
4. van Emde Boas, P.: Preserving order in a forest in less than logarithmic time. In: FOCS, pp. 75–84 (1975)
5. Farach-Colton, M., Ferragina, P., Muthukrishnan, S.: On the sorting-complexity of suffix tree construction. J. ACM **47**(6), 987–1011 (2000)
6. Fujishige, Y., Nakamura, M., Inenaga, S., Bannai, H., Takeda, M.: Finding gapped palindromes online. In: Mäkinen, V., Puglisi, S.J., Salmela, L. (eds.) IWOCA 2016. LNCS, vol. 9843, pp. 191–202. Springer, Heidelberg (2016). doi:10.1007/978-3-319-44543-4_15
7. Gawrychowski, P., Tomohiro, I., Inenaga, S., Köppl, D., Manea, F.: Efficiently finding all maximal α-gapped repeats. In: STACS 2016, pp. 39:1–39:14 (2016)
8. Glen, A., Justin, J., Widmer, S., Zamboni, L.Q.: Palindromic richness. Eur. J. Comb. **30**(2), 510–531 (2009)
9. Gusfield, D.: Algorithms on Strings, Trees, and Sequences. Cambridge University Press, New York (1997)
10. Hsu, P.H., Chen, K.Y., Chao, K.M.: Finding all approximate gapped palindromes. Int. J. Found. Comput. Sci. **21**(6), 925–939 (2010)
11. Kärkkäinen, J., Sanders, P., Burkhardt, S.: Linear work suffix array construction. J. ACM **53**(6), 918–936 (2006)
12. Kasai, T., Lee, G., Arimura, H., Arikawa, S., Park, K.: Linear-time longest-common-prefix computation in suffix arrays and its applications. In: Amir, A. (ed.) CPM 2001. LNCS, vol. 2089, pp. 181–192. Springer, Heidelberg (2001). doi:10.1007/3-540-48194-X_17
13. Kolpakov, R., Kucherov, G.: Searching for gapped palindromes. Theor. Comput. Sci. **410**(51), 5365–5373 (2009)
14. Manacher, G.K.: A new linear-time on-line algorithm for finding the smallest initial palindrome of a string. J. ACM **22**(3), 346–351 (1975)
15. Manber, U., Myers, E.W.: Suffix arrays: a new method for on-line string searches. SIAM J. Comput. **22**(5), 935–948 (1993)
16. Shi, Y.Z., Wang, F.H., Wu, Y.Y., Tan, Z.J.: A coarse-grained model with implicit salt for RNAs: predicting 3D structure, stability and salt effect. J. Chem. Phys. **141**(10), 105102 (2014)
17. Weiner, P.: Linear pattern matching algorithms. In: 14th Annual Symposium on Switching and Automata Theory, pp. 1–11 (1973)
18. Westbrook, J.: Fast incremental planarity testing. In: Kuich, W. (ed.) ICALP 1992. LNCS, vol. 623, pp. 342–353. Springer, Heidelberg (1992). doi:10.1007/3-540-55719-9_86
19. Willard, D.E.: Log-logarithmic worst-case range queries are possible in space $\Theta(N)$. Information Processing Letters **17**, 81–84 (1983)

Edit-Distance Between Visibly Pushdown Languages

Yo-Sub Han[1] and Sang-Ki Ko[2(✉)]

[1] Department of Computer Science, Yonsei University, 50, Yonsei-Ro,
Seodaemun-Gu, Seoul 120-749, Republic of Korea
emmous@yonsei.ac.kr
[2] Department of Computer Science, University of Liverpool,
Ashton Street, Liverpool L69 3BX, UK
sangkiko@liverpool.ac.uk

Abstract. We study the edit-distance between two visibly pushdown languages. It is well-known that the edit-distance between two context-free languages is undecidable. The class of visibly pushdown languages is a robust subclass of context-free languages since it is closed under intersection and complementation whereas context-free languages are not. We show that the edit-distance problem is decidable for visibly pushdown languages and present an algorithm for computing the edit-distance based on the construction of an alignment PDA. Moreover, we show that the edit-distance can be computed in polynomial time if we assume that the edit-distance is bounded by a fixed integer k.

Keywords: Visibly pushdown languages · Edit-distance · Algorithm · Decidability

1 Introduction

The edit-distance between two words is the smallest number of operations required to transform one word into the other [9]. We can use the edit-distance as a similarity measure between two words; the shorter distance implies that the two words are more similar. We can compute this by using the bottom-up dynamic programming algorithm [15]. The edit-distance problem arises in many areas such as computational biology, text processing and speech recognition [11,13,14]. This problem can be extended to a problem of computing the similarity or dissimilarity between languages [4,5,11].

The edit-distance between two languages is defined as the minimum edit-distance of two words, where one word is from the first language and the other word is from the second language. Mohri [11] considered the problem of computing the edit-distance between two regular languages given by finite-state automata (FAs) of sizes m and n and showed that it is computable in $O(mn \log mn)$ time. He also proved that it is undecidable to compute the edit-distance between two context-free languages [11] using the undecidability of the

© Springer International Publishing AG 2017
B. Steffen et al. (Eds.): SOFSEM 2017, LNCS 10139, pp. 387–401, 2017.
DOI: 10.1007/978-3-319-51963-0_30

intersection emptiness of two context-free languages. As an intermediate result, Han et al. [5] considered the edit-distance between a regular language and a context-free language. Given an FA and a pushdown automaton (PDA) of sizes m and n, they proposed a polynomial-time algorithm that computes the edit-distance between their languages [5].

Here we study the edit-distance problem between two visibly pushdown languages. Visibly pushdown languages are recognizable by visibly pushdown automata (VPAs), which are a special type of pushdown automata for which stack behavior is driven by the input symbols according to a partition of the alphabet. Some literature call these automata *input-driven pushdown automata* [10].

The class of visibly pushdown languages lies in between the class of regular languages and the class of context-free languages. Recently, there have been many results about visibly pushdown languages because of nice closure properties. Note that context-free languages are not closed under intersection and complement and deterministic context-free languages are not closed under union, intersection, concatenation, and Kleene-star. On the other hand, visibly pushdown languages are closed under all these operations. Moreover, language inclusion, equivalence and universality are all decidable for visibly pushdown languages whereas undecidable for context-free languages.

Visibly pushdown automata are useful in processing XML documents [1,12]. For example, a visibly pushdown automaton can process a SAX representation of an XML document, which is a linear sequence of characters along with a hierarchically nested matching of open-tags with closing tags. Note that the edit-distance between two visibly pushdown languages is undecidable if two languages are defined over different visibly pushdown alphabets since the intersection emptiness is undecidable [8]. Therefore, we always assume that two visibly pushdown languages are defined over the same visibly pushdown alphabet.

We show that the edit-distance between visibly pushdown languages is decidable and present an algorithm for computing the edit-distance. Moreover, the edit-distance can be computed in polynomial time if we assume that the edit-distance is bounded by a fixed integer k.

2   Preliminaries

Here we recall some basic definitions and fix notation. For background knowledge in automata theory, the reader may refer to textbooks [6,16].

The size of a finite set S is $|S|$. Let Σ denote a finite alphabet and Σ^* denote the set of all finite words over Σ. For $m \in \mathbb{N}$, $\Sigma^{\leq m}$ is the set of words over Σ having length at most m. The ith character of a word w is denoted by w_i for $1 \leq i \leq |w|$, and the subword of a word w that begins at position i and ends at position j is denoted by $w_{i,j}$ for $1 \leq i \leq j \leq |w|$. A language over Σ is a subset of Σ^*. Given a set X, 2^X denotes the power set of X. The symbol λ denotes the null word.

A (nondeterministic) finite automaton (FA) is specified by a tuple $A = (Q, \Sigma, \delta, s, F)$, where Q is a finite set of states, Σ is an input alphabet, δ :

$Q \times \Sigma \to 2^Q$ is a multi-valued transition function, $s \in Q$ is the start state and $F \subseteq Q$ is a set of final states. If F consists of a single state f, we use f instead of $\{f\}$ for simplicity. When $q \in \delta(p, a)$, we say that state p has an *out-transition* to state q (p is a *source state* of q) and q has an *in-transition* from p (q is a *target state* of p). The transition function δ is extended in the natural way to a function $Q \times \Sigma^* \to 2^Q$. A word $x \in \Sigma^*$ is accepted by A if there is a labeled path from s to a state in F such that this path spells out the word x, namely, $\delta(s, x) \cap F \neq \emptyset$. The language $L(A)$ is the set of words accepted by A.

A (nondeterministic) pushdown automaton (PDA) is specified by a tuple $P = (Q, \Sigma, \Gamma, \delta, s, Z_0, F)$, where Q is a finite set of states, Σ is a finite input alphabet, Γ is a finite stack alphabet, $\delta : Q \times (\Sigma \cup \{\lambda\}) \times \Gamma \to 2^{Q \times \Gamma^{\leq 2}}$ is a transition function, $s \in Q$ is the start state, Z_0 is the initial stack symbol and $F \subseteq Q$ is the set of final states. Our definition restricts that each transition of P has at most two stack symbols, that is, each transition can push or pop at most one symbol. We use $|\delta|$ to denote the number of transitions in δ. We define the size $|P|$ of P as $|Q| + |\delta|$. The language $L(P)$ is the set of words accepted by P.

A (nondeterministic) *visibly pushdown automaton* (VPA) [2,10] is a restricted version of a PDA, where the input alphabet Σ consists of three disjoint classes, Σ_c, Σ_r, and Σ_l. Namely, $\Sigma = \Sigma_c \cup \Sigma_r \cup \Sigma_l$. The class of the input alphabet determines the type of stack operation. For example, the automaton always pushes a symbol onto the stack when it reads a *call symbol* in Σ_c. If the input symbol is a *return symbol* in Σ_r, the automaton pops a symbol from the stack. Finally, the automaton neither uses the stack nor even examine the content of the stack for the *local symbols* in Σ_l. Formally, the input alphabet is defined as a triple $\widetilde{\Sigma} = (\Sigma_c, \Sigma_r, \Sigma_l)$, where three components are finite disjoint sets.

A VPA is formally defined by a tuple $A = (\widetilde{\Sigma}, \Gamma, Q, s, F, \delta_c, \delta_r, \delta_l)$, where $\Sigma = \Sigma_c \cup \Sigma_r \cup \Sigma_l$ is the input alphabet, Γ is the finite set of stack symbols, Q is the finite set of states, $s \in Q$ is the start state, $F \subseteq Q$ is the set of final states, $\delta_c : Q \times \Sigma_c \to 2^{Q \times \Gamma}$ is the transition function for the push operations, $\delta_r : Q \times (\Gamma \cup \{\bot\}) \times \Sigma_r \to 2^Q$ is the transition function for the pop operations, and $\delta_l : Q \times \Sigma_l \to 2^Q$ is the local transition function. We use $\bot \notin \Gamma$ to denote the top of an empty stack.

A *configuration* of A is a triple (q, w, v), where $q \in Q$ is the current state, $w \in \Sigma^*$ is the remaining input, and $v \in \Gamma^*$ is the content on the stack. Denote the set of configurations of A by $C(A)$ and we define the single step computation with the relation $\vdash_A \subseteq C(A) \times C(A)$.

- **Push operation:** $(q, aw, v) \vdash_A (q', w, \gamma v)$ for all $a \in \Sigma_c, (q', \gamma) \in \delta_c(q, a), \gamma \in \Gamma, w \in \Sigma^*$ and $v \in \Gamma^*$.
- **Pop operation:** $(q, aw, \gamma v) \vdash_A (q', w, v)$ for all $a \in \Sigma_r, q' \in \delta_r(q, \gamma, a), \gamma \in \Gamma, w \in \Sigma^*$ and $v \in \Gamma^*$; furthermore, $(q, aw, \epsilon) \vdash_A (q', w, \epsilon)$, for all $a \in \Sigma_r, q' \in \delta_r(q, \bot, a)$ and $w \in \Sigma^*$.
- **Local operation:** $(q, aw, v) \vdash_A (q', w, v)$, for all $a \in \Sigma_l, q' \in \delta_l(q, a), w \in \Sigma^*$ and $v \in \Gamma^*$.

An *initial configuration* of a VPA $A = (\widetilde{\Sigma}, \Gamma, Q, s, F, \delta_c, \delta_r, \delta_l)$ is (s, w, ϵ), where s is the start state, w is an input word and ϵ implies an empty stack.

A VPA accepts a word if A arrives at the final state by reading the word from the initial configuration. Formally, we write the language recognized by A_1 as

$$L(A) = \{w \in \Sigma^* \mid (s, w, \epsilon) \vdash_A^* (q, \epsilon, v) \text{ for some } q \in F, v \in \Gamma^*\}.$$

We call the languages recognized by VPAs the *visibly pushdown languages*. The class of visibly pushdown languages is a strict subclass of deterministic context-free languages and a strict superclass of regular languages. While many closure properties such as complement and intersection do not hold for context-free languages, visibly pushdown languages are closed under most operations including other basic operations such as concatenation, union, and Kleene-star.

3   Edit-Distance

The edit-distance between two words is the smallest number of operations that transform a word to the other. People use different edit-operations according to own applications. We consider three basic operations, insertion, deletion and substitution for simplicity. Given an alphabet Σ, let $\Omega = \{(a \to b) \mid a, b \in \Sigma \cup \{\lambda\}\}$ be a set of edit-operations. Namely, Ω is an alphabet of all edit-operations for *deletions* $(a \to \lambda)$, *insertions* $(\lambda \to a)$ and *substitutions* $(a \to b)$. We say that an edit-operation $(a \to b)$ is a *trivial substitution* if $a = b$. We call a word $\omega \in \Omega^*$ an *edit string* [7] or an *alignment* [11].

Let the morphism h between Ω^* and $\Sigma^* \times \Sigma^*$ be $h((a_1 \to b_1) \cdots (a_n \to b_n)) = (a_1 \cdots a_n, b_1 \cdots b_n)$, where $a_i, b_i \in \Sigma \cup \{\lambda\}$ for $1 \le i \le n$. For example, a word $\omega = (a \to \lambda)(b \to b)(\lambda \to c)(c \to c)$ over Ω is an alignment of abc and bcc, and $h(\omega) = (abc, bcc)$. Thus, from an alignment ω of two words x and y, we can retrieve x and y using h: $h(\omega) = (x, y)$.

We associate a non-negative edit cost to each edit-operation $\omega_i \in \Omega$ as a function $\mathsf{C} : \omega_i \to \mathbb{R}_+$. We can extend the function to the cost $\mathsf{C}(\omega)$ of an alignment $\omega = \omega_1 \cdots \omega_n$ as follows: $\mathsf{C}(\omega) = \sum_{i=1}^{n} \mathsf{C}(\omega_i)$.

Definition 1. *The* edit-distance $d(x, y)$ *of two words x and y over Σ is the minimal cost of an alignment ω between x and y: $d(x, y) = \min\{\mathsf{C}(\omega) \mid h(\omega) = (x, y)\}$. We say that ω is* optimal *if $d(x, y) = \mathsf{C}(\omega)$.*

Note that we use the Levenshtein distance [9] for edit-distance. Thus, we assign cost 1 to all edit-operations $(a \to \lambda), (\lambda \to a)$, and $(a \to b)$ for all $a \ne b \in \Sigma$. We can extend the edit-distance definition to languages.

Definition 2. *The* edit-distance $d(L_1, L_2)$ *between two languages $L_1, L_2 \subseteq \Sigma^*$ is the minimum edit-distance of two words, one is from L_1 and the other is from L_2: $d(L_1, L_2) = \min\{d(x, y) \mid x \in L_1 \text{ and } y \in L_2\}$.*

Mohri [11] revealed that the edit-distance between two context-free languages is undecidable from the undecidability of the intersection emptiness of two context-free languages. Moreover, he presented an algorithm to compute the edit-distance between two regular languages given by FAs of size m and n in $O(mn \log mn)$ time. Han et al. [5] considered the intermediate case where one language is regular and the other language is context-free. Given a PDA and an FA for the languages, it is shown that the problem is computable in polynomial time while computing an optimal alignment corresponding to the edit-distance requires an exponential runtime.

4   Edit-Distance Between Two VPLs

First we study the decidability of the edit-distance between two visibly pushdown languages. We notice that the edit-distance between two context-free languages is undecidable, whereas the edit-distance between two regular languages can be computed in polynomial time.

Interestingly, it turns out that the edit-distance between two visibly pushdown languages is decidable. Here we show that we can compute the edit-distance between two visibly pushdown languages L_1 and L_2 given by two VPAs by constructing the alignment PDA [5], which accepts all the possible alignments between two languages of length up to k. By setting k to be the upper bound of the edit-distance between given two visibly pushdown languages L_1 and L_2, we can compute the edit-distance between L_1 and L_2 by choosing the minimum-cost alignment accepted by the alignment PDA.

The alignment PDA is first proposed by Han et al. [5] to compute the edit-distance between a regular language and a context-free language. Given an FA A and a PDA P, we can construct an alignment PDA $\mathcal{A}(A, P)$ that accepts all possible alignments that transform a word accepted by the FA A to a word accepted by the PDA P. After we construct an alignment PDA for two languages, we can compute the edit-distance between the two languages by computing the length of the shortest word accepted by the alignment PDA. Furthermore, we can obtain an optimal alignment between two languages by taking the shortest word.

An interesting point to note is that the construction of the alignment PDA does not imply that we can compute the edit-distance. For example, the edit-distance between two context-free languages is undecidable even though it is possible to construct an alignment PDA with two stacks that accepts all possible alignments between two PDAs [11]. This is because we cannot compute the length of the shortest word accepted by a two-stack PDA, which can simulate a Turing machine [6]. Here we start from an idea that we do not need to consider all possible alignments between two visibly pushdown languages to compute the edit-distance and an optimal alignment. If we know the upper bound k of the edit-distance between two visibly pushdown languages, we can compute the edit-distance and an optimal alignment by constructing an alignment PDA that accepts all possible alignments of cost up to k between two visibly pushdown languages. This can be done because the stack operation of VPAs is determined by the input character.

Assume that we have two VPAs A_1 and A_2 over the same alphabet Σ. Then, the alignment PDA $\mathcal{A}(A_1, A_2)$ of A_1 and A_2 simulates all possible alignments between the two languages $L(A_1)$ and $L(A_2)$. Note that $\mathcal{A}(A_1, A_2)$ simulates two stacks from two VPAs simultaneously by reading each edit-operation. Whenever $\mathcal{A}(A_1, A_2)$ simulates a trivial edit-operation $(a \rightarrow a), a \in \Sigma$ which substitutes a character into the same one, the difference in height of two stacks does not change since two VPAs read characters in the same class. The height of two stacks becomes different when $\mathcal{A}(A_1, A_2)$ reads insertions of call (or return) symbols, deletions of call (or return) symbols, or substitutions between two characters in different classes. For example, the height of two stacks becomes different by 1 when $\mathcal{A}(A_1, A_2)$ read an insertion $(\lambda \rightarrow a)$ of a call symbol $a \in \Sigma_c$ since A_1 does not change its stack while A_2 is pushing a stack symbol onto its stack. The height of two stacks becomes different the most when $\mathcal{A}(A_1, A_2)$ reads an edit-operation that substitutes a call (resp. return) symbol into a return (resp. call) symbol since A_1 pushes (resp. pops) a stack symbol while A_2 pops (resp. pushes) a stack symbol. Therefore, if the upper bound of the edit-distance between two visibly pushdown languages is k, the maximum height difference between two stacks can be at most $2k$ whenever we simulate an alignment that costs up to k. Note that we can easily compute the upper bound of the edit-distance between two visibly pushdown languages by computing the shortest words from each visibly pushdown language. Let $\mathrm{lsw}(L)$ be the length of the shortest word in L.

Proposition 3. *Let $L \subseteq \Sigma^*$ and $L' \subseteq \Sigma^*$ be the languages over Σ. Then, $d(L, L') \leq \max\{\mathrm{lsw}(L), \mathrm{lsw}(L')\}$ holds.*

Now we give the alignment PDA construction for computing the edit-distance between two visibly pushdown languages. The basic idea of the construction is to remember the top stack symbols from two stacks by using the states of the alignment PDA. Intuitively, we store the information of the top $2k$ stack symbols from both stacks in the states instead of pushing into the stack of the alignment PDA.

Let $A_i = (\tilde{\Sigma}, \Gamma_i, Q_i, s_i, F_i, \delta_{i,c}, \delta_{i,r}, \delta_{i,l})$ for $i = 1, 2$ be two VPAs. We construct the alignment PDA $\mathcal{A}(A_1, A_2) = (Q_E, \Omega, \Gamma_E, s_E, F_E, \delta_E)$, where

- $Q_E = Q_1 \times Q_2 \times \Gamma_1^{\leq 2k} \times \Gamma_2^{\leq 2k}$ is the set of states,
- $\Omega = \{(a \rightarrow b) \mid a, b \in \Sigma \cup \{\lambda\}\}$ is the alphabet of edit-operations,
- $\Gamma_E = (\Gamma_1 \cup \{\lambda\}) \times (\Gamma_2 \cup \{\lambda\}) \setminus \{(\lambda, \lambda)\}$ is a finite stack alphabet,
- $s_E = (s_1, s_2, \lambda, \lambda)$ is the start state, and
- $F_E = F_1 \times F_2 \times \Gamma_1^{\leq 2k} \times \Gamma_2^{\leq 2k}$ is the set of final states.

Now we define the transition function δ_E. There are seven cases to consider as follows. The alignment PDA $\mathcal{A}(A_1, A_2)$ reads an edit-operation that

  (i) pushes on two stacks simultaneously,
  (ii) pushes on the first stack,
 (iii) pushes on the second stack,
 (iv) pops from two stacks simultaneously,
  (v) pops from the first stack,
 (vi) pops from the second stack, and
 (vii) not perform stack operation.

Assume that $x \in \Gamma_1^{\leq 2k}$ and $y \in \Gamma_2^{\leq 2k}$. Simply, x and y are words over the stack alphabet of A_1 and A_2 whose lengths are at most $2k$. For a non-empty word x over Γ_1, recall that we denote the first character and the last character of x by x_1 and $x_{|x|}$, respectively. We also denote the subword that consists of characters from x_i to x_j by $x_{i,j}$, where $i < j$.

Suppose that there are transitions defined in VPAs A_1 and A_2 as follows:

- $(q', \gamma) \in \delta_{1,c}(q, a_c)$,   [push operation in A_1]
- $q' \in \delta_{1,l}(q, a_l)$,   [local operation in A_1]
- $q' \in \delta_{1,r}(q, \gamma, a_r)$,   [pop operation in A_1]
- $(p', \mu) \in \delta_{2,c}(p, b_c)$,   [push operation in A_2]
- $p' \in \delta_{2,l}(p, b_l)$, and   [local operation in A_2]
- $p' \in \delta_{2,r}(p, \mu, b_r)$.   [pop operation in A_2]

By reading an edit-operation $(a_c \to b_c)$, we define δ_E to operate as follows:

- $(q', p', x\gamma, y\mu) \in \delta_E((q, p, x, y), (a_c \to b_c))$ if $|x| < 2k$ and $|y| < 2k$,
- $((q', p', x_{2,|x|}\gamma, y_{2,|y|}\mu), (x_1, y_1)) \in \delta_E((q, p, x, y), (a_c \to b_c))$ otherwise.

By the above transitions, we simulate the push operations on the stacks of A_1 and A_2 at the same time. We store the information of the top $2k$ stack symbols in the states instead of using "real" stack. If a state already contains the information of $2k$ symbols, we start using the stack by pushing the bottommost pair of stack symbols onto the stack.

We also define δ_E to operate as follows by reading an edit-operation $(a_c \to b_l)$:

- $(q', p', x\gamma, y) \in \delta_E((q, p, x, y), (a_c \to b_l))$ if $|x| < 2k$,
- $((q', p', x_{2,|x|}\gamma, y_{2,|y|}), (x_1, y_1)) \in \delta_E((q, p, x, y), (a_c \to b_l))$ otherwise.

Similarly, we define δ_E for an edit-operation $(a_c \to \lambda)$ as follows:

- $(q', p, x\gamma, \mu) \in \delta_E((q, p, x, y), (a_c \to \lambda))$ if $|x| < 2k$,
- $((q', p, x_{2,|x|}\gamma, y_{2,|y|}), (x_1, y_1)) \in \delta_E((q, p, x, y), (a_c \to \lambda))$ otherwise.

Note that the cases of reading $(a_l \to b_c)$ or $(\lambda \to b_c)$ are completely symmetric to the previous two cases. We also consider the cases when we have to pop at least one of two stacks by reading an edit-operation. First, we define δ_E for the case when we read an edit-operation $(a_r \to b_r)$ that pops from both stacks at the same time.

- $(q', p', \gamma_{\mathsf{top}}x_{1,|x|-1}, \mu_{\mathsf{top}}y_{1,|y|-1}) \in \delta_E((q, p, x, y), (\gamma_{\mathsf{top}}, \mu_{\mathsf{top}}), (a_r \to b_r))$ if $x_{|x|} = \gamma$, $y_{|y|} = \mu$ and the top of the stack is $(\gamma_{\mathsf{top}}, \mu_{\mathsf{top}})$,
- $(q', p', x_{1,|x|-1}, y_{1,|y|-1}) \in \delta_E((q, p, x, y), (a_r \to b_r))$ if $x_{|x|} = \gamma$, $y_{|y|} = \mu$ and the stack is empty.

When we simulate pop operations on $\mathcal{A}(A_1, A_2)$, we remove the last stack symbols stored in the state. Then, we pop off the top of the stack, say $(\gamma_{\mathsf{top}}, \mu_{\mathsf{top}})$, and move the pair to the front of the stored stack symbols in the state.

For the case when we have to pop only from the first stack, we define δ_E to be as follows:

- $(q', p', \gamma_{\text{top}} x_{1,|x|-1}, \mu_{\text{top}} y) \in \delta_E((q, p, x, y), (\gamma_{\text{top}}, \mu_{\text{top}}), (a_r \rightarrow b_l))$ if $|x| = 2k$, $|y| < 2k$, and the top of the stack is $(\gamma_{\text{top}}, \mu_{\text{top}})$,
- $(q', p', x_{1,|x|-1}, y) \in \delta_E((q, p, x, y), (a_r \rightarrow b_l))$ otherwise.

Note that $x_{|x|} = \gamma$ should hold for simulating pop operations on the first stack. We also define the transitions for the edit-operations of the form $(a_r \rightarrow \lambda)$ similarly. Again, the pop operations on the second stack are completely symmetric. Lastly, we define δ_E for the case when we do not touch the stack at all. There are three possible cases as follows:

- $(q', p', x, y) \in \delta_E((q, p, x, y), (a_l \rightarrow b_l))$,
- $(q', p, x, y) \in \delta_E((q, p, x, y), (a_l \rightarrow \lambda))$, and
- $(q, p', x, y) \in \delta_E((q, p, x, y), (\lambda \rightarrow b_l))$.

Now we prove that the constructed alignment PDA $\mathcal{A}(A_1, A_2)$ simulates all possible alignments of cost up to k between $L(A_1)$ and $L(A_2)$.

Lemma 4. *Given two VPAs A_1 and A_2, it is possible to construct the alignment PDA $\mathcal{A}(A_1, A_2)$ that accepts all possible alignments between $L(A_1)$ and $L(A_2)$ of cost up to the constant k.*

Proof. Let us consider the simulations of two VPAs A_1 and A_2 for an alignment ω. Given $h(\omega) = (x, y)$, the VPA A_1 has to simulate a word x while the VPA A_2 is simulating a word y. Suppose that x has $2k$ call symbols and y has k' call symbols, where $k' < 2k$, and no return symbols. Then, the stack contents of A_1 and A_2 should be $\gamma_1 \gamma_2 \cdots \gamma_{2k}$ and $\mu_1 \mu_2 \cdots \mu_{k'}$, respectively, where $\gamma_i \in \Gamma_1$ for $1 \leq i \leq 2k$ and $\mu_j \in \Gamma_2$ for $1 \leq j \leq k'$. See Fig. 1 for illustration of this example.

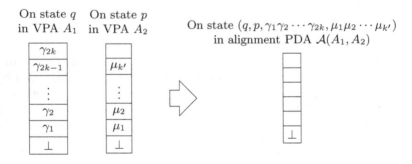

Fig. 1. Illustration of how we store the information of two stacks in the states of the alignment PDA $\mathcal{A}(A_1, A_2)$.

After this, we push the pair (γ_1, μ_1) of two stack symbols in the bottom of two stacks onto the stack of $\mathcal{A}(A_1, A_2)$ if we read an edit-operation $(a \rightarrow b)$ where a is a call symbol of A_1. Let us assume that A_1 pushes γ_{2k+1} by reading a and A_2 pushes $\mu_{k'+1}$ by reading b. Then, we push two stack symbols γ_{2k+1}

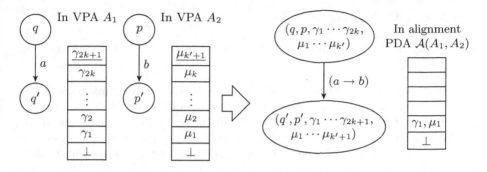

Fig. 2. Illustration of how we store the information of two stacks in the states of the alignment PDA $\mathcal{A}(A_1, A_2)$. Underlined stack symbols γ_{2k+1} and $\mu_{k'+1}$ are pushded by the current transitions of VPAs.

and $\mu_{k'+1}$ onto the simulated stacks stored in the state. See Fig. 2 to see what happens after reading $(a \to b)$.

In this way, we can make the stack of $\mathcal{A}(A_1, A_2)$ to be always synchronized. Note that we only push stack symbols onto the stack of $\mathcal{A}(A_1, A_2)$ when we need to push a stack symbol onto the stack where the simulated stack stored in the state is full. Therefore, the stack of $\mathcal{A}(A_1, A_2)$ should be empty if the maximum height of two stacks stored in the state is less than $2k$. When we read an edit-operation that pops a stack symbol from A_1 or A_2, we pop the stack symbols from the stack contents stored in the states. If the height of the stack in the state is $2k$ before we pop a stack symbol, we pop a stack symbol from the top of the real stack of $\mathcal{A}(A_1, A_2)$ and move to the bottom of the simulated stack stored in the state of $\mathcal{A}(A_1, A_2)$.

By storing stack information in the states instead of real stacks, $\mathcal{A}(A_1, A_2)$ accepts alignments where the height difference of two stacks during the simulation can be at most $2k$. We mention that $\mathcal{A}(A_1, A_2)$ also accepts alignments of cost higher than k if the simulation of the alignments does not require the stack height difference to be larger than $2k$.

Now we prove that the alignment PDA $\mathcal{A}(A_1, A_2)$ accepts an alignment ω, where $\mathsf{C}(\omega) \leq k$ if and only if ω is an alignment satisfying $\mathsf{C}(\omega) \leq k$ and $h(\omega) = (x, y)$, where $x \in L(A_1)$ and $y \in L(A_2)$.

($\Longrightarrow$) Since $\mathcal{A}(A_1, A_2)$ accepts an alignment ω, where $\mathsf{C}(\omega) \leq k$, there exists an accepting computation X_ω of $\mathcal{A}(A_1, A_2)$ on ω ending in a state (f_1, f_2) where $f_1 \in F_1, f_2 \in F_2$. We assume that $\omega = w_1 \cdots w_l$, where $w_i \in \Omega$ for $i \leq i \leq l$. Denote the sequence of states of $\mathcal{A}(A_1, A_2)$ appearing in the computation X_ω just before reading the lth symbol of ω as $C_0, \ldots, C_{l-1}$, and denote the state (f_1, f_2) where the computation ends as C_l. Consider the first component $q_i \in Q_1$ of the state $C_i \in Q_E$, for $0 \leq i \leq l$, and the first component $a_j \in \Sigma \cup \{\lambda\}$ of the edit-operation w_j, for $1 \leq j \leq l$. From the construction of $\mathcal{A}(A_1, A_2)$, it follows that

$\quad$ – $(q_{i+1}, \gamma) \in \delta_{A,c}(q, a_{i+1})$, $\qquad\qquad\qquad\qquad$ if $a_{i+1} \in \Sigma_c$

$\quad$ – $q_{i+1} \in \delta_{A,l}(q, a_{i+1})$, $\qquad\qquad\qquad\qquad\qquad$ if $a_{i+1} \in \Sigma_l$

$\quad$ – $q_{i+1} \in \delta_{A,r}(q, \gamma, a_{i+1})$, and $\qquad\qquad\qquad\quad$ if $a_{i+1} \in \Sigma_r$

$\quad$ – $q_{i+1} = q_i$. $\qquad\qquad\qquad\qquad\qquad\qquad\qquad$ if $a_{i+1} = \lambda$

for $0 \leq i \leq l - 1$. Note that the transitions of δ_E reading an "insertion opera-tion" ($\lambda \rightarrow b$) do not change the first components of the states. Thus, the first components of the state $C_0, \ldots, C_l$ spell out an accepting computation of A_1 on the word $x = a_1 \cdots a_l$ obtained by concatenating the first components of the edit-operations of ω. Using a similar argument for the word y obtained by concatenating the second components of ω, we can show that the computation yields an accepting computation of A_2 on y.

($\Longleftarrow$) Let $\omega = (\omega_{L(1)} \rightarrow \omega_{R(1)})(\omega_{L(2)} \rightarrow \omega_{R(2)}) \cdots (\omega_{L(l)} \rightarrow \omega_{R(l)})$ be an alignment of length l for $x = \omega_{L(1)}\omega_{L(2)} \cdots \omega_{L(l)} \in L(A_1)$ and $y = \omega_{R(1)}\omega_{R(2)} \cdots \omega_{R(l)} \in L(A_2)$. Let $\mathcal{C} = C_0 C_1 \cdots C_m, m \in \mathbb{N}$, be a sequence of configurations of the VPA A_1 that traces an accepting computation $X_{A,x}$ on the word x. Assuming that C_i is (q_i, γ_i), the configuration C_{i+1} is obtained from C_i by applying a transition $(q_{i+1}, \gamma_{i+1}) \in \delta_A(q_i, a, \gamma_i)$, where $a \in \Sigma \cup \{\lambda\}$. Note that $\omega_{L(j)}$ or $\omega_{R(j)}$ may be the empty word if $(\omega_{L(j)} \rightarrow \omega_{R(j)})$ is an edit-operation representing an insertion or a deletion operation. Suppose that the computa-tion step $C_i \rightarrow C_{i+1}$ consumes h empty words. Then in the sequence $\mathcal{C}$ after the configuration C_i, we add $h - 1$ identical copies of C_i. Then, we denote the modified sequence of configurations $\mathcal{C}' = C_0' C_1' \cdots C_l', l \in \mathbb{N}$. Analogously, let $\mathcal{D} = D_0' D_1' \cdots D_l'$ be a sequence of configurations of the VPA A_2 that traces an accepting computation $X_{B,y}$ on the word y.

$\quad$ From the sequences $\mathcal{C}'$ and $\mathcal{D}$, we obtain a sequence of configurations of $\mathcal{A}(A_1, A_2)$ describing an accepting computation on the alignment ω. For the deletion operations $(\omega_{L(j)} \rightarrow \lambda)$, the state is changed just in the first component and the configuration of A_2 remains unchanged. Recall that we have added the identical copies of configurations for simulating this case. The deletion operations can be simulated symmetrically. For the substitution operations $(\omega_{L(j)} \rightarrow \omega_{R(j)})$, the computation step simulates both a state transition of A_1 on $\omega_{L(j)}$ and a state transition of A_2 on $\omega_{R(j)}$.

$\quad$ This implies that two modified sequences of configurations of A_1 and A_2 can be combined to yield an accepting computation of $\mathcal{A}(A_1, A_2)$ on ω. $\qquad\qquad$ □

Let us consider the size of the constructed alignment PDA $\mathcal{A}(A_1, A_2)$. Let $m_i = |Q_i|, n_i = |\delta_{i,c}| + |\delta_{i,r}| + |\delta_{i,l}|$, and $l_i = |\Gamma_i|$ for $i = 1, 2$.

$\quad$ Note that each state contains an information of a pair of states from A_1 and A_2, and a stack information of at most $2k$ stack symbols of A_1 and A_2. If we represent a stack where the height of the stack is restricted to $2k$ with a word over the stack alphabet Γ_1, we have

$$l_1' = \sum_{i=0}^{2k} l_1^i = 1 + l_1 \cdot \frac{l_1^{2k} - 1}{l_1 - 1}$$

possible words. Similarly, we define l'_2 to be the number of possible words over Γ_2. Therefore, the number of states in $\mathcal{A}(A_1, A_2)$ is in

$$m_1 m_2 \cdot l'_1 l'_2 = m_1 m_2 \cdot \left(\sum_{i=0}^{2k} l_1^i \right) \cdot \left(\sum_{i=0}^{2k} l_2^i \right).$$

The size of the stack alphabet Γ_E is $l_1 l_2$ since we use all pairs of the stack symbols where the first stack symbol is from Γ_1 and the second stack symbol is from Γ_2. The size of the transition function δ_E is

$$m_1 m_2 \cdot n_1 n_2 \cdot \left(\sum_{i=0}^{2k} l_1^i \right) \cdot \left(\sum_{i=0}^{2k} l_2^i \right).$$

By Lemma 4, we can obtain an alignment PDA from two VPAs A_1 and A_2 to compute the edit-distance $d(L(A_1), L(A_2))$. Recently, Han et al. [5] studied the edit-distance between a PDA and an FA. The basic idea is to construct an alignment PDA from a PDA and an FA and compute the length of the shortest alignment from the alignment PDA. As a step, they present an algorithm for obtaining a shortest word and computing the length of the shortest word from a PDA. For the sake of completeness, we include the following proposition.

Proposition 5 (Han et al. [5]). *Given a PDA $P = (Q, \Sigma, \Gamma, \delta, s, Z_0, F_P)$, we can obtain a shortest word in $L(P)$ whose length is bounded by $2^{m^2 l + 1}$ in $O(n \cdot 2^{m^2 l})$ worst-case time and compute its length in $O(m^4 n l)$ worst-case time, where $m = |Q|$, $n = |\delta|$ and $l = |\Gamma|$.*

Now we establish the following runtime for computing the edit-distance between two VPAs.

Theorem 6. *Given two VPAs $A_i = (\Sigma, \Gamma_i, Q_i, s_i, F_i, \delta_{i,c}, \delta_{i,r}, \delta_{i,l})$ for $i = 1, 2$, we can compute the edit-distance between $L(A_1)$ and $L(A_2)$ in $O((m_1 m_2)^5 \cdot n_1 n_2 \cdot (l_1 l_2)^{10k})$ worst-case time, where $m_i = |Q_i|$, $n_i = |\delta_{i,c}| + |\delta_{i,r}| + |\delta_{i,l}|$, $l_i = |\Gamma_i|$ for $i = 1, 2$ and $k = \max\{\mathrm{lsw}(L(A_1)), \mathrm{lsw}(L(A_2))\}$.*

If we replace k with the length $2^{|Q|^2 \cdot |\Gamma| + 1}$ of a shortest word from a VPA from the time complexity obtained in Theorem 6, we have double exponential time complexity for computing the edit-distance between two VPAs. It is still an open problem to find a polynomial algorithm for the problem or to establish any hardness result. Instead, we can observe that the edit-distance problem for VPAs can be computed in polynomial time if we limit the edit-distance to a fixed integer k.

Corollary 7. *Let A_1 and A_2 be two VPAs and k be a fixed integer such that $d(L(A_1), L(A_2)) \le k$. Then, we can compute the edit-distance between $L(A_1)$ and $L(A_2)$ in polynomial time.*

As a corollary of Theorem 6, we can also establish the following result. A *visibly counter automaton* (VCA) [3] can be regarded as a VPA with a single stack symbol. It is interesting to see that we can compute the edit-distance between two VCAs in polynomial time when we are given t.

Corollary 8. *Given two VCAs A_1, A_2 and a positive integer $k \in \mathbb{N}$ in unary such that $d(L(A_1), L(A_2)) \leq k$, we can compute the edit-distance between $L(A_1)$ and $L(A_2)$ in polynomial time.*

Appendix

Context-free grammar (CFG). A context-free grammar (CFG) G is a four-tuple $G = (V, \Sigma, R, S)$, where V is a set of variables, Σ is a set of terminals, $R \subseteq V \times (V \cup \Sigma)^*$ is a finite set of productions and $S \in V$ is the start variable. Let $\alpha A \beta$ be a word over $V \cup \Sigma$, where $A \in V$ and $A \to \gamma \in R$. Then, we say that A can be rewritten as γ and the corresponding derivation step is denoted $\alpha A \beta \Rightarrow \alpha \gamma \beta$. A production $A \to t \in R$ is a *terminating production* if $t \in \Sigma^*$. The reflexive, transitive closure of $\Rightarrow$ is denoted by $\overset{*}{\to}$ and the context-free language generated by G is $L(G) = \{w \in \Sigma^* \mid S \overset{*}{\to} w\}$. We say that a variable $A \in V$ is *nullable* if $A \overset{*}{\to} \lambda$.

Proposition 3. *Let $L \subseteq \Sigma^*$ and $L' \subseteq \Sigma^*$ be the languages over Σ. Then,*

$$d(L, L') \leq \max\{\text{lsw}(L), \text{lsw}(L')\}$$

holds.

Proof. Assume that $\text{lsw}(L) = m$ and $\text{lsw}(L') = n$ where $n \leq m$. It is easy to see that the edit-distance between two shortest words can be at most m since we can substitute all characters of the shortest word of length n with any subsequence of the longer word and insert the remaining characters.   □

Proposition 5 (Han et al. [5]). *Given a PDA $P = (Q, \Sigma, \Gamma, \delta, s, Z_0, F_P)$, we can obtain a shortest word in $L(P)$ whose length is bounded by $2^{m^2 l+1}$ in $O(n \cdot 2^{m^2 l})$ worst-case time and compute its length in $O(m^4 n l)$ worst-case time, where $m = |Q|$, $n = |\delta|$ and $l = |\Gamma|$.*

Proof. Recall that we can convert a PDA into a CFG by the triple construction [6]. Let us denote the CFG obtained from P by G_P. Then, G_P has $|Q|^2 \cdot |\Gamma| + 1$ variables and $|Q|^2 \cdot |\delta|$ productions. Moreover, each production of G_P is of the form $A \to \sigma BC, A \to \sigma B, A \to \sigma$ or $A \to \lambda$, where $\sigma \in \Sigma$ and $A, B, C \in V$. Since we want to compute the shortest word from G_P, we can remove the occurrences of all *nullable* variables from G_P. Then, we pick a variable A that generates the shortest word $t \in \Sigma^*$ among all variables and replace its occurrence in G_P with t. We can compute the shortest word of $L(P)$ by iteratively removing occurrences of such variables. We describe the algorithm in Algorithm 1.

Since a production of G_P has at most one terminal followed by two variables, the length of the word to be substituted is at most $2^m - 1$ when we replace mth variable. Since we replace at most $|Q|^2 \cdot |\Gamma|$ variables to have the shortest word, the length of the shortest word in $L(P)$ can be at most $2^{|Q|^2 \cdot |\Gamma| + 1}$. Since there are at most $2|R|$ occurrences of variables in R and $|V|$ variables, we replace $\frac{2|R|}{|V|}$ occurrences of a given variable on average. Therefore, the worst-case time complexity for finding a shortest word is $O(n \cdot 2^{m^2 l})$. We also note that we can compute only the length of the shortest word in $O(m^4 n l)$ worst-case time by encoding a shortest word to be substituted with a binary number. $\square$

Algorithm 1. SHORTESTLENGTH(P)

Input: A PDA $P = (Q, \Sigma, \Gamma, \delta, s, Z_0, F_P)$
Output: lsw($L(P)$)
1: convert P into a CFG $G_P = (V, \Sigma, R, S)$ by the triple construction
2: eliminate all nullable variables
3: **for** $B \to t \in R$, where $t \in \Sigma^*$ and $|t|$ is minimum among all such t in R **do**
4:     **if** $B = S$ **then**
5:         **return** $|t|$
6:     **else**
7:         replace all occurrences of A in R with t
8:         remove A from V and its productions from R
9:     **end if**
10: **end for**

Theorem 6. *Given two VPAs $A_i = (\Sigma, \Gamma_i, Q_i, s_i, F_i, \delta_{i,c}, \delta_{i,r}, \delta_{i,l})$ for $i = 1, 2$, we can compute the edit-distance between $L(A_1)$ and $L(A_2)$ in $O((m_1 m_2)^5 \cdot n_1 n_2 \cdot (l_1 l_2)^{10k})$ worst-case time, where $m_i = |Q_i|, n_i = |\delta_{i,c}| + |\delta_{i,r}| + |\delta_{i,l}|, l_i = |\Gamma_i|$ for $i = 1, 2$ and $k = \max\{\text{lsw}(L(A_1)), \text{lsw}(L(A_2))\}$.*

Proof. In the proof of Lemma 4, we have shown that we can construct an alignment PDA $\mathcal{A}(A_1, A_2) = (Q_E, \Omega, \Gamma_E, s_E, F_E, \delta_E)$ that accepts all possible alignments between two VPAs A_1 and A_2 of length up to k. From Proposition 5, we can compute the edit-distance in $O(m^4 n l)$ time, where $m = |Q_E|, n = |\delta_E|$ and $l = |\Gamma_E|$. Recall that

$$m = m_1 m_2 \cdot \left(\sum_{i=0}^{2k} l_1^i \right) \cdot \left(\sum_{i=0}^{2k} l_2^i \right), \quad n = m_1 m_2 \cdot n_1 n_2 \cdot \left(\sum_{i=0}^{2k} l_1^i \right) \cdot \left(\sum_{i=0}^{2k} l_2^i \right),$$

and $l = l_1 l_2$. Note that

$$\left(\sum_{i=0}^{2k} l_1^i \right) \in O(l_1^{2k}) \text{ and } \left(\sum_{i=0}^{2k} l_2^i \right) \in O(l_2^{2k})$$

if $l_1, l_2 > 0$.

Therefore, the time complexity of computing the edit-distance between two VPAs A_1 and A_2 is

$$(m_1 m_2)^5 \cdot n_1 n_2 \cdot \left(\sum_{i=0}^{2k} l_1^i \right)^5 \cdot \left(\sum_{i=0}^{2k} l_2^i \right)^5 \cdot l_1 l_2 \in O((m_1 m_2)^5 \cdot n_1 n_2 \cdot (l_1 l_2)^{10k}),$$

where k is the maximum of the length of the two shortest words from $L(A_1)$ and $L(A_2)$. □

Corollary 8. *Given two VCAs A_1, A_2 and a positive integer $k \in \mathbb{N}$ in unary such that $d(L(A_1), L(A_2)) \leq k$, we can compute the edit-distance between $L(A_1)$ and $L(A_2)$ in polynomial time.*

Proof. If $l_1 = l_2 = 1$,

$$\left(\sum_{i=0}^{2k} l_1^i \right) \in O(k) \text{ and } \left(\sum_{i=0}^{2k} l_2^i \right) \in O(k).$$

If we replace l_1^{2k} and l_2^{2k} by k from the time complexity, we obtain the time complexity $O((m_1 m_2)^5 \cdot n_1 n_2 \cdot k^{10})$ which is polynomial in the size of input.

References

1. Alur, R.: Marrying words and trees. In: Proceedings of the 26th ACM SIGMOD-SIGACT-SIGART Symposium on Principles of Database Systems, PODS 2007, pp. 233–242 (2007)
2. Alur, R., Madhusudan, P.: Visibly pushdown languages. In: Proceedings of the 36th Annual ACM Symposium on Theory of Computing, pp. 202–211 (2004)
3. Bárány, V., Löding, C., Serre, O.: Regularity problems for visibly pushdown languages. In: Proceedings of the 23rd Annual Symposium on Theoretical Aspects of Computer Science, pp. 420–431 (2006)
4. Choffrut, C., Pighizzini, G.: Distances between languages and reflexivity of relations. Theor. Comput. Sci. **286**(1), 117–138 (2002)
5. Han, Y.-S., Ko, S.-K., Salomaa, K.: The edit-distance between a regular language and a context-free language. Int. J. Found. Comput. Sci. **24**(7), 1067–1082 (2013)
6. Hopcroft, J., Ullman, J.: Introduction to Automata Theory, Languages, and Computation, 2nd edn. Addison-Wesley, Reading (1979)
7. Kari, L., Konstantinidis, S.: Descriptional complexity of error/edit systems. J. Automata, Lang. Comb. **9**, 293–309 (2004)
8. Leike, J.: VPL intersection emptiness. Bachelor's Thesis, University of Freiburg (2010)
9. Levenshtein, V.I.: Binary codes capable of correcting deletions, insertions, and reversals. Sov. Phys. Dokl. **10**(8), 707–710 (1966)
10. Mehlhorn, K.: Pebbling mountain ranges and its application to DCFL-recognition. In: Automata, Languages and Programming, vol. 85, pp. 422–435 (1980)

11. Mohri, M.: Edit-distance of weighted automata: general definitions and algorithms. Int. J. Found. Comput. Sci. **14**(6), 957–982 (2003)
12. Mozafari, B., Zeng, K., Zaniolo, C.: From regular expressions to nested words: unifying languages and query execution for relational and XML sequences. Proc. VLDB Endowment **3**(1–2), 150–161 (2010)
13. Pevzner, P.A.: Computational Molecular Biology - An Algorithmic Approach. MIT Press, Cambridge (2000)
14. Thompson, K.: Regular expression search algorithm. Commun. ACM **11**(6), 419–422 (1968)
15. Wagner, R.A., Fischer, M.J.: The string-to-string correction problem. J. ACM **21**, 168–173 (1974)
16. Wood, D.: Theory of Computation. Harper & Row, New York (1987)

Data, Information and Knowledge Engineering

Model-Driven Development in Practice: From Requirements to Code

Oscar Pastor[(⊠)]

Centro de I+D+i en Métodos de Producción de Software, PROS,
Universitat Politècnica de València Camino de Vera s/n, 46022 Valencia, Spain
opastor@dsic.upv.es

Abstract. A crucial success factor in information systems development is the alignment of the final software product with business goals, business semantics and business processes. Developers should be freed from programming concerns and be able to concentrate on these alignment problems. To assess that the right capabilities are used, sound Conceptual Modeling (CM) techniques within a Model-driven system development (MDD) must be applied in order to provide a structured and systematic approach to systems development, where developers can successfully use model transformation technologies to derive models of a lower abstraction level that can be further refined, even generating software code automatically. From the experience got with the use of advanced MDD platforms, this keynote will show how to use a Capability-driven Development (CDD) strategy in order to integrate business process modelling (BPM), requirements engineering (RE) and object-oriented conceptual modelling with the objective of leveraging MDD capabilities. The current state of the art on modelling methods and code generation tools will be discussed to explore different ways to match an information system with business requirements. Concrete principles, concepts and common practices of MDD will be presented with a special focus on model-driven requirements engineering, meaning by it how BPM and requirements models can be embedded in a complete CM-based software production process.

1 Introduction

A sound software development process must guarantee that the final software product corresponds accurately to the system requirements and conforms to the organizational rules of the analyzed system. To assess the required traceability between source models and target products, precise conceptual models have to be elaborated, together with well-defined model transformations.

This "conceptual trip" between requirements and code involves different types of conceptual models, that work at different levels of abstractions (requirements models, business process models, conceptual schemas, code, …). The sound software development process commented before must determine what conceptual models to use, and what model transformations are to be defined. This Model-based Software Development Process presented in this paper has two main components: the notion of capability

© Springer International Publishing AG 2017
B. Steffen et al. (Eds.): SOFSEM 2017, LNCS 10139, pp. 405–410, 2017.
DOI: 10.1007/978-3-319-51963-0_31

applied in a CM context, and the use of the Model-driven Architecture (MDA) standard to structure the template of the proposed software process.

Firstly, the notion of capability is going to be used in order to characterize the relevant modeling components to be specified, especially at the earliest steps of a software process where goal models, organizational models, process models, requirements models, context models... are to be defined. In a business context, the notion of capability mainly refers to the resources and expertise that an enterprise needs to offer its functions. As pointed out by Zdravkovic et al. ([1]), it is a notion that has gained more and more attention in the last years because it directs business investment focus, it can be used as a baseline for business planning and it leads directly to service specification and design. It has been intensively argued that capabilities help to determine relevant changing business contexts and how to integrate applications designed for different execution contexts that are part of a common business process. This has an immediate application over the intention of providing a sound conceptual modeling framework for modeling requirements and business processes, using the most convenient method components and connecting with advanced model-driven development (MDD) practices.

Linking capabilities with a MDD approach can provide a rigorous approach where the relevant components of the software process are precisely identified with a clear purpose, and where the software components of the final software application are accurately connected with the source RE and BPM perspectives. This connection has not been analyzed in a clear and convincing way. This is why we focus here on this link between a CDD-based approach and the methodological guidance required to design a sound software production process.

Secondly, the Model Driven Architecture OMG standard (MDA) ([2]) is used in the definition of the desired software process, in order to provide a conceptual template intended to structure the different types of conceptual models to be used in the conceptual trip from requirements to code that we introduce.

This work aims to explore this integration aspect by using an open framework to model capabilities, assuming that different views require different modeling approaches. The holistic framework should make possible to incorporate the most accurate techniques for modeling a particular component, always following the conceptual path that MDA provides. Different conceptual models are needed to specify a conceptual map to be used for building a global software production process where the relevant different modeling views (i.e., requirements, conceptual schema, code) and their subsequent models transformations must be properly integrated.

According to this line of argumentation, after this introduction, we present in Sect. 2 the software development process that can be designed combining capabilities-based modeling with the MDA approach. In Sect. 3 we introduce a concrete instantiation of the proposed software process template, to close the work with conclusions and references.

2 The Software Development Process

We start from the definition of capability used in the FP7 CaaS project ([3]), as "the ability and capacity that enables an enterprise to achieve a business goal in a certain operational context". We use it to determine what essential system information must be captured in order to being able to design a complete and correct requirements model. A capability meta-model (CMM) determines the main conceptual primitives that characterize the corresponding, starting conceptual modeling platform. How to specify the different modeling perspectives that are present in this CMM becomes the essential decision to instantiate it in a particular method. Three main aspects must be considered (see Fig. 1): context, enterprise modelling and reuse and variability, each one requiring a particular conceptual modeling approach, but all of them integrated under the same, unified modeling perspective. These three aspects provides an effective conceptual coverage to face the RE - BPM connection problem that conforms the earliest step of the proposed software process.

To have an open architecture, it should be possible to select different modeling proposals to cover those modeling perspectives that are delimited with the meta-model. Once the most suitable modeling approaches are selected, a precise model transformation process must be introduced in order to guide how to represent correctly the information specified in these models in lower-level models finish by deploying the application code that constitutes the final product.

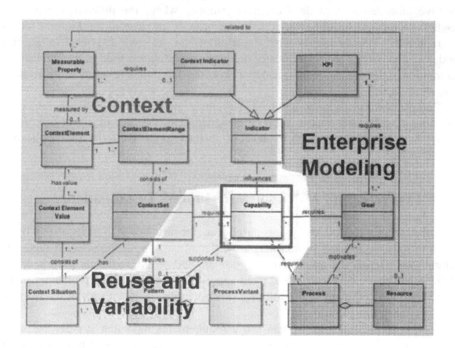

Fig. 1. The three main aspects of the capability meta-model

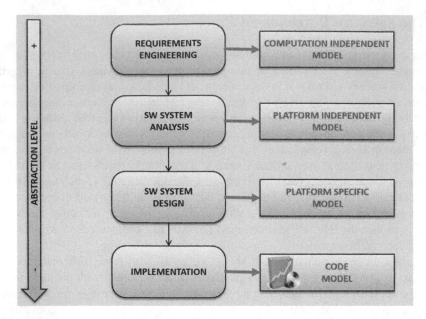

Fig. 2. A MDA-based template to characterize a software production process, based on conceptual modeling and model transformations.

This leads us to the second component of the presented approach: the MDA perspective, intended to provide a concrete template where the different components needed to put in practice the selected software process, are determined. Figure 2 shows it graphically. Depending on what capabilities are selected and what conceptual modeling approaches are subsequently used, what models are used to accomplish the elaboration of the different conceptual models at the different abstraction levels must be fixed.

Complementary, once the involved conceptual models are determined, the corresponding model transformation must be designed, with the final objective of keeping the system expressiveness while the level of abstraction moves to the final application code direction.

3   A Concrete, Full MDD Software Process Instantiation

Once the software process template is introduced, the next step is to materialize it into a concrete software process by fulfilling its different steps with the selected modeling components. Depending on the problem domain and on the modeling purposed, different approaches can be considered more appropriate for a particular problem, leading to the possibility of adapting the software process to the characteristics of the working problem under consideration.

As a concrete example, we can use a requirements modeling strategy based on Communicational Analysis for the CIM component, such as the one proposed in [4].

How to model organizational goals and system context within such an approach would make the modelers to analyze what kind of model extensions should be done. An example of such an effort can be seen in [5], where a well-known goal-oriented requirements modeling approach is used (i*, [6]), and how to transform it into a CA-based requirements model is explained.

Having a concrete CIM, the next step is include a PIM approach, and to define the link between the two models by designing an adequate conceptual models transformation. In our proposed example, an OO-Method conceptual model could be an appropriate answer. As OO-Method models are executable ([7]), this strategy will provide a software process where the PSM will be represented by the conceptual model compiler, and the final code will be the result of a complete model compilation process, what assures desired traceability between requirements and code.

In connection with the method engineering discipline, the proposed framework provides an effective solution to design a sound MDD-based software process able to:

- Provide a holistic perspective for the different method components that are required to go from requirements to code.
- Materialize a concrete starting point for capability-based design in the scope of RM/BPM by using as conceptual modeling strategy a communicational analysis-based approach.
- Connect the selected conceptual models for performing the RM/BPM steps with the model transformation properties of tools that can generate the final application code, making true the MDD goal of going from requirements to code following a process that is as much automated as possible ([8]). This strategy is based on using conceptual model compilers that can make true the statement "the model is the code" (instead of the conventional one "the code is the model").

4   Conclusions

This keynote presents an approach that combines a fundamental notion of capability from a conceptual modeling perspective, with a MDA-based software process template intended to select the most adequate modeling components that a concrete, materialized software process requires. Capabilities help to determine what kind of expressiveness to use, while MDA provides a framework to design a software process whose components at the different MDA levels are carefully selected according to the particular modeling needs of the system under consideration.

This association constitutes a sound basis to design a model-driven development approach intended to make true the objective of going from requirements to code following a precise strategy, where the right conceptual models are selected to be used in the right order –following the proposed MDA-based template- and with the corresponding conceptual model transformations that are defined to assess that traceability between requirements and code is fully achieved.

References

1. Zdravkovic, J., Stirna, J., Kuhr, J.-C., Koç, H.: Requirements engineering for capability driven development. In: Frank, U., Loucopoulos, P., Pastor, Ó., Petrounias, I. (eds.) PoEM 2014. LNBIP, vol. 197, pp. 193–207. Springer, Heidelberg (2014). doi:10.1007/978-3-662-45501-2_14
2. Object Management Group (OMG), Model Driven Architecture (MDA): The MDA Guide Rev 2.0. http://www.omg.org/mda/presentations.htm. Accessed October 2016
3. Bērziša, S., Bravos, G., Cardona Gonzalez, T., Czubayko, U., España, S., Grabis, J., Henkel, M., Jokste, L., Kampars, J., Koç, H., Kuhr, J., Llorca, C., Loucopoulos, P., Juenes Pascual, R., Pastor, O., Sandkuhl, K, Simic, H., Stirna, J., Valverde, F., Zdravkovic, J.: Capability driven development: an approach to designing digital enterprises. J. Bus. Inf. Syst. Eng. Spec. Iss. Adv. Enterp. Model. Springer (2015)
4. España, S., González, A., Pastor, Ó.: Communication analysis: a requirements engineering method for information systems. In: Eck, P., Gordijn, J., Wieringa, R. (eds.) CAiSE 2009. LNCS, vol. 5565, pp. 530–545. Springer, Heidelberg (2009). doi:10.1007/978-3-642-02144-2_41
5. Ruiz, M., Costal, D., España, S., Franch, X., Pastor, Ó.: Integrating the goal and business process perspectives in information system analysis. In: Jarke, M., Mylopoulos, J., Quix, C., Rolland, C., Manolopoulos, Y., Mouratidis, H., Horkoff, J. (eds.) CAiSE 2014. LNCS, vol. 8484, pp. 332–346. Springer, Heidelberg (2014). doi:10.1007/978-3-319-07881-6_23
6. Yu, E., Mylopoulos, J.: From E-R to "A-R" - modelling strategic actor relationships for business process reengineering. In: ER 1994, pp. 548–565 (1994)
7. Embley, D.W., Liddle, S.W., Pastor, O.: Conceptual-Model Programming: A Manifesto. Handbook of Conceptual Modeling, pp. 3–16 (2011)
8. Pastor, O., Molina, J.C.: Model-Driven Architecture in Practice - A Software Production Environment Based on Conceptual Modeling, pp. I–XVI, 1–302. Springer, Berlin (2007). ISBN 978-3-540-71867-3

Webpage Menu Detection Based on DOM

Julian Alarte, David Insa, and Josep Silva[✉]

Departamento de Sistemas Informáticos y Computación,
Universitat Politècnica de València, Camino de Vera s/n, 46022 Valencia, Spain
{jalarte,dinsa,jsilva}@dsic.upv.es

Abstract. One of the key elements of a website are Web menus, which provide fundamental information about the topology of the own website. Menu detection is useful for humans, but also for crawlers and indexers because the menu provides essential information about the structure and contents of a website. For humans, identifying the main menu of a website is a relatively easy task. However, for computer tools identifying the menu is not trivial at all and, in fact, it is still a challenging unsolved problem. In this work, we propose a novel method for automatic Web menu detection that works at the level of DOM.

Keywords: Information retrieval · Web template detection · Menu detection

1 Introduction

A webpage menu (in the following just menu) is a fundamental component in a website whose main objective is providing navigation among the main webpages that form the website. In this paper, we focus on HTML-structured webpages (ignoring those webpages built with alternative technologies such as Flash, or those whose structure is constructed by means of JavaScript). From an engineering perspective, a webpage is a set of Document Object Model (DOM) nodes. Thus, a menu is a subset of those nodes, and it provides essential information about the structure of a website, including its main sections, and implicit information about the sitemap of the website.

Our approach to menu detection is based on the DOM [4] structures that represent webpages. Roughly, given a webpage of a website, (1) we first compute the relevance (a weight) of each DOM node in the webpage, and then, (2) we use the relevance to identify those DOM nodes that are more likely to be part of the menu. (3) Finally, we analyse recursively the parents of those nodes to infer the complete menu. In practice, we input a webpage and we output the set of DOM nodes that correspond to the main menu.

This work has been partially supported by the EU (FEDER) and the Spanish *Ministerio de Economía y Competitividad* under grant TIN2013-44742-C4-1-R and TIN2016-76843-C4-1-R, and by the *Generalitat Valenciana* under grant PROMETEO-II/2015/013 (SmartLogic).

B. Steffen et al. (Eds.): SOFSEM 2017, LNCS 10139, pp. 411–422, 2017.
DOI: 10.1007/978-3-319-51963-0_32

2   Related Work

Menu extraction is a topic directly related to *template extraction*. Template detection and extraction are key topics due to their direct application to Web mining, searching, indexing, and Web development. *Content Extraction* is a discipline very close to template extraction. Content extraction tries to isolate the pagelet that contains the main content of the webpage. It is an instance of a more general discipline called *Block Detection* that tries to isolate every pagelet in a webpage. There are many works in these fields (see, e.g., [3,5,6,12]), and all of them are directly related to menu extraction.

Menu extraction techniques are often classified as page-level or site-level. In both cases, the objective is the same, detecting the menus of a given webpage; but they use different information. While page-level techniques only use the information contained in the target webpage, site-level techniques also use the information contained in other webpages, typically of the same website.

In the areas of menu extraction and template extraction, there are three main different ways to solve the problem: (i) using the textual information of the webpage (the HTML code) [7,9,12], (ii) using the rendered image of the webpage [2,8], and (iii) using the DOM tree of the webpage [1,11,13].

A webpage menu is a pagelet [1]. Pagelets were defined as a region of a webpage that (1) has a single well-defined topic or functionality; and (2) is not nested within another region that has exactly the same topic or functionality. One of the first template extraction approaches [1] proposed two algorithms that rely on the identification of identical pagelets occurring in a densely linked page collection.

Some works try to identify template pagelets analyzing the DOM tree with heuristics [1]. However, others try to find common subtrees in the DOM trees obtained from a collection of webpages of the website [11,13]. None of these methods tries only to isolate the menu pagelet, but they also try to find the whole template of the webpage. The main goal of [10] is not template extraction, but it is a webpage segmentation method based on detecting the layout of the webpage. Detecting the layout may help to detect the menu because the webpage is divided into functional blocks (i.e., header, footer, sidebar, main content, advertisements, images, etc.).

3   Menu Detection

Our technique inputs a webpage and outputs its main menu. It is a page-level technique, thus, it only needs to analyze the information contained in the target webpage. Because we work at the level of DOM, and due to the DOM tree properties, a menu can be represented with just one DOM node: the node whose subtree contains the menu. In our approach, we first identify a set of DOM nodes that are more likely to be the menu and then we analyze them to select the best candidate. Our approach is divided into three phases:

1. The algorithm visits some DOM nodes in the webpage and, for each node excluding the leaves, it computes and assigns the node a weight. Then, it selects a set of DOM nodes with the higher weight. We say that the webpage menu is a node of this set or an ancestor of it.
2. For each node in the set, we check its ancestors and we evaluate their weights. If the weight of an ancestor is higher than a computed value, we replace the node in the set obtained in phase 1 with that ancestor.
3. The menu node (the node that represents the menu) is extracted by comparing the set of selected DOM nodes. Recall that some of the nodes may be ancestors of the original DOM nodes selected in phase 1. For each node in the set, we analyse the average weight of its descendants. The one with the best average weight is the menu node.

These three phases are explained in the following sections.

3.1   Rating DOM Nodes

This section proposes a metric applied to DOM nodes that helps to identify a set of nodes that probably belong to the menu. Roughly, we explore the DOM tree of the webpage and we assign a weight to each DOM node that meets the following criteria: (1) It is not a leaf of the DOM tree. (2) It is an element node. Any other type (e.g., text nodes, comments, etc.) are not considered.

In order to provide a definition of menu, we first need to state a formal definition of webpage, website and node's hyperlinks.

Definition 1 (Webpage). *A webpage P is a pair (N, E) with a finite set of nodes N. Every node contains either an HTML tag (including its attributes) or text. The root node is the node corresponding to the* body *tag. E is a finite set of edges such that $(n \to n') \in E$, with $n, n' \in N$ if and only if the tag or text associated with n' is inside the tag associated with n, and there does not exist an unclosed tag between them.*

Given a node n in a webpage, we often use $descendants(n)$ to refer to those nodes that belong to the subtree of n. We use $characters(n)$ to refer to the total number of characters in $descendants(n)$ excluding those characters that belong to hyperlinks. And we use $target(n)$ to refer to the webpage pointed by the hyperlink of node n.

Definition 2 (Node's hyperlinks). *Given a webpage $P = (N, E)$ and a node $n \in N$, $hyperlinks(n)$ is the set containing all the hyperlink nodes in $descendants(n)$. $hyperlinks(P)$ is the set containing all the hyperlink nodes in N. $links(P)$ is a set of pairs $\{(P, target(n')) \mid n' \in hyperlinks(P)\}$*

A website is composed of webpages such that all of them are reachable from the main webpage. Hence, all of them (possibly except the main webpage) are pointed by at least one hyperlink in another webpage of the website (i.e., all webpages have an indegree greater than 0).

Definition 3 (Website). *A website S is a set of webpages such that $\exists\ P \in S,\ \forall\ P' \in S, P \neq P'\ :\ (P, P') \in links(S)^*$, where $links(S) = \cup_{Q \in S}\ links(Q)$ and $links(S)^*$ represents the reflexive and transitive closure of $links(S)$.*

We can now define webpage menu. Roughly, a menu is a DOM node whose subtree is the smallest subtree that contains at least two hyperlinks pointing to webpages on the same website and, moreover, because a menu provides navigation to the website, the same menu must appear in at least another webpage of the website. Formally,

Definition 4 (Webpage menu). *Given a website S, and a webpage $P = (N, E) \in S$, a webpage menu of P is a node $n \in N$ such that*

- $\exists\ n', n'' \in N\ |\ (n, n'), (n, n'') \in E^+ \wedge n', n'' \in hyperlinks(P) \wedge target(n'), target(n'') \in S$, *and*
- $\nexists\ m \in N\ |\ (n, m), (m, n'), (m, n'') \in E^+$, *and*
- $\exists\ P' = (N', E') \in S\ |\ n \in N'$.

Clearly, the webpage menu cannot be a leaf node because it must contain nodes with hyperlinks to different webpages of the website. On the other hand, the **element** node is the only kind of DOM node that can contain enumerations of hyperlinks. Thus, a webpage menu must be an internal DOM node of type **element**.

One of the main objectives of a template is to provide navigation to the webpage, thus almost all menus provide a large number of hyperlinks, shared by all webpages implementing the template. Hence, to locate menus we identify those DOM nodes with a high concentration of hyperlinks among their descendants. These nodes very likely belong to the webpage menu.

However, a high hyperlink density is only one of the properties of menus but, often, it is not enough to identify them. We now propose several other properties that must be taken into account to properly detect menus. All these properties are objectively quantifiable and, appropriately combined, they form a weighted arithmetic mean that can be used to uniquely identify menus.

Definition 5 (Node properties). *In a webpage $P = (N, E)$, every node $n \in N \wedge descendants(n) \neq \emptyset$ is rated according to the following properties:*

- **Node amplitude:** *The amplitude of node n is computed considering its number of children: $children(n) = |\{n' \in N\ |\ (n, n') \in E\}|$. It is defined as:*

$$Node\ amplitude(n) = 1 - \frac{1}{children(n)}$$

- **Link ratio:** *The link ratio of $n \in N$ is computed with the following function:*

$$Link\ ratio(n) = \begin{cases} 0 & \text{if } |hyperlinks(n)| < 2 \\ \frac{|hyperlinks(n)| + |descendants(n)|}{2 * |descendants(n)|} & \text{if } |hyperlinks(n)| \geq 2 \end{cases}$$

- **Text ratio:** *It is computed considering the amount of characters of a DOM node and its descendants:*

$$Textratio(n) = 1 - \frac{characters(n)}{\sqrt{characters(P)}}$$

- **UL ratio:** *It checks whether the HTML tagName of the node is "ul" or not.*

$$ULratio(n) = \begin{cases} 0 \text{ if } n.tagName \neq \text{"ul"} \\ 1 \text{ if } n.tagName = \text{"ul"} \end{cases}$$

- **Representative tag:** *It evaluates some attributes of the node:*

$$ULtag(n) = \begin{cases} 1 \text{ if } n.tagName = \text{"nav"} \\ 1 \text{ if } n.className = \text{"menu"} \\ 1 \text{ if } n.className = \text{"nav"} \\ 1 \text{ if } n.id = \text{"menu"} \\ 1 \text{ if } n.id = \text{"nav"} \\ 0 \text{ otherwise} \end{cases}$$

- **Node position:** *The position of n in the webpage P is evaluated using the function:*

$$Node\ position(n) = 1 - \frac{pos(n)}{|N|}$$

where function pos(n) is the position of node n in P, if all nodes are sorted with a depth first traversal.

The *Node amplitude* property takes into account the amount of children of a DOM node. The more children a node has, the higher the probability is that the node belongs to the menu. Usually, the menu nodes have a large amount of children that can be either 'link' nodes or 'element' nodes whose descendants contain 'link' nodes. We defined a function that promotes the nodes with more children and penalizes the nodes with less children. A node with a high amount of children will have a *node amplitude* value close to 1. However, a node with few children will have a *node amplitude* value close to 0.

The *Link ratio* property counts the amount of hyperlinks a DOM node and its descendants have. The more hyperlinks, the higher the link ratio is. We define a metric that examines all the descendants of a DOM node and counts the number of hyperlink nodes.

The *Text ratio* property evaluates the amount of text the descendants of a DOM node have in comparison to the total amount of text in the webpage. Usually, menu nodes do not contain text among their descendants except for the text of the hyperlinks. Therefore, we do not consider the text of the hyperlinks when counting the amount of text. The text ratio metric penalizes the nodes with more text in its descendants.

The *UL ratio* property is used to promote those nodes that use the UL[1] HTML tag because webpage menus are usually lists of links constructed with

---

[1] HTML Unordered List.

this HTML tag. In particular, we observed than more than 60% of the websites in our benchmarks use the *UL* tag for the node containing the menu.

The *Representative tag* property is used to promote the use of other particular HTML tags. We also observed in our benchmarks some other attributes that are frequently used in the webpage menu nodes. We have not considered them together with the *UL tag* because they are not as frequent. These HTML attributes are:

- *Nav* tag: HTML5 defines the *nav* tag to represent a set of navigation links.[2]
- Node's *id*: Some nodes representing the menu have the *nav* or *menu* identifier. For instance, *id= "nav"* or *id= "menu"*.
- Node's *classname*: Some webpages represent the menu with a node whose classname contains the *menu* or *nav* classes.

The *Node position* property is used to consider the fact that menus are usually located at the top or in the top left corner of the webpage. This means that the node containing the menu should be at the beginning of the DOM tree. We established a ponderation where the first nodes of the DOM tree get higher values than the last ones.

With these properties we can assign each node in the DOM tree a weight that represents the probability that this node is the main menu of the webpage. The exact ponderation used to combine all these node properties must be determined with empirical evaluation. Thus we conducted experiments to determine the best ponderation of these metrics. This is discussed in detail in Sect. 4.1.

3.2   Selection of Candidates

Once we have calculated the weight of all the nodes in the webpage, we select the heaviest nodes. These nodes are considered as candidates to be elected as the main menu. This process is simple: an algorithm visits all the nodes in the DOM tree, checks their weights, and selects the ones with highest weights. Only the nodes with a weight over a specified threshold are selected. This threshold has been calculated based on experimentation and it is worth 0.85.

3.3   Selection of Root Nodes

The selection of candidates only considers individual information based on the properties of the nodes. The candidates are nodes with a high concentration of links, with little or no text, etc. but they are not necessarily a menu. In fact, they are very often a part of the menu. For instance, in a menu that contains a submenu "Products" with a high density of hyperlinks, the DOM node representing the menu option "Products" is probably a candidate. Nevertheless, the DOM node representing the complete menu could not be selected as a candidate.

---

[2] We consider the *nav* tag because it is the specific tag (and recommendation) in HTML5 for representing menus. However, note that it can be changed if we want to focus on other technologies.

Algorithm 1. Selection of the root node

Input: A DOM node n and a threshold t.
Output: A DOM node $rootNode$ representing a candidate to be the whole menu.

begin
    $rootNode = n$;
    $currentNode = n$;
    $baseWeight = n.weight$;
    $found = false$;
    while ($\exists\ currentNode.parentNode \wedge found == false$)
      $parent = currentNode.parentNode$
      $nodeCount = |\{node \mid node \in parent.children \wedge node.weight > t * baseWeight\}|$;
      if ($2 * nodeCount > |parent.children|$)
        $currentNode = parent$;
        if ($parent.children > 1$)
          $rootNode = parent$;
      else $found = true$
    return $rootNode$;
end

The real menu is usually an ancestor of a candidate. It usually combines two or more candidates and possibly other nodes such as, e.g., images. This phenomenon usually happens in complex or large menus. Moreover, in menus with a set of submenus, the selection of candidates process usually detects only one of these submenus.

Algorithm 1 explores the ancestors of a candidate node to find the node that really represents the whole menu. The algorithm recursively explores each ancestor node of the candidate and checks whether more than half of their children, which are element nodes, have a *weight* higher than a given threshold t, called *root threshold*. When it finds a node for which this criterion does not hold, the algorithm stops and selects the last ancestor as the root node.

Example 1. Consider the DOM tree in Fig. 1. The "UL" node with a dotted border is one of the candidates because it has a *weight* higher than 0.85. Nevertheless, this node represents only a portion of the main menu, so we have to analyze its ancestors in order to locate the root node of the main menu.

By using Algorithm 1, we first explore its parent node (the "LI" node with grey background) and we check that more than half of its children have a *weight* higher than the *root threshold* multiplied by the weight of the candidate node "UL", so we can continue exploring its ancestors. Next, we explore the parent of the "LI" node, which is the "UL" node with black background. Again, we check that more than half of its children have a *weight* higher than the *root threshold* multiplied by the weight of the candidate node "UL", so we continue exploring its parent. Then, we do the same with the parent of the "UL" node (a "DIV" node with a dashed shape). In this case, the algorithm continues exploring the parent, but it keeps a pointer to the "UL" node as the menu node because the "DIV" node has only one child. Finally, we check its parent, which is another

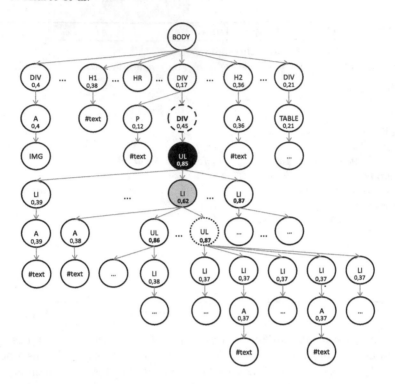

Fig. 1. Example of the selection of root node candidates

"DIV" node. It has two children, one is the "DIV" node with a dashed shape and the other is a "P" node. Both nodes have a *weight* lower than the *root threshold* multiplied by the weight of the candidate node "UL", so, in this case, the "DIV" node does not meet the criterion. The last node that satisfies the condition is the "UL" node (black background), thus the algorithm returns it as the root node.

3.4   Selection of the Menu Node

Algorithm 1 inputs one candidate and outputs a node that could be the main menu. Because we often have more than one candidate, the application of Algorithm 1 over the set of candidates produces another set of nodes. Hence, we need a mechanism to determine which of them represents the real menu of the webpage. This mechanism is implemented by Algorithm 2. For each node in the set, it counts the number of descendants that have a weight over a specified threshold, called *menu threshold*. Then, the average weight of these nodes is computed. The node with the highest average weight is selected as the menu of the webpage. We established this criterion because the menu node often has a high concentration of nodes with a high *weight*.

Algorithm 2. Menu node selection

Input: A set of DOM nodes N and a threshold *weight*.
Output: A DOM node *menuNode* representing the main menu.

begin
$\quad$ $max = 0$;
$\quad$ $bestWeight = 0$;
$\quad$ **foreach** $(n \in N)$
$\quad\quad$ $heavyChildren = \{child \mid child \in n.children \wedge child.weight > weight\}$;
$\quad\quad$ $nodeCount = |heavyChildren|$;
$\quad\quad$ $nodeWeight = \sum_{child \in heavyChildren} child.weight$;
$\quad\quad$ **if** $(nodeWeight/nodeCount > bestWeight)$
$\quad\quad\quad$ $menuNode = n$;
$\quad\quad\quad$ $bestWeight = nodeWeight/nodeCount$;
$\quad$ **return** $menuNode$;
end

4   Implementation

The technique presented in this paper, including all the algorithms, has been implemented as a Firefox add-on. In this tool, the user can browse on the Internet as usual. Then, when they want to extract the menu of a webpage, they only need to press on the "Extract Menu" button and the tool automatically (internally) rates the DOM nodes, analyzes them, and selects the menu node. The menu is then displayed on the browser as any other webpage.

Example 2. Figure 2 shows the output of the tool with a real webpage. The left image is the main webpage of the **foodsense.is** website. Once the menu is extracted, we can see it in the right image.

Fig. 2. Example of the detection of a webpage menu

4.1   Training Phase: Determining the Best Parameters Through Empirical Evaluation

In our theoretical formalization, we presented our technique in an abstract way. Some parameters of our algorithms, however, have been left open. In this section, we calculate the value of these parameters based on an experimental analysis. Firstly, we need to define a weighted arithmetic mean to combine the properties proposed in Definition 5. Moreover, Algorithm 1 explores the ancestors of a node to determine which of them is the webpage menu. This process depends on a parameter called *root threshold* that sets the stop condition. Another parameter to take into consideration is the one used to select the menu node among all the possible candidates in the set. Algorithm 2 explores the menu nodes in the set and, for each one, it computes the number of children with a weight over a specified threshold called *menu threshold*.

Our method to approximate the best combination of values for the two thresholds (*root threshold* and *menu threshold*) and for the weighted arithmetic mean of node properties, follows these steps:

1. First, prior to the development of our technique, we constructed a suite of benchmarks prepared for menu detection.[3]
2. Second, we executed our system with a training subset of the benchmark suite. For this, we evaluated the precision and recall obtained for each different combination of values for the properties and thresholds. We performed more than 1.5 million experiments, with a total computing time equivalent to 85 days in an Intel i7 4770k processor.
3. Third, we selected the best combination of properties and thresholds, and evaluated it against an evaluation subset of the benchmark suite.

Our suite of benchmarks is the first suite of benchmarks prepared for menu detection. This means that each benchmark has been labelled with HTML classes indicating what parts of the webpage belong to the menu. This allows any technique to automatically validate their recall and precision. Our suite is composed of 50 benchmarks, and it is not only prepared for menu detection, but also for content extraction and template detection (i.e., the template and the main content of the webpages are also labelled with specific HTML classes). This is one of the main contributions of our work. Any interested researcher can freely access and download our dataset from:

http://www.dsic.upv.es/~jsilva/retrieval/teco/

The suite is composed of a collection of Web domains with different layouts and page structures. To measure our technique, we randomly selected an evaluation subset and we performed several experiments with our menu detector, which implements the proposed technique. Once the algorithm detected the menu, we compared it with the real menu, and we computed the precision, recall and F1 scores of the algorithm. For each node, we computed its final weight evaluating different weighted arithmetic means (*weight = A * Node amplitude + B * Link ratio + C * Text ratio + ...*, where $A + B + C + ... = 1$). We repeated all the experiments with these possible values for the weighted arithmetic means used:

---

[3] We designed and implemented the suite of benchmarks before we constructed our technique to avoid their interference.

$$Node\ amplitude:\quad [0,00-0,20]\ \text{in steps of } 0,05.$$
$$Link\ ratio:\quad [0,05-0,40]\ \text{in steps of } 0,05.$$
$$Text\ ratio:\quad [0,25-0,60]\ \text{in steps of } 0,05.$$
$$UL\ ratio:\quad [0,00-0,20]\ \text{in steps of } 0,05.$$
$$Representative\ tag:\ [0,00-0,20]\ \text{in steps of } 0,05.$$
$$Node\ position:\quad [0,00-0,25]\ \text{in steps of } 0,05.$$

Moreover, for each possible weighted arithmetic mean, we also evaluated the *Root threshold* and the *Menu threshold* with the following values:

$$Menu\ threshold: [0,80-0,90]\ \text{in steps of } 0,05.$$
$$Root\ threshold:\quad [0,70-0,90]\ \text{in steps of } 0,10.$$

After having evaluated all possible combinations against all the benchmarks, the fastest combination that produces the best F1 metric is:

Menu	Root	Amplit.	Link	Text	UL	Repres.	Position	Recall	Precision	F1	Time
0,80	0,70	0,20	0,10	0,30	0,20	0,10	0,10	94,10%	97,91%	94,09%	4.77 s

Once the best combination was selected in the training phase, we evaluated our technique against a suite of 50 benchmarks (accesible in the website of the project). The technique achieved a precision of 98.21%, a recall of 94.13%, and a F1 of 94.46%. In 74% of the experiments, the menu was perfectly detected (F1=100%). The average computation time was 5.38 s.

5   Conclusions

Menu detection is useful for many systems and tools such as, e.g., indexers and crawlers. It is particularly useful for template extraction because many techniques use the menu to detect webpages that share the template.

This work presents a new technique for menu detection. This technique is a page-level technique and, thus, our algorithms only need to load and analyze one single webpage (the webpage from which we want to extract the menu). This is specially important from the performance point of view, because loading other webpages is costly.

We have proposed a set of features that should be considered in the menu detection process. We empirically evaluated these features to define a weighted arithmetic mean that can be used in the menu detection process. The obtained results are quite successful, almost 75% of the experiments perfectly retrieved the menu of the webpage, and we obtained an average precision of 98.21% and an average F1 metric of 94.46%.

References

1. Bar-Yossef, Z., Rajagopalan, S.: Template Detection via data mining and its applications. In: Proceedings of the 11th International Conference on World Wide Web (WWW 2002), pp. 580–591. ACM, New York (2002)
2. Burget, R., Rudolfova, I.: Web page element classification based on visual features. In: Proceedings of the 1st Asian Conference on Intelligent Information and Database Systems (ACIIDS 2009), pp. 67–72. IEEE Computer Society, Washington, DC (2009)
3. Cardoso, E., Jabour, I., Laber, E., Rodrigues, R., Cardoso, P.: An efficient language-independent method to extract content from news webpages. In: Proceedings of the 11th ACM Symposium on Document Engineering (DocEng 2011), pp. 121–128. ACM, New York (2011)
4. World Wide Web Consortium: Document Object Model (DOM) (1997). http://www.w3.org/DOM/
5. Gottron, T.: Content code blurring: a new approach to Content Extraction. In: Tjoa, A.M., Wagner, R.R. (eds.) Proceedings of the 19th International Workshop on Database and Expert Systems Applications (DEXA 2008), pp. 29–33. IEEE Computer Society, September 2008
6. Insa, D., Silva, J., Tamarit, S.: Using the words/leafs ratio in the DOM tree for content extraction. J. Logic Algebraic Program. **82**(8), 311–325 (2013)
7. Kohlschütter, C.: A densitometric analysis of web template content. In: Quemada, J., León, G., Maarek, Y.S., Nejdl, W. (eds.) Proceedings of the 18th International Conference on World Wide Web (WWW 2009), pp. 1165–1166. ACM, April 2009
8. Kohlschütter, C., Fankhauser, P., Nejdl, W.: Boilerplate detection using shallow text teatures. In: Davison, B.D., Suel, T., Craswell, N., Liu, B. (eds.) Proceedings of the 3rd International Conference on Web Search and Web Data Mining (WSDM 2010), pp. 441–450. ACM, February 2010
9. Kohlschütter, C., Nejdl, W.: A densitometric approach to web page segmentation. In: Shanahan, J.G., Amer-Yahia S., Manolescu, I., Zhang, Y., Evans, D.A., Kolcz, A., Choi, K.-S., Chowdhury, A. (eds.) Proceedings of the 17th ACM Conference on Information and Knowledge Management (CIKM 2008), pp. 1173–1182. ACM, October 2008
10. Sano, H., Shiramatsu, S., Ozono, T., Shintani, T.: A web page segmentation method based on page layouts and title blocks. IJCSNS Int. J. Comput. Sci. Netw. Secur. **11**(10), 84–90 (2011)
11. Vieira, K., da Silva, A.S., Pinto, N., de Moura, E.S., Cavalcanti, J.M.B., Freire, J.: A fast and robust method for web page template detection and removal. In: Proceedings of the 15th ACM International Conference on Information and Knowledge Management (CIKM 2006), pp. 258–267. ACM, New York (2006)
12. Weninger, T., Henry Hsu, W., Han, J.: CETR: content Extraction via tag ratios. In: Rappa, M., Jones, P., Freire, J., Chakrabarti, S. (eds.) Proceedings of the 19th International Conference on World Wide Web (WWW 2010), pp. 971–980. ACM, April 2010
13. Yi, L., Liu, B., Li, X.: Eliminating noisy information in web pages for data mining. In: Proceedings of the 9th ACM SIGKDD International Conference on Knowledge Discovery and Data mining (KDD 2003), pp. 296–305. ACM, New York (2003)

A Hybrid Model for Linking Multiple Social Identities Across Heterogeneous Online Social Networks

Athanasios Kokkos[1], Theodoros Tzouramanis[1]([✉]),
and Yannis Manolopoulos[2]

[1] Department of Information and Communication Systems Engineering,
University of the Aegean, Samos, Greece
{ath.kokkos, ttzouram}@aegean.gr
[2] Department of Informatics, Aristotle University of Thessaloniki,
Thessaloniki, Greece
manolopo@csd.auth.gr

Abstract. Automated online profiling consists of the accurate identification and linking of multiple online identities across heterogeneous online social networks that correspond to the same entity in the physical world. The paper proposes a hybrid profile correlation model which relies on a diversity of techniques from different application domains, such as record linkage and data integration, image and text similarity, and machine learning. It involves distance-based comparison methods and the exploitation of information produced by a social network identification process for use as external knowledge towards searches on other social networks; thus, the remaining identification tasks for the same individual are optimized. The experimental study shows that, even with limited resources, the proposed method collects and combines accurate information effectively from different online sources in a fully-automated way. The mined knowledge then becomes a powerful toolkit to carry out social engineering and other attacks, or for profit and decision-making data mining purposes.

Keywords: Online identities linkage · Online social network profiles data similarity and linkage model · Profile matching formulas · Machine learning

1 Introduction

The social web keeps generating swathes of publicly available personal data despite the documented implications of voluntarily exposing personal data on online social networks (OSNs). The methodologies to circumvent traditional privacy preserving countermeasures cover the use of either text analysis for author identification [1], re-identification algorithms on graph-structured data [2], or diverse linkages of the users' footprints in different online data sources [3], and so on.

This study focuses on the concept of online user profiling [4] that can be defined as the cross correlation of publicly available personal information for the successful identification and linking of online social profiles across heterogeneous social networking services that correspond to the same individual in the real world. The same problem in a wider setting is known as record linkage, entity resolution, profile matching, etc. [5].

© Springer International Publishing AG 2017
B. Steffen et al. (Eds.): SOFSEM 2017, LNCS 10139, pp. 423–435, 2017.
DOI: 10.1007/978-3-319-51963-0_33

A hybrid model is proposed that combines data analysis techniques (i.e. from record linkage to text mining) to select information from online data sources in an unsupervised fashion and to weave together the different online social identities of an individual. The model can be adopted in diverse data mining application domains, from security evaluation tools that focus on privacy risks assessments (e.g. physical identification, de-anonymization attacks, password recovery attacks), to data warehousing technologies for building repositories of OSN data from multiple heterogeneous online sources.

Section 2 develops around the proposed methodology for comparing and linking the users' social identities across heterogeneous OSNs. Section 3 describes the implementation and experimental performance efficiency of a prototype system to identify and link together the different profiles of targeted individuals. Section 4 analyses the advantages and limitations of the related work, and argues in favour of the proposed model. Section 5 summarizes and makes suggestions for future research.

2 The Proposed Model

The proposed model collects publicly available personal information from various OSNs. This personal information is inferred by exploiting their weaknesses e.g. using the email querying functionality offered by some networks, if the targeted individual (from now on called "the target") has been registered with an email address known to the attacker, and by exploiting hidden personal information extracted by applying machine learning techniques on openly available information on the OSNs e.g. the gender inference of a user on Twitter. Its effectiveness increases with every piece of accurate personal information collected during runtime, which, after its collection, is

---

Algorithm 1: MainRoutine (), Part I

Input: A list $O[1..m]$ of m OSNs to search for a target.

Output: The social identity $Q.v$ of a target Q in the physical world, de-
             fined as the union of all the OSNs profiles that belong to Q.

Let $U[1..t]$ be a list of t profiles of users of an OSN. Every such
   profile is a vector v of personal attributes;

Let $matchedInOSN[1..m]$ be a list of m flags (initially all FALSE) indicating if a matching profile has been found in the m OSNs.

Let $\Theta_{overall}$ be a predefined profile matching threshold (e.g., = 0.60);

$maxW = 0$; $MatchedProfile$ = NULL; $matched$ = FALSE;

1:   FOR $i = 1$ TO m DO

2:       The ith OSN is accessed and the names & types of the personal attri-
         butes that the OSN publishes for every user are dynamically re-
         corded.This way, an aggregated vector v of personal attributes in
         the form $v = (v_1, ..., v_d)$ is constructed after accessing all the OSNs;

3:   The attacker determines the weight coefficient for every personal
     attribute in a vector λ of weights in the form $\lambda = (\lambda_1, ..., \lambda_d)$;

4:   The attacker determines which personal attributes are mutually compa-
     tible, by providing values το a compatibility table $ACT(1..d, 1..d]$;

5:   For a target Q, the attacker provides the attributes' values of the
     personal profile $Q.v$ that are known from external sources;

Algorithm 2;

---

used dynamically to strengthen the search for the target from one OSN to the next. Should the profile of a targeted OSN user be uniquely identified, the proposed method takes into account this verified personal information to expand the set of valid data already available for that individual and uses it in combination with all the remainder of the known personal attribute values of that individual to search for her/his profile in other OSNs. The description of the model follows.

2.1 The Main Routine

The *pseudo*-code of the main routine of the proposed OSN identity identification and correlation model is presented in Algorithmic blocks 1 and 2, with the first initiating the process and the second being the main part of the process.

The algorithm in Lines 1–2 records the personal attributes published online in every OSN under consideration producing a vector v of personal attributes in the form $v = (v_1, v_2, \ldots, v_d)$. For example, if the first OSN provides the attributes (*username, firstname, lastname, work, education, bio/cv, hometown, country, image, friend*) and the second OSN provides the attributes (*username, fullname, gender, organization, summary, location, email, follows, followedby*), then the vector v has the form $v = (username, firstname, lastname, fullname, gender, work, organization, education, bio/cv, summary, hometown, country, location, email, image, friend)$. If an OSN provides the '*follows*' and '*followedby*' attributes (e.g. Twitter and Instagram) only the users that belong in both these sets will be considered as friends. This 'friends' selection can be approached from a different perspective.

	username	firstname	lastname	fullname	gender	work	organization	education	bio/cv	summary	hometown	country	location	email	image	friend
username	√	+	+	√												
firstname	√	√		√					√							
lastname	√		√	√					√							
fullname	√	+	+	√					√							
gender					√											
work						√	√		√	√						
organization						√	√		√	√						
education								√	√	√						
bio/cv		+	+	+		+	+	+	√	√	+	+	+			
summary						+	+	+	√	√	+	+	+			
hometown									√	√	√		√			
country									√	√		√	√			
location									√	√	+	+	√			
email														√		
image															√	
friend																√

Fig. 1. A sample of compatible personal attributes for the matching process (The existence of two or more '+' indicators in a horizontal line means that the attributes on the corresponding columns need to be combined to be compared against the attribute on the horizontal line).

username	firstname	lastname	Fullname	work	...	gender	...	country	...
	Federico García García	Lorca	Federico García Lorca García Lorca	poet	...	M Male	...	Spain	...

Fig. 2. A sample of personal information of an individual that may be available to the attacker.

In Line 3 the attacker evaluates the weight coefficient of every personal attribute in the vector v, to specify the attribute's importance in the profile identification process in relation to the other attributes. The attacker needs to provide the values to a vector λ of weights of the form $\lambda = (\lambda_1, ...,\lambda_d)$, where $\forall i \in [1, d]$: $\lambda_i \leq 1$, $\lambda_1 + ... + \lambda_d = 1$, and with the exception that $\lambda_{email} = \lambda_{image} = $ NULL. Practical experimentation can also fine tune these weights (e.g., $\lambda_{fullname} = 0.15$, $\lambda_{summary} = 0.01$). In Line 4 the attacker evaluates the attributes' compatibility by filling a three-value table as in Fig. 1: the last name of a target can be found in the *fullname* attribute; the full name of an individual can be constructed as the combination of the values of the attributes *firstname* and *lastname*, etc.

In Line 5 the attacker provides the values of the personal attributes of the target that are known from external sources (Fig. 2). Every personal attribute in the profile vector v of a target's digital identity is a list of values (implementation as non-normalized database relational table or as XML document).

Algorithm 2 implements the main process. For every OSN under consideration, it examines (Lines 8–10) whether it is possible to uniquely identify the target using the email functionality provided by some OSNs. If this test succeeds, the targeted profile

---

Algorithm 2: MainRoutine (), Part II

```
6:      FOR i = 1 TO m DO
7:         IF matchedInOSN[i] = FALSE THEN
8:            U[1] = IdentificationViaEmail(Q.v_email);
9:            IF U[1] <> NULL THEN
10:              Q.v = Q.v merge U[1]; matchedInOSN[i] = TRUE; matched = TRUE;
11:           ELSE
12:              Search the i^th OSN for retrieving t profiles U[1..t], one
                 of which may potentially correspond to Q;
13:              FOR j = 1 TO t DO
14:                 IF IdentificationViaAnImage(Q.v_image, U[j]).image) THEN
15:                    maxW = θ_overall; MatchedProfile = j; BREAK;
16:                 ELSE
17:                    S=IdentificationViaTheProfileAttributes(Q.v,U[j],ACT),
                       where S is a vector of personal attributes simi-
                       larity scores in the form S = (s_1,...,s_d), in which
                       ∀ k ∈ [1, d]: s_k ≤ 1, and s_email = s_image = NULL;
18:                    Calculate W = λ_1*s_1+...+λ_d*s_d, where W is the OSN-specific
                       normalised overall attributes similarity score bet-
                       ween Q.v and the profile U[j].It is noted that W≤1;
19:                    IF W > maxW THEN maxW = W; MatchedProfile = j;
20:              IF maxW >= θ_overall THEN
21:                 Q.v = Q.v merge U[MatchedProfile]; matchedInOSN[i] = TRUE;
                    matched = TRUE;
22:        IF (i = m AND matched) THEN i = 1; matched = FALSE;
23:     RETURN Q.v;
```

has been uncovered and all information published on that OSN is copied and enriches the vector v of personal information known to the attacker. Otherwise, in Line 12 of the algorithm the OSN is queried using its own search functionality (e.g., through its API), using prior knowledge obtained (e.g. using the values of the first and last names and the home town, or using any other combination of attributes). This search may select t profiles from the OSN, one of which may potentially correspond to the target. Therefore, these t profiles are considered for further examination.

Using a high image-similarity threshold Θ_{image} (e.g. ≥ 0.90), an image comparison function in Lines 14–15 (implemented on the basis of any known image similarity measurement [6]) can conclude whether any of the previously known to the attacker profile images for the target coincides with a profile image in any of these t profiles in the OSN under consideration. In the negative, in Line 17 a profile-comparison function – see Algorithm 3 – compares the prior knowledge obtained with the related information about every single one of the t profiles. Then in Line 18 an overall weighted similarity score W (normalized with regard to the attributes available on the OSN) between every selected profile from the OSN and the personal information known to the attacker is calculated; if the highest score W exceeds the corresponding predefined similarity threshold $\Theta_{overall}$, then in Line 21 this profile is recognized as the corresponding profile of the target in the OSN under consideration.

The process of Lines 6–21 is repeated for every OSN. Where the identification process has not yet yielded positive results (i.e., if $matchedInOSN[i]$ = FALSE), this process is repeated using the enriched information previously gathered from other OSNs. The process terminates if Line 22 indicates that no additional new information can be identified.

2.2 Identification *via* the OSN Profile Attributes

The identification of a profile in an OSN *via* the values of its profile attributes (Line 17 of Algorithm 2) is based on a record linkage method that computes the similarities between the known values of an individual's personal attributes and the corresponding attributes on a potential matched profile in the OSN. The *pseudo*-code of this profile linkage method is illustrated in Algorithm 3.

If the attacker knows the target's gender, the AttributeComparison function (Line 4 of the algorithm) checks whether the gender has been provided by the examined user in the OSN under consideration. If not, a text mining technique method for gender inference is used [7]. If this approach confidently concludes on the value of the OSN user's gender, then this value will be compared against the gender, and a corresponding similarity score of 1 or 0 will be provided. Should at least one friend of the target be known to the attacker, the AttributeComparison function for the *friend* attribute takes the form of Algorithm 4, discussed in the sequel.

Since fine-tuned and extensively tested similarity comparison methods in matching problems can perform poorly in new and different matching problems [8], the comparison performance of compatible text attributes with different representations was tested. In case of a name, the text similarity comparison function may need to overcome *lexical heterogeneities* between any two compared strings, as with 'Federico García

Lorca' and 'García Lorca'. This study developed and tested several string comparison functions, such as the similarity functions Jaro-Winkler [9] and Jaccard [10, 11]. Two versions were developed for the Jaccard function: a character-based similarity function and a token-based one; the first to compare strings using a character-based similarity metric; the second using a word-based similarity metric.

Algorithm 3: IdentificationViaTheProfileAttributes

Input: The digital identity of a target Q, defined as a vector $Q.v$ of
            personal attributes, some of which are known to the attacker.
            The profile of a given user U in an OSN as a vector $U.v$ of d
            attributes in the form $U.v = (v_1, ..., v_d)$, the values for some
            attributes of which are available in the OSN.
            An attributes' compatibility table $ACT(1..d, 1..d]$.

Output: The vector S of similarity scores between the corresponding d
            attributes of $Q.v$ and $U.v$, in the form $S = (s_1, ..., s_d)$, where
            $\forall\ i \in [1,d]: s_i \leq 1$, and $s_{email} = s_{image} = $ NULL.

Let $\theta_{attribute}$ be a predefined threshold to get rid of any random noise-
based attribute similarity (e.g., $\theta_{attribute} = 0.20$)

```
1:    FOR i = 1 TO d DO
2:        IF (Q.v_i <> Q.v_email) and (Q.v_i <> Q.v_image) THEN
3:            S.s_i = AttributeComparison(Q.v_i, U, ACT[i, 1..d]);
4:            IF S.s_i < θ_attribute THEN S.s_i = 0;
5:    RETURN S;
```

As illustrated in Fig. 3, both the character-based and the token-based similarity metrics produce the same results if the strings under comparison are identical (a score of 1.0 indicates a perfect match). In this case the character-based metrics perform more comparisons than the token-based metrics; in the case of the comparison of two strings distinguished by few different characters (e.g. two quite similar usernames), the potentially low similarity scores produced by the Jaccard token-based function make it unsuitable. The optimistically high scores, which both the Jaro-Winkler and Jaccard

Source of information	username	firstname	city	country	organization
The attacker's knowledge:	consba	Constantin	Linz	Austria	Johannes Kepler University
An OSN:	consbakery	Constantin	-	Linz, Austria	University of Southern California, Johannes Kepler University

(a)

Comparison function	username	firstname	city	country	organization
Jaro-Winkler(character-based):	0.78	1.0	0.0	0.41	0.61
Jaccard (character-based):	0.56	1.0	0.0	0.64	0.76
Jaccard (token-based):	0.0	1.0	0.0	0.33	0.43
Hybrid (2-grams & tokens):	0.55	1.0	0.0	0.50	0.50

(b)

Fig. 3. (a) Two vectors of personal attributes, (b) The results of the comparison of the compatible attributes of these vectors with four different text similarity comparison functions.

character-based metrics produced, are not always realistic. As the Hybrid method performed more accurately in most of the preliminary tests carried out, it was selected for the implementation of the attributes-comparison function in Line 3 of Algorithm 3.

With respect to the attribute's lexical heterogeneity, every personal attribute in the profile vector of a target's digital identity that is already known to the attacker might have more than one single value, e.g. for the *city* attribute's values, 'Paris, France' and 'Paris'. This means that the attributes-comparison function (Line 3 of Algorithm 3) needs to check for a match of every possible alternative known value for a personal attribute and to select the highest possible similarity score.

Besides lexical heterogeneity, a *structural heterogeneity* needs to be dealt with since most of the OSNs represent user profiles differently and use different database schemas. If an OSN provides values to the attribute *fullname* instead of the attributes *firstname* and *lastname* that might be known to the attacker, the attributes-comparison function needs to take into account the predetermined combinations of compatible attributes (Line 4 of Algorithm 1).

2.3   The Friends-Comparison Function

The *pseudo*-code of the function that examines whether the profile of any friend of a target matches the profile of an online friend of an examined user in an OSN is illustrated in Algorithm 4 (for simplicity, the friends of the friends of the target are not considered for examination by the algorithm). The function finally calculates and returns in Line 6 the ratio of the matched friends between the target and the examined user in the OSN.

```
Algorithm 4: AttributeComparison for the 'friend' attribute.
Input:      The list Q.vfriend[1..m] of profiles of the m friends of a target Q.
            The list U.friend[1..h] of profiles of the h online friends of a
                given user U in an OSN.
            The attributes' compatibility table ACT(1..d, 1..d).
Output:     The ratio of Q's friends matching with the U's friends.
            Let matched = 0 be the number of matched friends;
1:   FOR i = 1 TO m DO
2:       FOR j = 1 TO h DO
3:           S=IdentificationViaTheProfileAttributes(Q.vfriend[i],U.friend[j],ACT)
                where S is a vector of personal attributes similarity scores
                in the form S = (s1,...,sd), in which semail = simage = sfriend = NULL;
4:           Calculate W = λ1*s1+...+λd*sd, where W is the overall attributes
                similarity score between the profiles Q.vfriend[i] and
                U.friend[j]. It is noted that W ≤ 1;
5:           IF W >= θoverall THEN matched++;
6:   RETURN matched/m;
```

3 Experimental Study

3.1 The Model's Preparation Phase

It is assumed that an attacker who aims to construct the digital profile of a group of researchers appearing as authors in articles indexed by the DBLP service compiles a digital dossier by searching the OSNs: Facebook, Twitter, LinkedIn, Google+ and MySpace. A web crawler is developed to access these five OSNs and construct the vector $Q.v$ of personal attributes found online in these data sources for every target Q.

Then a SAX parser is developed to extract the first and last name as well as the publications and the co-authors of every researcher in the DBLP website, by using its XML-based API. The set of co-authors for every researcher is the primary source for finding real-life friends of the researcher. The parser also extracts all the web links that point to external digital libraries, such as the SpringerLink, the IEEE's Xplore, the ACM Digital Library (DL), the Elsevier's ScienceDirect, etc., and adds them to the list of external URLs for browsing to uncover more personal information about the targets. A crawling of the above major digital libraries is performed to gather additional identifiable personal information such as the city and country of residence, institutional affiliation/place of work, email, telephone number, postal address, postcode, etc. The more recent publications stored in the DBLP are considered first, since they might provide more accurate personal information (the SpringerLink and the IEEE's Xplore at the time activated processes to prevent webbots from crawling).

In the absence of gender information, the Baby Name Guesser service[1] is queried and the gender attribute is obtained *via* probabilistic estimation. If this response is accompanied by a high degree of confidence (e.g., 'John'/'Joanna'), it is considered that the researcher's gender is known to the attacker. The Geonames service[2] is queried to perform a cleaning process (e.g., by correcting misspellings) and a verification of the names of cities, countries and locations. The target group produced is a subset of 4,324 researchers for which as much identifiable personal information as possible was gathered *via* external web sources.

The weight coefficients of the importance of the available personal attributes were empirically selected (e.g., $\lambda_{firstname} = 0.15$, $\lambda_{lastname} = 0.15$, $\lambda_{gender} = 0.05$, $\lambda_{education} = 0.05$, $\lambda_{hometown} = 0.075$, $\lambda_{country} = 0.075$, *etc.*) by performing some preliminary tests and the values for the three thresholds appearing in the identification process were manually set as follows: $\Theta_{overall} = 0.60$, $\Theta_{image} = 0.90$ and $\Theta_{attribute} = 0.20$.

3.2 The Model's Execution Phase

The next step is to carry out a search, one at a time, for these 4,324 individuals on the five OSNs to uncover all the publicly available information from their profiles. An XML parser, a JSON parser, an HTML parser and an aggregator module were developed for crawling and collecting this accessible information from the OSNs APIs or *via*

---

[1] http://www.gpeters.com/names/.

[2] http://www.geonames.org/.

'screen-scraping'. The aggregator module performs additional data warehousing functionalities, such as data cleaning, data transformation, data integration, data mining (for
gender inference), etc. For every target, the final goal of the proposed model is to
identify and correlate at most one social identity from every OSN that possibly belongs
to this individual. In the performance evaluation phase, the *Accuracy* metric for measuring the effectiveness of the proposed model in every examined OSN is defined as:

$$Accuracy = \frac{\text{number of targets for which the model correctly identified their OSN profile}}{\text{total number of targets in the dataset}}$$

in which the model is considered to correctly identify an OSN profile or to correctly
point to no existing OSN profile if this is also validated by manual inspection.

Figure 4 shows the accuracy of the proposed profile identification model in every
examined OSN for the selected group of 4,324. The accuracy of the profile matching
algorithm on Facebook reaches 0.71, and consists of an almost equal percentage of true
positives (TP) and true negatives (TN). The cause of the unexpected error ratio of 0.29
is the rather low overall profile matching threshold $\Theta_{overall} = 0.60$, which was selected
for such a high number of user profiles of Facebook (which exceeded 1.71 billion as of
June 30, 2016[3]), with many users unavoidably sharing the same first, last, or their full
name, and other personal attributes, producing a rather high percentage of 28.1% of
false positives (FP). This result, however, leads to the expectation that, with an
exclusively customized-for-Facebook tuning of the attributes weight coefficients, the
model's performance can be markedly improved.

OSN:	Facebook	LinkedIn	Google+	Twitter	MySpace
Accuracy:	0.710	0.900	0.889	0.926	0.956

Fig. 4. The accuracy of the proposed profile identification model for the selected set of OSNs.

On LinkedIn the accuracy level of the model is 0.90, consisting of the majority (i.e.,
about 72%) of TP, as expected, due to the nature of the targeted group of individuals
which was selected on the basis of their occupation. Here, most of the targets take care
of ensuring that their profile fields are accurate and comprehensive, which contributes
to the profile identification process. In the case of Google+ the model's accuracy rate is
0.889, consisting however in the majority (i.e., about 65%) of TN. The number of FN
in Google+ (which is 3.1%) is higher than in Facebook (0.9%) and LinkedIn (0.3%),
which can be explained by the higher number of user profiles in Google+ with partial
or missing personal information.

On Twitter and MySpace the model also achieves very high accuracy ratings. In
these OSNs the number of TP is much smaller than the number of TN, which is
explained by the nature of the targeted group. Also, about 30% of the number of TP in

---

[3] https://newsroom.fb.com/company-info/.

432   A. Kokkos et al.

MySpace has been successfully encountered by a unique identification *via* a known email address. Notably, in most of these cases the values for `the remainder of the personal attributes (emails excepted) in the verified MySpace profiles would not correlate correctly with the profiles of the targets due to missing personal data or deliberate misinformation in the profiles. The percentage % of the targets with identified (by our model) online presence in one, two, three and four of the OSNs under consideration is recorded in Fig. 5. As expected, most of the researchers in the DBLP dataset, and who have an online presence in OSNs, maintain personal profiles mainly in LinkedIn and/or in Facebook.

	Presence in one OSN	Presence in two OSNs	Presence in three OSNs	Presence in four OSNs	Presence in five OSNs
Percentage of individuals in the dataset:	44.080%	9.968%	0.902%	0.046%	0%

Fig. 5. The identified presence of the targets in the five OSNs under consideration.

4 Related Work

The term record linkage [12] refers to the task of identifying tuples that represent the same entity in one or more, possibly heterogeneous, data sources. In recent years, this concept shifted to matching users' profiles across different OSNs, whereby the identification process detects and weaves together the multiple online social identities of the same entity. Different methodologies have been developed to establish whether a user profile in an OSN belongs to a targeted physical entity: by using the user's email address in [13]; the user's pseudonyms in [3]; the username in [14]; the < *username, name, location* > attributes in [2]; the Google search service together with the < *occupation, education* > attributes in [15]; the < *firstname, lastname, email* > attributes together with three friends in [16]; the < *instance-messenger-identifier, personal websiteurl, name, hometown, birthday, university, highschool, gender, email, friends* > attributes in [17]; machine learning techniques on several personal attributes and the friends' list in [18, 19]; the user's social behavior across time and the close to the user social network structure in [20], *etc.*

The linking task is made difficult by the high degree of heterogeneity of the information available. The methodologies with a limited degree of effectiveness are the simplified approach in [15], relying solely on Google search results on the basis of a predefined set of known personal attributes of the targets to uniquely identify their OSN profiles, and the approaches that rely on the similarity of one or of a small subset of personal attributes (e.g. [3, 14]). While the approach proposed in [13] is effective in a few individual cases, the OSNs which offer the desired *friends-finder* functionality using their known email addresses are not many because this feature threat ensuer privacy. Closer to the method proposed in this paper are the matching algorithm approach in [17] which takes into account a static predefined set of 10 attributes for the OSN profile identification process, and the work based on supervised learning on several profile attributes and the friends' list in [18]. The main advantages of our model are that: firstly, the set of personal attributes to be utilized in the identification process is practically unlimited(since every possible personal attribute on an OSN can provide valuable data input for the matching process in other OSNs); secondly, the selection of these attributes and the identification operation provided by the model are fully-automated tasks (not manual or supervised tasks for the attacker); and, thirdly, the amount of personal data available to the attacker increases during the identification process, which means that an examined OSN may be accessed several times during this process, every time with an increased pool of prior knowledge, increasing the likelihood of positive results.

Figure 6 summarizes the performance achievements of previous work, setting out the best reported performance ratings, including those achievable only under significantly restricted conditions. The proposed model appears at the bottom indicating that it outperforms most of the earlier work in OSNs profile identification and matching and, to the best of the authors' knowledge, it appears to be the first to address the problem by combining a number of different methodologies, such as machine learning techniques, a variety of linkage methods and, very importantly, by exploiting the verified knowledge produced during the runtime of the identification process in an unsupervised fashion.

OSNs' profiles linkage model	Accuracy	Precision[a]	Recall[b]
Narayanan &Shmatikov[2]	0.308	–	–
Irani et al. [3]	0.600	–	–
Balduzzi et al. [13]	0.049	–	–
Wang et al. [14]	–	0.862	0.685
Vosecky et al. [17]	0.930	–	–
Peled et al. [18]	0.959	–	–
Zhang et al. [19]	–	0.860	0.867
Liu et al. [20]	–	0,968	0.908
Wondracek et al. [21]	0.577	–	–
Goga et al. [22]	–	0.950	0.290
Human inspection [22]	–	0.960	0.400
This paper	**0.956**	**0.904**	**0.985**

Fig. 6. The best provided Accuracy, Precision and Recall by several OSNs profiles linkage models. ([a]*Precision* is defined as TP/(TP+FP) and represents the ratio of correct user profiles identifications in an OSN. [b]*Recall* is defined as TP/(TP+FN) and represents the ratio of correct user profiles identifications to the total number of existing user profiles to be identified in an OSN.)

5   Conclusions and Future Research

The model proposed for identifying and linking the multiple online social identities of the same physical entity across OSN services combines methodologies to collect, infer and integrate accurate personal information from heterogeneous OSN sources to build a warehouse of digital footprints that can be used in several application domains. This hybrid architecture is built upon four different methods for OSNs profiles matching, and operates using a limited amount of prior knowledge about the target. Every piece of accurate information from one OSN is exploited in other OSNs for the remaining matching tasks, dynamically increasing the model's efficiency. Additionally, the model is operational without any modification in any OSN[4] and in any language.

The empirical performance evaluation of the proposed framework with a dataset of 4,324 individuals indicated that it can successfully retrieve and link together the social identities of the targets across multiple OSN services, regardless of their different database schemas and of lexical and structural heterogeneity. It also indicates that this model outperforms most of the earlier work.

Scope for further exploration includes developing increasingly sensitive modules for measuring the similarity between OSN profiles attributes of textual, date, image, or any other specialized data type. For example, the traditional syntactic-based text similarity metrics might not be able to capture a valuable similarity between two attribute values that are semantically related [23] while lexicographically different (e.g. "MS Corporation" and "Microsoft Inc."). Besides, the effectiveness of our method could be increased by fine-tuning several operational parameters (such as the attributes weight coefficients and the similarity thresholds). An extension of the proposed model could aim to establish links with any information that may be of value for the purpose of targeting individuals from any existing online footprint that can be uncovered and from any trustworthy source.

References

1. Chaski, C.E.: Empirical evaluations of language-based author identification techniques. Forensic Linguist. **8**, 1–65 (2001)
2. Narayanan, A., Shmatikov, V.: De-anonymizing social networks. In: Proceedings 30th IEEE Symposium on Security & Privacy, pp. 173–187 (2009)
3. Irani, D., et al.: Large online social footprints - an emerging threat. In: Proceedings IEEE International Conference on Computational Science & Engineering - CSE, vol. 3, pp. 271–276 (2009)
4. Erlandsson, F., Boldt, M., Johnson, H.: Privacy threats related to user profiling in OSNs. In: Proceedings of IEEE International Conference on Social Computing, pp. 838–842 (2012)
5. Christen, P.: Data Matching: Concepts and Techniques for Record Linkage, Entity Resolution, and Duplicate Detection. Springer Science & Business Media (2012)
6. Flickner, M., et al.: Query by image and video content: the QBIC system. IEEE Comput. **28** (9), 23–32 (1995)
7. Kokkos, A., Tzouramanis, T.: A robust gender inference model for online social networks and its application to LinkedIn and Twitter. First Monday **19**(9) (2014)
8. Bilenko, M., Mooney, R., Cohen, W., Ravikumar, P., Fienberg, S.: Adaptive name matching in information integration. IEEE Intell. Syst. **18**(5), 16–23 (2003)

---

[4] Refer to e.g. the following list of over 200 OSNs at the time of writing: https://en.wikipedia.org/wiki/List_of_social_networking_websites.

9. Winkler, W.E.: String comparator metrics and enhanced decision rules in the Fellegi-Sunter model of record linkage. In: Proceedings of the Section on Survey Research Methods, American Statistical Association, pp. 354–359 (1990)

10. Jaccard, P.: Lois de distribution florale. Bulletin de la Socíeté Vaudoise des Sciences Naturelles **38**, 67–130 (1902)

11. Jaccard, P.: The distribution of the flora in the alpine zone. New Phytol. **11**(2), 37–50 (1912)

12. Winker, E.W.: Overview of record linkage and current research directions. Statistical Research Division U.S. Census Bureau (2006)

13. Balduzzi, M., et al.: Abusing social networks for automated user profiling. In: Proceedings International Workshop on Recent Advances in Intrusion Detection, pp. 422–441 (2010)

14. Wang, Y., Liu, T., Tan, Q., Shi, J., Guo, L.: Identifying users across different sites using usernames. Procedia Comput. Sci. **80**, 376–385 (2016)

15. Bilge, L., Strufe, T., Balzarotti, D., Kirda, E.: All your contacts are belong to us: automated identity theft attacks on social networks. In: Proceedings 18th ACM International Conference on WWW, pp. 551–560 (2009)

16. Zhou, C., Chen, H., Yu, T.: Learning a probabilistic semantic model from heterogeneous social networks for relationship identification. In: Proceedings 20th IEEE International Conference on Tools with Artificial Intelligence, vol. 1, 343–350 (2008)

17. Vosecky, J., Hong, D., Shen, V.Y.: User identification across multiple OSNs. In: Proceedings 1st IEEE International Conference on Networked Digital Technologies, pp. 360–365 (2009)

18. Peled, O., Fire, M., Rokach, L., Elovici, Y.: Matching entities across online social networks. Neurocomputing **210**, 91–106 (2016)

19. Zhang, Y., Tang, J., Yang, Z., Pei, J., Yu, P.S.: COSNET: connecting heterogeneous social networks with local and global consistency. In: Proceedings 21st ACM SIGKDD International Conference on Knowledge Discovery & Data Mining – KDD, 1485–1494 (2015)

20. Liu, S., Wang, S., Zhu, F., Zhang, J., Krishnan, R.: HYDRA: Large-scale social identity linkage *via* heterogeneous behavior modeling. In: Proceedings ACM International Conference on Management of Data- SIGMOD, pp. 51–62 (2014)

21. Wondracek, G., Holz, T., Kirda, E., Kruegel, C.: A practical attack to de-anonymize social network users. In: Proceedings IEEE Symposium on Security & Privacy, pp. 223–238 (2010)

22. Goga, O., Loiseau, P., Sommer, R., Teixeira, R., Gummadi, K.P.: On the reliability of profile matching across large online social networks. In: Proceedings 21st ACM SIGKDD International Conference on Knowledge Discovery & Data Mining – KDD, pp. 1799–1808 (2015)

23. Egozi, O., Markovitch, S., Gabrilovich, E.: Concept-based information retrieval using explicit semantic analysis. ACM Trans. Inf. Syst. **29**(2) (2011). article 8

Eco-Data Warehouse Design Through Logical Variability

Selma Bouarar[1]([✉]), Ladjel Bellatreche[1], and Amine Roukh[2]

[1] LIAS/ISAE-ENSMA, Poitiers University, Poitiers, France
{bouarars,bellatreche}@ensma.fr
[2] University of Mostaganem, Mostaganem, Algeria
roukh.amine@univ-mosta.dz

Abstract. The database (DB) is one of the active communities dealing with the non-functional requirements (NFRs) when designing advanced applications. The fulfillment of the NFRs is usually performed along the phases of DB life cycle in *an isolated way*. The physical design phase took the lion's share of these studies, because it is an important factor for a successful DB deployment in terms of *performance metrics*. By carefully analyzing these studies, we figure out that target DBs are assumed to be already deployed, meaning that their logical models are *frozen*. This assumption surely becomes questionable, since it ignores the chained aspect of the life cycle. Knowing that many variants of a logical schema may exist due to the presence of dependencies and hierarchies among attributes; it is worth studying the impact of this variation on the physical design. In this paper, we firstly identify the dimensions of the variability of a logical schema and their modeling. Secondly, we propose a methodology, by highlighting the efforts that designers have to make, to evaluate the impact of the logical schema variability on the physical design (by considering logical or physical optimization), where both energy consumption and query performance are considered. Finally, intensive experiments are conducted to evaluate our proposal and the obtained results show the real impact of variability on data warehouses (DW) eco-design.

1 Introduction

The development of advanced DB applications such as Business Intelligence goes through a well identified *life cycle* that includes: functional/non-functional requirements analysis, conceptual design, logical design, ETL (Extract, Transform, Load), deployment modeling, physical design and exploitation. Note that non functional requirements (NFRs) express desired qualities of the underlying DB applications. They cover both observable qualities such as DB performance and availability, but also internal characteristics such as maintainability and portability [1]. The physical design is the crucial phase of the DB life cycle, since it can be seen as a *funnel* of the other phases. It should be noticed that the majority of NFRs are evaluated during this phase that takes logical and deployment phases as inputs to be mapped to the target DBMS specific features and functions such as Oracle, DB2, PostgreSQL. Besides, optimization structures

© Springer International Publishing AG 2017
B. Steffen et al. (Eds.): SOFSEM 2017, LNCS 10139, pp. 436–449, 2017.
DOI: 10.1007/978-3-319-51963-0_34

like materialized views, indexes, and so forth are herein selected to satisfy one or several NFRs such as query performance and energy consumption [11,17].

Formally, the physical design problem ($\mathcal{PDP}$) is defined as follows: given: a DB/DW deployed in a given DBMS, a workload, a set of optimization structures ($\mathcal{OS}$) supported by the target DBMS, a set of constraints $\mathcal{C}$ related to these $\mathcal{OS}$ such as the storage cost, and a set of NFRs. $\mathcal{PDP}$ consists in providing *logical and physical optimizations* satisfying NFRs and respecting $\mathcal{C}$, and it is known to be NP-hard [13]. Note that logical and physical optimizations respectively include operations performed on query plans (e.g. join ordering) and access methods (e.g. indexes and materialized views) [8]. In order to further optimize the NFRs, the DB community spent a lot of efforts in varying the elements of each entry of the $\mathcal{PDP}$ and evaluate its impact on satisfying the desired NFRs. This is best illustrated by commercial and academic tools (e.g., *Tuning Advisor* of Microsoft SQL Server [7], and Parinda for PostgreSQL [12]) which offer designers the possibility to evaluate the performance of a workload by varying the supported $\mathcal{OS}$. Other efforts have been elaborated to evaluate the impact of DBMS storage layouts, used to store semantic DBs instances, on query performance [10].

Satisfying some requirements by configuring some variation points (entries) has been widely studied by the community of software engineering in the so-called *Variability Management* ($\mathcal{VM}$) field [2]. It is defined as the ability of a product or artifact to be changed, customized or configured for use in a particular context. An analogy can be immediately drawn between $\mathcal{VM}$ and $\mathcal{PDP}$. In fact, this latter owns different variation points (dimensions, entries), as depicted in Fig. 1. Each variation point is seen as a complex search problem, often using a mathematical NFR-driven cost model to evaluate and select "best" solutions.

Based on this Figure, we can easily identify the *dependencies* among these dimensions. Actually, varying the logical schema strongly impacts the following entries: *workload*, the $\mathcal{OS}$ and the *constrains*. Nevertheless, designers still intuitively fix a logical solution out of a panoply, hence omitting eventual more relevant alternatives ($\mathcal{VM}$ aspect). Bearing this in mind, we fix some objectives to handle this missing piece in $\mathcal{PDP}$ puzzle: (i) capturing variability, (ii) *studying the impact* of variability on dependent components, as well as *efforts in terms of modeling and coding* to be spent by designers to manage this variability, and (iii) validating our methodology.

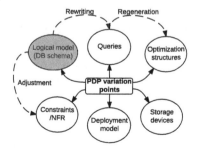

Fig. 1. Variation points of physical design problem.

To show the impact of the variability of the logical phase on the physical model, we consider the following entries of our $\mathcal{PDP}$: *(a)* a Star Schema Benchmark (SSB) as DW logical schema, *(b)* query performance and energy consumption as NFRs, *(c)* SSB workload, *(d)* materialized views and logical optimizations offered by the target DBMS as $\mathcal{OS}$, *(e)* the storage constraint dedicated to this $\mathcal{OS}$. To the best of our knowledge, our proposal is the sole that studies the variation of the logical dimension, and hence the majority of $\mathcal{PDP}$ dimensions, according to both energy and performance.

The paper is organized as follows: Sect. 2 provides some definitions about variability and its contributions in the context of DB design. Section 3 describes our methodology. Section 4 presents our results. Finally, Sect. 5 concludes the paper by summarizing the main results and suggesting future work.

2   Background

In order to cope with the upward diversity in DB design research, the need for managing variability is becoming real, if not urgent. In fact, designers need to be assisted in their choice, increasingly hard to make, against the rising variety. $\mathcal{VM}$ is defined as the ability of a product or artifact to be changed, customized or configured for use in a particular context. By analogy, physical design of a DB product, needs to be configured, using its entries, in order to reach high performance assessed in terms of NFRs.

Indeed, there is an impressive body of research on variability-aware DB physical design (Table 1), where variability can be either: **(i)** implicitly handled without borrowing the spectacular advances made by the SPL community in terms of variability management (DBMS Advisors are perfect examples of these approaches), or, on the opposite, **(ii)** explicitly handled [15], since designer can generate its tailored artifacts by choosing features using appropriate techniques such as SPL, FOP, AOP, etc.

Capturing Variability of Logical Design. There is a patent lack of considering logical design variability in $\mathcal{PDP}$. Yet while most problems can be solved by fine-tuning the physical schema, some performance/NFR problems are caused by a non-optimized logical schema. In fact, this latter is variable (can have many variants) thanks to the so-called *correlations*: Functional dependencies,

Table 1. Overview of variability-aware $\mathcal{DB}$ physical design studies.

Target	Technique
Query language	SPL [14]
Query optimizer	SPL [18] Optimization [7,12] (implicit)
Deployment Layout	[10,20] (implicit)
DBMS	Preprocessors (implicit), FOP [3], SPL [15] AOP [19], Component-based Approach [9]

Multi-valued dependencies and hierarchies. In case of DW (a particular DB) for instance, let $\mathcal{LM} = \{F, D_1, D_2, ..., D_n\}$ be the DW logical schema from which different other schemes (star and snowflake) can be generated. F for fact table, D_i for dimensions. The search space (referred to as product line scope in variability jargon) can be estimated around $\prod_{\{d=1\}}^{n} 2^{h_d-1}$ possible $\mathcal{LM}$s, such that h_d is the number of hierarchical levels of a dimension $d/d \in \{1..n\}$. The generation process is based on attributes correlations [4];

On the other hand, $\mathcal{VM}$ can be organized in two stages: (i) Modeling: concerned with capturing and modeling the commonality and variability among final products, and (ii) configuration tasked with developing final products by selecting and configuring shared artifacts and adding product specific extensions [2]. For several reasons, feature modeling is one of the most popular variability modeling techniques [2]. DB product feature model is depicted in Fig. 2. As for configuration stage, Software Product Lines (SPL) is one of the most famous approaches for implementing and automating software variability management. The basic idea behind SPL is that products are built from a core asset base, a collection of artifacts that have been designed specifically for use across the portfolio. We proposed a basic tool in [5] for modeling and configuring DB, to which, this new proposal, adding power as NFR, can be plugged.

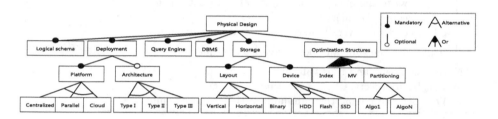

Fig. 2. Excerpt of the database feature model.

3   Variability Management in Physical Design

As we said before, our proposal considers the majority of dimensions of variability axes. To show the real impact on physical design and reduce the complexity of treating all dimensions at once, we incrementally integrate dimensions. We start by evaluating the impact of logical schema variation on physical design when executing a workload, without considering the impact on physical optimization: only optimizations offered by target DBMS (referred to as *logical optimization*) are considered. Secondly, we integrate the impact of logical variation on the problem of materialized view selection. To show the impact of the variability on the physical model, we consider our $\mathcal{PDP}$ with two objective functions, namely query performance and energy[1] consumption.

---

[1] For the rest of the paper, we will use interchangeably the terms *energy* and *power*.

3.1   Scenario 1: Impact of $\mathcal{VM}$ on Logical Optimizations

To study the impact of variability of the logical model on the physical phase, we consider a *naive scenario*, where logical optimizations (e.g. join implementations, join ordering, etc.) are delegated to the query optimizer of the target DBMS (Oracle 11gR2 in our case) and advanced optimizations structures such as materialized views are absent. We consider the query performance and energy consumption as two *objective functions* when executing the workload. In practice, for each variant of the initial logical schema of our DW, we compute both metrics. Note that each variant requires rewriting efforts of the initial workload. Algorithm 1 gives an overview of our approach:

Algorithm 1. Algorithm dedicated to Scenario 1.

Input: $\mathcal{DW}$ logical model: $\mathcal{DW} = \{F, D_1, D_2, ..., D_n\}$; $\mathcal{Q} = \{q_1, q_2, ..., q_m\}$;
Output: $\mathcal{DWl}$: $\mathcal{DW}$ logical schema having the *most suitable*
          performance/power-saving trade-off
Generate the different possible logical schemes;
for *each generated schema* **do**
    Calculate the size of the schema;
    for *each query in the workload* **do**
       Rewrite the query conforming to the target schema;
       Execute the query;
       Record the overall query power & its execution time;
    Calculate the time and power averages of queries;
Normalize power and time values;
Weight both objectives (power & time);
$\mathcal{DWl}$ = Schema having the minimum of the weighted sum;

Our algorithm provides us both metrics. In order to help DB designers choose the schema that best fits their requirements, we initially propose to use the weighted sum of the objective functions method that allows formulating the desired trade-off between target NFR. In this scalarization method, we calculate the weighted sum of the normalized objective functions so as to aggregate objectives and have an equivalent single objective function to be optimized. This method is defined as follows [21]:

$$minimize \quad y = f(x) = \sum_{i=1}^{k} \omega_i \cdot f_i(\overrightarrow{x}) / \sum_{i=1}^{k} \omega_i = 1 \tag{1}$$

Where ω_i are the weighting coefficients representing the relative importance of the k objective functions of the problem. For example, an eco-performing schema would have an $\omega_{pow} = \omega_{perf} = 0.5$) while a performance-oriented schema would have $\omega_{perf} > \omega_{pow}$, contrary to an eco-oriented schema ($\omega_{pow} > \omega_{perf}$). This technique is well suited when the *Pareto* front is convex, which is the case with our curve, as further illustrated in Sect. 4.

3.2   Scenario 2: Impact of $\mathcal{VM}$ on Physical Optimizations

In this scenario, we leverage the previous one by considering an optimization structure representing materialized views [13]. In our study, we do not delegate the selection of materialized views to advisors, we propose instead an algorithm selecting them according to our previous metrics. This selection is proven to be NP-hard problem, and has been subject to many studies [13]. The process of selecting views requires three main components [6]:

(a) A data structure to capture the interaction among queries, like the *And-Or view graph* or *Multi-View Processing Plan* [13]. It puts the algebraic operations of queries all together in a certain order as an acyclic graph. Starting from base tables as leaf nodes to queries results as root nodes, through intermediate nodes: unary operations (like selection/projection) and binary ones (like join/union). Getting the optimal order between intermediate nodes - join ones in particular- determines the efficiency of the structure.

(b) Algorithms (e.g. deterministic algorithms, randomized algorithms, etc. [6]) exploiting a such structure to pick the best configuration of materialized views.

(c) Cost models estimating different NFRs.

(a) The construction of the Data Structure. Our proposal has the ability to consider very large number of queries. This is due to the data structure borrowed from hyper-graphs [6] representing the global plan of the workload as well as the interaction among queries. The main steps of the process of selecting views are [6]:

– **Step 1:** Parse query workload to extract the different algebraic operations;
– **Step 2:** Construct the hypergraph He out of join nodes, such that every He represents a query and thus contains its different join nodes modeled as vertices;
– **Step 3:** Partition He into a set of connected components He_{sub} (disjoint sub-hypergraphs), to put interacting nodes together;
– **Step 4:** Order the nodes of each He_{sub} according to a benefit function that determines a pivot node at each pass;
– **Step 5:** Merge the resulting He_{sub} to generate the global structure.

Our contribution concerns the He construction, and the ordering of He_{sub} nodes (2nd & 4th steps). In fact, only star schemes are handled by the baseline approach [6], unlike ours that considers any multidimensional model (star, snowflake, constellation). The difference lies in that there henceforth exists some extra-join nodes not involving any-more the fact table (joins between dimensions and sub-dimensions, which we have called *extra-joins* against *fact-joins*), and this leads to a totally different situation. As depicted in Fig. 3, the 2nd and the 4th arrangements are impossible configurations in the baseline approach and frequent ones in ours. Indeed, we will have more than one starting nodes in one connected component.

However, the extra-joins introduce a partial order since they have to precede the fact-ones (sub-dimensions must be joined before their dimensions). This order must be considered when ordering nodes of He_{sub} (step4) so that: (i) the

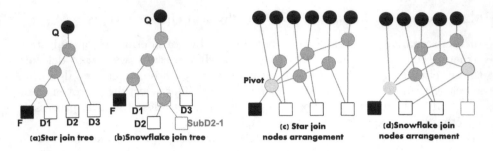

Fig. 3. Possible join nodes arrangement in a global plan.

mother dimension must always appear after its extra-joins, (ii) the outer extra joins must always figure before the inner ones. These rules are guaranteed thanks to the below benefit functions, the purpose of which, is to find the pivot nodes and thus order the He_{sub} nodes. Given: n_{f_i} a fact-join, n_{e_i} an extra-join, k the number of extra joins implied by a fact-join, nbr the number of queries using the node in question, $cost$ its processing cost $\Rightarrow$

$$
\begin{cases}
cost_{total}(n_{f_i}) = cost(n_{f_i}) + \sum_{j=1}^{k} cost(n_{e_j}) \\
benefit(n_{e_i}) = (nbr - 1) * cost(n_{e_i}) - cost(n_{e_i}) \\
benefit(n_{f_i}) = (nbr - 1) * cost(n_{f_i}) + \\
\qquad \sum_{j=1}^{k}(cost(nbr - 1) * cost(n_{e_j})) \\
\qquad - cost(n_{f_i}) - \sum_{j=1}^{k} cost(n_{e_j})
\end{cases}
$$

(b) Materializing Nodes and Schema Selection (Algorithm). Our approach, as summarized in Algorithm 2, is based on the *hyper-graph based* structure. In fact, if designer looks primarily for optimizing query performance, we will create this *structure* for each schema among the *top-k* performance-oriented schemes, materialize the pivot node of each one (the most advantageous node), execute queries for each schema and finally compare results. The schema having the smallest execution time of its queries will be the selected one. Otherwise, if designer needs to optimize both query performance and energy saving, the *structures* of the *top-k* eco-oriented schemes (or trade-off-oriented according to designer needs) will be generated.

Materializing the pivot node does not make sense anymore for saving power (because it is performance-oriented), nor all the join nodes because this would entail the highest power consumption [16]. Testing 2^n possible configurations, where n is the number of join nodes, to find *Pareto* solutions, is impossible especially in DW workloads involving a lot of joins. A Pareto solution is a set of nodes (a view configuration), that would give - when materialized - values that can not be improved without making at least power or performance worse off. They are the best alternative since there does not typically exist a solution that minimizes all objective functions at once. Evolutionary Algorithms (EAs) are indeed suitable for multi-objectives optimization problems where large search spaces can be handled and multiple alternative trade-offs can be generated in a single optimization run [21]. The general idea behind EA is to investigate a set of solutions that represent the Pareto optimal set as well as possible.

Algorithm 2. Algorithm dedicated to Scenario 2.

Input: NFR, $\mathcal{LM}$: a set of logical schemes /
$\quad\quad \mathcal{LM}_i = \{F, D_j, SubD_{jk}\}/j \in \{1..n\}, k \in \{1..n_k\}, \mathcal{Q}_i = \{q_{i_1}, q_{i_2}, ..., q_{i_m}\}^{\text{a}}$
Output: A set of join nodes to be materialized (view configuration)
for $\mathcal{LM}_i \in \mathcal{LM}$ **do**
$\quad$ Generate the Multi View Processing Plan corresponding to its queries $\mathcal{Q}_i$;
$\quad$ **if** *NFR = performance* **then**
$\quad\quad$ Each pivot node of each connected component of the structure is materialized;

$\quad$ **else** /* NFR = energy & performance */
$\quad\quad$ Annotate each join node by its execution time and power consumption;
$\quad\quad$ Apply an evolutionary algorithm to select candidate views to be materialized optimizing *performance* as well as *energy*;
$\quad\quad$ Apply the weigthed sum on these candidates to select one view configuration;

---

[a]$\mathcal{LM}$ and $\mathcal{Q}$ are generated from Algorithm 1.

(c) Energy Cost-Model. To evaluate the interest of the presence of a materialized view, without deploying, each time, the DB (schema and optimization structures), we adjust our mathematical cost model developed in [16]. In fact, this cost model has been constructed by assuming a DW with star schema. As a consequence, our adaptation consists in making it more generic to consider all variants of the logical schemes. This adaption mainly concerns the training phase that allows identifying the relevant parameters of our cost models using *polynomial* multivariate regression model [16].

4   Experimental Study

To evaluate the logical variability impact on physical design, we conduct intensive experiments related to our two scenarios. First, we present our development environment including hardware, software, datasets, and results.

Hardware Setup. Our machine is equipped with a "Watts UP? Pro ES²" power meter with one second as a maximum resolution. As commonly set up, the device is directly placed between the power supply and the DB workstation under test to measure the workstation's overall power consumption. The power values are logged and processed in a separate monitor machine (client-server architecture). We used a Dell PowerEdge R210 II workstation having an Intel Xeon E3-1230 V2 3.30 GHz processor, 10GB of DDR3 memory and a 2x500GB hard drive.

---

[2] https://www.wattsupmeters.com/.

Software Setup. Our workstation machine is installed with the latest version of Oracle 11gR2 DBMS under Ubuntu 14.04 LTS with kernel 3.13 to minimize spurious influences, with 8192 as block size. We also disable unnecessary background tasks, clear the system and oracle cache for each query execution. We also disable unnecessary background tasks, clear the system and oracle cache for each query execution.

Datasets. We use SSB datasets with a scale factor of 10. It illustrates decision support systems that examine large volumes of data, and execute different types of queries with a high degree of complexity. We have identified the main hierarchies for each dimension table of the SSB multi-dimensional model, applied our formula $(H(Customer)*H(Part)*H(Supplier)*H(Date) = 2^{3-1} * 2^{2-1} * 2^{3-1} * 2^{4-1})$, and generated the resulting 256 possible schemes thanks to attributes correlations. As for workload, we create 30 queries based on SSB datasets, in such a way that two main categories must always be handled: (i) queries with operations that exhaust the system processor (CPU intensive queries) and (ii) queries with exhaustive storage subsystem resource operations (I/O intensive queries). Note that the considered queries include: queries with single table scan, others with multiple joins with different predicates. They also contain sorting/grouping conditions and simple and advanced aggregation functions. These queries are rewritten according to every schema [4].

4.1 Evaluation of Scenario 1

As already mentioned, the scenario 1 involved logical optimizations. In our case, we use the default optimizations offered by Oracle 11gR2 DBMS query optimizer. To conduct our experiments, we have deployed the different 256 schemes obtained from varying the initial SSB schema of our DW. The initial queries of our workload are rewritten for each schema (7680 queries all in all) and executed. Execution time (from oracle) and power consumption (from power meter) are recorded. We first analyze one objective function *"power"*, depicted in Fig. 4 that confirms power variation according to logical schema and, even better, shows that star schema is far from being the most eco-model. We have noticed that the *co-normalization of the smallest dimension tables* (supplier (2000*SF) and

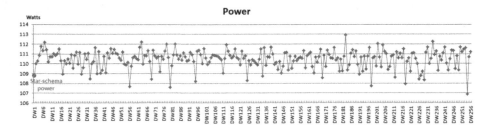

Fig. 4. Impact of logical design on DW power consumption.

dates (2556) in this case) in the presence of CPU-intensive operations clearly disadvantages power consumption, but neither the number of joins (IO costs) nor the number of CPU-intensive operations (e.g. aggregations/sorting) influence directly the power consumption. A possible explanation is that most of query time execution is spent in CPU processing because data is read quickly due to the files small size. On the opposite, when most of query time execution is spent in waiting until data is ready because of data swapping between memory/disk, less power consumption is recorded.

In a second place, we consider two objective functions representing query performance and power consumption. We then highlight the relation between them which takes the form of a convex as illustrated in Fig. 5. This reveals the existence of logical schemes optimizing both NFR (Pareto solutions), and meanwhile, approves our choice of weighting method in selecting schemes.

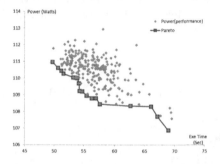

Fig. 5. Impact of logical design on DW power and performance.

On the other hand, normalization process reduces storage space, especially with large dimension tables and/or important size of hierarchies. Snowflake schemes are hence appropriate for space-constrained applications as depicted in Fig. 6. This storage gain could be also propagated to storage constraints of optimization structures. These experiments show the limitations of the initial SSB schema to satisfy our fixed NFRs.

Fig. 6. Impact of logical design on DW size.

4.2   Evaluation of Scenario 2

The previous experiments took almost 10 days (7680 queries) what reveals the
necessity of using a simulator (cost model) for these and future experiments. We
focus in this scenario, on the problem of selecting materialized views by considering the variation of the logical schema (256 schemes), unlike current studies
dealing with only one schema. To generalize this, we develop a Java-simulator
tool that generates the global plan, using our hypergraph-based approach, for a
given workload following any DW logical schema, and assessed the NFRs cost for
the different schemes/workloads using pluggable cost models. Our simulator is
equipped with *mathematical cost models estimating different metrics* (query performance, power consumption, etc.) [16]. Figure 7 presents our simulation results
of assessing performance (I/O) of the different workloads/schemes with/without
views. This attests to the relevance of: (i) materializing views to query performance, which is quite expected. This partially proves the coherence of our cost
model, (ii) the impact of logical variability on physical design.

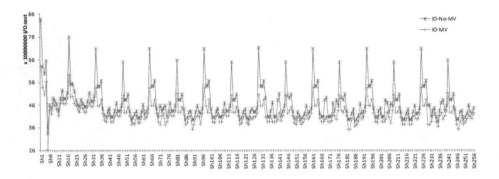

Fig. 7. Impact of $\mathcal{VM}$ on performance of physical optimizations.

Impact of $\mathcal{VM}$ on both Power and Performance of Physical Optimizations.
Rather than testing in combinatorial fashion all the configurations (256 schemes,
30 queries and n views generated by evolutionary algorithms, for each schema),
it would make more sense to first select three different logical schemes from our
first scenario (that can be hence done using our simulator): a performance, power
and trade-off oriented schemes. Using $MOEA$[3] integrated to our tool, we select
the set of *Pareto* materializable global plan nodes for each schema. For each
materialized view configuration generated by MOEA Framework, the simulator calculates performance and power consumption using cost models. Similarly,
it then needs to select a unique view configuration with the desired trade-off:
power-MV (*MV for materialized views*), time-MV, trade-off-MV, using weighted
sum method with corresponding ω_i. Note that I/O costs were converted to time
values (ms).

---

[3] Java library for multi-objective evolutionary algorithms. www.moeaframework.org.

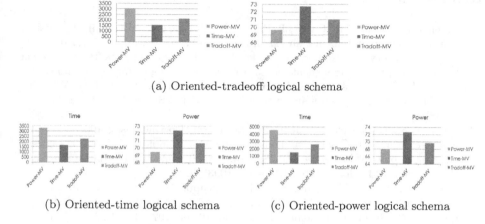

(a) Oriented-tradeoff logical schema

(b) Oriented-time logical schema   (c) Oriented-power logical schema

Fig. 8. Impact of $\mathcal{VM}$ on both Power and Performance of Physical Optimizations.

Our experiments (some of which are depicted in Fig. 8) show that (i) logical schemes intended to improve an NFR (performance/power), do not necessarily give the optimal values in the presence of optimization structures. That said, they do not give the worst values either, (ii) to orient a designer towards a given NFR at earlier stages, she/he must combine the suitable tradeoff of both logical schema and optimization structures, (iii) these results confirm the need for a holistic variability-aware design process where such interdependences have to be considered.

5 Conclusion

In this paper, we launched a think-tank about the impact of varying the logical model of a given DW on the physical design, according to two NFRs: efficiency of energy consumption and query performance. This think-tank is alimented by **(a)** a debate on the analogy between SPL and DB design, **(b)** tools to identify/model the dimensions of our problem variability, **(c)** the efforts that designers have to made to deal with this interesting issue. To show the consequences of varying the logical schema on the physical design, we handled two scenarios: **(i)** a physical schema without physical optimization and **(ii)** a physical schema with the process of selecting materialized views. These two scenarios are evaluated using the SSB benchmark and specific hardware to capture Energy. The obtained results shows the worthlessness of launching our think-tank that the frozen logical schema, and star schema in particular, is not always the best one to satisfy the fixed NFRs.

Currently, we are working on pushing back the variability to cover other phases of the life cycle such as ETL and conceptual modeling.

References

1. Ameller, D., Ayala, C.P., Cabot, J., Franch, X.: How do software architects consider non-functional requirements: an exploratory study. In: RE, pp. 41–50 (2012)
2. Apel, S., Batory, D., Kstner, C., Saake, G.: Feature-Oriented Software Product Lines: Concepts and Implementation. Springer Publishing Company, Berlin (2013)
3. Batory, D., Barnett, J., Garza, J., Smith, K., Tsukuda, K., Twichell, B., Wise, T.: Genesis: an extensible db management system. IEEE Softw. Eng. **14**, 1711–1730 (1988)
4. Bouarar, S., Bellatreche, L., Jean, S., Baron, M.: Do rule-based approaches still make sense in logical data warehouse design? In: Manolopoulos, Y., Trajcevski, G., Kon-Popovska, M. (eds.) ADBIS 2014. LNCS, vol. 8716, pp. 83–96. Springer, Heidelberg (2014). doi:10.1007/978-3-319-10933-6_7
5. Bouarar, S., Jean, S., Siegmund, N.: SPL driven approach for variability in database design. In: Bellatreche, L., Manolopoulos, Y. (eds.) MEDI 2015. LNCS, vol. 9344, pp. 332–342. Springer, Heidelberg (2015). doi:10.1007/978-3-319-23781-7_27
6. Boukorca, A., Bellatreche, L., Senouci, S.B., Faget, Z.: Coupling materialized view selection to multi query optimization: hyper graph approach. IJDWM **11**(2), 62–84 (2015)
7. Chaudhuri, S., Narasayya, V.: Self-tuning database systems: a decade of progress. In: VLDB 2007, pp. 3–14 (2007)
8. Garcia-Molina, H., Ullman, J.D., Widom, J.: Database Systems: The Complete Book, 2nd edn. Prentice Hall Press, Upper Saddle River (2008)
9. Geppert, A., Scherrer, S., Dittrich, K.R.: Kids: construction of database management systems based on reuse. Technical report (1997)
10. Jean, S., Bellatreche, L., Ordonez, C., Fokou, G., Baron, M.: OntoDBench: interactively benchmarking ontology storage in a database. In: Ng, W., Storey, V.C., Trujillo, J.C. (eds.) ER 2013. LNCS, vol. 8217, pp. 499–503. Springer, Heidelberg (2013). doi:10.1007/978-3-642-41924-9_44
11. Lang, W., Kandhan, R., Patel, J.M.: Rethinking query processing for energy efficiency: slowing down to win the race. IEEE Data Eng. Bull. **34**(1), 12–23 (2011)
12. Maier, C., Dash, D., Alagiannis, I., Ailamaki, A., Heinis, T.: PARINDA: an interactive physical designer for postgresql. In: EDBT, pp. 701–704 (2010)
13. Mami, I., Bellahsene, Z.: A survey of view selection methods. SIGMOD Rec. **41**(1), 20–29 (2012)
14. Rosenmüller, M., et al.: SQL à la Carte: toward tailor-made data management. In: BTW (2009)
15. Rosenmüller, M., et al.: Tailor-made data management for embedded systems: a case study on berkeley DB. DKE **68**(12), 1493–1512 (2009)
16. Roukh, A., Bellatreche, L., Boukorca, A., Bouarar, S.: Eco-dmw: eco-design methodology for data warehouses. In: ACM DOLAP, pp. 1–10 (2015)
17. Roukh, A., Bellatreche, L., Ordonez, C.: Enerquery: energy-aware query processing. In: ACM CIKM (2016, to appear)
18. Soffner, M., Siegmund, N., Rosenmüller, M., Siegmund, J., Leich, T., Saake, G.: A variability model for query optimizers. In: DB&IS, pp. 15–28 (2012)
19. Tesanovic, A., Sheng, K., Hansson, J.: Application-tailored database systems: a case of aspects in an embedded database. In: IDEAS, pp. 291–301 (2004)

20. Voigt, H., Hanisch, A., Lehner, W.: Flexs – a logical model for physical data layout. In: Bassiliades, N., Ivanovic, M., Kon-Popovska, M., Manolopoulos, Y., Palpanas, T., Trajcevski, G., Vakali, A. (eds.) New Trends in Database and Information Systems II. AISC, vol. 312, pp. 85–95. Springer, Heidelberg (2015). doi:10.1007/978-3-319-10518-5_7

21. Zhou, A., Qu, B.-Y., Li, H., Zhao, S.-Z., Suganthan, P.N., Zhang, Q.: Multiobjective evolutionary algorithms: a survey of the state of the art. Swarm Evol. Comput. **1**, 32–49 (2011)

Software Engineering: Methods, Tools, Applications

On Featured Transition Systems

Axel Legay[1]([✉]), Gilles Perrouin[2], Xavier Devroey[2], Maxime Cordy[2],
Pierre-Yves Schobbens[2], and Patrick Heymans[2]

[1] INRIA Rennes Bretagne Atlantique, Rennes, France
axel.legay@inria.fr
[2] PReCISE Research Center, Faculty of Computer Science,
University of Namur, Namur, Belgium
{gilles.perrouin,xavier.devroey,maxime.cordy,
pierre-yves.schobbens,patrick.heymans}@unamur.be

Abstract. Software Product Lines (SPLs) are families of similar software products built from a common set of features. As the number of products of an SPL is potentially exponential in the number of its features, analysing SPLs is harder than for single software. In this invited paper, we synthesise six years of efforts in alleviating SPL verification and testing issues. To this end, we introduced Featured Transition Systems (FTS) as a compact behavioural model for SPLs. Based on this formalism, we designed verification algorithms and tools allowing to check temporal properties on FTS, thereby assessing the correct behaviour of all the SPL products. We also used FTS to define test coverage and generation techniques for model-driven SPLs. We also successfully employed the formalism in order to foster mutation analysis. We conclude with future directions on the development of FTS for SPL analysis.

1 The Software Product Line Challenge

Software product line engineering (SPLE) is an increasingly popular development paradigm for highly customizable software. SPLE allows companies to achieve economies of scale by developing several similar systems together.

SPLE is now widely embraced by the industry, with applications in a variety of domains ranging from embedded systems (e.g., automotive, medical), system software (e.g., operating systems) to software products and services (e.g., e-commerce, finance). However, the benefits of SPLE come at the cost of added complexity: the (potentially large) number of systems to be considered at once, and the need for managing their variability in all activities and artifacts.

This added complexity also applies to the verification of the products' behaviour. A simple but cumbersome approach for product line verification consists in applying classical model checking algorithms [37] on each individual product of the family. However, for an SPL with n features, this would lead to 2^n calls of the model checking algorithm. This solution is clearly unsatisfactory and should be replaced by new approaches that take the variability within the family into account. Those approaches often rely on compact mathematical representations on which a specialized model checking algorithm can be applied.

© Springer International Publishing AG 2017
B. Steffen et al. (Eds.): SOFSEM 2017, LNCS 10139, pp. 453–463, 2017.
DOI: 10.1007/978-3-319-51963-0_35

The main difficulties are (1) to develop such a model checking algorithm, and (2) to propose mathematical structures that are compact and flexible enough to take the variability of the family and its specification into account.

In [10], we introduced *Featured Transition Systems* (FTS), an extension of transition systems used to represent the behaviour of all the products of an SPL in a single compact structure. We also showed how this representation can be exploited to perform model checking of product lines in an efficient way. In the rest of this paper, we briefly re-introduce FTS and summarize existing model checking algorithms for them. We also briefly show that FTS can be exploited to perform testing of software product lines. This is only a brief summary of the work that is presented at SOFSEM'17. More details can be found in our different papers cited below. Finally, we have to highlight that related work on product-line verification is vast and varied. To the best of our knowledge, effort in compiling related work on this topic can be found in the theses of Classen [5] and Cordy [11]. Beohar *et al.* recently compared the expressiveness of different SPL formalisms and found that FTS is the most expressive one [4].

2   Featured Transition Systems

Let us introduce Featured Transition Systems with a classical vending machine example. The example is a short version of the one we presented in [8]. In its basic version, the vending machine takes a coin, returns change, serves soda, and eventually opens a compartment so that the customer can take her soda, before closing it again. This behaviour is modelled by the transition system shown in Fig. 1(a). There exist other variants of this vending machine. As an example, consider a machine that also sells tea, shown in Fig. 1(b). Another variant lets the customer cancel her purchase after entering a coin, see Fig. 1(c). A fourth one offers free drinks and has no closing beverage compartment, see Fig. 1(d). This variability hints that the vending machines could be developed as an SPL,

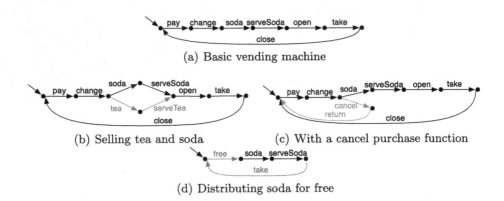

(a) Basic vending machine

(b) Selling tea and soda   (c) With a cancel purchase function

(d) Distributing soda for free

Fig. 1. Several variants of a vending machine.

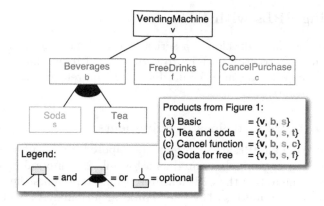

Fig. 2. FD for the vending machines of Fig. 1.

of which four features can be already identified: the sale of soda, the sale of tea, the ability to cancel a purchase and the ability to offer drinks for free.

By combining these features differently, yet other vending machines can be obtained. However, not every combination of features yields a valid system (e.g., a vending machine should at least sell a beverage). One can use variability models to represent the sets of valid products. In SPLE, feature diagrams [30,36] are the most common incarnation of variability models. The feature diagram for the vending machine SPL is shown in Fig. 2. This feature digram formally describes a set of vending machines; twelve of them. A model of the behaviour of a small example such as this would already require twelve, largely identical, behavioural descriptions, four of which are shown in Fig. 1.

FTS are meant to represent the behaviour of the myriad instances of an SPL in a single transition system. In fact, the main ingredient of FTS is to associate transitions with features that condition their existence. Consider again our vending machine example. Figures 1(b) and (c) show the impact of adding features *Tea* and *CancelPurchase* to a machine serving only soda: both add two transitions. *FreeDrinks* replaces $①\overset{pay}{\longrightarrow}②\overset{change}{\longrightarrow}③$ by a single transition $①\overset{free}{\longrightarrow}③$ and $⑦\overset{open}{\longrightarrow}⑧\overset{close}{\longrightarrow}①$ by $⑦\overset{take}{\longrightarrow}①$. The FTS of the whole vending machine SPL is given in Fig. 3. The feature label of a transition is shown next to its action label, separated by a slash. In these labels (and by conveniency in the rets of this paper), we use the abbreviated feature names from Fig. 2. The transitions are coloured in the same way as the features in Fig. 2.

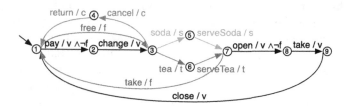

Fig. 3. FTS of the vending machine.

3   Verifying SPLs with FTS

Over the years, we have developed a series of model checking algorithms that exploit the compact structure of FTS to verify sets of requirements on product lines. We first recap the meaning for product line requirements, and then briefly summarise our results.

3.1   What Are Product Lines Requirements?

The requirements of an SPL are requirements imposed over a subset of its products. As such, they can be represented as a formula in temporal logic preceded by a Boolean formula over the SPL features, which represents the set of products whose behaviour must satisfy the temporal formula. As an example, in single systems one can check that "the system can never reach a bad state". The product-line counterpart of this property would be: "all valid products can never reach a bad state". The objective of an SPL verification algorithm is thus to discover all products that do not satisfy a given property, and a proof of violation (i.e. a counterexample) for each of them. One can also extend our queries to quantitative, real-time or even stochastic requirements. For example, the single-product property "is the probability to satisfy the safety requirement greater than 0.5" becomes "what are the products for which the probability to satisfy the safety requirement is greater than 0.5" in the product-line realm.

3.2   How to Exploit the FTS Structure to Model Check Requirements: A Sketch

Let us now illustrate how one can exploit the FTS structure to reason on a classical verification problem: finding all the reachable states. Consider again the vending machine FTS of Fig. 3. State ① is an initial state, and thus reachable by all products. From there, the transition ①$\xrightarrow{pay}$② can only be fired by products in $[\![v \wedge \neg f]\!]$. Transition ②$\xrightarrow{change}$③ can be fired for all products in $[\![v]\!]$, and so state ③ is reachable by the same products as state ②. Proceeding in this way, we compute in one step the reachability relation of s for all the products. The presence of the feature diagrams permits us to ignore products that are not part of the product line. We also observe that if we find a state s reachable by a set of products A and discover later that s can also be reached by a set of product $B \subseteq A$, then it is enough to consider the superset A.

Considering sets of products during the verification makes us move from an enumerative approach to a product line approach, which benefits from the common behaviour of the products. Interestingly, the theoretical complexity of our algorithms is higher than that of their enumerative counterpart. However, due to the structure of the FTS, experiments show that in practice the former is faster (see, e.g., [8] for extended comparisons). Observe that the efficiency of our approach also rely on efficient representation of sets of products. In [8], we showed that the best way is to represent them with Boolean formulas. We also showed that our approach remains efficient in quantitative settings, e.g. when properties are real-time [15] or in case the features are not Boolean [16].

3.3   Summary of Our Results

Let us now briefly summarize the results we have obtained over those six last years. Our first algorithms have mainly focused on extending model checking properties of Linear Temporal Logic (LTL) to FTS [8,10]. We then moved to CTL and symbolic algorithms [9]. We have then proposed extensions of FTS that allow us to reason on more quantitative aspect of systems. This includes real time to specify timing constraints in a timed automaton fashion [15], and probabilities that allows us to make quantitative hypotheses via a combination of FTS and Markov chains [34]. Behavioural relations such as simulation were also extended to FTS. There, one tries to compute the set of products for which two states are in simulation [12]. This allows us, among many other possibilities, to define a CEGAR-based abstraction for FTS [14]. In all those algorithms, the root has always been to efficiently represents pairs of (state,product).

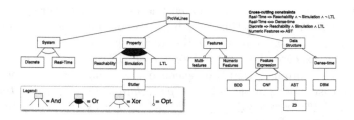

Fig. 4. Features of proveline

Tool. Some of our results have been implemented in ProVeLines: a product line of verification tools for QA on different types of product lines[1]. The structure of the tool is that of an SPL, whose corresponding feature diagram is presented in Fig. 4 (taken from [17]). One can observe that the tool provides several opportunities to describe both systems (discrete, real-time) and requirements (reachability, simulation, LTL). The constraints on the top left of Fig. 4 informs us that using the real-time specification for systems disables the possibility to use LTL and simulation algorithms. Otherwise, this would require the use of dense-time verification algorithms.

Any ProVeLines variant requires at least two artefacts from the user: an FD and an fPromela model. For the former, we use TVL [6,16], one of the latest incarnations of FDs, due to some of its advantages: high expressiveness, formal semantics and tool support. fPromela is a feature-oriented extension of Promela [27], which we defined as a high-level language on top of FTS. An fPromela model thus describes the behaviour of all the products defined by the FD [7,16].

---

[1] Note that prototype tools exist for other results we developed.

4   SPL Testing with FTS

FTSs, as concise models of SPLs behaviours, can also support model-based testing (MBT) activities. In our research we investigated two directions: *(i)* coverage and *(ii)* synergies between SPL testing and mutation analysis.

4.1   SPL Coverage Analysis

Extending Usual Coverage Criteria. Since FTS are extensions of transition systems, a natural research direction was to consider "usual" coverage criteria (e.g., all-states, all-transitions) for product-line test generation [21]. In our work, we modelled test cases in terms of sequences of actions. There are thus *abstract* by nature since in the FTS formalism, actions are simple labels without any input or output. Additionally, an Abstract Test Case (ATC) may not be executable. As we have seen, each transition can only be executed by the set of products that match the associated feature expression. If we consider a sequence of actions, we have to conjunct these feature expressions and check the satisfiability of the resulting expression to know which product(s) can execute this abstract test case. If the formula is not satisfiable, there is no product that can execute the behaviour described in this abstract test case. For example, ATC = {*pay, change, tea, serveTea, take*} leading to the run $①\xrightarrow{pay}②\xrightarrow{change}③\xrightarrow{tea}⑥\xrightarrow{serveTea}⑦\xrightarrow{take}①$, is executable by products in $[\![v \wedge \neg f \wedge v \wedge t \wedge t \wedge f]\!]$, which in turn trivially maps to the empty set. Such a negative test case can be useful to ensure whether an implementation does not allow more products than specified.

Thus, to be executable, an ATC can be executed by at least one product of the product line. We then extend this definition to executable test suites, by stating that they should contain only executable test cases. Equipped with such notions, we can defined product-line coverage as a function that takes a FTS and abstract test suite as parameters and returns a value between 0 and 1. This value represents the ratio between the number of actually covered elements (states, transitions, etc.) and the number of possible ones in the FTS, if the value is 1 then we obtain all-X coverage, where X is the set of elements under consideration for this coverage criterion. When such elements involve transitions, we impose that these transitions are executable by at least one product (see [21] for formal definitions). In our coffee machine, the following test suite both satisfies all-states and all-transitions coverage:

$$\{(pay, change, soda, serveSoda, open, take, close)$$
$$(free, tea, serveTea, take); (free, cancel, return)\}$$

We also experimented using another criteria that is not based on the model structure but on the capture of usage model that describes usages of the system [19]. There are two ways to capture such usages: either by extracting them from logs (such as Apache logs) [20], and assign more importance to more frequent usages or by assiging them directly using a dedicated modelling tool such as

MaTeLO [2]. Technically, these usage models take the form of a Markov chain that can be used to derive the most frequent test cases. There are then run on the FTS to derive the associated product-line coverage metrics. This scenario complements the one proposed by Samih *et al.* [35] who start by selecting a product prior to generate test cases using statistical testing techniques [38]. For more information about these dual scenarios, see [19].

Another interesting aspect that differs from "usual" coverage for single systems is the notion of *P-coverage*. P-coverage represent the ratio between the set of products executable by a given abstract test suite and the set of products derivable in the feature diagram that is $[\![FD]\!]$. Since ATCs relates the two types of coverage (products and their behaviours), their generation is de-facto a *multi-objective* problem. The compactness of the FTS formalism makes it easy for the SPL testing community to study different multi-objective scenarios and compare different criteria.

Multi-objective Coverage. Continuing previous line of work that considered coverage only a the structural (feature diagram) level [25,26,32], we initially started with a rather strange question: "what is the behavioural coverage of structural coverage?" [22]. The idea behind this question is that as some behavioural coverage criteria may be difficult to compute in practice because of their complexity, approximating them with less computationally expensive approaches at the feature diagram level can be of interest. To investigate this question, we measured the behavioural coverage (state, transitions and actions) of two FD coverage criteria: *(i)* pairwise coverage [29,32] that covers any two combination of features and *(ii)* similarity coverage that maximises distances between configurations [1,25]. Results [22] shown that it was indeed possible to cover large parts of behaviour by sampling few configurations (e.g. only 2 products were necessary to achieve all-transitions coverage for the Claroline SPL allowing more than 5,000,000 products). Nevertheless, the resulting test suites are not optimal and more experiments are needed to generalise our results.

Recently, we considered extending similarity at the behavioural level to design search algorithms that maximize both distances between configurations at the FD level and distance between test cases [23]. We considered various distances (Hamming, Anti-Dice, Jaccard, Levhenstein) and both single objective (operating on an initial random set of test cases) and bi-objective (also taking into account distance between products). We seeded our models with random faults to compare the various algorithms. In our models, being bi-objective is not necessary an advantage, and the efficiency seems largely influenced by the choice of the distance function we make. A threat to validity to these conclusions is the fact that our feature diagrams are not heavily constrained, favouring the accidental discovery of dissimilar products.

4.2   Mutation Analysis

A less expected application of FTSs in the field of software testing is mutation analysis [18,23]. Mutation analysis (see [28] for a comprehensive survey) is a technique that assess the quality of test suites by mutating software artifacts (program, models) called *mutants* and measuring the ability of such test suites to distinguish them from the original (we also say that a test case *kills* a mutant) ones. The underlying idea is to mimic a "competent programmer" that would introduce a few mistakes in the implementation of a system. The mutation score measures the ratio of the number of killed mutants divided by the number total mutants for a given test suite. The contribution of FTS to mutation testing is first to model mutants as families [18] and then to exploit the FTS formalism to perform shared execution of the mutants "all-at-once" to speed up analysis [23].

Mutants as SPL Variants. We studied mutation analysis at the model level, where the original system and its mutants can be expressed as transition systems. Model-based mutation complements program-based mutation as they tend to exercise different faults. To generate mutants automatically we design so-called mutation operators. For a transition system, these operators are model transformations that for example remove a transition or replace an action by another one. As we have seen, the features in a FTS add or remove transitions in a similar way. Building on this analogy, we sketched a vision of managing (model) mutants as a SPL to bring all the advantages of FTS and variability modelling to mutation analysis [18]. We describe mutations as features and organise them in a feature diagram, which allows a precise control on the type and number of mutants we allow for analysis. From a behavioural perspective, all the mutants are represented in a centralised model (the FTS), which each eases their management and storage.

Accelerating Mutation Analysis. As noted by Jia and Harman [28], one of the practical obstacles to the development of mutation testing is the cost associated to mutation analysis. Traditional mutation testing proceeds by running every test case on every mutant. Since we need to have a large number of mutants to assess test suites' sensitivity in a meaningful way, analysis time can be huge. In fact, this is equivalent as processing all mutants in isolation like the naive approach is doing for product line model-checking. Of course, an important justification of using the FTS formalism to model mutations is to avoid this naive approach and perform family-based mutation analysis [18]. We implemented this featured model-based mutation analysis recently [23]. The *Featured Mutant Model* (FMM) is thus comprised of a FTS modelling the mutant family and a feature diagram representing all the mutations supported by this family. To perform mutation analysis, we simply run test cases on the FTS. As we have seen, this yields a boolean formula describing all the mutants (in $[\![FD]\!]$) that are killed by this test case. Therefore, we only need to run each test case once on the FTS, rather than on the 2^n individual transition systems associated to this mutant family. Our experiments showed gains between 2.5 and 1,000 times than previous approaches. Additionally, the FMM favours *higher-order mutation*. Higher-order mutation consists in applying several mutation operators on the same model. In the FMM scheme, higher-order mutation is supported allowing certain features to be selected together in a mutant. If we want to restrict ourselves to the first order, we then need to specify that each feature excludes all the other ones. Computing the mutation score require enumerating the instances satisfying the union of formulas gathered for each test case and computing the total number of mutants from the feature diagram. Computing such values may be tricky for large models (even with BDD solvers) and optimisations require to be investigated [23].

4.3   ViBES: A Model-Based Framework for SPL Testing

All our research on model-based testing has been integrated in a framework called ViBES [24]. We designed an XML representation for FTS while the feature diagrams are encoded in TVL [6]. The framework is implemented in JAVA and provides a domain-specific language to create mutations operators and mutant families in a programmer-friendly way. The framework also contains the implementations of test coverage and generation techniques discussed above. Finally, the framework is open-source (MIT Licence) and can be downloaded here: https://projects.info.unamur.be/vibes/.

5   Conclusion

In ths paper, we summarised six years of efforts in harnessing the central problem of SPL analysis: the combinatorial explosion of the number of products to consider. To this end, we introduced featured transiation systems as a compact and efficient representation of the whole behaviour of a SPL. This unique representation of all the products served as a support to a family of verification algorithms itself implemented as a software product-line [17]. We also employed FTS for model-based testing activities such as coverage and test generation and prioritisation. The FTS formalism demonstrated its universality to readily be applide for mutation analysis of single systems, with substantial analysis speedups.

After having had a look on the past, let us have a look in the future. There are several research directions worth of investigation. First we would like to extend our verification algorithms to quantitative software product lines. This requires to extend the FTS formalism to specify quantities [31]. Another interesting information to specify in FTS is probabilities, in order to perform statistical model-checking activities [33]. Such extended FTS formalism is also of interest for testing [19,20]. As is the addition of inputs and outputs for ioco conformance [3]. With respect to mutation, we would like to formally investigate the mutant equivalence problem using exact or approximate simulation techniques [13].

References

1. Al-Hajjaji, M., Thüm, T., Meinicke, J., Lochau, M., Saake, G.: Similarity-based prioritization in software product-line testing. In: SPLC, pp. 197–206. ACM (2014)
2. ALL4TEC - MaTeLo.   http://all4tec.net/index.php/en/model-based-testing/20-markov-test-logic-matelo

3. Beohar, H., Mousavi, M.: Input-output conformance testing based on featured transition systems. In: 29th Annual ACM Symposium on Applied Computing, pp. 1272–1278. ACM (2014)
4. Beohar, H., Varshosaz, M., Mousavi, M.R.: Basic behavioral models for software product lines: expressiveness and testing pre-orders. Sci. Comput. Program. **123**, 42–60 (2016)
5. Classen, A.: Modelling and model checking variability-intensive systems. Ph.D. thesis, University of Namur (FUNDP) (2011)
6. Classen, A., Boucher, Q., Heymans, P.: A text-based approach to feature modelling: syntax and semantics of TVL. SCP **76**, 1130–1143 (2011)
7. Classen, A., Cordy, M., Heymans, P., Legay, A., Schobbens, P.-Y.: Model checking software product lines with SNIP. STTT **14**(5), 589–612 (2012)
8. Classen, A., Cordy, M., Schobbens, P.-Y., Heymans, P., Legay, A., Raskin, J.-F.: Featured transition systems: foundations for verifying variability-intensive systems and their application to LTL model checking. Trans. Softw. Eng. **39**, 1069–1089 (2013)
9. Classen, A., Heymans, P., Schobbens, P.-Y., Legay, A.: Symbolic model checking of software product lines. In: ICSE 2011, pp. 321–330. ACM (2011)
10. Classen, A., Heymans, P., Schobbens, P.-Y., Legay, A., Raskin, J.-F.: Model checking lots of systems: efficient verification of temporal properties in software product lines. In: ICSE 2010, pp. 335–344. ACM (2010)
11. Cordy, M.: Model checking for the masses. Ph.D. thesis, University of Namur (2014)
12. Cordy, M., Classen, A., Heymans, P., Schobbens, P.-Y., Legay, A.: Managing evolution in software product lines: a model-checking perspective. In: VaMoS 2012, pp. 183–191. ACM (2012)
13. Cordy, M., Classen, A., Perrouin, G., Heymans, P., Schobbens, P.-Y., Legay, A.: Simulation-based abstractions for software product-line model checking. In: ICSE 2012, pp. 672–682. IEEE (2012)
14. Cordy, M., Heymans, P., Legay, A., Schobbens, P.-Y., Dawagne, B., Leucker, M.: Counterexample guided abstraction refinement of product-line behavioural models. In: FSE 2014. ACM (2014)
15. Cordy, M., Heymans, P., Schobbens, P.-Y., Legay, A.: Behavioural modelling and verification of real-time software product lines. In: SPLC 2012. ACM (2012)
16. Cordy, M., Schobbens, P.-Y., Heymans, P., Legay, A.: Beyond boolean product-line model checking: dealing with feature attributes and multi-features. In: ICSE 2013, pp. 472–481. IEEE (2013)
17. Cordy, M., Schobbens, P.-Y., Heymans, P., Legay, A.: Provelines: a product-line of verifiers for software product lines. In: SPLC 2013, pp. 141–146. ACM (2013)
18. Devroey, X., Perrouin, G., Cordy, M., Papadakis, M., Legay, A., Schobbens, P.: A variability perspective of mutation analysis. In: SIGSOFT FSE, pp. 841–844. ACM (2014)
19. Devroey, X., Perrouin, G., Cordy, M., Samih, H., Legay, A., Schobbens, P.-Y., Heymans, P.: Statistical prioritization for software product line testing: an experience report. Software & Systems Modeling, pp. 1–19 (2015)
20. Devroey, X., Perrouin, G., Cordy, M., Schobbens, P., Legay, A., Heymans, P.: Towards statistical prioritization for software product lines testing. In: VaMoS, pp. 10:1–10:7. ACM (2014)
21. Devroey, X., Perrouin, G., Legay, A., Cordy, M., Schobbens, P.-Y., Heymans, P.: Coverage criteria for behavioural testing of software product lines. In: Margaria, T., Steffen, B. (eds.) ISoLA 2014. LNCS, vol. 8802, pp. 336–350. Springer, Heidelberg (2014). doi:10.1007/978-3-662-45234-9_24

22. Devroey, X., Perrouin, G., Legay, A., Schobbens, P., Heymans, P.: Covering SPL behaviour with sampled configurations: an initial assessment. In: VaMoS, p. 59. ACM (2015)

23. Devroey, X., Perrouin, G., Papadakis, M., Legay, A., Schobbens, P., Heymans, P.: Featured model-based mutation analysis. In: ICSE, pp. 655–666. ACM (2016)

24. Devroey, X., Perrouin, G., Schobbens, P., Heymans, P.: Poster: vibes, transition system mutation made easy. In: ICSE, vol. 2, pp. 817–818. IEEE Computer Society (2015)

25. Henard, C., Papadakis, M., Perrouin, G., Klein, J., Heymans, P., Traon, Y.L.: Bypassing the combinatorial explosion: using similarity to generate and prioritize t-wise test configurations for software product lines. IEEE Trans. Softw. Eng. **40**(7), 650–670 (2014)

26. Henard, C., Papadakis, M., Perrouin, G., Klein, J., Traon, Y.L.: Multi-objective test generation for software product lines. In: SPLC, pp. 62–71. ACM (2013)

27. Holzmann, G.J., Model, T.S.: Checker: Primer and Reference Manual. Addison-Wesley, New York (2004)

28. Jia, Y., Harman, M.: An analysis and survey of the development of mutation testing. IEEE TSE **37**(5), 649–678 (2011)

29. Johansen, M.F., Haugen, Ø., Fleurey, F.: Properties of realistic feature models make combinatorial testing of product lines feasible. In: Whittle, J., Clark, T., Kühne, T. (eds.) MODELS 2011. LNCS, vol. 6981, pp. 638–652. Springer, Heidelberg (2011). doi:10.1007/978-3-642-24485-8_47

30. Kang, K., Cohen, S., Hess, J., Novak, W., Peterson, S.: Feature-oriented domain analysis (FODA) feasibility study. Technical report CMU/SEI-90-TR-21 (1990)

31. Olaechea, R., Fahrenberg, U., Atlee, J.M., Legay, A.: Long-term average cost in featured transition systems. In: Proceedings of the 20th International Systems and Software Product Line Conference, SPLC 2016, pp. 109–118. ACM, New York, NY, USA (2016)

32. Perrouin, G., Sen, S., Klein, J., Baudry, B., Traon, Y.L.: Automated and scalable t-wise test case generation strategies for software product lines. In: ICST, pp. 459–468. IEEE Computer Society (2010)

33. Rodrigues, G.N., Alves, V., Nunes, V., Lanna, A., Cordy, M., Schobbens, P., Sharifloo, A.M., Legay, A.: Modeling and verification for probabilistic properties in software product lines. In: HASE, pp. 173–180. IEEE Computer Society (2015)

34. Rodrigues, G.N., Alves, V., Nunes, V., Lanna, A., Cordy, M., Schobbens, P.-Y., Sharifloo, A.M., Legay, A.: Modeling and verification for probabilistic properties in software product lines. In: Proceedings of the 16th International Symposium on High Assurance Systems Engineering (2015)

35. Samih, H., Bogusch, R.: MPLM - MaTeLo product line manager. In: Proceedings of the 18th International Software Product Line Conference: Companion Volume for Workshops, Demonstrations and Tools, SPLC 2014, vol. 2, pp. 138–142. ACM, New York, NY, USA (2014)

36. Schobbens, P.-Y., Heymans, P., Trigaux, J.-C., Bontemps, Y., Diagrams, F.: A survey and a formal semantics. In: RE 2006, pp. 139–148 (2006)

37. Vardi, M.Y., Wolper, P.: An automata-theoretic approach to automatic program verification. In: LICS 1986, pp. 332–344. IEEE CS (1986)

38. Whittaker, J., Thomason, G., Michael, A.: Markov chain model for statistical software testing. IEEE Trans. Softw. Eng. **20**(10), 812–824 (1994)

Domain-Specific Languages: A Systematic Mapping Study

Marjan Mernik[✉]

Faculty of Electrical Engineering and Computer Science, University of Maribor,
Smetanova Ulica 17, 2000 Maribor, Slovenia
marjan.mernik@um.si

Abstract. Domain-specific languages (DSLs) assist a software developer (or end-user) in writing a program using idioms that are similar to the abstractions found in a specific problem domain. Indeed, the enhanced software productivity and reliability benefits that have been reported from DSL usage are hard to ignore and DSLs are flourishing. However, tool support for DSLs is lacking when compared to the capabilities provided for standard General-Purpose Languages (GPLs). For example, support for unit testing of a DSL program, as well as DSL debuggers, are rare. A Systematic Mapping Study (SMS) has been performed to better understand the DSL research field, identify research trends, and any possible open issues. In this talk I will first introduce DSLs by discussing when and how to develop DSLs, then results from SMS will be presented along with open DSL problems such as lacking tool support for DSLs and difficulties in combining DSLs.

1 Introduction

"Domain-specific languages (DSLs) are languages tailored to a specific application domain. They offer substantial gains in expressiveness and ease of use compared with general-purpose programming languages in their domain of application [25].*"* As such, DSLs [10,13,19,25,26] become an emerging popular area of research within the field of Software Engineering (SE), and one of the more important constituents of software development methodologies such as: Generative Programming, Product Lines, Software Factories, Language-Oriented Programming, and Model-Driven Engineering (MDE) [29,30]. Software Language Engineering (SLE) [15] is a young engineering discipline with the aim of establishing systematic and rigorous approaches to the development, use, and maintenance of computer languages (including DSLs). As such, it is strongly believed that DSL development should be properly engineered. The following development phases are usually associated with DSLs: decision, domain analysis, design, implementation, deployment, testing and maintenance. Each phase has their own inputs and deliveries, which are discussed in more details in [6,25].

DSL researchers have published their works either under broader communities such as programming language research, or within specific application domains

© Springer International Publishing AG 2017
B. Steffen et al. (Eds.): SOFSEM 2017, LNCS 10139, pp. 464–472, 2017.
DOI: 10.1007/978-3-319-51963-0_36

for which DSLs were developed (e.g., embedded systems, high-performance computing, electronic commerce, robotics). Furthermore, DSLs can be developed in more varied ways than General-Purpose Languages (GPLs). For example, during the design phase a new DSL can be based on already existing language (language exploitation pattern [25]), or designed from scratch without any relationship to an existing language (language invention pattern [25]). Whilst, independently from a design phase a DSL can be implemented by different approaches (e.g., interpreter, compiler, preprocessing, embedding, extensible compiler/interpreter, COTS, hybrid [25]), each having its own merits [18]. Due to the fact that research on DSLs is spreading into many software development methodologies, vast areas of application domains, and different development approaches, it is hard to obtain a complete knowledge of the DSL research field, and foreseen DSL research trends. Therefore, the main objective of the Systematic Mapping Study (SMS) on DSLs [23] was of better understanding the DSL research field, identifying research trends, and possible open issues. In this invited talk the results of SMS for DSLs [23] have been summarized and open DSL problems are discussed.

2   Summary on SMS for DSLs and Its Results

A systematic review (SR) is a secondary study that reviews primary studies with the aim of synthesizing evidence related to a specific research question. Several forms of SRs exists [14], depending on the depth of reviewing the primary studies (e.g., performing quality assessment of the primary studies), and on the specificities of research questions:

- Systematic literature review (SLR): *"A form of secondary study that uses a well-defined methodology to identify, analyse and interpret all available evidence related to a specific research question in a way that is unbiased and (to a degree) repeatable* [14].*"*
- Systematic mapping study (SMS): *"A broad review of primary studies in a specific topic area that aims to identify what evidence is available on the topic* [14].*"*
- Tertiary review (TR): *"which is a systematic review of systematic reviews* [14].*"*

Hence, SLRs are more driven by specific research questions (e.g., is one particular approach better than other), whilst research questions in SMS are of a higher-level (e.g., which empirical methods have been used, which research topics have been addressed). A more detailed definition of SMS can be found in [28]: *"The main goal of systematic mapping studies is to provide an overview of a research area, and identifing the quantity and type of research and results available within it. Often one wants to map the frequencies of publication over time to see trends."*

SMS on DSLs [23] has been based on the guidelines presented in [14,28] and using good practices from previous similar SMSs. The protocol is available at [22]. The following simplified structure for performing SMS has been suggested in [28] and was used in study [23], as well:

– defining research questions,
– conducting a search for primary studies,
– screening primary studies based on inclusion/exclusion criteria,
– classifying the primary studies, and
– data extraction and aggregation.

The objective of study [23] was to obtain a comprehensive overview of DSL research since the survey paper on DSLs [25] was published more than 10 years ago. The following research questions were defined for elaborating on this overall goal.

RQ1 Type of contribution: What is the main contribution of DSL studies with respect to techniques/methods, tools, processes, and measurements? By answering *RQ1* we were able to assess whether the DSL community is more focused on developing new techniques/methods for particular DSL development phases, or on developing new tools for DSL development, or on DSL processes, or on DSL measurements.

RQ2 Type of research: What types of research methods have been used in DSL studies? By answering *RQ2* we were able to assess maturity within the field (e.g., whether DSL researchers have been using empirical or non-empirical research methods; whether they are using controlled experiments).

RQ3 Focus area: Which research topics have been investigated in DSL studies? By answering *RQ3* we were able to identify those DSL development phases (domain analysis, design, implementation, validation, maintenance) that are currently underrepresented.

The following elementary search string was used in [23]:

$$(\text{``}domain - specific\ language\text{''}\ OR\ \text{``}DSL\text{''})$$

$$AND\ year\ >\ 2005\ AND\ year\ <\ 2013$$

The search string was applied on the following set of DLs (Table 1) after following the protocol [22].

Table 1. Preliminary identification of relevant publications

Digital library	Accessible at	No. of publications
ISI web of science	http://sub3.webofknowledge.com	792
ACM digital library	http://dl.acm.org	361
		Σ 1153

The following inclusion criteria were used:

– study must have addressed DSL research,
– peer reviewed studies had been published in journals, conferences, and workshops,

- study must be written in English,
- study must be accessible electronically, and
- computer science literature.

The exclusion criteria were:

- irrelevant publications that lay outside the core DSL research field, which also excluded DSMLs, modelware, and MDE publications, visual/graphical languages (based on graph-grammars or other formalisms) or those mentioning DSL as future work;
- non-peer reviewed studies (abstracts, tutorials, editorials, slides, talks, tool demonstrations, posters, panels, keynotes, technical reports);
- peer-reviewed but not published in journals, conferences, workshops (e.g., PhD thesis, books, patents);
- publications not in English;
- electronically non-accessible; and
- non-computer science literature.

The inclusion and exclusion criteria were applied to the titles, keywords, and abstracts. In those case where it wasn't completely clear from the title, keywords, and abstract that a publication really addressed the DSL research then such publications were temporarily included but might be excluded during the next phase (classification phase) when the whole publication (not only the abstract) had been read. Hence, only publications that were clearly outside the scope were excluded during this phase. After the screening of 1153 publications (see Table 1) 713 publications satisfied the aforementioned criteria and entered into the next phase - classification, where an additional 323 publications were then excluded. Hence, altogether 390 primary studies were classified and the main findings were:

- The DSL community has been more interested in developing new techniques/methods (79.3%) that supported different DSL development phases, rather than investing in developing new DSL tools (6.9%). Primary studies about integration of DSLs into other SE processes have also been rare (10.5%), whilst studies about measuring the effectiveness of DSL approaches have been almost non-existent (3.3%). Indeed new DSL tools have rarely been developed over the past 10 years (an example of a new tool is Neverlang [31]). The matured tools (e.g., ANTLR [27], Stratego/XT [3]) have merely been enhanced with new features. Recent comparisons between DSL tools has have been discussed in [9]. Interestingly, a DSML tool Xtext [7] has been used for grammar-based DSLs as well. Hence, a small percentage (6.9%) should not be of great concern. On the other hand, it is quite clear that there is a lack of DSL research regarding processes and measurements. More emphasis should be placed in the near future on integrating DSLs into other SE processes, as well as about measuring the effectiveness of DSL approaches.
- The empirical research (72.8%) has prevailed over non-empirical research (27.2%). This is an indication of the maturity of DSL research. Opinion and philosophical/conceptual primary studies have been rare (about 2.1%) in DSL

research. The same is true for experience reports (9%). It can also be concluded that the presented ideas have also been implemented at least at the level of a prototype and hence only solution proposals have been rare (16.1%). Whilst the ratio between empirical and non-empirical research (72.8% vs. 27.2%) has been much higher than within some other research fields and hence satisfying, but this can't be claimed for the ratio between validation and evaluation DSL research (66.1% vs. 6.7%). There has been a clear lack of evaluation research into all types of contribution (technique/method, tool, process, measurement). A need for empirical evaluation in software modeling research is discussed in [4], where it was found that the rigour of empirically-validated research has been rather weak. In particular, the authors found only 4% of controlled experiments within the research works published during the period 2006–2010 at conferences on Model Driven Engineering Languages and Systems. This number is even slightly higher than the number we found (1.3% of controlled experiments) and further indicates, as in [4], that researchers within the DSL community are more interested in creating new techniques than they are in performing rigorous empirical evaluations (e.g., [20]).

- The primary studies usually discussed the following three DSL development phases: domain analysis, design and implementation, whilst validation and maintenance have been rarely presented. Indeed, in many primary studies we found a brief section on domain analysis identifying the main concepts of DSL under development followed by the design of DSL syntax and semantics and finalising with implementation details. On the other hand, there has been a lack of DSL research about domain analysis (only 1.3% of primary studies have concentrated solely on domain analysis). Of particular concern should be the lack of DSL research within the validation phase. DSLs had rarely been validated (e.g., by end-users) assuming that the developed DSLs were perfectly tailored for domains, as well as fitting end-users' requirements [11]. However, this is far from true. DSL under development should have been validated by empirical studies, involvement of end-users, or by the psychology of programming research. Recent attempts in this direction is work [1].

- Only 5.7% of primary studies that included domain analysis had used a formal domain analysis approach. Hence, formal domain analysis methods had been rarely used in DSL development and domain analysis had usually been done informally and probably in an incomplete manner. There is an urgent need in DSL research for identifying the reasons for lack of using formal methods within domain analysis and possible solutions for improvement. The first observation might be that information gathered during domain analysis cannot be automatically used in the language design process. Another reason might also be that complete domain analysis is too complex and outside of software engineers' capabilities. DSL researchers should look into available domain analysis tool and investigate how they can be accommodated for supporting the DSL domain analysis phase. Furthermore, only 1.3% of primary studies used in our SMS concentrated solely on the domain analysis phase. Investigating the domain analysis phase has clearly been insufficient.

- Only 16.8% of primary studies that included the design phase used formal approaches for describing syntax and semantics. Although internal DSLs, which rarely require formal description as they rely on (formal) description of existing language, comprised 47.8% out of 83.2% informal cases, the number of DSLs using formal syntax and especially semantic description had still been low. Again, the DSL community should identify the reasons and works towards improvement.
- Amongst the more frequently used implementation patterns have been the embedding approach (34.3%) and the compiler approach (28.1%). Other implementation approaches had been less frequently used: preprocessing (15%), COTS (7.9%), interpreter (7.9%), hybrid (3.9%), and the extensible compiler/interpreter approach (2.9%). Hence, this study doesn't support some claims that the embedding approach has prevailed over DSL implementation approaches (e.g., "*In fact, most of the common DSLs used today are designed as pure embedded programs within the structure of an existing programming language* [12]").

3   Some Open DSL Problems: Lack of DSL Tools and Composability of DSLs

Software tools are indispensable in any software development paradigm; software development using DSLs is not an exception. The construction of a DSL compiler or interpreter is only the first piece of the toolchain needed to assist software developers or end-user programmers. A DSL programmer also needs tools to easily discover the existence of software errors and locate them in a DSL program. The paucity of such tools can be one of the major factors that may prevent wider acceptance of DSLs in the software industry. Building DSL tools from scratch for each particular DSL can be time consuming, error prone, and costly. But, as can be observed in the case of functional languages [32], the lack of debuggers and profilers, inadequate support by Integrated Development Environments (IDEs), and poor interoperability with mainstream languages can be contributing factors for resistance of DSLs in the software industry. Up to now there has been little evidence about building debuggers, profilers, automated testing and refactoring tools for DSLs [23], although some attempts already exist [5,16,17,21,33,34]. Overall, the utility of a new DSL will be seriously diminished if supporting tools needed by a software developer are not available.

Any language description, formal or informal, should be amenable for refinement and composition. Unfortunately, this is usually not the case, making DSLs harder to adopt to frequent changes [24]. To be able to design and implement DSLs more easily, modular, extensible, and reusable language descriptions are needed. A language engineer may want to include new language features incrementally as a DSL evolves. Moreover, a language engineer may like to build a DSL simply by reusing different language description modules (language components, language fragments), such as modules for expressions, declarations, as well as to reuse and extend previous language descriptions. Thus, language description composition is a high level goal that still needs much work in the area of SLE. In the paper [8] it has been pointed out that language composition has not obtained enough attention, is still not well-understood, and associated terminology is confusing. All of these points suggest that research in this area is not yet mature. Language composability has been identified in [8] not as a property of languages themselves, but as a property of language description (e.g., how language specifications, formal or informal, can be composed together). To enable language composition, a language description has to be reused as is; that is, any changes to a language description are not allowed, but language descriptions can be extended or additional glue code can be written. This is much harder to achieve using informal language specifications [2] than using formal specifications. But, the challenge in formal language description is still to support modularity and abstraction in a manner that allows incremental changes to be made as easily as possible. Only then the vision of language-oriented software development will be achieved.

4   Conclusions

SMS on DSLs [23] is providing the DSL research community with an unbiased, objective and systematic overview of DSL research done during period 2006–2012. We strongly believe that within each research topic such SMSs should be periodically performed to make researchers aware of the amount of work done, the progress, and to find out possible gaps in the research. The main findings of our SMS on DSLs are:

- Research about DSL integration with other SE process is lacking, as well as measuring the effectiveness of DSL approaches.
- Clear lack of evaluation research, in particular controlled experiments.
- Amongst different DSL development phases the following phases have been insufficiently investigated: domain analysis, validation and maintenance.
- Lack of use regarding formal methods within domain analysis and in the semantic description of DSLs.

We encourage the DSL researchers to start addressing the identified gaps to enable practitioners to understand the effectiveness and efficiencies of DSLs.

References

1. Barišić, A., Amaral, V., Goulão, M., Barroca, B.: Evaluating the usability of domain-specific languages. In: Mernik, M. (ed.) Chapter 14, Formal, Practical Aspects of Domain-Specific Languages: Recent Developments, pp. 386–407 (2013)
2. Barrett, E., Bolz, C.F., Tratt, L.: Approaches to interpreter composition. Comput. Lang. Syst. Struct. **44C**, 199–217 (2015)

3. Bravenboer, M., Kalleberg, K.T., Vermaas, R., Visser, E.: Stratego/XT 0.17. A language and toolset for program transformation. Sci. Comput. Program. **72**(1–2), 52–70 (2008)

4. Carver, J.C., Syriani, E., Gray, J.: Assessing the frequency of empirical evaluation in software modeling research. In: Proceedings of the First Workshop on Experiences and Empirical Studies in Software Modelling, Paper 5 (2011)

5. Chiş, A., Denker, M., Gîrba, T., Nierstrasz, O.: Practical domain-specific debuggers using the moldable debugger framework. Comput. Lang. Syst. Struct. **44A**, 89–113 (2015)

6. Čeh, I., Črepinšek, M., Kosar, T., Mernik, M.: Ontology driven development of domain-specific languages. Comput. Sci. Inf. Syst. **8**(2), 317–342 (2011)

7. Efftinge, S., Völter, M.: oAW xText: a framework for textual DSLs. In: Workshop on Modeling Symposium at Eclipse Summit (2006)

8. Erdweg, S., Giarrusso, P.G., Rendel, T.: Language composition untangled. In: Proceedings of Workshop on Language Descriptions, Tools and Applications (LDTA 2012) (2012)

9. Erdweg, S., van der Storm, T., Völter, M., Tratt, L., Bosman, R., Cook, W.R., Gerritsen, A., Hulshout, A., Kelly, S., Loh, A., Konat, G., Molina, P.J., Palatnik, M., Pohjonen, R., Schindler, E., Schindler, K., Solmi, R., Vergu, V., Visser, E., van der Vlist, K., Wachsmuth, G., van der Woning, J.: Evaluating and comparing language workbenches: existing results and benchmarks for the future. Comput. Lang. Syst. Struct. **44A**, 24–47 (2015)

10. Fowler, M.: Domain Specific Languages. Addison-Wesley, Boston (2010)

11. Gabriel, P., Goulão, M., Amaral, V.: Do software languages engineers evaluate their languages? In: XIII Congreso Iberoamericano en "Software Engineering" (CIbSE 2010), pp. 149–162 (2010)

12. Ghosh, D.: DSL for the uninitiated. Commun. ACM **54**(7), 44–50 (2011)

13. Karakoidas, V., Mitropoulos, D., Louridas, P., Spinellis, D.: A type-safe embedding of SQL into java using the extensible compiler framework J%. Comput. Lang. Syst. Struct. **41**, 1–20 (2015)

14. Kitchenham, B., Charters, S.: Guidelines for performing systematic literature reviews in software engineering. EBSE Techical Report, Keele University (2007)

15. Kleppe, A.: Software Language Engineering: Creating Domain-Specific Languages using Metamodels. Addison-Wesley Professional, USA (2008)

16. Kolomvatsos, K., Valkanas, G., Hadjiefthymiades, S.: Debugging applications created by a domain specific language: the IPAC case. J. Syst. Softw. **85**(4), 932–943 (2012)

17. Kos, T., Mernik, M., Kosar, T.: Test automation of a measurement system using a domain-specific modelling language. J. Syst. Softw. **111**, 74–88 (2016)

18. Kosar, T., Martínez López, P.E., Barrientos, P.A., Mernik, M.: A preliminary study on various implementation approaches of domain-specific language. Inf. Softw. Technol. **50**(5), 390–405 (2008)

19. Kosar, T., Oliveira, N., Mernik, M., Varanda Pereira, M.J., Črepinšek, M., da Cruz, D., Henriques, P.R.: Comparing general-purpose and domain-specific languages: an empirical study. Comput. Sci. Inf. Syst. **7**(2), 247–264 (2010)

20. Kosar, T., Mernik, M., Carver, J.C.: Program comprehension of domain-specific and general-purpose languages: comparison using a family of experiments. Empirical Softw. Eng. **17**(3), 276–304 (2012)

21. Kosar, T., Mernik, M., Gray, J., Kos, T.: Debugging measurement systems using a domain-specific modeling language. Comput. Ind. **65**(4), 622–635 (2014)

22. Kosar, T., Bohra, S., Mernik, M.: Protocol of systematic mapping study on DSLs. http://lpm.feri.um.si/projects/DSL_SMS_Protocol.pdf
23. Kosar, T., Bohra, S., Mernik, M.: Domain-specific languages: a systematic mapping study. Inf. Softw. Technol. **71**, 77–91 (2016)
24. Mernik, M., Žumer, V.: Incremental programming language development. Comput. Lang. Syst. Struct. **31**(1), 1–16 (2005)
25. Mernik, M., Heering, J., Sloane, A.M.: When and how to develop domain-specific languages. ACM Comput. Surv. **37**(4), 316–344 (2005)
26. Mernik, M.: Formal and Practical Aspects of Domain-Specific Languages: Recent Developments. IGI Global (2013)
27. Parr, T., Patterns, L.I.: Create your own domain-specific and general programming languages. In: The Pragmatic Bookshelf (2010)
28. Petersen, K., Feldt, R., Mujtaba, S., Mattsson, M.: Systematic mapping studies in software engineering. In: Proceedings of the 12th International Conference on Evaluation and Assessment in Software Engineering (EASE 2008), pp. 71–80 (2008)
29. da Silva, A.R.: Model-driven engineering: a survey supported by a unified conceptual model. Comput. Lang. Syst. Struct. **43**, 139–155 (2015)
30. Sprinkle, J., Mernik, M., Tolvanen, J.-P., Spinellis, D.: What kinds of nails need a domain-specific hammer? IEEE Softw. **26**(4), 15–18 (2009)
31. Vacchi, E., Cazzola, W.: Neverlang: a framework for feature-oriented language development. Comput. Lang. Syst. Struct. **43**, 1–40 (2015)
32. Wadler, P.: Why no one uses functional languages. CM Sigplan Not. **33**(8), 23–27 (1998)
33. Wu, H., Gray, J., Mernik, M.: Grammar-driven generation of domain-specific language debuggers. Softw. Pract. Experience **38**(10), 1073–1103 (2008)
34. Wu, H., Gray, J., Mernik, M.: Unit testing for domain-specific languages. In: Taha, W.M. (ed.) DSL 2009. LNCS, vol. 5658, pp. 125–147. Springer, Heidelberg (2009). doi:10.1007/978-3-642-03034-5_7

Characterising Malicious Software
with High-Level Behavioural Patterns

Jana Šťastná[✉] and Martin Tomášek

Department of Computers and Informatics, Technical University of Košice,
Letná 9, 042 00 Košice, Slovakia
{jana.stastna,martin.tomasek}@tuke.sk

Abstract. Current research trends concerning malicious software indicate preferring malware behaviour over malware structure analysis. Detection is heading to methods employing malware models on higher level of abstraction, not purely on the level of program's code. Specification of applicable level of abstraction for investigation and detection of malware may present a serious challenge. Many approaches claim using high-level abstraction of malware behaviour but they are still based on sequences of instructions which form the malicious program. Techniques which rely on syntactic representation potentially fail whenever malware writers employ mutation or obfuscation of malicious code. Our work presents a different strategy. We utilised freely available information about malicious programs which were already inspected and tried to find patterns in malware behaviour, which are not bound to syntactic representation of malicious samples and so should withstand malware mutation on the syntactic level.

Keywords: Malware analysis · Behavioural patterns · High-level representation · Syntax-independent

1 Introduction

Malware classes and description of their notable members form many computer security publications, however, there are researchers, e.g. Obrst, Chase, and Markeloff, who indicate that malware ontology based on classes is not useful in some situations, e.g. for *"malware instances that exhibit either behaviours from multiple classes or novel behaviours not associated with any recognized class"* [11]. Hybrid malicious software that exhibits behaviour of several classes is however a quite common phenomenon these days. Gregio *et al.* emphasize that malware research community needs to address behavioural aspects of malware [7].

Instead of dealing with malware categorization, we believe looking at malicious characteristics and behaviour is more important. As a matter of fact, malware is placed into categories based on its behaviour and specific features. The problem is that distinguishing malware from harmless software is often done by checking whether the analysed sample corresponds to some malware signature.

© Springer International Publishing AG 2017
B. Steffen et al. (Eds.): SOFSEM 2017, LNCS 10139, pp. 473–484, 2017.
DOI: 10.1007/978-3-319-51963-0_37

Traditional malware signature is based on syntactic representation of malicious features taken from analysed samples - a concentrated representation of a harmful program. Malware authors adapted to detection techniques which use syntactic signatures by employing code obfuscation and mutation. Computer security specialists and malware analysts struggle with mutating malware which avoids detection. In our opinion, they need to adapt to the situation and instead of retaining research of malware's syntactic features, they should try to turn their attention to behavioural aspects of malware, which are harder to obfuscate and less likely to mutate in new variants.

From the long-term perspective our research aims at formulating malware models - behavioural signatures which will be independent from syntactic representation of malicious samples and withstand code mutation, obfuscation, and allow researchers to use any analytic tool they prefer to record malicious behaviour while letting them experiment with various detection mechanisms.

In this paper we address the problem of how detailed the behavioural analysis of malware has to be in order to find the features relevant for distinguishing various malware types or malware from harmless software (Sect. 2). We explored number of actions performed by 34 099 unique software samples (malicious and also harmless) and analysed whether those are manifested in some kind of pattern (Sect. 3). While we try to answer one question, several other emerge, so we outline them also (Sect. 4). As our contributions in this paper we state the following:

- We address malware behaviour research on an abstract level, by analysing number of general actions performed by malicious samples (Sect. 3.2).
- We experimentally demonstrate whether such high-level malware analysis can present characteristic features which differentiate malware infiltrations one from another, and we suggest a notation for describing these behavioural patterns (Sect. 3.3).

2   Related Work and Current Issues

There are several techniques for malware analysis and detection based on rather behavioural aspects, which are described in a survey [6] by Egele *et al.*:

- *Function call monitoring* allows to record which specific functions (e.g. Windows API and Windows Native API functions, system calls) were called by analysed sample.
- *Function Parameter Analysis* is focused on current values of parameters of called functions, and their relationship with return values of functions called previously.
- *Information Flow Tracking* examines usage or manipulation of specified data, which are tainted with labels, during execution of analysed program.
- *Instruction Trace* allows to examine details in behaviour of the sample at the level of machine instructions.

Mohd Shaid and Maarof summarised methods of observing malware behaviour [9], specifically as monitoring changes in resources of operating system at the time of malware execution, extraction of system call sequences, input and output requests initiated by malware, and network activity. They point out that some malware samples perform minimum network actions or do not exhibit them at all. That is why malware detection should not depend on one type of behaviour, otherwise it would be inhibited because of missing data.

It seems that extraction of malicious behaviour from system calls is a frequently used technique. In accordance with method used for system calls extraction, this type of detection technique is either static or dynamic. Static extraction of system calls was investigated e.g. in a work of Ding *et al.* [5]. They collected system calls from Windows PE file's header, specifically from import table. However, not all system API calls are necessarily listed in PE header. For example, encrypted or compressed malware does not have a complete list of used system calls in the PE header or the list may not correspond to real system calls usage. Authors [5] observed in their experiment that several frequent segments from system calls sequences appeared beside malware also in harmless samples, and discriminative power of these segments was quite high in both kinds of samples.

Wagener *et al.* described in their work [15] a method for creating models of malware behaviour. Before they started analysing a malware sample, they recorded the initial state of the virtual environment in which the sample was going to execute. After the experiment, they again recorded state of the system. By comparing the initial and final state of the system, they obtained a first overview of how the investigated sample affected the system. In addition to that, their analytic system generated reports about execution of the sample. At the end, they were able to extract executed system calls from the collected data and look for similarities among analysed samples based on system calls.

Dynamic system calls extraction is compared with the static technique in an experiment of Yuxin *et al.* [17]. They explain that static extraction is carried out in three stages: First the program is decompiled into assembly language, next control-flow graphs (CFG) are extracted from symbolic instructions and finally system calls are extracted from CFG. Dynamic method only analyses currently executed program's trace, which is a disadvantage, but it is able to reveal encrypted or compressed malware. Comparison of these two approaches showed that static extraction of system calls is more precise than dynamic extraction, but it consumes more time.

According to Lu *et al.* the modern way to represent malware behaviour is by creating a behaviour graph, which shows how information flow between system calls that the program executes [8]. Again, encryption and obfuscation of these information complicates usage of this technique.

An approach presented by Alam et al. [1] utilises control-flow graph (CFG) together with a certain level of code abstraction. A disassembled program's code is translated into optimized Malware Analysis Intermediate Language (MAIL). The optimization lies e.g. in elimination of dead-code segments. MAIL program is then annotated with patterns and from this representation CFGs are built for every function in the program. If a program matches predefined amount of control-flow graphs from representative malicious sample at a predefined threshold, then the program is detected as malicious. To test the system authors collected 1020 malicious metamorphic samples and 2330 harmless (benign) programs. We deem it contributory that a large amount of harmless samples was used, for this usually corresponds to a real-life situation of basic users. On the other hand, malicious programs belonged to only 3 families of metamorphic viruses. Samples used for training the detection engine were also chosen from the same set and their amount was rather low (first 25 samples, in the second stage 125 samples). In the end it is not surprising that the detection rate reached 99.6% and false positive ratio 4%. How successful it would be when testing malware from different families or even completely new kind of threat, we can only speculate.

Obfuscation and packing is a common problem which obstructs malware's code analysis. Based on statistics provided by Shadowserver, from total 73 267 493 malware samples[1] they acquired during time period of 90 days[2], 19 128 261 samples (which makes around 26%) were packed[3] by some of 10 mostly popular packers of that time period. Only those top 10 packers are listed for the statistic, so we expect that overall amount of packed samples was in fact higher since much more packing software exists, even if with smaller representation of samples. In some cases packers remain unidentified because malware writers implement custom packing solutions which do not correspond to any known tool, as noted also by Shadowserver.

Concerning problems with packers, results of our previous work [14] showed that distinguishing malicious software from harmless software based on the usage of packers is non-viable, since several packers are preferred not only by malware writers, but also by developers who provide their utility software on the internet. Moreover, we observed numerous samples which were obscured by one packer repeatedly in several layers or even diverse packers were employed to obstruct analysis even of harmless samples.

Moser *et al.* showed that it is possible to inhibit analysis of control-flow and data-flow in programs with obfuscation techniques which hide locations of data and data usage [10].

With these anti-analysis measures applied, techniques based on observing malware behaviour with static analysis, or methods employing other information obtained solely by static analysis, may not present results of desired quality. Defensive mechanisms of malware have to be considered in analysis and where static analysis may fail, dynamic analysis or combination of both approaches will handle malicious samples with no problem.

Also a level of abstraction on which malware behaviour is represented is a matter of debate. Bailey *et al.* question adequacy of malware behaviour extraction based on system calls. They claim that system calls are too low-level to pro-

---

[1] https://www.shadowserver.org/wiki/pmwiki.php/Stats/Malware.

[2] Data obtained 01/08/2016.

[3] https://www.shadowserver.org/wiki/pmwiki.php/Stats/PackerStatistics.

vide meaningful information, and that their level of abstraction is not suitable for comprehensive description of malware [2]. They describe malicious behaviour by analysing changes of the state of a testing system.

3   Searching Malware Analysis Data for Behavioural Patterns

Our intention is to study malware behaviour on as high level of abstraction as possible and employ lower-level data like system calls or program traces only when it becomes necessary.

3.1   Malware Behaviour Categories

Although dynamic analysis is not fully reliable, it allows to detect and observe actual behaviour, which is deeply hidden when analysing the same program through its obfuscated executable code. According to Wu *et al.*, operations that represent malware behaviour alter state (status) of the infected system [16]. Based on the type of alteration, they divided malware operations into 4 categories: (1) *File actions*, (2) *Process actions*, (3) *Network actions*, (4) *Registry actions.*

Unfortunately, Wu *et al.* do not describe the environment in which malicious samples were investigated nor the methods used to carry out the analysis. However, it turned out that these categories of malware operations are used also in the work of Bailey *et al.* [2] aimed at malware analysis and classification, Rieck *et al.* [12], Wagener *et al.* [15], and Bayer *et al.* [3]. The behaviour categorisation mentioned by authors above became inspiration for our research.

3.2   Collecting Malware Analysis Reports

To find out whether patterns of behaviour are present among malicious programs, we needed to analyse as many samples as possible. However, dynamic analysis requires that every sample is executed for at least several minutes and static analysis requires coping with obfuscation, packing and other anti-reversing measures. Since testing our assumption about behavioural patterns would take very long time in that manner, we addressed gathering malware behavioural data in a kind of crowd-sourcing approach.

Analytic reports available thanks to online malware analysis service *Totalhash* [4] were used as a resource. Thousands of files have been submitted there for analysis by malware researchers, analysts and also common users. Several similar services exist but Totalhash allows to browse the database as a list of reports in which every report is identified by a hash of analysed malware, so we did not have to identify which sample exactly we were looking for, while, on the other hand, different services require e.g. file name, name of malware signature, exact hash code or other identifier when looking for an analytic report. We built a software tool that automates collecting reports from Totalhash online database and helps us store, sort and analyse acquired data.

In order to look for malware behavioural patterns, we employed analytic reports of 34 099 unique malicious and harmless samples. This number may increase in future experiments.

Our exploration of malware behaviour commences with actions which correspond to general categories of behaviour observed in malware (Sect. 3.1). We attempted to detect patterns in number of actions executed by malicious samples in order to evince whether such general information about program's behaviour are relevant in malware recognition. In analytic reports we particularly focused on number of actions concerning: *file creation* (FC), *file deletion* (FD), *mutex creation* (MC), *process creation* (PC), *service creation* (SC), *service starting* (SS), *registry entries* (RE), *DNS* (D), *Winsock DNS* (WD), *HTTP get* (HG), *HTTP post* (HP), *TCP flows* (TF).

3.3   Malware Behavioural Patterns

Results of malware analysis collected with our helper application were stored in a database. To acquire desired data and test our hypotheses about behavioural patters in a short time, we employed database scripts to filter the data. Database environment *DataGrip*[4] by *JetBrains* was a great help for the task. First we listed names of malware signatures used for detection by one of antiviral engines (we chose specifically Eset Nod32 as one of several reliable engines) and then generated database queries which listed entries clustered by the name of the signature. Each cluster of entries comprised data of syntactically different malware samples but detectable by the same signature. For each cluster we observed number of actions executed - files created, files deleted, mutexes created, etc. and counted maximal, minimal and average number of occurrences of these actions. For example, if minimal and maximal number of file creations among samples from one cluster were equal, it indicated that malware samples associated with this signature are clearly defined by the number of file creations.

Our data suggest that not every sample of one malicious signature expresses behaviour with respect to some pattern. For several signatures their samples' behaviour (concerning number of executed actions) varies notably from sample to sample and in several cases none of considered actions were recorded. However, there are malicious infiltrations which are clearly defined by discovered behavioural pattern. For example, all samples detected with a signature labelled internally in our experiment[5] as signature A, performed 10 file creations, 2 file deletions, 4 mutex creations, 1 process creation, 3 registry operations, 3 DNS and Winsock DNS operations and 4 TCP flows, while the rest of observed actions did not occur. Numbers of actions performed are visualised in a chart (Fig. 1).

---

[4] https://www.jetbrains.com/datagrip/.

[5] We avoid stating the real signature label because disclosing such details may negatively influence employability of presented behavioural patterns in potential detection mechanisms.

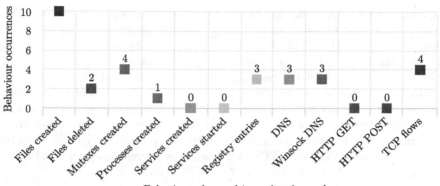

Fig. 1. Behavioural pattern of malicious programs with signature labelled internally as A. Every distinct analysed sample detected with the signature A performed exactly the same number of actions as presented in the chart.

It is important to note that the behavioural pattern illustrated in Fig. 1 matches samples of only one malicious signature, no other samples which correspond to other signatures match the behavioural pattern. Consequently, we can claim that the pattern is unique for the malware signature and can feature a high-level *malware behavioural signature* in the future.

Alongside patterns which assuredly correspond to some malware signature, we recognised partial patterns or patterns with limited variability of behaviour. Figures 2, 3 and 4 illustrate this case.

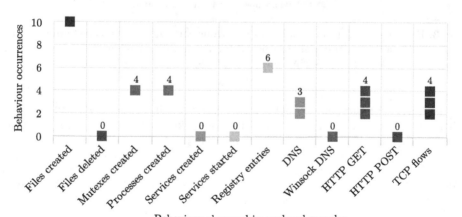

Fig. 2. Behavioural pattern of malicious programs with signature labelled internally as B. The pattern demonstrates slight variability of samples' behaviour regarding actions: *DNS, HTTP GET* and *TCP flows*

Concerning actions with variable occurrences, relationships between behaviour types are sometimes observable, e.g. samples from signature labelled B which performed 4 HTTP GET requests, exhibited also 4 TCP flows, and the same was observed with 3 and 2 occurrences of mentioned behaviour.

Indication that occasional variability in number of executed actions is not random was clearer in case of signature C. Variability is present in number of Files created, DNS, Winsock DNS and TCP flows (Fig. 3). After analysing samples belonging to the signature, we noted two sub-groups of samples according to behaviour variability: in the first sub-group samples showed 11 files created, 3 DNS, 3 Winsock DNS and 4 TCP flows, and the second sub-group had 12 files created, 8 DNS, 6 Winsock DNS and 7 or 5 TCP flows.

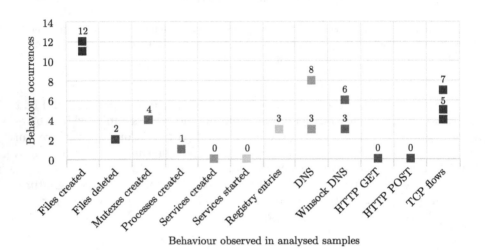

Behaviour observed in analysed samples

Fig. 3. Behavioural pattern of malicious programs with signature labelled internally as C. The pattern demonstrates slight variability of samples' behaviour regarding actions: *Files created, DNS, Winsock DNS* and *TCP flows*.

To describe unambiguous behavioural patterns and even groups of samples with non-random variability in number of behaviour occurrences, a behavioural pattern is denoted as 12-tuple p_{label} of elements

$$p_{label} = (n_{FC}, n_{FD}, n_{MC}, n_{PC}, n_{SC}, n_{SS}, n_{RE}, n_D, n_{WD}, n_{HG}, n_{HP}, n_{TF}),$$
$$n_{FC}, \ldots, n_{TF} \in \mathbb{N}^0, \tag{1}$$

where $n_{FC}, \ldots, n_{TF}$ are numbers of occurrences of behaviours according to the list from Sect. 3.2 and *label* is a name or an identifier of malicious signature with which is the pattern p_{label} associated.

Variants of number of behaviour occurrences are formulated by a set V_{label}:

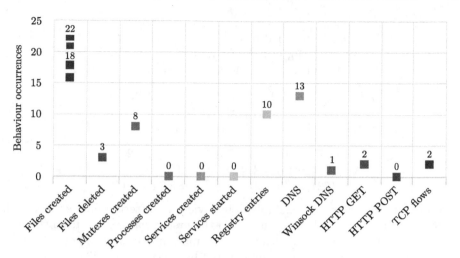

Behaviour observed in analysed samples

Fig. 4. Behavioural pattern of malicious programs with signature labelled internally as D. The pattern demonstrates moderate variability of samples' behaviour regarding only *Files created*.

$$V_{label} = \begin{cases} \emptyset, \text{ iff no variability in behaviour is present,} \\ \{v_1^l, v_2^l, \ldots, v_k^l | v_k^l = (x_1, \ldots, x_n), x \in \mathbb{N}^0, k, n \in \{1, 2, \ldots, 12\}, l \in \mathbb{N}^+\} \\ \text{otherwise.} \end{cases}$$

(2)

Elements of the set V_{label} are n-tuples v_k^l describing variants of related behaviour occurrences. Members of n-tuples x_n, where index n denotes n-th member from the n-tuple, can be substituted into the behavioural pattern p_{label}. When defining the variants we needed to consider that some of the behaviour actions can be related, so they change together. To cope with that, variables from the pattern can be divided into groups and each group will have its own description for values' variances. Index k identifies number of the independent group and l identifies number of the variant for the particular group. The more groups of values and their variants are defined in the set V_{label}, the less characteristic the behavioural pattern becomes.

For example, in the pattern p_B of sample B we identified 2 groups of variables: The first group ($k = 1$) has 2 variants which will be denoted as v_1^1 and v_1^2, the second group ($k = 2$) has 3 variants denoted as v_2^1, v_2^2 and v_2^3 (Fig. 2).

As an illustration, formulas 1 and 2 are used to describe behaviour of malware signatures A (Fig. 1), B (Fig. 2), C (Fig. 3) and D (Fig. 4) as follows:

$$p_A = (10, 2, 4, 1, 0, 0, 3, 3, 3, 0, 0, 4)$$
$$V_A = \emptyset$$

(3)

$$p_B = (10, 0, 4, 4, 0, 0, 3, v_1^l(1), 0, v_2^l(1), 0, v_2^l(2))$$
$$V_B = \{v_1^1, v_1^2, v_2^1, v_2^2, v_2^3\}$$
$$v_1^1 = (3) \quad v_1^2 = (2) \quad v_2^1 = (4, 4) \quad v_2^2 = (3, 3) \quad v_2^3 = (2, 2)$$
(4)

$$p_C = (v_1^l(1), 2, 4, 1, 0, 0, 3, v_1^l(2), v_1^l(3), 0, 0, v_1^l(4))$$
$$V_C = \{v_1^1, v_1^2, v_1^3\}$$
$$v_1^1 = (11, 3, 3, 4) \quad v_1^2 = (12, 8, 6, 7) \quad v_1^3 = (12, 8, 6, 5)$$
(5)

$$p_D = (v_1^l(1), 3, 8, 0, 0, 0, 10, 13, 1, 2, 0, 2)$$
$$V_D = \{v_1^1, v_1^2, v_1^3, v_1^4\}$$
$$v_1^1 = (22) \quad v_1^2 = (21) \quad v_1^3 = (18) \quad v_1^4 = (16)$$
(6)

When variable values for example in behavioural pattern p_C are substituted, in the first variation of substitution ($l = 1$) the first variable $v_1^l(1)$ from the pattern p_C is substituted by the first member (number in parentheses) of quadruple $v_1^1 \in V_C$, i.e. the variable $v_1^l(1)$ is substituted by the value 11. The second variable $v_1^1(2)$ is substituted by the second member of quadruple v_1^1, etc., until the last variable in the pattern is substituted. The pattern p_C after the substitution with the first variation will be as follows:

$$p_C = (11, 2, 4, 1, 0, 0, 3, 3, 3, 0, 0, 4)$$

In the second round of substitution ($l = 2$), variables in the pattern will be substituted by the members of quadruple v_1^2:

$$p_C = (12, 2, 4, 1, 0, 0, 3, 8, 6, 0, 0, 7),$$

and analogously for the last variation of substitution ($l = 3$) we use v_1^3:

$$p_C = (12, 2, 4, 1, 0, 0, 3, 8, 6, 0, 0, 5).$$

Three variants of behavioural pattern p_C describe which specific action occurred how many times in malicious samples detected by signature internally labelled as C. Formulas 1 and 2 can be employed to describe characteristic behaviour of any malicious signature. However, high numbers of independent groups of related behaviour denoted by k and numbers of variants for the particular group denoted by l lessen accuracy of the behavioural pattern, since $k \times l$ variants of behavioural pattern come into consideration.

4   Discussion

Number of samples which corresponded to one malware signature varied greatly. While there were signatures with hundreds or thousands of samples, other signatures had tens or even less than 10 representatives. As a consequence, behavioural patterns which we discovered among 34 099 samples are not equivalent in relevance. For further employment of patterns we suggest that a pattern relevance evaluation system should be designed. Alongside number of samples involved in formation of behavioural pattern also structure of the pattern needs to be considered. Types of behaviour which exhibit variability among samples decrease exactness of the pattern. Certain repetitions in variability are better than completely random variability and they are possible to delineate, even if it means increase in number of pattern's corresponding variants.

The problem that may potentially arise is that malware writers start to randomize number of performed actions in order to avoid the pattern - a variant of dead-code insertion - "dead-action insertion", e.g. creating empty or unused files just to perform different amount of file actions. We hope that similarly as dead-code insertion is detectable, also "dead-action insertion" would be possible to cope with, but it would probably require engaging additional information, e.g. purpose and usage of created files later in program execution.

Precision of presented behavioural patterns could be improved by combining dynamic analysis with static analysis. It is possible to figure out which actions can be potentially executed in the program by statically analysing its executable code. These techniques are currently well developed and also address code obfuscation, e.g. [13]. However, while using data from online analytic service, we can not influence how these data are obtained. Companies providing their analytic engines to the service also do not disclose which techniques they employ - it is a part of their know-how.

5 Conclusion

We believe that building malware behavioural models on patterns of program's executable code is a fast and perhaps simpler solution. The problem of malicious code obfuscation and mutation on the level of code is however a significant complication which, in the long term, may thwart reliability of detection techniques which are tied with program's code. We assume that we need to seek malware definitions and models, which are not bound to specific executable code patterns but are more abstract, so that they withstand code mutation and obfuscation. Despite Bailey's et al. scepticism about system calls [2], we do not exclude such information from our future considerations about malware models, if research proves they are required. Since not all malware samples that we analysed show behaviour with respect to some detectable pattern, it is most likely that we will analyse more details of behaviour, perhaps even on the level of system calls.

Behavioural patterns that we discovered are not yet suitable as malware behavioural signature but in the future they probably will form a part of such signatures. As it turned out, our approach to behaviour analysis is relevant for distinguishing malicious infiltrations. We encourage malware researchers to consider behavioural patterns presented here in their experiments and share their results with research community.

Acknowledgments. This work has been supported by the Slovak Research and Development Agency under the contract No. APVV-15-0055, and Grant No. FEI-2015-18: Coalgebraic models of component systems.

References

1. Alam, S., Horspool, R., Traore, I.: MARD: A framework for metamorphic malware analysis and real-time detection. In: IEEE 28th International Conference on Advanced Information Networking and Applications (AINA), pp. 480–489 (2014)
2. Bailey, M., Oberheide, J., Andersen, J., Mao, Z.M., Jahanian, F., Nazario, J.: Automated classification and analysis of internet malware. In: Kruegel, C., Lippmann, R., Clark, A. (eds.) RAID 2007. LNCS, vol. 4637, pp. 178–197. Springer, Heidelberg (2007). doi:10.1007/978-3-540-74320-0_10
3. Bayer, U., Habibi, I., Balzarotti, D., Kirda, E., Kruegel, C.: A view on current malware behaviors. In: Proceedings of the 2Nd USENIX Conference on Large-scale Exploits and Emergent Threats: Botnets, Spyware, Worms, and More, LEET'09, p. 8. USENIX Association, Berkeley (2009)
4. Cymru: totalhash (2016). https://totalhash.cymru.com/
5. Ding, Y., Yuan, X., Tang, K., Xiao, X., Zhang, Y.: A fast malware detection algorithm based on objective-oriented association mining. Comput. Secur. **39**, 315–324 (2013). Part B(0)
6. Egele, M., Scholte, T., Kirda, E., Kruegel, C.: A survey on automated dynamic malware-analysis techniques and tools. ACM Comput. Surv. **44**(2), 6:1–6:42 (2008)
7. Gregio, A., Bonacin, R., Nabuco, O., Monte Afonso, V., Licio De Geus, P., Jino, M.: Ontology for malware behavior: A core model proposal. In: IEEE 23rd International WETICE Conference (WETICE) 2014, pp. 453–458, June 2014
8. Lu, H., Wang, X., Zhao, B., Wang, F., Su, J.: Endmal: an anti-obfuscation and collaborative malware detection system using syscall sequences. Math. Comput. Model. **58**(5–6), 1140–1154 (2013)
9. Mohd Shaid, S., Maarof, M.: Malware behavior image for malware variant identification. In: International Symposium on Biometrics and Security Technologies (ISBAST) 2014, pp. 238–243 (2014)
10. Moser, A., Kruegel, C., Kirda, E.: Exploring multiple execution paths for malware analysis. In: IEEE Symposium on Security and Privacy 2007, pp. 231–245 (2007)
11. Obrst, L., Chase, P., Markeloff, R.: Developing an ontology of the cyber security domain. In: Semantic Technologies for Intelligence, Defense, and Security (STIDS), CEUR Workshop Proceedings, vol. 96, pp. 49–56 (2012)
12. Rieck, K., Holz, T., Willems, C., Düssel, P., Laskov, P.: Learning and classification of malware behavior. In: Zamboni, D. (ed.) DIMVA 2008. LNCS, vol. 5137, pp. 108–125. Springer, Heidelberg (2008). doi:10.1007/978-3-540-70542-0_6
13. Song, F., Touili, T.: Pushdown model checking for malware detection. STTT **16**(2), 147–173 (2014)
14. Stastna, J., Tomasek, M.: Exploring malware behaviour for improvement of malware signatures. In: IEEE 13th International Scientific Conference on Informatics 2015, pp. 275–280 (2015)
15. Wagener, G., State, R., Dulaunoy, A.: Malware behaviour analysis. J. Comput. Virol. **4**(4), 279–287 (2008)
16. Wu, L., Ping, R., Ke, L., Hai-xin, D.: Behavior-based malware analysis and detection. In: First International Workshop on Complexity and Data Mining (IWCDM) 2011, pp. 39–42. IEEE (2011)
17. Yuxin, D., Xuebing, Y., Di, Z., Li, D., Zhanchao, A.: Feature representation and selection in malicious code detection methods based on static system calls. Comput. Secur. **30**(6–7), 514–524 (2011)

AErlang at Work

Rocco De Nicola[1](✉), Tan Duong[2], Omar Inverso[2], and Catia Trubiani[2]

[1] IMT - Institute for Advanced Studies, Lucca, Italy
rocco.denicola@imtlucca.it
[2] Gran Sasso Science Institute, L'Aquila, Italy
{tan.duong,omar.inverso,catia.trubiani}@gssi.infn.it

Abstract. AErlang is an extension of the Erlang programming language which is enriched with attribute-based communication. In AErlang, the Erlang send and receive constructs are extended to permit partner selection by relying on predicates over set of attributes. AErlang avoids the limitations of the Erlang point-to-point communication making it possible to model some of the sophisticated interaction features often observed in modern systems, such as anonymity and adaptation. By using our prototype extension, we show how the extended communication pattern can capture non-trivial process interaction in a natural and intuitive way. We also sketch a modelling technique aimed at automatically verifying AErlang systems, and discuss how it can be used to check some key properties of the considered case study.

1 Introduction

Building distributed systems where large amounts of components interact according to sophisticated mechanisms is challenging [1]. Functional programming seems to address the size complexity of such systems, primarily by virtue of its great modularisability, which in turn promises to boost development efficiency and cut down maintenance efforts [2,3]. In addition, appropriate development frameworks based on functional programming may offer extra features and thus allow modelling richer classes of systems.

Erlang is a concurrent functional programming language originally designed for building telecommunication systems [4] and successfully adapted to broader contexts following its open source release. In particular, due to its native support for concurrency and distribution [5], and its lightweight concurrency model, Erlang is a good candidate language for building very large distributed systems [6]. The Erlang point-to-point interprocess communication model, however, turns out to be too rigid and not expressive enough to render some of the most increasingly often observed interaction features, including *anonymity* and *adaptation*.

Recently, attribute-based communication has been proposed for modelling complex interactions in distributed systems so to lift many of the limitations of point-to-point communication [7]. Communication no longer takes place between pairs of entities according to their identities, but between groups of them, only

© Springer International Publishing AG 2017
B. Steffen et al. (Eds.): SOFSEM 2017, LNCS 10139, pp. 485–497, 2017.
DOI: 10.1007/978-3-319-51963-0_38

considering among their features the ones that are visible to the rest of the system: their *attributes*. These typically encode characteristics that depend on the problem domain and that are relevant with respect to the communication pattern, local behaviour or system-level behaviour of interest. Predicate-based send and receive communication primitives then can use logic expressions over attributes, i.e., *predicates*, to dynamically select at interaction time the groups of communicating entities.

To investigate the full potential of the new communication paradigm, and more practically to make it possible to render more complex interaction, our first effort has been devoted to extend Erlang with attribute-based communication in our AErlang prototype [8].

In this paper, as a further step towards the same direction, we use our prototype extension to show how the extended communication primitives can indeed capture non-trivial process interaction in a natural and intuitive way. We adopt as a case study a classical algorithm that uses traditional component identification to solve a well-known matching problem. We then use AErlang to extend the traditional algorithm to two different attribute-based variants. The first variant provides anonymity, and the other hints at adaptive behaviour. Additionally, we argue that there may be further benefits when reasoning about system properties. We sketch a modelling technique aimed at automatically verifying AErlang systems, and discuss how it can be used to check some key properties of the considered programs.

The paper is organised as follows. We briefly overview AErlang in Sect. 2. We introduce the case study and present the two variants in Sect. 3, and verify some properties in Sect. 4. We conclude with related work and future research directions.

2   Attribute-Based Erlang

AErlang [8] instantiates attribute-based communication (AbC) [7] on top of the Erlang programming language, by extending its standard communication primitives (send and receive) to the corresponding attribute-based versions. Our prototype currently implements attribute-based send and receive along with environment handling, predicate declaration and evaluation. This allows programmers to write Erlang programs with the capability of attribute-based communication in an intuitive and natural way. In the following we briefly overview AErlang and its features, more details are provided in [8].

Processes, Attributes, and Predicates. AErlang processes are Erlang processes equipped with attribute environments. The attribute environment of a process is represented as a list of pairs, i.e., $[\{a_1,V_1\},\{a_2,V_2\},\ldots]$, where a_i is an Erlang atom denoting the attribute name and V_i is the corresponding value whose type is an Erlang term. Predicate expressions are represented as Erlang strings. Predicate terms can be attribute names, references to attribute values, constants or variables. A basic predicate is a comparison between two terms. Compound predicates are constructed from simpler ones using logical connectives.

Interface. The basic functionalities of AErlang are shown in Fig. 1. A top-level process starts AErlang by invoking the **start** function, which initializes our message-passing environment for attribute-based communication. Parameter **Mode** specifies the low-level message dispatching policy, and is essentially used to trade off between efficiency and reliability. The available policies (i.e., broadcast, pushing, and pulling) are explained later.

```
% initialization              % attribute-based send
start(Mode)                   to(Pred) ! Msg

% registration and unregistration   % attribute-based receive
register(Pid, Env)            from(Pred),
unregister()                  receive
                                  Pattern_1 -> Expression_1;
% environment handling            ...
setAtts(TupleList)                Pattern_n -> Expression_n
getAtts(NameList)             end
```

Fig. 1. AErlang interface.

To communicate by means of predicates, Erlang processes need to register to AErlang by invoking the **register** function, which takes as input the identifier of the Erlang process and its attribute environment. Registered processes can handle their own local environments by using functions **getAtts** and **setAtts**. A process can leave the attribute-based message-passing environment by calling function **unregister**. After unregistering, the process is no longer able to use attribute-based send and receive.

Processes exchange messages by using attribute-based send and receive. Differently from standard Erlang, in these constructs the source and destination process identifiers are replaced by predicates. The extended send primitive has the effect of sending a given message to all registered processes whose attributes satisfy the given predicate. On the other hand, attribute-based receive is used to receive a message from any sending process, provided that the message *and* the sender's attributes satisfy the predicate associated with the receive command. It is worth mentioning that this pair of communication primitives should be used at both sender and receiver sides to make the interaction possible.

Prototype Implementation. The design of AErlang follows a centralized architecture which consists of two main components: a process registry that stores process details, such as the process identifier and the current status, and a message broker that undertakes message dispatching.

As mentioned above, the behaviour of the message broker changes according to the dispatching policy selected when initializing AErlang: (i) *broadcast*, i.e., the broker broadcasts all the predicate-based messages from senders, then they are all filtered by the receiver according to sending and receiving predicates; (ii) *pushing*, i.e., the broker checks the sending predicates and forwards messages to selected receivers that will use the receiving predicates to decide whether to accept any incoming message; (iii) *pulling*, i.e., the broker checks the receiving predicates and forwards messages only from selected senders; the forwarded messages are then filtered by the receiver according to the sending predicates. Additional details can be found in [8].

In practice, the process registry is stored using an ETS (Erlang built-in term storage)[1] table and the message broker is a `gen_server` [2] process waiting for interactions from attribute-based communication primitives. To support these user-friendly constructs, we have used `parse_transform` [3] to translate the new syntax into valid Erlang code before it is actually checked by the compiler. The resulting messaging platform transparently mediates the communication, and at the same time guarantees seamless integration of attribute-based communication with common Erlang development practice.

3 Case Study

We now show how to use AErlang to implement a well-known algorithm that solves a classical matching problem, namely the Stable Marriage Problem (SMP) [9]. The problem is to find a matching between two disjoint equally-sized sets of men and women, where each person has a strictly ordered preference list of all members of the opposite sex. A *matching* is a one-to-one assignment between the men and the women. A matching is said to be *stable* if there exists no pair (m, w) such that man m prefers woman w to his matched partner and vice versa.

An algorithm to find a stable matching was proposed in [9] and can be informally summarized as follows. Each man actively proposes to the favourite woman extracted from his list of preferences; whenever a man is rejected, he tries again with the next woman in the list. Each woman waits for incoming proposals. If she is free then she becomes engaged, otherwise she compares the proposer with her current partner according to her preference list and rejects the least favored man. The algorithm terminates when there is no active man.

In the rest of the section, we present three algorithms to deal with stable marriage. The first one (Fig. 2) implements a classical solution where processes use their identity to communicate. A first extension replaces process identifiers with attributes to provide anonymity (non-adaptive program, Fig. 3). Finally, we introduce predicate lists to capture adaptive behaviour (Fig. 4).

Our AErlang implementation for the classical algorithm is shown in Fig. 2 (an AbC encoding can be found in [10]). Men and women are interacting processes associated with their own attributes: identifier, preference list, and current partner. Those processes are spawned by a top-level process that initializes AErlang. Their registration is done inside init functions. A simple initialization (for a problem size of four men and four women) is reported hereafter:

---

[1] http://erlang.org/doc/man/ets.html.

[2] http://erlang.org/doc/man/gen_server.html.

[3] http://erlang.org/doc/man/erl_id_trans.html.

```
smp() ->
 aerl:start(pushing),

 spawn(fun() -> man_init([{id,m1},{prefs,[w1,w2,w3,w4]},{partner,null}]) end),
 %% spawn other three men ...

 spawn(fun() -> woman_init([{id,w1},{prefs,[m2,m3,m1,m4]},{partner,null}]) end),
 %% spawn other three women...
end.
```

where {id,...} is the identifier of men or women, {prefs,[...]} is the preference list, {partner,null} is the current partner, initially nobody. Functions
man_init and woman_init register the spawned processes to AErlang; and call
functions man and woman, respectively. The code for man and woman is given in
Fig. 2. Process environments are handled by AErlang getter and setter functions
(lines 2, 3, 13, 17). A message tagged with propose means that the man is
proposing to the woman, while a no message means that the woman is rejecting a man. A woman takes her decision by using function bof to compare two
men. This function always returns true if parameter Part is an atom null, in
fact it means she was not engaged yet. A man specifies the sending predicate as
"id = this.partner" (line 4), and this has the effect of sending a message to
processes whose id equals to the value of attribute partner of the man. In the
woman code, we see that predicates can be over variables (line 20). This example
also shows two different uses of (receiving) predicates: (i) at line 10, a woman
wishing to consider any proposal uses "tt" as unrestricted receiving predicate;
(ii) at line 5, the predicate is instead over the message content "$X = no".

```
1   man() ->                                     9   woman() ->
2    [[H|T],Id] = aerl:getAtts([prefs,id]),     10    from("tt"),
3    aerl:setAtts([{partner,H},{prefs,T}]),     11    receive
4    to("id=this.partner") ! {propose,Id},      12     {propose,Y} ->
5    from("$X = no"),                           13      [L,Part]=aerl:getAtts([prefs,partner]),
6    receive                                    14      case bof(L,Part,Y) of
7     X -> man()                                15       true ->
8    end.                                       16        to("id = this.partner") ! no,
                                                 17        aerl:setAtts([{partner,Y}]),
                                                 18        woman();
                                                 19       false ->
                                                 20        to("id = $Y") ! no,
                                                 21        woman()
                                                 22      end
                                                 23    end.
```

Fig. 2. Classical stable marriage in AErlang.

The program presented in Fig. 2 uses attributes but in essence the communication is still point-to-point because the sending predicates always map to unique
receivers. In the following we propose a problem variant where partners are not
selected according to preference lists, but by considering the characteristics that
women and men mutually expect to find in their partners.

Intuitively, we use attributes to encode the characteristics of women and
men (e.g., the hair color), and then introduce predicates over those attributes to

express the partner selection preferences. For example, a man who is not interested in meeting dark-haired women might want to advertise his own interests using the predicate hair =/= dark, which has the effect of sending a proposal to all women whose hair is not dark.

Note that the increased expressiveness due to the use of predicates, still includes the classical case based on preference lists, because these can always be expressed by appropriate attributes and predicates. Hence, in general, the attribute-based version can be cast into many variants of the stable marriage problem which have been intensively studied in the literature [11].

It is worth to mention that men have no clue as to whether anybody will actually receive their proposals, and multiple women may receive the same proposal, a robust implementation for this algorithm would require that partners use extra acknowledge messages [12]. In this paper we do not consider these issues since our focus is to investigate the advantages of using attributes-based communication in capturing non-trivial process interaction.

Anonymity. A first version of our extended algorithm is explained hereafter:

1. A man sends a proposal message using a predicate to express his own preferences. The message includes the man's identifier and characteristics. If he receives a yes message, he becomes engaged, otherwise he remains single;
2. A woman that receives a proposal compares the characteristics of her current partner against the proposer, and chooses the man who better meets her expectations by sending him a yes, and a no to the other man.

Figure 3 shows the implementation of this extended version, where the preferences of men are used as sending predicates (lines 2–4), while the preferences of women are used to filter out uninteresting proposals by mean of function bof (lines 19, 23). An interesting property of this version is that it provides anonymity, in fact women and men have no knowledge at all about the presence of others, and therefore they do not use identifiers to explicitly specify their communication targets.

```
1   man() ->                                 17   woman() ->
2     [Id,Body,Wealth,Ps] =                  18     [Id,L,Part,Prior] =
3     aerl:getAtts([id,body,wealth,pred]),   19     aerl:getAtts([id,prefs,partner,prior]),
4     to(Ps) ! {propose,Id,Wealth,Body},     20     from("tt"),
5     from("tt"),                            21     receive
6     receive                                22       {propose,M,W,B} ->
7       {yes,Wid} ->                         23       case bof(L,Prior,W,B) of
8         aerl:setAtt(partner,Wid);          24         {true,New} ->
9         from("tt"),                        25           to("id = this.partner") ! {no,Id},
10        receive                            26           to("id = $M") ! {yes,Id},
11          {no,_} ->                        27           aerl:setAtts([{partner,M},{prior,New}]),
12            aerl:setAtt(partner,null)      28           woman();
13        end;                               29         {false,_} ->
14      {no,_} ->                            30           to("id = $M") ! {no,Id},
15        single                             31           woman()
16    end.                                   32       end
                                             33   end.
```

Fig. 3. SMP - *non-adaptive* version.

Interestingly, executing this program may result in some people left unmatched when the predicates of men are particularly demanding. This happens for example when a number of men are interested in a smaller subset of women, and hence, some of the men will inevitably be rejected. For the same reason, some women may not receive any proposal.

Let us consider a specific instance of size four, where women and men have the attributes and preferences shown in Table 1. In this dataset, men m1 and m4 both compete for woman w1, and it turns out that eventually m1 gets rejected since w1 prefers m4. Meanwhile, w2 remains single because her attributes do not satisfy any men's predicates. To handle these situations, we discuss how to extend the program in Fig. 3 so that men can progressively weaken their expectations upon being refused, thus increasing their chances of finding a partner. This leads to formulate an adaptive behaviour at the predicate level, as illustrated below.

Table 1. Attributes and predicates for women (left) and men (right).

id	Eyes	Hair	Preferences
w1	amber	red	wealth=poor and body=weak
w2	amber	dark	wealth=rich and body=strong
w3	green	red	wealth=rich and body=strong
w4	green	dark	wealth=rich and body=weak

id	Wealth	Body	Preferences
m1	rich	strong	eyes=amber and hair=red
m2	rich	weak	eyes=green and hair=dark
m3	poor	strong	eyes=green and hair=red
m4	poor	weak	eyes=amber and hair=red

Adaptive Behaviour. To achieve this behaviour, we introduce *predicate lists* for men. Given a preference predicate for a man m, the corresponding predicate list is iteratively constructed as follows. The first predicate fully reflects the desire of m in interacting with his favourite women, as before. Subsequent predicates are created by excluding from the previous predicate each of the favourite attributes one by one, according to a fixed order of preferences on the attributes. The last

```
1   man() ->
2     [Id,Body,Wealth,[H|T],Refusal] =
3     aerl:getAtts([id,body,wealth,
4                       preds,refusal]),
5     aerl:setAtt(preds,T),
6     Ps = concat(H,Refusal),
7     to(Ps) ! {propose,Id,Wealth,Body},
8     from("tt"),
9     receive
10      {yes,Wid} ->
11          aerl:setAtt(partner,Wid),
12          from("tt"),
13          receive
14            {no,Wid} ->
15                New=blacklist(Wid,Refusal),
16                aerl:setAtt(refusal,New),
17                man();
18      {no,Wid} ->
19          New=blacklist(Wid,Refusal),
20          aerl:setAtt(refusal,New),
21          man()
22    end.

23  woman() ->
24    [Id,L,Part,Prior] =
25    aerl:getAtts([id,prefs,partner,prior]),
26    from("tt"),
27    receive
28      {propose,M,W,B} ->
29        case bof(L,Prior,W,B) of
30          {true,New} ->
31            to("id = this.partner") ! {no,Id},
32            to("id = $M") ! {yes,Id},
33            aerl:setAtts([{partner,M},{prior,New}]),
34            woman();
35          {false,_} ->
36            to("id = $M") ! {no,Id},
37            woman()
38      end
39  end.
```

Fig. 4. SMP - *adaptive behaviour* version.

predicate may not include any preference, so to guarantee that the man can eventually have the chance to interact with at least one woman. For example, assuming that a man gives more importance to the colour of the eyes rather than hair, the predicate list for this man would be: 'eyes=amber and hair=red', 'eyes=amber', 'hair=red', 'gender=w', where *gender* is another attribute representing gender of people which is not shown in Table 1.

Figure 4 shows the AErlang program that uses predicate lists. The behaviour of women is unchanged, while the behaviour of men is slightly altered: a man extracts a predicate from the top of his predicate list, and sends a proposal message using this predicate. After receiving a rejection, the man adds the identifier of the woman who rejected him to a blacklist. He then proceeds with the next predicate and excludes all women in the blacklist. Before a send (line 6), the man's predicate is combined with a predicate for excluding all the women who rejected him in the past. `Refusal` is initially an empty string, and is updated when the man receives a `no` message by using function `blacklist` (lines 15, 19).

4   Formal Verification of the Case Study

Attribute-based communication can potentially offer further benefits when reasoning about system properties. To support this claim, as a proof-of-concept, we sketch a technique that from the two programs seen in the previous section (Figs. 3 and 4) generates models to be formally and automatically analyzed.

System Modelling. Our verification approach consists in modelling AErlang processes (including a standalone process for the message broker) as UML state machines, and then using the UMC verification framework [13] for property checking. UMC is particularly suited for our purpose because it uses doubly-labelled transition systems on which it is possible to express state- as well as event-based properties to model components attributes and actions[4].

Message Broker. The message broker is modelled by class `MessageBroker` (Fig. 5). It stores attributes of processes in vector `attributes`, and their names in vector `components`. There is only one possible transition that loops back to the initial state, to model the fact that the message broker is ready to accept incoming signals at any time. This transition is triggered by the `send(pred,msg)` signal by class objects corresponding to other AErlang processes, in our case they are spawned from `man` and `woman` functions. A `receive` signal is then triggered for each object whose attribute environment satisfies predicate `pred`, if any. For simplicity, we assume that `pred` is a vector $[[a_1,v_1], \dots, [a_n,v_n]]$ representing the predicate $a_1 = v_1$ and $\dots$ and $a_n = v_n$.

---

[4] UMC's project homepage: http://fmt.isti.cnr.it/umc.

```
Class MessageBroker is
Signals: send(pred,msg)
Vars: components:obj[],attributes:obj[[]];
Transitions:
    s1 -> s1 {send(pred,msg)/
        for i in 0..components.length-1 {
            count:int := 0;
            for j in 0..pred.length-1 {
                for k in 0..attributes[i].length-1 {
                    if attributes[i][k] = pred[j] then {count:=count+1;}
                } };
            if count = pred.length then {components[i].receive(msg)} }
    }
end MessageBroker
```

Fig. 5. UMC class for component MessageBroker

Women and Men. For each function woman and man (as seen in Fig. 4) we create a UMC class (Fig. 6) whose variables are the process attributes along with a class instance of the message broker (for invoking send). Each class has a receive signal to be called by the message broker. We model attribute-based send with transitions without trigger signals, and gather the resulting actions within this transition. The transition for an attribute-based receive is triggered by signal receive. The receive(msg) signal is used to receive message msg.

The behaviour of a man is modelled by three transitions. The first one has no trigger signals but is guarded by the non-emptiness of plist. The other two are triggered by signal receive, that returns the message if the given condition over its first element holds. With these transitions, we model exactly the same basic actions that a man performs in the corresponding AErlang program.

```
Class Man is
Signals: receive(msg)
Vars: id, wealth, body, partner,
      plist, refusal, mb
Transitions:
    s1 -> s2 {-[plist.length>0]/
        pred:obj:=[refusal]+plist.head;
        plist:=plist.tail;
        mb.send(pred, [propose,id,wealth,body])
    }
    s2 -> s1 {receive(msg)[msg[0]=no]/
        refusal[msg[1]-1]:=msg[1]}
    s2 -> s2 {receive(msg)[msg[0]=yes]/
        partner:=msg[1]}
end Man
```

```
Class Woman is
Signals: receive(msg)
Vars: id, eyes, hair, partner, current,
      f_wealth, f_body, mb
Transitions:
    s1 -> s1 {receive(msg)[msg[0]=propose]/
        -- calculate new priority of proposer
        -- based on preferences f_wealth, f_body
        if new > current then {
            mb.send([_id,partner], [no,id]);
            partner:=msg[1];
            current:=new
        }
        else {mb.send([_id,msg[1]], [no,id])}
    }
end Woman
```

Fig. 6. UMC classes for women and men.

The behaviour of a woman is represented by a single transition, triggered by the message broker forwarding a propose message. Again, the actions within this transition mimics the initial program. For conciseness we omit the bof function that compares two men. Interested readers can find implementation details of running AErlang programs and their encoding in the online archive[5].

Property Checking. We are now ready to check some key properties of our two programs (Figs. 3 and 4) with respect to the dataset shown in Table 1:

- *"at the end of the execution, everybody is engaged"* (P_1)
- *"at the end of the execution, the matching is stable"* (P_2).

To check whether P_1 holds we add some abstraction rules to our model:

```
Abstractions {
    State w1.partner=$1 -> w1($1)        State m1.partner=$1 -> m1($1)
    ...                                  ...
}
```

which have the effect of extracting relevant information about the partners into observable system state labels. Property P_1 can then be expressed by the formula:

```
AF AG (not w1(null) and not w2(null) and ...  and not m4(null))
```

which amounts to saying that from the initial state, all the execution paths eventually lead to the state where all the observed values of **partner** are non-null.

Checking P_2 is equivalent to check if the matching contains blocking pairs. We introduce an extra transition for class `Woman` to communicate **partner** values to the `MessageBroker` class. Once every woman has a partner, the `MessageBroker` class performs the stability check. In our case, a man `m` is considered to prefer a woman `w` to another woman `w'` if the predicate satisfying attributes of `w` appears before the predicate satisfying attributes of `w'` in the predicate list of `m`. A woman `w` prefers a man `m` to another man `m'` if the attributes of `m` are closer to `w` preferences than the attributes of `m'` (see Sect. 3). A Boolean variable `stable` is used to store the result of this check. Similar to the previous property, we introduce an abstraction rule to observe the value of `stable`. Property P_2 can then be expressed as:

```
AF AG (not w1(null) and ... and not m4(null) and stable(true)).
```

The results of the verification of the two properties are summarised in Table 2. P_1 and P_2 turn out to be true for the adaptive program (Fig. 4), and false for the non-adaptive one (Fig. 3). Certainly, these results prove an interesting fact: if the men are willing to relax their expectations, nobody stays single in the end.

---

[5] https://github.com/ArBITRAL/sofsem-code/blob/master/archive.zip.

Table 2. Formal verification results.

Program	Observed final state labels	P_1	P_2
Non-adaptive version	m1(null), m2(4), m3(3), m4(1), w1(4), w2(null), w3(3), w4(2), stable(false)	False	False
Adaptive version	m1(2), m2(4), m3(3), m4(1), w1(4), w2(1), w3(3), w4(2), stable(true)	True	True

5   Related Work

The AbC calculus has already been instantiated on an imperative programming language. AbaCus [10] is a run-time environment supporting AbC communication primitives in Java language. AbaCus relies on a message forwarder for message dispatching in a broadcast manner. Our prototype, instead, builds on a distributed, concurrent, and functional language and different message dispatching policies are made available aiming at trading off between efficiency and reliability. Currently, we do not have any evaluation for this trade off; it will be the subject of investigations in the near future.

Existing tools to verify Erlang code [14,15] could be used for exhaustive validation of AErlang implementations. Etomcrl [16] translates Erlang programs into process algebraic specifications and applies a third-party model checker for checking programs properties. McErlang [17] is a model checker written in Erlang that reimplemented a part of Erlang runtime system for facilitating verification. It supports a large subset of Erlang including distribution and fault-tolerance. Soter [15] can be used for infinite-state model checking for a variant of Core Erlang. For AErlang verification, our choice has been to rely on UMC because it permits us to naturally obtain system models capturing the behaviour of AErlang programs and to carry out formal analysis at this level. In fact, UML state machines are particularly suitable to model AbC components and the formal model based on doubly labelled transition systems (L2TS) and on the ACTL logic of UMC permit naturally expressing properties of AbC programs.

6   Conclusion and Future Work

In this paper we have reported a practical application of our AErlang prototype, that enables attribute-based communication in Erlang. Although it only implements a restricted set of primitives, we have demonstrated the usefulness of our prototype in implementing a traditional solution for a well-known problem. We have also shown how natural it is to have two alternative, more flexible, solutions that guarantee anonymity and adaptivity. Remarkably, for both new solutions the key features were conveniently captured at the level of predicates, while keeping the changes to other parts of the code essentially negligible.

We have argued that the benefits of attribute-based communication may have a potential impact when reasoning about system properties. To support this intuition we have shown how to exploit a model checker for verifying some properties of the two flexible attribute-based program variants. We have exploited the tight correlation between UML state machines and attribute-based communication systems. In the near future, we plan to generalise and automate the translation from the AbC syntax (thus not necessarily only from AErlang) to the UMC specification language, in order to further investigate the advantages of attributes from a formal verification perspective to a deeper extent. In particular, judiciously combining attributes and predicates with doubly-labelled transition systems may help pruning the state space and extending the verification of other properties. Another research direction will aim at understanding whether attributes can be exploited to enable the joint verification of functional and non-functional properties (such as performance, reliability, security).

Acknowledgments. We thank Franco Mazzanti from ISTI-CNR, Pisa for providing valuable insights on modelling in UML and for supporting us in using the UMC framework.

References

1. Sommerville, I., Cliff, D., Calinescu, R., Keen, J., Kelly, T., Kwiatkowska, M., Mcdermid, J., Paige, R.: Large-scale complex it systems. Commun. ACM **55**(7), 71–77 (2012)
2. Hughes, J.: Why functional programming matters. Comput. J. **32**(2), 98–107 (1989)
3. Hu, Z., Hughes, J., Wang, M.: How functional programming mattered. Nat. Sci. Rev. **2**(3), 349–370 (2015)
4. Blau, S., Rooth, J., Axell, J., Hellstrand, F., Buhrgard, M., Westin, T., Wicklund, G.: AXD 301: a new generation ATM switching system. Comput. Netw. **31**(6), 559–582 (1999)
5. Armstrong, J.: Erlang. Commun. ACM **53**(9), 68–75 (2010)
6. Thompson, S., Cesarini, F.: Erlang programming: a concurrent approach to software development (2009)
7. Abd Alrahman, Y., De Nicola, R., Loreti, M.: On the power of attribute-based communication. In: Albert, E., Lanese, I. (eds.) FORTE 2016. LNCS, vol. 9688, pp. 1–18. Springer, Heidelberg (2016). doi:10.1007/978-3-319-39570-8_1
8. De Nicola, R., Duong, T., Inverso, O., Trubiani, C.: http://cs.gssi.infn.it/files/AErlang/AErlang-Technical-Report.pdf
9. Gale, D., Shapley, L.S.: College admissions and the stability of marriage. Am. Math. Mon. **69**(1), 9–15 (1962)
10. Abd Alrahman, Y., Nicola, R., Loreti, M.: Programming of CAS systems by relying on attribute-based communication. In: Margaria, T., Steffen, B. (eds.) ISoLA 2016. LNCS, vol. 9952, pp. 539–553. Springer, Heidelberg (2016). doi:10.1007/978-3-319-47166-2_38
11. Iwama, K., Miyazaki, S.: A survey of the stable marriage problem and its variants. In: Proceedings of the International Conference on Informatics Education and Research for Knowledge-Circulating Society (ICKS 2008), pp. 131–136. IEEE Computer Society (2008)

12. Aknine, S., Pinson, S., Shakun, M.F.: An extended multi-agent negotiation protocol. Auton. Agents Multi-Agent Syst. **8**(1), 5–45 (2004)
13. ter Beek, M.H., Fantechi, A., Gnesi, S., Mazzanti, F.: A state/event-based model-checking approach for the analysis of abstract system properties. Sci. Comput. Program. **76**(2), 119–135 (2011)
14. Guo, Q., Derrick, J., Benac Earle, C., Fredlund, L.Å.: Model-checking Erlang – a comparison between EtomCRL2 and McErlang. In: Bottaci, L., Fraser, G. (eds.) TAIC PART 2010. LNCS, vol. 6303, pp. 23–38. Springer, Heidelberg (2010). doi:10. 1007/978-3-642-15585-7_5
15. D'Osualdo, E., Kochems, J., Ong, C.-H.L.: Automatic verification of Erlang-style concurrency. In: Logozzo, F., Fähndrich, M. (eds.) SAS 2013. LNCS, vol. 7935, pp. 454–476. Springer, Heidelberg (2013). doi:10.1007/978-3-642-38856-9_24
16. Arts, T., Earle, C.B., Derrick, J.: Development of a verified erlang program for resource locking. Int. J. Softw. Tools Technol. Transf. **5**(2-3), 205–220 (2004)
17. Fredlund, L., Svensson, H.: McErlang: a model checker for a distributed functional programming language. In: Proceedings of the 12th ACM SIGPLAN International Conference on Functional Programming (ICFP 2007), October 2007

Software System Migration to Cloud-Native Architectures for SME-Sized Software Vendors

Frank Fowley[1], Divyaa Manimaran Elango[1], Hany Magar[1], and Claus Pahl[2(✉)]

[1] IC4, Dublin City University, Dublin 9, Ireland
[2] Faculty of Computer Science, Free University of Bozen-Bolzano, Bolzano, Italy
Claus.Pahl@unibz.it

Abstract. Independent software vendors (ISVs) are often faced with the need to migrate their software products as software-as-a-service (SaaS) solutions to the cloud. We document and evaluate four case studies by considering various factors that the respective companies need to consider in a cloud migration process. We look at migration project as a software re-engineering activity, involving project planning, cloud architecture design and architecture transformation. Specifically for software vendors, a cloud migration opens opportunities such as the possibility of modernising their software through re-engineering their product architecture. However, small and mid-size enterprises(SMEs)often do not have the required cloud expertise to plan and implement a cloud migration.

While many experience reports exist, there is new impetus in the domain resulting from the drive towards cloud-native architecture and other developments particularly in the cloud PaaS space. This allows software modernisation as part of a wider software evolution strategy. We present such a modernising architecture evolution process here. While there is a higher initial cost, the benefits of cloud-native architectures turn out to be advantageous in the long run.

Keywords: Cloud migration · Architecture evolution · Software modernisation · Cost models · Cloud native · ISV · SME

1 Introduction

Migration to the cloud is done by Independent Software Vendors (ISVs) either because they see advantages of providing their products as Software-as-a-Service solutions through the cloud or are forced through change in customer demand and requirements to do so. The problems for companies aiming to migrate to the cloud is that it is often difficult to scope and determine the costs of a migration project [2] because of

- misconceptions about benefits and risks of cloud-based provisioning of software,
- unclear expectations resulting from different cloud service and deployment models.

From a software engineering perspective, which is at the core of the ISV's business, problems emerge. What of the existing architecture is migratable? What is the extent of re-engineering necessary to make migration work? What target architecture is most beneficial? Specifically for software vendors, a cloud migration opens opportunities such as the

© Springer International Publishing AG 2017
B. Steffen et al. (Eds.): SOFSEM 2017, LNCS 10139, pp. 498–509, 2017.
DOI: 10.1007/978-3-319-51963-0_39

possibility of modernising their product through re-engineering their legacy software architecture through the replacement of existing code/architecture, but also of supporting tools/services, and development processes. Sample concerns include webification or the use of software product lines for bespoke products. Re-engineering might also simply be necessary due to non-suitable licenses for some components or the need to upgrade due to interoperability concerns. SMEs, even though technology providers, often do not have the required cloud expertise to plan and implement a migration.

Many experience reports investigate cloud benefits and risks for companies. Only a few look at the software vendor perspective, where not only the existing on-premise IT system needs to be moved, but where in addition

- Development and continuous maintenance and re-engineering in the cloud needs to be considered as this is part of the core business for software developers.
- the costing needs to consider the costs for deploying software in the cloud, but also to develop a monetisation model that reconciles these costs with income to be generated from an entirely different revenue model for the software product.

Moreover, specifically in the cloud PaaS space there is a lot of activity that merits a fresh look at software development and provisioning in and through the cloud. This includes the trend towards cloud-native architectures [4] as a new architectural style suitable for the cloud that help to better control quality and costs [23].

We present an incremental, pattern-based migration process that includes early experimentation and performance testing [21]. We analysefour case studies by considering various factors that the respective companies need to consider in this context. These case studies are from different sectors, including banking, document management, food and insurances. We have been involved in the migrations as consultants in various stages from initial feasibility analysis to full multi-stage system migration. The trend towards cloud-native architectures is essentially a componentisation of the application architecture in terms of cloud infrastructure and platform services such as storage (infrastructure) or databases and integrationware (platform). We illustratehow re-engineering towards cloud-native architectures addressestechnical ISV concerns, but also costing to estimate and manage expenses for a cloud-deployed solution.

We start with an introduction of a process model towards a cloud-native architecture in Sect. 2. We then introduce and discuss the use cases in Sect. 3. In Sect. 4, we look at experimentation to determine the scope of the migration and re-engineering project and in Sect. 5, we note observations, before discussing related work and concluding in Sects. 6 and 7.

2   Migration Framework–Towards Cloud-Native Architectures

As part of our studies, we have surveyed several consultants and solution providers in the cloud platform (PaaS) space to define a common PaaS-specific migration process [6]. Figure 1 shows this process tailored to ISV needs. Central in this process are software architecture concerns (such as stateless architectures) and re-engineering to modernise software (driven by different reasons as discussed above).

PaaS Provider

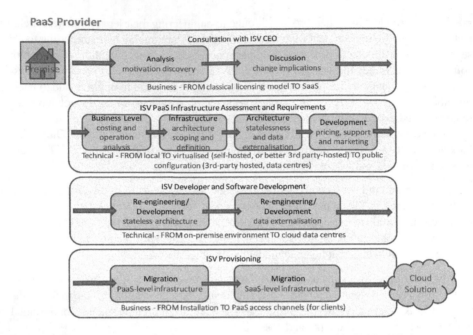

Fig. 1. PaaS Migration Process with four main Stages and individual Tasks.

For the architectural migration, we use a pattern-based approach using individual migration patterns to define the migration process in several steps. We use a catalogue of migration patterns that describe simple architectural transformations for specific scenarios (e.g., for simple cloudification in an IaaS solution). Each pattern defines a re-engineering step [6]. The 15 patterns can be broadly categorized into: (i) relocations of a single component into the cloud, (ii) replacements of a component by a cloud-native service, (iii) distribution of several components across several cloud service providers.

Many patterns directly address the introduction of a cloud-native service [22]. A sample pattern is the Multi-cloud Relocation (Fig. 2), specified as follows:

- Definition: A component re-hosted (or relocated) on a cloud platform is enhanced by using the environmental services of the other cloud platforms.
- Problem: Enhancing the availability of an application without the significant architecture change, and without incurring capital expenditure for on-premise hardware.
- Solution: Leverage cloud platform environment services to improve availability, e.g., live migration from existing platform to the target in case of service outage.
- Benefits: As component re-hosting in multiple cloud platforms and improve availability and avoid vendor lock-in.
- Risks: Cloud providers do not provide the necessary services to enable application to run in multiple cloud platforms without re-architecting or rewriting the code.

The combination of patterns defines a staged process as a migration path which in the individual steps is driven by selection criteria (e.g., time to market or introduction of new capabilities) [18, 19]. Migration paths are sequential compositions of these patterns on a

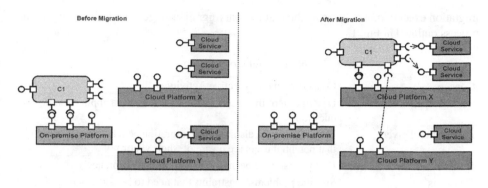

Fig. 2. Multi-Cloud Relocation

source architecture [17]. A cloud-native architecture as the target of this stepwise migration is build up from individual services provided in the cloud, such as the cloud services indicated in the pattern above. Step-wise migration into cloud could happen as follows, if a fully cloud-native solution is aimed at:

- The on-premise system can be packaged into VMs as a first non-native solution, i.e., license fees occur as usual. A business problem is scaling out, i.e. adding more VMs, means adding more license fees for every replicated component. A technical problem is copies of data storage that are not in sync if multiple VMs are in use.
- In order to address the problems, we can refactor and extract storage, i.e. use data-as-a-service. This alleviates the technical problem of different copies of data.
- Another step is to package the whole DBMS into single machine, which alleviates the licence fee issue for DBMS and simplifies data management. However, the business problem that other licence fees still occur multiple times remains.
- The final step(s) are then to fully move to PaaS services (e.g., Azure SQL server), which alleviates as far as possible licensing fees issue.

This results in a so-called cloud-native architecture, which is generally characterised as scalable and elastic due to cloud service support such as scaling engines, clusterable and multi-tenant due to cloud virtualization principles being applied, and pay-per-use and self-service as two other cloud principles. This has better scalability characteristics as platform tools can be used to manage performance. It also allows better licensing and cost management. Thus, this addresses both technical and business problems.

3   Use Cases – Documentation of Four ISV Cloud Migrations

3.1   Description Framework

We document the use cases in two ways. Firstly, in a pre-migration view looking from an analytical, pre-migration perspective at the companies, following the concerns from Table 1. Table 1 provides a list of concerns that should be elicited prior to migration [1]. Then, for the migration execution, we report on the main actual migration stages that follows largely the process outlined in Fig. 1.

Table 1. Migration Concerns

Concern	Concern of the Respective Activity
Setting/Application	Description of the sector &classification of the application in question
Expectation/Driver	The drivers and a distinction of migration benefits and expectations that potential users are aware of (their vision)
Ignorance	Factors that have been overlooked (their 'ignorance')
Concerns	Specific problems/constraints that need to be addressed

The migration execution follows the process of Fig. 1, with the actual architecture migration follows the migration path defined through the pattern application.

3.2   Pre-migration Analysis

Following Table 1, we summarise the case studies as in Table 2. The factors already indicate a need for re-engineering. A SaaS product requires cloud metering services to be added to monitor consumption. Internationalisation is typically part of an expansion strategy that needs to be supported by scalability. Cost as a concern requires equally individually monitorable and adaptable services.

Table 2.   Use Cases – Pre-migration categorisation of factors

	UC1 – Banking	UC2 – Insurance	UC3 – Food	UC4 – Doc. Managemen
Setting and Application	*Sector*: Financial services *Application*: comprehensive (ATM, Internet banking)	*Sector*: Insurance product *Application*: multiple products with policy database, CRM and telephony (call centre) support	*Sector*: Food. *Application*: Sector-specific ERP system	*Sector*: Business Solution *Application*: Document processing
Expectation Drivers	Cloudification, Internationalisation, SaaS product	Internationalisation, Scalability	Internationalisation, SaaS product	SaaS product
Concerns	Data location, Vendor lock-in	Data location	Data location	Data location
Ignorance	Implications of different layers	Cost	Cost	Implications of different layers

As a staged migration process, we carried out the following tasks as described in Table 3, following the outline from the process presented in Fig. 1.

Table 3. Migration Tasks.

	UC1 Banking	UC2 Insurance	UC3 Food	UC4 – Doc. Management	*Notes on* *Architecture*
Technology Review	Available technologies and solutions for cloud-based transaction, card and customer storage and processing	Available technologies and solutions for cloud-based insurance storage and processing	Available technologies and solutions for cloud-based ERP solutions	Network concerns for high-speed up/download, services for in-cloud document processing	*Components such as storage, high-performant networks, ERP systems or transaction processing indicate re-engineering focus*
Business analysis	Investigate security and monitoring/auditing options for cloud-based banking processing	Investigate security and monitoring/auditing options for cloud-based insurance processing (focus data integrity and location as products offered cross-boarder)	Investigate legal (rather than linguistic) localisation requirements regarding the deployment (the ERP system is provided to customers across Europe, but also China)	Business analysis to investigate security/data privacy regulations	*Indicates the benefits of cloud-native architectures*
Migration & Architecture	Focus on feasibility and efficacy of process-aware migration of banking admin and operations management systems into scalable cloud architecture	Focus onimplementing business process-aware migration of insurance admin & operations management (policy, accounts, CRM, telephony) into distributed cloud architecture	Focus on feasibility and efficacy of process-aware migration of ERP system features (15 core modules) into scalable cloud architecture	Development of a 2-staged incremental migration plan (IaaS and PaaS) to migrate a document scanning, storage and processing to scalable cloud architectures	*Defines the scope of a re-engineering process towards a cloud-native architecture*
Test& Evaluation	Evaluate scalability of cloud-based integrated banking service configurations	Evaluate scalability of distributed cloud-based integrated insurance service configurations	Evaluate scalability of cloud-based integrated ERP service configuration for different markets	Testing of cloud-specific properties: Scalability, Performance, Integration, Security	*Explains why a cloud-native architecture is useful for technical and cost reasons*

3.3   Migration and Architecture Case Study

We detail two activities from the 'Migration and Architecture' task for the Document Management case study. This illustrates the re-engineering process in more detail.

The first decision was to consider the configuration and management of both IaaS and PaaS solutions for the Document Image Processing system (DIP) using MS Azure as the default platform. Both solutions were part of a stage plan to make a first virtualized version quickly available and then re-engineer properly in a second phase. The creation of a virtualised DIP system for deployment on a cloud IaaS solution thus preceded the componentisation at PaaS level. Here specifically storage, document processing components and integration with other services was considered. This is essentially a stepwise architecture evolution towards a cloud-native architecture.

Securing all parts of the system in both IaaS and PaaS configuration is another task. Data (document) protection and tenant isolation is a strong requirement, as are authentication, authorization, backup and recovery management. These requirements need decisions regarding a private cloud setting (for isolation) and the use of additional services for ID management and backup/recovery. Our patterns allow this to be modelled. Security policies need to be defined for the cloud and security mechanisms configured.

4   Experimentation for Migration, Testing and Evaluation

Experimentation plays a major role during the migration and architecture re-engineering to address the Testing and Evaluation task. Experimentation of prototypes of the partly or fully cloud-native re-engineered architectures is required to evaluate options in a realistic setting. As for instance scalability was an important concern, driven by the business aim of the companies to expand, at early stages we did feasibility tests to validate a proposed architecture [7]. A motivation for experimentation was also to carry out a cost-vs-performance experiment, i.e., to consider sometimes different options and compare them technically, but rank them under consideration of the costs they would create. In the introduction of cloud-native architecture, we have already pointed out the importance of financial concerns (e.g., licences) in the re-engineering process.

A key question for ISVs is to validate a cloud-based business model with expenses and revenues prior to fully embarking on a cloud-based architecture. There is always a trade-off between the quality, e.g., performance of services in the cloud, the income they generate and the cost that these incur.

In Fig. 3, storage services are compared in terms of performance and consumption (which is essentially a cost metric). It allows to decide which cloud-native service to use from the options considered in the test. What experimentation shows in general is:

- the difference between PaaS/IaaS/SaaS solutions (as consumer and provider)
- scalability of different target architecture options
- integration and interoperation problems
- how to structure and cost a staged migration (plan derivation)

Experimental feasibility and validation studies have played a key role in our migration process to validate re-engineering options before fully implementing these. How to do experimental feasibility studies is outlined here. We have defined source and possible target architectures and have selected critical components that can be replaced by cloud-native service, e.g. high volume data processing to test scalability of storage (DB) or communications infrastructure to test integration/communications scalability.

This experimentation often results in a prototype evaluation of a partly cloud-native cloud architecture. Rather than just cloudifying a system in a virtual machine, we often

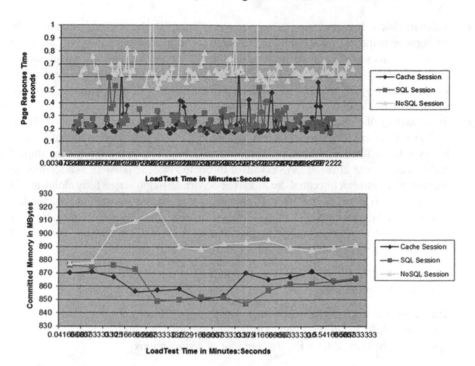

Fig. 3. Experimental results for storage component options (performance at the top and consumption at the bottom)

selected a component such as data storage and have experimented with different cloud-native storage options, including for instance a mix of traditional RDBM and other table/blob storage formats as we have done for the document management system.

Partial experimentation with cloud-native prototypes allows to consider a fully cloud-native architecture to be discussed with realistic technical (e.g. scalability) and cost assumptions (storage, access). Only realistic costs for cloud operation allow a charging model for their own product to be developed and validated.

5   Observations

Surveys of the participating companies in the migration projects have revealed the following expectations and uncertainties. The drivers to consider a migration are the following expectations of improvement in relation to [6]: time to market improvement, inclusion of new capabilities, reduce operational cost, leverage investments, free up on-premise resources, scalability to support expansion, integration and access. These depend much on the sector and product type. The observations on clarifying concerns are essentially confirmed by all use cases considered.

While there was a clear business case at a high level to consider a cloud-based SaaS product, some problems emerged during the migration:

- Clarity of vision: Business reasons to go to cloud did exist, such as internationalisation and improve company value (being in the cloud). Technical reasons to go to cloud that accompany this were also clear (e.g., scalability to support expansion). Awareness of general concerns (business and technical) and barriers did exist, such as data protection. This was not always matched by full clarity about architectural options and possible cloud monetisation models.
- Understanding of cloud (all have impact on architecture and process selection): Technical concerns were understood, such as scalability or data protection as a requirement. However, the difference between provisioning models and cloud layers and their impact on the management effort at I/P/SaaS level in comparison. A possible vendor lock-in resulting from some architectural decisions (basic virtualisation versus fully cloud-native implementation) was not clear either. The business concern that was incompletely understood was the business model, i.e., the required revenue model change. In legal/governance terms, awareness of data protection and location issues was there, but needed further clarification of architectural impact of this.

Our solution to rectify the lack of understanding was a combination of experimentation as part of a migration:

- exploration and documentation of scenarios through the migration patterns
- experiments help to clarify cloud architecture and quality options
- experiments help to address business model misconceptions

Experiments help identifying architecture options and the costing of migrated software solutions. The architecture/cost mapping can be summarised as follows in Fig. 4. Components can be scaled, but this has a direct cost for the provider. This can increase the quality and can result in a higher cost for the user, depending on the pricing model used. More demand (for quality services) need to be fed back into a scaling engine to adapt the component and its infrastructure accordingly.

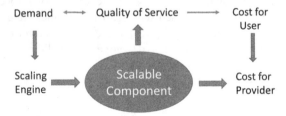

Fig. 4. Architecture-Quality-Cost Dependencies

The use cases have differed only with respect to two concerns: firstly, data protection requirements, which are stronger in the banking, insurance and financial services industry due to legal constraints. There are also legal constraints in the food section. These result in traceabilty requirements (answered through monitoring etc.) rather than data location decisions as for financial services.

Going for cloud-native has not been a goal for all use case companies from the outset. Many seek initially a simple cloudification to obtain some crucial cloud benefits quickly, without being aware of or considering the long-term cost perspective. The software solutions under consideration (see Table 3) are all reasonable complex and possible optimisations of their complex architectures would justify the cost for modernisation in the long-term from a software maintenance perspective. In order to properly manage the new revenue streams coming from the cloud-based delivery of the SaaS product against the expenses of development and operation, a cloud-native solution has clear advantages due to better control and more transparency of the actual costs.

The costs for running the software in the cloud (essentially the TCO Total Cost of Ownershop) can be predicted through experimentation with prototypical migration of central components. Based on this TCO estimation, a guide exist to analyse the economic viability of the software product in conjunction with the development of suitable payment models for the software product in question, be that pay-per-use, pay-per-user or another licence-oriented payment model for the end user.

6   Related Work

Cloud migration methodologies exist – see [2, 20] for an overview of academic research. In industry, many consultants and service providers also offer support. For IaaS migration, with the existence of VM packaging standards such as OVF, some simplifying mechanisms exist that allow virtualised software to be easily migrated into and between clouds. Case studies do exist here, such as Li et al.'s coverage e of a partial migration [16]. For the SaaS space, many service providers offer tool support, e.g., data loaders that exist for instance for many products in the CRM space.

Less clear is the solution in the platform (PaaS) space. Here, general strategies for software evolution and re-engineering apply [11]. Methodologies and tool support are provided to determine the impact of changes, refactor code and analyse the semantic equivalence to software before and after evolution.

Specific to the cloud is Son's proposal for service selection [3] that takes resource efficiency into account, i.e., already considers a mix of performance and cost concerns. Gilia [13] also addresses service selection in this context. However, as Arshad et al. [5] and also Al-Roomi et al. [9] note, more attention needs to be paid to costing/pricing models for cloud services [10]. Wang et al. [14] also look at pricing strategies for companies to operate a sustainable business model in the cloud. Xiong et al. [7] have made this interlinkage clear in their investigation of performance and cost trade-offs.

Menychtas et al. [12] suggest a model-driven approach to migration on-premise software to SaaS, but none of these specifically target cloud-native architectures at the PaaS level as we have done here. We have also used case studies to empirically support the value of cloud-nativeness in the cloud migration process. While we have considered SMEs in general, Giardino et al. [15] have also noted the difficulties that many companies, in their case start-ups, caused by technological uncertainty arising from new technology environments.

7 Conclusions

Independent software vendors (ISVs) are a specific group of cloud users that require a deeper understanding of architecture and cost concerns. In the cloud, an IaaS or PaaS deployed software product is made available as a SaaS solution to their customers. Particularly, for SMEs without cloud experience this knowledge does often not exist. For ISVs, the re-engineering of their software product for the cloud has turned out a critical aspect. Two important aspects here are:

- Cloud-native: More than for many in-house used cloud migrations, there is a need to componentise the product properly and implement this as far as possible as a cloud-native solution to enable an effective SaaS provisioning.
- Cost model: Cloud-native architecture allows to better control the costs for the provided software and align this with the charging and billing model for their product.

While cloud-nativeness is at the core an architectural concern, the fact that cloud-native makes cloud-based software more predictable in terms of licensing costs and also costs for scalability makes the link to cost an absolutely crucial one. Our solution towards cloud-natives is a structured migration process with two core components:

- A pattern-based approach to determine and analyse migration plans
- Early-stage experimentation as a means to address quality and cost considerations

The mapping between costs for developing and operating software in the cloud and income generated from providing the same software to customers through the cloud remains still a major challenge. Through experimentation with selected components, costs can be estimated in relation to varying demands and targeted quality of service.

What we have demonstrated through the use cases is the usefulness of cloud-native architectures for both quality considerations as well as cost calculation and management. However, due to the widely varying charging mechanisms, the development of a generic model remains an open challenge that we aim to address in the future.

Acknowledgement. The research work described in this paper was supported by the Irish Centre for Cloud Computing and Commerce, an Irish national Technology Centre funded by Enterprise Ireland and the Irish Industrial Development Authority.

References

1. Pahl, C., Xiong, H., Walshe, R.: A comparison of on-premise to cloud migration approaches. In: Lau, K.-K., Lamersdorf, W., Pimentel, E. (eds.) ESOCC 2013. LNCS, vol. 8135, pp. 212–226. Springer, Heidelberg (2013). doi:10.1007/978-3-642-40651-5_18
2. Jamshidi, P., Ahmad, A., Pahl, C.: Cloud migration research: a systematic review. IEEE Trans. Cloud Comput. **1**(2), 142–157 (2013)
3. Son, J.: Automated Decision System for Efficient Resource Selection and Allocation in Inter-Clouds. The University of Melbourne (2013)

4. Balalaie, A., Heydarnoori, A., Jamshidi, P.: Migrating to cloud-native architectures using microservices: an experience report. In: European Conference on Service-oriented & Cloud Comp (2015)
5. Arshad, S., Ullah, S., Khan, S.A., Awan, M.D., Khayal, M.: A survey of Cloud computing variable pricing models. Eval of Novel Approaches to Software Engineering (2015)
6. Jamshidi, P., Pahl, C., Chinenyeze, S., Liu, X.: Cloud migration patterns: a multi-cloud service architecture perspective. In: Workshop Eng Service Oriented Applications (2014)
7. Xiong, H., Fowley, F., Pahl, C., Moran, N.: Scalable architectures for platform-as-a-service clouds: performance and cost analysis. In: European Conference on Software Architecture (2014)
8. Pahl, C., Xiong, H.: Migration to PaaS clouds - migration process and architectural concerns. In: International Symposium on Maintenance *and* Evolution of Service-Oriented and Cloud-Based Systems (2013)
9. Al-Roomi, M., Al-Ebrahim, S., Buqrais, S., Ahmad, I.: Cloud computing pricing models: a survey. In: International Journal of Grid and Distributed Computing, vol. 6(5) (2013)
10. Sharma, B., Thulasirm, R., Thulasirman, P., Grag, S.: Pricing cloud compute commodities: a novel financial economic model. In: International Symposium Cluster, Cloud and Grid Comp (2012)
11. Rashid, N., Salam, M., Sani, R.K.S., Alam, F.: Analysis of risks in re-engineering software systems. Int. J. Comput. Appl. **73**(11) 5–18 (2013)
12. Menychtas, A., Konstanteli, K., Alonso, J., et al.: Software modernization and cloudification using the ARTIST migration methodology and framework. Scalable Comput. Pract. Exp. **15**(2), 131–152 (2014)
13. Gilia, P., Sood, S.: Automatic selection and ranking of cloud providers using service level agreements. Int. J. Comput. Appl. **72**(11) 45–52 (2013)
14. Wang, W., Zhang, P., Lan, T., Aggarwal, V.: Datacenter net profit optimization with deadline dependent pricing. In: Conference on Information Sciences and Systems (2012)
15. Giardino, C., Bajwa, S.S., Wang, S., Abrahamsson, P.: Key challenges in early-stage software startups. In: XP Conference (2015)
16. Li, H., Zhong, L., Liu, L., Li, B., Xu, K.: Cost-effective partial migration of VoD services to content clouds. In: Cloud Computing (CLOUD) (2011)
17. Jamshidi, P., Pahl, C., Mendonca, N.C.: Pattern-based multi-cloud architecture migration. software - practice and experience (2016)
18. Fang, D., Liu, X., Romdhani, I., Jamshidi, P., Pahl, C.: An agility-oriented and fuzziness-embedded semantic model for collaborative cloud service search, retrieval and recommendation. Future Generation Computer Systems, vol. 56 (2016)
19. Fang, D., Liu, X., Romdhani, I., Pahl, C.: An approach to unified cloud service access, manipulation and dynamic orchestration via semantic cloud service operation specification framework. J. Cloud Comput. **4**(1) 14 (2015)
20. Gholami, M.F., Daneshgar, F., Rabhi, F.: Cloud migration: methodologies: preliminary findings. In: European Conference on Service-Oriented and Cloud Computing – CloudWays 2016 Workshop (2016)
21. Affetti, L., Bresciani, G., and Guinea, S.: aDock: a cloud infrastructure experimentation environment based on Open Stack and Docker. In: International Conference on Cloud Computing, pp. 203–210 (2015)
22. Fowley, F., Pahl, C., Jamshidi, P., Fang, D., Liu, X.: A classification and comparison framework for cloud service brokerage architectures. IEEE Trans. Cloud Comput. (2016)
23. Fowley, F., Pahl, C.: Cloud migration architecture and pricing - mapping a licensing business model for software vendors to a SaaS Business Model. In: European Conference on Service-Oriented and Cloud Computing ESOCC – CloudWays 2016 Workshop. Springer (2016)

Using n-grams for the Automated Clustering of Structural Models

Önder Babur[1]([⊠]) and Loek Cleophas[1,2]

[1] Eindhoven University of Technology, 5600 MB Eindhoven, The Netherlands
{o.babur,L.G.W.A.Cleophas}@tue.nl
[2] Stellenbosch University, Matieland 7602, South Africa

Abstract. Model comparison and clustering are important for dealing with many models in data analysis and exploration, e.g. in domain model recovery or model repository management. Particularly in structural models, information is captured not only in model elements (e.g. in names and types) but also in the structural context, i.e. the relation of one element to the others. Some approaches involve a large number of models ignoring the structural context of model elements; others handle very few (typically two) models applying sophisticated structural techniques. In this paper we address both aspects and extend our previous work on model clustering based on vector space model, with a technique for incorporating structural context in the form of n-grams. We compare the n-gram accuracy on two datasets of Ecore metamodels in AtlanMod Zoo: small random samples using up to trigrams and a larger one (∼100 models) up to bigrams.

Keywords: Model-driven engineering · Model comparison · Vector space model · Hierarchical clustering · n-grams

1 Introduction

Models and metamodels, i.e. abstract representations of typically domain-specific knowledge, are utilized in Model-Driven Engineering as central artefacts to deal with the increasing complexity and size of software systems [12]. The advance of MDE in the academic and industrial context has led to a similar issue: increase in size, complexity and number of models. Of particular interest for this work, it is difficult to manage a large number of models, whether they be assets of an industrial software product line or family, part of an online model repository, etc. In order to tackle this issue, many researchers have developed fundamental model operations to identify the relations among models and integrate them. Among those are model comparison and matching; with applications to model merging and versioning.

The research leading to these results has been funded by EU programme FP7-NMP-2013-SMALL-7 under grant agreement number 604279 (MMP).

B. Steffen et al. (Eds.): SOFSEM 2017, LNCS 10139, pp. 510–524, 2017.
DOI: 10.1007/978-3-319-51963-0_40

Most of these approaches employ complex techniques for pairwise comparison of models (a notable example based on graph matching can be found in [10]). Another interesting dimension of model comparison is for the case of a large dataset with many models; it has been pointed out in [6,11] to be different from pairwise comparison. Recent efforts such as [1–3] have proposed using clustering techniques to analyse and compare a large number of (meta-)models; with the common goal of identifying groups/subgroups and outliers among (meta-)models (e.g. for model repository management).

We aim to develop a model clustering technique which incorporates the structural context in a generic way and acts as a compromise between contextless techniques such as in [1] and expensive pairwise ones such as in [10] (see [3] for a performance comparison of such a clustering approach vs. EMFCompare). While using bigrams (i.e. n-grams with $n = 2$) as in [2,3] is promising, it is noteworthy to investigate the general case of using n-grams and its effect on clustering precision. The scope of this work is concisely captured in two research questions:

- **RQ1.** How can we incorporate structural context into a vector space model (VSM) for automated model clustering?
- **RQ2.** How do the proposed techniques affect clustering precision, for small and larger datasets?

In this paper, we extend our previous work in [2] with n-gram extraction and comparison. We propose extracting fixed-length n-grams from models, to populate a VSM via extended and configurable comparison schemes. The resulting VSM is fed into the agglomerative hierarchical clustering algorithm implemented in the R statistical software[1]. We compare the clustering efficiency using n-grams on two datasets as subsets of the Ecore metamodels in AtlanMod Metamodel Zoo[2]: random samples (20–30 models × 50 runs) using up to trigrams (i.e. $n = 3$) and a larger one (107 models) up to bigrams. We conclude that n-grams lead to higher accuracy on average, though not monotonically with increasing n.

Related Work. Structural comparison has been studied in context of pairwise model comparison in a lot of studies, e.g. in [10]. These techniques in general develop elaborate pairwise techniques involving graph comparison/isomorphism and aim to reach high accuracy for a small number of models to compare (typically two). On the other hand, there are a few techniques which consider multiple models without pairwise comparisons, such as N-way merging in [11].

Recent approaches such as [1–3] propose using hierarchical clustering for a large set of (meta-)models. Both use similar Information Retrieval (IR) techniques for extracting term vectors out of models and using various similarity measures such as cosine distance. The use of structural relations among model elements is proposed in [2,3] encoded as bigrams of model elements; in [3]

---

[1] https://cran.r-project.org/.
[2] http://web.emn.fr/x-info/atlanmod/index.php?title=Ecore.

via external pairwise comparison operation provided by EMFCompare[3]; while ignored in [1] altogether with the exclusive use of unigrams (i.e. $n = 1$). A final application of n-grams is given by Bislimovska et al. [5] in the context of model indexing and searching.

2 Preliminaries

We outline here the underlying concepts of our approach (see [1] for details). Information Retrieval [7] deals with effectively indexing, analyzing and searching various forms of content including natural language text documents. As a first step for document retrieval in general, documents are collected and indexed via some unit of representation. Index construction can be implemented using VSM with the following major components: (1) a vector representation of occurrence of the vocabulary in a document, named *term frequency*, (2) *zones* (e.g. 'author' or 'title'), (3) weighting schemes such as inverse document frequency (idf), and zone weights, (4) Natural Language Processing (NLP) techniques for handling compound terms, detecting synonyms and semantically related words.

The VSM allows transforming each document into an n-dimensional vector, thus resulting in an $m \times n$ matrix for m documents. Over the VSM, document similarity can be defined as the distance (e.g. Euclidean or cosine) between vectors. These can be used for identifying similar groups of documents in the vector space. This unsupervised machine learning (ML) technique is called clustering. Among many clustering methods [7], there is a major distinction between flat clustering, where a flat cluster labelling is performed, and hierarchical clustering, where a hierarchy of proximities is produced.

Finally, n-grams [8] are used in computational linguistics to build probabilistic models of natural language text, e.g. for estimating the next word given a sequence of words, or comparing text collections based on their n-gram profiles. In essence, n-grams represent a linear encoding of structural context.

3 Motivation for Structural Comparison

As previously mentioned, model comparison taking structure information into consideration has been studied in many pairwise comparison approaches (see [13] for an overview). In this section we would like to motivate the problem from a model clustering perspective. Several approaches in [1] and [3] propose extracting identifier names as independent features to be used in a VSM. This effectively ignores all the structural context of the model. Figure 1(a) illustrates one of the shortcomings of using just unigrams for model clustering. It is trivial to see that an approach as in [1] would treat those three models as the same.

Another point can be made, given the case that we extract model fragments from three different models (Fig. 1(b)). The case depicts that the second fragment has the vertex I inserted, while the third fragment has B replaced by its

---

[3] https://www.eclipse.org/emf/compare/.

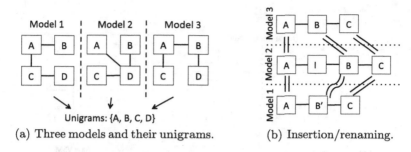

(a) Three models and their unigrams.   (b) Insertion/renaming.

Fig. 1. Motivating examples for using n-grams.

synonym B'. Ideally we would like our clustering technique to treat these three model fragments as strongly similar beyond the unigram similarity of independent $A, B/B'$ and C.

One way of encoding the structural context would be in the form of n-grams of model elements; simpler and cheaper to compare than e.g. subgraphs. This approach has been mentioned in [2] and [3] for $n = 2$. We would like to investigate the general case of using n-grams and their effect on clustering accuracy.

4   Extending the Framework for n-grams

In this section we describe our approach for clustering structural models based on n-gram representations. Since this work builds on top of our existing model clustering framework [1], we start with the basic introduction of that framework. The base framework (refer to [1] for details) is inspired by IR-based and statistical techniques for comparing document as summarized in Sect. 2. The approach starts with the extraction of model element identifiers and types from a set of input models, with a metamodel-based traversal of models using EMF Dynamic API[4]. The resulting data, i.e. typed unigrams, are used to populate a VSM after some NLP steps such as tokenization, filtering and synonym checking. As a result, each model is represented in the VSM as a point in a high dimensional space and similarity of models is reduced to a distance calculation. Hierarchical clustering is applied on top of these distances. The framework allows configuring several matching schemes (e.g. whether types are ignored, synonyms are checked) and weighting schemes (e.g. idf or type weights).

This work extends the framework in various ways as depicted in Fig. 2, with modified features in red and disabled features in grey. The underlying concepts of our approach are introduced in Sects. 4.1 to 4.3, while from Sect. 4.3 onwards we describe the components in the workflow. The steps of this modified workflow can be summarized as follows:

---

[4] http://www.eclipse.org/modeling/emf/.

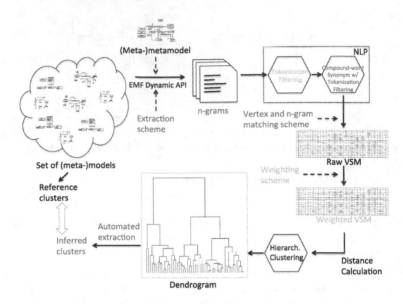

Fig. 2. Overview of the modified model clustering framework. (Color figure online)

1. Obtaining a set of models with the same kind, e.g. Ecore metamodels,
2. Generating n-grams with an $n > 0$ and extraction scheme (Sect. 4.3),
3. Picking a vertex matching scheme: synonym matching using a compound-word similarity measure (Sect. 4.5) and type matching [1],
4. Picking an n-gram matching scheme (Sect. 4.4),
5. Calculating the term frequency matrix (Sect. 4.5),
6. Picking a distance measure and calculating the vector distances,
7. Applying hierarchical clustering over the VSM,
8. Automatically extracting the clusters and comparing them against the reference clusters.

4.1   Models as Labelled Graphs

Leaving the fully formal definition for later, we consider Ecore models as $M = \langle E, V \rangle$, where E is the set of name-type pairs $e = (n_1, t_1)$ and V is the set of edges (t_2, e_s, e_t) with consecutively the edge type (i.e. label of the edge on the underlying labelled graph), source and target of the edges. We consider only a subset of the Ecore, and *ENamedEntity* subclasses such as *EPackage, EClass,*

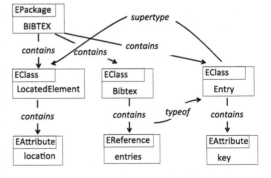

Fig. 3. Graph representation of an Ecore metamodel.

EAttribute as vertices; and structural containment, reference type and super-type relations as edges. Thus we omit several parts including: *EAnnotations*, OCL constraints and various attributes such as *abstract* for classes, multiplici-ties for *ETypedElements*, types of *EAttributes* and so on. This restriction yields the domains for the corresponding types: $t_1 \in \{EPackage, EClass, \ldots\}$ and $t_2 \in \{contains, typeof, supertype\}$. Traversing the model and filtering/extracting the desired elements is relatively straightforward using the Dynamic EMF API. Figure 3 shows a simple graph representation of an Ecore metamodel.

4.2   Revisiting Unigrams

Given the above definition for the simplified graph representation, the unigrams as studied in [1] are simply the set of vertices (name-type pairs) of the extracted graph. All the structural information captured in V is discarded. Checking the similarity of unigrams is just vertex similarity; the framework implements type/synonym matching, and weighting schemes (see [1] for details). For check-ing the similarity for compound-word names, tokenization and expansion of the unigrams for the tokens is applicable and effective to be used with regular syn-onym checking mechanisms for simple words.

4.3   Extracting n-grams

We define n-grams using paths of length $n-1$ on the extracted model graph: an n-gram is a sequence of vertices $v_1, \ldots, v_n$ with $n \geq 1$ where for each (v_i, v_{i+1}) there exists some $e \in E$ with type t such that $e = (t, v_i, v_{i+1})$. We further add the restriction that the involved paths have to be *simple* paths, thus having no cycles. With this basic definition, there exists an upper bound for the longest n-gram that can be extracted from non-cyclic paths in the model.

Note that this is a simplified first-attempt formulation of n-grams where edge labels are considered only for the calculation of paths, and are not part of the n-gram itself. We treat edges simply as *relations*, to denote that there is structural association between the vertices. Extending this simple formulation, possibly for other type of structural models as well, is left as future work.

The above formulation treats the graph in a naive and general-purpose man-ner. While we have implemented this naive extraction of n-grams in the frame-work for genericness, we propose a domain-specific extraction exploiting the actual semantics of the Ecore meta-metamodel. Involving the three types of edges, the following shows how we tackle Ecore models:

– **Rule 1:** Edges of type *contains* are processed regularly in the path traversal.
– **Rule 2:** EReference types can be considered a placeholder for basic associa-tion (e.g. consider UML associations). We thus fork the path traversal upon encountering *typeof*. One way we include the n-gram up to the EReference vertex and terminate the traversal in order to retain the information encoded by the relation label, if any. The other way we further advance the traversal jumping over that vertex.

– **Rule 3:** For *supertypes* we exploit the inheritance semantics and fork the path traversal recursively for every *supertype*. This way we cover for instance the implicit associations of a subclass with the attributes of its superclass.

In Table 1, we list some illustrative results (types omitted for simplicity) of n-gram extraction from the example in Fig. 3. Note the application of Rules 2,3 for a domain-specific extraction.

Table 1. n-gram extraction: some examples.

n	n-grams	Rules
3	(BIBTEX, LocatedElement, location)	1
	(BIBTEX, Bibtex, entries)	1,2
	(BIBTEX, Bibtex, Entry)	1,2
	(Bibtex, Entry, key)	1,2
	(Bibtex, Entry, location)	1,2,3
4	(BIBTEX, Bibtex, Entry, LocatedElement)	1,2,3
	(BIBTEX, Bibtex, Entry, location)	1,2,3

4.4 Defining n-gram Similarity

Now we would like to generalize the similarity scheme that was previously applicable for unigrams only, to n-grams. Given two n-grams P_1, P_2 with size n, we can think of the following similarity schemes:

– strict matching with all vertices equal: 1 if for every $1 \leq i \leq n$, $V_1^i = V_2^i$, 0 otherwise.
– semi-relaxed matching: sum of vertex similarities, times context multiplier:

$$nSim(P_1, P_2) = ctxMult(P_1, P_2) * \sum_{i=1}^{n} vSim(V_1^i = V_2^i) \tag{1}$$

$$ctxMult(P_1, P_2) = \frac{1 + |\text{nonzero } vSim \text{ matches}|}{1 + n} \tag{2}$$

– relaxed matching, and using the maximum similar subsequence:

$$nSim'(P_1, P_2) = ctxMult'(P_1, P_2) * score(mss(P_1, P_2)) \tag{3}$$

$$ctxMult'(P_1, P_2) = \frac{1 + length(mss(P_1, P_2))}{1 + n} \tag{4}$$

The function in Eq. 3, which call *maximum similar subsequence (mss)*, is a slight modification of the longest common subsequence algorithm, particularly the standard implementation with dynamic programming [4]. We extended the matching of equal elements to incorporate the relaxed vertex similarity schemes. The function is given in Algorithm 1.

Context multipliers given in Eqs. 2 and 4 are introduced so that larger percentages of matches contribute to higher similarity. We have implemented variations of this multiplier in the framework, i.e. normalization (adding 1 to numerator and denominator, inspired by [9]) and power (1 for linear and 2 for quad- ratic, inspired by the implicit quadratic multiplier in [11]). According to this formulation the multiplier in Eq. 4 is a normalized linear one. Readers should assume the third scheme (Eqs. 3, 4) is used for the rest of the paper.

4.5   Other Modifications to the Framework

Compared to [1], one major modification to the framework is on the NLP techniques. The previous technique uses tokenization and filtering to expand unigrams. For instance the unigram with the compound name *(LocatedElement, EClass)* would be expanded to two separate unigrams *(Located, EClass)* and *(Element, EClass)*. Afterwards synonym checking is performed on the names of expanded unigrams using

---

Algorithm 1. Maximum similar subsequence.

function $mss(P_1, P_2)$
  $n_1 \leftarrow$ size(P_1)
  $n_2 \leftarrow$ size(P_2)
  initialize array $score[n_1 + 1][n_2 + 1]$
  initialize array $length[n_1 + 1][n_2 + 1]$
  for $i = n_1 - 1$ **to** 0 **do** {decrementing}
    for $j = n_2 - 1$ **to** 0 **do** {decrementing}
      if $vSim(E_i, E_j) > 0$ **then**
        $score[i][j] = score[i + 1][j + 1] + vSim(E_i, E_j)$
        $length[i][j] = length[i + 1][j + 1] + 1$
      else
        $score[i][j] = max(score[i + 1][j], score[i][j + 1])$
        $length[i][j] = max(length[i+1][j], length[i][j+1])$
      end if
    end for
  end for
  $m, n \leftarrow i, j$, where $score[i][j] = max(score)$
  return $(score[m][n], length[m][n])$

---

algorithms for single-words. While this works efficiently for unigrams, adopting this directly for n-grams has some problems. Expanding an n-gram of size n, with compound-word names of average t tokens leads to a combinatorial explosion (by t^n) of features in the VSM. An example would be the bigram *(LocatedElement, EClass)-(geographicalLocation, EAttribute)* expanding into { *(Located, EClass)-(geographical, EAttribute), (Located, EClass)-(Location, EAttribute), (Element, EClass)-(geographical, EAttribute), (Element, EClass)-(Location, EAttribute)* }. For unigrams, it has been reported in [1] that tokenization helps in reducing the vector space as larger datasets tend to have a higher percentage of common tokens. For n-grams, however, this is not the case given the limited dataset: there are not enough common tokenized n-grams in the Ecore dataset used in this paper and as a result the vector space explodes. For this reason, we have integrated a simple compound-word vertex similarity measure syn_{multi}. Given two vertices with compound names l_1 and l_2, the similarity is the total sum of maximum synonym matches for each token pair, divided by the largest of the token set sizes:

$$syn_{multi}(l_1, l_2) = \frac{\sum_i \underset{j}{argmax}(syn_{single}(T_1^i, T_2^j))}{max(|T_1|, |T_2|)} \tag{5}$$

$$T_{1,2} = filter(tokenize(l_{1,2})) \tag{6}$$

This technique, supported by a cached lookup for synonyms or an in-memory dictionary, greatly improves the performance of checking synonyms (for n-grams with $n > 1$) over the *'tokenize & expand'* approach previously proposed.

Another parameter we have built into the framework, is the calculation of term frequencies, rather than incidences. During our experimental runs we have encountered the fact that allowing synonym checks and relaxed type checks leads to multiple non-zero matches across n-grams of different models. Hence two different calculations strategies are integrated into the framework when populating the VSM. Given a model M consisting of n-grams $\{M_1, \ldots, M_n\}$ and vector space cell for the n-gram S_j:

- **incidence:** $valueAt(M, S_j) = \underset{i}{argmax}(nSim(M_i, S_j))$,
- **frequency:** $valueAt(M, S_j) = \sum_{i=1}^{n} nSim(M_i, S_j)$.

We have empirically evaluated both calculations and observed higher accuracy with the latter strategy in the scope of the experiments in this paper. The readers should thus assume the latter is applied throughout this paper. A final modification to the framework is the use of automatic extraction of clusters from the dendrogram. This will be detailed in the next section.

5   Case Studies and Results

In order to quantitatively compare the accuracy of using n-grams with $n = 1$ versus $n > 1$, we have designed two case studies. Before moving on to the case studies themselves, we would like to list exhaustively the parameters of the framework for these experiments. Note that we have deliberately aimed to disable the features which are of relatively less importance for this work; to minimize the overall set of parameters and focus on the ones related to the application of n-grams. The framework settings are:

- n-gram extraction scheme: Ecore-specific scheme (Sect. 4.3), with $n = \{1, 2, 3\}$ for the first experiment, and $n = \{1, 2\}$ for the second one.
- NLP features: compound-word synonym checking using internal tokenization/filtering (Sect. 4.5) with basic NLP processing such as stemming and Levenshtein distance.
- Type matching: relaxed for model elements with different types, i.e. allowing non-exact type matches.
- n-gram similarity: the above vertex similarity settings (synonym and type matching), with relaxed matching for equal order n-grams and maximum similar subsequence (Sect. 4.4, Eqs. 3, 4).
- VSM calculation: Raw VSM with term frequencies (Sect. 4.5).
- Hierarchical clustering: `hclust` function is used with average linkage and cosine distance (from lsa package[5]) to obtain the dendrogram.

The last step of the framework is enhanced in this work with the automatic extraction or *'cutting'* of the dendrogram. For this we design two scenarios. In scenario 1, the user is assumed to be able to guess the number of clusters

---

[5] https://cran.r-project.org/package=lsa.

in the dataset, say n, with $\pm 20\%$ accuracy. For all the integers in the range: $[floor(0.8 * n), ceiling(1.2 * n)]$, we apply the standard `cutree` function of R to perform a straight horizontal cut on the dendrogram. As an external measure of cluster validity, we employ the $F_{0.5}$ measure (see [1] for details and the cluster labels for ground truth).

For scenario 2, we assume that the number of clusters cannot be guessed; rather a dynamic cut using the `cutreeDynamic` function in the `dynamicTreeCut`[6] package in R has to be performed. For this function we use the permutation of the following parameters for `cutreeDynamic`:

- maximum cut height $\in \{0.6, 0.7, 0.8, 0.9\}$; where to cut the tree into subtrees, with height corresponding to the cosine distance in the range $[0.0, 1.0]$.
- minimum cluster size $= 2$; not to end up with isolated single data points as clusters,
- deep split $\in \{0, 1, 2\}$; the extent to which subtrees should be further cut into smaller subtrees, i.e. clusters.

5.1   Case Study 1 - Random Small Datasets

This case study aims to measure the accuracy of n-grams for relatively small datasets using up to tri-grams ($n = 3$). Given the subset of AtlanMod Meta-model Zoo already specified in [1], consisting of 107 metamodels from 16 different domains (ranging from conference management to state machines) we extract random subsets of smaller sizes. The only restriction is that we pick individual cluster items of size ≥ 2 from each domain/cluster, hence avoid having a

Table 2. $F_{0.5}$ measures of the runs with regular cut.

Run	Unigram	Bigram	Trigram
1	0.693 ± 0.049	0.637 ± 0.154	**0.783 ± 0.036**
2	**0.913 ± 0.064**	0.891 ± 0.034	0.868 ± 0.049
3	0.796 ± 0.057	**0.799 ± 0.136**	0.781 ± 0.121
4	0.542 ± 0.064	0.688 ± 0.185	**0.757 ± 0.045**
5	0.576 ± 0.152	0.547 ± 0.118	**0.634 ± 0.012**
6	0.691 ± 0.052	0.679 ± 0.094	**0.707 ± 0.037**
7	**0.958 ± 0.027**	0.956 ± 0.026	0.936 ± 0.044
8	**0.872 ± 0.180**	**0.872 ± 0.180**	**0.872 ± 0.180**
9	0.912 ± 0.08	0.892 ± 0.077	**0.936 ± 0.035**
10	0.512 ± 0.12	**0.582 ± 0.137**	0.460 ± 0.031
...	...	...	...
Avg	0.665± 0.203	0.682 ± 0.197	**0.700 ± 0.175**

dataset with too many isolated outliers. We run this random procedure 50 times, obtaining 50 datasets of size 20–30. Doing this, we aim to avoid coincidental results for specific corner cases. For each dataset we run the framework with the same settings for unigrams, bigrams and trigrams.

---

[6] https://cran.r-project.org/package=dynamicTreeCut.

We list the $F_{0.5}$ measures of the runs in the format *mean ± standard deviation* for the random runs: Table 2 for the regular cut scenario and Table 3 for the dynamic cut scenario. In both tables, the last row gives the averages over 50 runs. One immediate observation is that bigrams and trigrams do not universally improve accuracy over unigrams; counterexamples for this are run 10 in Table 2 and run 8 in Table 3. Secondly, it also

Table 3. $F_{0.5}$ measures of the runs with dynamic cut.

Run	Unigram	Bigram	Trigram
1	0.693 ± 0.061	**0.771 ± 0.060**	0.726 ± 0.074
2	0.706 ± 0.055	0.758 ± 0.093	**0.822 ± 0.107**
3	0.548 ± 0.250	0.524 ± 0.142	**0.574 ± 0.125**
4	0.464 ± 0.143	**0.693 ± 0.188**	0.589 ± 0.135
5	**0.520 ± 0.141**	0.469 ± 0.084	0.515 ± 0.047
6	0.694 ± 0.090	0.813 ± 0.068	**0.865 ± 0.069**
7	0.671 ± 0.148	**0.938 ± 0.061**	0.749 ± 0.058
8	0.887 ± 0.079	**0.958 ± 0.040**	0.928 ± 0.097
9	0.742 ± 0.089	**0.880 ± 0.071**	0.814 ± 0.025
10	0.517 ± 0.117	**0.542 ± 0.197**	0.493 ± 0.137
...	...	...	...
Avg	0.599± 0.200	**0.679 ± 0.205**	0.672 ± 0.182

cannot be claimed that picking higher n (e.g. trigrams vs. bigrams) leads to monotonically higher accuracy. Indeed the goal of having so many random runs is to come up with an approximate judgment on n-gram accuracy for Ecore models. Bigrams and trigrams perform differently (in comparison with each other) for the two scenarios; nevertheless in the average case for both scenarios, n-grams with $n > 1$ perform better than with $n = 1$.

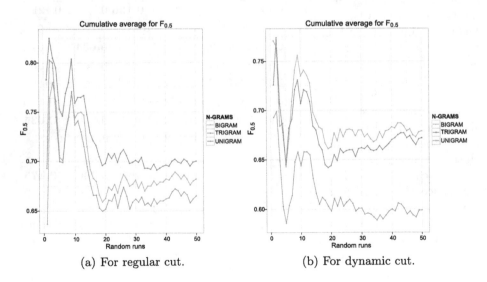

(a) For regular cut.   (b) For dynamic cut.

Fig. 4. Cumulative averages for $F_{0.5}$ over random runs.

We further supply the line chart of the cumulative mean $F_{0.5}$ measure over the 50 runs in Fig. 4 for the two scenarios. The points on the diagram correspond to the cumulative mean $F_{0.5}$ values of all the random runs up to k (x axis). This indicates a conclusive *stabilization* after a few runs. This improves our confidence in the measurement, eliminating the chance of e.g. alternating averages over the number of runs.

5.2 Case Study 2 - Larger Dataset

With the first case study giving us some insight, we turn to cluster the whole 107-model dataset. We restrict the upper bound for n-grams to bigrams, as trigrams reduce the performance to the point where at least multi-core processing, or high performance computing would be required. Nevertheless, as shown in Fig. 5, bigrams lead to a considerable increase in the accuracy of the clustering algorithm. The results are

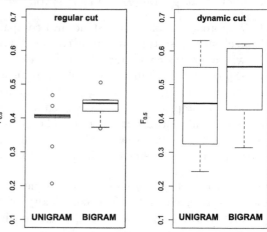

Fig. 5. Unigram vs bigram $F_{0.5}$ measures.

given in a boxplot of the $F_{0.5}$ measures with all the parameter permutations for unigrams (left plot) and bigrams (right plot). It is fairly easy to see that bigrams improve the worst case, mean and median; while there is a negligible decrease in the best case (right plot only). Our findings here reinforce our confidence on the average behaviour of bigrams, as pointed out in the first case study.

6 Discussion

The two case studies indicate using n-grams with $n > 1$ is a promising technique for incorporating structural context into model clustering. Our technique allows the extraction of model elements together with (part of) their context in the form of n-grams (**RQ1**) to overcome some difficulties of using just unigrams and losing the context information for model elements (Sect. 3). We have relaxed many of the framework parameters and in principle strived for reasoning based on average measurements in order to avoid getting stuck on corner cases and specific parameter settings. The clustering accuracy is shown in two case studies to improve over unigrams on average (**RQ2**). Consequently we deduce that:

- On average, n-grams with $n > 1$ lead to higher accuracy than $n = 1$.
- The accuracy does not monotonically increase along with increasing n.
- Given the increasing complexity of clustering with larger n, using unigrams remains the most scalable but inaccurate approach, while bigrams can be considered as a safe middle ground for relatively large datasets.
- Depending on the type of the input models, size and nature of the dataset, and for accuracy-oriented tasks, n-grams with $n > 2$ can be employed. However, a preliminary consideration and experimentation should be performed as the accuracy is not guaranteed to increase on average.

Our approach incorporates structural comparison to the N-way model comparison/clustering setting. It can be considered a compromise between the work in [1], which ignores context, and approaches such as [10] which can exploit full structural context for pairwise model comparison. There are further advantages of using this technique, stemming from the underlying framework. For example, the individual steps of the workflow such as the graph-based n-gram extraction and clustering algorithms are generic and extendible for other types of structural models (e.g. UML class diagrams). Furthermore using R brings in strong tool support in terms of clustering, analysis and visualization techniques.

Complexity of Using n-grams. The complexity of clustering is omitted here; readers are referred to [7]. The complexity of VSM construction for n-grams is proportional to $|n\text{-}grams|^2 * compare_n$; i.e. the number of extracted n-grams and cost of comparing each n-gram. $compare_n$ is $\mathcal{O}(n^2)$ with the maximum similar subsequence implementation in Sect. 4.4. The number of extracted n-grams in turn is proportionate with size of the input dataset N, average size of models (underlying graph) s and a factor f_n which depends on the n chosen. The formal complexity analysis of f_n would involve measuring the average number of attributes, references and supertypes, plus the graph-theoretic path calculations up to n. This may be difficult to calculate in the domain-specific extraction scheme (Sect. 4.3) we adopt for this paper. Another approach would be to have a larger and more representative dataset of Ecore models and deduce it empirically using regression on the above mentioned metrics. We leave these as future work, and report here a rough empirical observation on our dataset.

We can safely assume that the number of n-grams for one model is $\mathcal{O}(s)$ in the case of unigrams; where s is the model size. For a rough comparison of the n-gram sizes, we crawled $17000 +$ Ecore models from GitHub[7] and ran our n-gram extraction algorithm on them for $n = 1, 2, 3$. Figure 6 shows the number of bigrams and trigrams (y axis) versus unigrams (x axis) per model. Here we note some simple observations. Unigrams per model tend to be on average in the range of 100 s, with bigrams in the 1000 s and trigrams growing up to 10000 s. There are of course cases with many unigrams and disproportionately few bigrams/trigrams, i.e. presumably flat models with few supertypes/references, and also cases with the opposite; presumably smaller-sized models with complex inheritance hierarchies and cross-references.

---

[7] https://github.com.

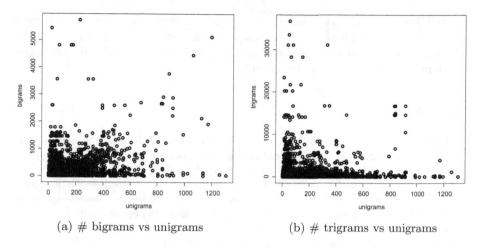

(a) # bigrams vs unigrams   (b) # trigrams vs unigrams

Fig. 6. Empirical observation on the number of n-grams per model.

Threats to Validity. While we aimed for a transparent methodology avoiding coincidental conclusions for corner cases, there are some threats to validity for our work. Firstly, using n-grams should be validated on other and larger datasets of different model types (e.g. UML class diagrams). Secondly, we take only the average accuracies into consideration to conclude the usefulness of using n-grams with $n > 1$, while individual cases (Sect. 5.1) are shown to reduce the accuracy. A meta-analysis is required to find out the reasons, and if possible come up with some heuristics for picking an optimal n considering certain characteristics of the dataset (e.g. size or homogeneity/compactness of clusters and complexity of models in terms of inheritance).

7   Conclusion and Future Work

In this paper, we have presented a technique using n-grams, originating from computational linguistics, for clustering structural models. This work builds on top of our model clustering framework, extending its features to incorporate structural context into clustering. We have indicated a shortcoming of previous approaches, i.e. ignoring the context of model elements, and have proposed a flexible technique, which can be considered as the compromise between context-less clustering approaches and advanced pairwise structural techniques. We have tested our approach on an Ecore dataset from AtlanMod Metamodel Zoo. With carefully devised case studies, avoiding coincidental conclusions for corner cases, we show that n-grams improve the clustering accuracy on average. Picking an $n > 1$ is shown to increase complexity and using larger n is suggested for smaller datasets and precision-oriented tasks, though after preliminary consideration as precision is not guaranteed to increase monotonically along with n.

As future work, we want to address the points listed as threats to validity. The approach can be tested on larger datasets, and on different structural models such as UML class diagrams. We are in the process of obtaining further datasets from the industry. Moreover, a meta-analysis of different settings can also be performed, to find out the correlations of n-gram accuracies with dataset size, homogeneity, nature of model types, etc.

References

1. Babur, Ö., Cleophas, L., van den Brand, M.: Hierarchical clustering of metamodels for comparative analysis and visualization. In: Proceedings of the 12th European Conference on Modelling Foundations and Applications, 2016, pp. 2–18 (2016)
2. Babur, Ö., Cleophas, L., Verhoeff, T., van den Brand, M.: Towards statistical comparison and analysis of models. In: Proceedings of the 4th International Conference on Model-Driven Engineering and Software Development, pp. 361–367 (2016)
3. Basciani, F., Rocco, J., Ruscio, D., Iovino, L., Pierantonio, A.: Automated clustering of metamodel repositories. In: Nurcan, S., Soffer, P., Bajec, M., Eder, J. (eds.) CAiSE 2016. LNCS, vol. 9694, pp. 342–358. Springer, Heidelberg (2016). doi:10.1007/978-3-319-39696-5_21
4. Bergroth, L., Hakonen, H., Raita, T.: A survey of longest common subsequence algorithms. In: Seventh International Symposium on String Processing and Information Retrieval, 2000, SPIRE 2000, Proceedings, pp. 39–48. IEEE (2000)
5. Bislimovska, B., Bozzon, A., Brambilla, M., Fraternali, P.: Textual and content-based search in repositories of web application models. ACM Trans. Web (TWEB) 8(2), 11 (2014)
6. Klint, P., Landman, D., Vinju, J.: Exploring the limits of domain model recovery. In: 2013 29th IEEE International Conference on Software Maintenance (ICSM), pp. 120–129. IEEE (2013)
7. Manning, C.D., Raghavan, P., Schütze, H., et al.: Introduction to Information Retrieval, vol. 1. Cambridge University Press, Cambridge (2008)
8. Manning, C.D., Schütze, H.: Foundations of Statistical Natural Language Processing, vol. 999. MIT Press, Cambridge (1999)
9. Mass, Y., Mandelbrod, M.: Retrieving the most relevant xml components. In: INEX 2003 Workshop Proceedings, p. 58. Citeseer (2003)
10. Melnik, S., Garcia-Molina, H., Rahm, E.: Similarity flooding: a versatile graph matching algorithm and its application to schema matching. In: 18th International Conference on Data Engineering, 2002, Proceedings, pp. 117–128. IEEE (2002)
11. Rubin, J., Chechik, M.: N-way model merging. In: Proceedings of the 2013 9th Joint Meeting on Foundations of Software Engineering, pp. 301–311. ACM (2013)
12. Stahl, T., Völter, M., Bettin, J., Haase, A., Helsen, S.: Model-Driven Software Development: Technology, Engineering, Management. Wiley, New York (2006)
13. Stephan, M., Cordy, J.R.: A survey of model comparison approaches and applications. In: Modelsward, pp. 265–277 (2013)

Author Index

Printed in the United States
By Bookmasters